DEADLY SECRETS

THE SINGAPORE RAIDS
1942–45

Lynette Ramsay Silver

SALLYMILNER
PUBLISHING

First published in 2010 by
Sally Milner Publishing Pty Ltd
734 Woodville Road
Binda NSW 2583 AUSTRALIA

© Lynette Ramsay Silver 2010

Design: Anna Warren, Warren Ventures Pty Ltd
Editing: Anne Savage
Printed in China

National Library of Australia Cataloguing-in-Publication entry

Author: Silver, Lynette Ramsay, 1945-
Title: Deadly secrets : the Singapore raids 1942-45 / Lynette Ramsay Silver.
ISBN: 9781863514101 (pbk.)
Notes: Includes index.
            Bibliography.
Subjects: Krait (Ship)
            Operation Jaywick.
            Operation Rimau.
            World War, 1939-1945–Campaigns–Singapore.
            World War, 1939-1945–Naval operations, Australian.
Dewey Number: 940.545994

10 9 8 7 6 5 4 3 2 1

Dedication

For Denis and Bettina, who believed that truth should out,
and for Neil, who made sure that it did.

Contents

Acknowledgements

The author gratefully acknowledges the invaluable support and assistance of the late Denis Emerson-Elliott and Bettina Reid; information supplied by the late Geoffrey Brooke, Tony Emerson-Elliott, Elizabeth Ennis, John 'Lofty' Hodges, Brenda McDuff; Marjorie de Malmanche, Archie Mitchell, Ron Morris, Don Ramsay, Geoffrey Rowley-Conwy, Clarrie Willoughby and Kelvin Wright; Arafin bin Akup, Mahat Kunil, Abdul Achap, Aloysius Weller, Tan Yong Meng and Colonel Brian Nicholson in Indonesia and Singapore; Betty Bradbury, Redmond Faulkner, Don Russell, Arthur Suters, Glenn Darlington, and Ray Evans in Australia; Jeremy Atkinson and Jonathan Moffatt in England; Dr Godfrey Oettle, Professors John Hilton and Denise Donlon for their forensic assistance; John Erikson in the USA and Don Munro for insight on the Schow family; various personnel connected to Ruston Diesel, Gardners and Sons, Greaves Cotton Bombay and Duetz.

Gratitude is expressed also to Clive and Madeline Lyon, Greg and Robert Pace, Maureen Devereaux, Jean Bates, Lyn Snowden, Max Manderson, Beverley Wain, Henry Hawke, Alan Stewart, Ila Roff, Jeff Willersdorf, Katherine Willersdorf, the Perske family, Ian Cameron, Julie Edwards, Norman Dean, Tony and Virginia Frazer, John Sachs, Wesley College Archives Department, Ted Butler, Margaret Reynolds, Allan Miles, Denis Harman, Robert Mullock, Robert Gregg, Val Grimson, Peter Woods of RVCP and David Hope for additional biographical and/or photographic material, especially Joanne Bosma and Maria Jackman for the wealth of information on Roland Fletcher and Bruno Reymond; to Bill Young, Bert Rollason, Frank Martin, the late Carl Jensen and the late Chris Neilsen for their input on Outram Road Gaol; to Moss Berryman for additional information regarding Jaywick and to Dr Barbara Orchard for her introduction to the Emerson-Elliotts. Many thanks also for the valuable research assistance of Peter Macmillan, Derek Emerson-Elliott, Keith Andrews in the UK, Janine Smith of the Defence Library in Sydney, Nick Fletcher of the Australian War Memorial, the Director and Staff of Changi Museum, Vanessa Perez and Di Elliott. The deepest gratitude is acknowledged to Neil Silver, whose on-going financial, moral and practical support was integral to the writing of this book.

Secret agencies and abbreviations

The secret organisations and units operating in Australia, Britain and Singapore during World War II included:

- Allied Intelligence Bureau (AIB): umbrella organisation in Australia for all covert Allied units, except SOA.
- Department of Information (DOI): Australia's propaganda organisation.
- Economic Research Bureau (ERB): cover name given by SOE to the Oriental Mission's propaganda arm.
- Far Eastern Bureau (FEB): organisation in Singapore to organise, publish and distribute propaganda.
- Far Eastern Combined Bureau (FECB): cover name for the Admiralty run intelligence gathering organisation in the Far East.
- Far Eastern Security Section (FESS): a division of the Far East Combined Bureau, to report and pass on reports of anti-British activity.
- Inter Allied Services Bureau (IASB, ISD): cover name for SOE (Australia).
- Inter Services Research Bureau (ISRB: cover name for Special Operations Executive (SOE).
- Joint Intelligence Bureau (JIB): military equivalent of Standing Committee on Intelligence (SCI).
- M Special Unit: The administrative arm of Allied Intelligence Bureau, to cater for AIF recruits. Also a holding unit for the same personnel. Non-operational.
- Malayan Political Advisory Bureau (MPAB): set up in 1924 by the Inspector General of Police to disseminate internal security information to government and military departments.
- Military Intelligence Section 5 (MI5): Britain's internal Security Service.
- Military Intelligence Section 6 (MI6): Britain's Secret Intelligence Service or SIS.
- Ministry of Information (MOI): Britain's propaganda organisation.
- Number 101 Special Training School (101 STS): Oriental Mission's specialised training facility in Singapore.
- Oriental Mission (OM): cover name for SOE's Singapore Section.
- Special Branch (SB) of Singapore and Malay Police Forces, which collected intelligence.
- Secret Intelligence Bureau (SIB), the forerunner of Secret intelligence Service (SIS)
- Secret Intelligence Service (SIS) also known as Military Intelligence Section 6 or MI6. Previously the Foreign Section of Secret Intelligence Bureau (SIB).

- Services Reconnaissance Department (SRD): cover name for Special Operations Australia (SOA).
- Special Operations Australia (SOA): the Australian equivalent of SOE, answerable to General Thomas Blamey.
- Special Liaison Unit (SLU): cover name for personnel who worked on Y intercepts.
- Special Operations Executive (SOE): an offshoot of SIS, dedicated to subversion and sabotage in occupied countries, answerable to Winston Churchill. Previously Section D of SIS. Code-named Inter Service Research Bureau (ISRB).
- SS: Security Service or Directorate of Military Intelligence Section 5 (MI5). Previously the Home section of SI
- Standing Committee on Intelligence (SCI) – replaced MPAB in 1931.
- Station IX: The Frythe, at Welwyn, where experts developed weapons, gadgets, etc. to assist SOE in its covert wor
- Station X: Bletchley Park, home to Directorate of Military Intelligence Section 10, which worked on cracking enemy codes.
- Y: the code for intercepted signals, and name of the section which intercepted and decrypted them. Also code named Special Liaison Unit (SLU
- Z Organisation: a deep cover group, parallel to SIS, which took over when SIS's European network was compromised in 1939. Headed by Colonel Z, code name for Sir Claude Edward Dansey.
- Z Special Unit: the administrative arm of Special Operations Australia, to cater for AIF recruits. Also a holding unit for same personnel. Non-operational.

PROLOGUE

The man with the
black leather briefcase ...

Central Station, Sydney
17 June 1996

It is a cold, drizzly, overcast day. Miserable, in fact. The cavernous roof over the country train platform offers only partial protection from the drifting rain, whipped along by a stiff southerly wind which tugs annoyingly at my damp trench coat. Hugging my arms to my chest for warmth, I peer through the gloom, willing the train from Canberra to be on time.

It is.

Despite the depressing weather, I am in high spirits, and aglow with anticipation. I have come to Central Station to meet Denis Emerson-Elliott, British Secret Service, a former and long-serving member of the organisation known popularly as MI6 and a wartime special agent. As an officer in the Royal Australian Navy from 1942–45, he served with the Department of Naval Intelligence and was also personal assistant and confidante of the Director, Commander R M Long. Denis Emerson-Elliott is a man who knows many secrets, some of which he is willing to share with me. In short, I am about to meet a latter-day spy.

The train, which is actually a rail motor, consists of only two carriages. Mr Emerson-Elliott, to whom I refer mentally as MI6, has supplied details of the seats he and his son Tony are occupying, so I have ascertained which end of their carriage to wait. I have no idea of what either man looks like but I do know that MI6 sounds terribly British, from the guarded conversations he has had with me over the phone.

The meeting he has arranged is quite unexpected. He called a few days ago to say that he is travelling to Perth by train and, as he has several hours to wait before the Indian Pacific departs, it would be an ideal opportunity for us to meet. He has matters to discuss which will be of interest to me and, because of what he has to say, it must be face to face. I have given him a brief physical description of myself. His response to this was to advise that he will be carrying a black leather briefcase.

The train glides to a stop. The carriage door opens and out steps a rather portly, middle-aged man – bespectacled, balding, and looking slightly rumpled. He is puffing a little as he manhandles two travel-worn, composite-cardboard suitcases through the narrow doorway.

Denis Emerson-Elliott, retired secret service agent, 1995

Plastered with old shipping labels and bound with strong leather straps, the dun-coloured bags look like props from a 1950s British film. As he plods across the platform, the stiff breeze ruffles his unruly greying hair, flicking strands across his shiny pate.

Right on his heels is an elderly gentleman, spare of build, his hair slicked back smoothly from an angular, somewhat aquiline face. In stark contrast to the younger man, he is immaculately dressed and looks exceedingly dapper, in spite of the long train journey. Highly polished brown brogues, neatly laced with a double bow, are topped by tailor-made sports trousers, the carefully pressed creases amazingly knife-edged. His upper body is clad in a well-cut Harris tweed jacket, long-sleeved shirt, fine wool vest and a woollen, Windsor-knotted tie. A high-quality wool overcoat is folded carefully over one arm. For identification purposes, the soft, black leather briefcase, clutched under the other arm is superfluous. This has to be MI6.

I step forward, hand extended, and say, 'Good morning. You must be the Emerson-Elliotts.'

To which the older man replies, in beautifully modulated tones, 'And you must be Lynette.'

The introductions over, MI6 asks me how I recognised them so quickly. Somehow managing to maintain a straight face, I whisper conspiratorially, 'It's the black leather briefcase – it's a dead giveaway.'

After locating the Left Luggage room, where a smiling but somewhat red-faced Tony gratefully divests himself of his burden, MI6 suggests that some refreshment might be in order. Chilled to the bone from my vigil on the platform, I readily agree and allow him to lead the way. To my surprise, he does not select one of the smaller, intimate cafes scattered along the concourse, which are quiet and cosily inviting. Instead he heads for one on the far side – filled with a chattering early lunch-time crowd. I doubt there will be a spare table, but MI6 spots one and makes a determined beeline for it. Left in his wake, Tony and I thread our way through the throng, to find he has successfully made claim by placing his briefcase and overcoat on one of the chairs.

Old habits die hard – especially if you have spent all your life in the Secret Service. The table Denis Emerson-Elliott has chosen is in the far corner of this busy, noisy cafe. The chair he has selected for himself allows him to have his back to the wall, at the same time affording a direct line of sight to the door. Mindful that MI6 was a spy for many years, I had worn my trench coat as a bit of a joke, but it now appears I am appropriately dressed for the occasion.

A harried waitress hands us a menu. We order tea and toasted sandwiches for three, with a rock cake, liberally sprinkled with sugar and cinnamon, for Tony. The waitress apologises and says that, owing to the crowd, there is a bit of a backlog and our order will not be ready for about twenty minutes. We don't mind, because we have plenty to talk about and a few hours to kill. I initiate the conversation by asking MI6 about his life in Singapore before the war, and his subsequent evacuation.

It is not surprising that we develop an instant rapport. I have spent years immersing myself in war-time events which he is now describing from first-hand experience. Tony regards us with astonishment. We are like two old friends, reliving the glorious days of the Empire and reminiscing about former colleagues, many of them secret agents, whom I also 'know' through my research.

While his father is chatting, Tony takes a ballpoint pen from his pocket and, on a spare paper napkin, makes a sketch for me of the evacuation ship which brought his family to Australia – Empire Star. Despite his being only a small boy at the time, the drawing is extraordinarily detailed.

Finally, our waitress appears. After passing out the sandwiches and carefully arranging the tea cups in front of him, MI6 picks up the steaming pot and, with a charming smile turns to me and says, 'Well, my dear, enough of Singapore for the time being. How about a spot of tea while we discuss Operations Jaywick and Rimau? I am sure you will find it most interesting, for what I am about to tell you, you will not find recorded anywhere else.'

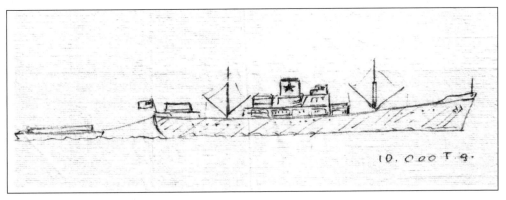

Tony Emerson-Elliott's sketch of Empire Star

1.

War comes to Singapore

February 1942

From the cockpit of his Zero fighter plane, a lone Japanese pilot surveyed the coastal road ahead. Making its way towards the Changi-Singapore road was a solitary Singer sedan, looking for all the world like a small black beetle. It wasn't much of a target, but as a loyal servant of the Emperor it was the pilot's duty to eliminate all the enemies of Japan. Bringing the car carefully into the cross-wires of his machine-gun sights, he depressed the firing button. A stream of lead spurted instantly from the nose of the Zero, homing in remorselessly on the unsuspecting occupants.

The vehicle had set off a few minutes earlier from Whitelawns – a sprawling beachside bungalow with twin castle-like turrets linked by a broad verandah and set amidst lush and well-tended tropical gardens. At the wheel was Lieutenant Denis Emerson-Elliott, Royal Naval Volunteer Reserve. As always he appeared calm, due to his training and natural demeanour, but his mind was racing at a frenetic pace. His anxiety was well founded. On 8 February, less than twenty-four hours previously and despite all predictions to the contrary, vast numbers of Japanese troops had poured from Malaya across the narrow Straits of Johor, overwhelming the defenders to gain a firm foothold on Singapore Island – the brightest jewel in Britain's Far Eastern empire and a supposedly impregnable fortress.

Hostilities had broken out two months previously, on 8 December, when a Japanese invasion force had accomplished what all but a handful of military experts deemed to be impossible – storming ashore at Kota Bharu, on Malaya's far north-eastern coastline, at the height of the monsoon. This shock had barely been digested at Malaya Command Headquarters in Singapore when, two days later, news was received that HM battle cruiser *Repulse* and HM battleship *Prince of Wales* had been sunk by enemy aircraft in the Gulf of Siam.

Dispatched on the orders of British Prime Minister Winston Churchill as a show of strength, the two warships had sallied forth with a small flotilla from the safety of Singapore, home to the world's most modern naval base and protected by batteries of huge guns. Left without air cover when their aircraft carrier escort had run aground in Jamaica, the two great grey goliaths, the pride of the Royal Navy, were sitting ducks for enemy planes. Attacked by

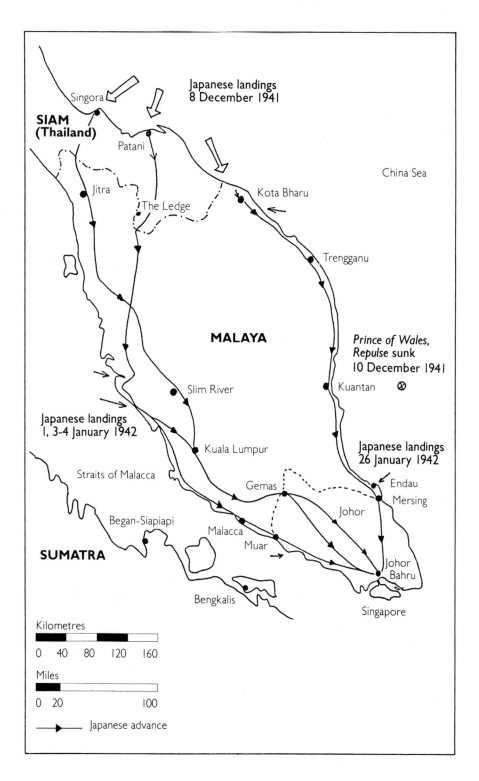

The Japanese advance through Malaya

four high-level bombers and 51 torpedo bombers, the vessels did not stand a chance. Five torpedoes struck *Repulse*, which sank shortly after midday. Less than an hour later *Prince of Wales* succumbed to torpedoes and a well-placed bomb. As 845 officers and men slid to a watery grave, the accompanying destroyers could do nothing but search for survivors.

Seemingly unstoppable, the Japanese had then consistently steamrolled their way south towards Singapore through Malaya's vast jungles and rubber plantations. In stark contrast to the Allied army, hampered by large amounts of personal and unnecessary military gear, the invaders carried only bare essentials. Living off the land with apparent ease, they had covered thousands of kilometres in a bare seven weeks, making excellent use of the well-paved British roads and often pedalling along on bicycles purloined from the locals.

The enemy's competence had come as a great surprise to the defending troops. During training they had been assured by senior officers that the short-statured Japanese – being myopic, equipped with inferior weapons and flying aeroplanes made from recycled pots and pans – were not a serious threat, especially since Singapore was protected by mountainous jungle-clad Malaya to the north and by massive gun emplacements on the seaward approaches. Although the Japanese had made threatening noises in the latter part of 1941, there was no cause at all for alarm, according to the Commander-in-Chief Far East, Air Vice-Marshall Brooke-Popham. In late October, just over three months before, he had issued a statement of reassurance, declaring:

> I bring you good news – there is no need to worry about the strength of the
> Air Force that will oppose the Japanese should they send their army and navy
> southward ... the Air Force is on the spot, and is waiting for the enemy – clouds
> of bombers and fighters are hidden in the jungle, and are ready to move out on to
> camouflaged tarmacs of our secret landing fields and roar into action at the first
> move of the Japanese towards this part of the world ... the planes are the most
> modern planes Britain, Australia and America are producing.

In the face of such official confidence, air-raid drills were deemed unnecessary and, since it was a widely known fact that Japanese pilots could not fly in the dark, no blackout precautions were taken. It was pure and utter propaganda. Not only was the Allied air force severely under strength, the aircraft that were available were for the most part obsolete.

It did not take long for Allied soldiers thrown into action to discover that their adversaries were well-equipped, well-trained, well-disciplined and extremely well-versed in the art of jungle warfare. And, as British and Australian air force personnel soon learned, the quality of the enemy aircraft, piloted by airmen who definitely had no problems flying in the dark, far outstripped anything available in Malaya.

Although the Allied troops outnumbered the enemy, it was a very uneven contest. Many of the Indians, who comprised a high percentage of the combined Allied forces, were teenagers. Raised in a hurry to come to the defence of the Empire, most were untrained and were often indifferently led by inferior British officers. In the face of a vastly superior enemy, they simply collapsed. Many of those not killed or wounded fled, divesting themselves of their weapons and uniforms and seeking refuge among the local population. Others who surrendered expecting to become prisoners of war became corpses, slaughtered by an enemy which gave no quarter.

As retreat followed retreat the Allies were pushed further down the Malay peninsula, the speed of the enemy advance forcing them to abandon valuable equipment, fuel and supplies, which the Japanese quickly appropriated. Towns and cities fell like ninepins but despite the general collapse there were some pockets of determined resistance, especially by units whose commanders had insisted on jungle training. With Malaya Command believing any attack must come from the sea, jungle warfare training had been considered entirely unnecessary. Consequently, it had been restricted to the Australian Imperial Force (AIF) under the fiercely independent Major-General Gordon Bennett and to the Argyll and Sutherland Highlanders, led by Lieutenant-Colonel Stewart, whose ideas on jungle training were considered by his superiors to be those of a 'crank'. When one junior British officer showed some enterprise by organising a training exercise in the jungles of Johor, his efforts were ignored completely by his commanding officer. He did not even turn up to observe, much less lead the exercise – he was too busy playing cricket.

Consequently, when the Japanese invaded, the majority of the Allied forces, trained for desert and open warfare, were ill-equipped to handle jungle conditions. However, the highly trained Ghurkas, as was expected, fought with their legendary ferocity and some of the better-trained British units displayed dogged persistence before falling back. So too did the jungle-toughened Australians, who pulled off a morale-lifting victory when large numbers of Japanese troops pedalled their way into a well-prepared ambush at Gemas.

But perhaps the greatest battle of all was an epic fighting retreat by two under-strength Australian battalions sent to repel 10,000 crack Imperial Guards, escorted by tanks and with air support, who had landed on the west coast at Muar. With the main Allied army currently withdrawing down the central trunk road in great peril of being cut off by this outflanking manoeuvre, the Australians were given the seemingly insurmountable task of holding up the enemy advance. They achieved their goal, but the fighting which ensued was desperate. The five-day action through rubber plantations, jungle and swamp had ended at the village of Parit Sulong where the Australians, valiantly protecting their large number of wounded, were forced to fight hand-to-hand to stave off total annihilation. With no hope of relief and their supplies exhausted, some of the survivors finally managed to escape encirclement to rejoin the main Allied army, now safely past the danger point. The Australian commander, Lieutenant-Colonel Charles Anderson, was awarded a Victoria Cross but the losses sustained were immense – both battalions virtually wiped out and the seriously wounded, left in an ambulance convoy at the village in the expectation that they would be protected by the Red Cross flag they displayed, roped together and massacred.

However, while every soldier who came face to face with the Japanese realised the Allied troops were up against a vastly underestimated foe, the civilian authorities, including Singapore's governor, Sir Shenton Thomas, continued to live in a fool's paradise. Sir Shenton, who was approaching retirement and had accepted what was generally regarded as a plum job to finish his career, was more social than military in his inclinations. Consequently, although he held the position of Commander-in-Chief he failed to impress the military, who saw him as somewhat shallow. He was kept abreast of the war situation by Malaya Command but elected to ignore most of it by placing a complete embargo on all war news. The publication of any details of the fighting or the massive civilian casualties was absolutely forbidden on the grounds that the civilian population might become demoralised – the same reason advanced by the General Officer Commanding, Britain's Lieutenant-General Arthur Percival, for not installing fixed defences along Singapore's vulnerable northern coastline.

There was little chance of the civilian casualty figures being made public. Those killed were buried in mass graves with indecent haste, many of them unidentified. While the sauna-like heat made swift disposal essential, it helped hide the truth about the mounting death toll. Relatives of the deceased were also prohibited from inserting the usual death notices in the paper, on the grounds that the long lists would make for depressing reading. With the civilian authorities doing everything in their power to suppress anything which could possibly

Grief-stricken Chinese women with the body of a small child, following an air raid on Singapore city

18

*Whitelawns,
near Changi, the
palatial home of
the Emerson-Elliott
family*

be construed as bad news, it was little wonder that the majority of Singapore's population believed that the pitched battles in Malaya were nothing more than minor skirmishes.

This air of unreality had begun on day one of hostilities, when Singapore suffered its first air raid. Kota Bharu had been invaded a scant three hours earlier, yet the military chiefs in Singapore had not invoked a blackout and the city was ablaze with lights. And so, as the citizens of Singapore slumbered on, oblivious to the danger, waves of enemy aircraft released their deadly loads unchallenged. While most of the bombs fell on Chinatown, officially killing sixty people, the now wide-awake Europeans living outside the attack zone watched the show from their living-room windows, believing it was a spectacular and most realistic air force exercise.

Out at Whitelawns, which faced the South China Sea near the village of Mata Ikan, a little to the south of the new Changi Prison, and was therefore not only 20 kilometres from town but also off the beaten track, Denis Emerson-Elliott had been woken from a sound sleep at around 4 am by a strange, ululating noise which he took some time to identify. It was the sound of unsynchronised twin-engined aircraft and, judging by the density of the vibrations, there were a lot of them. He quickly woke his wife Norma and led her out onto the dew-sodden grass, where they directed their gaze to an unmistakable glow in the west – the lights of Singapore city, 20 kilometres away. To his horror, the thrum of the aircraft engines became louder and was shortly overlaid by a far more chilling sound – the distant crump of exploding bombs – but the lights did not go out.

While the raid was in progress, the phone rang. It was the naval base, instructing Denis to proceed at once to his ship, an ex-fishing trawler which had been converted to a minesweeper to carry out patrols around Singapore. The instructions were brief and to the point. He was to proceed to the harbour at once and implement standing orders to round up and impound all Japanese vessels in port. After briefly discussing the need to construct an air-raid shelter with Chu Lun, the family's gardener and general factotum, Denis set off at once in his rather sporty, two-door Fiat Marvelette. There was no time to waste.

Up until this fateful day, Norma and her husband had, like many of their friends, enjoyed a lifestyle which those outside Singapore believed only existed in the pages of a Somerset Maugham novel. With the tropical heat not conducive to rushing about or indulging in any kind of unnecessary labour, life for the privileged white community was slow-paced. In European households all menial tasks were performed by legions of servants or staff, all of whom worked for low wages, while the heat and humidity were avoided if possible by organising one's day to suit the climate. But a relaxing lifestyle did not mean that one could relax one's standards. Despite the heat and cloying humidity those wishing to play cricket at the magnificent and exclusively 'white' Cricket Club, situated on the western end of the city's padang or village green, could only do so in traditional cream flannels. During the day, men wore collars and ties, the women silk stockings, hats and gloves, and in the evening everyone dressed for dinner. At Whitelawns, Denis and Norma typically eased into the working day with a horse ride along the beach, followed by lunch at the exclusive Tanglin Club and a short rest during the mandatory siesta period. A little more work in the latter part of the afternoon and it was time for an icy-cold gin sling or two and then, more often than not, a formal dinner on the terrace of the Singapore Swimming Club, or at Raffles Hotel.

Norma Emerson-Elliott

On 8 December 1941, Denis had no time for any of this. His day was fully occupied in seizing a number of Japanese fishing boats and other craft and towing them to an internment pen for safekeeping. Those in and around the harbour were taken to Telok Ayer Basin, where fishing boats awaiting repair were already moored. Here they were signed over to A H 'Dickie' Dickinson, the Inspector-General of Police, who wore several hats. Besides being the chief law enforcement officer he also controlled the Local Defence Forces and, since 1939, had kept tabs on all enemy aliens, particularly Malaya's 7,900 Japanese immigrants who were believed, one way or the other, to work for Japanese Intelligence.

Following a well-orchestrated plan, of

which Denis and his ship formed a vital part, Dickie had moved with lightning speed that morning to ensure no fishing vessels left port and that the 1200 Japanese whom he knew were in Singapore were rounded up. Newly seized vessels were added to those impounded at their moorings and their crews, if still on board, handed over to the relevant authorities. Other craft captured out to sea by larger naval vessels, including the Australian corvettes HMAS *Goulburn*, *Burnie* and *Maryborough*, were boarded by armed sailors and escorted to the naval base, situated at Seletar on the Straits of Johor, on the island's northern coast.

Meanwhile, questions were being asked about the previous night's air raid. Why, for instance, had no sirens sounded, and why had the city's lights not been switched off as soon as the attack began? As RAF radar operator Harry Grumber later explained, the seventeen aircraft had shown up on his screen while they were still 55 minutes from their target, but he was unable to take any action as he was under instructions from the governor to sound no warning, lest it frighten the population. By the time Sir Shenton decided it would be prudent to raise the alarm after all, another 35 minutes had passed. When Harry called Air Raid Patrol Headquarters on his direct line to relay the order, he was told that HQ was powerless to sound the sirens as the chief warden, who had the keys controlling the alarm switch, was at the late-night movies.

While Harry tried without success to have the city lights doused, the final 25 minutes before the Japanese attacked was wasted in a fruitless search to locate the warden and his keys. Although the pilots of three antiquated Brewster Buffalo fighters from an Australian squadron were on full alert, with their planes' engines warmed and running, they were not ordered into the air, because the British Air Force chief, Air Vice-Marshall Pulford, was worried that incompetent anti-aircraft gunners might shoot them down.

Although some patrons were put out to discover that their favourite eatery, the restaurant in Robinson's department store at Raffles Place, had fallen victim to enemy bombers, the early morning raid did not perturb the rest of the populace unduly, especially since most of the damage was confined to the Chinese quarter. There were no more raids over the next three weeks of December so, after the initial shock had worn off and people had ceased to enter the bombed area to gawp at the destroyed buildings, life settled back into its normal routine with the usual round of dances, parties, shopping excursions and coffee mornings. It was almost as if, by ignoring the entire affair, the air raid had not occurred and the Japanese did not exist.

Any residual anxiety concerning the landings in northern Malaya was soon dispelled by an official communiqué broadcast over the radio by the governor. Declaring that the Japanese had been repulsed at Kota Bharu, where only a small number of bombs had fallen harmlessly on the airfield, he said the few enemy troops on the beach had been machine-gunned, and all Japanese surface craft had retired at high speed. To further boost morale he stated that although the bombing of Pearl Harbour had given the enemy an appearance of victory, the United States had now entered the war and would, before long, put an end to Japan's militaristic dreams.

The Japanese were back in January, bombing Singapore numerous times, but the majority of civilians remained unfazed, standing about in the open to watch aerial dogfights and swarming in increasing numbers to view damage from the latest raid. At Whitelawns, Denis Emerson-Elliott's small sons, four-year-old Tony and Derek, aged two-and-a-half, stood on the lawn in their pyjamas as the hostilities unfolded before their very eyes. Immediately out to sea they saw Japanese planes attack and set on fire an oil tanker, the massive flames illuminating the entire horizon. Once the aircraft departed the two boys had the unusual experience of watching their father at work as his ship searched for survivors. A short time later, while on another patrol, Denis's vessel was sunk off Pangahrang Point, just to the north of Changi village. Fortunately Denis was able to swim ashore.

Since a number of military targets, including the huge naval guns, were at nearby Changi, an air-raid shelter had been constructed at Whitelawns following the first attack. Shelters had also been built in the gardens of the city's more affluent citizens, mainly for their novelty value, but very few blast walls or public refuges were erected. The main problem with building air-raid shelters, apart from general apathy, was that the watertable beneath the city was very high and any excavation was soon flooded. The sturdy British bungalows afforded some shelter but for those who lived in Chinatown, where entire streets were levelled, on the sampans along the river, or in the Malay kampongs (villages), there was no protection at all. The flimsy, often makeshift homes, if not blown to bits in the initial blast, collapsed into smouldering heaps of timber, atap (palm leaf) and rubble, killing thousands whose bodies were not recovered.

Although the bombing eventually forced the closure of many factories and workshops,

Tony (seated on the pony) and infant Derek, with their nursemaids and groom at Whitelawns

milk was still being delivered. As soon as the 'all clear' sounded, the shops re-opened, inviting well-heeled matrons to view the latest range of 'snappy' day and afternoon frocks recently imported from America. Raffles Hotel, where an orchestra was engaged to play from 8 pm until midnight, was still the place for Singapore's young things to go dancing each evening or to enjoy a leisurely curry tiffin at the midday break. Over at Government House normal protocol remained in force, with guests adhering to a strict dress code and observing all the niceties of gracious living. When shells began to rain on the far side of the island with an intensity to rival anything experienced on the Western Front in World War I, Sir Shenton was most put out. The shelling disturbed his bath.

Such was the feeling of invincibility that at the end of January, when the Allies were finally forced to pull back across the causeway linking Malaya to Singapore, a rumour circulated that it was just a clever ploy to lure the enemy onto the island, allowing the British to fight them on their own patch. Sir Shenton did not help matters by suggesting that citizens with green thumbs should start planting vegetables, lest supplies from the traditional Chinese market gardens begin to dry up. Should any person take up his suggestion, fertiliser would be supplied, free of charge.

With the governor, along with most civilians, believing, or pretending, there was nothing to worry about, Norma Emerson-Elliott had stubbornly refused to listen to any suggestion put to her by her husband, or anyone else, that she should quit Singapore for a safer destination, even though she had the boys to care for and was pregnant with her third child.

The military chiefs, however, were now becoming concerned about the number of women and children on the island. After overcoming their initial disbelief that the Japanese had dared take on the mighty British Empire, they were now urging the evacuation of all 'useless mouths'. Ostrich-like, Sir Shenton refused to pass on the instructions, neglecting not only to inform the civilians that evacuation had been recommended, but that all evacuees would be transported to a safe port, free of charge. Norma, like many others, believed that the Allied forces massed on the island would, as the governor was reported to have remarked, 'shove the little men off'. So why should anyone leave, particularly those who enjoyed an enviable lifestyle? Although there was virtually nothing she could contribute to the war effort, Norma had also been profoundly influenced by the governor's exhortation shortly after hostilities began that European women should stay and fight, 'shoulder to shoulder with their dark-skinned sisters'. Consequently, throughout December and January, ships ferrying troops and materials to Singapore had been returning to their home ports virtually empty.

Unaware of the free passage being offered, those who had sensibly decided to evacuate had paid large amounts to the enterprising shipping companies still issuing tickets. Burns Philp confidently advertised that their first-class tickets to Melbourne, carrying a price tag of £1,000, were interchangeable for the return voyage. Other would-be evacuees who had heard about the free passages turned them down on the grounds that they wanted to go to England, not Australia or India or New Zealand. Consequently, on 8 February, the day the Japanese crossed the Straits of Johor, Singapore was still full of defenceless women and children.

The next morning, news that the enemy was on Singapore Island itself spread, and reality began to set in. Denis Emerson-Elliott, who had humoured his wife up until this point, decided it was time for direct action. After partaking of a frugal breakfast in the cramped cabin of his new command, a navy fairmile (a Harbour Defence Vessel) moored in Keppel Harbour, he managed to obtain a three-hour pass for the afternoon along with an invitation for Norma and the boys to join a party of evacuees being organised by John Wilson, the Anglican Bishop of Singapore.

With the roads in the city jammed with military and emergency vehicles, debris from falling bombs and shelling, fallen power poles, and panic-stricken civilians running hither and thither, time was of the essence. Jumping into the Fiat, he drove as fast as possible to Whitelawns, where he managed to persuade the still reluctant Norma that the time really had come to go. After hurriedly packing a few belongings, including the boys' silver christening cups and a handful of photographs, which she stowed in the boot of the family's Singer sedan, Norma took the front passenger seat beside her husband. Jammed into the rear were two nursemaids dressed in starched white uniforms, complete with veils, and clutching their small charges firmly to their bosoms. Squashed in alongside them was Amah, the family's matriarchal and highly protective housekeeper, who had insisted on supervising the evacuation. With the car already filled to over-capacity there was no room for Chu Lun, Amah's husband, who wanted to come partway to see them off. He solved the problem by pedalling alongside on his bicycle, steering with one hand and clinging grimly to the frame of the open front passenger window with the other.

The car was still on Tanah Merah Besar Road, less than two kilometres from home, when it was spotted by the Japanese Zero. The plane was just above the treetops when the machine-gun opened up. The noise was deafening as the heavy calibre bullets raked the vehicle along the passenger's side, tearing off the front door and puncturing the front and back tyres. As the plane was possibly running short of fuel, or the pilot was intent on finding richer pickings elsewhere, he fortunately did not attempt a second run.

Bringing the car to an abrupt stop, Denis checked his passengers. Miraculously, no one was hurt, not even Chu Lun, who had let go of the vehicle before the bullets hit only to go into an uncontrolled slide, hitting a tree and smashing his bike in the process. Nevertheless, the evacuation attempt was clearly off. After nursing the damaged Singer back to Whitelawns, Denis returned to his ship in the Marvelette, leaving Chu Lun to bemoan the loss of his unrepairable bicycle, his only mode of transport.

The next day, 10 February, dawned hot and oppressive. Denis had intended to return to his family early that morning, but was ordered to sea at first light to ferry evacuees out to a line of ships lying off Keppel Harbour. There was little cloud cover and enemy planes were soon overhead, dropping bombs with impunity all along the wharves and on any vessel in or near the harbour waters. Denis and his crew spent a harrowing day dodging bombs as they rescued scores of evacuees whose transfer craft had been attacked. Bodies and bits of bodies were everywhere. As his small ship ploughed resolutely through the debris-strewn water, Denis tried to blot out the vision of children the same age as his own, floating face down, their blond hair fanning out like halos. With everyone concentrating on saving the living there was no time to check identities, and for the remainder of that long and terrible day he was haunted by the fear that his own family was among the 500 civilians killed.[1]

On land the situation was no better. With the enemy now on the island the Allies had been retreating towards the city, eventually forcing all the military, plus the million or so civilians and refugees from Malaya, into a an ever-decreasing circle. That morning General Archibald Wavell, Commander-in-Chief of all American, British, Dutch and Australian forces in the area, had arrived from his headquarters in Java. Rapidly appraising the situation, he ordered the Royal Air Force to plough up all the airfields, destroy all remaining ammunition, fuel and other supplies, and leave at once for the Dutch East Indies. An American pilot serving with the RAF, Arthur Donahue, flew the last Hurricane fighter plane to Java that afternoon.

Wavell's assessment that the battle was not going well and that he did not hold much hope of any prolonged resistance was now shared by the general public, who had only to look about them to see what was happening. To the north, clouds of billowing smoke from the massive oil storage tanks at Kranji and Bukit Timah, set on fire as part of a scorched earth policy, spiralled menacingly into the air, covering everyone in an oily sludge every time it rained. The destruction of other oil reserves and military supplies soon followed. Downtown, piles of paper currency from banks and treasury reserves were put to the torch, while monsoon drains were awash with thousands of litres of liquor as bond stores and cellars were hurriedly emptied. This, combined with the constant shelling, air raids, the nauseating stench from hundreds of unburied corpses and the sound of small arms and machine-gun fire, was more than sufficient warning. People were now attempting to leave the island in droves.

The panic, which had begun shortly after the artillery barrage began, was at fever pitch. Clifford Pier, directly opposite the imposing Fullerton Building which, among other things, housed the General Post Office, was the closest embarkation point to the city. Here the situation was chaotic, with terrified men, women and children clamouring for a place aboard a ship – any ship at all. Displaying great equanimity, the staff of the P&O shipping line were still selling tickets – not from the city office, which had been bombed, but from the manager's house. Here hopeful passengers who had turned up their noses when previously offered tickets to 'unsuitable' destinations, stood in long, snaking lines for hours in the scorching heat, small children clinging fretfully to their mothers' skirts. With berths at a premium, those who tried to short-circuit the system by attempting to board ships without tickets were sent back down the gangway, jostling with those trying to force their way up.

Official travel passes had been issued, but only to selected white civil servants and the families of defence personnel, and to some Eurasians who had sufficient documentation at hand to satisfy the bureaucrats that they were of part-British extraction. Despite the governor's declaration only weeks before that the brown-skinned sisters were as precious to the Colonial Administration as the white, and that all citizens would be treated equally, the Malay, Indian and Chinese civil servants, along with the Oriental wives of British citizens, did not stand a chance. Under this 'Europeans only' policy, loyal Chinese and Malay maritime employees suddenly found that their services had been terminated, on the orders of the Royal Navy, and their jobs given to Europeans, many of whom were completely unqualified to hold the position. With no hope of evacuation, the non-Europeans ran in all directions, mingling with stragglers and a number of army deserters looking for booty and a way to escape the island. Looters were everywhere, right across the city, even normally law-abiding housewives rushing from one bombed-out warehouse and shop to another, loading up with food and any goods they thought might come in useful.

Denis had no worries that his wife and family would qualify for immediate evacuation. Apart from the fact that he had a written invitation for them to join the bishop's party, he was definitely white, Anglo-Saxon and very Protestant – Church of England. Norma, whose family had fled the Russian revolution, was undeniably 'White Russian', and related to nobility. Furthermore, Denis was not just any naval lieutenant. His commission with the RNVR was a blind, a cover. So too was the profitable import-export business he had run before the outbreak of war. Mr Emerson-Elliott, the respectable, wealthy businessman and more recently urbane naval officer, was a long-serving member of His Majesty's Secret Service.

Singapore city against a background of billowing smoke from the burning oil reserves

2

Secret business

1938–1941

Denis was actually Leonard Emerson, born in Lambeth, London, on 20 April 1905. After attending school in London and then Taunton in the county of Somerset, he entered the University of Aberdeen, Scotland, where he lived with a Professor Garden and his family while studying agricultural science. It seems that the professor had links to British Intelligence and it was through him that Denis and others were recruited. A keen sportsman, young Emerson was a skilled cricketer and rugby player, representing both the university and, later, the London Scottish Rugby Club. In the mid-1920s, he married Doris Rathbone and they had a daughter, Patricia, but the marriage did not meet with the approval of the Emerson family. The couple parted, and Denis left rather mysteriously for Srinagar, Kashmir, for reasons which were not disclosed.

In 1929, with a passport issued by the British Government now identifying him as Leslie Denis Elliott, he sailed on the P&O liner *Kalyan* for Malaya where he worked (for official purposes) as an agricultural scientist on an experimental plantation owned by Dunlop Rubber Estates. He remained with Dunlop for a number of years before joining Guthries, a Scottish trading company, where he was known as 'Laddie' to his close friends, mainly from Deeside, near Aberdeen, his old stamping ground. According to his latest passport, his name was now Leslie Denis Emerson-Elliott, born in Taunton in 1908. In 1934, and at his request, Doris divorced him. Within eighteen months or so he met Nona Brayer-Roberts, a beautiful Russian girl. Her mother was Julia Orlov, daughter of Vasily Orlov, a member of the Russian nobility who lived in Astrakhan, at the mouth of the Volga River.

Denis, while on a 'mysterious' visit to Kashmir

Julia, who was born in 1900, had two long-term relationships. The first was with Carl-Gustav Brayer, whom she married in 1918, following the birth of Nona in August the previous year. When the revolution began the family fled to India, where Daisy was born in Bombay in 1924. From here they moved to Malaya and Singapore where a third child, another daughter, arrived in 1925. Shortly afterwards Carl-Gustav disappeared, never to be seen again.

Now in Kuala Lumpur, Julia met and married Ernest Roberts, a tea merchant and tin-miner from Deeside who was a friend of Professor Garden. It was through Roberts, a member of the 'Deeside set', that Denis met the teenaged Nona, who had added her stepfather's name to her own. Although Denis was twelve years older than Nona, it was a great and rather unconventional love match, especially in a society where couples did not live together before marriage. When they moved to Singapore, where they were not known and where Denis, officially, ran a highly profitable import-export business, Nona was introduced as Norma Emerson-Elliott, Denis's English wife, born also in Taunton. She appears to have had no problem in either changing her name or her origins, possibly because she was already involved, either directly or indirectly, with intelligence gathering through her stepfather. In 1941 the couple, now proud and doting parents of two sons, were quietly married at St Andrews Cathedral, Singapore, with Archdeacon Grahame-White officiating.

By this time Denis had been working for undercover agencies including Britain's Secret Intelligence Service (SIS) for a number of years. Founded in England in 1909 as the Secret Service Bureau (SIB), in response to a widely held public belief that all Germans were spies, it was headed initially by Major Vernon Kell. A joint initiative of the British Admiralty and the War Office, SIB was split into a Foreign Section (navy) which specialised in foreign espionage under the leadership of Captain Sir George Mansfield Smith-Cumming, and a Home Section (army) which concentrated on internal counter-espionage activities, under Kell.

Before the Great War, the budget allocated to the Foreign Section was severely restricted, and its few agents tended to regard espionage as 'capital sport'. However, with the outbreak of hostilities an injection of funds greatly expanded the service, allowing more agents to be recruited. Among them were the well-known writers Compton Mackenzie, John Buchan and W Somerset Maugham. However, the best known full-time operative was Sidney Reilly who, decades later, would become known to television viewers as 'Reilly, Ace of Spies'.

In 1919 Smith-Cumming's Foreign Section took over the Government Code and Cypher School and, in 1921, became the Secret Intelligence Service or Directorate of Military Intelligence, Section 6 – MI6, the name by which it would become popularly known. Kell's Home Section was now the Security Service or Directorate of Military Intelligence Section 5 – MI5. The numbers 1 to 19 were used to designate the various directorates, though 13 and 18 were not allocated. Section 6's director, who generally dropped the Smith from his name, had the habit of signing himself simply as 'C' – and always in green ink. This idiosyncrasy evolved as an identification code, which was used by all future SIS/MI6 directors when signing documents to retain anonymity.

In this post-World War I period a network of MI6 station commanders, working under diplomatic cover as 'Passport Control Officers', was also established. Based in British embassies in their various cities, their main role was to keep an eye on Communists in Europe and the East, but particularly Russian Bolshevists. In 1923 Cumming died and was replaced by Admiral Hugh Sinclair. In 1925, having unsuccessfully tried to have MI5 absorbed into MI6 to strengthen the fight against bolshevism, Sinclair established his own counter-espionage section. By 1938, with a new war in Europe looming, several new subsections of MI6 were created, including Section D, whose operatives were to conduct political covert and paramilitary missions in time of war. To this end, in the European spring of 1938, Sinclair used his own funds to purchase the sprawling Victorian mansion, Bletchley Park, to be used as an intelligence station. The property, known as Station X (the Roman numeral for Section 10), would house cipher experts intent on cracking and reading enemy codes. However, Sinclair did not live long enough to see D Section or Bletchley Park reach their potential. He died in November 1939.

One of his colleagues had been Lieutenant-Colonel Sir Claude Edward Dansey, whose code name was Z. Known also as Colonel Z, Dansey was a long-serving member of SIS. While assigned as station chief in Rome, where he had kept a close watch on Mussolini's Fascist movement, Dansey had become concerned that MI6 had collected no worthwhile intelligence in Europe, where war appeared to be a distinct possibility. He also saw that because of budget cuts many agents were now retired military personnel on pensions who drew little or no salary, thereby creating an environment apathy and incompetence. However, his greatest concern was that the position of Passport Control Officer had been compromised years ago – everyone knew that whoever held this diplomatic post was the head of MI6 in that particular city.

Taking the initiative, Dansey began to rely on a network of businessmen which he had built up over the years and who, being outside the bureaucratic system, were not affected by the petty jealousies and favour seeking prevalent at the time. With no one doing anything about the passport control officer system, Dansey set about establishing a hidden structure running parallel to MI6 which he named Z Organisation, after his own code name. By 1936, Z Organisation had over two hundred operatives, who collected intelligence for the sheer thrill of it. Forbidden to take extreme risks, to record anything on paper, take photographs or carry any type of spy equipment, these businessmen and journalists used their own credentials as cover, with film-maker Alexander Korda visiting sensitive locations on the pretext he was scouting for film locations.

Shortly before World War II broke out, Dansey was given the job of heading covert intelligence operations. A few months later hostilities began and the intelligence disaster he had long predicted occurred. Operations in The Hague, the major collection point for intelligence gathering, were penetrated by Nazi agents and the retired British officers in control captured. Within a few days the Nazis knew everything and the structure was destroyed. Dansey immediately brought his Z Organisation out of deep cover. Within weeks his men were providing more and much better intelligence than had been the case under the old structure. Dansey was promoted to the post of deputy director to MI6's new director, Lieutenant-Colonel Menzies, who had succeeded Sinclair.

Stewart Graham Menzies (pronounced 'Mingis') had joined MI6 at the end of the Great War. Said to be the illegitimate son of the then Prince of Wales (the future King Edward VII), he was born in 1890 into a wealthy family with considerable interests in whisky distilleries. Under Menzies' directorship, intelligence and counter-intelligence departments were expanded; he also supervised the code-breaking efforts at Bletchley Park.

On 22 June 1940, Henri-Philippe Pétain, deputy premier of France, signed an armistice with Nazi Germany. The country was now split into an occupied zone under Nazi rule and an unoccupied zone controlled by the pro-German Vichy French under Marshal Pétain. General de Gaulle and his Free French went into exile, determined to fight on. Just over a week later, a meeting was held at the British Foreign Office to discuss what steps could be taken to assist them. On 2 July Hugh Dalton, recently appointed to the Ministry for Economic Warfare (established to oversee covert activities), wrote to Foreign Secretary Lord Halifax suggesting the establishment of a new organisation to 'co-ordinate, inspire, control and assist the nationals of possessed countries, who must themselves be the direct participants'. A fortnight later, on 16 July and after much discussion, Dalton was directed by Prime Minister Winston Churchill to 'set Europe ablaze'.

The means by which this was to be achieved was by Special Operations Executive or SOE, which would not only undertake covert missions in occupied countries but also prepare for resistance after the expected invasion of Britain. Answerable to Churchill, it was a highly secret organisation, funded under an arrangement through the Foreign Office, about which no questions could be asked. Indeed, the minute setting up SOE stated it would be 'very undesirable' for any questions to be asked at all, let alone answered. The new organisation comprised MI6's Section D, a propaganda section named EH (after Electra House, where it was situated), and MIR (Military Intelligence Research), which was pretty much a one-man outfit concentrating on irregular warfare methods.

SOE was divided into three sections: SO1 for propaganda, SO2 for active operations and SO3 for planning. After a short stint in a couple of totally unsuitable temporary premises, SOE, code-named Inter-Allied Liaison Department, moved into 64 Baker Street, a large office building in south-east Marylebone referred to as 'the Home Station'. Baker Street was a well-known address – Number 221B (which did not exist) was home to the fictional

Sherlock Holmes. When requiring 'undercover' work to be carried out, the famous detective occasionally called on the assistance of a band of street urchins, 'the Baker Street Irregulars' – a name soon adopted to describe those recruited to SOE.

It was an apt term. Dalton believed that activities in which SOE was to be involved required the mind of a subversive – a rebel who understood what was required to demoralise and bring the enemy to its knees. Many different methods would be needed, ranging from assassinations and liquidating traitors to military and industrial sabotage, which encompassed organising labour strikes, disseminating constant propaganda and provoking boycotts and riots – all of which, he believed, could be better achieved by civilian minds, rather than military.

As was the case with other pre-war secret services, recruitment initially was by word of mouth, but later became better organised, with formal 'job' interviews and reasonable fluency in a second language a mandatory requirement. Training was carried out at special schools established on secluded country estates sited from Beaulieu, on England's southern coast, to the Scottish Highlands. Courses covered included security, unarmed combat and silent killing, espionage trade-craft (which incorporated disguises, how to live secretly in an occupied zone, mechanical gadgets and secret ink), resistance to interrogation, parachuting, signalling and sabotage. Using the code-name Inter-Services Research Bureau (ISRB), SOE also established Station IX at The Frythe, a former hotel at Welwyn outside London. Here mechanically minded and inventive personnel developed specialised equipment and gadgetry, including radios, weapons, explosive devices and booby traps, for use by agents and covert raiding parties. In a former roadhouse in north London known as The Thatched Barn, film director Elder Willis ran the Camouflage Section, where ex-prop makers fashioned ingenious devices concealed inside papier-mâché or plaster shapes. By the end of the war, SOE would train 11,500 agents, 7,500 of whom operated in occupied Europe, particularly in France, where 500,000 Frenchmen armed by SOE agents conducted 3,000 acts of sabotage against the local railway system. It is estimated that the organisation supported close to one million operatives, world wide.

SOE, mindful that the MI6 network had collapsed the previous year, built its own network, initially parachuting agents into occupied territory 'blind' until more sophisticated methods evolved. SOE operations, being more overtly offensive and often involving an alliance with anti-establishment groups such as Communists, soon clashed with the more discreet methods employed by MI6, which preferred to work quietly, using influential people and authorities to gain its intelligence.

When security increased in occupied countries because of SOE's activity, restricting MI6 operations, a turf war between the parent and its high-profile offspring broke out. MI6 chief Stuart Menzies denounced SOE as 'amateur, dangerous and bogus' and tried to exert massive internal pressure to shut the organisation down. Some senior members of the armed forces, accustomed to abiding by the gentlemanly rules of the Geneva Convention, did not approve of the type of warfare carried out by SOE, either. Bomber Command, which believed the best way to win the war was by bombing Germany out of existence, voiced its objections through Air Chief Marshal Charles Portal, who declared:

> The dropping of men dressed in civilian clothes for purposes of attempting to
> kill members of the opposing forces is not an operation with which the Royal Air
> Force should be associated ... There is a vast difference in ethics between the time-
> honoured operation of the dropping of a spy from the air and this entirely new
> scheme for dropping what one can only call assassins.

Churchill, however, thought differently. With the prime minister as its protector, SOE was inviolate.

Irrespective of their background or origins, those who worked with SOE were united by the one aim – overthrowing the enemy, by fair means or foul. Some, who spoke a foreign language fluently, such as Australia's Nancy Wake (known as the White Mouse) operated behind enemy lines for extended periods. Others were flown or parachuted in to perform a specific task such as sabotage, or to assist local resistance groups. Yet others collected intelligence abroad or at home. Among the latter were the high-profile actors Laurence Olivier, Noel Coward, David Niven and Anthony Quayle.

By the time the Japanese entered the war, SOE, with its European operations established, was in a position to expand into Singapore where other agencies had been involved in counter-intelligence against the Japanese for many years. From 1914 inspectors-general of police, aware of the development of an extensive Japanese spy network, had been keeping close watch through their Special Branches (SB) on 'immigrants' engaged in mining, rubber, fishing, trade, commerce, banking and agriculture. Small businesses, such as barber shops, were always a good source of local gossip for Japanese agents, as were Japanese-run brothels. Information gleaned from a great variety of sources was constantly relayed to Japan by these nationals, along with detailed charts of the coastlines, mapped by 'fishermen'. The Special Branches reported regularly on the 'Japanese menace', but were only able to take action when allowed to do so, since Foreign Office policy required all matters regarding Japan to be treated with kid gloves, following the repeal of the Anglo-Japanese Treaty.

In 1924 the Malayan Political Advisory Bureau, headed by the Inspector-General, was established to disseminate internal security information to government departments and the military. By 1931 the Bureau had been replaced by a Standing Committee on Intelligence which, with its military equivalent (the Joint Intelligence Bureau), produced monthly intelligence summaries. Two years later, disturbed by the growth in overt and covert activities by Japanese agents (including the purchase of information on the Singapore Naval Base, the structural plans of key bridges and important railway junctions, and the acquisition of large rubber plantations in strategic areas), the Singapore and Federated Malay States Police Forces formed Japanese Sections in their Special Branches.

Throughout this period there was no MI6 representative at the Foreign Office in Singapore, although there was one in Hong Kong. However, MI5's 'man in Singapore', who reported directly to Kell, had been maintaining a presence there as 'Defence Security Officer'. In October 1936, that man was Colonel Hayley Bell, aged 58, who had extensive experience in the Far East, spoke seven Chinese dialects as well as Russian, and had a direct intelligence link to the British army, which bypassed the local top brass. Mervyn Wynne, Head of Special Branch, also sent reports without the knowledge of his superiors.

Also appointed to Singapore that year was Major K Morgan, Indian Army, now heading the Japanese Section of the Special Branch at Police Headquarters. As Morgan jealously guarded and kept his information to himself, Bell went his own way. Working with hand-picked agents, including businessmen such as John Becker and mining engineer Robert 'Pat' Garden, whose jobs took them frequently all around Malaya and to adjacent countries, he exposed the full extent of the Japanese spy network, as well as the cosy relationship Japan appeared to have developed with Malaya's near neighbour Siam (now Thailand). Even more alarming, Bell's investigations revealed not only great deficiencies in defence but also that the most likely place for a Japanese invasion was the north-eastern coast of Malaya and southern Siam during the north-east monsoon, a time-frame previously considered to be most unlikely.

Bell's intelligence, which was also critical of local and military administration, was not well received locally. The governor, the defence chiefs (apart from the Navy, which had immediately set about rectifying its areas of weakness) and the pro-Thai British Minister in Bangkok, all of whom who dismissed parts of the report as sensationalist, would much rather not know that such a disturbing document existed. Sir Shenton Thomas had reportedly proclaimed Bell's wariness of Japan as a preposterous notion, declaring 'who but a fool, Hayley Bell, thinks Japan wants Singapore'. General Officer Commanding General Dobbie was, however, concerned about the lack of defences in Malaya and applied for funding to build some. A measly £60,000 was allocated; when Dobbie was recalled to England all work stopped, with only one third of the money spent.

In 1938, after Bell's perceptive analysis regarding invasion strategy had been proven by independent exercises, his full report was forwarded to England, advising that the security of the naval base depended entirely on holding northern Malaya and the southern state of Johor. The report was evidently as unpopular in Britain as it had been locally. In 1939, when Bell was recalled to England at the request of Sir Shenton, the excellent counter-espionage organisation he had set up was disbanded, giving the Japanese spy network virtually free rein.

That year MI6, which had been operating on a fairly small scale in Hong Kong, moved to Singapore with the appointment of a businessman and former Inspector General of Police in Singapore, Godfrey Denham. Denham occupied an office in the police CID building next to MI5's Colonel Johnston, whose assistant he claimed to be. He was actually in control of a huge area, stretching from the Dutch East Indies to Japan and from the Philippines to Burma. With only a handful of agents, all European, working for MI6, he set about creating a network of 'native' agents who could easily melt into the local scene. The Police Inspector General, Dickie Dickinson, one of the very few to know Denham's true role, facilitated this by introducing him to the chief secretary of the local Communist Party, Loi Tek.

At about the same time as Denham arrived, the Far East Combined Bureau, previously stationed in Hong Kong, took over offices and accommodation in a secluded section of the Singapore Naval Base. Although this organisation, which was in contact with MI6, was run by the Admiralty, officers from the army and the air force, who reported directly to their own senior officers, were 'attached', along with liaison officers from the Australian, French, Dutch and American military. A vital component of the Far East Combined Bureau was Y Section, which detected, intercepted and decrypted enemy wireless signals. Mainstream intelligence was gathered over a vast area, throughout the Far East and the Pacific and Indian oceans. Local sources included the offices of the Chief Censor, the Director of Information, the Controller of Enemy Property, Special Branch, MI5's Defence Security Officer, diplomats, consulates, and agents in the private sector, most notably Reuters' newsagency and Cable & Wireless, which tapped and monitored telegraphic transmissions. In December of that same year, the Far East Combined Bureau also established the Far Eastern Security Section (known as FESS). Using the same sources as the Bureau, its brief was 'to collect, co-ordinate and pass to the authorities concerned reports of anti-British activity in the area'.

A few days later, in very early January 1940, a Special Liaison Unit from Bletchley Park arrived in Singapore to handle and control all special intelligence gleaned from Y (intercept) sources. The intelligence obtained from decrypted enemy signals was known as 'Ultra' and was so secret that extraordinary precautions were taken to keep it that way, even to the extent of employing technicians not above the rank of sergeant, in order to maintain a very low profile. Ultra messages were destroyed as soon as they were read and understood, and no recipient was permitted to forward one. Should any action be taken as a result of information received, it must be done in such a way as to give no hint to the enemy that his signals were being read. If this was impossible, no action could be taken.

In September 1940 the military in Singapore, along with the security and intelligence services, suffered a severe setback when SS *Autonedan* was intercepted en route from London by the German raider *Atlantis* in the Indian Ocean and relieved of the contents of the strong room. This included top-secret reports from MI6 and Naval Intelligence, as well as advice from the chiefs of staff that no planes or ships could be spared to reinforce Singapore and Malaya – even though, without them, a Japanese invasion could not be repelled. The defenders would have to make do with what they had. The Germans forwarded the report to the Japanese, who had long believed that the Allied powers had an integrated defence plan for the area. On receipt of this priceless information they discovered that this was a myth and that the vision of Singapore, the fortress, an illusion.

Rather late in the day, the Ministry for Economic Warfare decided that an SOE presence was warranted in Singapore, to improve on the espionage, counter-espionage and other ground intelligence operating in the Far East. A Royal Marine, Lieutenant-Colonel Alan Warren, was sent out in March 1941 to assess the situation and two months later SOE Far East opened, with offices in the Cathay Building, Singapore's only skyscraper. A civilian agent, Valentine St John Killery, who had worked for many years in the Far East for Imperial Chemical Industries, was appointed to head the operation, which had been given the cover name Oriental Mission (OM). With him were a fellow businessman from ICI, Basil Goodfellow, and Major Jim Gavin, Royal Engineers, who had previously commanded SOE's Special Training Centre in the Scottish Highlands. Sir George Sansom, a recognised Britain-Japan expert, was brought from Tokyo, where he was attached to the British Embassy, to advise and assist them.

With SOE London well aware from experience in Europe of the value of agents working on the 'inside' in occupied zones, part of the Oriental Mission's brief was to train and to organise local 'stay behind' parties, in the event of an invasion. To facilitate this, Operation Puma established a training school known successively as Scapula, the School of Demolitions and, finally, Number 101 Special Training School. It occupied a mansion and estate belonging to J B David, a wealthy Armenian merchant, situated at Tanjung Balai – a headland connected to Singapore Island by a long narrow spit at the mouth of the Jurong River, on the western side of the island. In October, in view of the likelihood of war with Japan, SOE ordered the school's CO, Captain Ambrose Trappes-Lomax, to proceed to Australia, an order which was postponed as Singapore's priority was greater. At about this time, Denis Emerson-Elliott officially joined the ranks of SOE. Known also as BB007, his true role was protected by commissioning him into the Royal Naval Reserve, with the rank of lieutenant.

As SOE's credo was that only those who needed to know, needed to know, neither the General Officer Commanding, Lieutenant-General Arthur Percival, nor Sir Shenton Thomas, were aware of their planned activities. Percival found out by accident, and informed Sir Shenton. After weeks of discussion, the idea was rejected on the grounds that the scheme would be a drain on available manpower and, in any case, white men would not be able to move freely in occupied territory. Any suggestion that Chinese might be employed was brushed aside – Sir Shenton and the general agreed that should the concept of stay-behind parties become known among the non-European community, it would not be good for morale. In late December SOE finally won the argument but the delay had greatly devalued the potential of the project.

Working closely with SOE and the Oriental Mission, particularly its propaganda arm (code-named the Economic Research Bureau), was another propaganda division of the ironically titled British Ministry for Information. Known as the Far Eastern Bureau, which had no connection to the Admiralty's similarly named Far East Combined Bureau, it was headed by barrister Robert Heeley Scott. He was well versed in the aims of MI6 and SOE, having worked for the British Foreign Office for years – in Manchuria in 1931, Shanghai from 1932–37 and Chungking in 1938. From there he had gone to Tokyo, where he had carried out propaganda, until his transfer to Singapore. Assisting Scott in his new role were Sir George Sansom and an Australian journalist, John Galvin, who had been given the task of recruiting staff. Galvin, after stints in Australia and London, had transferred to China in 1937, and in 1940 was carrying out propaganda and other covert work for MI6 through the Far Eastern Bureau, using journalism as a cover.

Galvin and Sansom decided the best vehicle for their propaganda would be with a reputable Australian newspaper, with international links. Galvin returned to Australia where, with the help of Prime Minister Robert Menzies, he was referred to Warwick Fairfax and the *Sydney Morning Herald*. In an agreement facilitated by Sydney businessman and MI6 agent George Proud (of the well-known Sydney jewellery family), Fairfax and his general manager agreed to send correspondents to Singapore, Manila and Chungking to disseminate propaganda. In return, the newspaper received top-secret payments of a hefty £1,250 per quarter. Although the British did not consider that any substantial service had been provided after 1942, the payments continued until the end of the war as a gesture of goodwill.

Staff recruited by Galvin to manufacture and distribute propaganda included a number of Australians: Lionel Wigmore, who would become an official war historian, worked from April 1941 in Singapore with the Department of Information, the antipodean equivalent of the British Ministry for Information; his colleague John Proud of the Royal Australian Navy (RAN) and also a member of the jewellery family; Ian Morrison, who lived in Singapore and was correspondent to *The Times*, London; Rohan Rivett, of the Malaya Broadcasting Corporation; Lorraine Stumm, wife of an Australian Air Force pilot stationed in Singapore, who was employed by the *Malaya Tribune*; and Galvin's friend, journalist Stanley Smith, who would later head covert operations in China. There were a number of others, such as Rivett's colleague Giles Playfair and a young Chinese woman, Doris Lim, who had been raised in Shanghai and spoke English with an American accent. 'Wanted' by the Japanese, she had worked for British intelligence in north China, escaping just before the city of Tientsin was overrun by enemy troops.

Using the Malay Broadcasting Service and the local and international press, the SOE recruits at the Oriental Mission's Far Eastern Bureau began to wage psychological warfare against Japan by distributing and publishing material designed to boost the Allied image and to instil mistrust, doubt and fear about the wisdom of Japan's entering into hostilities against the combined might of the Allied forces. Their efforts were overseen by Australian Ted Sayers, acting director of the Department of Information and president of the Australian Journalists' Association. Two weeks after his appointment, Sayers became the Director of Economic Research with the Ministry for Economic Warfare (SOE). Using his cover as the Far Eastern representative of British Overseas Features, he was now responsible for placing as much propaganda as possible in as many media outlets as possible.

Using on-the-spot 'observers' and information obtained from 'well-informed circles', the newspapers and radio stations distributed a vast amount of pro-Allied and anti-Japanese propaganda, including Brooke-Popham's fantastic claims about Allied air power. The articles, which continued to be published until the very fall of Singapore, commented on a range of topics, such as Japan's ability to wage war at sea, suggesting that while the Japanese may have developed 'some specialities', they had not kept pace with Western inventions and it would therefore be foolhardy to take on the might of the British Navy. One report, ostensibly from Manila, referred to a growing feeling that Japan had deserted its Axis partners, because there were doubts that Germany could win the war. Since reputable news agencies were distributing this material, the reports were believed by many people, including Norma Emerson-Elliott. The feeling of false security the reports created, combined with general apathy, was a recipe for disaster.

The Japanese, however, were not fooled at all.

3

Exodus

10–15 February 1942

It was not until late in the afternoon of 10 February, his job of impounding enemy-owned and enemy-registered vessels finally completed, that Denis Emerson-Elliott was able to head for home. He arrived in the Marvelette just as night fell, the last rays of the sun setting behind the billowing clouds of smoke bathing the house and garden in lurid shades of pink and bronze. To his surprise the house was empty, but before he had time to worry Chu Lun appeared, informing him that Norma and the children had gone with Archdeacon Grahame-White to Bishopsgate, home of Bishop Wilson, where the evacuation party was assembling.

The archdeacon, a family friend, had arrived at Whitelawns in a Model T Ford that morning to find Norma now in two minds about evacuation. She was fully aware of the danger she faced. Her home was close to Changi, a legitimate enemy target which had already been bombed and strafed repeatedly. However, to Norma's way of thinking, to accept voluntary evacuation was akin to running away and, as Denis was not leaving, she felt strongly that she too should stay.

Puffing quietly on one of his trademark small cigars, Grahame-White sat in the shade of the verandah and listened to her impassioned arguments, looking as if he had all the time in the world. His exterior appeared cool and calm but his stomach was churning with anxiety. Here was this attractive woman, mother of two small children and expecting a third, voicing heroic and patriotic sentiments while enemy patrols were advancing as she spoke and enemy shells and bombs were exploding not far away. Fortunately, patience, common sense and persuasive argument finally won the day.

Leaving Amah to bury the family silver and other valuables in the garden for safekeeping, Denis drove to Bishopsgate to say good-bye to his family. To his dismay, he discovered that the entire party had left that afternoon to board one of the ships in Keppel Harbour. Which one, the bishop's staff did not know. This was disquieting news. Had Norma and the boys managed to get away in time? Were they on the docks when the bombs fell? Or on one of the transfer vessels? Could two of the lifeless little bodies floating in the sea be his children, after all?

With no way of finding out, as the bishop himself was not at home, Denis reported to Fort Canning where he had been reassigned as one of four duty officers. Occupying a hill overlooking the city and waterfront, the complex consisted of blocks of impressive three-storeyed colonial-style buildings and a massive and greatly fortified underground bunker which housed, among other things, secret naval communications. The fortress, which had its own independent generators, water and air supplies, was protected from gas and blast attack by special doors and from bombing and shelling by the heavily reinforced walls and roof. With isolated enemy patrols now on the outskirts of the city Denis was not surprised to learn that General Percival had moved his headquarters, formerly at the Syme Road barracks, to Fort Canning and that Malaya Command was now directing operations against the Japanese from the bunker.

Late the following afternoon, Wednesday 11 February, Denis was hard at work when he was called to the office of his immediate superior, Captain George Mulock. The two men, heavily involved in naval intelligence and the SIS and SOE networks, knew each other well.

Disposition of troops on Singapore Island, 8 February 1942

Aged sixty, the captain had been brought out of retirement in 1939 to take up the role of Extended Defence Officer. More recently he had also held the post of Captain of Auxiliary Vessels, an appointment he had relinquished to Commander Bayly on 1 February only to find himself back in charge nine days later. With the naval base now in Japanese hands and many naval personnel evacuated, his successor had fled to the safety of Java, ignoring direct orders from Admiral Spooner to return at once. Mulock, who was in charge of evacuating key military personnel and civilians, ordered Denis to join the evacuation ship *Empire Star* as an 'additional officer', immediately.

In peacetime, the Blue Star Line's 11,000-tonne refrigerated cargo liner transported frozen meat from Australia and New Zealand to Britain. With the outbreak of war, it also carried war materiel. The vessel, loaded with motor transport, anti-aircraft guns, Bren-gun carriers, light tanks and 2,000 tonnes of ammunition, had been in port for almost a fortnight, having arrived on 29 January as part of Convoy BM11, a fleet of five merchant ships bringing 17,000 troops of the British 18th Division to reinforce Singapore. With the docks in Keppel Harbour being constantly bombed, *Empire Star* had been ordered to anchor offshore in the Dangerous Goods area, where she was forced to remain until 6 February when, under cover of darkness, she eased into Keppel Harbour. With the skipper, Captain Selwyn Capon, unable to find any dockworkers willing to unload her, the crew had no option but to do the job themselves. They were only partway through the task when enemy bombers arrived, forcing a hurried return to the former anchorage. There *Empire Star* remained, miraculously undamaged by repeated enemy air strikes until 9 February when, with the Allied ammunition dumps near the causeway now in grave danger of falling to the enemy, she was ordered to a berth at Number 4 wharf, with instructions to unload the precious and desperately needed ammunition at all costs. As shells whistled overhead and bombs fell all around, the crew toiled for a day and a night to complete the mammoth task.

With the cargo finally offloaded, *Empire Star* was now ready to leave for Australia, via Tanjung Priok in Java, the port servicing Batavia (now Jakarta). Ostensibly, Denis was boarding the ship to take her through the minefields, although this task was already in the capable hands of Captain George Wright of the Singapore Pilots Association, who had been on board for hours. One of ten pilots operating in Singapore, he had excellent knowledge of the minefields as well as the harbour waters. The vessel was supposed to have sailed at noon but with Singapore's future looking bleak, Air Vice-Marshal Pulford had ordered the evacuation to Java of all members of the RAF still in Singapore, including himself. *Empire Star*, therefore, was ordered to delay departure in order to reload much of the cargo destined for the RAF and to embark a number of British and New Zealand air force personnel, along with more civilian evacuees. Mid-afternoon, Charlie Johnstone, an Australian pilot serving with the RAF, was among the airmen told to pack a small bag and report to a hotel in Singapore before marching to the harbour, the city roads by this time being all but impassable.

Captain Wright was concerned about the delay, which would put the time of departure back by several hours. Protected to the south by Blakang Mati Island (now Sentosa), Keppel Harbour was only 228 metres wide and, since all the tug-boats been destroyed by bombs or deserted by their crews, the 160-metre-long ship would have to clear the dockside area without assistance – a task best accomplished on an ebb tide. To further complicate the situation, the harbour remained under constant attack from shelling and waves of enemy bombers targeting the oil storage tanks on Blakang Mati and nearby Brani Island.

Who engineered the need for an 'additional officer' on board the vessel, creating a spot for Denis, is not clear, but before Singapore fell SOE was very anxious to evacuate as soon as possible anyone involved in covert activities, which included all those supervising the insertion of 'stay-behind-parties' and the elimination of enemy agents and other 'undesirables' by a special 'death squad'. Mulock gave Denis papers to deliver to the ship's captain, stressing that he must destroy his car before boarding to prevent it from falling into enemy hands. Should he not be able to leave for any reason, he must try to return to Fort Canning, where his personal safety, and those of other key personnel, was guaranteed by armed Sikh guards. As Denis turned to leave the office, Mulock caught his eye and said 'Oh, and by the way Denis – I think you will find Norma and the children are aboard the ship, so take particular care with those minefields!'

He had an hour to reach Number 4 wharf at Keppel Harbour, about six or seven kilometres away. Normally, this would have been more than ample time to cover the distance, but with the city now a complete shambles he realised it could be a near-run thing. The Marvelette had covered less than two kilometres when Denis saw a row of lamp posts, directly ahead, falling like wheat stalks before the scythe. Having had virtually no sleep for days, his tired brain did not connect the toppling lamp posts with an air raid – until he saw people from the vehicle in front sprinting across the road to take cover in the deep monsoon drain. Following their lead, he flung himself into the drain as a stick of bombs lifted the road surface where he had left his car, saving him the bother of having to dispose of it later.

With the danger past, at least for the time being, he set out on foot for the harbour, aware that time was running out. As he made his way along the desolate streets, the familiar landmarks now reduced to rubble and the sun blotted out by clouds of billowing black smoke, a Bren-gun carrier slithered to a stop beside him. Denis was in luck. The carrier was in the hands of an anti-aircraft gun crew stationed at Number 4 wharf, the gunners having left their post only temporarily in a fruitless search for more ammunition. Picking his way around bomb craters and manoeuvring around festoons of telegraph and phone lines dangling from teetering poles, the driver dropped his passenger at the dockyard gates without further incident.

It was now a little before 6.30 pm. Denis threaded his way through debris and abandoned vehicles, some with their engines still running, and onto the wharf. Embarkation appeared to be almost complete with just a small crowd bravely waiting to farewell friends and relatives, along with a hundred or so troops. But as he drew nearer he realised that, although the gangway had not been raised, the mooring lines were off and the vessel was drifting away from the wharf. Grabbing the outstretched hand of the fortunately positioned and aptly named bosun, Mr Power, he took a flying leap to land safely on the end of the gangway.

The premature departure had been caused by a last-minute, and successful, attempt by a number of Australian troops to board the vessel. Earlier that afternoon, following a rumour that *Empire Star* would be the last ship to leave Singapore, hordes of civilians and Allied military of all descriptions had arrived at the wharf, clamouring to join those already on board. The latter included a group of about sixty Australian Army Service Corps (AASC) personnel who had embarked much earlier that day on the orders of their senior officer, 35-year-old Captain John Wooldridge. Once on board, they were allocated space by the ship's crew and RAF personnel and put to work by the ship's captain, draining petrol from the vehicles on deck to lessen the risk of fire if they were attacked.

As the air raids and shelling increased, streets became impassable

Exodus

For the remainder of the morning a steady stream of officially designated civilians, including women and children, plus another twenty of Wooldridge's men, made their way on board for the expected noon departure. On learning that sailing was to be delayed to await the arrival of even more women and children, army nurses, Air Force personnel and other designated evacuees, the Australians and members of the crew scrounged for provisions in the bombed warehouses. Mindful that youngsters would soon be arriving, the enterprising scroungers included toys and undelivered Christmas gifts in their haul.

As the afternoon wore on, more and more evacuees, and would-be evacuees, crowded the wharf. With harassed officials hard-pressed to keep even a modicum of control, it was absolute chaos. One group of nursing sisters from 10 Australian General Hospital was encountering difficulty in boarding until the colonel accompanying them produced a pistol to press his point, while other women and children, rounded up by the police and instructed to report immediately to the ship, were admitted without passes. Anyone else without the proper authority had to dodge the military police manning the gangway. It wasn't hard to do. Some simply walked on board with the crew and military personnel collecting food and other supplies. Others shinned up mooring lines and scrambled up rope ladders while yet others joined the general melee heading for the gangway – all this to a background of crackling flames, smoke and unbelievable noise and confusion. As the docks were still being attacked the anti-aircraft gun, which still had ammunition at this stage, fired constantly, the recoil shuddering the wharf with every round. Norma's party of women and children, who had been taken ashore when the air-raid warning sounded, sat out the worst of the bombing in a completely inadequate sandbagged shelter, the mothers waving Chinese paper fans in an attempt gain some relief from the claustrophobic heat, and at the same time trying to appear calm as the planes dived constantly overhead.

Overseeing the evacuation was Kenneth Atkinson, Royal Navy, Dockyard Captain and also Captain-in-Charge Singapore. Moving between the docks and the command bunker at Fort Canning, Atkinson had continued to carry out his duties with his usual efficiency despite the bedlam around him. It was some time before the expected evacuees arrived, the congested roads making progress difficult. A group of Australian nurses who had left 13 Australian General Hospital at St Patrick's College, Katong at midday finally arrived, only to have their embarkation further delayed by the air raids. At about 4 o'clock the New Zealanders from 488 Squadron under the command of Squadron Leader Ross put in their appearance, followed by Charlie Johnstone's group and, at 5.30, by three NCOs from RAF Seletar Air Base. Shortly afterwards about twenty Australian soldiers, in full uniform and carrying their weapons, jostled their way up the gangplank.

Captain Capon, standing on the bridge, was not pleased by this unexpected incursion and ordered them to leave. When they refused he called the military police on board. Although the

Captain Kenneth Atkinson, RN

provosts threatened to open fire, the group's spokesman and leader, aged about twenty-four, stood his ground in the belief they should be evacuated. The MPs, unwilling to force a showdown, retreated. In an attempt to put a stop to any further incidents, Capon ordered the ship to leave its berth at once, effectively putting an end to any further embarkation. There were no wharf hands to handle the mooring lines, but Captain Wright had briefed a group of British soldiers who had offered their assistance. Apart from letting go the ropes a little too soon, causing a slight panic in the engine room, the soldiers performed creditably, and the ship reversed into the current, running at about three knots, without incident.

Denis, having made his dramatic flying leap onto the ship, was making his way to the bridge when he heard rifle shots at close quarters. The fire was directed at Australian Archie Mitchell and a group of about fourteen of his AASC mates, who had been instructed by Wooldridge to report to the ship. They had eventually located the wharf, and the vessel, only to find she had cast off. Seeing other Australians from their unit on board, they had hopped into an abandoned bumboat and paddled out to the ship to a rope ladder lowered over the side by troops on the deck. As they clambered up, bullets whistled over their heads, forcing crew members handling the mooring ropes on the forward deck to duck for cover. Although the Australians still on the ladder were prime targets, no one was hit and there were no further shots.

Stories later circulated that the bullets had been fired by troops on the wharf farewelling their friends, or showing annoyance at being left behind. Others assumed that Archie and his companions were deserting. None of these assumptions was true. Crewman Red Faulkner, watching embarkation proceedings from the top of the gangway, saw that some distinctively kilted Argyll and Sutherland Highlanders ordered to guard the wharf were responsible. It is unlikely that the Scots, renowned for their discipline as much as their fighting abilities, had missed their targets because they were firing in a fit of pique or their aim was off. It is far more likely that, in the mistaken belief that the Australians were deserting, they chose to fire high either because they did not wish to kill fellow soldiers in cold blood or because some of the

Australians on the ladder might have been amongst those responsible for extricating what was left of the Argylls from a perilous situation less than forty-eight hours previously.

Capon had been instructed by Naval Control not to clear the harbour before midnight, so the ship made her way slowly to an anchorage in the nearby Eastern Roads. As she moved to the mooring the entire area was rocked by a massive explosion as an ammunition dump on Bukom Island blew up, turning the sky into a mass of fire and black smoke. At around midnight the ship weighed anchor again. The night was inky black, with none of the buoys lit and a strong current sweeping across the minefield. The buoy marking the entrance to the minefield was also missing. Using the glimmer of light cast by the fires raging ashore, George Wright was able to judge the channel entrance accurately, guarded by the minefield on one side, and a reef on the other. At this point the pilot's official duties ceased. However, as Wright had also been instructed to leave Singapore, Captain Capon accepted his offer to guide the ship to the entrance to the wide, cliff-lined Durian Strait, where they were to await the arrival of three other vessels: the Blue Funnel Line's SS *Gorgon* with 358 evacuees on board and two escorts, the Royal Navy's cruiser *Durban*, carrying just 57 passengers, and HMS *Kedah* with more than three hundred. The latter, now classified as a patrol boat, was a coastal vessel of just on 2,500 tonnes, the largest vessel belonging to the Straits Shipping Company.

With none of the lighthouses functioning, navigation could have been tricky had Wright not mentally noted the position of the fires blazing on shore. Using them as reference points he brought the vessel safely to the rendezvous. During the night fifteen more ships joined the convoy – the British destroyers *Jupiter* and *Stronghold*, each with 150 evacuees, and thirteen small merchant vessels ranging from 200 to 6,000 tonnes.[1]

Early next morning, just as they were about to get underway, three British sailors who had survived the sinking of *Prince of Wales* and six Australian infantrymen came aboard. Infantryman Private Roy Cornford and his five companions had been cut off in the fighting on the western side of the island on 8 February. After a three-day slog through thick jungle they had eventually reached the coast, where they met up with the sailors. Finding an oarless sampan, they scouted around for a few planks of wood and were paddling in what they thought was the direction of Singapore when they spotted the convoy. As they came alongside *Empire Star* a crane lowered a heavy rope cargo net, allowing the men to clamber on deck.

Soon afterward one of the naval vessels delivered some more Australians, picked up from a small boat. There were now well in excess of 2,000 people crammed on a ship whose decks and holds were all but filled with vehicles and equipment. Normally, *Empire Star* carried just sixteen passengers. Besides the 88 crew and 'distressed British seamen' (four from the bombed-out *Empress of Asia*), there were 1000 British airmen, 500 British soldiers and sailors, 60 Australian nurses, about 140 Australian soldiers, approximately 70 specialised signal staff, 29 authorised civilians (including four Salvation Army officers)[2] and about 200 civilians. The 128 women and 36 children were crammed into the few cabins and a small saloon. Norma and the boys, who had now been on board for more than thirty-six hours, had been assigned a cabin with several others. To help amuse the children, Captain Capon authorised the distribution of toys and other items collected from the warehouses. Denis's sons received quite a swag of stuff, but the gift which really took young Derek's eye was a brightly coloured comb.

The convoy left at about 6 am. Initially the ships were protected from air attack by a thick haze but this soon lifted. *Durban*, in the lead, had just cleared the Durian Strait when, at 8.50 am, they were spotted by a reconnaissance aircraft. It took just twenty minutes for the dive-bombers to appear – a formation of seventeen Mitsubishi aircraft, which peeled off in waves for the attack.

Being a Defensively Equipped Merchant Ship (DEMS), *Empire Star* was well-armed and provided with Royal Navy gunners. Anticipating that attack was extremely likely, Capon had already deployed them and his crew members to battle stations. The available firepower was strengthened considerably by AASC soldiers who, although they were not front-line troops, set up Bren guns in the three lifeboats on the boat deck and assisted the RAF manning various machine-guns. Others stood by to assist the crew with firefighting. Military personnel not engaged on deck were either taking cover behind the trucks where they let loose with rifle and pistol fire, or sheltering in the holds along with most of the nurses and male civilians. Picking off the weakest first, the planes concentrated their attack on the smaller craft at the rear, sinking some and disabling others. The four ships at the front were targeted next but the concentrated anti-aircraft fire forced the enemy to release their bombs at an altitude of about 1,000 feet, thereby reducing their accuracy. *Gorgon*, whose machine-gunners were credited with shooting down an enemy plane, last seen losing height and with its port engine on fire, emerged from the encounter unscathed. *Empire Star*, the largest vessel in the fleet and the last to be attacked, did not.

As six dive-bombers hurtled towards the ship, the guns on board opened up. RAF gunners manning a Hotchkiss gun on the starboard side brought down one plane and another, smoke pouring from the tail, was forced to abort its attack, but nothing could stop the onslaught. *Empire Star* took three direct hits, killing twelve of the military outright. Fifteen others and two of the ship's crew were very badly wounded. One of the aft lifeboats, where six Australians had stationed themselves with their Bren guns, took almost a direct hit, killing five of them and critically injuring the other. A young crewman, Tony Higgins who was not yet seventeen, helped the wounded man to the engineer's mess, which was doing duty as an operating theatre. Two of the dead were cousins, Jim and John Bowman, who came from country New South Wales and lived only 20 kilometres from each other. They were army transport drivers. They had enlisted in the AASC on the same day and had consecutive service numbers.

At the height of the bombing, with pieces of shrapnel and bullets whistling everywhere, another Australian soldier manning the ship's rear machine-gun was badly wounded. With no thought for their own safety, two Australian Army nurses, Margaret Anderson and Veronica Torney, left their cover and ran to the wrecked wooden turret. As they lifted the limp and bleeding man to the deck the planes turned for a strafing run. Without hesitation Sister Anderson threw herself across the wounded man in an attempt to prevent him from further injury as the bullets slammed and ricocheted around them. The aircraft then peeled off, allowing him to be dragged to safety. After some basic instruction from the teenaged Tony Higgins, who was able to fire off a few rounds himself before being hunted below by the chief steward, another Australian volunteer took over a second gun.

Gorgon was the only one of the four leading ships to emerge from the encounter intact. *Kedah* had minor splinter damage, but *Durban* had six or seven killed and another seventeen injured. The six-inch gun was also out of action, as was some of the navigating gear. *Empire Star* had suffered the most. Two of the bombs had penetrated the decks, causing a great deal of damage. One which fell on the poop deck killed several soldiers and injured about eighteen, with three more allegedly blown overboard. One badly wounded airman dragged himself to the railing and toppled into the sea. Australian pilot Charlie Johnstone, taking cover in the nearby well-deck, went to the aid of the seriously injured but all were beyond help. Most had lost limbs or been disembowelled. One, who was still alive, was on fire and screaming for help. Knowing full well that it would hasten his death but unable to let him suffer, Charlie found a bucket of water and threw it over him.

The bomb which wiped out the Australian gunners also wrecked the chief engineer's quarters and the galley, killing an RAF officer sheltering there. Fortunately it missed the holds, which had only one escape exit each – a narrow steel ladder. Roy Cornford, who was in the hold and only three metres from where the bomb exploded, was enveloped in clouds of choking dust, smoke and fumes, so thick that despite the strafing he was forced to seek refuge on the deck behind one of the vehicles. For those cowering in the second hold the noise of the bomb which exploded above them was so tremendous that an Australian nurse had both her eardrums ruptured.

By 9.30 the first attack was over, allowing nurses and RAF medical officers to set up a casualty clearing station in the main saloon to attend to the wounded, while parties under the direction of the ship's first officer, Joseph Dawson, set about extinguishing the fires. During the lull Roy Cornford and his mate were given the task of collecting identity discs from the corpses of their countrymen before pushing them unceremoniously over the side. Twenty-two-year-old George Heads, the ship's cook, did the same with the shattered body of a young airman, while Charlie Johnstone, after disposing of the severed limbs of the other victims, put what remained of the dead into bags for burial later. Red Faulkner hosed off what was left.

Denis Emerson-Elliott meantime had left the bridge and gone below to check on the condition of the hull following a couple of very near misses. The iron plates were still sound but below decks it was an absolute shambles, with casualties and blood everywhere. Although pale and distressed, the Australian nursing sisters were quietly and methodically attending to their patients. The wounded, including those seriously injured, now totalled thirty-seven. Despite their best efforts, the soldier shielded by Margaret Anderson, and the critically wounded soldier from the lifeboat, both died, bringing the death toll officially to fourteen. Throughout the attack the nursing sisters had maintained their composure, singing wartime songs and that Australian favourite, 'Waltzing Matilda', to keep up morale and prevent panic from setting in among the passengers. While still below Denis was approached by the young soldier in charge of the group of Australians who had boarded the ship and refused to leave. Explaining that he had done what he had thought was best for his men, he confided that he was a little concerned about the reception they would receive at their destination. Assuring him that he should not worry too much about it, Denis returned to the bridge – and only just in time. At 10 am the enemy returned.

This time it was a squadron of twenty heavy bombers, which circled the convoy at long range before splitting into three flights. Augmented by an additional nine aircraft, they maintained continuous high-level bombing attacks on all the ships from a height of 6,000– 10,000 feet. At 1.10 pm the attack was strengthened by another twenty-seven aircraft which concentrated their bombs on *Durban* and *Empire Star*, the two most attractive targets.

Throughout the terrifying three-and-a-half hours that this second attack lasted, Selwyn Capon kept his head, manoeuvring his ship from side to side as George Wright and the ship's third officer, James Smith, relayed information on the movement of the enemy planes as well as the probable angle of attack. Faced with an assault at one stage by all twenty-seven aircraft, Capon outwitted them by ordering full astern and then changing direction. Although some of the bombs exploded only three metres from the vessel, lifting her hull from the water with great shuddering vibrations, the ability of Smith and Wright to pre-empt the attackers' next move, combined with superb seamanship by Capon, brought the vessel through safely. At 1.30 pm the bombers broke off the attack. It was all over.

As *Durban* was having problems with her navigating equipment, *Kedah* took over the lead as they headed into the Bangka Straits, followed by *Empire Star* and *Gorgon* with *Durban* bringing up the rear. The afternoon was spent clearing away debris and organising food and water. This posed something of a problem on *Empire Star* as the galley was smashed and no plates, mugs or eating utensils were available. After setting up distribution points around the ship, volunteer mess orderlies doled out army biscuits, tinned bully beef and tinned vegetables into whatever the evacuees could find – steel helmets, handkerchiefs, even scraps of paper. Most of the troops had water bottles, but the civilians and nurses drank the tea which the crew brewed from cigarette tins, empty lolly jars and such like. Washing facilities were tubs of salt water placed at intervals around the decks, while sanitary arrangements consisted of a screened-off section near the deck railing, hosed down with sea water every hour.

The remaining dead were buried at sunset. Unlike the previous disposals over the side, there was no need for unseemly haste. Prayers were said for the safe delivery of the ship and the souls of the departed. As the bodies, weighted in their canvas shrouds, were consigned to the deep beneath the flag of the Empire for which they had given their lives, the survivors sang the well-known hymn 'Abide with me'.

Some of the Australians who had died, including Sister Anderson's patient, were buried as 'unknown', their identification discs having disappeared. Many years later, labouring under the misapprehension that every Australian aboard *Empire Star* had wilfully deserted, British writer Peter Elphick alleged that the lack of identification discs was deliberate. No attempt was made to ascertain whether the discs, which should have been attached to the mangled bodies, could possibly have been lost or destroyed. Or why deserters who had fled Singapore would volunteer to man guns, thereby exposing themselves to very great danger. Or why troops who believed their evacuation was authorised would remove the one thing which identified them, should they be killed. Neither were the physical characteristics of the Australian discs worn at that time considered. Unlike the metal discs issued later, these were flimsy affairs, made of composite cardboard strung onto leather thongs in the expectation that the troops' final destination would be the dry deserts of the Middle East, not the steamy jungles of Malaya. Very few tags lasted long. Unable to withstand the heat and humidity the thin leather became weak, making them liable to break at the slightest provocation.

On arrival in Batavia, all the Australians on board were marched from the ship and subjected to an investigation, allegations of desertion and boarding the vessel at gunpoint having reached the ears of senior Australian commanders. While there were undoubtedly some unauthorised troops on board, and some very rough types among them, it was found that the Australians had no case to answer. After a few days' detention all were released. Some who were assessed as being of no further use to the army were sent home but the rest volunteered to remain and continue the fight, until they too were captured. Post-war, the army's legal division examined the question of whether Wooldridge should face a court martial, but decided to bring no charges. Roy Cornford and others experienced no animosity from either the crew or the British personnel on board and were unaware until Peter Elphick's 'revelations' in 1995 that they had ever been branded deserters. There was never any complaint lodged in the ship's log, or made to Denis Emerson-Elliott or to anyone else by Capon, who thanked the Australians for the defence of his ship.

The exoneration of the troops, coupled with testimony repeatedly corroborated by senior war correspondents, Denis Emerson-Elliott, George Wright, Red Faulkner, RAF officers, Australian nurses and others, did not stop the rumour-mongers or put and end to the scuttlebutt, which now included the fantastic allegation that the last group who had pushed their way on board had shot dead Dockyard Captain Kenneth Atkinson in the process. In 1987 British writer Richard Gough even included a full description of this non-event in his book *Escape from Singapore*. When challenged and presented with irrefutable evidence that Atkinson had gone down with his ship *Ying Ping* in the Bangka Straits, three days after his supposed murder, Gough confessed that while he had not actually witnessed the event, 'he had imagined it had happened that way'. Vice-Admiral Sir John Hayes, another 'eyewitness', also admitted he had not actually seen the murder but it was 'a very well-known fact at the time'. Singapore identity Captain Percy Bulbrook added even more spice to the tale, drinking out for years on his claim that he had seen the pocked-mark wall and bloodstains at Tanjong Priok where every fifth Australian had been taken out and shot.

As *Kedah's* skipper Commander Sinclair plotted a course close to Sumatra's coast, well away from the main shipping lane, the remainder of the voyage to Tanjong Priok where the convoy docked twenty-four hours later was mercifully uneventful. Ships which kept to the main route ran into serious trouble. A convoy of tankers which had sailed from Palembang under the protection of *Jupiter* and *Stronghold* was bombed and set ablaze while the ammunition ship *Derrymore*, which had miraculously survived the attacks the previous day, was torpedoed 50 nautical miles from the safety of Java. Further north, the Japanese were concentrating on other hapless vessels bottled up in the Bangka Straits, aptly named 'bomb alley'. These ships, many of them no bigger than motor launches, were facing not only enemy aircraft but also the might of the Japanese navy, which had chosen the waterway for a rendezvous prior to an attack on Palembang in southern Sumatra. Although Dutch Intelligence had warned Singapore on 10 February of the impending move, the signals could not be decoded as the code books at Fort Canning had been prematurely destroyed. Discovering this, Mulock and Lieutenant Commander Copely drove immediately to Government House and ordered Sir Shenton to hand over his copy. They stood over him while he rooted through his desk, but he had apparently 'mislaid' it. Consequently, almost every vessel which had left Singapore after *Empire Star* departed was intercepted.

At 8.30 pm on 15 February, General Percival unconditionally surrendered all Allied forces in Singapore to the Imperial Japanese Army. The following day, deciding that any further repairs to his vessel could be completed in Australia, Capon left Tanjung Priok with another merchant ship, *Plancius*, with 3,000 evacuees on board. Escorted by the faithful *Durban* the vessels cleared the Sunda Straits separating Sumatra from Java and entered the Indian Ocean where *Empire Star*, now with just ninety-seven on board, headed for Fremantle alone, leaving *Durban* to shepherd *Plancius* to Colombo. On arrival in Fremantle, a voyage which would take ten days, Denis Emerson-Elliott was to report immediately to Naval Intelligence. With Singapore lost to the enemy, SOE Far East was in disarray until such time that its key personnel, if they had survived, could regroup.

Two who would not escape the clutches of the Japanese were Denis's friends Colonel John Douglas Dalley and Captain George Mulock, both of whom had many secrets to protect. Dalley, Director of Intelligence for the Federated Malay States Police Force and attached to SOE's 101 Special Training School, also commanded the Singapore Overseas Chinese Anti-Japanese Volunteer Army. Normally referred to as Dalforce, this unit had been formed on Christmas Day, when the governor and Percival had finally given permission to establish and train a Chinese volunteer force at 101 School to operate as guerrillas behind enemy lines – the 'stay behind parties' – and to allow some Communists who were in political detention to be released to Dalley. Commanded by Chinese and British officers drawn from the Straits Settlement and Malay Volunteer Forces, Dalley's recruits, also referred to as Chinese Irregulars, came from all social classes, ranging from coolie labourers and rickshaw pullers, to students and businessmen.

On 5 February, the Dalforce recruits, following an intensive five-day training course, were sent to the front line. They were armed with an assortment of rifles and shotguns plus ammunition amounting in some cases to just five rounds apiece, the arms intended for their use having gone down with *Empress of Asia*, destroyed by an enemy air strike as she approached Singapore. On 9 February one Dalforce company, which had been assigned a position on the mudflats near Kranji, found itself up against a Japanese machine-gun battalion whose objective was to seize the causeway. When their handful of ammunition was expended the Chinese fought hand to hand with bayonets and parangs. Not one of them survived. It was left to a British officer and five other ranks to report the bravery of these Chinese Irregulars, whose courage equalled that of any Victoria Cross winner.

Members of the ill-fated Dalforce

Dalley had started out with 200 volunteers in December. By the time the battle for the island began he had 4,000. However, he had lost many men and on 13 February he assembled the remnants of his force at their headquarters in Kim Yam Road and ordered them to disband. Most fled to Malaya where they formed the Malaya People's Anti-Japanese Army. Within a few hours of dismissing his men Dalley himself was ordered to leave Singapore.

Like Dalley, who was on the Japanese 'wanted' list, Mulock knew he must do everything possible to avoid falling into enemy hands. Although his position was not as perilous as that of Dalley, whose involvement with the Chinese – long-time and bitter enemies of the Japanese – made him a marked man, Mulock was one of the few to know that the British had broken the enemy's codes. He was also custodian of the navy's top-secret decoding machine. His orders were explicit. As there were no more ships available the organised evacuations were at an end. Mulock was to evacuate himself and other key personnel immediately and, once clear of the harbour, he was to throw the machine into the sea. Under no circumstances was this vital piece of equipment to fall into enemy hands, lest they discover that the Allies had been deciphering many of their coded signals for a considerable time.

On the night of 14 February Mulock and his party reached the docks. They boarded *Osprey*, the launch assigned to them, only to be challenged by armed troops who tried unsuccessfully to board. As it moved from the wharf shots were fired but no one was hit. The vessel, designed to carry ten, had thirty-eight on board. Included in Mulock's party were SOE's Frank Brewer, some of Dalley's officers and staff, a very senior Australian diplomat, Vivian Bowden, and two of his colleagues. As *Osprey* was vastly overloaded, once they were safely out of range all passengers were transferred to *Mary Rose*, a 13-metre diesel-engined launch.

They cleared the outer harbour on 15 February without any problems and were heading towards Palembang when, in the early hours of 17 February, they were caught in the searchlights of two Japanese patrol boats, which threatened to open fire. There was no option but to surrender but as no white flag was available a pair of underpants was hoisted. *Mary Rose* was escorted to Muntok on Bangka Island, where the prisoners' baggage was examined. They were then herded into a hall where the 62-year-old, snowy-haired Bowden, who spoke Japanese and had already remonstrated with the guard over the baggage, informed their captors of his status. The guard took exception to this latest interference, punching Bowden, threatening him with a bayonet and removing his watch. He was then was marched outside, forced to dig a shallow grave, and shot dead.

During the fracas which cost Bowden his life Mulock had his nose broken with a rifle butt. He and Dalley were extremely fortunate. Although prisoners, both would survive the war – Dalley going on to become head of the Malayan Security Service and Mulock to enjoy his much deferred retirement.

Exodus

Mervyn Wynne, head of the Singapore Special Branch, his Malayan counterpart H B Sym, and D Matheson, another Special Branch policeman, also died after falling into the hands of the Japanese in Sumatra. Their colleague, the secretive Major Morgan of the Japanese Section, was also captured. He survived internment but his health was so shattered he never worked again.

As he leaned against the deck rail of *Empire Star* watching the sun set across the Indian Ocean, Denis had no idea of the tragic scenes occurring to the north, beyond the horizon. All he could do was hope that he and any colleagues who managed to flee Singapore in time could once more put their combined talents to use against an enemy which to date had outwitted them. His spirits would have lifted had he known that, as he and his family were sailing to the safety of Australia, events were already unfolding which would not only resurrect the network but also hit the Japanese where it hurt most – in Singapore. The means by which this would be achieved had yet to be formulated but the key figure had already emerged. He was an old friend of Denis – an Australian by the name of Bill Reynolds.

4
Escape

12–24 February 1942

On 12 February, while *Empire Star* was engaged in a struggle for survival in the Bangka Straits, William Roy Reynolds, master mariner and mining engineer, stood on the wharf at Singapore's Telok Ayer Basin, deep in thought. High above, the smoke from the oil fires, burning now for three days and contaminating the air with their bitter acrid fumes, had reduced the normally brilliant noonday sun to a watery, fuzzy disc. The protected waters of the basin were calm but beyond it the harbour heaved in a confused tangle of twisted and splintered wreckage. Behind him majestic colonial buildings, many miraculously undamaged but with proud facades blighted by filthy, oily sludge, looked down on wrecked city streets packed with frightened people. The rangy Australian seethed with barely repressed rage at the sight. By now there should have been very few civilians on the island.

Bill Reynolds harboured no illusions about the Japanese. Unlike other civilians up-country he had been prepared for the invasion he knew must come and, many months before, had taken the precaution of evacuating his wife and daughter to Australia where his son was attending boarding school. When the Japanese finally invaded Malaya most of the Europeans in Ipoh, where he lived, were caught completely unawares and departed with alacrity for Singapore, while locals sought refuge in limestone caves. Reynolds, however, had not fled. A lance-corporal in the Perak Volunteer Defence Corps, he had reported for duty to the area commander at Ipoh where he was employed by the giant English tin mining firm, Anglo-Oriental Mining Company.

After the first bombs fell on the town a week later Reynolds was ordered to organise the compulsory evacuation of all civilians. It had been an administrative and logistical nightmare with various officials, without any reference to each other, issuing a series of conflicting orders. This, coupled with the terror created by the air attacks, had turned what was supposed to be an orderly evacuation into absolute chaos. On December 23, after a direct hit on an ammunition train had set oil tanks ablaze, the few Europeans left in Ipoh, including all Volunteers, were ordered to move south. Reynolds, who had no intention of leaving vital supplies and equipment intact for the enemy, refused to go.

The 49-year-old Australian, who had spent years in and around mines, was a demolitions expert. Armed with a swag of dynamite, he joined the Royal Engineers operating in the northern command zone, who assigned him to an Indian unit. As the Japanese rolled across Malaya like an unstoppable wave, Reynolds and his like-minded friends from 3 Field Company, Bombay Sappers & Miners, managed to keep one step ahead, blowing up bridges, public utilities such as telephone exchanges, power and telegraph stations, and private concerns including the tin mining plant belonging to Reynolds' employer at Malim Nawar just to the south of Ipoh. Tin was in short supply so the destruction of this establishment was vitally important, especially since orders to demolish the Eastern Tin Smelting Works at Penang, where 4000 tonnes of tin were stockpiled, had been received far too late, providing the resource-starved enemy with a great windfall.

By 7 January Reynolds had reached Kuala Lumpur. From here he worked his way further south, blowing up everything he could along the way. By the time he arrived in Singapore on 19 January he had been in action long enough to no longer believe in the so-called invincibility of the island. If the Japanese crossed the Straits of Johor, which it seemed they had every intention of doing, the only method of escape would be by boat. Unless a miracle occurred he feared Singapore would become another Dunkirk.

However, unlike the massive evacuation of the British Expeditionary Forces from the French channel port in 1940 by thousands of naval and volunteer civilian craft, Reynolds knew that Singapore could hold out no hope of rescue from the outside. If the one million plus civilians and troops were to be evacuated, it would have to be organised from within. So with this in mind he immediately offered his services to R J 'Old Man' Farrar, the Chief Man Power Officer, who suggested several agencies. To Reynolds' intense disappointment no one wanted him, least of all the senior British naval personnel stationed on HMS *Laburnum*, a former World War I Flower Class sloop permanently moored at Telok Ayer. Now an engineless hulk, the vessel had been converted into naval offices which housed a number of officials including the officer organising evacuations – Denis Emerson-Elliott's friend and colleague, George Mulock.

Reynolds' proposal that he try to restore to working order the motley and rapidly deteriorating Japanese fishing vessels, impounded by Denis the previous December, evoked not the slightest bit of interest. Indeed, the naval officer involved was dead against the idea and dismissed Reynolds peremptorily, telling him to go about his business and informing him that 'nobody can put the engines in order'. It appears that Mulock and his staff, in common with most of the military, still held out hopes that Singapore would repel the invaders should they attempt to cross the Straits of Johor, described by Winston Churchill as 'a splendid moat'.

At the end of January, nine days after Reynolds' visit to *Laburnum*, the Royal Navy's complacency was shattered when its magnificent naval base was subjected to heavy bombing. The attack prompted an evacuation of such haste that almost the entire base, including a massive amount of valuable supplies and equipment, was left intact. When Bill Reynolds arrived a few days later to assist with demolition works ordered in a belated attempt to prevent the vital facility from falling into enemy hands, the speed with which the naval personnel had departed was plainly evident in plates piled with putrefying food and cups half-full of stale tea, scattered along hurriedly vacated mess tables.

On 30 January, two days after the navy abandoned the base, the hard-pressed Allied army abandoned Malaya and began its retreat across the Straits of Johor. They were protected at the rear by battle-hardened troops – 250 Argylls, part of the 8th Australian Division and members of 2 Battalion Gordon Highlanders who, although they were garrison troops, had been dispatched to Malaya late in the campaign. As the 30,000 battle-weary troops accompanied by thousands of frightened refugees trudged onto the island, the army engineers waiting to blow the causeway in the hope of delaying the Japanese advance heard the sound of bagpipes. Along the road, with heads held high and backs erect and looking anything but defeated, came the Australians and the Gordons, followed by the Argylls, marching defiantly to the stirring strains of 'Heilan' Laddie' and 'A Hundred Pipers'.

At the very end of the column was Drummer Hardy. Noticing that his batman, who had never been known to run, was moving with no sense of urgency, Brigadier Stewart, the Argylls' CO, exhorted him to get a move on. However, Stewart's psychological pep talks, that there was nothing exceptional about the Japanese, had been heeded by the bandsman, who had not run from the enemy to date and could see no valid reason why he should do so now. Despite Stewart's bellowed admonishments to hurry up and shake a leg, Hardy stubbornly maintained his carefully measured pace. With the rearguard watching his every step and the engineers waiting, hands poised over their demolition plungers, the lone figure of Drummer Hardy finally crossed the causeway. In so doing, this lowly-ranked soldier earned for himself an undying place in history, not simply for being the last man to leave Malaya but also its most unlikely hero, who dismissed protests over his lack of haste with a laconic: 'Japs are only Japs, and it is undignified for an Argyll to take any notice of them'.

Hardy's contempt for the Japanese, while undeniably the stuff of which legends are made, did not stop them crossing the 'splendid moat' on 8 February, just over a week later – not via the partially blown causeway, which was soon repaired, but in hundreds of small boats. Storming ashore in wave after wave, 20,000 fanatical troops overran three sparsely positioned and under-strength Australian battalions which had been given the impossible task of holding the entire north-west coast.

On 10 February, with the Japanese well entrenched and the situation deteriorating rapidly, Reynolds returned to the wharf at Telok Ayer Basin. Still sitting there were the thirty abandoned Japanese fishing boats which, unfortunately for their owners, had been in port when Denis had received Dickinson's orders to impound them. Reynolds looked them over

THE SKIPPER

DON RUSSELL

Bill Reynolds, through the eyes of artist Don Russell, and in real life

carefully. As Captain Mulock's staff had scathingly pointed out, most of the vessels were not capable of going anywhere. Some had vital engine components missing while others were so battered from the bombing and shelling they would not have made it past the protected harbour waters. Casting his eye over what was left of the fleet, looking even more dilapidated and weather-worn than before, Reynolds began to formulate a plan. Provided he could kick one of these ramshackle tubs into life, he might be able to make a break before he became an unwilling guest of the Emperor of Japan.

For those who did not know Reynolds, a lanky, almost gauntly lean man whose weatherbeaten features added at least ten years to his age, he seemed a most unlikely candidate to make a dash across enemy-controlled waters. But the chameleon-like Australian, well-drilled in undercover work and fluent in both Malay and Japanese, was better equipped than most to undertake such a mission.

Not just a demolitions expert but also a skilled engineer and sailor, Reynolds had spent the best part of the last twenty years in Borneo, Burma, Malaya and the many hundreds of islands which formed the Netherlands East Indies. The sea had always been in his blood.

Born in 1892 at Brighton on Melbourne's Port Phillip Bay, he had spent much of his life in Williamstown, a busy little port which was home to his grandparents and many seafarers. Bill had inherited his love of the sea from his paternal grandfather, who had sailed a yacht single-handedly from Portland in far western Victoria to Sydney. His father, however, was not a sailor – he worked for the Victorian Railways and his work took him around the state. While the family was living at Sale, in East Gippsland, he was killed by a train as he crossed the lines at the station. His untimely death had taken Bill, not much more than a lad, out of the schoolroom and into the merchant marine.

Highly intelligent and a brilliant mathematician, he had risen steadily in the service, obtaining his master's ticket in Dundee, Scotland. With the British Empire still embroiled in World War I, Bill joined the Royal Naval Reserve in September 1917, serving initially as a sub-lieutenant and then as lieutenant on the depot ship HMS *Zarina* in Portsmouth and then on *Attentive III* with the Dover Patrol, on England's south-east coast. In April 1919 he was appointed commander of *Firmament*, a fishing vessel classified as a 'drifter' which, with three others (*Filey, Flame* and *Flash*), had been undertaking minesweeping and anti-submarine duties for the navy. With hostilities over, *Firmament* was assigned to salvage and harbour reconstruction duties in Zeebrugge, a Belgian port which had been used by the Germans as a submarine base until it was blocked by a British naval raid in April 1918.

Seven months after the Armistice was signed, bringing to an end the war 'to end all wars', Reynolds was demobbed. He returned to Australia almost immediately, taking with him his

Captain William Roy Reynolds, Master Mariner   *Bessie Reynolds*

Scottish-born bride, 21-year-old Bridget (Bessie) O'Brien, whom he had married in Dover on Boxing Day the previous year. The Reynolds family was not happy about the marriage – Bill had been expected to marry a local girl from Williamstown. The couple settled in Melbourne, where Bill Junior was born in October 1919. When the baby was about two years old Reynolds returned to the Merchant Marine. For the next few years, based mainly in Hong Kong, Captain Reynolds sailed all over the world, carrying mixed cargo from one exotic port to another, sometimes accompanied by his wife and child. He also ferried Muslim pilgrims between the Far East and Jidda on the Arabian Gulf, where they disembarked for the overland journey to the holy city of Mecca, birthplace of the prophet Mohammed. While the pilgrims were ashore Reynolds continued his voyage, delivering and picking up cargo from Mediterranean ports such as Barcelona and Genoa until it was time to return to Jidda for the voyage home.

Reynolds loved the sea but by the end of 1925 he had had enough. For the past two years he had experienced a run of very bad luck. His problems had begun on 29 July 1923 on board SS *Ferrara* when, due to the incompetence of the vessel's third engineer, fire had broken out in the engine room. Despite Captain Reynolds' best efforts the outbreak could not be contained and the ship, to which he had just been appointed, had to be abandoned off the island of Sabang, Northern Sumatra.

A bare eight months later, in March 1924, he lost a second ship, SS *Frangestan*. Laden with a cargo of cotton and linseed and with 1221 pilgrims and fifteen European passengers on board, the vessel caught fire in the Red Sea en route to Jidda. As the cause was the spontaneous combustion of the cargo, Reynolds was exonerated of all blame. Furthermore, he was commended for evacuating everyone safely, including his thirty-nine crew members, and for his innovative attempt to pipe carbon dioxide, which was another part of the cargo, into the burning hold in an attempt to save the vessel. But although he had emerged with his reputation not only intact but enhanced, he decided enough was enough. Both ships were a total loss and the investigations before marine courts of inquiry had taken weeks. It was not just the stress and worry which prompted him to quit; he also knew his prolonged absences from Bessie and Bill Junior, now at school, were not conducive to harmonious family living. Evidently with few qualms, he resigned command of his next vessel, SS *Setstan*, in September 1925 and returned to Australia.

His career now took a new direction. He was offered a position with Thompson's, a foundry firm in the Victorian town of Castlemaine with which he had personal connections – his sister Lillian had married into the Thompson family. The company, which had mining interests in Pahang (Malaya) and Borneo, was in need of a dredge master. The family's idyllic life in these tropical outposts came to an end after only three years when Thompson's, like many other firms, was hit hard during the Great Depression and went into liquidation.

SS Frangestan, *lost in the Red Sea when fire broke out in the cargo, en route to Jidda*

Bill told his wife that he had been offered 'good support' in England and perhaps they should go there but, as they now had another child, Rosemary, born in Pahang in 1926, Bessie was keen to return to Melbourne. Before long they were off again – Bill had accepted a job to manage the Taungpila mine at Tavoy in lower Burma (in which the prominent Australian politician Edward G 'Red Ted' Theodore had an interest). From here, in about 1932, he went to Malaya to work for Anglo-Oriental.

On the surface it appeared that Reynolds, at the height of a world economic depression which saw many unemployed, had fallen on his feet. However, it is likely that he was also working for MI6, which used reputable British companies throughout South-East Asia as fronts. Anglo-Oriental, for instance, which produced 15 per cent of the world's tin, was backed by prominent British businessmen and was typical of the firms which co-operated with the Secret Service. He may, in fact, have been involved with MI6 for some time – as far back as World War I – hence the 'good support' which had been offered to him from an unspecified source in Britain. If he were working for British Intelligence, his career in mining, and particularly his time in the merchant marine, sailing in and out of ports all over the world, would not only have allowed him to collect information from many sources, it would also have provided an excellent cover.

While it is not possible to prove any very early connection with MI6, Reynolds was most certainly working for the organisation in Malaya in the early 1930s. Denis Emerson-Elliott was at this time with Guthries, a firm which was a 'friend' of the Secret Service, and it wasn't long before he and Reynolds were well acquainted. It was hard not to like the affable Australian who, at 193 centimetres, towered over his more diminutive friend. Although Bill's formal education had been cut short following the death of his father, he was well read, enabling him to hold his own in any company, including vice-regal. A congenial host and bon vivant, he also revelled in an opulent and refined way of life which was in complete contrast to the rough-and-tough image he projected to the sea-going fraternity. But it was not Bill's capacity to fit easily into any social scene, or his skill as a raconteur which attracted Denis – it was his well-developed spirit of adventure.

His favourite sport in Malaya was tiger hunting, which Denis also enjoyed. And what better place to indulge in this dangerous but thrilling activity than this colonial outpost, with its vast tracts of virgin rainforest? Mounted on elephants, Bill and Denis ventured to

*Denis Emerson-Elliott
at a jungle camp in
Malaya*

many remote locations in search of their quarry, staying with the indigenous Saki people who lived deep in the jungle. Reynolds was a fantastic shot – so good that when reports reached district officers of rogue tigers terrorising villagers, more often than not it would be Reynolds who was dispatched to track them down and dispose of them. Until the Japanese put paid to everything, Reynolds enjoyed an enviable lifestyle with Bessie and their children in their palatial homes in Ipoh and Penang.

Although his main aim following the invasion of Malaya was demolition, Reynolds was also working for MI6. On reaching Kuala Lumpur as he moved south from Ipoh, he and an unidentified Australian had stayed in a house opposite the palatial home of Mr H Harrison, who had been given the task of arranging billets for the local defence corps. There was no lack of accommodation. Empty bungalows abandoned by their owners stood in rows, their contents including wine cellars still intact and their servants still on call, hoping that their way of life might yet be restored. Precisely what Bill and his friend were doing in Kuala Lumpur was not disclosed. All Harrison knew was that they were on some kind of secret mission.

Having finally reached Singapore, it was against a backdrop of noise and devastation at Telok Ayer that Reynolds summed up his situation. In light of the present circumstances, rounding up a crew willing to sail with him to freedom did not appear to be much of a problem although supplies, fuel, weapons and ammunition might be more tricky. The major difficulty would be to get hold of an vessel seaworthy enough to make a dash across enemy-patrolled waters but inconspicuous enough to avoid attracting attention. With all other craft commandeered for official evacuees, his choice was narrowed down to the moth-eaten Japanese boats deemed by the Navy to be beyond salvation. Since orders had been issued to scuttle or burn any vessels not required for evacuation purposes, it was a case of strike now, or never.

The impounded vessels at Telok Ayer were still under the control of Dickie Dickinson and his deputy, F D Bisseker. Reynolds knew both men well. Dickinson, among other things, controlled the Local Defence Forces of which Reynolds was a foundation member. His mining colleague Bisseker had been responsible for bullying the authorities to organise a Civil Defence Unit, of which he was deputy director, as well as Director of Labour and Transport. Unlike the naval officials who had abandoned *Laburnum* for the safety of the bunker at Fort Canning, or quit Singapore completely, these stalwart civilians were still at their posts. Reynolds thus had no trouble at all in obtaining permission to salvage any vessel which took his fancy, especially since there was no one left in authority on the now almost deserted *Laburnum* to tell him otherwise. Giving them all the once-over, he finally settled on a vessel which appeared a little less disreputable than the rest.

The small, nondescript, narrow-gutted craft, not much more than a motorised sampan, was hardly an inspiring choice. From the pungent odour wafting from her holds and permeating every timber it was obvious that *Kofuku Maru*, registered number 2283, was a fishing boat. It was no wonder that Mulock had written her off. As Reynolds was first to admit, she didn't look much of a ship. Neither did she live up to her name (*Happiness* or *Good Fortune*), painted in bold block letters on her bow. But Reynolds realised that her down-at-heel appearance was the very reason she was still at the wharf. Had she looked less derelict and smelled less foul, she would have been appropriated long before because, although Japanese owned and operated, to European eyes she did not look particularly Asian. In fact, she looked very similar to driftnet fishing boats operating out of English ports in East Anglia, including Bill's old command *Firmament*, for her design and construction had been 'borrowed' by the Japanese, masters of adapting Western ideas to meet their own needs.

Kofuku Maru, built in 1934 in Nagahama, a small port on the island of Shikoku in Japan's Inland Sea, was classified as a fish carrier and was typical of vessels made at the Hamagami shipyards, one of about five operating there at the time. Her owners were the Fujisawa family, headed by Kotaro Fujisawa whose given name, containing 'Ko' meaning 'fortune', evidently inspired the ship's name. The design on which she was based was very flexible, allowing adaptation for driftnet fishing and fish carrying as well as conversion to ferries for passengers and goods.

Constructed by artisans who passed their skills from one generation to the next and who used no formal plans, *Kofuku Maru* was smaller than her English counterparts – just 21 metres long and barely 3.5 metres in width. She was also a great deal less comfortable, being almost bereft of crew facilities apart from a seat which doubled as a bunk, squeezed into the poky wheelhouse, roughly two metres square. Above the seat was a fold-down chart table which, when in use, restricted space to such an extent that the helmsman was obliged to move to one side, making it impossible to steer with any degree of accuracy. And when the table was in the down position for the charts to be consulted, it was only 30 centimetres above the bunk, forcing anyone trying to sleep to be ejected. Apart from this inconvenient bunk there was only one other berth – in the noisy, smelly engine room. In the stern a small tub of sea water served as a bath while the lavatory, known as the 'head' in nautical circles, was nothing more than a bucket on a rope. Right alongside this most unhygienic and completely exposed 'sanitary' arrangement was a tiny galley, consisting of a small petrol stove and a primitive vented oven.

Immediately behind the wheelhouse was a long low platform, the engine-room housing, into which six glass side-panels had been set to provide light for the engine room below. The sturdy German-made Deutz four-cylinder diesel engine, a 1927-34 model, had been well maintained by its previous engineer. Beyond the engine room, set into the 2 centimetre thick decking planks, was a small storage hatch and, beyond that, the stern. For'ard of the wheelhouse, ranged in a row towards the bow, were four small hatches leading to four cork-lined, insulated holds in which 17 tonnes of fish could be stored. Beyond, almost in the bow itself, was a single mast which, if necessary, could be lowered out of the way to rest in a cradle-like crutch on top of the wheelhouse. There was no sign of any sail. In any case, as a sail was used merely to keep the vessel square to the wind while drifting over the fishing grounds, it was useless as a means of propulsion.

Apart from the wheelhouse the only protection from the elements on deck was a tatty canvas awning, stretching from wheelhouse to stern. Its maintenance was evidently not a priority since the ship had been used as a shuttle service to provide supplies to, and carry fish from, the Anambas Islands fishing fleet, rather than operate as an offshore fishing boat.

Dickie Dickinson, whose job was to monitor the activities of all Japanese nationals, had found the constant wandering by Japanese fishing vessels to and fro across South-East Asian waters highly suspicious. Concerned that they could be used to guide enemy warships into British-held territory, he had kept a very close on all fishermen, as well as their boats.

It appears that his distrust of alien craft and their crews, at least in the case of *Kofuku Maru*, were well-founded. The appearance of the vessel's name and official number (39331), on a Japanese government document issued in 1939, indicates that espionage may have been of far more importance than fish carrying. This suspicion is strengthened by the fact that shortly before the Japanese attacked Malaya, two of *Kofuku Maru*'s sister ships, *Shofuku Maru* (*Small Fortune*) and *Fukufu Maru* (*Fortune of Wind*) – both of which had carried a 'seaman' who looked too aristocratic to be a simple fisherman and had left Singapore without permission – had been in areas on both the east and west coasts, where attacks had been launched.

Shofuku Maru and yet another sister ship, *Fukuyu Maru* (*Fortune of Excellence*), both of which had been 'arrested', were not at Telok Ayer Basin. Intercepted out to sea by ships of

Fukuyu Maru, *sister ship of* Kofuku Maru

the Royal Australian Navy, they had been escorted to the naval base where they had been scuttled. The three vessels were like peas in a pod. The similarity in their looks and names was such that years later, when *Kofuku Maru* gained a degree of notoriety, disputes would arise over who had captured her, in the mistaken belief that she was the first Japanese ship captured by the RAN in the Pacific Zone. (See Appendix 2.)

Spy ship or not, *Kofuku Maru* looked little different from any run-of-the-mill Japanese fishing boat. Not only were her crew facilities spartan, she had only basic equipment on board. Apart from a compass, navigational aids were non-existent, making it essential that a sharp lookout be maintained through the three wheelhouse windows whose frames, along with two clip-back doors, had been painted a grubby shade of white. There was no wireless and no aerial. Indeed, the only installations of any height aft were three pipes protruding through the canopy – two to extract exhaust from the engine and the generator motor, and the other to serve as a ventilation shaft for the engine room. There was no windlass either, and no ground tackle. Perhaps the ship's only real attribute, apart from the engine which was capable of a top speed of eight-and-a-half knots, was her unexpected seaworthiness. The black-painted Formosan teak hull, clad below the waterline with a type of copper-based material known as Muntz metal, was so solidly put together that the 47-tonne vessel could be run ashore and careened, rather than dry-docked, for repairs.

With his vessel selected and permission obtained to salvage it, Reynolds headed into the twisting narrow streets of nearby Chinatown. He re-emerged some time later with one Ah Tee and seven other Chinese in tow, rounded up from a local boarding house. For the next twenty-eight hours, while the oil fires continued to light up the sky and exhausted troops digested Churchill's latest message to fight to the bitter end, the workers on *Kofuku Maru* toiled unceasingly, reconditioning the engine, scrounging fuel oil and generally readying the ship for sea. As *Empire Star* waited in the Roads on the night of 11 February, Reynolds, his work complete, combed Singapore in search of provisions. It was no easy task, but he managed to acquire quite a load and by 10 o'clock next morning was ready to leave.

The boat did not head out to sea but instead sailed a short distance to Blakang Mati Island to pick up two Englishmen, also Perak Defence Force Volunteers. Alec Elliott, a 51-year-old engineer who came from Swindon in south-east England, and Londoner Harold Papworth, aged twenty-four, had been billeted on the island by the Straits Trading Company Works to assist with the demolition of tin smelters at nearby Pulau Brani (Brani Island).

Kofuku Maru was just one boat among many leaving that morning. Apart from the *Empire Star* convoy which was coming under attack in the Bangka Straits, numerous vessels of all shapes and sizes were attempting to make a run for it. The numbers had been bolstered by the overnight dropping of twenty-nine wooden boxes, each containing a letter from General Percival's Japanese counterpart, General Yamashita, urging surrender. While refusing to consider such a move at present Percival had, nevertheless, issued orders to destroy as much military hardware as possible and to evacuate more women, children, nursing sisters, technical and shore-based naval staff.

Towards noon, at the height of the attack against the *Empire Star* convoy, *Kofuku Maru* headed across Singapore's outer harbour. As she neared the Singapore Strait, twenty-seven enemy bombers plastered the area with high explosive. The boat managed to avoid annihilation by scuttling into the shelter of St John's Island, about 6 kilometres from Blakang Mati, where Reynolds made himself useful by shouting directions to troops attempting to make a getaway in sundry motorised craft.

Many others were not so lucky. To the south the bombers were pounding the flotilla of ships which had followed *Empire Star* into the Durian Straits. Two old Yangtze River gunboats, *Grasshopper* and *Dragonfly*, were escorting two paddle-steamers and a gunboat. By the time the bombers had unleashed their load all these vessels had been either sunk or blown to bits, killing all but 50 of the 400 passengers. On the harbour itself the survival rate was just as poor.

A few days beforehand, Australian naval officer Lieutenant Gordon Keith had just reached the T-piece jetty in the Roads, where his ship HMAS *Wollongong* was moored, when the air raid siren wailed. He reported:

It gave scant warning of the raid. The Jap bombers were already visible, coming in from seaward as I quickly took shelter behind sandbags. Hundreds of sampans and launches were tied up between the shore and the jetty, which ran parallel to it. Movement ceased everywhere. The swarming populace went to earth or into hiding. Alone in the expectant stillness, a sturdy Chinaman stood at his work, slowly rowing a sampan towards the shore with rhythmical strokes. The planes passed overhead and bombs exploded across the anchorage and among the shipping in rapid succession. As though by the wave of a magical wand, the Chinaman and his sampan were transformed into a mass of flame and brown smoke. Only a small, dark stain on the placid waters of the bay remained to mark their passing.

At 1.30 pm, with the raids over for the time being, Reynolds eased *Kofuku Maru* from her hiding place and looked towards the Durian Strait. Deciding from the distant pillars of smoke smudging the horizon that the southern approach to Java was fraught with danger, he changed course to the east via the less direct but much safer route down the Riau Strait. While the other vessels which risked 'bomb alley' generally came to grief, Reynolds and his crew encountered no more trouble as they crossed the 40 kilometres of sea separating Singapore from the Riau Archipelago. About seven hours later the boat arrived at the sprawling, ramshackle town of Tanjung Pinang on the south-western side of Bintan Island. To Reynolds' consternation the Dutch, believing the boat was Japanese, placed it under immediate arrest.

The mistake was sorted out just after 9 am the next day, when the Dutch controller discovered Reynolds was not the enemy. Having just weathered an air raid, he was even friendlier when the Australian offered to evacuate 266 dependants of the local garrison to Rengat, a moderately-sized settlement some 200 kilometres upstream from the mouth of the Indragiri River in Central Sumatra. By the time they left at seven that evening, Reynolds had managed to pack fifty refugees onto his boat and crammed the remainder on board *Silver Gull*, a disabled island trader which *Kofuku Maru* took in tow. It was now Friday 13 February – Black Friday – a date which Reynolds and thousands of others would have cause to remember for the rest of their lives.

After sailing all night under cover of darkness Reynolds reached the island of Ichwavg, where he ordered everyone to disembark and rest for the day under the trees, out of sight of enemy planes. While the two vessels rode quietly at anchor among the mangroves, Reynolds and his crew took on much-needed fresh water. As night fell they were off again, sailing without lights to avoid detection. Dawn next day saw them in Amphitrite Bay, close to the Indragiri estuary. Once in the river they kept going, arriving at Chenako at 4 pm. At this point the Indragiri narrowed considerably and, with jungle closing in on both sides, it was impossible to tow *Silver Gull* any further. Facilities at Chenako consisted of one hut and a telephone, so the refugees transferred to motor lorries to cover the last 50 kilometres upstream to Rengat, where there was a small hospital and telephone communication to the west coast.

Considering that they had spent the past two days in extremely cramped and uncomfortable conditions, the passengers were in amazingly fine shape. Not so lucky, they later learned, was a mixed convoy which had left Tanjung Penang for Sumatra twenty-four hours later. Of the nine vessels, including four under tow, it seems that only one – a Chinese boat crewed by a handful of Australian soldiers – had made the crossing safely. The Australians were more fortunate than they could possibly have imagined. About thirty of their countrymen who had arrived in the town too late to be evacuated were later captured and massacred by the Japanese.

As *Kofuku Maru* and *Silver Gull* were making their way slowly to Sumatra, the situation in Singapore had deteriorated to such an extent that General Percival now issued orders to clear the harbour of all remaining craft and to evacuate as many people as possible. While the hundreds of women, children, medical staff and non-combatants were being loaded onto a thirteen-vessel convoy, the dock area was once again heavily bombed, making it almost impossible to maintain any semblance of order. Evacuees stampeded the nearest vessel, some people didn't arrive at all while others, taking advantage of the general confusion, grabbed any places that were left. Some civil servants, ordered to remain at their posts by the governor, also joined the rush. Among them was Rex Nunn, head of the Public Works Department, who claimed that as a group captain in the RAF Volunteer Reserve he had vital documents to deliver on behalf of the governor. He and his wife, who had refused earlier evacuation, were well away before this subterfuge was detected – but like all those who left that day, they were about to sail into the heart of the Japanese fleet.

The British surrender two days later did not put a stop to the exodus. All those determined not to become prisoners of the Japanese left for Sumatra that night in anything that could float. While high-ranking officers and civil servants made the journey in luxury launches belonging to local sultanates, others were forced to adopt far more humble modes of transport. Under the command of Major Geoffrey Rowley-Conwy, a group of British gunners and engineers, generally regarded as being among the more intellectual members of the army, learned by frustrating trial and error how to keep their Chinese-style junk off the mud flats and in the water. Other enterprising escapees resorted to more desperate, and unscrupulous, methods. An Australian army captain, on finding himself alone in his bid for freedom, roused an elderly Chinese man from his bed and forced him into a dinghy at gunpoint. He later boasted that he was rowed all the way to Sumatra, a few waves of his pistol giving the unfortunate oarsman's tired muscles the necessary bursts of adrenalin to keep going. These desperate and daring souls entered the Japanese-infested waters off Sumatra at about the same time that Reynolds, having avoided the enemy by the slenderest of margins, was navigating the channels which criss-crossed the mangrove-clustered mouth of the Indragiri.

To enter the river was to venture into a completely different world. The languid, tropical peace of this little-used waterway, linking the heart of Sumatra's jungle-covered interior

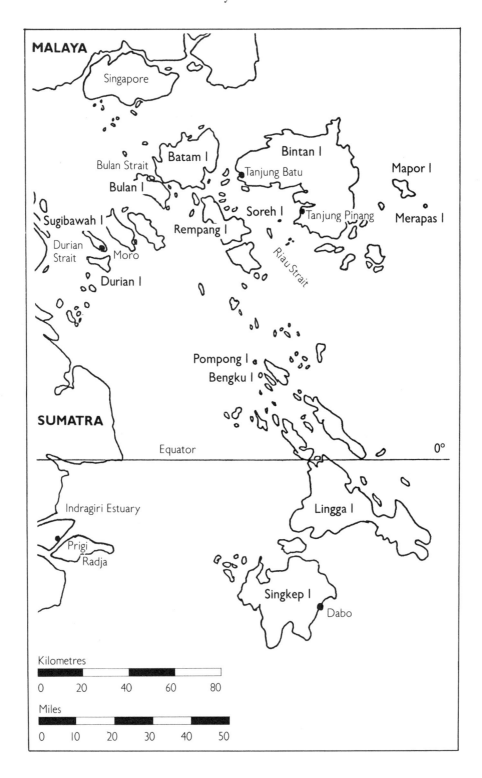

The SOE escape route from Singapore to Sumatra

with the sea, was totally at odds with the carnage taking place 300 kilometres beyond the horizon. For those who could appreciate it, the river downstream was an artist's delight, the dark tones of the mangroves creating a perfect foil for masses of purple water hyacinths, so prolific at times that they threatened to block the river's flow. Upstream, well away from the wide open estuary and the village of Prigi Radja, the river gradually narrowed, the shadows cast by overhanging branches relieved here and there by shafts of brilliant sunlight, filtered and diffused by the density of the jungle canopy. Beyond the muddy banks, on which the occasional crocodile lazily sunned itself, the lush foliage stretched endlessly, interrupted only in the west by the purple, mist-enshrouded peaks of distant mountains.

The war had shattered the serenity of this beautiful and untamed wilderness on 14 February, when the villagers at Prigi Radja heard the sound of heavy distant gunfire. What this meant was not apparent until the first survivors arrived at the village, bringing garbled tales of terror and death, of large numbers of people clinging to wreckage in the sea or marooned on islands off the coast. Communication along the river was erratic at the best of times, and it was not until the following day that the Dutch Controller at Rengat, Mr von Brenkel, heard of the scale of the disaster. From the Durian Strait in the north to the Bangka Strait in the south, scores of Allied craft had been attacked by Japanese planes and surface vessels. It was reported that as the result of one engagement, near the island of Pompong at the northern end of the Lingga group and almost 60 kilometres from the river mouth, hundreds of survivors were in dire and urgent need of assistance.

With almost all his Bintan Island refugees handed over to the Dutch authorities at Chenako, Reynolds had continued upriver to Rengat, arriving at 10 pm. What he intended to do from here is not clear, but it seems likely that, having come as far as they could in *Kofuku Maru*, he and his crew planned to make their way across the mountains to the west coast port of Padang and board an evacuation ship. Whatever his plans might have been, they were shelved when von Brenkel, his secretary Mr Kaag and sundry officials who had come down to the wharf to take charge of the fifty refugees still on board, told Reynolds of the plight of the bombed evacuees at Pompong Island. On learning that a group of British officers had already opened up an escape route across the mountains, Reynolds volunteered to mount a rescue operation. Disregarding completely the fact that, in order to reach the castaways, he would need to cross enemy-controlled waters, he began immediately to round up fuel, mattresses, blankets and provisions. Once loaded, *Kofuku Maru* and her crew, which now included an Ipoh planter named Paddy Jackson and a Royal Naval reservist, set off downriver at 2 am.

Kofuku Maru was followed by *Numbing*, a 60-tonne coastal launch skippered by Major Rowley-Conwy. After abandoning the junk, which they had finally and irretrievably run aground while still within sight of Singapore, Rowley-Conwy and his artillerymen, with the help of local fishermen, had reached Rengat, where Controller van Brenkel had given them

Numbing to assist with the rescue operations, unaware that their nautical skills left much to be desired. They ran it aground so often that when the hull began to leak the Controller finally gave them *Plover*, a nine-metre wood-burning steam launch. Being a much smaller craft with less powerful engines, they were able to spend more time in the water and less time in the mud.

It was not just the inexperienced who ran into trouble. Reynolds was making good time but around mid-morning, in his haste to reach the castaways, he took an ill-advised shortcut and judged one of the bends too finely, running aground. Despite every effort to free their vessel they remained stuck fast in the mud until about 4 pm, when they floated off on the high tide. After a near collision with a small Dutch trader, *Tanjung Pinang*, they finally made Pompong Island at 3 am.

Just over three hours later, the first rays of the sun revealed a shoreline littered with wreckage, much of it charred and splintered – grim testimony to the events which had so recently occurred. Off one end of the island was the wreck of *Kuala*, her superstructure poking pathetically above the water, while nearby was a mast, all that could be seen of *Tien Kwang*, a small coastal vessel which had been scuttled. Of *Kung Wo*, the third ship in this group, there was no sign at all.

The much larger HMS *Kung Wo*, an auxiliary minelayer of around 4,500 tonnes, had arrived during daylight hours on 13 February, well before the other two, and so was the first to be attacked. The ship was already damaged, having suffered a direct hit while moored at the Singapore naval base a few days previously. A bomb dropped in this second attack penetrated two decks before exploding, ripping a hole in the side. *Kung Wo*'s 500 passengers abandoned ship, many of them to be swept away and drowned in the ferocious tidal movements and currents swirling round the islands. While the survivors who had spent the night on nearby Bengku Island were wondering what to do next, two auxiliary patrol vessels, formerly the small coastal ships *Tien Kwang* and *Kuala*, anchored at Pompong Island about five kilometres away.

Kuala, the larger of the two, normally plied between Singapore and Penang. She had left Singapore at 7 o'clock the previous evening with 500 passengers on board, including 120 RAF personnel, assorted key citizens, a raja's son and Doris Lim, the Chinese secret agent who was on the enemy's wanted list. Not all the intended refugees had made it on board. While *Kuala*, tied up alongside HMS *Laburnum*, had been embarking passengers the area had come under attack, killing many evacuees and setting fire to abandoned vehicles on the wharf. Among the smaller *Tien Kwang*'s 300–400 passengers were patients evacuated from Alexandra Hospital and medical staff, PWD employees and RAF personnel who operated secret radar equipment

Unaware of the fate of *Kung Wo*, at daybreak the two ships' captains dispatched boatloads of volunteers to go ashore on Pompong and cut foliage with which to camouflage the vessels, now sheltering 200–300 metres offshore. The work was only partially completed when seven bombers returned to finish off *Kung Wo*. One plane dive-bombed the ship, which sank almost immediately. The others, circling round, spotted the two much smaller vessels and mounted a concentrated attack on *Kuala*, which received three direct hits to her upper bridge, stoke-hold and engine room. With the ship in flames, the enemy planes then turned their attention to *Tien Kwang*. She was hit, but the damage appeared to be relatively slight.

On board the stricken *Kuala* all hell had broken loose. One of the bombs had penetrated a cabin where four hospital matrons were having a discussion, killing three of them. The fourth, Matron Jones from Singapore General Hospital, was injured by shrapnel and had a large piece lodged in her lower back. The shrieks of the injured mingled with the hiss of escaping steam, only to be drowned out by deafening explosions as bombs exploded in and around the ship and machine-guns strafed survivors in the water. Ignoring their own safety, medical staff still able to function worked feverishly, trying to sort out those who could be saved from those who had no chance of survival, while sailors tried to assess the damage. As the fires began to spread the stupidity of replacing trained Malay and Chinese seamen with untrained Europeans became painfully evident. Having no idea of what to do and with the layout of the ship a mystery, the substitute crews were useless as a firefighting force, particularly since a bomb had knocked out the firefighting equipment. As the bombing and strafing continued, and the smoke made breathing difficult, many passengers leapt into the sea.

One forced to make this decision was Edith Stevenson, a missionary nursing sister who had been working at Queen Alexandra Hospital in Singapore. As she summoned the courage to jump, she saw that below her:

There were non-swimmers holding onto bits of wreckage. I saw one woman grab a dead body only to let go when the truth dawned. Another lady, a nursing sister who, judging by her uniform was from the Government Hospital, was swimming very well and getting clear of the crowded area when a Japanese plane blew her to bits … The top deck seemed a long way from the water. However, there was no alternative. Time was short and the way to the lower deck was either blocked by dead bodies or frantic survivors. Blood from the casualties made the deck slippery. Without further hesitation, I left my small case of valuables on deck and slid overboard. It seemed better to die by drowning than be roasted alive. The heat from the fire on board was unbearable.

Those who ultimately survived were among the last to leave. Although injured by the blast which hit the bridge, *Kuala*'s captain, Lieutenant Franklin Caithness, managed to rescue five women who had taken shelter in a nearby cabin before freeing a jammed gangway to allow more survivors to abandon ship. Fortunately as the planes had by this time departed, most of those who took to the water made it to the safety of the rocks on Pompong under their own steam or were rescued by the foliage-collecting life-boats. Others, cowering in perforated life-boats or clinging to wreckage, were also helped ashore by the stunned working parties.

Some who were caught in the tidal flow tried desperately to reach the island. Sister Stevenson, who had swum free of the burning ship, tried in vain with another nurse and a male passenger to tow an overloaded life raft to shore. What at first seemed very easy proved to be an impossible task. One minute they could almost touch the undergrowth around the island. The next, as if by magic, the raft was swept out to sea. Believing they could swim to the island, her two companions abandoned the raft, only to be carried away themselves.

That some of the castaways who reached Pompong were alive was miraculous. Marjorie de Malmanche, an English nursing sister, was among the last to leave *Kuala*. She had slid down a rope and into the sea only to discover that the only life-boat in sight was crammed to capacity and surrounded by dozens of others clinging to the sides:

> I made for it and hung on with the others. There was only one oar, which was being used, not very effectively, by an elderly woman. I saw the two doctors [Australian Marjorie Lyon and Englishwoman Else Crowe] sliding down into the sea.

As the heavily laden boat had made its way laboriously towards the shore the bombers attacked *Tien Kwang*. Marjorie and her companions watched in horror as many of those now in the water were blown to pieces. One of the planes then focused on the hopelessly overcrowded lifeboat.

> There was an unpleasant whistling sound, and, looking up, I saw a bomb falling straight for us. We all cringed towards the side of the boat, and the next minute were caught up in a huge wave which flung us onto the rocky beach of the island. Everybody scrambled over the rocks and ran up the steeply wooded hillside. Halfway up, the planes came again, and we crouched behind trees for protection. Bombs fell, and our boat and the rocks went up in smoke.

About 700 evacuees were now marooned on Pompong. Fortunately, among them were seasoned military personnel who quickly assumed command. While doctors and nurses carried the wounded to a clearing about 30 metres above sea level, *Kuala*'s chief engineer, Lieutenant Marshall, built a canopy of vines and branches to protect them from the sun. Leaving the military to round up all available stores, a small party led by Bruce Smith, who worked for Singapore's Drainage and Irrigation Department, set off to look for water. According to the information they had, Pompong was without either water or edible fruit. Fortunately, although this proved to be correct in regard to the food situation, Smith used his expertise to locate a small spring on the other side of the island.

The following morning, 16 February, the food situation was eased somewhat when three Malay fishermen arrived with coconuts and freshly caught fish. They also brought the disturbing news that Singapore had fallen and that enemy troops were now moving into the nearby islands. After showing Mr Nunn, the PWD head who had authorised his own evacuation, where an outrigger canoe was hidden, they offered to guide a small party to Singkep Island, where survivors rescued from other sunken ships had been taken, and where help could be obtained from the pro-British Amir Silahili.

A ten-man party comprising eight wounded RAF airmen, one sepoy and Ivor Salmond, an English businessman who spoke Malay and Dutch, set off. Fourteen hours later, Salmond was pouring out their tale of woe to the sympathetic amir, whose authority extended across a hundred islands and who was known by the rather daunting Dutch title of 'Hoofd der Onderafdeeling Blakang Diak'. Immediately pledging his help, he sent word to the Dutch Controller at Dabo before personally assuming control of the rescue, rounding up motor tonkans (wooden ocean-going boats) from a nearby island and instructing the skippers to pass all refugees on to the Indragiri escape route.

In the meantime, at Pompong the idea of salvaging *Tien Kwang* was scrapped when the engineers discovered she was damaged below the waterline and the engines would not start. After being stripped of anything of value, the sea-cocks were opened and the ship scuttled to avoid attracting enemy aircraft. It was a vain hope. Before long the planes returned and strafed the beach. In order to keep casualties to a minimum Nunn split the survivors into three groups.

Food stocks were limited, and help was a long time coming. It was not until two days had passed that the first rescue boats, sent north by Amir Silahili, reached Pompong and Bengku. By the time Reynolds learned that help was needed, many of the more able-bodied had been rescued and taken south to Singkep. From here they were eventually ferried to the Djambi and Indragiri rivers and on to the escape route, where they joined hundreds of other castaways who owed their lives to the shuttle service run by Chinese and Malay fishermen.

Among them was Edith Stevenson. After her two companions had been swept away she had tied herself to the raft with her belt and had continued to tow it, alone. The eight people on the raft – three Indian soldiers, two RAF corporals, an Anglo-Indian woman, an Australian woman who couldn't swim (and whom Edith had saved earlier), and an elderly man, Singapore's chief censor – refused to make room for her so, when darkness approached, she was still in the water and near to exhaustion. Suddenly, a speck appeared on the horizon.

It was a native fishing boat. Pulling alongside the raft, the Malays cut Edith free and lowered her into their small craft, only to have the ingrates on board the raft yell 'Leave her – she can swim!' After caring for everyone in the village nearby, the fishermen passed them on to Amir Silahili's rescue organisation.

The first European rescue vessel to arrive at Pompong was *Tanjung Pinang* which, after picking up 208 women and children, had been on her way up the Indragiri when she almost collided with *Kofuku Maru*. After successfully dropping off half her passengers there, she set sail for Java with the rest, but never arrived. It was later learned that the ship had been caught in a searchlight beam on the night of 18 February and attacked. Eleven survivors took to a makeshift life raft but only two, Margot Turner and Englishwoman Molly Watts-Carter, who were picked up by a Japanese cruiser, are known to have survived.

The remaining castaways, their food and water now severely rationed, were about to enter their third day when, at 3 am, *Kofuku Maru* arrived. As he made his way ashore in the pale dawn light Reynolds, now sporting a bushy grey beard which gave him the air of a geriatric pirate, could see several figures tending the wounded at a roughly constructed first-aid post. Mounds of freshly turned sand surmounted by crude wooden crosses stretched in rows along the narrow beach. There would have been many more, had it not been for the efforts of the medical staff, especially Dr Marjorie Lyon, a leading obstetrician who was herself wounded, and fellow Australian Sister G Dowling. They were assisted by Marjorie de Malmanche and Patsy Brennan and Brenda McDuff, two nursing sisters from Batu Gajah Hospital near Ipoh. Brenda, whom Reynolds knew, had the surprise of her life when he strode onto the beach to greet her with a cheery 'Hello, Mrs Mac'. Using the most rudimentary equipment and with only basic emergency supplies these women, described by Reynolds as 'stout hearted', had somehow managed to keep thirty seriously wounded patients alive.

As it was far too risky to attempt evacuation until nightfall, Reynolds sailed around to the opposite side of the island, where a large camp had been set up near the spring. To the horror of the 400 or so castaways who were anxiously scanning the horizon, *Kofuku Maru* came into view at the same time as an enemy plane flew overhead. To their great relief the aircraft flew off, the pilot evidently believing, from the familiar shape of the vessel, that it was nothing more than a Japanese fishing boat. Promising the hundreds who had to remain behind that he would be back, Reynolds embarked a small number of women and the less seriously wounded before returning to the makeshift hospital to organise the evacuation of the gravely ill. Obstetrician Dr Elsie Crowe, a close friend of Marjorie Lyon, had been bombed while in the water, suffering a fractured skull and other serious injuries. Marjorie had saved her from drowning and had kept a close watch on her ever since. Dr Crowe and Sister Warre, who was comatose from shrapnel lodged in her brain, were carried on makeshift stretchers constructed from tree branches to *Sirius*, a small rowing boat Reynolds had managed to acquire. From here Paddy Jackson, the planter from Ipoh, and a couple of British naval officers, including Surgeon Williams, helped them board *Kofuku Maru*. Even with the tireless assistance of the medical staff, it was not until midnight that *Kofuku Maru*, with her seventy-six refugees, nine of whom were hideously injured with gangrenous wounds, was able to head for the safety of the Indragiri River.

The voyage, described by Reynolds as 'shuffling' and Sister Brenda McDuff as 'very uncomfortable', was nightmarish. Sister Dowling, with the help of Reynolds' medicine chest, was able to give the seriously wounded some measure of comfort, but the rest had to make do as best they could, themselves. With no accommodation other than the bare wooden deck and with virtually no protection from the elements, the evacuees were sardined into small areas of decking, already strewn with an assortment of ropes, gear, chains and miscellaneous items. Dr Crowe and the other stretcher cases were placed side by side on the larger sections but the rest were forced to sit, knees tucked under their chins, in the small spaces which normally served as walkways. Space was so tight that the able-bodied had to take turns to stand and stretch their legs. One consolation was that there was no queue for the bucket on the rope – the passengers were so dehydrated and undernourished that no one needed to use it.

Fifteen long and wearisome hours after leaving Pompong, Reynolds nosed his ship alongside a rickety jetty at Tambilahan, a fishing village between Prigi Radja and Rengat, which had several warehouses to shelter the refugees as well as a market and small dispensary. From here all those not badly injured made the remainder of the journey in great style, in well-appointed cabins on *Mapia*, a luxuriously appointed Dutch coastal boat. Dr Crowe, Sister Warre and a Greek family, accompanied by Marjorie Lyon and Marjorie de Malmanche, were placed on a fast motor-launch belonging to the Dutch controller and transferred at once to Rengat, where Dr Lyon operated successfully on both her patients. On finding that an entire ward of the hospital was full of injured British soldiers, the doctor, Brenda McDuff and Paddy Clarke volunteered to remain behind to look after them. Meanwhile, back at Tambilahan, Reynolds had handed over the seriously injured to Lieutenant-Colonel Albert Coates, a brilliant Australian surgeon from Melbourne serving with 10 Australian General Hospital.

Coates had left Singapore on the evacuation ship *Sui Kwong*, an auxiliary patrol vessel of just under 800 tonnes, at about midnight on 13 February. Sixteen hours later the vessel was attacked. Fortunately Coates was among those rescued by *Tenggaroh*, a luxury launch owned by the Sultan of Johor, which was taking a number of senior Allied personnel, including Coates' fellow officer Colonel Broadbent, to the Indragiri to join the escape route. On learning that many wounded would be arriving shortly, Coates and two of his medical staff, Sergeants Glancy and Hughes, remained behind at Tambilahan and converted the dispensary to an aid post instead of continuing to the west coast along the escape route.

When *Kofuku Maru* turned up just on dusk four days later, Coates was roused from

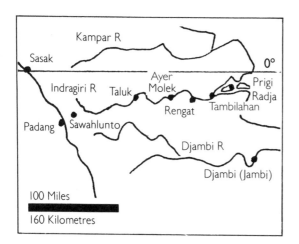

The SOE escape route along the Indragiri River, Sumatra

his work by the sound of Reynolds' distinctly Australian voice bellowing from the water 'Colonel Coates! Here is a new load of customers, plenty of them. Get your saw sharpened up!' That night, after the patients had been transferred with great difficulty from the ship and up the spidery, ladder-like steps onto an equally spidery jetty, they were carried to a primitive room which Coates called his 'operating theatre'. Using the most basic surgical instruments, which included a chopper donated by a local, and with Sergeant Benjamin Glancy acting as anaesthetist (Sister Dowling being 'all in'), Bertie Coates performed seven major operations that night. A brigadier and a squadron leader died, but they managed to save the life of Matron Jones after removing the bomb splinter from her spine.

Reynolds did not hang around to witness to the life-saving surgery performed by Coates, who gave him a note to deliver to General Broadbent advising that he would remain at Tambilahan with the wounded until he was no longer needed. As soon as Reynolds had seen his last patient safely on shore and had arranged transport for the others, he was off again to Pompong, where he discovered that three Malay tonkans had reduced the number of people awaiting evacuation by two-thirds. Among the ninety-six still waiting anxiously for his promised return were Mr Nunn and his wife who, still refusing to leave her husband, was now the only woman left on the island.

Save for the lonely graves, Pompong was now deserted but Reynolds did not pause to rest. Learning from reports flooding in to the Indragiri that many others were awaiting rescue elsewhere, he delivered his passengers and set sail again immediately, visiting Moro (Monkey), Sugibawah, Bengku, Singkep, Pompong and Lingga islands to collect stragglers rounded up by Malay fishermen. Because *Kofuku Maru* was very obviously a Japanese fishing boat, his decision to hoist Chinese colours as he neared the islands reassured both castaways and locals who, with his identity established, spared no effort to help him. *Kofuku Maru* was now an integral part of the escape route.

Escape

Returning from one of his trips on about 24 February, Reynolds noticed a small sailing craft negotiating the waters of the Indragiri estuary. Thinking that the two occupants might be in need of a tow or other assistance, he altered course. As *Kofuku Maru* drew alongside, her wash adding to the chop already on the water, those on board the larger vessel were startled to see a figure, shorts around its ankles, pitch headlong over the side of the small craft. Seconds later, and to the obvious amusement of the boat's other occupant as well as *Kofuku Maru*'s now very interested gallery, a head emerged, spluttering waterlogged expletives in an accent that was very obviously Welsh. Mustering what dignity he had left, a very wet Welshman, now minus the shorts into which he had been changing at the time of Reynolds' inopportune arrival, clambered back on board. His companion, a captain in the Gordon Highlanders, assured the would-be Good Samaritan that they were perfectly all right and were making for Prigi Radja, where they intended to find a powered boat to take them to Rengat. Satisfied that the officer had the matter well in hand, Reynolds headed upriver.

Some hours later, with his latest group of castaways safely delivered, Reynolds had just finished securing *Kofuku Maru* to the wharf at Rengat when he heard the chug of a small diesel engine. This was followed almost immediately by a substantial bump, which rocked the ship on her mooring lines. Never one to suffer fools gladly, especially in matters nautical, Bill Reynolds stormed out of the wheelhouse. Even without his beard, the tall, mahogany-tanned figure, clad in a pair of scruffy, filthy shorts and an equally disreputable shirt, was a most intimidating sight. Without pausing to see who or what had rammed his ship Reynolds let forth with a stream of colourful abuse which, after years at sea, he had refined to an art form. After a lifetime of practice, Reynolds was also a master of the Australian vernacular, delivered with such fluency that, in his earthy two-minute tirade, he did not repeat himself once. It was not until he had finished that he bothered to look down and see who was responsible for what he considered to be an outrageously poor exhibition of seamanship. Glaring through his horn-rimmed spectacles, he was astonished to see that the object of his tirade was the Gordon Highlander whom he had met in the river estuary that very morning. To his further astonishment he discovered that, far from being reduced to a quivering mass of jelly by the vitriolic outburst, the officer was sitting calmly at the tiller, glancing from Reynolds to his companion, standing in the bow, with an expression of quiet bemusement. IVAN

The face that the Australian now viewed from his superior perch was in some ways not unlike that of a fox – finely boned, sharp and alert – with close-cropped, slightly reddish brown curls hugging a neat skull. The grey-green eyes which met and held Reynolds' furious stare sparkled with barely suppressed mirth. Not in evidence at the moment was the ready, gap-toothed smile which could transform an often pensive expression. Although the Gordon Highlander was over 180 centimetres tall, the muscular spareness of his build at first glance suggested frailty, an impression reinforced by slender, artistic-looking fingers and quick,

Ivan Lyon

bird-like movements often found in those possessed by a restless, nervous energy. But any appearance of frailty was deceptive. This man had a mind honed like fine-tempered steel and resolution to match, with a sense of purpose and determination quite capable of forcing his whippet-like body well beyond its own, or any one else's, normal limits of endurance.

He was SOE's Ivan Lyon, a very close friend and colleague of Denis Emerson-Elliott. For the first time in his life, Bill Reynolds had met his match.

5

A meeting of like minds

January–February 1942

Captain Ivan Lyon, 2 Gordon Highlanders, was descended from a long line of military men whose roots extended far back in Scottish history. His ancestor David Lyon had lost his life at the Battle of Flodden in September 1513 and generations of Lyons had served their monarch and country ever since. His great-great-grandfather was Clan Chief Ranald McDonald, whose cousin Flora had attained immortality by saving Bonnie Prince Charlie from certain death at the hands of the English. And it was Ranald himself who produced the surety bond for the Prince's troops, enabling him to march on London.

Hundreds of years later the family, which was also very distantly related to Elizabeth Bowes-Lyon, daughter of the Earl of Strathmore, consort of King George VI and mother of Queen Elizabeth II, was still upholding these fine traditions of gallantry and bravery. Ivan's grandfather, Francis, had served with the prestigious Horse Artillery during the reign of Queen Victoria, only to die prematurely when a high-explosive shell had exploded unexpectedly during an experiment. His son Francis, Ivan's father, had been wounded during the Siege of Ladysmith in South Africa while serving with the artillery in the reign of the same monarch. On the recommendation of his commander, Field Marshall Sir George White, VC, he had been awarded a Distinguished Service Order.

The outbreak of the Great War saw Francis in action again, this time rising to the rank of brigadier-general. On 17 August 1915, while he was at the Western Front, his wife Jane gave birth to a son, Ivan, at Sevenoaks. After the war the general accepted a posting as military attaché in the Balkans and then Brussels, where he remained until his retirement. It was during this period that Ivan learned to speak French. On returning to England the family settled at Gorsehanger Farm at Farnham, a small town in Surrey not far from the famous army establishment at Aldershot. Ivan, whose elder brother had died in infancy, was the third born. Now the eldest son, he was a natural leader to the surviving siblings – two sisters and a brother. A somewhat solitary child, he was happy with his own company and could spend long periods deep in thought. His formal education had begun at West Down Preparatory, a boarding school which catered mainly for bright pupils wishing to enter Winchester College. In 1929, in a complete break with the family tradition of enrolling sons at Eton, Ivan was sent to Harrow, which boasted Winston Churchill among its notable old boys.

It was at Harrow that Ivan learned to sail, embracing it with such passion that he was out on the water at every opportunity. He particularly enjoyed single-handed yachting, which suited his temperament and, at the age of seventeen, was awarded a trophy for a solo voyage in a small dinghy across the North Sea to Denmark. Although he performed creditably enough on the academic front, he was far more interested in physical challenge than intellectual exercise. Winter holidays were spent skiing in Austria and Switzerland and by the time he finished school he was an accomplished skier. An athletic all-rounder, he also carved a name for himself with long-distance running, another solitary sport and one suited to lean, wiry people.

As he grew into adulthood Ivan developed a taste for all things military, particularly war history, an interest actively encouraged by his father who was keen to see him follow in the footsteps of his forebears. Ivan's natural inclination, reinforced by the responsibility of living up to the high standards of conduct and achievement set by his family, developed in him a keen sense of duty, a love of Empire and, equally importantly, a rigid code of gentlemanly behaviour.

When he announced that he intended to join the navy on leaving Harrow, it came as no surprise, although he had spent four years as a band member in the school's army cadet corps. There was no objection from his father, as several Lyons in the past had acquitted themselves well as sailors. However, he was thwarted from a career on the high seas, not because of any problems with his intellectual capacity or fitness level, but because Ivan, by this time a rather individual thinker, did not give the expected answers to questions posed by the members of the Naval Board at Dartmouth.

Taking the initiative, his father offered his son the choice of entering the artillery or joining the Gordon Highlanders. The latter was another departure from family tradition, the Lyons being generally artillery men, but the bravery of the Gordons in 'going over the top' on the Western Front had greatly impressed the general, whose two friends, Sir George White (his commander in the Boer War) and Field Marshal Sir Ian Hamilton (the Gordons' Commander-in-Chief at the time) had also chosen this regiment to pursue their military careers. After weighing up the prestige of intellectual superiority, universally associated with the exacting science of the artillery, with the snappily immaculate image projected by the kilt-swinging Gordons, Ivan opted for the latter, telling his mother it was 'easier to be smart than clever'. In 1934, having made his choice and with family finances sufficient to supply him with a small private income to make army life more comfortable, Ivan, already a gentleman, marched off to the Royal Military College at Sandhurst to learn how to be an officer.

Ivan may have been in the army but it didn't keep him away from the water. In the summer of 1935 he and two of his fellow officers paddled a small canoe down the Danube

Lyon on parade with the Gordon Highlanders

to Budapest. On this highly successful trip, which he planned and organised, he learned many things including tolerance, how to live harmoniously in very close quarters and, most importantly, flexibility, since the best thought-out project could be easily upset by poor weather or disrupted by events outside his control. At the end of that year, his military training over, Ivan was posted to Redford Barracks where soldiering for the next twelve months consisted of guard duty, ceremonial parades and lessons on how to handle a cantankerous Lewis gun. Any spare time during the day was filled with cross-country running, while long evenings were enlivened by vigorous highland dancing. It was in the comfortably old-fashioned Redford Barracks that Ivan found a most congenial soul mate – Francis Moir-Byres, a self-sufficient officer whose passion for sailing matched his own.

When the time came to chose between spending the next six years in the confines of the familiar barracks or somewhere overseas, both Ivan and Francis jumped at the chance to extend their horizons. In the winter of 1936–37 they left England on the troop ship *Dorchester*, bound for Singapore via Gibraltar, Malta and Port Said. The two friends spent many hours lolling against the deck rail, discussing a great variety of subjects, ranging from the antics of *Two Flappers in Paris* (a racy book bought from an Arab street-pedlar) to the disturbing political situation in Europe. As the days ran into weeks, Francis realised Ivan's ability to make snap decisions was not because he was a superficial thinker, but because he was able to think laterally. His agile mind not only allowed him to tackle a problem or approach a new idea from a different angle, it also skipped far ahead and grasped the crux of the matter while others were still plodding along. When he was confident the solution had been found he delivered it succinctly, quietly and calmly, his well-modulated tones more powerful and impressive than louder, more insistent voices.

Unable to resist the lure of the sea, as soon as Francis and Ivan were settled into their new home at Selarang Barracks on the Changi peninsula they obtained a loan from the battalion sports fund and purchased *Vinette*, a three-tonne, six-metre sloop. It came with a rather cantankerous outboard motor. As neither man was mechanically minded, one day in total frustration they heaved it over the side, leaving them at the complete mercy of the winds. Both were experienced sailors, but they quickly discovered that sailing in Singaporean waters required a brand new set of skills. To avoid being swept out into the South China Sea by strong rips it was essential they learned the intricacies of the capricious local wind patterns and swirling tidal flows. From sheer necessity they also became skilled meteorologists, reading the weather with uncanny accuracy and developing the ability to detect the onset of fierce tropical storms, known as 'sumatras', which blew up with little warning.

It did not take long for the two young men and their yacht to come to the attention of policeman John Dalley and MI5's 'man in Singapore', Colonel Hayley Bell, who drew them into their circle of agents. Dalley and Bell, being unconventional thinkers, appealed to Ivan enormously, and he to them.

By August 1937 the two sailors felt confident enough to undertake a 'pleasure' cruise to Kota Bharu. Armed only with an army prismatic compass, a navigational book giving some coastal information and such charts as they had managed to scrounge, they spent a month travelling from one small village to the next, making friends with the locals, practising their Malay and slaking their thirst with fresh green coconuts, for which Ivan had an absolute passion. At Trengannu they met up with John Dalley and another, far more bizarre character – Morganson, the local harbour master, who was renowned for his ability to knock back whisky at a rate which would have killed lesser men. Morgie, as the enormous Dane was commonly known, looked as if he had stepped from the era of pirates and square-rigged sailing ships and was part of Bell's and Dalley's intelligence network. Ivan, always attracted to characters who were larger than life, found him fascinating company.

As *Vinette's* keel drew just over one metre, the adventurers were able to enter many shallow coves protected by sandbars and normally accessible only to small native fishing craft. Aided by good weather, they penetrated 100 illegal kilometres beyond the border into Thailand. Their presence ashore aroused no particular interest so they stayed overnight, taking in a movie at the small local cinema. It was a World War I film, and to their amusement they found that the 'baddies' were all wearing British helmets, while the heroes were easily identifiable by their German headgear.

On the way back, after visiting the beautiful Redang Islands, they reported to Dalley at

Trengannu before arranging to have *Vinette* shipped back to Singapore, for they were running short of time and the monsoon winds, which had given them a good run up the coast, were against them, and freshening. On their return they submitted a comprehensive intelligence report to Hayley Bell, who was at that time collecting evidence to convince Whitehall of the need to establish adequate defences. He was most interested to learn that Ivan and Francis believed that, should the Japanese attempt to extend their empire into Malaya, they would do so from the north-east, during the monsoon – an opinion which was in absolute concurrence with Bell's, and was used to reinforce his argument for defensive measures to be taken.

Ivan, bored out of his mind by garrison duties and irritated by the shallow social scene, grasped every opportunity to 'escape'. His next adventure took him to Australia, as a crewman on the twelve-tonne ketch *Kewarra*. Owned by J Gagan, a prominent Australian, the vessel was on a pleasure cruise to Darwin via the Dutch East Indies. When Ivan reached Darwin he met and fell instantly in love with a daughter of the famous Durack pastoral family. The lady was evidently equally smitten, for when Ivan returned to Singapore by freighter he informed Francis that he was engaged. Although the betrothal was at this stage 'unofficial', the relationship between the pair was intense enough for the powerful and wealthy Durack family to dispatch an uncle to Singapore. Under instructions to give the prospective bridegroom the once-over, he arranged to meet Ivan and Francis at the Seaview Hotel. Although they all got on famously, the revelation that Ivan, whose yachting activities kept him short of cash, could not obtain a marriage allowance from the army ultimately went against him. The 'old conk', as Ivan had secretly dubbed the uncle, farewelled his hosts cordially, but his report to the family on Ivan's financial position ultimately put paid to any chance he may have had of marrying the young heiress.

Sailing occupied the bulk of his spare time and Ivan nurtured a secret hope that he might quit the army and sail around the world, an ambition which his fiancée had offered to help finance. Being always on the move, he also continued to star as a distance runner, played a passable game of rugby and became proficient at ju-jitsu. He even had a stab at learning to fly when the army offered to pay for the tuition of any officer who gained an A Class pilot's licence. Francis obtained his wings but Ivan failed in his quest to become an airborne officer, mainly due to his propensity for trying to land when still 15 metres above the ground. But although flying eluded him, he did manage to make a lasting impression on the members of the pukka Singapore Swimming Club.

In a fit of exuberance one night, after consuming a large curry washed down by copious quantities of Tiger beer, Ivan, Francis, and their friend George Elsmie visited a tattooist in Serangoon Road in the heart of the Indian quarter. Francis's good sense prevailed, but George and Ivan succumbed to temptation, George opting for a large Chinese dragon tattooed on his forearm. After three agonising hours Ivan emerged with a large, brilliantly-hued tiger's

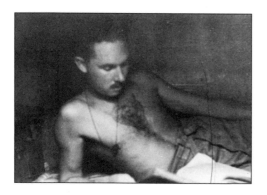

Lyon and his infamous tiger tattoo

head emblazoned on his chest in red, blue and yellow. Francis considered it to be a real work of art, as did Ivan. Believing that such a magnificent masterpiece deserved a wider viewing audience, they decided to try it out on the unsuspecting public at the Singapore Swimming Club. After ensuring they had everyone's attention by mooring *Vinette* directly in front of the Club, they swam ashore. Ivan's entrance was nothing short of spectacular. As he emerged bare-torsoed from the water, every eye was on that magnificently lurid tiger, snarling at them as Ivan flexed the muscles of his chest.

Ivan enjoyed partying almost as much as outdoor sports, attacking both with equal enthusiasm. He also adored the company of beautiful women, both Oriental and European, even though he was 'engaged', and he loved to dance. An expert in the art of sword dancing as well as the highland fling, he did not require any encouragement other than a drop or two of his favourite tipple to entice him onto the dance floor. On one occasion, when his naturally high spirits were boosted by the more liquid variety at an RAF cocktail party, he discarded his clothing and cavorted around on the manicured lawn, demonstrating his dancing prowess in a manner which was long remembered. The next day, when it was tactfully suggested that an apology might be in order, Ivan somehow managed to turn what might have been an embarrassing situation into a social event. A fearful Francis, waiting with trepidation in the car outside the senior RAF officer's office, was invited inside where he found, to his astonishment, Ivan and his new best friend enjoying a most convivial pre-luncheon drink.

It was a mixture of pink gins, sailing and an eye for beautiful women which in 1938 led Ivan to Gabrielle Anna Georgette Bouvier. While enjoying a congenial drink with Colonel Willy Graham, their CO, he and Francis learned that an exceptionally beautiful French girl lived on the prison island of Poulo Condore in French Indo-China, where her father was governor. With Ivan's current love conveniently forgotten, he and Francis began planning for an almost immediate departure for the island to check out this story and to take advantage of the south-west monsoon. *Vinette* was restocked and a radio receiver installed so that they could obtain a daily weather report and other information from a friend, Captain Stanley Wilson, a wireless buff. At the last minute there was a change of plan, for Francis's father advised he was coming to visit his son while they intended to be away and Ivan could no longer leave Singapore on the previously agreed date. They solved the dilemma by deciding that, since Francis had a few days free before his father arrived, he and a crew of two should sail *Vinette* to Mersing on Malaya's east coast, where Ivan would take over and continue on, alone.

Although Ivan had learned a fair bit about navigation when he sailed to Australia on *Kewarra*, his navigation skills, according to Francis, were still 'bloody awful'. Undaunted that he was unable to use the stars to determine his longitude, he set sail for Poulo Condore with a watch, compass and charts his only navigational aids. Blessed with the luck usually associated with the Irish, he found his lack of navigational know-how no handicap. After sailing for several days in the general direction of the island he decided, by dead reckoning, that he was in the right area. A floating grapefruit box told him he was on a shipping route and a butterfly that he was not far from land. Taking a cross-bearing from the nearest point of Indo-China and the established shipping lane he plotted, and then found, Poulo Condore. He immediately went ashore and introduced himself to the governor, Commandant Georges Bouvier. As he seldom had any visitors, let alone someone who dropped by and spoke fluent French, the governor invited Ivan to dinner.

While effecting repairs to *Vinette*'s storm-damaged hatch and sails, a task he managed

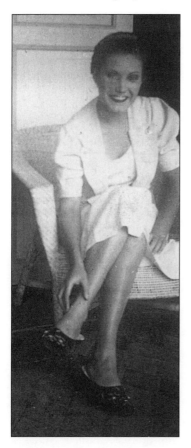

Gabrielle Lyon, c. 1939

to stretch out for five days, he fell head over heels in love with 24-year-old Gabrielle Bouvier, a ravishingly beautiful, dark-eyed brunette and the sole reason for his voyage. The feeling was not reciprocated initially, for although the charming Frenchwoman was attracted to Ivan's good looks and ready wit, she thought he drank too much and was far too wild. She was also very wary of any romantic involvement. Born in Cayenne, France, in January 1914, by the time she was nineteen years old she was the mother of a small daughter and had gone through a harrowing marriage and divorce. Gabrielle had not, however, reckoned with the Lyon charm. Returning to Singapore determined to marry her, Ivan set about achieving this aim with the same enthusiasm and dedication he tackled everything else in life. Fortunately he had by this time received a letter from his Australian fiancée to say the engagement was off – she could no longer wait for him and was going to marry someone else. Following a well-orchestrated plan, which even involved his giving up drinking, Ivan wooed his newfound love relentlessly, by letter and in person, until she eventually capitulated. In early 1939 she agreed to become his wife.

Initially the priest refused to conduct the ceremony, on the grounds that Gabrielle was a divorcee, but when Ivan threatened to sack his church he adopted a more reasonable stance and married them in Saigon on 27 July 1939.

Gabrielle's arrival in Singapore created a sensation. Not only was she a stunningly beautiful and cultured woman, she was also a brilliant cook and a marvellous hostess, attributes which helped make the newlyweds in great demand socially. In the coming months the regiment, which saw very little of Ivan normally, saw him even less. When at home he scarcely ventured outside the door of the charming house Gabrielle had found for them on the beach near Changi, after moving from married quarters off Orchard Road. The new house was not far from the home of Denis and Norma Emerson-Elliott. With Denis and Ivan in the same 'business' and Denis always enjoying the company of unconventional people, it did not take long for them to become acquainted. This professional association soon blossomed into a deep friendship, to the degree that Ivan and Gabrielle were the only guests invited to the Emerson-Elliotts' very private wedding.

When not at home Ivan was involved in secret intelligence work, which had begun in August 1938 when he was seconded from his normal army routine to undertake special missions for Hayley Bell. The transfer, which gave him great freedom of movement, had coincided with, and greatly facilitated, his voyage to Poulo Condore. The variety of the job and the odd hours suited him, for counter-espionage and laying traps for Japanese agents had far more appeal than irksome garrison duties and regimental life. One of his tasks was to test the possibility of invasion through Malaya and Thailand. Using *Vinette*, he accessed remote areas of these countries' coastlines and made forays inland on foot to investigate routes which the enemy might take. At one stage he spent weeks trying to trace the origins of suspicious signals being transmitted from Singapore City. He amassed a great deal of information, but the phantom radio operator evaded capture despite several police raids.

The disbanding of Bell's intelligence network in mid-1939 coincided with Ivan's marriage, and he had been lured into a more stable job in the censorship office of the Intelligence Bureau. When it was realised he was fluent in French, he was appointed aide-de-camp to General Catroux, formerly Governor-General of Indo-China. He was then attached to the staff of Sir Geoffrey Layton, naval commander of the China Station, operating as a liaison officer with the Free French – a role which encompassed organising and liaising with agents operating secretly in Indo-China, which was controlled by the pro-Japanese Vichy French.

Six months later Gabrielle was also working for the Free French. In June 1940 she accepted the post of secretary to Monsieur Brizay, head of the Free French in Singapore, an organisation secretly sponsored by SOE. One of the liaison officers at Gabrielle's workplace was Pierre Boulle, who was being trained to carry out demolitions in Indo-China by SOE – a mission that was aborted when agents advised the situation there was too dangerous. Boulle was captured on a subsequent mission but survived the war to become the bestselling author of the wartime novel *The Bridge on the River Kwai*.

In July 1941 the Japanese occupied French Indo-China prior to the invasion of Malaya. Gabrielle's father now became a vital link in the secret intelligence chain, passing on information to Ivan about the movement of Japanese troops, and other useful intelligence. He did this for some time but eventually the Vichy French discovered his activities and denounced the Bouviers as traitors. They were badly beaten and died as a result. Back in Singapore, it was perhaps poetic justice that their daughter Gabrielle, who was broadcasting to Indo-China, acted as interpreter for the police Special Branch when they arrested Commandant Maurice Lenormand, the chief Vichy agent, and also questioned him before he was sentenced to death for treason. He escaped the gallows, for he was still in Outram Road Gaol awaiting execution when Singapore fell and was subsequently released by the Japanese. He was fortunate to have been tried at all. Other Vichy French sympathisers were simply arrested and shot.

On 12 September 1941, less than two months after the occupation of Indo-China, Gabrielle gave birth to a son, Clive. He was delivered by Colonel (Dr) Bloom, Royal Army Medical Corps, and Sister Marjorie de Malmanche, who knew both mother and father well. Ivan, whose job involved a great deal of travel and was in Batavia at the time of the birth, was overjoyed. He hurried home, but despite his added family responsibilities he now embarked on even more dangerous work – for SOE. On 10 September Ivan, who had come to the attention of Valentine St John Killery in July and been watched closely ever since, was 'taken on' officially by SOE. With Denis Emerson-Elliott and others, he now began secretly planting arms dumps for stay-behind parties in Malaya, despite General Percival's orders to desist. While in Singapore he spent much of his time at SOE's 101 School, where he so impressed Colonel Alan Warren with his ability to get on with the job that the colonel informed Malaya Command that they 'could keep everybody else, provided he had Ivan to work for him'. Given a completely free hand in the manner of dress, weapons and modus operandi, Warren, Ivan, John Dalley and several other like-minded individuals were responsible for the assassination of a large number of enemy agents.

One agent caught red-handed who was not assassinated immediately by the 'death squad' was Captain Patrick Heenan of the Indian Army, working as a liaison officer with the RAF. Arrested in Butterworth, Malaya on 10 December 1941 for transmitting signals to the enemy, he was escorted from nearby Penang to Singapore by Ivan, who handcuffed him to the Argylls' Private David Gibson with instructions to shoot him if he tried to escape. Once in Singapore, Heenan was questioned by Special Branch, court-martialled and found guilty of treason – a verdict which demanded the death sentence. Like Vichy agent Maurice Lenormand, he was transferred to Outram Road Gaol to await execution. Unlike the Frenchman, he was not set free by the Japanese. According to the military police guarding him, on 13 February he became very cocky, boasting that he would soon be free and they would be prisoners. Goaded beyond endurance, it is said that they cut cards to decide who would have the pleasure of killing him, and took him to the dockside. Here 'a sergeant' executed him with a single bullet to the back of the head, and dumped the body into the harbour.

As no other British officer was murdered at the docks, it may well be that the tall, good-looking Heenan was mistaken for another striking, well-presented officer – Captain Atkinson – alleged to have been murdered by Australians on board *Empire Star*. Whether this mistake in identity occurred, and whether it was by accident or design, is a question which remains unanswered. However, many years later Denis Emerson-Elliott, who knew all about Heenan's arrest and activities, conceded that the story of Atkinson's murder may have been invented by MI6 to explain away Heenan's violent end and that Heenan's death may, indeed, have been at the hands of MI6 or SOE itself.

Once it was obvious that the Japanese would occupy all of Malaya, Ivan Lyon arranged a passage to Australia for Gabrielle and Clive on SS *Narkunda*, formerly a P&O liner and now a troopship. With his family out of harm's way, Ivan turned his attention to help infiltrate Chinese guerrillas behind enemy lines. Such was the urgency and importance of this work, which saw SOE insert ten groups successfully, that on 30 January 1942 he and Frank Brewer were still busily organising supply dumps for one party while Denis Emerson-Elliott was assisting another. Although a reluctant Denis had been compelled to make his terrified labour force complete the task at gunpoint, for Ivan's group it had been an even more hair-raising experience.

Fighting against traffic streaming chaotically into Singapore, they had arrived in Johor Bahru with three trucks laden with supplies to discover their Chinese contact nowhere in evidence. The labourers, who by this time were feeling extremely anxious, wanted to bury the lot in a swamp near the road but Ivan would not have a bar of it. He ordered them to drive to a rubber plantation where battle-stained and weary troops were trying to dig slit trenches for a last-ditch stand against the Japanese. Ignoring an officer's opinion that they were crazy to go any further, the SOE team moved about two kilometres further up the road, where they found a small copse suitable for their needs. The Japanese were close, very close, so Ivan too used his pistol to persuade his workers to keep going. It was not until the enemy was just 300 metres away that he pulled his men out, hurriedly covering the partially established dump before beating a hasty retreat to join the crocodile of troops crossing the causeway. Later that evening, after attending a regimental dinner at the Gordons' mess, Ivan reported to 101 Special Training School to find a message from Alan Warren ordering him to report to SOE HQ at the Cathay Building the following morning.

While Ivan had been scuttling about Johor caching supplies, it had become obvious to Colonel Warren that, unless something was done to provide a safe route, movement in and

The Cathay Building, Singapore's only skyscraper and HQ of SOE Far East

out of Singapore would soon be extremely difficult. Somehow he must find a way to keep his stay-behind parties supplied and evacuate them to safety, if need be. After considerable thought, he concluded that the solution lay with Sumatra, the back door to both Malaya and Singapore. To infiltrate Malaya, he would set up a base on Sumatra's north-eastern coast where there was an old pirate haunt, a fishing village with the melodious name of Began-Siapiapi. From here he believed he could smuggle men and supplies across the Straits of Malacca and into Malaya. To move in and out of Singapore, a base would be established at Rengat on the Indragiri River. With the cooperation of the Dutch administrators, equipment and troops could be moved across the mountains from the deep-water anchorage at Emmahaven, near Padang on the west coast. A third base, its location as yet to be determined, would provide a major supply point between Singapore and the Indragiri, facilitating the establishment of food dumps on various islands, and from which personnel could be redirected. Should Singapore fall, the route could be reversed to move troops, stage by stage, to safety.

With his idea fast becoming concrete, Warren had turned his attention to the selection of personnel capable of organising such a mission. Having already earmarked two SOE men – policeman John Davis and Richard Broome, a district officer from Ipoh – for the behind-the-lines operations from Began-Siapiapi, the names of Ivan Lyon and SOE naval officer Brian Passmore, both of whom had good knowledge of the waters in and around Singapore, sprang to mind.

He called Passmore, who considered the offer. However, Passmore had already been approached by Davis and Broome, who wanted him to find a diesel-engined junk and take them to Sumatra where, apart from infiltrating enemy territory, they hoped to be able to bribe local fishermen to rescue a number of Argylls reportedly stranded on some islands off Malaya's west coast. When Passmore decided that rescuing marooned Argylls and infiltrating guerrillas into Malaya sounded far more exciting than setting up food dumps on palm-fringed islands, Warren was forced to cast about for an alternative recruit among SOE ranks. He settled on Lieutenant Herbert Alan 'Jock' Campbell, a bustling, slightly balding 37-year-old planter who, like many of those involved in secret intelligence, had lived and worked in Malaya for some time. In 1927 he had joined Socfin, a large French consortium involved in rubber and palm oil plantations, by 1939 rising to the ranks of company director. In 1941 he was also appointed Inspector of Palm Oil Plantations by the Colonial Office. Fluent in French, Malay and Tamil (a Ceylonese language spoken by many estate workers), Campbell boasted a military career spanning an impressive twenty years, beginning with the Officer Training Corps at Edinburgh University in 1922, progressing to the King's Own Scottish Borderers (a territorial or militia unit) in 1924 and then, in Malaya, to several local volunteer units. In late December 1941, while enlisted with the Johor Volunteer Engineers, he was formally recruited by SOE and commissioned as a major in the British Army's 'general list'. However, because of his previous peacetime enlistment in Scotland, he was permitted to adopt the uniform of the King's Own Scottish Borderers, a regiment whose members wore trews, close-fitting tartan trousers, instead of the more traditional kilt.[1]

By the time Ivan reported to the Cathay Building on 31 January and accepted Warren's offer, the colonel's plan was almost finalised. Campbell was to organise the Sumatran end, leaving Lyon, with his excellent local knowledge, to select a conveniently situated island en route to the Indragiri and stock it with food, weapons and medical supplies. As the latter would be of more use in the hands of someone with some medical knowledge, Lyon suggested Welshman Ron 'Taffy' Morris, a chirpy, good-humoured ex-coalminer, a corporal in the Royal Army Medical Corps, currently attached to 101 Special School.

The following day, 1 February, Lyon and Campbell sounded out Morris and 101's Lance-Corporal E Baker, Royal Engineers. As SOE's Ambrose Trappes-Lomax, now promoted to major, had announced that the school was relocating to Rangoon in Burma, both men were keen to join the operation. As they had a day or two before they were needed, Morris drew a weapon from the armoury and, against all regulations (since medical staff were not supposed to carry arms), spent a short but gleeful period practising on the nearby range. He

Jock Campbell   *Ron 'Taffy' Morris*

and Baker then moved into the Union Jack Club and on 3 February reported to Ivan on SOE's recently acquired *Hong Chuan*, a small, steam-driven coastal trader. With the harbour under constant attack, the four Malay-Chinese crew members wasted no time in loading provisions for the supply dumps. The sealed 4-gallon (18-litre) tubular metal cans, designed to provide sustenance for twelve men for twenty-four hours, each contained tins of corned beef, ship's biscuits and a 'for medicinal purposes only' bottle of Scotch whisky.

For the next day or two the small vessel cruised through the islands of the Riau Archipelago, where Lyon and Campbell made contact with kampongs (villages) and fishing pagars – essentially stilt houses, often temporary, surrounded by fish traps and built out to sea. At each centre they spoke to the headman, and at the village of Moro on Sugibawah Island and other strategic spots they left many emergency ration tins and instructions on how to reach the next island in the chain. Using some of the apparently unlimited cash carried by Campbell they recruited a network of fishermen willing to collect and ferry troops, and/ or refugees, to Lyon's halfway house, which he decided to establish on uninhabited Pulau Durian (near Sugibawah) at the northern end of the Durian Strait. With its inconspicuous approaches, a precipitous overhang as protection from attacking aircraft, and a rather steep, jungle-covered hill providing an excellent vantage point, Durian was perfect for their needs.

Anchoring in the shadow of the cliffs, Lyon and the others began the laborious task of

Refugee Route
est. by Lyon

lumping the supplies up a narrow dirt track to the top of the hill, a job not made any easier by the heavy rain squalls that lashed the island without warning. With the supplies safely stowed in a small atap hut built by the ship's crew, they moved on to Prigi Radja. Realising that the twin conical hills beyond the village provided a distinctive and useful landmark, Lyon and Campbell persuaded the headman to look after a supply dump and direct any refugees upstream to Tambilahan, their next port of call. From here they went to Rengat which, contrary to their expectations, was quite a good sized centre with docks, a proper quayside and some rather large warehouses.

Lyon returned to the Cathay Building late on 5 February to learn that Gabrielle and Clive, along with 742 other adult passengers, had arrived safely in Fremantle on 24 January. This was indeed welcome news. By this time the situation in Singapore had deteriorated to such an extent that soon there would be only one method of escape – through Sumatra. Since the head of SOE Basil Goodfellow now wanted *Hong Chaun* to set up a further supply dump at the small but conspicuous island of Pulau Salu, 16 kilometres south-west of Singapore. The following afternoon Lyon, Campbell, Morris and Baker hitched a ride on SS *Krain*, an 845-tonne Straits Steamship Company vessel which normally plied between Singapore and British North Borneo. Her skipper, who had just dismissed his Asian crew, had agreed to evacuate key staff from 101 School to Rangoon on the condition that SOE provide the necessary manpower.

The vessel came under attack, resulting in some minor casualties, but fortunately the resourceful Morris had managed to locate a quantity of medical supplies and have them delivered to the ship in a borrowed truck. Once they were underway he further demonstrated his usefulness by ferreting around in the galley for whatever food he could find and producing a large pot of Maconnachie stew. After dropping off Lyon and Morris at Pulau Durian, and Campbell and Baker at Prigi Radja, *Krain* proceeded to Tanjung Priok in Java to pick up SOE's Jim Gavan before sailing for Rangoon.

Ashore on Pulau Durian, Ivan began to advertise their presence by weaving amongst the nearby islands in a five-metre sailing dinghy, informing the headmen that 'the army' was in occupation of the island and that all vessels from Singapore should be directed there. When night fell he and Morris, their chores complete, shared a bottle of medicinal whisky while they listened to the crump of the enemy's heavy artillery barrage and watched the flashes from the explosions light up the sky over Singapore. They took turns to keep watch for the remainder of the night, lest the Japanese attempt to infiltrate Singapore from the south via the Durian Strait.

When the black oily haze from the ruptured oil tanks spread across the horizon the following day they realised they might soon see some activity. Within thirty-six hours, ships which had taken the risk of leaving in daylight were running the gauntlet of waves of Japanese bombers. On 12 February they watched as *Durban* raced through the strait, fighting off attack after attack from bombers focusing their attentions on *Empire Star* and *Kedah*. The smaller boats which followed supplied Ivan with his first customers, followed by survivors from vessels which had run aground. Many of the arrivals were injured so Morris was kept busy, removing chunks of splintered wood and shrapnel, and suturing jagged wounds. As he moved among his patients he dispensed words of comfort in his soft Welsh lilt, taking special care with the small children orphaned by the attacks or the subsequent sinkings. For those beyond earthly help he could do nothing, save bury them in a small clearing nearby.

Not everyone required medical assistance. Vessels which managed to reach Durian unscathed were loaded up with rations and castaways and redirected to Prigi Radja, where Campbell was waiting. On 17 February two ships and the launch *Joan* arrived, bringing news that Singapore had surrendered. This information coincided with a marked increase in the volume of traffic and news from local people that some vessels had been sunk by surface craft, not aircraft – the first indication that the evacuees entering the Bangka Straits had run into an enemy fleet.

While Ivan Lyon was directing proceedings on Durian, in northern Sumatra there had been some changes to Warren's plan. Shortly after Lyon left Singapore, updated intelligence had prompted the colonel to broaden the scope of his operation. In order to make contact with Freddie Spencer Chapman, who was operating behind the lines, Chinese guerrilla parties would now be infiltrated into Malaya in the 80-tonne motor tonkan *Hin Leong*, which Brian Passmore had requisitioned in such a hurry that its load of sugar, soy sauce and rice was still in the hold. On February 8 the vessel, with the cargo partially removed to make room for arms, ammunition, explosives and canned provisions, put to sea.

Besides the crew of four there were two lorry-loads of Chinese guerrillas; SOE Lieutenants Frank Vanrenan and Ronald Graham who, like Jock Campbell, were ex-planters; Broome and his Chinese cook Lo Gnap Soon; Davis, accompanied by his orderly Jamal bin Diam; and Lieutenant Allen Lind, naval reservist and ex-insurance broker from Batavia whom Warren had recruited as he spoke fluent Dutch. Vanrenan and Graham had been part of a much larger group operating behind the lines with Spencer Chapman and mining engineer Pat Garden (now part of the official SOE team). Having lost contact with the group, the pair had been forced to return to Singapore and were anxious to return to Malaya to join the rest of the party.

Lind took the ship from the harbour without any trouble, only to return several hours later when he could not find the passage through the minefield. Back in port they were joined by Warren who, with the situation worsening, had decided to liaise personally with the Dutch on secret matters. Having cleared the minefield on Lind's second attempt, they reached Began-Siapiapi where Warren sold the rest of the cargo, using the proceeds to hire three junks and their local crews. Everyone then set off in various directions – one junk to begin the search for the stranded Argylls; another, with Vanrenan and Graham on board, to Port Selangor to look for Spencer Chapman; and the third to Sapang, south of Port Swettenham, to infiltrate the thirty guerrillas along with Davis and Broome, who were disguised as Malays.

When the junk dispatched to rescue the Argylls returned empty, having failed to find any trace of them, the rest of the party moved to the small seaport of Labanbilik where the Dutch informed Warren that Singapore had fallen. It was only matter of time before the enemy landed on Sumatra's west coast, so Warren decided to investigate the possibility of establishing another operation there. Since this would require the purchase of additional supplies and a ship of some kind, Passmore set off on a 400-kilometre journey north by taxi to Medan, where there was a branch of an English bank. He had no trouble obtaining the money. The manager was so happy to dispose of the cash before the Japanese could arrive and help themselves that he handed over 14,000 guilders.

While Passmore was away General Wavell, now at his headquarters in Java, ordered Warren to Padang where large numbers of troops were allegedly assembled. Realising that this would give him the opportunity to set up his new base, Warren set off at once with Lind as his interpreter, leaving Passmore and his companions to wait for the other junks to return. In the meantime the Dutch Controller in Medan had learned that a party of British officers was down the coast. Believing this warranted his personal attention, he arrived in full diplomatic regalia, including cocked hat and gold, oakleaf-encrusted uniform, accompanied by the police commandant. As a result of this meeting at which Jamal, a member of the Malay Police Force, acted as interpreter, Passmore was given a letter instructing all Dutchmen to assist the party. It was also agreed to swap *Hin Leong* for two lorries, four police drivers, a police corporal and two accumulator batteries, needed to operate the radio set. The boat was almost unseaworthy but this did not worry the Dutch, who simply wanted to scuttle the vessel to blockade the river. Before handing over the ship Passmore stripped it of everything of use, including the canned provisions, mattresses, radio, compass and swags of explosives which Warren, who revelled in blowing things up, had brought with him.

When Broome and Davis arrived back from Began-Siapiapi after successfully inserting the guerrillas, they brought worrying news that Vanrenan's and Graham's junk had returned without them. It appeared that the vessel, anchored offshore to wait for them, had aroused the suspicions of the Japanese and the crew had panicked and fled, leaving the SOE men stranded. Not until after the war was their fate established. Finding they had been abandoned, and unable to locate Chapman, they had turned inland, blowing up everything they could find and leaving a trail of such devastation that the Japanese took entire villages hostage. Believing local guerrillas to be responsible for demolishing a troop train, the Japanese made an example of a village of about two hundred people, shooting all the men and mutilating all the women.

In the interests of avoiding further bloodshed the SOE men gave themselves up on 25 March, after convincing the Japanese that they had been cut off from the British forces. They were imprisoned in Pudu Gaol in Kuala Lumpur, where they were reunited with Bill Harvey, a member of Chapman's group, who had also been captured when separated from his main party.

The three men, who had no intention of remaining in gaol, managed to make contact with Chapman. After much careful planning and with the help of Australian POWs in the gaol, they managed to escape in mid-August 1942, only to be recaptured a fortnight later. This time the Japanese were not as benevolent. On 16 September they were taken to a nearby cemetery where they, and others who had also attempted to escape, were executed.

When it was realised that the chances of Vanrenan and Graham returning were slim, the party was ordered to abandon the base and join Warren at Padang, with Passmore's letter of introduction ensuring VIP treatment all the way.

While Reynolds and others were rescuing the survivors from the islands near Pompong, and Passmore was riding around northern Sumatra in a taxi, Lyon and Morris were still on Durian Island. By the end of February the numbers of survivors requiring food and rest before being transported the 112 kilometres to Jock Campbell at Prigi Radja had been reduced to a mere trickle, so Lyon made arrangements with local fishermen to take any stragglers to the Indragiri, and pinned detailed instructions on how to reach Prigi Radja to the wall of the hut. Leaving the campsite to the dead buried in the clearing, they clambered down the steep path to the shore, slipped the sailing boat from its mooring and set off in a south-westerly direction towards Sumatra.

Around midnight as they drifted quietly down the strait, a Japanese destroyer, anchored off their port bow, loomed from the darkness. They veered immediately to starboard, only to have an equally alarming shadow suddenly scan the water's surface with a brilliant searchlight. Ripping down the sail, the pair lay flat on the bottom of the boat, which floated past both vessels undetected. Their relief, however, was short-lived, for they were suddenly caught in the tail of a violent storm which sent their small craft roller-coasting over crests of mountainous waves to plummet even more sickeningly into the troughs on the other side. This helter-skelter ride in total darkness terrified Morris, but perturbed Ivan not at all. He sat in the stern, hand firmly on the rudder, casually glancing at the luminous dial of his compass from time to time. Already astonished, Morris was even more astounded when Ivan, announcing that he was going to take a nap, removed the rudder and curled up like a cat. Morris, who had never felt less like sleeping in his entire life, could scarcely believe it. However, the sight of Ivan's quietly slumbering figure reassured the Welshman, inspiring him with such confidence that he, too, fell asleep. They awoke the following morning to find themselves alone on a restlessly heaving ocean and not a skerrick of land in sight. Indeed, they saw nothing but water and

95

Fearless Ivan

scudding grey clouds until midday when, with an aim as true as a well-sighted arrow, Ivan steered the boat through the mouth of the Indragiri River.

Finally reaching Rengat, it was not until the enraged Australian emerged from the wheelhouse that Ivan realised the elderly looking pirate who had enquired about their welfare downriver was the skipper of the boat he had just rammed. His extended and colourful enquiry about who had taught them to sail amused both Ivan and Morris, who decided they would like to become more closely acquainted. With his taste for unorthodox and flamboyant characters, Lyon was fascinated by Reynolds, who obviously feared neither man nor beast.

When the outburst had subsided, Lyon introduced himself and suggested that with the sun well over the yardarm it was high time for a drink. As they downed their medicinal whiskies, the conversation turned to possible means of escape. There were only two options – across the mountains to Padang, the route Ivan and Morris intended to take, or across the Indian Ocean via the Japanese-infested Straits of Malacca. The latter was risky, possibly suicidal, but Reynolds believed it was possible and for this reason had been stockpiling provisions for several days, always taking on more fuel and supplies than he needed for his rescue work. Reynolds told Lyon that he was confident that his ship, being a Japanese fishing boat, could run the blockade by simply sailing through it.

When Lyon heard that the Australian's scruffy little vessel had attracted not the slightest attention from the enemy to date, he too was convinced that the Malaccan route was viable. Even better, they agreed that if *Kofuku Maru* could get out of Japanese waters unchallenged, she could surely get back in. Fired with enthusiasm at the possibility of being able to continue the fight, Lyon and Reynolds made a pact. Provided both survived, they would meet again in India. Leaving his new-found friends to make arrangements with Campbell to travel overland to Rengat, Reynolds took on more supplies and the next day, 25 February, headed downriver in search of more survivors.

Although he had rescued hundreds of castaways, Reynolds found it ironic that so far he had not been able to convince a single soul to sail with him to India. Not even the outrageous rumour that *Kofuku Maru* was a spy ship, filled with sophisticated equipment, had elicited the slightest interest, although Dr Coates, now in Rengat with his patients awaiting transport to Padang, and a British officer, Colonel Dillon (neither of whom harboured any illusions about the ship), were sorely tempted. While Coates had been delighted to accept Reynolds' gifts of tobacco, gin and a slouch hat, and to treat a neck injury for crewman Ah Tee earlier that day, he told the Australian that his duty lay with his patients. Dillon too had responsibilities to his men, so he also declined the offer to join Reynolds, whom he fondly described as 'a real old pirate'.

By 6 March, there were so few evacuees moving along the Indragiri that two dedicated Argylls, Sergeant Major J McLaren and Captain Gordon, who had been running a ferry service along the upper reaches of the river, shut up shop and Reynolds, his rescue work at a standstill, agreed to a request by van Brenkel to collect intelligence while dropping off much-needed supplies to outlying islands. Although it was expected that Sumatra and the rest of the Dutch East Indies would soon be occupied by the enemy, as soon as the necessary paperwork was completed *Kofuku Maru* took on 199 sacks of rice and headed for the Riau Archipelago.

Before he left Sumatran waters, probably in deference to his superstitious Chinese crew, Reynolds renamed his boat. Inspired by the purple water-hyacinths growing in profusion along the Indragiri, he discarded the Japanese name in favour of British Privateer *Suey Sin Fah*, which not only had a good ring to it but also suited the mission he was about to undertake. Despite the rather swashbuckling prefix, the remainder of the title, meaning 'star-shaped flower', pleased the crew who regarded it as 'good joss'. With everyone happy, Reynolds painted out *Kofuku Maru 2283* and arranged for a large sign, bearing the new name in bold block letters, to be displayed on the roof of the wheelhouse when nearing civilisation.

The voyage from the Indragiri estuary across the Berhala Straits was incident free, but Reynolds ran into serious trouble in the Riau Straits. Challenged by a Japanese patrol boat near Tanjung Pinang, *Suey Sin Fah* was forced to make a fight of it. With the aid of a Lewis machine-gun, Thompson submachine-guns and rifles which Reynolds had had the foresight to acquire, *Suey Sin Fah*, although peppered by automatic arms fire, came off best in the ensuing altercation, eventually forcing the aggressor to flee to a small strait to the south.

Far from being intimidated by the incident, an exhilarated Reynolds stuck to his original route, sailing deeper into enemy territory to Karimoen Island, virtually on Singapore's doorstep. But while Reynolds was in his element, his Chinese crew members were not. Every one of them deserted at the next port of call, Tanjung Batu on Pulau Koendoer, where there was a large Chinese community. Although left with just Elliott and Papworth to help him handle the ship Reynolds, mindful of his intelligence-gathering role, decided to return to the Indragiri via Dabo on Singkep Island – a plan he was forced to abandon on discovering the Japanese had already landed there. However, he was able to evacuate 120 Chinese women and children from a hospital on the northern part of the island before continuing up the Berhala Strait, where he assembled a flotilla of nine small boats carrying mostly military personnel. Unfortunately, before his fleet could reach the safety of the Indragiri they were attacked, the superior enemy force sinking eight of the small boats and forcing the ninth to run aground. *Suey Sin Fah* was undamaged, but Reynolds sustained injuries to his feet and legs. On reaching Rengat he learned that the Japanese were advancing rapidly and that this trip, his tenth, was his last. In the month he had been engaged in rescue operations, Bill Reynolds had rescued at least 1519 people.

While he and his two exhausted crew members rested, repairs were carried out on *Suey Sin Fah*'s stern, which had been rammed by the motor vessel *Pearlfisher*, an incident which had undoubtedly evoked another colourful outburst. Fortunately, the repairs were almost complete when Controller van Brenkel's secretary, Mr Kaag, arrived on the afternoon of 12 March to inform Reynolds that the Japanese were heading up the Djambi River valley and would be at Rengat within the next forty-eight hours.

Clearly, the time had come to depart, but not before blowing up all the craft still at Rengat to prevent the enemy from giving chase downstream. Reynolds, back in the demolition business, placed explosives on more than sixty vessels, ranging from *Tenggaroh*, the Sultan of Johor's luxury yacht, to an almost brand-new Catalina tanker which had been taken from the RAF base at Blakang Mati and was filled with high-octane spirit. Only one boat, the most lowly of the lot, was saved from what must have been a satisfyingly spectacular conflagration. This was a three-metre dinghy named *Supply* – a name long associated with Australian colonial history. As Reynolds stowed her aboard *Suey Sin Fah* he noted with admiration that the tiny craft, in common with her namesake which had voyaged from England to Sydney with the First Fleet in 1787, had been sailed all the way from Singapore by a bunch of 'very tough guys'.

His demolition work completed, Reynolds began scouring Rengat in search of a crew. There were evidently few European applicants – three of the four newcomers were Chinese. Accepting the role of stewardess/cook was a remarkable young woman, Cantonese-born Looi Pek Sye, aged twenty-five, who had escaped from Ipoh with her three-year-old daughter Lam Kwai ('Twin Seasons'). Ah Chung, aged thirty-two, who hailed from Shanghai, and 34-year-old Ah Kwai from Tien Tsin agreed to act as motormen. After obtaining clearance from British Headquarters in India, Reynolds took on as sick-berth attendant the sole European, Frank McNeil, Royal Navy, a 23-year-old Londoner who had arrived with a party from Singkep. With his crew organised, Reynolds recorded their details in the first of his three daily 'Log Books' – cheap ABC-brand exercise books, which he had ruled into precise columns to record, in a meticulously neat hand, the time, course, rain, wind, sea, temperature readings and detailed remarks of the voyage.

That evening at 7.15, with the assistance of Pilot Amman, *Suey Sin Fah* set off down river as soon as the tide began to ebb. They had been underway for scarcely an hour when McNeil claimed he had fallen and injured his pelvis. He appeared to be in such pain that Reynolds immobilised him on top of the engine-room housing and made for Chenako in the hope that the telephone line to Rengat was still in operation. On discovering that the overland track linking the two settlements was impassable due to heavy rain, Reynolds continued downstream to Tambilahan.

It was after 5 am before McNeil, prostrate on a stretcher carried by Elliott and Papworth, finally reached the dispensary-cum-aid post. Three hours later, to Reynolds' utter amazement, the stricken patient reappeared, walking unassisted and exhibiting no trace of the pain which had so afflicted him a short time previously. During the subsequent 'cross examination' McNeil admitted he had feigned the injury, as only a madman would attempt such a voyage. Reynolds, suffering himself from wounds to his feet and legs, was ropable. After a few choice words, the mildest of which was 'coward', Reynolds made arrangements to have McNeil transported back to Rengat at the earliest opportunity. The malingerer should have stayed with the madman. Within a few hours of McNeil's return to Rengat, the Japanese were in occupation.

Despite the unscheduled stop at Chenako, *Suey Sin Fah* made good time downriver, giving Reynolds plenty of time to prepare for the journey across the open sea. For the rest of that day, Friday 13 March, and for the whole of the next, everyone was kept busy. The local controller, who provided information on the most suitable route, arrived with a lifeboat and sail salvaged from the ill-fated *Kuala*. While the crew bunkered oil, stowed gear and secured the sail to foremast, gaff and boom, Reynolds visited the aid post to have his injuries dressed before adjourning to the controller's office to obtain the latest military intelligence. The news was not good. Although there were some isolated pockets of resistance, the Japanese had occupied most key centres in Sumatra, and Padang had been surrendered without a fight, trapping thousands of refugees awaiting evacuation. To avoid a similar fate, Reynolds must leave at once.

Just after 7 am on 15 March, *Suey Sin Fah* left Tambilahan with Pilot Amman on board. Nudging the jetty at Prigi Radja just long enough to allow Amman to leap ashore, Reynolds headed for northern Sumatra, with no charts and no navigational equipment other than a compass. Believing that a minefield lay ahead, he anchored off Danut village for the night, only to discover the next day, after spending the best part of an hour creeping close to the shoreline, that the report was false. Resuming full speed, the vessel had a trouble-free run across smooth seas to Sungei Pakning village. The local Malays were surly and unresponsive but the Chinese, who were very friendly, willingly imparted what information they had, informing Reynolds that low-flying aircraft had been passing over the village on a daily basis and that Allied soldiers had been strafed at Sungei Siak estuary six days previously.

Although no planes had been sighted in the area for the past two days, at first light Reynolds weighed anchor and headed for Bengkalis where, two hours later, he was tying up at the jetty under the watchful eye of Controller Warnaar. The controller was helpful, but Reynolds suspected his suggestion that the ship proceed to once to Began-Siapiapi, to hide among the Chinese fishing vessels there, was motivated more by a desire to be rid of them rather than any real concern for their personal welfare. To Warnaar's consternation, his visitor chose to remain in port, resting the crew, cleaning the engine and checking that the machine-guns and rifles were in good order.

It was evidently the size of *Suey Sin Fah*'s arsenal that prompted the Dutchman, towards evening on 17 March, to ascertain Reynolds' intentions if enemy vessels entered the harbour. His reply that he would 'engage them in action' was not what the controller, hoping to negotiate with the Japanese, wanted to hear. A 'heated discussion' ensued which saw Reynolds reluctantly agreeing that, should he engage the enemy, he would do so in the Brouwer Strait. Although it was a very narrow waterway, separating Bengkalis Island from the mainland, it was evidently far enough away to be regarded as 'international' waters. With extremely bad grace Reynolds made a further promise not to fire at enemy aircraft while in port.

That night, his motormen Ah Chung and Ah Kwai deserted. The next evening at 8 o'clock a very nervous Warnaar visited the ship, his anxiety over an enemy reconnaissance plane flying overhead that morning increased tenfold by news that enemy troops were advancing down the Sungei Siak to take Bengkalis. Terrified by the thought that *Suey Sin Fah* might be captured in a Dutch port, he ordered Reynolds to leave by midnight, 'an armed merchant ship being difficult to explain away'. Reynolds, who had acquired the services of two Malays to act as motormen in return for towing the motor launch *Rasak* to Began-Siapiapi, conceded that this was not an unreasonable request. However, he was prevented from leaving by an unexpected sumatra which blew up just before midnight, not only lashing the town, but creating heavy seas and further delaying their departure until the next evening, 19 March. They spent the next day sailing, *Rasak* still in tow, but decided to hide during the daylight hours of 20 March tied up at a charcoal-burner's jetty in mangrove-lined Allah Muda Creek. The decision not to sail during daylight was justified when a reconnaissance plane flew over at 1500 feet at around 11 am, prompting a call to action stations. Fortunately, they were not detected. When night fell they proceeded to Began-Siapiapi, which they reached shortly after 8 am and where Reynolds took on oil and provisions and engaged two Malays – one as a motorman, and the other, Saitaan bin Abdulhamid, a 17-year-old youth from Kuala Lumpur, to fill the role of deckhand. The arrival of the armed British Privateer was not exactly welcomed by Controller Vischer, who politely suggested later that evening that *Suey Sin Fah* depart as soon as it was convenient. Reynolds had not yet committed himself to a firm departure time but the matter was taken out of his hands the next day when Vischer, shortly after a reconnaissance aircraft had flown over, informed him that all communications with Rengat had been cut and they should leave. They were about to comply when the local police inspector arrived and arrested the newly acquired motorman, wanted by his wife for desertion.

With the Japanese expected to arrive in the morning, the controller ordered them to leave at once, forcing Reynolds to put Elliott in charge of the engine. Anxious to be rid of the ship, which was seen as a distinct liability, the police supplied a mechanic to start the engine, a complicated procedure which involved the use of compressed air. To the controller's immense relief, they finally cast off from their mooring at the mouth of Sungei Rokon at 9.30 am the next day, 22 March.

With enemy aircraft constantly patrolling the skies, Reynolds continued his previous policy of sailing by night and anchoring by day at one of the many fishing pagars scattered off

Reynolds with the 'crew' of
Suey Sin Fah *after their safe*
arrival in India

the coastal villages near Tanjung Pertandagan. With *Kuala's* lifeboat sail hoisted, they looked exactly like innocent fishermen going about their daily business and none of the patrolling aircraft bothered to come down for a closer look. The fishermen, whose traps they temporarily borrowed, kept them abreast of the movements of Japanese troops, now occupying every large centre.

Blessed by generally fine weather and a favourable current, by 24 March they had cleared the Straits of Malacca and, now beyond the range of enemy patrols, were no longer compelled to sail only at night. The next day they were off Diamond Point on Sumatra's northerly tip and twenty-four hours later were well into the Indian Ocean, steaming towards Nagapattinam in southern India at a speed of eight knots. Apart from the glow of fires burning in the fishing village of Nus as they passed north of the Nicobar Islands, Reynolds saw no sign of life and nothing remotely worthy of note. From 25 March the log made for very boring reading, with repetitive entries of 'fine/clear/cloudy, smooth/slight/choppy, no enemy aircraft' giving way to the even more terse 'similar weather conditions'. At exactly 3.40 on the afternoon of 31 March, sixteen days after leaving the Indragiri, *Suey Sin Fah* anchored in the Nagapattinam Roads. After a feat of amazing seamanship and navigation, which had found Reynolds out by only 32 kilometres in his distance reckoning, they had finally reached their destination.

Captain Reynolds was ordered ashore immediately by the Port Officer, with instructions to board the 5 pm train for Madras, about 290 kilometres to the north, for a debriefing by the Senior Naval Officer. There was no risk of *Suey Sin Fah* disappearing while her skipper was away. With no air in the starter bottles and the compressor used to refill them defective, the engine could not be fired without outside assistance.

His debriefing in Madras over, Reynolds returned to Nagapattinam, restarted the engine and sailed to the dockyard in Madras, where *Suey Sin Fah* was to be slipped and completely overhauled. He had plenty of time to organise repairs, for it was not until the third week of April that Ivan Lyon appeared to fulfil his half of the pact made on the far-off Indragiri River.

6

A plan evolves

March–September 1942

When Reynolds departed on 25 February in search of more survivors, Lyon and Morris had turned their attention to crossing the mountains to Padang before the Japanese arrived. Fortunately a now well-worn path had been established by Campbell and Baker, who had enlisted the help of the local controller to organise food stocks, accommodation and petrol dumps at Taluk, Peranap and Sawahlunto. Similar arrangements were made at Tambilahan and their base at Prigi Radja, where Campbell took charge of operations until, with the Japanese closing in, they decided it was time to move on. Before they departed Campbell left signed instructions for any latecomers with the headman, who also promised to provide transport upriver.

The headman did a fine job but the number of refugees using the escape route had been very much underestimated, with military personnel and civilians fleeing from Singapore in such large numbers that the camps were soon filled to capacity. Besides the hundreds making their way from Prigi Radja, there were hundreds more who had used an alternative route along the Djambi Valley – mainly evacuees who had been passed on by Amir Silahili or who had found their way to the river after eluding the Japanese in the Bangka Straits. To make things more difficult, not everyone was well behaved. Food supplies, handed out freely by villagers, were often stolen by parties of deserters, along with household goods, causing ructions between evacuees and the locals.

Despite the thousands moving from one camp to another, and problems with some of the evacuees, the escape route worked. Disembarking from larger craft at Rengat, the escapers moved upstream to Ayer Molek on *Faith*, *Hope* and *Charity* – two flat-bottomed barges drawn by an ancient, steam-driven, wood-fired launch. From here they turned inland, crossing the mountain ranges in whatever vehicles could be provided, with some completing the final stage of the journey from Sawahlunto to Padang in the comparative comfort of a mountain train.

Morris and Lyon were more than ready to leave Rengat with its swarms of voracious mosquitoes, only kept at bay by puffing constantly on smoky cigarettes throughout the night. Their ordeal ended when Campbell appeared with their transport – an open tourer which he had somehow managed to acquire. Huddling in the back seat beneath a ground sheet in a futile effort to ward off the chilling rain, they were jolted from side to side as the car groaned its way to an altitude of almost 2000 metres and then down the other side. It was best not to look, for at every hairpin bend the headlamps shone alarmingly into inky nothingness. They finally reached the coast where Warren had arranged for a submarine to pick them up, only to discover the rendezvous had failed, forcing them to back-track a considerable distance. By the time they arrived at Padang on 2 March, the quiet, usually sleepy seaside town was bursting with troops and civilians.

From here the refugees moved to the port of Emmahaven, 5 kilometres away, where they risked constant bombing attacks to crowd onto a variety of vessels ranging from fast naval destroyers to flimsy native traders. On 4 March a group of Rowley-Conwy's gunners were among 102 officers and men who sailed on a 1200-tonne cargo boat carrying 900 tonnes of bombs. Subsisting on rations intended to last three to four days, they would not reach Colombo for another ten, with nothing to guide the captain other than a compass and school atlas.

The following day Warren, who had been pressured into taking command of the town by the Dutch, learned that one of two ships about to depart had space for fifty refugees – men only, as the captain refused to carry any women. Taking advantage of the captain's misogyny he ordered all SOE's 'other ranks', including Morris, to leave. As the vessel threaded its way past the bombed-out wrecks of less fortunate vessels, Morris wondered if he would even see Lyon again.

His fears were well founded. The Allied troops still in Padang had little chance of escape, with rumours of the enemy advance only adding to the general anxiety. At his headquarters at the Eendracht Club, Colonel Warren was forced to monitor news broadcasts from Ceylon for information, as the Dutch consul had rather prematurely destroyed all the code books. The news received on 7 March was not good – it was believed that *Rooseboom*, the last boat to leave, had been hit by torpedoes en route to Java, and the evacuation ship *Chilka*, finally dispatched from India a week late, was now a further two days overdue. Both had been sunk.

Rooseboom, a small coastal vessel which usually sailed between Java and Sumatra, had left several days before with Brigadier Archie Paris and a group of Argylls, including the unflappable Drummer Hardy, plus Mr and Mrs Nunn and a large number of other military and civilians. The ship was only three days from Padang when she was torpedoed. At first it was thought that the two Javanese sailors picked up by Morris's ship were the only survivors. However, another 135 people either in or clinging to a lifeboat built to hold twenty-eight had also survived. As it drifted aimlessly under the scorching tropical sun many, including the brigadier, died from the combined effects of thirst, exposure and starvation. They were among the more fortunate. Others, including Drummer Hardy, were murdered by a group of British Army deserters from Liverpool who had indulged in unspeakable acts of cannibalism before they themselves were forced over the side. After drifting for four weeks, only four were left alive – two mad Javanese crewmen, SOE agent Doris Lim, and Sergeant Walter Gibson, the last of the Argylls. A short time after staggering ashore on an island off the Sumatran coast, Lim and Gibson were captured. Gibson survived the war but Doris Lim, who survived forced labour in a cement factory, married a local man who murdered her in March 1945.

That night there was more bad news. The enemy was now a mere 96 kilometres away. As the Dutch, hoping to negotiate, wished to appear neutral, all assistance for further evacuation was withdrawn, a boom was placed across the harbour, and all vessels were closely watched lest any be appropriated. For those with sufficient ready cash it was still possible to purchase a boat, but the prices were exorbitant and far beyond the means of would-be buyers who possessed only the clothes they wore.

There was, however, one boat available – *Sederhana Djohanes* (Lucky John), a native prahu fully provisioned and moored a short distance up the coast. Spotted by Warren in the Padang River, it had been purchased with what remained of the 14,000 guilders Passmore had obtained from the Medan bank manager. When he, Davis and Broome arrived in Padang, Warren, who had hopes of operating behind enemy lines, had taken them straight to the boat, where they unloaded the lorry-load of supplies and equipment brought from the *Hin Leong*. The prahu's sails were threadbare but Broome and Passmore managed to purchase a gross of sail-making needles, a small quantity of strong thread and a roll of canvas, before sailing the boat to a new hiding place.

As the enemy drew ever nearer, Warren realised that sea-borne raids were no longer feasible, and that *Sederhana Djohanes* could be used an escape vessel for a lucky few. There was no question of his leaving, for not only was he the only officer willing to take command, he was also disturbed by reports of rape and theft, and of soldiers selling their weapons to raise cash. In addition, some of his fellow officers had 'done a bunk', leading to a general feeling of disrespect among the lesser ranks. The non-arrival of Colonel Dillon, who was still making his way up the Indragiri, and the outright refusal of more senior officers to take responsibility meant that Warren himself must stay to keep law and order.

With Warren remaining behind, there was room for eighteen on the ship. Absolute secrecy was essential. Not only might the Dutch put a stop to the escape attempt, but should word leak out to the hundreds of people praying for evacuation there would be a general stampede. Since all the SOE 'other ranks' had been evacuated and only six places were required for his officers, Warren filled the remaining spots with those whom he felt could contribute best to the war effort. The chosen few assembled at the Eendracht Club for a very short briefing: they were to proceed up the coast and then sail 2400 kilometres across the Indian Ocean to Ceylon (Sri Lanka). As secrecy had to be preserved at all costs, no one was permitted to return to his billet to collect even a few possessions in case suspicions were aroused. Under cover of darkness the small band left the town, any noise from the departure of their two-wheeled, horse-drawn carts masked by the intermittent rain squalls. As their Malay drivers strained to see through the inky blackness of the stormy, moonless night, the passengers' apprehension, already heightened by the driving rain, was exacerbated by the disturbing thought that if they lost sight of the barely discernible red oil-lamps of the vehicle in front, they would become lost in the jungle.

The nerve-wracking journey ended at 2 am at Perjalanan, a small, palm-fringed fishing village. It had stopped raining and the moon now bathed the beach in a silvery light which, had circumstances been otherwise, would have been regarded as very romantic. Moored about 800 metres from the shore was the 20-metre *Sederhana Djohanes*, a nondescript trader of about 25 tonnes. Almost the entire deck space, except for a small patch at each end and the narrow walkways along the sides, was covered by a steeply pitched roof, constructed of planks coated with sheet copper and then atap, creating a strong and waterproof shelter. The bowsprit was extremely long, as was the tiller, and the copper-clad hull, which had no keel, resembled a broad, shallow saucer. Above the deck, supporting sails so thin that the stars could be seen through them, were two masts – one 8 metres tall, the other 15 metres. While the sailors in the group conceded that it was an ideal craft for benign local waters, they were not at all confident that the prahu was capable of sailing across thousands of kilometres of open sea, buffeted by roaring monsoonal winds and tropical squalls.

It was not until 3 am on 9 March that they were ferried from the beach to join those already on board. When they awoke some hours later they found that the vessel was well underway and that Ivan Lyon was at the helm. He had pinned to the mainmast a pendulum and a piece of paper, on which he had drawn two oblique lines. 'If the pendulum swings past those lines,' he told them, 'we'll turn over.' Besides Lyon, the SOE contingent comprised Davis, Lind and Passmore, Richard Broome, who was in overall command, and Jock Campbell, who had the job of controlling the water and provisions. To the annoyance of those who believed that any spare places should have been filled by 'more useful' white personnel, Davis and Broome were accompanied by their loyal servants, Jamal and Lo Gnap Soon.

Also on board was a merchant mariner who, with Ivan, was essential to their escape – navigator Garth Gorham, *Kung Wo*'s swarthy-skinned second officer who had a magnificent black beard, a fiery eye and ill-concealed contempt for anything remotely pertaining to the Royal Navy. After surviving the sinking at Pompong he had reached Padang and was about to board a ship for India when Warren grabbed him. Navigating *Sederhana Djohanes* was not going to be easy – all Gorham had by way of aids were an unreliable wristwatch, a tatty Sumatran Pilot Book, some hurriedly hand-copied navigational tables, a chart of Sumatra's west coast and a tiny wind map of the Indian Ocean, torn from a pocket dictionary. He also had a sextant but its usefulness depended on the ability of the dilapidated radio and two batteries (included in the exchange deal brokered by Passmore for *Hin Leong*) to hold out long enough to give accurate time signals.

The other nine passengers were Major 'Doc' Davies, Royal Army Medical Corps; naval lieutenants 'Holly' Holwell and Richard Cox; Lieutenant Geoffrey Brooke, another *Kung Wo* survivor; Captain Spanton, a cheery, freckle-faced army officer who had joined forces with the rather pessimistic Bill Waller (an unfortunate army Major on Percival's staff who had been given the humiliating task of signing the surrender orders when Singapore fell) to row part of the way to Sumatra in a flat-bottomed boat, given to them by a Chinese waiter at Raffles Hotel. Cox, Brooke, Spanton and Waller had all been picked up in the Indragiri by two men also on board – Major Rowley-Conwy, now sporting a rakish trilby hat, and his friend Douglas Fraser, a civilian who had arrived on a motorcycle and 'joined' the gunners on Singapore Island, and whom Rowley, as he was always called, had recently 'promoted' to the rank of lieutenant. The last passenger was Lieutenant Clarke of the Intelligence Corps who, because of his part-Japanese parentage and fluency in that language, was nicknamed 'Tojo'.

Broome split his team into two watches and ran through the list of equipment and provisions on board. First and foremost was the armament, comprising two Lewis guns, a few rifles and some revolvers, all with adequate supplies of ammunition. Food stocks included cases of bully beef, potatoes, carrots, condensed milk, canned fruit, coffee, butter and biscuits, plus bags of porridge, sugar and rice, some coconuts and a few limes and bananas. Drinking water was stored in two 200-litre oil drums, with another 360 litres in earthenware jars and petrol tins. Medical supplies were basic but adequate – morphine, various drugs, antiseptic, bandages and, should constipation be a problem, a bottle of castor oil. The nicotine addicts were well catered for with cigarettes, cigars and pipe tobacco, while two well-thumbed editions of *Esquire*, a well-known 'gentleman's' magazine, and a copy of Daphne du Maurier's classic thriller *Rebecca* would help pass the time. Also stowed carefully away were five precious bottles of 'for medicinal purposes only' whisky.

Provided the stores, water in particular, were carefully rationed, Broome calculated that they should have enough to last the distance. His plan was to hug the coastline until they were on about the same latitude as Ceylon, in the hope that they could pick up the north-east monsoon. Should everything go to plan and the winds prove favourable, the voyage should take about three weeks. To help them negotiate the treacherous Sumatran coast, the prahu's former crew, an old man and two boys, had agreed to sail with them until they were past the worst of the treacherous coastal strip, by which time the new crew should be able to handle the boat. Lyon, being the only one with any experience with small craft and also fluent in Malay, was soon engaged in animated discussion with the elderly sailor.

Aided by fair weather and a stiff breeze they covered 60 kilometres on the first day, their progress halted by a number of small islands which forced them to anchor for the night. At first light next morning they were under way again, bowled along by a strong easterly, only to have the boom crack and the worn mainsail rip apart from the strain. As the wind strengthened and the seas heaved beneath the prahu's protesting timbers, the anxiety levels increased, but only among the Europeans. After binding the boom the Malays, who were used to such conditions, expertly steered the vessel through murderously sharp coral reefs to the sheltered waters of a small island, where local fishermen supplied two lengths of giant bamboo to replace the boom. Here the old man announced that this was as far as he was prepared to go. Shaking hands and wishing them well, the old rascal then demanded another fortnight's wages plus money to cover the hire-car fare home.

At this point, the leadership shifted subtly from Broome to Lyon, for it was obvious that the fate of all on board depended on the skills of this capable man. He needed all the expertise that he had acquired on his long, single-handed voyages, for *Sederhana Djohanes* was difficult to handle, displaying a tendency to sail backwards if the wind were not in the right quarter. When it was, it would more often than not be too much for the sails which, with a sickening rip, would split from top to bottom, forcing Ivan to heave-to while the amateur sailmakers, to the accompaniment of much swearing and pricked fingers, sewed on yet another patch.

The day after the Malays left, they were near a small island when they heard the sound of a marine engine. Fearing the worst, the boat's company went into a well-rehearsed drill. In the hope of the vessel being mistaken for a local trader, Jamal took the tiller and Lo made himself conspicuous while the remainder took cover, armed with every available weapon, but it was just a tug, towing a small barge. As it flew no flags, the men remained hidden, watching its progress until it became obvious that the fair-haired, pink-skinned figure at the helm was

Lyon and his fellow escapees on board Sederhana Djohanes, *March 1942*

Dutch. Lyon went off in the dinghy to investigate and discovered he was an acquaintance from Padang, bound for Sibolga, a large port about 130 kilometres to the north. He agreed to give them a tow and a length of thick rope to replace the frayed halyard in return for a bottle of medicinal whisky. It was a fair exchange for, when the tow was severed the next day, *Sederhana Djohanes* was 110 kilometres closer to their destination.

On about the fifth night they were hit by a violent storm. Tired bodies which had battled with an equally fierce tempest not twenty-four hours previously now had to muster the strength to keep the boat afloat. With the patched mainsail and jib in danger of ripping yet again, Broome climbed the mast while Rowley crawled along the bowsprit, inching their way up and out despite mountainous seas until they managed to retrieve both sails intact. During this hair-raising procedure, watched by the others from the shelter of the covered area, only one man remained on deck. It was Ivan Lyon. Wrapped in a ground sheet, water streaming down his face and tiller in hand, he was in his element, enjoying every minute of his absorbing contest between himself and nature.

The storm was starting to abate when they heard a new noise – of waves pounding on rocks – a sound that should not be heard so far out to sea. Ivan pulled as hard as he could on the tiller and, with agonising slowness, her timbers straining under the load, the boat slid narrowly past a reef of jagged coral. Any relief was short-lived. The vessel had barely righted when they heard the sound once more – this time dead ahead. Lyon, who only just averted an impaling on rocks which would have torn the hull to pieces, realised they were encircled by a coral reef. As nothing could be done until daybreak, he calmly gave orders to drop anchor, returned to his place at the stern, wrapped his ground sheet round himself and, head upon his knees, fell sound asleep.

The sun's rays early next morning confirmed they were indeed trapped within a reef. The problem was how to get out. Time and again they edged toward what looked to be a channel, only to find their progress blocked. Ivan finally realised there was only one solution – to pole the boat along, like a Venetian gondola. It took hours of back-breaking labour before *Sederhana Djohanes* was clear of the coral, whereupon they ran into yet another storm. Hands raw and bleeding from poling were not nimble enough to retrieve the mainsail in time, and it split the full length of the recently mended seam. The upside was that the wind was so strong it whipped the boat along at a record speed of seven knots. As the bare poles raced beneath a leaden sky, sore and blistered fingers grappled with yet another bout of sewing.

The favourable winds were all too often offset by periods of dead calm under a cloudless blue sky, radiating heat in such great waves that water was rationed to one small cup per man. It was during such a time, becalmed during a period of intensely hot weather, without a whisper of air and with only a few drops of water to moisten parched lips, that the morale of some fell to the lowest possible level. With no sign of any rain, and with the sails hanging flaccid against the masts, some of the men wanted to attract the attention of a Japanese merchantman, believing that surrender was preferable to floating aimlessly with no apparent hope of salvation. Ivan, however, was made of sterner stuff. Exhibiting the same powerful determination as that other great sailor, Captain William Bligh, 150 years before, he cocked his pistol and held it steady, while Campbell continued to dole out the meagre water ration. There would be no thought of surrender. This display of absolute and ruthless determination later prompted Bill Waller, one of those whose morale had dissolved, to declare 'Ivan Lyon is one of the most courageous men I have even known.'

Fortunately the threat of 'mutiny' was a one-off, with monotony generally relieved by singing, by discussing anything and everything, and by devouring every page of the *Esquire* magazines. However, it was not the titillating ladies which evoked drawn-out sighs of great longing – it was a glossy, full-page advertisement; a reminder of those halcyon days before the war; a tantalising, life-sized photograph of polished cut-glass tumblers, filled with tinkling ice, bubbling, thirst-quenching tonic water – and gin.

It was not until 28 March that both the monotony and the heat were broken, with the simultaneous arrival of a steady breeze and an enemy fighter plane. The men took their appointed places just seconds before the boat was raked with machine-gun fire. Bullets sprayed across the deck, thudding into the hull and the roof and ricocheting around the interior of the shelter. The unflappable Jamal and Lo held their positions until Davis yelled at them to take cover. But despite the obvious need to leave the exposed deck, Jamal had no intention of being rushed – it was probably the way in which he nonchalantly adjusted his sarong before calmly moving below that convinced the Japanese pilot that the boat was manned by harmless Malay fishermen. An inspection when the 'all clear' was announced showed that, although the vessel had received five long bursts of machine-gun fire, no one had been hurt and there was no damage, other than perforation of the already ragged sails. Most importantly, the water containers were all intact. Their luck held. The following morning when the plane returned they were safely hidden beneath low cloud. The aircraft flew back and forth, heard but unseen, as the pilot tried unsuccessfully to find a gap in the cloud layer.

The monsoon continued to blow in their favour, but the more benevolent winds were often interrupted by periods of dead calm or violent squalls. Spirits on board sagged a little when a time-check from the rapidly fading battery-powered wireless revealed that Gorham's old watch, their only method of reckoning longitude, was out, and they were 176 kilometres further from their destination than he had calculated. This mild bout of depression was soon replaced by adrenaline-producing fear when, just 320 kilometres from Ceylon a plane, thought to be friendly, came down for a closer look. As it banked, the sun reflected a bright red rondel – the unmistakable emblem of Japan. Fortunately, all the pilot did was look, but the incident was sufficiently alarming for everyone to abandon Western clothing in favour of sarongs.

The final days dragged slowly, as fickle winds alternately filled and deflated sails that now resembled an ancient patchwork quilt, held down by ropes that had been spliced and re-spliced. Never a smart-looking boat, *Sederhana Djohanes* was looking decidedly tatty. The crew did not look much better – almost five weeks on reduced rations with no fresh fruit or vegetables had resulted in dramatic weight loss, and many were suffering from a variety of complaints, mainly skin-related. Morale was generally good, but it fluctuated according to the strength and direction of the winds. On 12 April, Ivan calmly announced, 'There is a cloud over there which might be land.' When Gorham's binoculars confirmed this was indeed the case and that the mauve triangle just visible above the cloud layer was definitely Ceylon's Friar's Hood Mountain, the ship reverberated with whoops of joy. Only one man remained apparently unmoved – Lyon was almost sorry that the voyage was nearing its end.

The next morning two tankers were sighted. As the signal lamp was not working properly, a makeshift distress signal was hoisted but to the disappointment of all, especially the fiercely pro-merchant navy Gorham, the vessels did not respond. Only later did they learn how narrowly disaster had been avoided: shortly afterward the same ships, which were Japanese, intercepted an escape party led by Colonel Dillon. He had eventually arrived in Padang, but did not take over from Warren. The latter selflessly remained behind to face ultimate capture, leaving Dillon free to escape in a prahu, *Setia Berganti*, purchased from the fishing village of Sasak, further up the coast. They were in sight of their destination when all on board were taken prisoner. Others of those whom Lyon and Reynolds had taken such pains to rescue were never seen again.

Apart from a distant tanker which also passed them by, for the next two days Lyon's party saw no more ships. The land temporarily disappeared from sight, reappearing to reveal, on closer inspection, an uninhabited coastline so treacherous that landing was impossible. However, spirits soared almost immediately when a ship was sighted coming straight toward them. The distress signal was again displayed, the message reinforced by the hoisting of the Union Jack upside down. While everyone else waved and yelled, Brooke, his signal lamp completely dead, climbed onto the roof of the shelter and, in classic British understatement, semaphored 'Sixteen British officers from Singapore request assistance please'.

Covering them with a large gun mounted on the stern, *Anglo-Canadian*'s skipper motioned for the small boat to come alongside. The inquisitive faces watching proceedings from the freighter's deck must have thought them a very odd bunch. Some had donned identifiable uniforms carefully preserved for the occasion, others wore tattered rags or sarongs. All were burnt mahogany brown from weeks at sea and, even more amazingly, they were sailing a native prahu which looked as if it might break apart and sink at any moment. Fascination turned to laughter when, during the scramble up the Jacob's ladder, Waller fell into the sea and Gorham lost his sarong, forcing him to greet his rescuers stark naked.

Left: *Lyon climbs the bowsprit of* Sederhana Djohanes *as* Anglo-Canadian *alters course to pick them up, 14 April 1942*
Right: *The abandoned* Sederhana Djohanes, *after her 2670-kilometre voyage from Sumatra*

With all safely on board the ship's engines throbbed into life and *Sederhana Djohanes* slipped astern, her sails flapping like a decrepit banner as her battered hull rode the swell. *Anglo-Canadian*'s captain, deciding she posed a threat to other vessels, ordered the 12-pound gun to open fire. When the smoke cleared, those watching from the railings saw a pathetic, stricken thing, the mast in tatters, the hull holed but, amazingly, still afloat. In the end, no one saw her demise, for the range was opening fast. Last sighted, she was still bobbing along, a brave tribute to an incredible voyage which had lasted fifty-two days, and carried them across 2656 kilometres of open sea.

The adventurers were still in high spirits when they arrived in Bombay (now Mumbai) where, for the next four days, they revelled in the luxury of the Taj Mahal Hotel, the country's finest, before going their separate ways. Broome and Davis departed to an ancient fort to undertake special training before insertion by submarine into Malaya to join SOE's stay-behind parties; 'Lieutenant' Fraser, still technically a civilian, was sent to an officers' gunnery course before attachment to Force 136, which saw him parachuted into Malaya to operate with the Chinese guerrillas, his civilian status never questioned; Rowley-Conwy went off to active service in Burma and the naval officers returned to England to receive new commissions from the Admiralty. For almost all, the traumatic days spent crossing the Indian Ocean would soon become an unpleasant memory.

The exception was Ivan Lyon. From the day they had been strafed by the enemy plane, his agile mind had been racing along in top gear, fuelled by the outrage of the attack, by his fury with High Command for losing Singapore, by the humiliation of defeat and by his overwhelming sense of guilt. Guilt that so many of his fellow soldiers were dead or in Japanese hands. Guilt that when he was most wanted he had not been there to fight the battle which had brought the mighty British Empire to its knees. Tormented by these thoughts, by his rage over Singapore's loss and by his hate and contempt for the enemy, exacerbated by the memory of the bullets thumping into *Sederhana Djohanes'* deck, he had sat at the tiller for days, searching for a way to strike back.

The Japanese might be in occupation throughout the Far East, but Lyon realised that no army or navy could possibly patrol and guard tens of thousands of miles of coastline. The British had lost Malaya and Singapore because they had played by the book. If the Japanese were to be defeated, it would require the use of irregular warfare – the kind of unorthodox methods which SOE employed. By the time he reached Ceylon, an idea germinated on the far-off Indragiri had formed into a viable plan – a plan for a daring operation that could be carried out, provided he had the help of one particular man.

When Ivan arrived in Bombay and found both Reynolds and his ship safe and sound, he wasted no time in outlining his proposal to the Australian and, as he now discovered, fellow secret agent. Basically, it involved sneaking back into Singapore with a team of highly trained operatives to secrete incendiary devices on shore installations and place top-secret, delayed-action, magnetic limpet mines on the hulls of enemy vessels. Reynolds' Japanese fishing boat would provide the undercover transport from India to the islands near Singapore, hiding among the mangroves of Sumatra's Kampar River estuary while the saboteurs, in small, two-man kayaks or folboats carried out the assaults. With a time-fuse attached to the explosive devices, Lyon was confident that the raiders would be well away before the targets blew up.

The idea appealed enormously to Reynolds. He was convinced that such a daredevil stunt was not only possible, but that they could get away with it. In 1925, while ferrying Muslim pilgrims to Jidda, he had decided that he too would like to go to Mecca. Completely ignoring the fact that this holy Islamic city was strictly off-limits to all Arab 'non-believers', let alone an Anglo-Saxon of Roman Catholic persuasion, the infidel disguised himself as an Arab, mingling successfully with the crowds and risking his life in what he dismissed as an 'interesting excursion'. Having proved it was possible to enter Mecca disguised as an Arab, he could not see why it was not feasible to penetrate Japanese-held Singapore in a Japanese fishing boat. The problem was that no one, apart from Reynolds and Lyon, thought so.

Although SOE's India Mission had been set up in Domba House, New Delhi, from where it would run the highly effective Force 136, it did not as yet have the resources or network to assist. Mainstream military organisations, which did, dismissed the plan put forward by Lyon, a relatively junior officer, as a pipe-dream. It was not until early May that Ivan, his list of contacts exhausted, walked into the Delhi office of his old sailing friend Bernard Fergusson, recently appointed to General Wavell's planning staff. Still smarting over Singapore's loss, Wavell, who liked off-beat ideas, heard Ivan out and gave it his seal of approval. Here, at least, was someone willing to take the offensive. When the two admirals, Sir Geoffrey Layton, Commander-in-Chief Ceylon, and Geoffrey Arbuthnot, Commander-in-Chief East Indies, also gave the plan the nod, things began to move. Wavell, however, had one proviso. With the

Indian Ocean, Burma, Malaya and indeed the entire Far East a hive of Japanese activity, the mission would have a better chance of success if it originated from Australia.

On learning he must travel to Australia, Ivan, who had only just made arrangements for Gabrielle and Clive to sail to India, sent an urgent message for them to remain in Fremantle. Unfortunately, they were already on their way to Bombay on board *Nankin*, which had left Fremantle at 8 am on 5 May, carrying general cargo and 162 passengers, thirty-eight of whom were women and children. Five days out of Fremantle the ship disappeared without a trace, evidently the victim of a submarine or surface raider. It appeared there were no survivors. Ivan, who was at an onboard function when told the devastating news, finished his drink and quietly left.

Clinks Gab is dead

Pushing aside his personal sorrow he turned to the task at hand, which now had the full support of SOE London and the backing of Wavell, who gave him a letter of introduction to open doors in Australia which might otherwise be closed. After securing the services of Jock Campbell, who was working in Assam and southern India as a Tamil interpreter, Lyon flew to Ceylon where, with some difficulty, he succeeded in rescuing Ron Morris from bed-pan duty at No 55 Combined Ceylonese Military Hospital in Colombo. To allow him to carry arms legitimately, Morris was also transferred, on paper, to the Indian Army Corps of Clerks. At the beginning of June, after making arrangements for his first two recruits to follow him to Australia on *Athlone Castle*, Lyon had a final conference with Bill Reynolds.

Before they parted company, Lyon to Australia and Reynolds to supervise a complete overhaul of *Suey Sin Fah*'s engines, each had one last task to perform – Reynolds to rename his ship yet again, and Lyon to devise a code name for the proposed mission. Reynolds settled on *Krait* (pronounced 'Krite'), a small but deadly Indian snake. As any reader acquainted with the books of Rudyard Kipling knows, the krait is a skinny, nondescript-looking snake whose appearance is so innocuous that it is rarely noticed – until it attacks. The analogy was brilliant. Like the cunning little reptile, MV *Krait* would creep as close as possible to its unsuspecting Japanese victims to deliver a blow of such speed and potency that the enemy would not know what had hit it. Reynolds was so pleased with the new name that he went straight to the nearest bazaar and purchased a hand-wrought brass krait, captured in the strike position, for the ship's mascot.

krait

Lyon, motivated by an overwhelming desire to lessen the shame of Singapore's loss and to help wipe away the humiliating smell of defeat, chose for his mission the far more obscure 'Jaywick'. Contrary to post-war opinion that the tiny English port of Jaywick had prompted the choice, Jay Wick originated not from East Anglia but the Far East. Besides being a well-known and powerful deodoriser, used to sweeten the air of Singapore's lavatories, the humble but indispensable Jay Wick was the subject of a long-standing joke shared by Ivan and his sailing friend, Francis Moir-Byres.

'Airlie', SOA HQ at 260 Domain Rd, South Yarra, Melbourne

Where Jaywick comes from (*)

On their trip from Trengannu to Thailand, they had been attempting to manoeuvre *Vinette* across one of the sandbars when a basket of eggs, suspended from the galley roof, had broken free in the rough conditions. Smashing to the floor in one slimy mess, the contents had then seeped into the bilge to rapidly decompose. In the oppressive tropical conditions below decks, the stench was so overpowering that for the rest of the voyage there was not a single day when Ivan had not moaned 'If only we had a Jay Wick – that would get rid of the pong'. Working on the assumption that if the powerful and magical Jay Wick could eliminate odours as foul as raw sewage and rotten eggs, it could surely obliterate the smell of defeat from the nostrils of the British Empire, Ivan left his private joke for Francis and posterity. Provided everything went to plan, *Krait* would take Operation Jaywick to Singapore.

While Lyon was making his way to Australia, SOE was organising a new intelligence organisation which would facilitate his proposed mission. The preliminary stages for the formation of SOE (Australia) had been under way for some weeks. Using the cover name Inter-Allied Services Department (IASD or, more usually, ISD), Ivan's SOE colleagues Major Edgerton Mott and Major Ambrose Trappes-Lomax had set up headquarters in Airlie, a magnificent mansion at 260 Domain Road in the upmarket Melbourne suburb of South Yarra.

Trappes-Lomax had arrived in Fremantle from Java on 11 March and, as orders from the previous October posting him to Australia were still standing, he was called to Australian General Headquarters by the Chief of the General Staff, General Sturdee. Mott had flown with General Wavell to Java before Singapore's surrender. He had left Batavia shortly before it too fell to the enemy and was attempting to reach Australia in a fishing boat when he was picked up by the Australian Navy corvette, HMAS *Maryborough*. On informing London of

Left: *Lieutenant Denis Emerson-Elliott, in his office at the Department of Naval Intelligence*
Right: *Commander R M Long, Director of Naval Intelligence*

his whereabouts on his arrival in Fremantle on 10 March, he was instructed to proceed to Melbourne where, being senior to Trappes-Lomax, he became adviser on Special Operations (SO) to Lieutenant-Colonel Caleb Grafton Roberts, Director of Military Intelligence (DMI). The SOE officers were given a small office in Victoria Barracks where they were in close contact with the Director of Naval Intelligence (DNI), Commander Rupert M Long, also known as 'Cocky' (a soubriquet which he loathed). Long, who had visited Singapore for a high-level secret intelligence conference at Fort Canning on 14 November 1941, had met both Mott and Denis Emerson-Elliott, now working on Long's staff in Western Australia.[1]

Long, who was exceptionally well-informed on SO matters and had been instrumental in establishing the pre-war network of Coastwatchers on the islands to Australia's north, worked with Mott to lay the groundwork for the establishment of SOE in Australia. On 27 March, Mott, High Court Judge Sir Owen Dixon and propaganda specialist Commander John Proud were flown to Canberra for a conference with a Dutch secret service expert. Proud had close connections to secret intelligence, along with Dixon, who had married Alice Brooksbank, sister of W H Brooksbank, who was Civil Assistant to Commander Long and had helped build the Naval Intelligence network.

On 7 April Mott conferred with Generals Blamey and Sturdee. Blamey, who believed a Special Operations organisation was imperative, also believed that a civil cover organisation, as proposed by Long and Mott, was not necessary and that control should be vested in America's General Douglas MacArthur, with Blamey in 'immediate control' and Mott as director. The organisation's role would be to insert trained operatives into enemy territory to harass lines of communication, carry out general sabotage, attack shipping and organise local resistance. The cost, estimated by Mott to be £100,000 per annum, would be met every six months by the various Allied governments. Blamey submitted an outline of the scheme and the budget estimate to Sturdee, who in turn submitted them to MacArthur who gave his approval on 17 April.

Mott, now promoted to lieutenant-colonel, was ordered by Blamey to immediately set the wheels in motion. It was easier said than done. It was not until 17 May that he was able to obtain suitable office accommodation at Airlie, allowing him and Trappes-Lomax to move out of the shoebox room at Victoria Barracks and organise their staff. Operatives were recruited and sent to the Guerrilla Warfare School near Foster on Wilsons Promontory, established by SOE's Freddie Spencer Chapman in 1941 and where, by arrangement with the Director of Military Training, ISD had its own section. Frustratingly, although the new SOE organisation was GHQ approved, Mott found it difficult to get anyone in authority to make any decisions regarding tasks or priorities.

By June ISD, known internally among SOE staff as 'Force 137', was functioning on a proper basis and planning began to get underway. A communications system was established, consisting of a Beam Station run by the Dutch at Craigieburn outside Melbourne, a relay station at Cairns for dealing with New Guinea and the islands to Australia's north, and another at Darwin, manned by Dutch personnel, to handle transmissions with the Netherlands East Indies. With operations planned for New Guinea, Timor and the Aroe Islands, personnel with local knowledge of these destinations were recruited. Among them was Harry Manderson, a prominent journalist who had established and close connections to SOE, chosen to head the Timor Section. A rather mild-looking, bespectacled civilian, Manderson, or 'Mandy' as he became known, had, among other things, business interests in Timor oil and knew the country well.

However, most of ISD's recruits came from the three Australian services, particularly the Army. There was no problem finding suitable applicants, but the training program at Foster soon ran into problems – security was difficult to police; there were no holding arrangements for operatives awaiting the commencement of the course; and the cold Victorian climate was detrimental to the health of soldiers who had been serving in hot tropical zones.

With Foster's climate proving unsuitable, plans were put in train during June for the establishment of a new training school at Fairview, a large hickory, kauri and red-cedar mansion designed by the French architect Louis Severin, built in 1896 on a hillside estate on the outskirts of Cairns in far north Queensland. The property, formerly owned by the grandfather of the famous aviator, Charles Kingsford Smith, had already been earmarked by ISD, which had selected it for their wireless relay station. Known officially as 'Z Experimental

Station' or ZES, and colloquially as 'The House on the Hill', the site was ideal, being well away from prying eyes, particularly as many of the local civilians had been evacuated further south. No reason was given for the choice of Z Experimental Station as the name, but it seems likely that it was inspired either by Sir Claude Edward Dansey's (code name Colonel Z) undercover, and short-lived, Z Organisation in England or by General Blamey whose signals, prefixed by a Z, ensured immediate attention.

To provide a holding unit for the large number of Australian Army recruits, and a cover unit for the civilians, Sturdee created an administrative body called 'Z Special Unit'. Despite its swashbuckling and somewhat melodramatic title, Z Special Unit was purely administrative, its role being to administer to the Australian Army component of ISD and provide a holding unit for these recruits, who always remained on the war establishment of their parent unit.

Z Special Unit had no war establishment of its own, no war equipment table and no colour patch. Non-Australian personnel and RAN and RAAF recruits, being much fewer in number, did not use Z Special Unit for holding purposes or administratively, but remained under the administration of their own branch of the services. Although Z Special Unit, being non-operational, was unable to plan or carry our missions in its own right, it was an extremely handy tool as it had *carte blanche* from General Blamey to draw whatever was required from ordnance stores. Under the control of ISD, which also supplied all the funding, it held a unique role in the Australian Army.

On 6 July ISD was taken over by a new organisation – Allied Intelligence Bureau, or AIB. The Americans at GHQ, wanting to keep a tight rein on what they considered to be the sometimes maverick tendencies of the Dutch and British agencies, and also believing, quite rightly, that the British and Dutch were more interested in regaining their colonial empires than furthering MacArthur's plans to retake the Philippines, had issued a directive to amalgamate all irregular units. All Inter-Allied units – SOE (Australia); SIS; two field intelligence organisations (the Netherland East Indies Field Intelligence Section, known as NEFIS, and Commander Long's Coastwatchers); and the Propaganda Section (Far East Liaison Office or FELO) – were now under the umbrella of AIB. To Mott's horror, in one fell swoop ISD had lost its independence, its specialised funding and control of its exclusive administrative arm Z Special Unit.

Mott, whose chain of command had been Blamey and then MacArthur, discovered there was now another level of command – AIB's Controller, 44-year-old Lieutenant-Colonel Roberts, formerly the Director of Military Intelligence, and son of Tom Roberts, the famous Australian artist. Roberts, who had a reputation for working at a snail's pace, was controller in name only, for his deputy, Colonel Allison W. Ind, United States Army, was also the Finance Officer. This arrangement gave GHQ indirect control since, as Ind later pointed out, without American approval any proposed mission 'would die from financial anaemia'.

On 6 July, the same day as ISD lost its independence, Ivan Lyon arrived in Melbourne. Despite high hopes, he had discovered shortly after his arrival in Australia that he needed more than Wavell's letter of introduction to get his mission up and running. He had started out well enough, with the most encouraging reactions from Lieutenant-General Gordon Bennett and Fremantle's Naval Officer in Command, Commodore Collins, at a meeting on 4 July brokered by Denis Emerson-Elliott. Heartening too had been his follow-up conference with Mott, who immediately saw the plan's potential and contacted GHQ. To Lyon's and Mott's utter dismay, Wavell's letter made no impression on MacArthur's influential right-hand man General Charles Willoughby, who informed them that US plans for the future did not include Singapore. The attitude of the Australian Army was not much better. General Blamey, according to Lyon, was 'rude and obstructive', possibly because Lyon had with him a letter of introduction, extolling the plan, from Blamey's arch-enemy, General Bennett. There was some support from General Northcott, who thought the Jaywick concept might have possibilities in Timor, but the bottom line was that the Australian Army was unwilling to back any venture deep in enemy territory.

Had Ivan Lyon been less determined, he may have given up. However, as he had no intention of abandoning his plan he used his personal ties with Victorian Governor Sir Winston Duggan, with whom he was staying, to obtain an audience with the Governor-General, Lord Gowrie. Unlike the Americans, Gowrie understood the significance of Wavell's letter and by 17 July Ivan was in conference with the head of the Australian Naval Board, Admiral Royle, and Commander Long who, conversant with the workings of SOE and aware of the value of undercover work, embraced the plan with enthusiasm.

Lyon did not have to worry about currying favour with AIB's Finance Officer. Jaywick, also known as 'Jock Force', was to be an SOE/RAN mission. The navy had agreed to provide guidance and support, but in all other respects Jaywick was to be controlled and funded by SOE, which had already sent £3000 of the estimated £11,000 required. As soon as Campbell and Morris arrived on 2 August they set to work spending some of it – Campbell in his role as administrator and Morris as general factotum. With *Krait*, which had been delayed by engine trouble, due to arrive sometime after 4 August, Lyon's priority was to find an able second-in-command (2IC) to select and train the volunteer recruits.

It was quite a tall order. The applicant, besides being extremely physically fit and skilled in guerrilla tactics, needed to be at home on the sea and in the jungle, able to assume command in an instant, be resourceful, innovative, fearless and, if necessary, absolutely ruthless. At dinner one evening, the name of Donald Davidson was put forward by his brother-in-law, equerry to Lyon's host, Governor Duggan. Lyon not only knew the name, he knew the man. Lieutenant Donald Davidson, aged thirty-four, was 'close' to MI6, so close that, like Denis Emerson-Elliot and many other MI6 'friends,' in April 1940 he was commissioned into the Royal Naval Volunteer Reserve. With the rank of sub-lieutenant Special Branch (Intelligence) he had been assigned to the staff of the Rear Admiral at the Naval Base. Three months later he was promoted to lieutenant and was given the job of Assistant to the Staff Officer (Operations), Singapore.

Lieutenant-Commander Donald Davidson

Davidson, whose roots, like Lyon's, were Scottish, was the son of a clergyman, the Anglican vicar of Woodford Kettering in Northamptonshire. Left motherless at a tender age, Donald was not only the youngest but the most difficult of six children so, in 1914, not long after his sixth birthday, he was packed off to boarding school. In 1926, at the age of just eighteen and spurred by a well-developed spirit of adventure, he sailed to Australia where he found employment in outback Queensland, initially as a jackeroo at Ooraine Station, Dirranbandi, and then at Booka Booka, near Charleville, where he spent some time as ringbarking contractor. Realising after working for two years on low wages that the possibility of his ever owning a sheep station was remote, he headed for Thailand where he obtained a position with the Bombay Burmah Trading Company, supervising timber-getting in the teak forests.

Apart from revelling in the freedom and variety of the outdoor life, Davidson was fascinated by the ecology of the jungle, rediscovering his boyhood passion for nature and building up such a substantial collection of butterflies and moths that it was acquired by the Victoria and Albert Museum in London. He was just as home with the elephants which worked in the teak forests and other large creatures, actively seeking excitement by stalking tigers, often without a gun, for the sheer thrill of following their padmarks in the dew-soaked grass. He spent six years in this exotic wilderness, his only contact with the outside world were letters carried by runners to and from Bangkok.

After returning from leave in 1935, most of which he had spent paddling down the Danube, he was transferred to Burma. At his new posting on the Irrawadi River he spent his free days building a boat and his nights studying navigation. But he now had a companion with whom to share his campfire – a wife. Nancy was a long-standing girlfriend who, tired of waiting for him to make a firm commitment and annoyed that he had severed their relationship during his home leave, had taken the initiative and sailed for the Far East, where they married on the spot.

With war clouds gathering in early 1940, Davidson had tried unsuccessfully to enlist in the Burmese Frontier Force before joining the RNVR in Singapore. In 1941, his wife gave birth to a daughter on the same day and in the same hospital as Lyon's daughter was born. By this time Donald had met both Ivan Lyon and Denis Emerson-Elliott. Unable to reveal his connections to the Secret Service to anyone outside the circle, he claimed to anyone who inquired that he had gone to Singapore intending to join the AIF, but had stopped off at the mess at the Naval Base to play a game of dice and come out with a commission. It was a story believed by his wife who, at the end of December 1941, was evacuated with their infant daughter Caroline to Australia on the Blue Funnel Line's SS *Ulysses*.

Davidson, who left Singapore with other naval staff just before the surrender, was reunited with his family in March 1942. 'On loan' to the Royal Australian Navy, he was languishing in Melbourne bound to a desk job when Ivan renewed their acquaintance and offered him the job of training commandos for a highly secret mission. Within days they had the names of about forty sailors from Flinders Naval Depot (HMAS *Cerberus*) who had volunteered for 'adventurous' work which Lyon, dressed for the occasion in his Gordons kilt, warned them 'could be a bit dangerous'. With the applicants interviewed and reduced in number to a more manageable seventeen, Davidson, with the help of Sub-Lieutenant Bert Overell, put them through a gruelling course at the Army Physical and Recreational Training School at nearby Frankston. Physical fitness was no stranger to Overell, a tall young man of twenty-two, blessed with a wide smile and dashing good looks. After serving in an army cadet unit

Lieutenant Bert Overell

from 1937, he had joined the AIF in 1941 and been sent to Officer Training School, to be discharged after about four months to accept a commission in the RANVR as an intelligence officer. Davidson, who was even fitter than Overell, broke the obstacle course record, but the challenge proved too great for three of the sailors, who did not measure up physically, mentally or emotionally and were sent back to normal duties. The rest were granted eight days' leave and ordered to report to the Garden Island Naval Base in Sydney before noon on 6 September, to undertake more specialised training at 'Camp X'.

While Davidson and Overell were knocking their volunteers into shape, Lyon, Morris and Campbell had met in Sydney on 26 July. Unhindered by the usual red tape and with an apparently limitless cash supply from SOE, they established their headquarters in a furnished upstairs flat at 15 Onslow Gardens, Potts Point. Here they were joined by Morris, their general factotum, and an intelligent, charming, well-educated and attractive army corporal, Bettina Reid, grand-daughter of Australia's first prime minister, Edmund Barton. Reid, who came from a privileged background, had 'come out' in England, making her debut at Buckingham Palace, where she met Ivan's distant relative Queen Elizabeth. An independent young woman, she toured Europe before returning, unaccompanied, to Australia at the end of 1938. She married in 1940. Her husband, who joined the AIF, was now a prisoner of the Germans. She had no financial need to work but as she was highly motivated to 'do her bit' she enlisted in early 1942. Being well connected as well as efficient and astute, she was appointed Jaywick's 'typist' by Military Intelligence. In reality she was the mission's unofficial Intelligence Officer and in time would not only become privy to almost every facet of Jaywick's planning and organisation but also Ivan's most trusted and valued confidante.

Leaving Morris, Campbell and Reid to organise the flat, and with money now channelled into a secret bank account at the Kings Cross branch of the Bank of New South Wales, Lyon headed into the wilderness around Broken Bay to the north of Sydney in search of a suitable site for Camp X. He settled on a clifftop high above Refuge Bay, a small and protected cove on the south side of the Hawkesbury River estuary. Screened by thick scrub and substantial trees, it had a permanently running stream which cascaded 25 metres to a small sandy beach below and a 180-degree view of the seaward approaches from the top of the sandstone precipice. Accessible only by water from Coal and Candle Creek or by a three-kilometre hike across

Camp X, high above Refuge Bay. Visiting warships, regarded as 'fair game', were 'attacked' during training exercises

rugged country from a defence road leading to an army post at West Head, the area was well concealed and remote.

The camp was only partially ready by the time Davidson's train pulled into Sydney's Central Station. Morris, who formed the welcoming committee with Lyon and Campbell, had never met the new 2IC and was looking forward to the encounter with great interest. The tall, fit-looking figure striding down the platform in immaculate naval uniform was, at first glance, an impressive sight. Morris's critical gaze travelled from the highly polished black shoes, past the jacket displaying the golden braid of the 'Wavy Navy' (as the Naval Reserve was popularly known), only to stop dead at the left eye-socket. There, firmly tucked between eyebrow and cheekbone, was a monocle. As Morris gazed in wonderment at this unexpected and incongruous eyepiece, Davidson missed his footing – his body shooting in one direction and cap, briefcase and precious monocle in the other. The displaced cap had concealed a receding hairline that made Davidson look older than his years. It was some time before Morris realised that the monocle was pure affectation, and that Davidson's love of the ridiculous was offset by a single-minded dedication to duty that equalled that of Lyon.

Trainer

7

Jaywick begins

September 1942–August 1943

Even with Davidson helping, Morris and Leading Seaman Johnson, who was on loan for a month, were still readying the camp when the recruits arrived on 6 September. Their new home at this stage consisted of just eight canvas-and-pole tents, a cookhouse which was the domain of Allan 'Bluey' Hobbs, and Taffy Morris's well-stocked Q-store. Beyond the tented area was a rocky outcrop which, to Morris's initial consternation, was home to a variety of venomous snakes and huge goannas (monitor lizards). Bathing facilities were a large rockpool while sanitary arrangements comprised a wooden toilet seat mounted on top of a narrow split in the rocky outcrop. This rather precarious perch was rendered even more so if Morris, who used the area at the base of the drop as an incinerator, set fire to the rubbish without checking whether anyone was seated topside. As yet there was no sign of the proposed parade ground, flagpole or boxing ring, which would be built by the recruits as part of their training program.

With Jaywick's attack scheduled for 15 February 1943, the first anniversary of Singapore's fall, training began immediately. The punishing program, carried out for eighteen hours a day in all weathers and at any time of day or night, was not designed for the faint-hearted. Davidson's objective was not only to train silent saboteurs but to bring every member of the

Ann ferrying goods and personnel to the secluded beach below Camp X

team to the peak of fitness and endurance. Meanwhile, Lyon explored the area on foot and in *Ann*, a six-metre launch and the camp's sole method of transportation, to suss out challenging routes – a task which saw him arrested and held for several hours by sentries manning one of the more remote army posts on the estuary until his bona fides were established.

Davidson's first edict, apart from no cigarettes, beer or women, was that access to the beach was via a bosun's chair and the return journey by rope, hand-over-hand up the cliff face, commando-style. The second was to go naked or near-naked whenever possible to build up a tan – why, he did not say. Besides hardening their bodies and using muscles they never knew existed, the men also learned how to fade into the landscape and to carry out any task silently, from canoe paddling, to stalking, to killing. Swimming, an important part of the training program, was carried out regularly in the bay, with one of the team stationed on a rock with a shotgun should any shark put in an unwelcome appearance. Curious boat-trippers were sent packing by firing one or two shots across their bows.

A thorough knowledge of weapons was mandatory – Bren, Oerlikon, Lewis and Owen guns, plus rifles, pistols, mortars and grenades. To ensure that all were thoroughly conversant with the mechanical workings of each type, as well as how to use them, weapons experts Sergeants Clarrie Willoughby and Arthur 'Sam' Suters, recruited by Jock Campbell from Ingleburn Army Camp, were put in charge of training. With no rifle range handy, their targets were sandstone boulders on the cliff face of a nearby inlet and weighted buoys in the bay. There was also anti-aircraft training at the army range at Malabar and at the Globe trainer at Woolloomooloo. By the time Clarrie and Sam had finished with them, the raiders were not only excellent marksmen but also able to strip and reassemble their weapons in the dark.

More covert killing would require the use of the garrotte and specially crafted knives, including stilettos, sheaths, parangs and an ingenious knuckle-duster variety, all supplied to Davidson's detailed specifications. Their chief instructor was Davidson himself, an expert exponent of the use of the knife, as the splintered wood panels on his bungalow door in Burma could attest. Stealth was essential, and by trial and error Lyon and Davidson explored ways to prevent betrayal by sound or smell. Soft japara (a fine, oiled cotton) or bare skin replaced normal army-issue uniform, reducing noise made by clothing to a minimum; pungent, tar-soaked ropes exchanged for cords made from odourless materials; and feet toughened by going unshod whenever possible. Thick woollen socks, worn to counter barnacle-covered rocks, were

Arthur 'Joe' Jones, armed with a knife, honing his attack skills at Camp X, late 1942

wrung out on reaching the shore and thrust into dry sandshoes which, unlike water-logged footwear, did not squelch with every step. The most important and most difficult art was that of endless patience and stealth, instilled by hours of tactical manoeuvres, lest a sudden movement lead to detection.

Since noiseless, undetectable movement on water was just as important as on dry land, intensive training in the small two-man craft to be used to mount the attack was vital. Similar to the traditional animal-hide and whale-bone kayaks of the Inuit people, the team's folboats, constructed of black, rubberised canvas stretched over a lightweight wood-and-bamboo frame, were collapsible, portable and very manoeuvrable. For ease of access the folboats, along with boxes of gelignite for demolition practice and 'fish bombing' to supplement the canned and dried food rations, were stored in a large cave which Davidson had discovered immediately behind the waterfall.

Refinements in equipment and technique introduced by Davidson and Lyon were used to decrease the risk of detection while on the water. Finely-honed single-bladed paddles eliminated the telltale flashes of light reflected by the twisting movement of double-bladed paddles, while 'freezing' the canoe end-on to the observer reduced an already low profile to such a degree that the canoeists were all but invisible, even at quite close range. By the end of their training the men were so skilled that they could successfully sneak up on Lyon, stationed in *Ann*, and also paddle past the searchlight battery on nearby Juno Head and other defence posts around Broken Bay unseen by the lookouts.

But an ability to reach the target was only the beginning. The real skill came in blowing it up, and then getting clean away. Assisting Davidson in teaching this daunting task were Overell, who had completed a ten-day sabotage course at ZES to the complete satisfaction of Major Trappes-Lomax, and 42-year-old Major Francis George Leach Chester, British Army.

Born in Johannesberg, South Africa, in 1899, to British parents who later settled in Kenya, Chester was educated in England. After graduating from Sandhurst in 1916 and serving with King Edwards Horse, he left Africa in 1923 for British North Borneo, where he purchased a rubber plantation near Tawau, in the far south-east corner of the country. In 1940, with Germany now at war with England, he obtained a commission in the Kings African Rifles, raised from the British colonies in East Africa and commanded by officers seconded from the British Army. After seeing action in Abyssinia, in May 1942 he went to India, joined SOE and met Ivan Lyon. Fluent in Malay and trained in internal sabotage and propaganda, Chester had the perfect credentials for Jaywick and, in September 1942, after serving with SOE in Burma, was assigned to the mission at Lyon's request. His transfer was given top priority and, after flying via Cairo, Miami, Chicago, San Francisco, and Hawaii, he arrived at Refuge Bay at the end of October. Commonly known as 'Gort' because of his uncanny resemblance to Field Marshal Viscount Gort, Chief of the British General Staff,

Jaywick's five original officers (L to R): 'Gort' Chester, Ivan Lyon, Bill Reynolds, Donald Davidson, Bert Overell, January 1942

Chester, like his high profile namesake, he had a round head, a hairline receding to the point of baldness, bushy eyebrows and a lush moustache.

To blow up the ships, Lyon had obtained a brand-new weapon from SOE's 'department of dirty tricks' in London – a delayed action, magnetic limpet mine which adhered to the hulls of iron ships in the same way as a limpet shell clings to the rocky seashore. Packed with four kilograms of explosive, each limpet was capable of blowing a one-metre hole in the hull of an ordinary ship. The manoeuvrability of the lightweight folboats, which could each carry nine limpets, made them ideal for the job. While the bowman held the boat steady by attaching a magnetic hold-fast to the hull of the ship, his partner, using a collapsible 183-centimetre rod, clamped the mines into position below the water line. When three limpets connected by a detonating cord were firmly attached, the raiders proceeded to the next target.

To test the operatives' skill, night practice raids were mounted against any naval vessel that entered the bay. The level of expertise was such that even when the ships' companies were alerted, the canoeists usually managed to approach their targets unobserved and, to the chagrin of more than one Officer of the Watch, climb aboard and chalk 'Surrender sailor' on the ships' guns and elsewhere. Other vessels boarded had items purloined, often from the captain's locked cabin, before the successful raider pressed the alarm button, rousing the entire ship to action stations. The saboteurs enjoyed similar success with land-based raids directed at the hapless soldiers manning the army post at West Head. After paddling from Refuge Bay and scaling the towering, scrub-covered cliffs, they infiltrated the camp, using chalked 'brands' to 'poison' the water supply, blow up guns, knock out the searchlight battery, demolish the signals hut and dispose of anyone not awake to their tactics.

Ivan and Gort, who flitted in and out of the camp attending to their many tasks, were delighted with the progress. And so were the top brass, including very senior naval officers and also Lord Gowrie, who arrived by motor launch on 5 December with an impressive retinue to

126

inspect the camp. Although there was now a path, accessed by rope ladders from the beach, the vice-regal party rode up in style in the bosun's chair. After watching an unarmed combat demonstration, Gowrie accepted an invitation to launch a plywood experimental canoe, designed and built by Davidson with the help of one of the recruits, apprentice cabinet-maker Fred Marsh. Possibly the smallest and most humble craft ever to be launched by such an esteemed personage, it was christened HMAS *Lyon*.

Although women were banned from the camp, Corporal Reid was another, very unexpected visitor. Normally, she drove from Potts Point or from HMAS *Penguin*, the naval base at Balmoral (where the stores were stockpiled), to the small jetty at Coal and Candle Creek where supplies, equipment and personnel were transferred to *Ann*. One beautiful summer day Gort Chester, who was on his way back to the camp, suggested she might like to undertake an 'inspection', evidently believing that Lyon would organise the bosun's chair for the ascent. But Ivan made no concession to the fact that Reid was a woman, or that she was wearing her normal army uniform, including a slim-fitting skirt. If she wanted to see the camp, which she did, it was by rope ladder or nothing. Her determination to reach the top earned her the distinction of being the first, and only, woman to visit Camp X.

Towards the end of the training period all those involved in the operational side, including Lyon, Davidson and Overell, were required to undertake a series of three-day, high-level endurance tests. Sustained only by iron rations, or 'hard tack', all team members were expected to be sufficiently fit to cover 80 kilometres a day on foot using roads or tracks; 60 over rougher terrain; 50 by folboat on rivers or 50 on land and water combined, carrying, if necessary, the dismantled folboats in special bags. The route of the final test was demanding – Refuge Bay to Palm Beach, across the Hawkesbury Estuary to Lion Island, then Ocean

Original Jaywick recruits at Camp X, taken on the road to West Head. (Back row) Andrew Huston, Norris 'Norrie' Wright, Fred Marsh, Leslie 'Tiny' Hage, John Mackay. (Front row) Arthur Jones, Ernest 'Snow' Kerr, Stan McCabe, Paul 'Mick' Cameron

Beach, Brisbane Water and Narara Creek, overland to Ourimbah and then into the water again to paddle to Tuggerah, well to the north of Gosford. Although they participated in normal training exercises, the only people excused from this fearsome endurance regime were Gort, who was now in charge of food, stores and signals; Leading Telegraphist Don Sharples, whose expertise in Morse transmission made up somewhat for his undisguised distaste for rigid discipline, and Morris, whose role as medical orderly and general hand did not require him to meet the same level of physical fitness.

It was during one of the shorter tests that Davidson met his match. Rather than paddle all the way back to Refuge Bay, he had arranged for a truck to pick up the men and their folboats. As they sloshed wearily through the mud flats to the rendezvous point near the Hawkesbury River bridge a young soldier, rifle in hand, emerged from the gloom near the truck and challenged them with a 'Halt. Password'. The canoeists took absolutely no notice so he issued a sterner warning, firing over their heads and clipping a tree. To a man, they hit the ground. After recovering his composure Davidson announced authoritatively that he was 'an officer of the Royal Navy on exercise', which was met with a re-cocking of the rifle and a laconic 'You'll be a bloody dead one unless I get a password'. With no room for argument Davidson called 'Snake'. 'Gully', echoed the soldier, followed by 'Pass, friend'. Their credentials proven, it was a much chastened team which returned to camp.

Although Lyon, who was rather reserved, had a good rapport with the men, he was always careful to maintain the fine line which separated a commander from his troops. Davidson, being 2IC and with the trainees twenty-four hours a day, was more gregarious by nature and allowed a little more latitude. His full name was Donald Montague Noel, but he always signed himself DMN – initials which the trainees, not privy to his full name, evidently had trouble recalling. To make life easier he told them all they had to remember was 'Duff Monkey Nuts' Davidson – a memory aid which was not explained but which stuck so firmly that it was still remembered sixty years later.

It was just as well that Davidson did not actually require *Krait*'s presence for training purposes. Worried by the delay, Commander Long had sent a message to Colombo on 17 July

Davidson applying camouflage paint outside his tent at Camp X

asking, 'Has Lyon's sampan sailed?' and requesting an ETA. When the rescheduled date of arrival of 4 August was put back owing to engine trouble, Campbell signalled SOE in India, reminding them that Jaywick's latest departure date was 1 December. With no satisfactory response forthcoming and in an effort to make up for lost time, a further flurry of signals from Lyon to Reynolds ensued, asking if he could be in Broome, Western Australia, by early November. The reply that Reynolds hoped to have *Krait* in Sydney by the end of September was evidently not good enough for Jock, who dispatched yet another message seeking details of the route, a definite arrival date and confirmation that the ship had actually sailed. She hadn't. On 3 October SOE advised that major engine trouble had so disrupted the schedule that assistance was now being sought to transport *Krait* and Reynolds to Sydney on the first available cargo ship.

Alone in India, Bill Reynolds was despairing that *Krait* would ever reach Australia. In Madras he had learned that, in addition to a major engine overhaul, the main bearings and big ends needed to be re-metalled, the inlet port re-welded and the circulating pump repaired. As such major repairs could only be carried out by specialists at the South Indian Railway Workshops, in October Reynolds sailed to Mandapam where he handed the ship over to Lieutenant-Commander Seaton. The former submarine engineer, now the Marine Superintendent, delivered more bad news – the clutch required attention. This work could not be done in Mandapam, so Reynolds had to take the vessel to Bombay where a new squad of mechanics from the Royal Indian Naval Dockyard took over. Perhaps the only advantage gained by this latest move was that Reynolds was able to replace the faulty air compressor and the auxiliary motor by persuading Greaves Cotton, the distributors in India for the English manufacturers Ruston Hornsby, to part with two brand-new motors held in their Bombay warehouse.

Back at the Potts Point flat, Jock Campbell had become so alarmed by the constant delays that on 29 October he urged the DNI, Commander Long, to scrap all plans to use *Krait* for the mission. Jock's suggestion that a seine-net trawler or pearling lugger might be a suitable substitute may have received Long's approval had India not signalled that *Krait* was now on board P&O's SS *Shillong Shillong*, and that the vessel would be ready on arrival in Sydney. The elation this news evoked was shattered when India advised that the steamship would not sail for another fortnight. Concerned that any further delays would throw out the timetable completely, Campbell sought and received affirmation that *Krait* would be ready for immediate service – an assurance which was retracted the following day, leaving Lyon and Campbell with no option but to hope that somehow Bill Reynolds would manage to complete all repairs while the ship was in transit.

As soon as India confirmed that *Shillong Shillong* had actually left Bombay, on 24 November, Long instructed Denis Emerson-Elliott to inspect *Krait* on arrival in Fremantle and report on her state of readiness. Although busy interrogating Chinese-speaking prisoners who had been aboard *Kormoran*, the German raider which had sunk the cruiser HMAS *Sydney* off the West Australian coast, Denis was keen to see his old friend Reynolds and the ship. He found them both in fine form, *Krait* perhaps a little too fine. The erstwhile fishing boat was no longer decrepit, nor disreputable. The dockyard workers in Bombay had done such a good job sprucing up the exterior of the ship that, 'unless she is roughed up', Denis reported, 'she will stick out like a sore thumb'.

The ship berthed in Sydney on Christmas Day, but there was no reception committee. The super-fit, highly efficient Jaywick team, apart from Morris and Sharples who remained behind to guard the camp, had been given three days leave and the dockyards were idle – the festive season being of greater priority than the war. Although Davidson dispatched recruits Clifford Monk and Norrie Wright to assist Reynolds with the ship on 2 January, by the time the holidaying labour force returned to work and arranged for *Krait*'s removal it was 4 January. For the next eight days the RAN engineers at Garden Island worked almost round the clock, repairing damage sustained to the hull by lifting equipment during the transfers and refitting the interior to accommodate the mass of stores and equipment.

At Camp X, training continued with a vengeance. The operational team now numbered ten. One recruit suffering from dysentery had been posted to HMAS *Penguin* on 1 January, another to HMAS *Warramunga* the same day, while Davidson had taken advantage of the Christmas break to dismiss another. Branded a potentially disruptive influence, he had also shown a tendency to panic when, during one period of excitement, he had put a mortar bomb upside down in the firing tube. Equally damning, when asked by Vice-Admiral Sir Guy Royle to show him the newfangled Owen gun during a camp inspection, he somehow accidentally managed to discharge it, ploughing up the ground between the terrified Royle's feet. Although Davidson had no qualms about instructing Naval Intelligence to ship the miscreant 'off to some far place where he could do no harm through talking too much', he didn't go far. He remained where Davidson had dumped him – HMAS *Penguin*, at nearby Balmoral.[1]

Davidson was only too aware of the need to maintain the level of fitness and keep up morale, especially when it was learned on 13 January that *Krait*, having finally been cleared to leave port, had not made it past Middle Head. After taking on supplies at Balmoral the ship had been forced to put into the nearby Army Water Workshops at Chowder Bay with a cracked cylinder head and poor engine timing. Storming ashore, his patience pushed to the limit, Reynolds poured out his troubles to Staff-Sergeant Don Ramsay, an electrical engineer and a World War I veteran about the same age as Reynolds. Taking pity on him, Ramsay put his 'boys' to work at once.

Four days later, at 9.15 on the morning of 17 January, fully six weeks overdue, the ship rounded Challenger Head and dropped anchor in Refuge Bay to a tumultuous reception.

Jaywick begins

Krait finally arrives at Refuge Bay, 17 January 1943

Bursts of machine-gun fire echoed round the ancient sandstone cliffs, drowning out the raucous cheers and shouts of welcome. Unable to wait a moment longer Fred Marsh, 'co-owner' of HMAS *Lyon*, and his mate Andrew Huston took the plywood canoe and paddled out to meet the ship. When the excitement finally died down, Morris and the younger team members spent the rest of the day transferring the folboats and gear to the already cramped holds and stowing miscellaneous items into every other available nook and cranny. There had been some minor improvements, but as the exterior had now been suitably scruffed up she was very similar in appearance to the grubby little boat that had sailed up and down the Indragiri.

At six the following morning, after farewelling Campbell who, with the help of two recruits who had not made the final cut, remained behind to dismantle the camp, Reynolds gave the order to weigh anchor and they were finally on their way. On board were Reynolds, Morris, Sharples, Hobbs, the recently recruited Stoker Manson, Lyon, Davidson, Chester, Overell and the eight men finally selected for the operation.

An unexpected addition was Taffy Morris's cat Cleopatra, a beautiful white Persian. She had arrived at the camp one day, quite out of the blue, to give birth to a litter of kittens on Morris's pyjamas. One of them, the oddly-named Tiddles, found a new home on HMAS *Gympie*, where she was greatly indulged until her unexpected death in June 1943. As a member of the ship's crew, she was buried at sea in Cairns Harbour with full naval honours, including the traditional rifle volley. After the rest of the litter had been given to new homes, Cleopatra had remained and was now Taffy's inseparable and much cosseted companion. When a leading seaman joined the ship in Brisbane, the total number of humans on board would be eighteen. It was a tight squeeze. With stores for six months, fuel, weapons, explosives, equipment and radio gear, space was at a premium, so much so that there was no room for a lifeboat. *Supply*, left behind at Garden Island, had been replaced by two rafts.

As *Krait* was only 21 metres long and scarcely three metres at the widest point, conditions on board were barely tolerable. The hold closest to the engine room was now filled with fuel drums, the for'ard one with limpets and explosives, and No 2 hold, immediately behind it, with food. The remaining hold, about three metres by three metres and accessed by a steep wooden ladder, was designated the 'officers' mess'. It contained an AT5/AR8 wireless transmitter and receiver, manufactured by Amalgamated Wireless Australasia (AWA), positioned under the steps; a chart table; Taffy Morris's medical supplies; sundry batteries and three bunks, arranged in a U shape. Two were stacked with stores and supplies and anything else which did not have a proper home, including a copy of *The Sheik*, a racy novel chosen to help alleviate possible boredom. On top of the wheelhouse was a lumpy pile of tarpaulin-covered miscellaneous items, while the greater part of the engine-room housing accommodated drums of kerosene, extra diesel fuel, fresh provisions and a weapons box.

Apart from the uncluttered bunk in the officers' mess, the engineer's berth, the chart-table-cum-bunk in the wheelhouse and the top of the water tank (reserved for the cook), there were no proper sleeping arrangements. With all available space on deck jam-packed with water tanks, even more fuel containers, ropes and tools, anyone not on watch or occupied with other duties was obliged to bed down on the small space left on the engine-room housing or use one of the three hammocks slung above it.

The bucket on the rope had not gone, it had just been reassigned. The toilet facilities now involved 'sitting out' over the stern, with bucket and rope at hand for washing the nether regions. To reach the designated area the men had to make their way through the poky galley, which often meant climbing over the unfortunate cook, crouched in his confined space trying to prepare meals. There was a big improvement with the awning, however, which had been completely revamped with sturdy marine ply, clad in strong, khaki-coloured bituminised paper, stretching from wheel house to stern. Further improvements were the installation of faded canvas side-blinds, providing shelter from the weather and a screen from prying eyes, and two flaps which had also been cut in the roof, greatly facilitating watch-keeping.

It soon became obvious why Lyon, in his detailed personal reports to Reid, who was holding the fort at Potts Point, had dubbed *Krait* the 'Reluctant Dragon'. They were only five hours out of Refuge Bay when the Deutz engine suddenly died. Reynolds coaxed it back to life by bleeding the fuel lines of a large amount of air, only to have it break down again almost immediately, this time from an overheated clutch. To everyone's mortification Reynolds now hoisted the sail, turned the ship before the wind and radioed for assistance. Help was not long in coming. To prevent *Krait* being blown out of the water by overzealous shore batteries or naval patrol boats, the DNI had circulated a detailed description of the vessel and alerted all depots between Sydney and Darwin to keep a lookout for her. As an added precaution two wooden planks bearing the name KRAIT in bold block letters had been attached to the wheelhouse roof. Had the Navy had its way, the sign on the wheelhouse would have been *Audacious*, a name they evidently preferred and, since it appeared on documentation as 'Audacious (also known as Krait)', a name they had attempted to use.[2]

To prevent further embarrassment, before the minesweeper HMAS *Peterson* arrived from Newcastle to give them a tow, Reynolds had the crew lower the sail, only to lose what small headway he had. Unable to manoeuvre, *Krait* collided with the larger vessel, damaging her bow. After considerable effort a line was eventually secured and the ship taken in tow, whereupon the king-post, which was riddled with dry rot, parted company with the deck. While *Krait* was subjected to further indignity by being towed by the stern, Reynolds continued to struggle with the clutch. About three kilometres from port, and just in time to save them from the humiliation of being dragged stern-first into the harbour, the engine spluttered back into life.

In an effort to make a better impression Reynolds, stern rope in hand, took a flying leap onto the wharf. Unfortunately, his momentum was stopped mid-flight when the rope fouled, jerking him up short and spearheading him into the harbour. When he surfaced, spluttering and covered in oil but still clutching the rope, to discover that his spectacles, his one and only pair, had been consigned to the deep, the entire dockyard rocked under the torrent of his abuse. When the ship was finally repaired, his disposition was not improved in the slightest by the news that enemy submarines had been reported off the coast and all vessels were confined to port until at least 20 January. The delay was put to good use by Lyon, who returned to Sydney to finalise a few matters before catching up with the ship by train.

By normal military standards the inclusion of Reynolds, or indeed any civilian, in any mission was extremely irregular. For SOE, which actively recruited civilians, it was the norm. Reynolds had actually been offered the usual 'cover' of a commission as lieutenant in the Royal Australian Navy but had turned it down – Bill Junior was also in the navy and he had no intention of being of lesser rank than his son. In any case, there was no incentive for him to enlist. Not bound by any financial constraints, SOE had a completely free hand when negotiating pay for civilians. Reynolds remuneration was set at £75 a month, about two and a half times the going rate, and far outstripping any 'danger money' paid to anyone in the military.

By the time they reached Brisbane at the end of January, Reynolds felt he had earned every penny. The 'Reluctant Dragon' had stuttered her way up the coast of New South Wales, with problems as diverse as choked bilge pumps, a faulty generator, a seized front-end bearing, blocked lubricating pipes and seized air compressor forcing her to make unscheduled stops at Trial Bay, near Kempsey, and Coffs Harbour. *Krait* was a rather unstable vessel in anything other than a dead calm sea and as the swell increased off the north coast so did the

Krait, *with Bill Reynolds at the helm, makes her way up the Brisbane River, January 1943*

incidence of seasickness among the sailors, much to the amusement of Reynolds, Davidson and the army personnel, who were unaffected. The sailors' already low morale plummeted even further when Cleopatra, to Morris's acute distress, was washed overboard and drowned in heavy seas.

With engineers announcing that repairs to the ship would take at least a month, Lyon sent everyone off to a cottage by the beach at Surfers Paradise to improve their tans and for further fitness training while he booked into Brisbane's Anne Hathaway Hotel, an establishment 'fully representative of truth, temperance and bad sanitation'. While Reynolds turned his full attention to *Krait*, Lyon caught up on the latest intelligence and organised the making of native-style sarongs. The cotton fabric, a checked pattern in various shades similar to that worn by Lo Gnap Soon on *Sederhana Djohanes*, was supplied by Overell's, a general drapery store on Brunswick Street owned by Bert Overell's family. On 6 February Jock Campbell arrived from Sydney with a volunteer civilian engineer, Mr Hazewinkel, who confirmed Reynolds' gravest fears. Before *Krait* could put to sea a complete engine overhaul would be necessary. Although he had a stockpile of spare parts in Sydney, salvaged by Lever Brothers from their trading centres in the Pacific before the Japanese arrived, many other components would need to be made especially. The delay, he calculated, would be about a month.

The Jaywick team returned from their break at the seaside prior to the 2 March departure to find that the two small petrol stoves in the galley had been replaced by a safer, more efficient model and that the entire foredeck had been coated with a bullet-proof, marine-glue compound. There had also been a change of personnel. Stoker Manson, although an 'able and attentive watch keeper', had no experience with diesel engines. Unable to deal with the most basic mechanical repairs, he had been replaced by Leading Stoker James Patrick 'Paddy' McDowell, who could. Born in Belfast, Ireland in 1900, Paddy was a tough, scrawny, chain-smoking, bandy-legged former merchant mariner who, after emigrating to Queensland, had enlisted in 26 Militia Battalion in 1933. During the previous war he had served on Q-ships – the code name given to armed merchantmen used as decoys against German submarines and surface craft. Loaded with timber to help keep them afloat if holed by shells or torpedoes the ships, usually tramp steamers and colliers, looked defenceless enough – so defenceless, Paddy told his young shipmates, that submariners were often tricked into surfacing without firing their torpedoes. Completely vulnerable upon the surface, it was not until the Q-ships opened fire with guns concealed behind collapsible structures that the enemy understood their mistake. Although Paddy realised from the amount of gear and fuel on *Krait* – enough to travel 13,000 miles – that this was no pleasure cruise, he said nothing. In any case, where they were going was of small concern. His sole interest was focused entirely on his oily, smelly engine.

Operative Norrie Wright, who had left the ship in Newcastle to return to normal duties, had not been replaced but there was an additional crew member on board. Leading Seaman Kevin 'Cobber' Cain, a strong, silent, practical sailor who had seen overseas service on four ships, had yet to be confronted with a knot he couldn't tie, a seam he couldn't caulk or a rope he couldn't splice. Cain went about his shipboard duties with the minimum of fuss, noticed much and said little. He also enjoyed a quiet life, and was prepared to resort to fisticuffs to achieve it. However, as he was normally even-tempered, it was a rare occasion that he felt the need to flex his well-developed muscles. One look from this handsome, dark-haired sailor who had the build of a professional wrestler was more than sufficient to subdue the most belligerent aggressor.

They were at Tin Can Bay, about a third of the way to Townsville, when double disaster struck – an oil-pipe burst, and Davidson went down with malaria. The patient required temporary hospitalisation and was taken ashore along with Paddy by forestry workers from nearby Fraser Island. Having located the necessary spare parts, Paddy returned to the ship with mechanics recruited from Walker's Shipyard in Maryborough, the nearest town of any size, to help him with the repairs. A day later, with Davidson back on board, *Krait* sailed for Lindeman Island where they anchored for the night.

The following morning Paddy was warming up the engine when Morris, who was in the bow, heard a violent explosion behind him. Unlike most of the crew, who sensibly abandoned ship, he hurried to the engine room. Peering through a skylight he saw that a piston had speared through the engine casing, and the connecting rod had wrapped itself round the camshaft, spewing chunks of hot metal everywhere. At this point Reynolds lost his temper with operative Don Russell, who had been in the engine room assisting Paddy. Evidently pushed beyond the limits of endurance, he put an end to the quarrel by flattening Russell, almost as tall as Reynolds himself, with a hefty blow to the jaw. When the excitement had died down Paddy inspected the damage. He was not a happy man. His precious engine had self-destructed and was beyond salvation.

On 13 March, after suffering the indignity of being towed all the way, *Krait* arrived in Townsville where Reynolds was expecting to face an enquiry regarding his altercation with Russell. However, although he had prepared some kind of defence for 'striking a seaman' and 'using unseaman-like methods of coercion', the case fizzled out. Ironically, it appears that it was the state of *Krait*'s engine, rather than Reynolds' purely civilian status, which let him off the hook.

On 27 March it was decided at a high-level meeting in Melbourne that unless another engine could be located Jaywick would have to be postponed indefinitely. There was no prospect of a replacement engine arriving in the foreseeable future so the stores and useless engine were removed. With no cargo or engine to act as ballast the ship was towed with some difficulty to Cairns. With the Navy giving an undertaking to allow any sailors not engaged elsewhere to rejoin the mission, if and when it was resurrected, the Jaywick team was accommodated at ZES to isolate them from mainstream military personnel and to maintain their fitness level and training. While they were busy Davidson had a temporary change of scenery with a transfer in April to HMAS *Assault*, a shore base at Port Stephens, north of Newcastle, followed by a month at sea on HMAS *Manoora*. In June he was back at *Assault*, this time to conduct courses in unarmed combat with the help of Jaywick's operatives.[3]

Reynolds, being a civilian, had by this time joined the ranks of the unemployed. He returned to Bessie and his family in Melbourne determined one way or another to get back into the war. His refusal to accept the naval commission in India was now a mixed blessing. One the one hand it had prevented him from being court-martialled. On the other, he was now an ordinary and very middle-aged citizen. He was also very determined. By exploiting all his contacts he managed to convince the United States that he had skills essential to the war effort. After a series of protracted meetings, which saw him flying back and forth from Melbourne to Brisbane for discussions with MacArthur at his headquarters in Lennon's Hotel, Reynolds became part of a highly secret and very irregular outfit – the US Bureau of Economic Warfare.

This American equivalent of SOE specialised in recruiting people with expert local knowledge to operate behind enemy lines in the South-West Pacific. One of their long-term agents, even older than Reynolds, was Irish-born Edward Farrell, who had flown with the Royal Flying Corps in World War I and whose spirit of adventure and business interests had taken him deep into New Guinea and the surrounding islands. Both men knew the risks were high, but so too was the monetary reward. It was an elated Reynolds who, after successfully negotiating his contract, astounded Bessie by tipping a pile of US currency onto the quilt of their matrimonial bed with the announcement, 'There will be plenty more where this came from'.

However, although he now had a job, and a highly paid one at that, Reynolds was a realist. Once he left Australia, he did not officially exist. Aware that all financial assistance would cease should he fail to return from one of his missions, and with all his property in Malaya lost to the enemy, he took steps to ensure his family's future security by lodging, on the advice of his solicitors, a claim with the British Admiralty for salvage rights to *Krait*. Unaware that that legal proceedings would soon be in train to claim compensation for a vessel to which neither they, nor SOE, had any right, Lyon and Campbell, with the help of Denis Emerson-Elliott, began combing Australia for a replacement engine.

It was Denis who finally located one – a 103-horsepower, six-cylinder Gardner 6L3 diesel. Unfortunately, it was in Tasmania, thousands of kilometres from Cairns. Worse, having just taken delivery of a commodity which was in extremely short supply, Gardner's Tasmanian agents, A G Webster & Sons, were not about to simply hand it over. However, Lyon held the trump card – a reorganisation of special forces which had taken place in April assured him of success.

SOE (Australia)/ISD had vanished in February, along with its director, Major Edgerton Mott, who had become frustrated by problems with the command structure, a tendency by GHQ to regard SOE (Australia) as merely another intelligence-gathering organisation, and interference from AIB's Controller Caleb Roberts, who was under the control of GHQ. A conventional soldier, known for his slowness and uncharitably described by SOE chief Major-General Sir Colin Gubbins as 'a remarkably stupid and unimaginative officer', Roberts could not grasp that SOE was a highly secret and extremely irregular organisation which indulged in some very dubious activities, such as 'bumping off [German] missionaries and other undesirable persons'; carrying out covert missions in supposedly neutral Timor; and associating with Chinese Communists. Mott, who had been led to believe that SOE (Australia) was to have a free hand, had pointed out rather forcefully to Roberts that he should be left in peace to get on with the job and only required 'general direction and backing'. This lack of involvement by anyone outside the organisation was to ensure that everyone, including GHQ, would at all times be 'in a position to disown, if necessary, any activities which are officially undesirable but unofficially very much required'. Unfortunately, neither GHQ nor Roberts subscribed to this viewpoint. On 17 February, GHQ issued orders to relieve Mott from the command of ISD. The order was signed by General Sutherland, who claimed that Mott was 'recalcitrant', that he had failed 'in co-operation and in obedience' and that his performance was 'unsatisfactory'. On 24 February, without informing either Mott or Blamey until it was a *fait accompli*, Roberts replaced Mott with Australian Major Oldham, Mott's own 2IC. Mott, while awaiting transportation home to England, filled in his time before his departure in April by writing bitter letters to Generals Sutherland and Blamey about his treatment, and the high-handed way in which Oldham had been appointed. It did him no good. To ensure that he did not dabble in matters which were no longer his concern, orders had been issued that he was 'not to undertake or be connected with any secret activities in the SWPA'.

For two months the future of special operations was in great doubt. This included Jaywick, about which the top brass was having second thoughts. Despite almost a year of very expensive training, preparation and planning, they now believed that to attack enemy shipping in the way Lyon intended was impossible. It was obvious that unless something could be done to change their minds, Jaywick would be cancelled.

Salvation was to come from a most unexpected quarter – an Australian geologist by the name of Sam Carey who had been working in New Guinea before being stationed at ZES as ISD's liaison officer. On 15 December 1942, when air reconnaissance photographs indicated a heavy build-up of enemy shipping in Rabaul Harbour, Blamey had sent for Carey who suggested a raid on shipping along almost the same lines as Jaywick, the only difference being that, after the attack, Carey intended to hide on Vulcan Island until the heat was off. This small volcanic island, thrown up by the 1937 eruption, was in the centre of Rabaul Harbour and was riddled with small caves.

Blamey had given Carey the go-ahead to select men, mostly old New Guinea hands, for training. However, with the ructions caused by Mott's departure Carey's mission, code-named Operation Scorpion, was so far behind its intended strike date of 3 March that it was decided to launch Jaywick and Scorpion simultaneously. Prior to this, the Americans at GHQ had not been informed of the Scorpion plan, evidently because Rabaul was Australian Mandated Territory and therefore not regarded as 'overseas'. However, the secrecy could not last – Carey needed submarine transportation, which meant asking GHQ for help. The request was denied. The US Navy had recently lost a submarine in St George's Channel and the area was now considered 'too hot'. While Carey was waiting to hear the outcome of an alternative proposal to drop his team off in the open sea and then paddle the rest of the way, he was ordered to report to Oldham in Melbourne. It was now that Ivan Lyon, also summoned to Melbourne, learned that GHQ had thrown a spanner in the works – both raids were off. According to Oldham, unless something were done to change the belief that limpet attacks were not feasible, the whole idea would have to be abandoned.[4]

Picking up the broad hints, Lyon volunteered to carry out a dummy raid in Australia. His offer was refused. Oldham knew that with submarine transport unavailable only one raid could be mounted. He was also aware that whoever led a dummy operation would be in very hot water. Rabaul, being a key base for the Japanese offensive through the Solomon Islands, was a far more important a military target than Singapore, which had no longer had any strategic value, but Singapore was the sentimental favourite. It was also streets ahead from the point of view of propaganda, a fact recognised by both Lyon and Oldham. Properly handled, a raid on Singapore would not only force the Japanese to redeploy their troops to cover their coastal bases, it would create an enormous morale boost for Britain and Australia.

Carey knew exactly what was expected of him. Without any orders being issued, or indeed any specific words being spoken, Carey left SOA HQ knowing full well he must mount a mock raid so convincing it would put Jaywick back on track. Carey also realised that Oldham had been extremely clever. If the raid were botched, Carey would carry the can. If it were successful, Oldham would take all the credit. However, as delivering anything less than his best had never been Carey's style, he decided to pull out all stops. Scorpion would raid Townsville Harbour.

On 13 April, at 11 pm, Carey and his team of nine men left ZES in Cairns and slipped from the southbound train just north of Townsville. They reached Black River, intending to paddle down it, only to find the upper reaches were dry. Thirty-six hours of strenuous porterage and paddling saw them reach Magnetic Island, where they rested. After plotting their targets, which were ten kilometres away and guarded by a minefield, through a powerful telescope, the Scorpion team set off, worried that the brightly moonlit night would make their approach risky. However, it was all too easy. While one folboat headed towards the roadstead, the other four teams drifted through the narrow entrance and past the control post unobserved to enter the harbour proper. Once inside they attached their dummy sand-filled limpets, linked by parachute cord 'fuses' to fifteen vessels, including two American Liberty ships, five freighters, two destroyers and the corvette HMAS *Katoomba*. The port was busy and well lit but there was only one challenge issued – by a sailor, hanging over the rail of a ship anchored in the Roads, who had yelled, 'What are youse blokes doing out there?' 'Just paddling around,' the raider replied, which elicited no further response other than a cheerful, 'Good night mate.'

By seven the next morning, with forty-five mines clinging to fifteen ships, Carey's men had paddled into Ross Creek, dismantled their folboats in full view of workers passing over a nearby bridge, and eaten their breakfast. While the rest of the team went upriver out of harm's way, Carey booked into the Officer's Club and went to bed to await the inevitable. Three hours later, all hell broke loose. With its cargo unloaded, the Dutch freighter *Akaba* was now riding high in the water, so high that the parachute cord was visible above the water line. When a closer inspection revealed it was linked to some kind of metal devices, probably explosives, orders were issued for an immediate evacuation of all personnel and the removal of all suspect ships from the harbour. As a further precaution a convoy about to sail for Port Moresby was instructed to remain in port.

The gangplanks were soon crowded with scurrying sailors as more and more strange objects were detected. Rumours were now circulating like wildfire that Japanese submarines had invaded Townsville and that all the ships in the harbour would soon blow up. As the entire wharf area emptied in response to the emergency, worried naval officers tried in vain to establish what had happened. No one had seen a thing and the sentries were adamant that nothing could possibly have entered the harbour. Telegraph wires ran hot as messages were relayed between Townsville, the Admiralty, Naval HQ and MacArthur's office in Brisbane. When they finally reached Colonel Ind, now the GHQ-AIB Liaison officer, the mystery was solved. Sam Carey had to be the culprit. Scorpion's modus operandi and Carey's close proximity to Townsville could not be simply coincidence. 'Find Captain S W Carey,' he advised Townsville, and the hunt was on.

It was not hard to find and arrest Carey, who had booked into the club under his own name. After being paraded before a succession of increasingly senior army officers, to whom he admitted nothing, he was finally passed to Lieutenant Asher Joel, RANVR. Joel may have been of junior rank, but he had had one great advantage over the more senior army officers – he worked for secret intelligence. His rise had been meteoric. After serving for less than two months in the AIF as a lowly lance-corporal he had been recruited for secret intelligence by Long, entering RANVR in early October with the rank of sub-lieutenant. Three months later he was a full lieutenant, and his status had moved from 'pay lieutenant' (a common cover for those recruited for secret intelligence work) to 'special duties'. Without further ado Carey confessed to Joel, declaring 'Sir, my name is Carey and I beg to report that last night, with my raiding party, I sank the following ships', and then proceeded to rattle off verbatim the names of the fifteen destroyers, corvettes and freighters targeted. Joel was impressed, and so too was the commander of HMAS *Arunta*, the first of the latest Tribal-class destroyers and the pride of the RAN.

With Carey's credentials established by Joel, the destroyer captain invited the entire Scorpion team on board for pre-dinner drinks. Overhearing his host ribbing Townsville's naval officer-in-command Commander Wheatley about the incident, Carey realised that no one on *Arunta* realised that she also had been limpeted. In full view of a very amused and attentive audience Dick Cardew, Carey's 2IC, took a small boat alongside the ship and removed the limpets which had been clinging to the hull for the best part of twenty-four hours. Many thought the escapade a great lark, but most of the local naval and port authorities were not amused. How humiliating that ten men had managed to penetrate the harbour defences, prevent a supply convoy from leaving and terrify half of north Queensland! But Carey had proved his point. On 16 April, courtesy of Sam Carey, Jaywick was given a reprieve. Apart from proving that raids on enemy ports, most likely no better defended than Townsville, had every change of success, he had also demonstrated a need for far greater security – a point appreciated by the Security Service. The local chief, after informing his superior in Brisbane on 17 April that 'the time bomb contraption' did not contain any explosives and that as 'Captain Carey was acting with authority, no further action is contemplated', requested immediate action be taken to improve security at the docks.

That same month AIB was reorganised into five sections: Philippines Regional Section, an almost completely autonomous US operation; Netherlands East Indies Regional Sections (NEFIS III), mainly a Dutch organisation; North East Regional Section (NEA) which included Coastwatchers and concentrated on collecting intelligence in the SWPA to the east of the Dutch New Guinea border; SIS (affiliated with SIS in London) which concentrated on espionage, especially in the Netherlands East Indies; and, finally, Special Operations Australia (SOA), to carry out intelligence and the 'execution of subversive and highly specialised sabotage, chiefly by under cover methods'. The propaganda group FELO was not included in this restructure as it had been detached from AIB the previous September.

In late May SOA was code-named Services Reconnaissance Department or SRD to maintain secrecy and to avoid compromising its similarly named British equivalent, SOE. As SOA now came under the direct control of General Blamey and was virtually autonomous, it needed its own administrative unit. This problem was solved when Blamey removed Z Special Unit from the control of AIB and handed it over to the exclusive use of SOA. Another unit, M Special Unit, was then created to cater for the needs of Australian soldiers serving with AIB. There is no explanation as to why M was chosen, but it may have been inspired by SOE's 'Colonel M'.

To further maintain secrecy, personnel recruited to SOA were subsequently given a 'secret number' which was used in the place of names in signals and in some correspondence. To differentiate who was assigned to which role within SOA, the secret numbers were prefixed with letters. All army operatives used AK (Also Known), navy personnel AKN and RAAF AKR. Signallers were AKS, headquarters staff AKX, instructional and camp staff AKV, Ordnance were AKO and females (very few), AKQ. As Jaywick's status was SOE/RAN, no one on this mission was allocated a secret number. Lyon, Chester and Campbell used their old SOE 'BB' numbers, but were later assigned new ones, Lyon being AK161 and Chester AK232. Bob Page, one of the first army operatives to be allocated an SOA number, was AK4 and Davidson, one of the first sailors, was AKN3.

With Z Special Unit able to draw whatever was needed from army stores Denis Emerson-Elliott had no trouble in securing the Tasmanian engine, which had been earmarked for the army, for *Krait*. He also located Bert Bevan-Davies, Gardner's expert in Victoria, who later described Ivan Lyon as 'a man among men and the most charismatic man I have ever met'. Told only that the marine diesel engine might need to run non-stop for a month, Bert spent hours with Ivan, familiarising him with spare parts, matching them to the specification manuals and observing similar engines working at marine establishments until Ivan knew the workings of the engine as well as any mechanic. Determined that should *Krait* fall into enemy hands she would not betray her origins, Ivan and Bert stayed up night after night until every trace of the Gardner name was removed, not only from the engine but from every spare part as well. When the task was complete Ivan shook hands with Bert, saying, 'If all goes well you will know what you helped to prepare. If not, you will never know.' As soon as £2250 sterling was handed over as part-payment to the Hobart importer, Bert packed the now anonymous engine, with its mountain of equally anonymous spare parts, into a wooden crate and loaded it on a ship bound for Cairns.

Five weeks later, when Paddy McDowell went down to the wharf at Cairns to collect the new engine, he discovered that, while the engine itself was intact, all the tools for its installation had been 'well ratted'. Apparently the sight of such hard-to-come-by supplies, clearly visible through the damaged sides of the packing crate, had proved too great a temptation for roaming scroungers. The tools were soon replaced and the engine transported to Smith Creek, a quiet, out-of-the-way tributary of the Barron River where *Krait* was transformed from engineless hulk to ocean-going vessel. As soon as the shipwrights and engineers, sent up especially from Walker's at Maryborough, had strengthened the bed-plate to ensure that the shaft alignment was correct, the new engine was lowered carefully into place.

It was now well into July. With the schedule so tight, the new engine-room housing was a poor substitute for the original which had been demolished and removed at Townsville, along with the useless engine. The new housing was a nondescript timber affair with two vertical hatches, propped up by a pair of battens, replacing the detailed joinery and the glass side-panels of the previous construction. The only apparent advantage was that the hatches could be dropped quickly to create a blackout when necessary, but this also reduced the air-flow to zero, making the engine room not only stuffy but unbearably hot. Both the new timber work and the wheelhouse had been painted an indeterminate shade of brown which matched the equally drab checked curtains strung across the grimy wheelhouse windows.

The cramped conditions, sauna-like heat and thousands of cockroaches which had infested the ship did not bother Paddy, who was too busy to notice. As soon as the engine was installed to his exacting requirements, *Krait* was slipped and a new propeller fitted. Then and only then was Paddy ready for a test run. With a mixture of excitement and apprehension he put *Krait* into the water and started her up. He was ecstatic. Compared to the sound of the old Deutz, which Paddy scathingly compared to 'a brass band in a railway cutting', the Gardner purred.

While Paddy had been busy with the engine and Lyon had been fine-tuning the operational plans and consulting with Commander Long in Sydney, Davidson and 'the boys' had returned from HMAS *Assault*. Fit as fiddles from weeks of obstacle course and unarmed combat training, they sharpened up their sabotage skills by attaching sand-filled limpets to the Liberty ships in Cairns harbour. As the captains had been tipped off, there was fortunately no repetition of the panic which had gripped Townsville following the Scorpion 'raid'. Also, at long last it looked as if their luck had changed. They had been inundated with good news: Jaywick was back on the rails, Ivan had been promoted to the rank of Major, and Ivan, Morris and Reynolds had been decorated by the King for their rescue work in Sumatra. It was an understandably elated Major Ivan Lyon, MBE, who now gave his full and undivided attention to Operation Jaywick.

The mission had been substantially altered. With the installation of the long-range engine there was no longer any need to call in to Darwin for fuel or set up a special supply dump on Hope Island, as had been planned. The attack on land installations had also been scrapped, resulting in the loss of Overell and 'Tiny' Hage. Gort was now operational so his old position (in charge of *Krait* while the raiders were gone) was filled by Lieutenant Walter Witt RAN. There would now be six canoeists – three officers and three men – with two reservists.

By August there were four more changes to personnel. Hobbs the cook had quit. He had wanted to be released for some time, in fact since the previous September, when he had gone on strike at Camp X to force the issue, only to be sweet-talked into staying by Jock Campbell. When they learned that Hobbs was no longer available, he and Lyon searched in vain for an Asiatic who could carry out the dual role of decoy-cook, in much the same way as Lo Gnap Soon had done on *Sederhana Djohanes*. After calling unsuccessfully for unmarried volunteers from 7 Australian Division, training on the nearby Atherton Tablelands, Lyon was approached by Scottish-born Corporal Andrew 'Andy' Crilly, a small, curly-haired army engineer who had recently been posted to 2/14 Battalion after treatment for appendicitis.[5] Crilly, who had enlisted in 1941 and had seen action the following year at Milne Bay in New Guinea, was evidently hankering for a bit of excitement. Having established that a cook was needed for a hazardous mission he landed the job, as there was no other applicant. His admission that his culinary skills stretched only to making pancakes and boiling water was of no consequence. As Lyon pointed out, the only 'cooking' required was to prepare two meals a day by opening up a few cans and heating the contents, or soaking dehydrated mutton, onions, carrots and potatoes in salt water and boiling them until they were tender. As Andy 'forgot' to tell his CO that he had a new job, he was posted as a deserter by the battalion when he failed to show up for duty. But by that time he was far beyond the clutches of the military police. Bags packed, he was on board *Krait*, where he had the distinction of being one of only two members of the team who belonged to the AIF.

The other was Lieutenant Robert Page, replacing Gort, recalled to Melbourne by Oldham who had decided to make better use of his talents by assigning him to lead Operation Python into British North Borneo. With Gort booked on the southbound train on 19 July, Lyon had to find a replacement – an officer who was fit, and conversant with folboats and limpet mines. Bob Page, who had taken part in the Scorpion raid and was now at ZES, fitted the bill perfectly.

Raised in New Guinea and son of a highly decorated World War I soldier, the dark-haired, slimly built Page, with the good looks of a matinee idol, was an instant success. Cultured, well educated and charming, he also had a great sense of humour. A second year medical student and a sergeant in the Sydney University Regiment, he had enlisted in April 1941 and had been posted to 2/4 Pioneers. At the end of 1942, having attended bomb disposal school and a mortar course, he was seconded to 23 Infantry Training Battalion where he remained until recruited by Carey for Scorpion.

His motivation in joining SOA was entirely personal. His father, Harold Page, Assistant Administrator of New Guinea, had been captured in early 1942 following the fall of Rabaul. Determined to try and find him, Bob was fired by the fanciful notion that if he volunteered for special duties in New Guinea he might somehow be in a position to effect a rescue. Having lived in New Guinea until the age of thirteen and spent many vacations there while attending school in Sydney, he was familiar with the territory. When Scorpion was cancelled, dashing his hopes of finding his father, he joined Jaywick whose area of operation, so the rumours went, was also New Guinea. Not only had Bob Page no idea of Jaywick's true target, he was also unaware that *Montevideo Maru*, the ship carrying his father, 200 other civilians and 849 Australian prisoners from Lark Force, had been torpedoed and sunk by an American submarine in July the previous year. There were no Allied survivors.

There was also a new navigator and new telegraphist. The latter post had gone to Leading Telegraphist Horrie Young, a rather pale-faced, seriously minded young man, and a wireless-mad naval reservist. Born in Perth in 1921, he had joined the Post Master General's Department on leaving school and had also trained in the late 1930s as a cadet telegraphist with the Naval Reserve. He was serving at HMAS *Assault* when 'a very strange character' (Davidson), clad in jungle greens and wearing jungle boots and with the similarly outfitted Jaywick team in tow, had arrived from north Queensland to observe 'beach commandos' training for action and to 'demonstrate unarmed combat'. Don Sharples, who had been assigned to Young's mess, had mentioned that he was not at all keen to remain at his current posting which involved going on 'a small ship up in the islands to browse around', even though there was a financial incentive of an extra four shillings (a 50 per cent loading) per day. It was a cold and rainy July. Lured by the thought of the substantial cash bonus Young, who was 'fed [up] to the neck' with the Newcastle weather, swapped drafts with Sharples and headed north.

The role of navigator had been harder to fill. Reynolds, who was preparing to head into Dutch Borneo on a solo mission for the Americans, was no longer available. Several names were submitted to Commander Long, who realised he knew one of the applicants. In

December 1912 he and Hubert Edward 'Ted' Carse, barely teenagers, had been accepted as midshipmen at the Naval Training College at Jervis Bay on the NSW south coast. They had both agreed to serve for twelve years after they reached the age of eighteen, but by the time Carse turned twenty-one he had developed a dislike for authority and an almost insatiable taste for beer. Unlike Long, who remained in the service, Carse left the navy in 1921 when only seven years into his twelve-year commitment to become a schoolteacher. It was not a successful career change and within two years he was back at sea again, serving as an able seaman on a British merchant ship and then as third mate on a tramp steamer to Brazil. In an effort to break his heavy drinking habit his brother, a Catholic priest, found a job for him on a pearling lugger in the Torres Straits, hundreds of kilometres from the nearest pub. Pearling was followed by collecting bêche-de-mer, cleaning in a Sydney factory, unsuccessful gold prospecting in the outback, running an illegal backyard betting shop, more cleaning and, finally, imitation jewellery retailing. Long's career had been far more illustrious, with a posting to London and promotion to lieutenant-commander in 1928. He remained in the service until 1934, well beyond his release date, but in April 1940 re-enlisted and became DNI.

In September 1942, after a spat with his wife, Carse, previously rejected for enlistment on health grounds, decided once again to try and join the navy. A heavy smoker as well as drinker, he suffered from a 'weak' chest and looked a lot older than his forty-two years – three years beyond the upper limit for normal enlistment. Although the requirements had been lowered since his last application in an attempt to recruit more men, he knew it was unlikely he would be accepted, so this time he wrote to his old, and now well-placed classmate, asking for a job. Long, who was well aware of Ted's drinking problems and patchy employment record, told Denis Emerson-Elliott that he felt sorry for him. Motivated to some extent by a degree of loyalty from the old days and also believing he might amount to something if he were given some responsibility, Long arranged a probationary commission with naval intelligence, where he could keep an eye on him.

Carse, a fairly unobtrusive type, managed to keep out of trouble and in February 1943 was 'loaned' to ISD. Two months later, lured by the promise of an interesting assignment, he arrived at ZES where he was given the task of trying to turn Indonesian recruits who spoke no English into sailors, as well as assisting with Scorpion's folboat training. Although he was in command of the beaten-up training boat *Gnair*, which had been used by Lark Force soldiers to escape from Rabaul in 1942, by July he was beginning to regret his hasty decision to re-enlist when he was given the job of victualling *Krait*. Learning that a mission might be in the offing and that a navigator was required Carse, who had vowed never to volunteer for anything again, put his name forward. With *Krait* due to depart in a matter of days, a navigator was urgently needed. As Carse had spent a considerable time sailing in the waters to Australia's north, the normally hard-headed Long overrode concerns raised by

Denis Emerson-Elliott, saying that he had decided to give Carse a chance to prove himself.

Neither his appearance nor demeanour impressed Taffy Morris, used to associating with officers who not only looked but acted the part. With his less than immaculate uniform, his generally down-at-heel air and with a lifetime of intemperate drinking habits clearly etched on his weather-worn face, Morris thought Carse would have been more at home on a tramp steamer. However, his opinion carried no weight. The DNI had given the appointment his blessing and Lyon, acting on the recommendation, had already signed him on. As Carse was a naval officer, Lyon decided he could also take charge of the *Krait* crew while the raiders were absent, making the recently appointed Lieutenant Walter Witt redundant.

At one minute to midnight on 4 August, merely nine days after Paddy McDowell had collected the engine from the Cairns waterfront, *Krait* was ready to sail to Townsville to retrieve the stores offloaded the previous March. These included food and stores for four months; emergency rations, tents, ground sheets and gear for the raiding party; medical supplies; a mountain of cigarettes; 400 gold Dutch guilders; Japanese occupation dollars which the children of SOA's Harry Manderson had crumpled repeatedly to simulate a worn appearance; plastic explosive, limpet mines and detonators; boxes of gelignite; weapons consisting of two Lewis guns, two Brens, eight Sten guns, eight Owen guns, fourteen .38 calibre revolvers, two hundred hand grenades, commando knives, coshes, parangs and ammunition for the various weapons. New folboats were to be collected at Exmouth Gulf, but Davidson had packed the old ones as a precaution.

As the navigational instruments had not yet arrived, navigation during the 36-hour voyage was largely a matter of point-to-point coasting. While the ship was in port being victualled, the instruments, with the exception of the azimuth mirror (used to take precise compass bearings) arrived, allowing Carse to make better time on the return voyage to Cairns. After spending an entire day tarring the ropes and sail, purchasing a small dinghy, stowing a spare propeller and making a few mechanical adjustments, at 8.30 pm on 9 August *Krait* left for her next port of call, Thursday Island, on the tip of Cape York Peninsula.

At long last, Operation Jaywick was under way.

8

The Jaywick raid

August–October 1943

The fourteen-man team which finally set sail for Thursday Island was a very diverse group indeed: Ivan Lyon, skilled amateur sailor and a most unorthodox but very professional soldier; his deputy Donald Davidson, former jackeroo and teak forester; Carse the navigator, reforming alcoholic with a friend in high places; the dashing Bob Page, a partially qualified medico fired by idealism; Taffy Morris, the Welsh medical orderly and former coalminer who loved to sing; Cobber Cain, the eminently practical sailor with muscles reminiscent of a comic-book super-hero; Andy Crilly, engineer turned cook on the lookout for adventure; telegraphist Horrie Young, quiet, reserved and seemingly far too pale and introspective to be part of a sabotage mission; engineer Paddy McDowell, Irish-born Scot and World War I veteran who loved engines with a passion; and the five sailors who had volunteered for special duty twelve months previously.

Their ages ranged from eighteen to twenty-three, and the only thing they had in common was that they were super-fit, highly trained and blessed with the indestructible enthusiasm of youth. Wally Falls, whose family owned a dairy farm in Casino, northern New South Wales, was the eldest and was known as 'Poppa'. Extremely strong, he was blessed with good looks, an engaging smile and an amazingly placid nature. At the other end of the scale was Fred Marsh, only eighteen and always the life and soul of any party. Usually called 'Boof' because his nuggetty body was topped with a rather square-shaped head covered in a mass of blond curls, Fred the cabinet-maker was a quintessential larrikin whose predilection for engaging in practical jokes was offset by his outstanding prowess in unarmed combat. While in the camp at Refuge Bay he had placed a dead snake in Wally Falls' bedding, a prank which was not discovered until 5 o'clock the next morning when Wally woke everyone with blood-curdling yells. Fortunately for Marsh, he was unable to discover who was responsible.

Andrew Huston, who was responsible for Boof's nickname, was Marsh's complete opposite. Aged nineteen but looking much younger than his best mate, the lithe, olive-skinned Queenslander was dubbed 'Happy', because during training he wasn't. However he also displayed an iron-willed determination which Davidson recognised and admired, especially when he discovered that in order to gain selection Andrew had first to learn to swim and to fight.

Also aged eighteen, Mostyn 'Moss' Berryman was as quiet and reserved as Boof was noisy and outgoing. Possibly the most intelligent of the five, Moss had a talent for figures and had been training as a stockbroker before enlistment. His ability to go about his work quietly and efficiently, and with a minimum of fuss, had been noted by Davidson, who had him marked as officer material. Equally quiet was Arthur 'Joe' Jones from West Australia, who was slightly senior in rank to the other four. A former grocery store assistant, he had joined the navy at the age of nineteen. After serving briefly on HMAS *Perth*, he had been posted to HMAS *Manoora* for convoy duty in the Indian Ocean, stopping off in Singapore on 6 December 1941, two days before Malaya was attacked. After returning from Noumea when his sphere of operation shifted to the South-West Pacific, he was undertaking a gunnery course at Flinders Naval Depot before transferring to Defensively Equipped Merchant Ships when he volunteered for special duties. Dark-haired and with skin that tanned easily, Joe Jones was of sufficiently small stature to pass as Asian. Now aged twenty-one, and the only recruit who had sea experience, he had a sense of calm stability about him which the critical Morris found very reassuring.

Without the azimuth mirror to check his position, navigating a path through the islands of the Coral Sea was so difficult that, as soon as the moon set that night, Carse dropped anchor lest they run aground on one of the many reefs. Even with the moon out and lookouts posted he still had trouble and on the fourth night out from Cairns ran aground near Chapman Island. Fortunately no damage was done, and the ship proceeded the following day to Thursday Island to take on additional water and fuel. Lyon immediately went ashore where his friend Denis Emerson-Elliott, recently appointed as Intelligence Officer for the area, supplied him with details of the outward journey and a copy of SOA's latest intelligence summary before arranging for RAAF air cover. Although they would not be entering enemy territory to reach Exmouth Gulf in West Australia, their next port of call, Denis advised that enemy bombers and float planes had been attacking shipping in the vicinity of Cape Wessel on the Gulf of Carpentaria. With the memories still fresh of those who had tempted fate by sailing from Singapore on Black Friday 1942, Lyon put *Krait*'s departure back by twelve hours to Saturday 14. That same day SOE in India finally received official approval for the mission from the Commanders-in-Chief Eastern Fleet and India Command, fully fifteen months after Wavell had sanctioned Ivan's plan.

As it turned out, the covering aircraft were not needed – there was no sign of the enemy. There was, however, one untoward incident, later dubbed the Battle of Carpentaria. It occurred when a jammed bullet, which Cobber Cain was trying to free from a Lewis gun, exploded. In the chain reaction which followed the projectile ricocheted off a spare magazine and smashed a tomato sauce bottle to pieces before burying itself in the roof. The initial horrified reaction to the assumption that an artery or two had been severed soon dissolved into laughter when it was discovered that the bloody gore splattered everywhere was only tomato sauce. The goo was wiped away, revealing two casualties – Berryman, peppered with shards of glass, and Morris, who had been standing on a fuel drum keeping watch through the flap, almost on top of the exploding bottle. While the multitude of glass splinters was mostly uncomfortable, of greater concern was Morris's ankle, badly lacerated by flying metal. Eagerly grasping the unique opportunity to show off his medical skills, Page probed about. As the ship pitched and tossed, he tried to reconnect the ends of a badly contused artery with a blunt and oversized needle while his patient, spread-eagled on the engine-room housing and held down by two of his shipmates, tried to wipe away the pain with judicious swigs of medicinal brandy and bursts of tuneless whistling.

It took about ten days for the wound to close over. Morris, having refused point-blank to be put ashore in Darwin, was still recovering from his ordeal when the ship almost ran aground on the reefs encircling Adele Island, Western Australia, into which Carse had inadvertently strayed. Although how *Krait* had crossed the reef without coming to grief was a complete mystery, they avoided ultimate disaster when, after a painstaking and worrying search, they managed to find the one and only way out, described by Davidson as 'very foul'.

The seas were calmer on the west, creating the opportunity to make a couple of modifications to the ship – Paddy fitted a silencer to the extremely noisy exhaust and the crew chipped off and dumped the thick bituminous bullet-proof coating from the bow. In all but the smoothest seas, *Krait* had been behaving like a drunken whale, making handling difficult and threatening to capsize at any moment. Once free of the two tonnes of overburden, the freeboard rose from 23 centimetres to 34 centimetres, making her ride higher and far more easily and allowing them to proceed to Potshot, the US Naval Base at Exmouth Gulf, at top speed.

For the four days that *Krait* was moored alongside the American repair ship *Chanticleer*, the men enjoyed the lavish hospitality of generous hosts who arranged berths ashore for half the crew, allowing those left on board to enjoy far more room. In between bouts of turkey and cranberry sauce, followed by lashings of ice cream, they refuelled and restocked the ship, painted the deck a flat, camouflaging grey and removed the KRAIT signs from the wheelhouse roof. To help improve wireless reception and transmission, US Navy divers fitted a large copper sheet to *Krait*'s hull. The communication plan, organised by AIB and reviewed by 7 Fleet's Intelligence Officer, Captain A H McCollum, confirmed that Jaywick's call sign would be VHKO and that a 24-hour listening watch, on various frequencies, would be maintained by the naval wireless station at Coonawarra.

Included in the stores' replenishment were bags of rice, sugar, flour and potatoes; cases of dried fruit, ships' biscuits, dehydrated vegetables and mutton; tins of meat and vegetables, sausages, beef, fruit, tomatoes, salmon and sardines; orange juice, lime juice, soap, dripping,

A fully erected folboat with rations and equipment for two men

tea, coffee, butter, condiments and milk; khaki singlets, shorts and shirts; white canvas shoes and black socks; towels and blankets; knives, forks, spoons, mugs and plates; an emergency medical chest; 1000 gallons of diesel, 80 gallons of lubricating oil, twelve of petrol, eight of kerosene, 600 of water and an additional two gallons of rum.

While the crew was busy with *Krait*, Lyon and US Admiral Christie flew to Yanrey, an outback cattle station owned by the de Pledges, who had looked after Gabrielle and Clive in Perth and were able to provide Ivan with first-hand news of his lost family. Admiral Christie, who was aware of Jaywick's destination, was so impressed by the young officer accompanying him that years later he was able to recall the conversation with absolute clarity.

They returned to Potshot to find Davidson in a fine old temper. He had unpacked the stores brought from Melbourne and left by Gort Chester as he passed through on his way to Borneo. The swag of plastic explosive to augment the cases of gelignite was fine, as were the spare parts for *Krait*, compasses, anti-glare glasses, mail, a telescope and a pair of binoculars, but the four new folboats had been made with little or no reference to his exacting specifications. The dowelling framework fitted badly, the stitching on the canvas was shoddy and none of the improvements Davidson had asked for had been incorporated. It was a great disappointment for the new models were not only much stronger and longer (5 metres instead of 4), they were also so roomy that they could accommodate another man, if necessary. With the only other option the worn-out training folboats, Davidson hauled the men away from their rest and recreation and put them to work modifying the frames while he composed a tersely worded report for his superiors. On 31 August, the day they were supposed to leave Exmouth, Davidson's 'loan' to the RAN expired and he reverted to the control of the Royal Navy.

With the problems finally rectified and a trial run carried out to Davidson's satisfaction,

Krait left her final mooring alongside the US supply ship *Ondina* late in the afternoon of 1 September bound, so the Americans thought, for Melbourne. But the joy in receiving Admiral Royle's top priority message 'Bug in. Good hunting', and the news that Young was the father of a baby boy, evaporated when, on moving astern, the coupling key of the intermediate propeller shafting broke. The entire mission, along with the propeller, might have foundered there and then had *Chanticleer* not been able to return to port just a few hours later. While the Jaywick team once more enjoyed the generous hospitality of the ship's company, *Chanticleer's* engineers and mechanics worked on *Krait* non-stop. The following afternoon at two o'clock they declared the job complete, cautioning Lyon that as the repairs were at best temporary the ship should proceed at once to the nearest shipyard. Paddy, however, told Lyon he was confident the weld would hold. So, with one final wave *Krait* was off, not south to Fremantle to undergo further repairs as the Americans assumed but north, to Java and the Lombok Strait, the first leg of an 8000-kilometre journey. Hoping to make up for lost time, the crew hoisted the sail in the hope of nudging a knot or two more from the ship.

They had barely left the sheltered waters of Exmouth Gulf when they ran into mountainous seas, forcing them to lower the sail in a hurry. Whipped up by Force 7 westerly winds, huge waves battered the port side, upending Horrie Young from his hammock. Bruised and dazed, he would have gone overboard had Boof Marsh not grabbed him. As Lyon fought desperately to bring the ship around, water swirled in and around the wheelhouse and poured waist-deep across the deck, threatening to carry away anyone and anything not tied down. Morris, clinging desperately to a railing near the engine room, was sure his final moment had come. Even without the decking armour the vessel rolled heavily, lunging from one massive wave to the next until it did not seem possible she could remain afloat. As the waves hit the ship broadside, the list increased to 45 degrees to starboard, as tonnes of water, pouring over the port gunwale, could not escape as the scuppers were rusted. Just when it seemed that the ship would capsize, one of the crew grabbed an axe hanging above the lockers and smashed away the starboard scupper boards. As the water was released *Krait*, with agonising slowness,

At Exmouth Gulf September 1943: (Back row) Wally 'Poppa' Falls, Kevin 'Cobber' Cain, Ivan Lyon, Ted Carse, James 'Paddy' McDowell. (Front row) Andrew 'Happy' Huston, Moss Berryman, Horrie Young

righted herself. Within one hour she was out of the worst of it and in twenty-four hours the swell had completely abated, allowing order to be restored and routine to return to normal.

The next day Lyon mustered everyone onto the foredeck and divulged their destination – the subject of speculation for months. If the rest of the crew, who had put their money on Surabaya, Java, were surprised that the target was Singapore, Taffy Morris was astounded. Never in his wildest imaginings had he considered that Ivan would have the audacity to return there, especially since it was so far behind enemy lines. He scarcely had time to recover from the shock before Lyon began outlining the operational plan.

Essentially, he told them, the success of the mission depended on their ability to masquerade as native fishermen operating a Japanese fishing boat. To achieve this subterfuge the Japanese flag would be flown, sarongs would replace their shorts and shirts and all exposed skin converted to a deep shade of brown by applications of a spirit-based makeup, formulated especially by the Australian cosmetic house Helena Rubinstein. If they came under surveillance all but three men were to take up concealed action stations. The three nominated to remain in sight were those who might, at a distance, pass for local fishermen: Lyon, whose light build, darkly waving hair and deeply tanned skin made him look so like a Malay that it was a long-standing family joke that one of his ancestors must have had an illicit dalliance somewhere along the line; Carse, also of spare build, with a face so tanned and deeply lined it was a toss-up which he resembled most – a Lascar pirate or an Arab; and olive-skinned, dark-haired Joe Jones, who had a distinctly Oriental look about him. With the decoys making themselves conspicuous, it was thought that any observer would assume that the ship was simply a local vessel going about her normal business. Carse, keeping a nervously watchful eye on the sky, hoped that that such subterfuge would not be necessary. As each throb of the engine took them closer to Lombok Strait his anxiety was reflected in his log: 'the sea remains calm and, glory be praised, the scattered clouds of this morning are becoming more and more numerous, showing every indication of poor to bad visibility for the day of days, or rather night of nights'.

Although most of the others were quite tanned, any further attempt to convert them to brown-skinned Malays with artificial stain was a total failure. If used neat, it was far too dark. If thinned down, it streaked. Not only did it adhere to everything except the human skin it was supposed to cover, it also stung abominably when applied to eyelids and to more delicate parts of the anatomy. With blue eyes impossible to disguise and fair hair absolutely resistant to colour change in spite of repeated applications, the donning of the specially made sarongs was, for the most part, academic. Those with darker complexions fared better than the rest, as their tanned skin made the streaks less noticeable, but nothing could be done to reduce the bulk of men like Falls and especially Cain, whose round face and generous chest measurements – the subject of much ribald teasing – gave him the appearance of a benignly smiling, mahogany-coloured Eastern god. As Carse noted in the ship's log, the rest of the crew 'resemble blackamoors. A more desperate crowd I have never seen'. Despite the shortcomings it was still hoped that the general effect, and the displaying of the Japanese ensign, would keep enemy patrol boats from coming too close.

If they did become inquisitive Davidson had concocted an ambitious contingency plan. Two breathing tubes made of water-pipe had been clamped to a modified gas mask through the bottom of the ship's new wooden dinghy, to which a harness and four limpets clinging to tin plates had been secured. With Davidson hidden beneath the dinghy, a coolie-hatted Jones was to paddle up to the enemy vessel and hold up an empty carboy, buying time by indicating that they needed fresh water. As soon as Davidson had attached the limpets, Jones was to paddle as fast as possible to the other side of the ship, thereby putting the hull between himself and the explosive devices. As the charges went off, those on board *Krait* would rake the decks with machine-gun fire. The only casualty besides the enemy was expected to be Davidson who, as he cheerfully pointed out, would be killed by the underwater concussion.

At 7.30 on the morning of 6 September, to the sound of noisy cheering and banter from the sarong-clad throng, Lyon ordered Young to break out the red and white flag of the enemy on the stern flagpole. Sewn in absolute secrecy by Mrs Manderson, wife of Harry the Timor expert, the formerly pristine ensign, along with another spread out on the wheelhouse roof, had been reduced to filthy rags by liberal doses of engine oil and a general scruffing around the deck.

The following day as they neared the Lombok Strait, security, which had always been tightly controlled, became absolute. Although the labels on tinned food had already been replaced by numbers for ease of identification and other stores had been selected to make sure they were of Japanese origin or design, all rubbish had to be collected in tins, weighted and sunk. Smoking was strictly forbidden, lest butts and matches float away and betray their

Members of the team applying brown dye, en route to Lombok Strait

presence to surface craft and submarines. However, to the relief of the nicotine-dependent Carse and McDowell, and the less dependent Morris, this edict was modified to allow smoking during the day and under the awning at night provided the blinds were down, a concession which saw the canvas shades lowered immediately, and permanently. As mirrors might flash in the sunlight, all shaving was relegated to below decks while the use of toilet paper was absolutely prohibited. When the authorised replacement, a jar of smooth pebbles per man, was exhausted, it would have to be sea water, via the bucket on the rope, native style.

The tension rose as the men, now in local attire, scanned the horizon to the north for the first glimpse through the tops of the clouds of Agung and Rinjani, the conical volcanic mountains on Bali and Lombok islands, either side of the strait. Despite an afternoon entry in the log that *Krait* was headed directly for Lombok, the peaks failed to materialise – they were way off course. At midnight on 7 September, many hours after they should have been entering the strait, they were at the western end of Bali Island, instead of to the east. After a radical course alteration and 270 kilometres later, the navigator finally located Nusa Besar Island, guarding the western approach to the strait, only to discover that the tide was against them. Despite a Dutch chart which showed there was a suitable anchorage near Nusa Besar, where they had planned to hide, there was now far too much activity on the island and in any case the water was far too deep, forcing them to continue. With the flood tide flowing fast, at times *Krait* was actually going backwards. For almost three hours, as the crew watched the headlamps of enemy vehicles move along the same stretch of coastal road, the vessel made no headway, at all. Between midnight and 4 am, with the engine still on full speed ahead, they covered less than ten kilometres. Even when the tide finally turned the situation improved only marginally. According to the pilot book a thick haze should have reduced visibility considerably, but the day dawned bright and clear, with the first rays of the sun illuminating every rock and tree on Mount Agung on the western side of the strait. The eastern shore, where a searchlight spotted the previous evening indicated a military base at Ampenan on Lombok Island, was fortunately shrouded in a light haze which afforded some protection. Consequently, it was due entirely to good luck, or possibly divine intervention, which allowed Carse at 10 am on 9 September to write in his log, 'Thank Christ. We are through the strait ... This war is certainly hard on the nervous system'.

There were many surface craft about, but the promised haze had finally descended, cheering Carse considerably. No one took the slightest notice as *Krait* sailed north towards the Kangean Islands before changing course to the west, into the Java Sea and then the Karimata Straits, south of Borneo. Had they attracted unwelcome attention and things become sticky, Lyon, whose action station was in the wheelhouse, would have pushed a plunger, detonating the box of plastic explosive near Young's wireless set and the gelignite bundles stowed around the hull, blowing them all to kingdom come. However, there was no call to action stations –

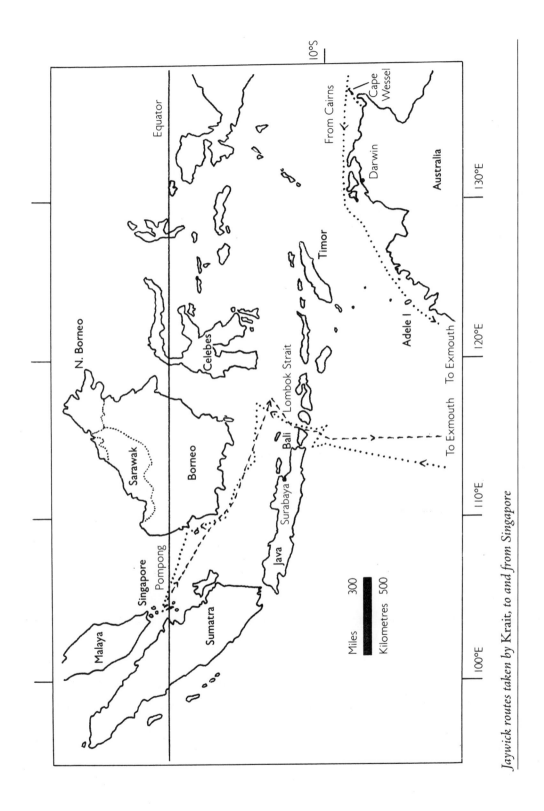

Jaywick routes taken by Krait, to and from Singapore

the journey was so uneventful that Ivan reported it was 'almost dull', an assessment endorsed by Bob Page, who sought to relieve his boredom by handing out pills and vitamins to his human guinea pigs to see what effect they had. With the exception of Carse, whose eyes were affected by the glare, and Morris, whose wound had not yet completely healed, they were all fit and healthy, apart from the occasional barked shin caused by stumbling against equipment in the dark.

Despite the monotony, morale was high: although two planes had been spotted in the distance, there had been no trouble from the Japanese; the weather, while extremely hot, had remained fine and the seas calm; news from the wireless reported that Italy had capitulated and, perhaps most importantly, Crilly could actually cook. Apart from his ability to turn rock-hard, pellet-like dehydrated food into appetising dishes in his microscopic galley, his pancakes were superb – a talent demonstrated so often that he was dubbed 'Pancake Andy'. There were only two meals a day – at around 7 in the morning and evening, with a mug of lime juice, to prevent scurvy, and two or three ships' biscuits at noon. Water was rationed to one water bottle every three days, supplemented by the lime juice, and a cup of tea with each meal. The beer given to the crew as parting gifts had long since run out but there was a generous issue of rum every evening. Morris, who did not care for the taste, arranged to have his share put aside.

The engine was also performing well, apart from a faulty feed-line when south of Lombok, and was now purring sweetly under the tender ministrations of Paddy and his new offsider, Boof Marsh, who had displayed a surprising degree of mechanical flair. The log also recorded that Paddy had worked diligently to train the others 'should anything happen to him'. However, nothing did, and such was Paddy's devotion to his mechanical baby that Boof rarely had chance to show off his skill.

On 14 September near Pelapis, off Borneo's south-western tip, they sailed through a fleet of small local craft. Their disguise passed the test – at the sight of the Japanese flag, the boats dispersed in all directions. The following day, after crossing the equator, they encountered the first rain since leaving Exmouth Gulf, enabling them to replenish water supplies and have a most welcome shower. The second downpour, a wild sumatra which hit about midnight, caused great unease among the uninitiated and struck terror into the heart of Jones, on watch on top of the wheelhouse, when a huge tanker appeared from the gloom and cut across their bow. The next morning brought fine weather and the beautiful palm-fringed islands of the Lingga Archipelago with their picturesque kampongs and native tonkans, so streamlined in design that, in comparison to the cumbersome-looking Chinese junks, they appeared almost European.

After passing through the Temiang Strait they reached Bill Reynolds' old stamping ground, the island of Pompong, to discover that it was now frequented by visiting fishermen, making it unsuitable as a base. Not bothering to anchor, *Krait* continued around the point, where disappointment turned to apprehension when a mast suddenly appeared. Altering course 180 degrees, Carse called for full speed and ran for shelter, only to discover from the keen-eyed Berryman, positioned on the masthead, that it was the wreck of *Kuala*, the mast poking pathetically from the water the solitary reminder of the disaster which had occurred such a short time before. In the hope that Bengku Island, where *Kung Wo's* survivors had gathered, might offer better shelter, they sailed south-east. Davidson and a couple of others were in the dinghy, searching for a way through the seemingly impassable reef encircling the island, when a low-flying enemy float-plane approached Krait from astern. Evidently from a naval base on nearby Tjampa, it had not been spotted by the rear lookout, whose attention was on the dinghy. As the aircraft descended to 30 metres to check them out everyone, including the lookout up the mast, dived for cover. Fortunately the pilot flew off, evidently reassured by the Japanese flag on the wheelhouse roof and, as Lyon had fortunately ordered fresh stain to be reapplied after the rainstorm, the coolie-hatted brown bodies manning the dinghy.

After this near miss Lyon directed that only those on lookout duty, or performing an authorised task, were to be on deck during daylight hours. There was a further ruckus when the lookout atop the mast lost his towel and hat, invoking Lyon's wrath and forcing them to turn back to look for, and fortunately retrieve, both articles. Unable to find a better place they spent that night at Pompong, anchored off a deserted cove which they christened Fishermen's Bay, intending to sail the next night for Lyon's old camp on Durian Island some 70 kilometres distant. The following morning, in order to make *Krait* less conspicuous against the horizon, they decided to lower the mast into its cradle. As the wireless aerial was strung from the mast, communications were maintained by running the antenna wire under the railing which ran round the sides of the ship. Unskilled in a task which local fishermen performed with ease, while dismantling the mast the men lost control and gravity took over. Fortunately for Huston, who would have been squashed flat had the mast hit the deck, it came to rest on the wheelhouse roof, crushing some of the timber. They were just clearing away the debris when an elderly Malay man and two boys paddled towards the island in a small kolek, evidently intent on doing some fishing. To the horror of the younger and more naive crew members, Lyon's first reaction was to shoot them, lest the mission be compromised, but as they had not given *Krait* a second glance he agreed to raise the anchor and leave. As it was far too early to proceed to Durian, they detoured to the north.

At about 3 pm, while off the west coast of Rempang Island, Lyon noticed the small, hilly, uninhabited and jungle-covered island of Panjang. Unable to stop and investigate further, or to alter course to Durian without attracting the attention of a Japanese observation post on nearby Galang Island, he ordered Carse to continue towards Bulan Strait to give the appearance that they were bound for Singapore. However, the observation post was so strategically placed that they were forced to hold this course, so that when night fell they were far away from their intended destination. Unsure whether Durian was still uninhabited and unwilling to run the risk of running aground on uncharted reefs in the dark, Ivan abandoned Durian as a base and issued orders to return to Panjang.

Carse, who had been apprehensive ever since they had left what he referred to as 'THE STRAIT', let alone penetrated deep into enemy territory, was relieved by Lyon's decision to go no closer to Singapore. Nightfall could not come soon enough for the navigator. After a day of moving about aimlessly, waiting and praying for dark and becoming decidedly edgy, his log book entry recorded that 'no lovers ever longed for darkness as we do'. When the sun finally went down that night he muttered yet another heartfelt 'Thank God' that he had survived another day.

As the new base at Panjang was some kilometres from Durian, the old plan for Krait to hide in Sumatra's Kampar River estuary while the raiding party was away was also scrapped. Indeed, as it was unrealistic to expect Krait to remain undetected in the one place for the best part of a fortnight, no matter how well concealed, Lyon also abandoned any thought of selecting a permanent hiding place. Believing that a moving vessel was less likely to attract attention, he decided that Krait should wander about the waters of southern Borneo until it was time for the raiding party to return to a revised pick-up point – Pompong Island.

They arrived back at Panjang at 10 pm, Lyon having navigated the way safely through the darkness by the lights on fishing pagars, the positions of which he had memorised. However, even with Cobber Cain sounding the depth with a lead line and Carse taking Krait as close as he dared, it was another three hours before they found a beach sheltered enough to attempt a landing. Once Davidson and Jones had completed a reconnaissance and declared the site suitable, Marsh and Berryman, who had been nominated as the reserve attack team, took turns to ferry the stores and the six operatives ashore in the dinghy. At about 3 am, with all supplies and equipment stowed safely above the high-water mark, it was time for Marsh, still on board, and Berryman who paddled the final load to the beach, to shake hands with the three teams who were to carry out the raid – Lyon and Huston, Page and Jones, Davidson and Falls. Both reservists were bitterly disappointed to be left behind, Fred more overtly so. His frequent and voluble prayers, in which he had begged the Almighty to strike one of the chosen six with a malady serious enough to force a replacement, had gone unanswered. With Singapore now so close that the city lights created a glow on the horizon, it was with difficulty that the two reservists bade their comrades farewell.

The raiders did not expect to make contact with them, or indeed anyone, until Krait returned to Pompong Island after dusk on 1 October. Even then, there was no guarantee that the group would be reunited. If anything went wrong and the rendezvous was not kept by any or all of the raiding teams, Carse was to return to Australia immediately. If Krait failed to meet the deadline, Lyon and the others would have to make their way to India as best they

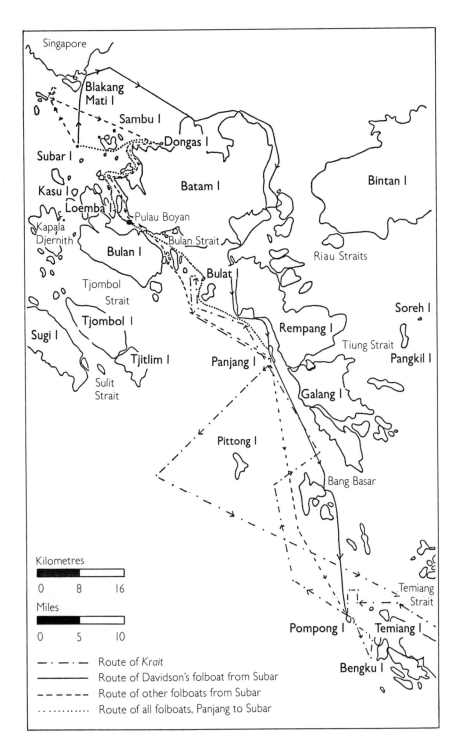

Singapore

Blakang
Mati I

Sambu I

Dongas I

Subar I

Kasu I

Loemba I

Pulau Boyan

Batam I

Bintan I

Kapala
Djernith

Bulan Strait

Bulan I

Riau Straits

Bulat I

Tjombol
Strait

Rempang I

Soreh I

Tjombol I

Tiung Strait

Sugi I

Pangkil I

Tjitlim I

Panjang I

Galang I

Sulit
Strait

Pittong I

Bang Basar

Kilometres

0   8   16

Miles

0   5   10

Temiang
Strait

Pompong I

Temiang I

— · — · — Route of *Krait*
———— Route of Davidson's folboat from Subar
– – – – Route of other folboats from Subar
· · · · · · · Route of all folboats, Panjang to Subar

Bengku I

Routes taken by the folboat teams and Krait, *after arrival at Pompong Island* could. As *Krait*, an indistinct shadow on an inky black sea, faded from sight to begin fourteen days of perilous wandering, Lyon and his men wondered if they would ever see her again. And for the second time in as many years, Taffy Morris was thinking exactly the same thing about Ivan Lyon.

Before *Krait* had time to disappear completely, the beach party had hefted the stores out of sight and established a camp in the jungle beside a hidden freshwater pool and spring. For the next two days they rested and relaxed, maintaining their fitness and cavorting in the water with a family of otters for whom they named the bay. Apart from the physical jerks which Davidson insisted upon as they had been so long at sea, the only other energy exerted was to secrete a supply dump for the return journey among rocks on the cliff face. Not a soul came near, and the only sign of the enemy was the rhythmic chug of a patrol boat each evening as she passed on her rounds.

After spending the whole of 20 September checking their stores and equipment, they blackened their hands and faces and donned the clothes reserved for the attack: a khaki shirt beneath a blue-black, two-piece tracksuit-type garment made of waterproofed japara; two pairs of black cotton socks; black sandshoes with reinforced soles; black webbing supporting a .38 revolver and 100 rounds of ammunition; a sheath knife; a rubber cosh; assorted first aid gear and a compass in zippered pockets and, in Davidson's case, his monocle. Apart from the explosives and equipment needed for the attack, supplies of water, vitamins, salt, commando cookers, canned solid fuel, mosquito nets, binoculars, parangs and canvas to serve as a ground sheet, were stowed into the folboats.

About to push off for the first leg of the journey, they heard the sound of the patrol vessel. Reacting instinctively, all froze. Fortunately, with their black suits rendering them invisible against the dark background and the black folboats riding low in the water with their 315-kilogram loads, they remained undetected. Once the sound of the engine died away they set off in an arrowhead formation, with Davidson and Falls leading, for the 20-kilometre paddle to Pulau Bulat in the Bulan Strait. At midnight, after a rather difficult reconnaissance in the darkness, they dragged their folboats to the base of a cliff and fell into a deep sleep on the sandy beach.

Early next morning they were partway through the task of moving their equipment to a less exposed position when a small boat, the red-and-white flag of Japan fluttering in the breeze, anchored only metres away. The crew, it appeared, had decided that it was an ideal place to have breakfast. Stranded between the shoreline and the nearest cover, the raiders kept perfectly still. After what seemed an interminably long meal, during which time not one of the Japanese even so much glanced in Jaywick's direction, the boat's engine was restarted and, with much noisy chatter from the crew, disappeared.

The men had only just recovered from this alarm when they looked up to see a lone

Lyon, Huston, Page, Falls and Jones cool off at Pulau Bulat, prior to the attack

fisherman paddling a small kolek straight for the beach. Falls and Jones were preparing to silently dispatch him when he saved himself from a premature death by diverting to a nearby island. The rest of the day passed uneventfully, allowing them to swim, rest, eat their iron rations and observe the many vessels passing through the straits.

The journey that night was difficult and their progress slow. Forced to make wide detours around fishing pagars, and then mistaking the lights on a junk for an enemy patrol boat, they were caught in a tide race. While trying to steady his folboat by hanging onto the bough of an overhanging mangrove, Lyon lost his grip and his folboat shot backwards, colliding with Page's and damaging the framework. Exhausted from the night's exertions, they sought refuge in the sandfly-infested and mosquito-ridden mangroves of Pulau Boyan as dawn approached. With a village nearby and boats passing by in a constant stream they spent a miserable day in the mud, unable to move or speak above a whisper after Lyon fortunately overheard a villager talking about 'three canoes'. A thunderstorm saved them from further torment in the afternoon, making such a racket and so reducing visibility that they were able to refill their water bottles and relieve pent-up tension by dancing about and singing. The shower was particularly welcome for, although the japara suits were a great barrier against mosquitos, the tightly woven fabric did not breathe, making them not only very hot but also incredibly smelly.

Aided by a favourable tide that night they were soon out of the straits. As they rounded the western end of Batam Island, one of two large islands guarding the northern entrance to the Riau Straits, they could see the lights of the oil storage facility on Pulau Sambu, only eight kilometres from Singapore Harbour.[1] According to the plan, they were to establish an observation post on Pulau Kapal Kechil or Hill 120, a small island rising 36 metres (120 feet) from the sea. However, it was now only 8.30 pm on 22 September, five full days before the target date and three days ahead of schedule. Unable to bring the time of the attack forward,

Lyon decided to put the five spare days to good use by gathering intelligence, rather than hide out on Hill 120.[2]

As it turned out, it was a sensible move. Although Hill 120 is elevated and in 1943 offered good cover, there was a village on the only accessible beach and part of its all-important view of Singapore was blocked by the tiny but also elevated Subar Island, just a short distance away. Although Subar affords a good view of Singapore Harbour, it is waterless, rocky and, being poorly vegetated, very hot and exposed. Covered in low scrubby bracken and ribbon-like grass, with one or two scraggy fig trees clinging tenaciously to the rocks just above the water line, Subar provided no shade and virtually no cover for six men and their equipment for five days. Lyon's decision to gather intelligence sent them past Sambu and its huge and brightly illuminated oil tanks to the island of Dongas, a further 13 kilometres to the east. Superbly positioned, this steep, jungle-covered island overlooks the Singapore Roads and, in good visibility, Keppel Harbour itself. At night, the headlights of cars travelling along Beach Road in front of Raffles Hotel could be seen, and by day the wireless masts on top of the old SOE HQ at the Cathay Building and at Paya Lebar were clearly discernible. As there was plenty of water in a disused well, dense foliage in which to hide and no sign of life apart from dozens of yellow-and-black iguanas which scuttled away into a mangrove swamp on the southern side of the island, Dongas was the perfect observation post. Well hidden from both land and sea, the raiders used a powerful telescope to keep close watch on everything in and east of Singapore city for the next two days. From the absence of patrol boats, the free movement of medium-sized local craft and, above all, the large number of merchant ships in the Roads, Lyon realised that no minefields had been laid.

Although the scheduled attack day was still forty-eight hours away, a convoy of thirteen ships entered the Roads that afternoon. With 65,000 tonnes of shipping anchored opposite Dongas the temptation was too great to resist. At 8 o'clock that night, loaded with limpets, the raiders set off from the island towards their selected targets. They started out well enough, but the same tidal movements which had swept castaways to their deaths the previous year now made it impossible for the Jaywick men to reach their objective. At 1 am they abandoned the attempt, finding that the return journey was almost as difficult, particularly for Lyon and Huston, whose damaged folboat kept veering to the left and so reducing their speed that, when dawn broke and unsure of their position, they were forced to seek cover among some rocks on the nearest island. They spent an unpleasant and sleepless day in the rain only to discover they had been on Dongas all the time. At about 7 pm, by which time Lyon and Huston had been reunited with the others and fortified themselves with a hot meal, the party moved off to Hill 120.

When reconnaissance revealed Hill 120's shortcomings, including a pack of a dozen village dogs which chased the recce party away, they moved to Subar, where the extreme heat and lack of shade was offset to some extent by the view of the attack area. Apart from a Japanese transport plane which passed overhead on its approach to one of Singapore's airfields, everything was quiet. That night at around seven, with their target areas selected, Davidson and Falls, followed twenty minutes later by the other two parties, launched their folboat and slid away into the darkness. Just 13 kilometres across the sea lay Singapore – and the Japanese.

The raiding parties had no illusions about the enemy or what they must do if captured. As there was no telling what secrets might be revealed under the influence of 'truth serum' drugs or the 'extreme interrogation' techniques employed by the dreaded Kempeitai (secret police), each man had been issued with a suicide pill – a small, bakelite-covered glass capsule, filled with deadly potassium cyanide. Perfectly harmless in its unbroken state, the capsule could be held in the mouth or even swallowed without any ill effect. But the capsule was not meant to be swallowed whole. If capture were inevitable, the raiders had been instructed to bite the glass and release the cyanide. Death would be instantaneous. However, as Lyon had left the choice to each individual, he, Davidson and Page had an alternate plan. If the worst came to the worst, they would shoot 'the boys' and then kill themselves.

But any thought that this might be a suicide mission was far from the minds of the raiders. As they neared their respective targets, Davidson and Falls in folboat 2 peeled off and headed for the boom and Keppel Harbour. Apart from almost being run down by a steamer, they had no trouble reaching the boom, which was not only open but unmanned. Once inside the harbour they found only a 'camouflaged oddity' and an old hulk at the wharf area so, noting that the Empire Docks were far too well lit, headed for the Roads where they had previously observed at least nine large ships. At 10 pm, before reaching the targets, they and the others prepared the timers, which had a seven-hour delay.

Davidson and Falls finally settled on three 6,000-tonne cargo vessels, two of which were heavily laden. With clockwork precision they paddled silently up to the first and went through their well-rehearsed drill – holdfast, limpet, contact, fuse, release. Despite hours and hours of practice there was an inordinate delay before Davidson clamped the first limpet into place. It was not until the folboat passed through a patch of light that Falls realised why – ever the practical joker, Davidson had halted proceedings to clamp his monocle to his perfectly good eye.

They were dealing with their final target when the sound of the clock on Victoria Tower, alongside the Cricket Club and Supreme Court, chimed the hour of one – the warning that it was time to go. They headed off at once for Batam Island where Davidson would later fill his notebook with details of all the vessels and installations they had observed. Like the other four men, he and Falls would meticulously report the type, size and tonnage of the ships they had limpeted as well as anything else of interest. This, combined with information already

Folboat attack courses for Operation Jaywick

recorded on topography, villages, shipping routes, aircraft movements and enemy posts and installations, would create a useful intelligence report.

While folboat 2 had been paddling around the ships in the roadstead, the other two teams had headed off together. Apart from a searchlight based on Blakang Mati coming uncomfortably close, they experienced no trouble and at about 9.30 parted company near Pulau Jong for their respective targets to the west of Keppel Harbour – Lyon and Huston in folboat 1 to Examination Anchorage and Page and Jones in folboat 3 to Pulau Bukom. Reaching the Anchorage, Lyon and Huston looked in vain for the ten ships which they had seen so clearly through the telescope that afternoon: with the area totally blacked out they were now impossible to detect. After eventually finding a ship, which he then rejected as he believed it might have been one assigned to folboat 3, Ivan decided to place all nine limpets on a tanker. A multi-compartmented target, it would be extremely difficult to sink, but Lyon hoped at least to do some damage.

They made a direct approach to the stern, assisted by a red lamp serving as an anchor light, and were about halfway through their task when Huston looked up to see a man apparently staring at them from a porthole not three metres away. He must have been gazing idly into space because, after looking in their direction for some time, he withdrew his head and lit his bedside lamp, much to the relief of Huston and Lyon who completed attaching the remainder of the limpets and set off for Dongas, 19 kilometres away.

At about 10 pm, an hour after leaving Lyon and Huston, Page and Jones reached the wharves at Pulau Bukom. Although the place was ablaze with light and swarming with Japanese it was as if they were invisible. First spending a good hour examining various targets, they placed the first three limpets on a freighter anchored not far from the wharf, holding onto the anchor chain for a rest while enemy troops strutted back and forth and welders worked on another vessel just behind them. After snacking on some chocolate the pair moved onto the next target – a 4000-tonne freighter tied up alongside the wharf. While members of her crew leaned over the side, chatting and smoking cigarettes, the two Australians paddled around to the far side where, by the reflected light from the wharves, they attached limpets 4, 5 and 6. Greatly emboldened, they then paddled 450 metres to their final target – a rusting, heavily-laden cargo ship. Fortunately this ship was in relative darkness, which allowed Jones to scrape away at the rust to expose enough new metal to attach the magnets. With their limpets expended, they dumped the superfluous equipment into the sea and made straight for Dongas, anxious to put as much distance between them and the Japanese before the alarm was raised.

Lyon and Huston reached Dongas at around 4.15 am, followed by Page and Jones thirty minutes later. They hid their folboats and climbed up the steep slope to their vantage point in time to hear the first explosion at 5.15. As Singapore and the rest of the Japanese empire

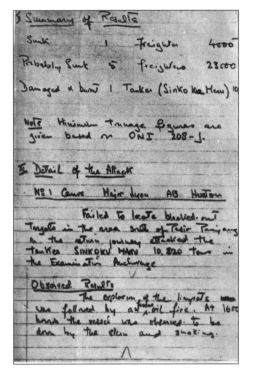

A page from Lyon's hand-written report of the attack

now ran on Tokyo time, it was still very dark. During the next thirty minutes they heard six more blasts, confirming that all the limpets had detonated. At this stage they couldn't see a thing. Fifteen minutes after the first explosion, sirens had wailed and the lights went out, enveloping Sambu and the city in total darkness. As everyone within earshot was now wide awake, the four men quickly took cover.

When dawn broke, the villagers in Kampong Patam on nearby Batam Island were jubilant, laughing and shouting and prancing around miming the effects the explosions, now clearly evident as the first rays of the sun flooded the harbour with light. From their lookout, the raiders could see the bows of a ship pointing skywards, beyond the billowing clouds of smoke belching from the burning tanker. It appeared that Jaywick had achieved a success rate of 100 per cent, bagging a total of 37,000 tonnes of shipping and creating total chaos. Even without the telescope, it was plain that the Japanese had no idea what had happened. Some ships left their anchorage and sailed about aimlessly; patrol boats swarmed everywhere like angry ants, following no particular pattern and achieving nothing; and aircraft searched the skies above the Malacca Straits looking for something – what, they were not quite sure. All this frenzied activity was accompanied by a great cacophony of sound, as dozens of ships' sirens wailed continuously. Worried that there might be a search of Dongas, which was a very small island, the four men moved to a new hiding place among the nearby mangroves on Batam Island There they remained for the rest of the day, perched on mangrove roots just above the waist-deep mud.

Davidson and Falls, who had a head start and were returning to Pompong via the Riau Straits, were skirting the coastline beyond Dongas in search of a place to hide when they heard the explosions. Because of the distance and their position, they heard only five and would not know any details of the reaction in Singapore or the fate of the others until they all met at Pompong in five days' time. In their excitement they became careless and were surprised by a kolek which rounded the point and caught them in the open. Fortunately, on seeing the two strange white men in an even stranger canoe, the occupants did a quick about-face and fled. Believing that this area of Batam was too far removed from civilisation to worry about the

Nasusan Maru, *a ship similar to this vessel was one of two ships which the Japanese were unable to salvage, following the attack*

locals raising the alarm, the pair decided to stay put until nightfall. As soon as it became dark they headed down the Riau Straits, spending the next day at Pulau Tanjung Sau. Early the following morning they reached Otter Bay at Panjang Island, having negotiated a circuitous and tricky route past a large number of fishermen and fish traps and evaded a patrol boat near Tanjung Klinking by hugging the bay. Retrieving the stores left in the cliff-face cache, they rested and treated themselves to a gastronomic feast. At seven that night, after scribbling a short note to Lyon that said 'We are proceeding to RV' on a strip of paper which they placed with the remainder of the stores, they left on the final leg of their journey.

They had paddled only 6 kilometres when a violent sumatra blew up, electrifying the night sky and whipping the sea to a fury. Caught in the open, they were forced to ride out the storm for two hours, by which time the wind and rain had eased sufficiently to allow them to seek shelter on the nearby island of Abang Besar. They were spotted by two Malay fishermen

Lyon observing shipping in the Singapore Roads from Dongas Island, September 1943

Lyon on Dongas Island. His camouflaged folboat is barely discernible

also seeking shelter who, on realising the strangers were white, turned tail and fled.

Because of the delay caused by the storm, it was no longer possible to reach Pompong in one hop. However, it was not far and they completed the final sector in relative ease, arriving after a six-hour paddle at 1 am on 1 October, seventeen hours before dusk, the earliest pick-up time. As darkness fell that night, they waited anxiously for the first sight of *Krait*. It had been fourteen days since they had last seen her – fourteen days in which anything could have happened. Would she make Pompong on time? Would she turn up at all?

At 15 minutes after midnight on 2 October, the anxiety and waiting were over. A darker shadow on a dark sea, *Krait* slipped into the bay. Silently, the two men paddled out to the ship. They were spotted by the lookouts, but when the folboat was about three metres away Davidson's sense of humour got the better of him, calling out in hideously fractured English for all on board to put up their hands and surrender. The reception was tumultuous, with dozen questions fired off at once. But the big question was – where were Lyon and the others?

Unlike Davidson and Falls, after leaving the mangroves they had an incident-free run from Dongas. Spending the first day hiding in a Chinese graveyard at the end of the Bulan Strait, they retraced the route of the incoming journey to Otter Bay, where they were saturated by the same storm that was giving Davidson and Falls a difficult time, just a few kilometres away. As Lyon refused to touch the cache of stores, which were emergency supplies left there in case they were compelled to make their own way home, he did not see the note left by Davidson. With a second storm brewing and sustained only by their iron rations, they delayed their departure until dawn on 1 October, leaving them 45 kilometres to cover, most of it in daylight, in order to meet the 'between dusk and dawn' pick-up arrangement. As they were used to paddling long distances this timetable would have presented no problem had Lyon and Huston, saddled with the damaged folboat, not been forced to expend a huge amount of energy just to keep it on course. Even so, they did extremely well. Page and Jones had a one-hour start, but Lyon and Huston caught up to them, enabling them to cover the final leg together. After a superhuman effort against a whirling tidal race, they arrived at Pompong on the morning of 2 October, three hours before dawn. Although dead tired they paddled about the bay looking in vain for *Krait* before collapsing exhausted, onto the beach. When they awoke at 6.15 they spotted her, about three kilometres away and heading down the Temiang Strait. They had been at the southern end of the bay, and *Krait* had been anchored at the north. Somehow, in the darkness, they had missed each other.

Daybreak revealed a recently vacated campsite, indicating that the other two had made it back safely. While Lyon believed that Davidson, aware that the others could be held up by adverse weather conditions, would bring *Krait* back at a later date, he could not rely on it. Anticipating a possible lengthy stay, he ordered Page to organise the building of a hut to provide shelter until the change of the monsoon, when they would pirate a local boat and sail to India. There was no village on the island, but an old Malay who paddled up with his son in a kolek traded his freshly caught fish for tobacco and promised to keep them supplied with vegetables and fish. He was keen to do business. Since the Japanese had become their masters, trade for the local people was at a standstill. With food supplies assured, the four men were about to spend their second night on the island when, a little after 8 o'clock on the evening of 3 October, *Krait* returned.

It was Davidson who was responsible. Having paddled Lyon's damaged folboat from Dongas to Subar, he knew that even in calm conditions making Pompong on time would be difficult. And, although the orders had been specific, Davidson knew that Lyon had no problem amending his plans to suit the circumstances. He went to the wheelhouse to talk to Carse. Would they blindly follow Lyon's orders and abandon their comrades, or would they attempt a second rendezvous the next night? Carse, whose nerve had failed, wanted to leave at once but with the assistance of a well-positioned pistol, Davidson persuaded the reluctant navigator to change his mind – a course of action which had the complete approval of Cobber Cain, who witnessed the exchange.

To add to Carse's nervousness, Davidson subsequently decided that the pick-up would be delayed a further twenty-four hours, until dawn to dusk on the night of 3–4 October. If it failed they would sail back to Panjang to see if Lyon had found the note. If there were still no sign of them, the search would be abandoned. This contingency plan was scrapped when the ship returned to Pompong to find the four men waiting on the beach. After a joyful reunion, considerably enhanced by the distribution of a generous rum ration, the newcomers learned what *Krait* had been doing for the past fourteen days.

All in all, it had been a boring but tension-filled fortnight, sailing the shallow waters of southern Borneo and wondering when, and if, the raid had taken place and if anyone had survived. Despite a constant vigil, Horrie Young had heard nothing on his radio that might have put an end to the waiting. The weather had not helped either. When it was not raining and squally, it had been extremely hot – too hot to walk in bare feet on the deck – and the water ration had run dangerously low.

After leaving the raiding party at Panjang, *Krait* had headed south-west, passing to the north of Pittong and Tortell islands. Anxious to keep well away from the Panjang base, Carse held this heading for some time before changing course 90 degrees for the Temiang Strait. With only eight men to crew the ship and provide a 24-hour watch, they were all so tired that Carse was soon wondering if a few benzedrine tablets might be in order. But as night came, and with it the open sea, Temiang and its many islands, around which too many dangers lurked, were left far behind, allowing them to relax a little.

While the relief after the non-stop strain of the previous day or so was welcome – Carse equated it to spending 'an evening at home' – it was not long before they realised that if there was something worse than too much activity, it was too little. Not only was there the boredom of sailing nowhere in particular, they also had no idea of what was happening outside their immediate environment. This uncertainty affected them in different ways. Horrie Young, hunched over his wireless below decks, dismissed the period as 'uneventful' while Moss Berryman, on constant lookout duty atop the wheelhouse, simply regarded it as 'boring'. On the other hand Carse, who said little, found the strain almost unbearable. As the days progressed, his comments in the log reflected this anxiety, with one entry comparing the waiting as far worse than that experienced by an expectant father outside a delivery room.

While some coped better than others, the general sense of isolation was exacerbated by the need to stay out to sea whenever possible, far away from inhabited islands and local craft. As one day merged seamlessly into the next and the date of the attack grew nearer Young, now excused from most of his other duties, increased his listening watch. He listened diligently but there was little of interest, apart from a BBC item that the war was not going well for the enemy in Europe. There was no local news and no mention on the Japanese propaganda stations that the raiders might have run into trouble.

On 23 September, after five interminably dull days, they were jolted from their lassitude when Carse, who had been navigating by dead reckoning, mistook the Borneo coast for low-lying cloud and hit the bottom, 200 metres from the shoreline. Extricating themselves with considerable difficulty, they anchored for the night in deeper water, but were tossed around by such a strong swell that by morning they had drifted 11 kilometres. The searing heat of the past few days had now been replaced by gale-force winds and seas. After a day being buffeted about, a very relieved Horrie Young gave thanks that the time had almost come to turn the ship in the direction of Singapore. Throughout that night, acutely aware that the early hours of 25 September was the earliest date for Lyon to launch the attack, Young listened more keenly than ever for any news of the raiding party. It was not a comfortable task. He had been severely sunburned on his rear end and could not sit down but, if nothing else, his vigil took his mind off this tender bottom and also off his stomach which, because of reduced rations, was rumbling more than usual.

Food and water in particular were running low, Andy's pancakes were now a mouth-

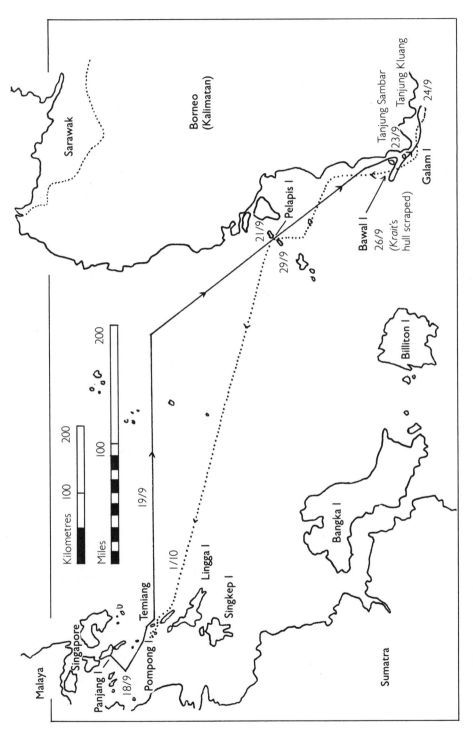

Route taken by Krait while the raiding party was absent, 18 September–1 October 1943

watering memory, and steamed puddings had been replaced by a handful of raisins and a hard tack biscuit, washed down by a cup of water. Fortunately it rained the next night, replenishing the water supply and bringing relief from the heat. When the following day dawned bright and clear with calm seas, the crew spent a pleasant afternoon in the dinghy and in the water, scraping some of the weed from *Krait*'s hull, which Carse had ordered to be done as Paddy had calculated the drag was reducing their speed by at least half a knot. It was 27 September, attack day, but there was still no news on the radio. Finally at 7 pm Carse, now 'heartily sick' of 'hanging round the coast of Borneo' for what were 'the worst sixteen days of my life', set a course back to Pompong Island.

The voyage was less than pleasant. Carse, who had become increasingly anxious about the return passage through the Lombok Strait, had been consuming far more rum than his daily ration. Had Berryman and Marsh, who had discovered his little secret, realised what it would later cost them, they might have turned a blind eye. Without his crutch the navigator became increasingly irascible over what he perceived to be relaxed attitudes to routine duty by the 'younger' members of the crew, who evidently found jobs such as cleaning rifles and keeping watch very tedious. In addition to delivering a tongue-lashing regarding their lack of responsibility, he entered derogatory remarks in the log to the effect that no one under the age of twenty-five should ever be selected for a voyage such as this. As Young spent almost all his time below decks with the radio, and Morris, Paddy, Cobber Cain and Crilly could hardly be classified as 'younger members', Carse's remarks appear to be directed solely at Berryman and Marsh who, being under the navigator's direct control and the most junior members of the crew, seem to have been unfairly targeted.

At 3 pm on 29 September Carse confidently calculated that in another forty-seven hours they would be back at Pompong, 460-odd kilometres away. To meet this target they needed to sustain a rather ambitious average speed of 6.2 knots, but he had not allowed for a change in the weather. At 8 o'clock on the morning of 1 October, while they were still off Lingga Island, the blue skies gave way to leaden clouds and a sea so chopped by wind-whipped waves that *Krait* almost came to a standstill. Consequently, at seven that evening, when they should have been at Pompong, they were still south of the Temiang Strait, with a good five hours' sailing to go. It was not until 15 minutes past midnight, at least six hours after sundown, that they finally reached the rendezvous.

Carse's plan to make a fast pick-up and disappear within the hour had been completely thwarted, firstly by the unwelcome realisation that only one folboat had made it back on time and secondly by Davidson's forceful insistence that they wait for the others. But now that the last four were safely back on board, *Krait* was able to turn towards the Temiang Strait and home.

Compared to the outward journey which Lyon found so dull, the homeward voyage through the Java Sea was mind-numbingly so. They saw only one sail as they passed through the Karimata Strait on 6 October and, apart from a minor engine problem three days later caused by a broken spring on a fuel valve, nothing at all happened. Indeed, it was so monotonously tedious, and so warm, that while on lookout duty on top of the wheel house, Happy Huston nodded off, curled up in a coil of rope. Unfortunately for him, Bob Page reported him to Lyon. Huston, who was given 'three days water and dry biscuits besides additional punishment', was just welcoming the return to normal diet on 11 October when they reached the dreaded Lombok Strait.

They had spent the entire day in nervous anticipation. The anxiety was heightened as darkness approached with the onset of a fresh south-easterly wind which made conditions choppy, especially as they neared the northern narrows where confused seas broke over the ship and flooded the officers' mess. They entered the strait at 11 pm. Unlike the outward journey the tide was running with them this time and they fairly raced along, allowing everyone, except Falls and Jones who were on lookout duty and Young, monitoring his wireless, to relax. Lyon and Page went below, Davidson joined Carse in the wheelhouse and the others took the opportunity to catnap behind the awning.

The moon had risen, but low clouds scurrying before the wind had reduced visibility somewhat. Suddenly, the lookouts positioned on the wheelhouse roof spotted something moving from the eastern shore. Whatever it was, it was big enough to create a bow-wave and was moving fast. Lyon, summoned from below, ordered everyone to action stations and to ready their weapons. There was no question of being taken alive. Although flying the flag of the enemy was a perfectly legitimate ruse, it would not be viewed in that light by the Japanese and, in any case, international law required that they show their true colours before firing. There was also the matter of their disguise – as all uniforms and identification tags had been left in Australia, they would be classified as 'spies', and therefore outside the protection of the normal rules of warfare. If *Krait* were stopped it would be death – either mercifully by their own hands, or decapitation by the enemy after hideous torture and interrogation. There was no possibility of their implementing the contingency plan – the seas were far too high and the current far too strong to launch the dinghy.

Within minutes, their worst fears were confirmed – it was a patrol boat, heading straight for them. Just as it appeared she would ram the small wooden craft, the larger vessel altered course to run on a parallel heading off *Krait*'s port bow. Altering course slightly to display the Japanese flag flying from the stern, *Krait* continued on. The larger vessel, which was not flying any flag, was not overly large by naval standards, but her silhouette indicated she was either a Japanese minesweeper or torpedo boat, both of which were capable of overtaking *Krait*, about one-third her size. While Andy Crilly, a devout Catholic, crouched in his galley praying, Moss Berryman stared at the rapidly approaching ship through the sights of his

A sketch of Minesweeper 17, which Davidson identified as being very similar to the patrol vessel which paced Krait *in the Lombok Strait, 11 October 1943*

Bren, certain that the chances of his tucking into a plate of his mother's apple pie and cream again were extremely remote.

Below decks Davidson calmly checked the wiring of the cases of gelignite and the plastic explosive, more than sufficient to blow the ship and everything in it to smithereens. Lyon, now in the wheelhouse with Carse, stood by to distribute the suicide pills and to depress the plunger, if necessary. No one else moved a muscle. They watched in absolute silence as the sleekly built enemy ship, now close enough to distinguish individual crew members standing on the bridge, began to pace *Krait*. For the next five minutes or so, she was held under close scrutiny. There was no attempt to hail her, or to signal her to stop. Perhaps the officers on watch were searching for a second signal flag, which local vessels should have been displaying, concluding that the reason none was flying was because there was no mast. Whatever the reason, it was a nerve-wracking few minutes. Just when it appeared that death was inevitable for the entire Jaywick team the Japanese vessel broke off its pursuit, altered course abruptly and powered away at full speed.

Why she did so is still the subject of debate but the most plausible reason is that, as it was close to midnight and the change of watch, the commanding officer was probably more interested in retiring to the comfort of his bunk than bothering with a scruffy little fishing boat flying a Japanese flag. After this terrifying encounter with what was officially identified by Davidson as a 60–70 metre minesweeper or corvette, but which Young and other crew members were convinced was a 3000-tonne destroyer at the very least, their passage through the remainder of the strait was uneventful. According to Carse, who was fed up with 'skulking the by-ways and corners of the sea', the final homeward leg was 'like sitting before a nice fire'. Always discomforted by the sight of the enemy flag fluttering at the stern, he was mightily relieved the following day when Lyon ordered the offending article to be taken down.

Less than twenty-four hours later, while still within range of enemy bases, a radio signal was transmitted by Young without Lyon's authorisation. That there was any transmission at all on this particular date has in recent years been vigorously denied, despite the fact that two books published in 1960, both based largely on interviews given by surviving crew members in 1958, only fifteen years after the mission, state categorically that there were two transmissions – one on 13 October and another two days later. Referring to the 13 October transmission Brian Connell, a British writer who had unlimited access to Taffy Morris with his 'lively descriptive mind' and 'happily retentive memory', recorded that 'during the night Young opened up his wireless transmitter for the first time during the trip. He tried to contact Darwin to announce their arrival but failed to raise the shore station'.

Australian author Ronald McKie, who relied heavily on Carse, Young and Jones to provide his narrative, gave more detail. According to Young, not only had the transmission on 13 October occurred, but Lyon had insisted on foolishly breaking radio silence. Quoting Young, McKie recorded that 'Young encoded Lyon's message and quickly tapped out Coonawarra's call sign three times ... Young felt sure a close watch would be kept on *Krait*'s signals, but Coonawarra didn't reply, and he cursed them at long range for their inefficiency'. Lyon's motive, according to Young, who 'warned him of the danger of breaking the radio silence again', was to let Admiral Christie know that Lombok was patrolled.

For thirty years no one involved in the Jaywick mission challenged the claim that two transmissions had occurred. It was not until 1990, when research undertaken for *The Heroes of Rimau* by the present author indicated that Young had transmitted a message 'authorised' by Carse, that contention arose. Evidently forgetting that he had told McKie about two signals, Young stated in an article entitled 'More About *Krait* – The ship's operator tells the story', published in *Amateur Radio* in January 1991, that 'only one message was transmitted during the entire voyage. It was sent on the afternoon of 15 October 1943 when the vessel was some 100 miles [160 km] clear of Lombok Strait, heading back to Exmouth Gulf'. According to Young, the Coonawarra station failed to respond, but the message was acknowledged by Fremantle, allowing Young to transmit 'For ACNB [Australian Commonwealth Naval Board] Priority immediate. Mission completed. For Admiral Christie Lombok now patrolled – ETA pm 17th'.

In an interview for the National Film Archives some years later, Young reverted to the story which had appeared in McKie's book – that two signals were sent, two days apart. In regard to the transmission of the first, he claimed he had told Lyon 'it would be unwise, because we were barely 80 miles from Lombok at the time'. However, in response to further questioning by the interviewer, some doubt appears to have crept in: 'Lyon would have been the man. He had the code book. He would have had to have composed the message and I would say in conjunction with Carse, and I believe it was Lyon who gave me the message to transmit'. Carse, being in command of *Krait* while the raiders were away, would, of course, also have had a copy of the code.

In 2005, in an article appearing in *Duty First*, the journal of the NSW Royal Australian Regiment, Young repeated this story, adding that Admiral Christie had arranged with Lyon to transmit a message if Lombok were patrolled. The code-word 'Potshot' was to be included in the text. Again, after confirming a message was transmitted on 13 October while in range of enemy aircraft, Young again expressed doubt as to who authorised the message and whom he allegedly warned, stating 'I believe it was to Major Lyon I spoke about the wisdom of persisting with the call'.

That a message was sent and received on 15 October has never been in dispute and a copy of the transmission, since it was received and decoded, is held in Australian Archives. According to Taffy Morris, the reason for giving the ETA was to avoid being fired on by accident as they neared the Australian coastline, *Krait*'s silhouette having been altered considerably by the removal of the mast. Harry Manderson, writing to Lyon's mother after the war, remarked that the message passed to SOA by Commander Long was not only typical of Lyon, it was possibly the most succinct and laconic signal ever received from the leader of a successful operation – 'Mission completed'.

There has never been any suggestion that Young sent the 13 October signal of his own volition. In 1990, using information provided by Reid and naval personnel, Carse was named as the instigator of the first signal, a fact confirmed later by Denis Emerson-Elliott. Despite the inconsistencies in Young's statements, including an outright denial in 1991 that such a signal existed, there is no doubt whatsoever that the 13 October transmission was not only unauthorised, but was also described by Lyon as 'disobeying signal orders'. However, it does not appear that he was aware, at the time of transmission, that this signal had been sent. Had he known, Young would have been disciplined on the spot.

Lyon, an absolute stickler for security, was furious when he found out and discussed the matter personally with Reid on his arrival back in Australia. As he and Davidson were determined to press charges, they sought an interview with Commander Long with a view to court-martialling Carse for cowardice and severely reprimanding Young. Both men would have been aware of the action Lyon intended to take. Normal military protocol demanded that personnel to be disciplined were informed before the misdemeanour was brought to the attention of more senior officers. Lyon was extremely angry about the wireless transmission, but the push to court-martial Carse for lack of moral fibre appears to have been driven more by Davidson, who was personally involved in the incident. According to Reid, Lyon normally 'would never damn people (in writing) whose courage had failed' and had been very angry when Jock Campbell had disclosed that her cousin, Bill Waller, had been one of those on *Sederhana Djohanes* wanting to surrender to the Japanese in the Bay of Bengal.

Denis Emerson-Elliott, who had been transferred to Melbourne from Thursday Island on the express orders of Commander Long to take up the post of his Personal Assistant, was on duty when Lyon and Davidson arrived at the Department of Naval Intelligence:

> I was in the office of the DNI when Ivan and Donald Davidson called. They were
> both extremely angry. I realised that whatever had upset them was very serious, as
> it took a lot to get Ivan riled. I explained the DNI was not in, and asked them what
> was the matter. They then told me they wanted to see him, and would wait, as they
> intended to court martial Carse for cowardice and to severely reprimand Young for
> sending an unauthorised signal.

Confirming that Carse had helped himself to the rum supply, Emerson-Elliott observed that although he was an able enough navigator, he was not up to it psychologically:

> Several attempts had been made to get him off the drink over the years and had
> failed. He was a poor choice, as he had always been a heavy drinker. He could not
> function without alcohol and lost his nerve, which is why Davidson had to pull the
> pistol on him.

Mindful of the raid's great propaganda value, and the impact that the daring and heroism of the raiders would have on the public, not only in a few days, but in the years to come, Emerson-Elliott, despite his poor opinion of Carse, did his best to defuse the situation:

> I tried to calm them down and dissuade them from taking such action, as I knew
> that very soon the raid would be big news around the world and, if it got out,
> which it would, that the navigator had been court martialled and the telegraphist
> reprimanded, it would leave a nasty taste in the mouth.
> I tried to talk them out of it, but they were adamant. They waited for the DNI
> and went into his office. They were with him for about an hour. The DNI convinced
> them not to do it, for the same reasons I had said. It was only because of this that
> Ivan, very reluctantly, backed down.

Emerson-Elliott also revealed that Young's breach of discipline in sending the signal, which had been at Carse's behest, was discussed at some length. The telegraphist's case, however, was helped by the fact that the signal, although unauthorised, had resulted in 'no damage' being done. According to Emerson-Elliott, Young's claim that Lyon had insisted on breaking radio silence when still in range of enemy bases is not only ludicrous, but 'indefensible':

Apart from the fact that Lyon had reported the incident to the DNI and wanted Young officially reprimanded, thereby bringing the issue into the open, there was no way Lyon would ever have agreed to the transmission of a signal so close to enemy territory, unless it were a dire emergency. There was nothing in the signal of such urgency that it could not wait for another two days. Lyon was so annoyed over this security breach that he said he would not consider Young for another mission, even if he wanted to go.

While the contentious signal was made public in 1960 by Young, the incident in the wheelhouse was known only to a handful of people, one of them Cobber Cain. For years he had smarted over the image in McKie's book, painted largely by Carse and supported by Young, portraying Ivan Lyon as an overwrought, overly superstitious, highly-strung British officer, putting their lives at risk by breaking radio silence and hellbent on carrying out a very dodgy mission for personal reasons. It was a portrait which had gone unchallenged. By the time Carse and Young were interviewed by McKie, all the senior officers, including Lyon and Davidson, were dead.

The pick-up orders allowed for one rendezvous only, a fact stressed by Lyon as he left the ship. However Carse claimed that the original plans called for a second rendezvous date, forty-eight hours later, so he had no problem in returning to Pompong for the rest of the raiding party. He may have succeeded in carrying off this untruth had Cain not broken his silence in 1990, in the hope that some of the damage done to Lyon's reputation could be reversed – the same motive which prompted Bettina Reid to also come forward. Following this revelation Young denied that the incident in the wheelhouse had occurred and that he had sent an unauthorised signal.

In 1960 Connell had commented on Carse's anxiety, quoting at some length the nervous remarks appearing in his log, and McKie had emphasised the navigator's well-known love of alcohol. However, similar assertions made thirty years later, by which time the public perception of Jaywick was one of untarnished heroism, did not go down well with Young, who publicly defended Carse as being calm, cool, collected and unflappable, despite overwhelming evidence to the contrary. Although it was Cain who first passed on the information about the wheelhouse incident which he witnessed, it was Taffy Morris, whose poor opinion of Carse was no secret, who was blamed for breaking ranks – and ranks were indeed broken, despite the denials. Not only had Berryman confirmed that Carse had been sampling the rum, but Cain had informed both Andrew Huston's sister and at least one other Jaywick crew member of the wheelhouse incident. In the late 1980s, before the 1990 story appeared in print, this same information was passed to a film producer who had bought the rights to McKie's book. His informant was a member of the Jaywick crew, acting as the film's consultant. Although it would have added drama to the production, finally screened under another producer in 1988, the wheelhouse incident was not included because the program was aimed at commercial television and the original producer, after a great deal of thought, had settled on a 'feel-good' ending.

The radio security breach was no secret among naval intelligence staff, who were aware that Carse, possibly to make himself appear more important than he actually was, had 'authorised' the 13 October message to alert Potshot that Lombok was patrolled. That a request for information had been made was confirmed in 2003 by Arthur Jones, who was on board *Krait* when an American officer visited the ship at Exmouth Gulf. It was widely known that Carse was very put out that he, a naval officer, was subservient to a British army officer on an ocean-going exercise and, in consequence, was keen to exert his authority as 'Officer Commanding, Krait'. Although he had been in charge of the ship while the raiders were absent and had used this authority to the fullest when reprimanding the young crew members, his position overall was navigator, and it rankled. This rancour became apparent in later years, when Carse, in speaking to the press, assumed the mantle of overall command, placing Lyon in a subordinate position. Whatever Carse's motive, it was a futile exercise, as the wireless station could not be raised.

The ETA at Potshot, calculated as the afternoon of 17 October, was ambitious. *Krait* arrived early on the morning of the 19th, after completing a journey of almost 6,500 kilometres in forty-eight days. Their safe return sparked diverse emotions. While Young was simply thankful that the 'nightmare' was over and Berryman looked forward to a large slice of apple pie, for Boof Marsh it was the immense satisfaction that they had 'flown the Rising Sun' and got away with it. For Morris, it was the opportunity to engage in some lively trade with alcohol-starved Americans, by exchanging the four one-litre bottles of rum he had amassed from his unclaimed ration for three sacks of cigarettes.[3]

After the high tension of the past six weeks, *Krait*'s arrival back in Australia was something of an anticlimax. As the mission was still top secret until all debriefings had been completed, the victorious raiders returned to a high-level but low-key welcome at Potshot, the true nature of their mission unknown to everyone except Admiral Christie who, after hosting a small dinner for Lyon and Page, recorded in his diary: 'Last night I had the great honour of entertaining Major Lyon of the Gordon Highlanders and Captain Page of the Australian Army – almost a single-handed endeavour of extremely bold pattern. My hat is off to them.'

Krait was in need of urgent repairs so almost the entire team cooled its heels at Potshot for the best part of three weeks. The exceptions were Morris, who sailed to Fremantle on *Chanticleer* to receive proper medical attention for his ankle, and Lyon and Page, who flew to Melbourne and Sydney for preliminary debriefings with the top brass. Lyon also took the opportunity to give a full and very candid report to Reid, including the names of the two members of his team with whom he was displeased, and why. Although the existence of Jaywick was known only to a few, the official congratulations in both Melbourne and Sydney were so embarrassingly effusive that both Lyon and Page were glad to deliver their reports and escape to the relative sanity of the Northern Territory. They reached Darwin on 3 November, three days ahead of *Krait*, which had sailed from Exmouth under Davidson's command.

Security was still very tight, so the ship tied up in the secluded East Arm of the harbour, about five kilometres by sea and twenty by road from Darwin township. Here on a small island linked to the mainland by a causeway was a secret establishment run by AIB, known only by its cover name Lugger Maintenance Section, or LMS. The base, housed in the former Quarantine Station and surrounded by mangroves, was used primarily as a staging post and supply depot for Allied undercover units. However, it also organised and repaired water craft and processed personnel evacuated or rescued from enemy-occupied islands to Australia's north. Originally the brainchild of Colonel Mott, who established the base in November 1942 when Cairn's ZES started to burst at the seams, LMS had passed to AIB's control during the organisational shake-up in early 1943. Such was the security at this remote northern base that none of the many who passed through it, nor any of the RAAF personnel attached to the adjoining flying boat base, had any idea that LMS was anything other than a Quarantine Station.

It was possibly the remoteness of the base, many kilometres from the nearest pub, that caused Paddy McDowell to go on a bender. Whatever the catalyst, he broached the ship's remaining liquor supply and became rip-roaringly drunk. Unfortunately, although Lyon was the first to admit that Paddy was a fine engineer, the ruction caused by this woeful lapse of self-control resulted in Lyon reluctantly informing SOA that he had no further use for his services. The ship he had so lovingly tended remained in Darwin. She was retained by AIB which, impressed by Jaywick's success, had concluded that sea-borne raids, using ships which were common to South-East Asian waters, were the way to go. As a result, plans were already in train to build a number of Indonesian-style fishing boats to carry other raiding parties deep into enemy territory.

Paddy's drinking spree did not, however, have any bearing on Lyon's report on Operation Jaywick. The engineer's devotion to duty was fully recognised and late the following year he would become the proud possessor of a Distinguished Service Medal (DSM), an honour also to be bestowed upon operatives Wally Falls, Arthur Jones and Andrew Huston. Lyon, Page and Davidson, being officers, would receive a Distinguished Service Order (DSO) while Taffy Morris and Crilly would each be awarded the Military Medal. Lyon was actually recommended for a Victoria Cross by Prime Minister Curtin, a recommendation seconded by Lord Selbourne in London. However, in October 1944 the Australian Governor-General would be informed that the recommendation had been downgraded to a DSO. According to the panel in England, Lyon's action, 'though an extremely gallant one did not quite reach the

Formal photograph of the victorious Jaywick team with Jock Campbell, taken at Meigunyah, Brisbane on 11 November 1943. (Back row) Berryman, Marsh, Jones, Huston (Centre row) Crilly, Cain, McDowell, Young, Falls, Morris (Front row) Carse, Davidson, Lyon, Campbell, Page

very high standard of outstanding gallantry required for the award of a Victoria Cross'.

The decision on what awards, if any, were to be conferred upon the sailors was left up to 'naval channels'. This included Long, who was only too aware of what had transpired on board *Krait*. The problems with the two Jaywick members who, in Lyon's view, 'did not come up to scratch', and Carse's acerbic comments in the log book regarding the younger members of the party, ensured that the other five could receive nothing more than a Mention in Dispatches (MID). It appears that Cobber Cain, the fifth crew member, was lumped together with the other four, while Marsh's and Berryman's case was probably not helped by their downgraded official classification on the operational documents as '2nd engineer' and 'deck hand'. For many years post-war the reason why the medical orderly, cook and engineer had received gallantry medals and the five sailors had not, was vigorously debated among ex-servicemen, with the general consensus being that 'the army had it in for the navy'.

However the awards were many months away and no one at this stage, apart from the officers, had any idea of the regard in which Operation Jaywick was held by the top brass. Indeed it was not until 11 November that there was any real celebration for the team members. On the 10th, with the interrogations in Darwin completed, they were flown to Brisbane where, reunited with Taffy Morris, they commemorated Armistice Day and celebrated their successful mission with a slap-up party, also attended by Jock Campbell and Harry Manderson, held in the historic homestead Miegunyah. But far from becoming front page news, Jaywick remained absolutely top secret.

In early November, when intercepted and decoded enemy signals revealed that the Japanese 'did not know what had hit them', orders were issued at the highest level to 'take maximum precautions to ensure secrecy' and inform only a 'minimum number of high ranking officers' that Jaywick had taken place. These instructions, carried out to the letter, ensured that it was impossible for anyone outside the top military and intelligence echelons, or the Japanese, to know the truth.

When Lyon and Long found out they were furious. Propaganda had been Jaywick's main aim, but this decision ensured that the chance to create panic in every port in Japanese-occupied territory was lost, along with the opportunity to lift the morale of the Western world at a time when Allied successes were few and far between. The ships attacked were of no military significance. Only two of the seven attacked remained sunk; the rest would soon be salvaged and put back into service. Had Jaywick been used as Lyon, Long and those who understood the value of propaganda intended, the mission would have fulfilled its potential. This unexpected security embargo now reduced Operation Jaywick, one of the most daring raids in history, to nothing more than an exclusive sideshow.

A celebratory drink on the steps of Meigunyah, 11 November 1943. (Front) SOA's Harry Manderson, Ted Carse, Bob Page. (Row 2) Horrie Young, Moss Berryman, Arthur Jones. (Row 3) Ron Morris, Wally Falls, Cobber Cain, Ivan Lyon. (Rear) Jock Campbell, Paddy McDowell, Andy Crilly, unknown guest.

Lyon was so angry about the security clampdown that he refused point-blank to dine with General Blamey who, as head of SOA, was now keen to be associated with the success of the mission. Telling Reid 'If I had to sit opposite that man, I would choke', Lyon sent Bob Page in his place.

Tragic as this loss of propaganda was, a far greater tragedy was unfolding elsewhere. Horrie Young hit the nail very firmly on the head when he recorded in his diary: 'curious to know what the Japs will have to say – probably say it is internal sabotage and shoot a couple of hundred Chinks'. He was appallingly close to the truth.

Operation Jaywick was now a very deadly secret, and the price paid for it would be one of the bloodiest of the entire war.

9

The Double Tenth massacre

10 October 1943–September 1944

By September 1943 the Imperial Japanese Army, which had so confidently stormed ashore on Singapore Island the previous year, was not quite so cocksure. The first flush of victory had passed and, as the war progressed, some losses were being encountered. Since April, when the Japanese had been forced to withdraw from Guadalcanal, news from the front had not been favourable. Japanese forces had been annihilated on the Aleutian island of Attu, Burma generally was at a stalemate and the British were advancing in the Akyab area. This loss of momentum was more than just a military blow – it made Japanese propaganda, promoting a united Asia under benevolent Japanese patronage, far less effective. Aided by BBC broadcasts picked up on clandestine radio sets, those subjected to Japanese rule began to suspect that the all-powerful conquerors might have feet of clay after all.

The hatred traditionally felt by Singapore's large Chinese population for the Japanese had increased immeasurably with the murder of thousands of educated and prominent civilians, and the easy-going Malays had become increasingly disenchanted by the demands to hand over entire food crops for the garrison troops. There was more discontent when food rationing was enforced, followed by restrictions on clothing and other staple products. As the most basic necessities became scarce a black market flourished, pushing prices to exorbitant heights. A bag of rice that once could be bought for 20 yen now cost 500 yen, beyond the reach of many.

Fired by the knowledge that SOE agents were operating with the guerrillas in Malaya, anti-Japanese feeling began to give way to action. In July 1943 godowns were inexplicably burned to the ground. In August a Japanese transport ship mysteriously caught fire and sank off Malacca. Then a boat factory was torched on the Malay peninsula and telephone wires cut, severely disrupting communications. As the 'incidents' increased so did the rumours that the British would soon be back.

Feeling under threat, the Japanese began to see ghosts behind every tree – a soldier injured in a street fight must be the victim of nose-thumbing enemies of the Imperial Japanese Army and a Japanese official killed when crossing the road the target of anti-Japanese subversives. With what was perceived to be a general breaking down of law and order, accompanied by acts of sabotage, the Japanese were certain there was an organised ring sowing seeds of discontent and masterminding espionage. But who was behind it? Who controlled it, organised it, financed it, planned the next move?

Dismissing the local Malays as 'followers', the Japanese concluded that the ringleaders must be Eurasian and Chinese sympathisers in town, and the Europeans who had held prominent posts before the war and were now imprisoned in Changi Gaol. For some reason the thousands of Allied POWs were not on the list of suspects, but as Blakang Mati Island was in the heart of the area being attacked, prisoners stationed there were no longer allowed to supplement their food ration by indulging in 'fish bombing' with their Japanese guards.

A brand-new gaol, or Civilian Internment Camp as it was known, situated on the Changi peninsula to the east of the city, housed about 3000 people, of whom 400 were women and children. While most inmates remained within the confines of the prison, certain civilians with particular skills, such as doctors, engineers and technical staff, were permitted to work in town. The internal camp administration was rarely bothered by the Japanese and, as the prisoners had to provide their own blankets, medical supplies, clothing and other items as well as augment the barely adequate basic ration, they were permitted regular trips into Singapore by lorry, under armed escort. As this exercise took an entire day there was ample opportunity for such work parties to mingle with the many indigenous Singaporeans sympathetic to their plight. Before long, all those who went on buying excursions, as well as those permitted to work outside the camp, were able to bring back far more than bags of rice and a few rolls of bandages.

Anyone too ill to be treated at the camp was taken to the former mental asylum, now the Miyaka Hospital, in an ambulance driven by Englishman John Long. While his patients underwent treatment he waited in the hospital canteen run by Choy Koon Heng, a former bookkeeper with the Borneo Company, and his wife Elizabeth, who until Singapore's fall had taught at St Andrew's School. The couple, who provided clothing and money to the internees and passed on letters, also formed a close alliance with Long, collecting items for a camp news sheet along with information on the fate of POWs. More importantly, they also recorded troop and shipping movements and the locality of enemy airfields for secret dispersal to other camps, in the hope that the intelligence would reach Australia or India and so speed up the day of liberation.

With this in mind the Singapore Re-establishing Committee was formed at the civilian camp, with Stanley Middlebrook as chairman, to formulate a plan of action for when the British returned. It was dangerous work and some of it punishable by death, but the conspirators attracted not the slightest attention until December 1942, when some English-speaking, pro-Japanese Sikh guards replaced the previously lax and inattentive Japanese sentries. The Japanese were particularly interested in Robert Heeley Scott, formerly Head of the Far Eastern Bureau, whom they knew had close connections to SOE, MI6 and the Foreign Office. Scott's background was also known to the Japanese and his record, in their view, was a bad one, encompassing, as it did, postings in Manchuria, Shanghai, Chungking and Tokyo, and his most recent posting in Singapore.

The Japanese had been keeping a close eye on Scott for some time. He and a number of Ministry for Information and Malayan Broadcasting staff had managed to get away on 12 February 1942 on *Giang Bee*, a coal-burning cargo boat crammed with at least 400 passengers that normally catered for only twenty-five. Scott acted as one of the stokers while his Chinese cook took over the galley. The ship's captain, stopped by enemy destroyers off Sumatra the following day, was attempting to evacuate his passengers in inadequate life-boats and on rafts when the Japanese opened fire, killing at least two hundred. Scott was captured and transferred to Singapore, where he spent several months in solitary confinement in the tower of Changi Gaol. Well aware of the risk he posed to anyone who came in contact with him, he was extremely cautious when participating in camp activities. Apart from editing the camp news sheet and volunteering for the rice-collecting party in order to collect information from his many contacts, Scott's prime contribution, along with Long, Dr Fergus McIntyre, former police magistrate Lionel Earl, and William Cherry, the government printer, was the control and operation of the camp radio.

Following the increase in surveillance of the detainees, in June 1943 Major Sumida Haruzo, recently appointed to a senior post with the local Kempeitai, brought in experienced interrogators from as far afield as Thailand to investigate the recent acts of sabotage. This force, numbering somewhere between forty and sixty-four personnel, was split into four subsections under Lieutenant Yamada. With the aid of undercover agents planted in the Civilian Internment Camp and infiltrated into the regular civilian population, they were ordered to amass sufficient evidence to bring about arrests by December and so put an end to the spy network. In anticipation of an influx of prisoners, additional interpreters were recruited and a new Kempeitai substation opened in a civilian residential building in Smith Street to supplement the dungeons at Kempeitai headquarters, which occupied the former YMCA building on Stamford Road and Singapore's Central Police Station on South Bridge Road.

The Kempeitai had made scarcely any inroads into their secret investigations when, on the morning of 27 September, Ivan Lyon and his Jaywick men blew up the ships in Singapore Harbour. With the civilian internees already in their sights, the Japanese immediately assumed that this outrageous act of sabotage was an inside job masterminded by prominent civilians held at Changi who had transmitted the necessary information to the raiding parties. At no stage did they ever consider the saboteurs might have come from the outside – after all, Singapore was an island, surrounded by Japanese-controlled territory and therefore impregnable to attack, the same fallacious belief held by the British such a short time before.

Initial disbelief gave way to outrage when the full implications of the attack were realised. At a conference held at Army HQ it was concluded that the explosions had not been caused by torpedoes but by something which had been detonated on the ships, most likely by enemy agents using small boats. The prime suspects, according to the Johor branch of the Kempeitai, were British soldiers operating from Johor and working in conjunction with foreign spies in Singapore and at the civilian internment camp. The commander of the Southern Army, General Terauchi, issued an immediate order to Major Sumida to 'clean up the enemy elements in Singapore and Prai [Penang area] and take measures promptly to counteract any acts against the Japanese forces'. Anxious not to incur the wrath of his general, Sumida gave the secret investigations, now known as Dai Ichi Kosako (Number One Work), top priority. By the second week of October Sumida was ready. Convinced that the existence of an internal sabotage unit had been proved beyond all doubt, the Kempeitai swooped on the hapless local population and then upon the Changi camp.

The unfortunate Chinese had already paid dearly for their loyalty and patriotism. On 21 February 1942, less than a week after the surrender, the Japanese had ordered all men between the ages of eighteen and fifty to assemble at noon at five different locations. The well educated, anyone affiliated with political or secret societies and anyone displaying any type of British influence, such as Western-style clothing or wearing spectacles, were especially targeted, along with the volunteer forces, particularly John Dalley's Dalforce. Rounded up with ruthless efficiency, these 'undesirables', including Elizabeth Choy's teenaged brother, were executed by the thousand in what the Japanese sanitisingly referred to as Operation Cleanup.[1]

Twenty months later, on a warm October morning in 1943, a reign of terror began that was to last for almost a year. Civilians and internees were hauled from their beds in the dead of night, never to return. No one was safe, from the humblest coolie to John Wilson, Bishop of Singapore. The Number One Work was destined to become a hideous and terrifying monster from which there was no escape. The nightmare that began on 10 October – the 'tenth of the tenth' – was destined to go down in history as the 'Double Tenth Massacre'

Anxious to solve 'the mystery of the oil tankers', in the firm belief that 'the state of peace and order and this serious incident were related and that a thorough measure should be taken to prevent the recurrence of such serious incidents', Sumida cast his net wide. He and his men were authorised to:

1. Obtain information about the sinking of the ships and arrest people suspected of being concerned with it

2. Investigate the Changi Camp and arrest suspected persons there

3. Arrest persons suspected of being engaged in sabotage

4. Arrest all other enemy elements not included in the above.

Scott had received the news on 28 September that ships had been blown up the previous day and some of the Australian POWs, including Queenslander Norm Dean of 2/26 Battalion, who had recently returned from the Burma-Thai railway and was in a new camp at Adam Road, had actually heard the sound of the explosions. Their suspicion that something of great importance had occurred was confirmed when their rations were suddenly cut in half – the usual Japanese reaction to bad news. Information from the POWs had reached the internees in the camp in dribs and drabs but the knowledge was confined to a handful of people, none of whom had any idea what had caused the explosions. Scott and Long could only suppose that British stay-behind parties operating from Malaya were responsible.

The first inkling that something was amiss came on 9 October, when the internees were warned there would be a full parade the next day. No reason was given but shortly after dawn all were herded into the main yard. The Camp Commandant and a large number of Kempeitai appeared, followed by armed soldiers who blocked off all passages and the entrances to buildings. Names were read out and about a dozen people, headed by Robert Scott, were taken inside the gaol where they were violently interrogated. The remainder were forced to stand in the hot sun for the entire day without food or water, while the Japanese conducted a thorough search, looting and destroying personal belongings. When they finished at about 8 pm they had part of a radio belonging Walter Stevenson as well as other wireless components, a box belonging to an ex-banker filled with cash, and various bits of paper including notes taken down from a BBC broadcast. None of the news sheets was found, nor the remainder of the wireless set. As a result of the search and the preliminary interrogations more names were added to the list, including Stevenson and Dr Stanley, bringing the total number of suspects to nineteen. All were transferred to either Smith Street or the YMCA Building, along with a large number of townsfolk also caught in the web.

Like their Gestapo brothers in Germany, the Kempeitai were masters at extracting confessions by whatever means were most expedient. To be suspected was automatically to become guilty and, once a prisoner was deemed guilty, it was the task of the Kempeitai to ensure that the crime was admitted. When Robert Scott asked Sumida what would happen if he refused to say anything, he was told 'it is essential that you make a confession. Under our law you cannot be tried until you confess. For that reason I have the authority to use any degree of force to extract a confession and so have my subordinates'. In this way, some of the most horrific crimes known to civilisation were perpetrated in the name of Japanese justice.

Standard torture took the form of a beating, which varied in intensity from open-handed slaps to savage attacks with iron bars, belt buckles, bamboo canes, truncheons, metal sword scabbards, knotted ropes, chairs and the butt of a revolver. To increase the pain, victims were often suspended by their fingers or thumbs or given the 'log treatment', where they were forced to kneel on sharp lengths of wood or metal, with other sharp pieces placed behind the knees. The interrogator then jumped on the victim's thighs, inflicting terrible wounds to the knees, shins and ankles as well as to the flesh of the upper legs. Fingers were bent backwards, joints dislocated and nails hammered into the soles of feet. Lighted cheroots and cigarettes were ground into the most sensitive parts of the body, men and women alike, while women were often singled out for electric shocks, the bare wires positioned on their most intimate parts.

Many were subjected to water torture. The first method involved forcing water into the mouth of the prisoner who, by sheer necessity, was forced to swallow huge amounts or drown. When the stomach was fully distended the interrogator would order an underling to jump on it. The other method was to strap the prisoner to a seesaw-like contraption which was then lowered into a tub of water, submerging the head until the prisoner was close to asphyxiation. If no confession were forthcoming, the process was repeated. Other prisoners, the Chinese in particular, had their abdomens or hands doused in petrol or methylated spirits and set alight.

If the suspect still failed to confess, the interrogators moved to the next stage: psychological torture. Prisoners, told that execution by shooting or decapitation was imminent, were permitted to write their final letters before being blindfolded and led outside, where further preparations were carried out with such hideous realism that the victims often fainted. In some cases, terrible threats were made against family members. In others, prisoners were offered pistols to put an end to their suffering, only to have it snatched away at the last moment.

The Kempeitai's strength lay in the ability of the interrogators to discover the individual prisoner's breaking point. Some people, tortured to a state of semi-consciousness, would confess to anything to gain respite from their agony. Others were given a taste of some particularly painful torture and then treated kindly in the hope that they would talk freely. After a few days' confinement in appalling conditions, the promise of a hot bath and a good meal was sufficient to break the resolve of some who under normal circumstances might have held out. By cajoling and beating, by constant physical violence, threats of decapitation and other psychological torture, the Kempeitai managed to wear down all but the most resolute.

John Long, who had worked for Asiatic Petroleum (Shell Oil) and was deputy director of American Rubber Products, was brought in for questioning on 16 October, a week after the initial arrests. As a tanker had been attacked he was high on the list of suspects but, in spite of lengthy interrogations and horrendous torture, he admitted nothing. Once, in an effort to gain some relief he made some 'confessions' which he immediately retracted, saying he had lied, but the Kempeitai were too quick for him, arresting and torturing the unfortunate Choys, his friends who ran the hospital canteen.

The YMCA Building on Stamford Road, Singapore, one of the Kempeitai interrogation and torture centres

Mr Choy, accused of sending wireless sets and money into the camp, was arrested first. A fortnight later on 15 November Elizabeth was lured to the YMCA building on the promise that she could see her husband, only to be arrested herself. Both were determined not to crack, but when Mr Choy was forced to watch his wife being beaten and subjected to electric shock, followed by the log treatment for both of them, they 'admitted' that they had received a letter from Robert Scott. After a further severe beating Mr Choy 'confessed' that he had been sinking ships. Encouraged by these confessions, which had been written out in advance, the Kempeitai pressed on. They could not, however, force the Choys to reveal any more details or implicate others. Although separated and told they would be beheaded, both Elizabeth and Koon Heng Choy remained silent.

Mr Choy was then interrogated for weeks about a message allegedly passed to John Long. Refusing to betray his friend, he withstood the punishment meted out each day with tight-lipped determination, caving in only when Long wrote a note urging him to 'confess', thereby saving his life and salving his conscience. Tried on 3 May, he was sentenced to twelve years' hard labour. His wife, who believed he had been executed when he was taken away, was held for almost 200 days, during which time she was not permitted to wash. 'If they were going to execute me,' she later said, 'so be it. But we knew nothing. I said that we would die with honour.'

The fortitude exhibited by the Choys was not rare, but was indicative of the stoicism of the Chinese. Not intimidated in the slightest by the Kempeitai, they risked punishment and death time and again to assist Allied POWs. As a grateful Corporal James Brodie of 2/9 Australian Field Ambulance declared: 'Too much cannot be said in praise of the Chinese. During the occupation they risked their lives to give us smokes and food. Often they were bashed but their spirit never wavered.'

Some Europeans were as equally stoic. Sixty-one-year-old Bishop Wilson, who had

Survivor Elizabeth Choy inspecting an exhibit depicting the suffering of Singapore's civilians, Changi Museum, Singapore

chosen to remain with his flock when *Empire Star* sailed, withstood the most brutal treatment, although beaten and tortured until he could no longer walk. Doctor Cuthbert Stanley, aged forty, also showed extraordinary courage. Arrested on 10 October, he was interrogated by one of the more brutal members of the Kempeitai after his name, along with those of Long and Scott, had been mentioned by Dr McIntyre, a 57-year-old Australian osteopath. Convinced that Stanley possessed information vital to the investigation, the Kempeitai held him in a filthy cell until 13 November, when he was benignly questioned. No information was forthcoming, so he was given the log treatment for five days, all the while being savagely beaten. When he was no longer able to walk he was carried to the interrogation room in a rattan chair. As he would still not crack he was electrocuted and horribly burnt, then returned to his cell on a stretcher. Threatened with more of the same the next day he finally 'confessed'. He was so overcome with remorse for his 'confession' that he threw himself from the first floor verandah, intending to put an end to his life. He missed the concrete and hit an earth mound, breaking both his fall and his pelvis. The Japanese doctor called in to see him declared he was 'not sick enough' to be taken to hospital. The Kempeitai continued to torture him in this condition, his screams of agony reverberating around the YMCA and clearly audible on the ninth floor of the Cathay Building, some distance away. When Dr Stanley was dumped on the floor of his cell for the last time, his poor pain-wracked body was in a dreadful state. He was clad only in his vest, his face and feet pulped and bleeding, his skin scarred and burnt, his flesh rotten and putrefying. It was only when he became delirious that the Kempeitai allowed him to be admitted to hospital where, mercifully, he died thirty minutes after admission. Unyielding until the end, his secrets died with him.

The degree of resistance to torture surprised the Japanese but they continued, nevertheless. They had information about the camp organisation and radios but they still had no evidence against Scott, whom they believed was closely connected to the shipping incident. When a beating which lasted without let-up for six nights and seven days failed to break him, they persevered on and off for another three weeks before moving on to less resolute victims. Confessions were obtained under torture but, to the interrogators' consternation, were just as readily retracted. By November the Japanese were no further advanced in finding out who had blown up the ships. The strong were prepared to die before admitting anything; the confessions of those who were more easily broken were useless. This lack of success did not prevent the round-up from continuing, or the displaying of the severed heads of Chinese victims on posts along city streets in order to increase the pressure. How many Chinese died is not known. In all, sixty European internees from Changi were arrested and interrogated. Many, including Colonial Secretary Hugh Fraser, did not survive the ordeal. But it was not simply the torture which ended their lives – it was imprisonment itself.

At both the YMCA and Smith Street, prisoners were crowded twenty to a cell – European, Asian, Japanese, men and women alike. In the basement of the YMCA, heavy wooden cages had been constructed, accessed by a small door through which food was pushed. The cages were so small that the prisoners could not lie down in comfort. No bedding or blankets were provided and a bright light burned day and night. Women were not spared and no concessions were made. Besides Elizabeth Choy, Mrs Cornelius, the wife of a man suspected of passing money to the internees, and a number of other women were arrested, including Dr Cecily Williams, who had contact with the men's camp in her professional capacity; Mrs Dorothy Nixon, who was on the camp committee; Mrs Lean Ah Beck from town; and Mrs Bloom whose husband, the British Army's Dr Bloom, had delivered Lyon's and Davidson's children. 'Freddie' Bloom, as she was known, was an American journalist who had been teaching herself Braille, which the Japanese assumed was some kind of secret code used to send messages to the saboteurs. Although closely questioned about her relationship with Scott, Elizabeth Ennis, a nursing sister who had been a nanny to his two children and had been given permission to visit the men's wing to see him, was not arrested.

When not being interrogated, prisoners were required to sit upright in rows, legs crossed, from 8 am until 10 pm. Apart from an enforced session of heavy exercise from which no one was excused, no movement was permitted, except to use the lavatory – an open pedestal in the corner. A list of rules which inmates were required to recite daily was posted on the wall: no talking, grumbling, preaching or walking about. The prisoners, however, did manage to communicate after internee John Dunlop taught them basic sign language. They had to take extreme care not to get caught, since any infraction of the rules resulted in a heavy beating.

The filthy floor was infested with cockroaches and at night the mosquitoes swarmed unchecked. Even without the insects sleep was almost impossible. Since interrogations were conducted around the clock, there was scarcely thirty minutes in any one day free of the shrieks of the tortured. Roll calls were conducted throughout the day and night, in an effort to wear down resistance and reduce the prisoners to a state of total exhaustion. Food was insufficient to sustain life over an extended period – a small amount of rice with an occasional bit of vegetable matter or unidentifiable meat, eaten with the fingers twice a day, plus weak black tea served in a filthy, rusted cup. Water was available only from the lavatory pedestal, which was also used for washing. Neither soap, towels, sanitary requirements for the women nor changes of clothing were provided, although some prisoners were detained for months.

Disease was rife. Scabies and sores were commonplace but it was dysentery which accounted for many lives, the Japanese refusing to move prisoners to hospital until death was imminent. Some did not manage to make it that far. Mr Cornelius, a Eurasian from town, was arrested with his wife on 10 October for allegedly supplying $200 to internees. First beaten up at home, he was taken to the YMCA for further interrogation ten days later. After being severely tortured he was carried back to his cell, where he muttered 'Christ, what a beating', before collapsing. A Japanese doctor came, took a look and threw some water over him. In the morning he was dead. Even then the Japanese paid him no attention. It was not until late afternoon that they finally arrived. Amid much laughter and joking they removed his body, now stiff with rigor mortis, breaking his outstretched arms in order to manoeuvre the body through the door.

In spite of all the arrests and the many thousands of hours of interrogation, the Japanese still had no idea who was responsible for blowing up the ships in the harbour. The final arrests took place in early April 1944, six months after the first suspects were detained. Among them were two Eurasian men from the city, Edward and Reginald Ebert. The former, charged with espionage and spreading sensational rumours, received fifteen years while Reginald, found guilty of merely spreading rumours, was given six. None of the internees arrested at that time – Wulfram Penseler, general manager of the Australian Gold mine at Raub, New Zealander Hilary Rendell and A W Ker, director of American Rubber Products – survived. The bodies of Rendell and 45-year-old Norman Coulson, the municipal engineer and an early arrest, were sent back to camp following their deaths in gaol. Four other internees who survived the interrogation were also sent to trial – Robert Scott, Lionel Earl and William Cherry for their wireless activities, and Robert Calderwood. All received sentences of up to six years with hard labour. In all, over thirty of the one hundred civilians arrested were tried and sentenced to gaol. Towards the end of 1944 three Dutch POWs also came under the microscope – Captain Cornelis Woudenberg, a Pioneer in the NEI Reserve, and two other ranks, J W Zaayer and Charles Redy. The officer was charged with espionage, breaching military security and assisting the enemy to attack, and the ORs with assisting the enemy. Why they were singled out is not known but, as they were serving with volunteer units, their pre-war occupations may have been connected with the Dutch petroleum industry.

The poor food, inhumane treatment and lack of sanitation took a dreadful toll in the year that the investigation lasted. In May 1944, while those arrested in April were undergoing interrogation, intercepted enemy signals revealed that the Japanese believed 'two Chinese and one Malay had rowed out in a sampan and exploded a bomb, sinking a ship' – a piece of intelligence which prompted nothing more at SOA than the observation 'interesting to note the Japanese ideas on how it [the raid] was carried out'.

Although there was insufficient evidence to pin anything on him, the Kempeitai held John Long, their major suspect, for almost a year without trial. Along with other detainees, he was sent to Outram Road Gaol. Within its forbidding walls, constructed in the style of many nineteenth century British prisons, were held all those, Japanese miscreants included, who had the misfortune to come under the jurisdiction of the military police.

Ringed by solid stone walls and containing a large number of cells, Outram Road was tailor-made for the needs of the occupying forces, which had moved in almost as soon as the British moved out – the transition from His Majesty's prison to Japanese gaol greatly facilitated by the departing tenants who had thoughtfully left the keys to every cell hanging neatly on a rack in the main office. Since 1942 the number of inmates who had gone into Outram Road alive, and come out dead, was considerable. The majority of Chinese inmates didn't stay long – just long enough for their executions to be arranged.

Throughout 1942 and 1943 conditions in the gaol were so appalling that by comparison

Entrance to the Kempeitai's punishment gaol at Outram Road Singapore

the camps at Changi were considered to be 'like heaven'. Indeed, some prisoners, teetering on the fine line that divided life from death, owed their survival solely to the fact that the Kempeitai, who were anxious not to have too many deaths in custody, packed them off to the camp hospitals when their demise appeared imminent. If they died in hospital, the blame could be apportioned to incompetent Allied or internee medical staff.

The first European POW to be sentenced to Outram Road was Corporal John McGregor, a soldier from Western Australia who had escaped from the Changi POW Camp with Lieutenant Penrod Dean shortly after the surrender. As the Japanese equated escaping with desertion, upon recapture they were tried before a military court held in Singapore's Supreme Court building and sentenced to death. The court subsequently commuted their sentences to two years' solitary confinement.

Conditions in the gaol were even worse than at the YMCA and Smith Street. Washing facilities were non-existent, every cell was infested with mice, cockroaches, bugs and lice, and the lavatory was an open bucket. Contact with other prisoners was not permitted and when not sleeping the prisoners were forced to sit at attention. To ensure they did so, regular checks were made through the Judas hatch in the heavy iron door.

Not all those interrogated over the shipping incident went to Outram Road Gaol. Death had already claimed or was about to claim them. Fifteen internees, along with Mr Cornelius and an untold number of Chinese and Malays, lost their lives directly or indirectly as a result of the Kempeitai's Number One Work. Others sustained physical and psychological injuries that would remain with them for life. Buried in hurriedly dug, unmarked graves were the remains of innocent men and women whose only crime had been to attract the attention of the Japanese. It would be many months before the outside world learned of the terror, suffering and bloodshed from the purge which began on the tenth day of the tenth month, 1943. Meanwhile, military chiefs in Australia and India, who knew from intercepted signals that the locals were being blamed and that terrible reprisals must be taking place, remained silent.

This knowledge was not confined to those privy to the secrets of the intercepts. Occasionally it was deemed essential, or useful, to make use of such information as long as it could not be traced back to its real source. To assist in this subterfuge, especially in intelligence summaries compiled by AIB and SOA for distribution, the source was attributed to 'captured enemy documents'. If additional credibility were required, a second source nominated was 'enemy radio broadcasts' which, as everyone knew, were monitored. Quoting a 'captured document', secret intelligence was able to advise those on its exclusive distribution lists: 'In Singapore on the morning of 27 Sep six ships of 2000 to 5000 tons (three tankers among them) were sunk by bombs due to a clever plan by Malayans working under supervision of Caucasians directing behind scenes'. Naturally, the public and defence personnel generally knew nothing of this.

The absolute secrecy clamped down on Operation Jaywick ensured that not a single word could leak out to release the innocent from their torment. Throughout 1944, while bruised and battered bodies were subjected to even greater punishment, the Japanese continued to scratch their heads over the loss of the ships in the harbour.

Back in Australia, Ivan Lyon was busily planning yet another raid.

10

Lyon's tigers

March–September 1944

This time Ivan had all the help he needed. On learning that the Japanese were unaware that Allied forces had attacked Singapore, Lord Louis Mountbatten, Supreme Allied Commander South-East Asia, urged SOA to consider further raids against Singapore Harbour, Saigon and the recently repaired Singapore Naval Base. The chances of the Americans agreeing to clandestine operations in their patch were not good, however. Keen to maintain superiority over its junior Allied partners, and to give the impression of winning the war single-handedly in the eyes of the American electorate, the United States was very suspicious of maverick organisations such as SOE and SOA. On the other hand, Australia and Britain, fully aware that 'the main weight of attack on Japan will be delivered by commands that are overwhelmingly American', were just as keen to 'increase the representation of the point of view and the interest of the British Commonwealth in this area', believing that SOA-SOE activities could exercise 'a degree of influence out of all proportion to the magnitude of the operations undertaken'. In other words, with an eye on post-war re-occupation, Australia and Britain wanted to indulge in a bit of flag-waving in territories they had previously controlled.

As a result, activities organised by SOE and SOA assumed an importance 'out of all proportion', with operations and their unsuspecting personnel becoming pawns in a massive battle of political wills as the two governments took on the might of the United States in an effort to retain their foothold. US authorities, unable to control the infrastructures of covert Allied organisations other than their own, insisted that General MacArthur must have total power in deciding what operations could take place in his zone.

Therein lay the stumbling block. Before reaching MacArthur, all plans were vetted by General Willoughby, who had already rejected Jaywick, thereby forcing Lyon to seek assistance from the RAN. Keeping well away from the Philippines, an area regarded as sacrosanct by the United States, SOA examined Mountbatten's proposal and came up with a new operation. Code-named Hornbill, it was to be a larger and more ambitious version of Jaywick involving folboats, limpets, submarines and, in place of *Krait*, a new mode of transport known as 'country craft' – converted seine-net fishing trawlers modified to resemble Asian vessels. Operating out of a base in the Nantuna Islands off the west coast of Borneo, these diesel-driven, pseudonative-style boats would enter enemy waters and drop off sabotage teams, coastwatching parties and intelligence agents in folboats. When the time came for the pick-up, the powerful diesel engines would ensure a fast getaway.

Because of Hornbill's complexity, the overlap in command areas between Mountbatten and MacArthur, and the need for submarines, which were in short supply, it was essential for the British and American chiefs to be in complete agreement. Lord Louis had no trouble gaining MacArthur's approval. The success of Jaywick, from which the Americans had excluded themselves, ensured that ears which had previously been closed were open. After meeting Lyon in Brisbane, MacArthur had been won over, declaring that raids similar to Jaywick were invaluable as 'the effect on [the] enemy war effort by such attacks are greater than in any other theatre'. Keen to enter areas outside the range of normal military activity, he ordered his Joint Chiefs of Staff in Washington to ensure that submarines were made available – a decision that delighted SOA's new director, Lieutenant-Colonel John Chapman-Walker.

As the first two targets were to be Singapore and Saigon, Lyon was the natural choice as party leader. With a nucleus of trained and experienced operatives on hand and the British submarine *Porpoise*, currently undergoing a refit, already assigned to Hornbill at Lord Louis Mountbatten's personal direction, Lyon was dispatched to England in March 1944 to inspect *Porpoise* and check on SOE's latest sabotage equipment.

He was met at the Baker Street headquarters in London by Major Walter Chapman, who presided over an Aladdin's cave of ingenious devices ranging from explosives to blow up anything from a fuse box to a train, to bombs disguised to look like everyday objects and cleverly concealable weapons, suitcase transmitters and disguises. Listening carefully as Lyon outlined Hornbill's plan, the tall bespectacled engineer announced that what the Singapore missions needed was a brand-new invention – a form of underwater transport called a 'Sleeping Beauty'.

Sleeping Beauty, or SB, was the code name for a highly secret, very sophisticated, one-man submersible craft designed by SOE inventor, Major Quentin Reeves. Known officially as a Motor Submersible Canoe, the idea was first conceived by Royal Marine Major 'Blondie' Hasler, who had led a raiding party of ten Royal Marines in 'cockle' canoes from the Bay of Biscay to place limpets on German shipping moored in Bordeaux Harbour. Only two of the five canoes made it to the target, 100 kilometres from the drop-off point, where six ships were limpeted. The mission, known as Operation Frankton and carried out on the night of 11–12 December 1942, was later immortalised in book and film as *Cockleshell Heroes*.[1] As Hasler had lost eight of his men, six of whom were captured and executed and two drowned, he was keen for future targets to be approached underwater.

Constructed from mild steel and aluminium, the SBs were almost four metres long and

A Sleeping Beauty, about to submerge

measured seventy centimetres at the widest point. The operator, wearing an underwater suit and breathing apparatus, controlled the craft with a joystick, approaching the target either completely submerged or with his head above the water. There was no periscope so the driver 'porpoised' to the surface at regular intervals or used an underwater compass to maintain his bearing. Buoyancy was controlled by flooding two tanks positioned either side of the operator's legs, but submersion was limited to two hours – the limit of the oxygen supply. The half-horsepower produced by four standard six-volt car batteries produced a top speed of 4.5 knots on the surface and 3.5 when submerged. The range at full speed was 19 kilometres, 38 kilometres when cruising, and the craft was so manoeuvrable that chief test pilot Sub-Lieutenant Grigor Riggs could loop the loop while under water. Unaffected by Force 5 winds and virtually impossible to capsize, the SB could also be sailed or paddled if the batteries failed, but because it weighed 270 kilograms this was found to be rather impracticable.

With an enthusiastic Chapman in tow, Lyon went to Staines Reservoir, just outside London, for a first-hand demonstration and a test drive. He was extremely impressed but it was a follow-up demonstration in Portsmouth Harbour, when the 20-year-old Riggs showed how easy it was to approach and mine naval ships while remaining completely underwater, that convinced Lyon he must have Sleeping Beauties for Hornbill. Wanting them was one thing; getting them out to Australia and to the Natunas was quite another. According to the Royal Navy's Commander Newton, it was unlikely any submarine commander would agree to carry them inside the hull as the time taken to unload at the target area would leave the submarine exposed upon the surface for too long. But *Porpoise* could carry them externally in the mine-laying casing – a square, tunnel like structure which ran the length of the hull. Supplies packed in special containers had been carried this way to the beleaguered island of Malta for some time.

After inspecting the submarine, docked at Rothesay on the Firth of Forth, Lyon returned to London. Thwarted by 'security' from contacting *Porpoise*'s Commander Hubert Marsham, with whom he hoped to thrash out details, Ivan was forced to leave the design and manufacture of the SB containers in the hands of others – who were unfortunately short on practical experience. After a considerable delay the first of fifteen very expensive J containers, weighing in excess of 2.5 tonnes, was produced by a private manufacturer, the engineers at the naval dockyards being too hard-pressed to undertake the work. Because of its weight the prototype, as soon as it reached the end of the rails in the mine casing, pitched forward and jammed. Modification of the casing was obviously required, but because of time constraints Lyon was informed that this work would have to be carried out in Australia.

While Lyon was sorting out the problems with the J containers, a talented young lieutenant from the Malay Volunteers was trying to talk his way into active service in Room 238 of the Victoria Hotel, on London's Northumberland Avenue. The officer conducting the interview at this unlikely venue was Colonel Edgerton Mott, ISD's former director, who was now working at SOE. Before him stood Harold Robert (Bobby) Ross, 26-year-old son of a British Army doctor and a plantation owner's daughter. Although born in Madras, India, Ross was raised in England after his father, a lieutenant-colonel, resigned his commission and returned to civilian life. Intelligent and a good sportsman, Bobby Ross had attended Wellington College in Berkshire before taking up a scholarship in 1936 to enter Cambridge University, where he studied anthropology and zoology for his Bachelor of Arts degree, graduating with first class honours in both. After spending a short time in both Germany and Iceland, at the end of 1939 he sailed for Kuala Pilah, Malaya, to take up a post with the Colonial Administrative Service. A member of his school and university cadet corps, he joined the Federated Malay States Volunteer Force (FMSVF) at Port Dickson in early 1941. After a year serving as a private with a machine-gun company in 3 Battalion, he transferred to the artillery, only to have his career as a gunner come to an abrupt end on the night of 15 February 1942.

Six hours after the surrender, Ross and seven companions had joined General Bennett's party as it left Singapore in a slow-moving tonkan. When the general transferred to a fast motor launch, the others had continued to Padang and from there sailed to India, where Ross spent three months at the Officer Training School at Belgaum before returning home. Discharged in June 1942, he obtained a posting with the Colonial Administration to Nigeria, where he had spent an anthropologically interesting but militarily boring time as a district officer. By January 1944 he was ready for something different and returned to England to enlist.

Ross's credentials were tailor-made for the type of work undertaken by SOE, which initially had envisaged deploying him in India: reasonable fluency in colloquial and everyday Malay; a thorough understanding of the people and cultures of South-East Asia; the ability, from the months spent in Nigeria, to find his way across uncharted territory; a fundamental grasp of the engineering principles involved in road and bridge engineering in tropical climates and, last but by no means lest, a well-developed spirit of adventure. Mott, who doubtless saw a great similarity between Ross and Lyon, sent him to SOE's training school before assigning him to Hornbill.

By 24 April Lyon had every reason to be in good spirits. Hornbill had been sent to GHQ for final approval and the gallantry wards for Jaywick had been published in *The London Gazette*. While Ivan Lyon, DSO, MBE, took time out to visit family and friends before flying back to Australia on 1 May, Major Walter Chapman succeeded in extricating himself from his desk and attaching himself to Hornbill. At Gorsehanger Farm, one hour after farewelling the son whom she had not seen for seven years, Mrs Jane Lyon learned from the Red Cross that Gabrielle and her grandson Clive, believed dead these past fourteen months, were alive and well.

Lyon had returned to Sydney and was discussing his trip with Reid when the wonderful news finally reached him. Following the recent capture of the German raider *Thor*, it had been learned that Gabrielle's ship *Nankin* had indeed been attacked and, although the vessel's Captain Stratford had put up a brave fight, he had surrendered to prevent loss of life. All the prisoners had been transferred to other enemy vessels and taken to Japan. Although Gabrielle and Clive were now behind barbed wire in Fukushima Internment Camp Number 12, they were safe, and Commander Long, passing on the good news, was hopeful that their release could be secured through a prisoner exchange. Interviewed on Melbourne radio, Lyon's only comment was, 'War is a grim business, isn't it?'

Overjoyed, Ivan turned his full attention to Hornbill which, because of the SBs, had not only been substantially altered by SOA's planning department but was now extremely complex. At a briefing held on 30 May Lyon discovered that the country craft, loaded up with SBs, folboats and assault boats, were to sail independently to the Natunas for a rendezvous with SB operators and maintenance crews, transferred by submarine. The country craft would then sail to within 70 kilometres of Singapore where each two-man team would transfer to an assault boat packed with equipment, including a folboat, towing the SB the rest of the way. Once within striking distance of the target, one operative would carry out the attack in the SB while the other waited. When the SB returned it would be sunk, along with the assault boat. The men would then paddle the folboat back to the mother ship. The fifteen assault boats, which were so heavy it required six men to lift them, were to be operated 'with or without engines'. How a heavy assault boat, further encumbered by a 270-kilogram SB dragging behind on the end of a tow rope, was to be controlled and paddled by two men without the assistance of an engine, was not disclosed.

A fortnight after the planning department had given the green light to this fantastically ambitious and logistically outrageous project, it received multiple bad news. The country craft, affected by striking workers in Melbourne, would not be ready for delivery before the onset of the monsoon; the additional submarines promised by the Americans were unavailable and, in any case, it was now doubtful whether enough fuel could be transported by submarine to keep the country craft working at such a range. The final straw was that the stores from England would not arrive in time to be transported to the Natunas before the proposed attack date. Since the timing of the monsoon made it impossible to put back the dates of the raids, the modus operandi would have to be changed if Hornbill were to go ahead.

Any thought of using the Natunas and country craft was scrapped, along with the assault boats, and the project split sensibly into two far more manageable sections. One, code-named Kookaburra, would cover raids from Johor in the west to Sarawak (Borneo) in the east, on dates yet to be decided. The other operation was to concentrate solely on raiding Singapore Harbour. Unlike Jaywick, which had been designed as propaganda, the aim of this mission was to cause real damage to the enemy by sinking thirty ships and damaging thirty others. Its commanding officer was Ivan Lyon, on whose chest was tattooed the head of the creature which would give its name to the operation – Rimau, the Malayan word for tiger.

The final planning conference for Operation Rimau took place on 6 July. Although not nearly as complicated as Hornbill, it was far from simple. Using *Porpoise*, they would establish a rear base, Base A, before sailing to a known junk route where, to compensate for the lack of country craft, they would pirate a local vessel and capture the crew. While the submarine returned to Australia with the prisoners the Rimau team would sail the junk, with SBs on board, to a rendezvous point close enough to Singapore to launch the attack. A small group left on board would prepare the folboats for a fast getaway and dispose of any incriminating evidence. Once the raiding party returned, the SBs and junk would be sunk and the entire team would paddle back to Base A where, a fortnight later, *Porpoise* would pick them up. Although the revised plan was still very complex and Lyon was worried about its complicated structure, he knew that if Singapore were to be attacked it would have to be before the change of the monsoon. Despite his misgivings that the project was 'too big', he gave his assent.

The question of who would command the junk while the raiders were absent was decided by the late appointment to the team of Major Ronald 'Otto' Ingleton, a 28-year-old Royal Marine. A former architect from Wanstead, Ingleton had joined the Marines at the outbreak of war and by October 1940 had his commission. In 1944, after serving in a technical and organisational capacity with an armoured support group, Major Ingleton, by then a married man, left for Ceylon with Detachment 385, a special assault force which was part of the recently formed Small Operations Group. After a brief but intensive course he was seconded to SOE, which immediately appointed him to Rimau as observer for Mountbatten's South-East Asia Command (SEAC). He evidently owed the post to Mountbatten and to Blondie Hasler of SB fame, now instructor and developmental officer for Small Operations Group. With Rimau the first mission to make use of SBs, both men were particularly interested in the outcome. Too late, someone at the planning conference realised that, as Ingleton weighed 108 kilograms, an SB would sink under his weight. Since his appointment had been confirmed and he was already on his way to Australia with seventeen Free Frenchmen recruited for the intended raid on Saigon, Lyon, who had met him and been impressed by his technical expertise, assigned him to take charge of the waiting junk.

With Rimau given the green light, things began to move very quickly. Within twenty-four hours of the final planning conference Donald Davidson had nominated eleven SOA men suitable to join the mission. All had been training for some months at SOA's new and highly secret establishment on Fraser Island off the Queensland coast.

The restructuring of covert organisations the previous year meant that ZES, which was taken over by the Dutch Section of AIB, was no longer available to SOA for training. As special operations (apart from Jaywick, which was SOE/RAN) were in limbo for months, the lack of a proper training school had not been a problem until August 1943, when Chapman-Walker put forward a proposal for thirteen sabotage missions, code-named Falcon. In anticipation that one hundred men would be required for the project, a tropical training establishment which offered both security and specialised facilities had become top priority.

Fraser Island, which offered seclusion, large freshwater lakes and plenty of scope for folboat training, jungle craft and sabotage, was ideal. Given SOA's predilection for choosing obscure names, the decision to call its new establishment Fraser Island Commando School (FCS) is something of a mystery. The school, under canvas and under the command of Jock Campbell, opened for business in October 1943 with an initial intake of thirty soldiers recruited from battalions fighting in New Guinea. In January, when Jock was succeeded by Donald Davidson, who arrived with the first contingent of naval personnel, the school was still very much a tent city. Lieutenant Walter Witt, who had been removed from the Jaywick mission when Carse took over his appointed role, was most unimpressed with the camp facilities, especially the latrines. Accustomed to the amenities offered on a large cruiser, he was disconcerted to discover that on Fraser Island the army expected everyone to sit in a line over pit latrines 'like the front row at the stalls'.

In February a highly specialised intelligence branch known as the School of Eastern Interpreters was formed, dealing mainly in espionage techniques, advanced Malay and communications. As the course required students to have practical experience in undercover work, including built-up areas, in June it was moved from Fraser Island to a new site at Mount Martha, outside Melbourne. By this time Davidson, who had gone to Melbourne in March to oversee the conversion of the country craft, was back again at FCS as chief instructor, the unresolved labour problems having made his task redundant.

The island itself and the adjacent mainland, which was sparsely populated, were perfect for land–sea exercises, while the island's interior with its patches of dense rainforest provided a good jungle-training ground. In the absence of any naval vessels in the nearby deep-water anchorage, a steel transportation barge and the wreck of SS *Maheno*, sunk during a cyclone in December 1935, were used for limpet practice. It was ironic that *Maheno*, a former passenger liner which had been bought for scrap by a Japanese firm and was under tow when the cyclone hit, was now being used as a dummy target for an attack on Japanese vessels. As operational experience improved, more time was devoted to the teaching of Malay for which civilian instructors were employed. Apart from the language lessons the training syllabus was similar to that used at Refuge Bay. Security was absolute, with any breach leading to a quick expulsion, and interaction between trainees kept to a minimum by strictly isolating each intake from the next.

The eleven men selected by Davidson were sent by train to Perth on 7 July. Six days later they and twenty others arrived at Careening Bay Camp on Garden Island, a naval base about 20 kilometres south of Fremantle. The camp, virgin bush just six weeks earlier, had been hurriedly constructed and was still in a raw state, much to the discomfort of its 52-year-old commandant, Lieutenant-Commander Michael Cox, who had come out of retirement in 1940 and been placed on the 'emergency list'. The thirty-one new arrivals were joined by signallers, engineers and other potential operatives, all of whom had been assigned for special duty. Heading the list were operatives Lyon, Davidson, Page (now a married man), Falls, Huston and Marsh, along with Major Ingleton, just arrived from Colombo. The five Jaywick veterans had volunteered immediately. Davidson and Page declared 'We cannot let Ivan go on his own', perhaps summing up the feeling of the entire group. Happy Huston was not the least surprised that Lyon had been selected to lead another raid, or that he had been asked to take part in it. On 27 April, when Davidson had written to congratulate Huston on his DSM, he had signed off with a cryptic 'Hoping you are having a good leave. I have not lost you yet'. Granted a month's leave after the Jaywick mission, Arthur Jones, along with the other four operatives, had transferred to Fraser Island but had become bored. Although Marsh, Huston and Falls had decided to stay when Davidson assured them another operation was in the offing, Berryman and Jones elected to return to general service. Jones was posted to HMAS *Lonsdale* on Melbourne's Port Phillip Bay. Once there, he discovered he had made a poor choice – if Fraser Island was boring, sentry duty at the base was mind-numbingly so. He contacted Davidson and asked to be allowed to return, discovering to his great disappointment that his place had been given to someone else. Jones decided to complete the gunnery course he had abandoned in order to join Jaywick and served out the rest of the war on armed merchant ships.

As part of their training, the Jaywick veterans who had accepted Davidson's invitation were sent to Richmond RAAF base near Sydney to attend a parachute course. With them was John 'Lofty' Hodges, a very tall and very experienced combat soldier who had been seconded to SOA from 2/17 Battalion in 1943 and was now on the short list for Rimau. Accommodation was in canvas tents which, since the base come under control of the air force, were not only roomy but featured comfortable stretchers instead of the rough, straw-filled palliasses so favoured by the army. To add variety to the course the air force had arranged for boxing and wrestling lessons with well-known title-holders Eddie Scarff and Ron McLauglin, who had enlisted in the RAAF. To the sailors' dismay, however, the physical fitness program also included drill under the watchful eye of a regimental sergeant-major. Marching around parade grounds, left-wheeling and right-wheeling, was part and parcel of army life, but drill had never been high on the navy's list of priorities. The half-hearted efforts of the Jaywick men became a source of constant amusement for Hodges, and complete frustration for the RSM, Warrant Officer Norman Teudt. So too was the sailors' habit of draping wet laundry in a most unregulation fashion over the guy ropes of their tents – a transgression which finally ended when Teudt, pushed to the limit of his endurance, bellowed one memorable day, 'If youse blokes keep hangin' yer washin' on the tent lines, I'll ****!!@@ conFISTICate it!'

Parachute training completed, the graduates earmarked for Rimau moved on to Careening Bay. Although only ten more SB operators were needed, each member of the party including the technical experts had to be fit enough to paddle back to Base A from the junk, a distance of more than 100 kilometres, in twelve days. While there was a pool of sixty prospective SB operators, some did not make it beyond the preliminary screening. First to go was anyone with false teeth – the breathing equipment had to be held firmly in the mouth. As the final selection could not take place until the SBs arrived, Davidson, using four hurriedly constructed dummies, put the remainder through a tough elimination program. By 21 July, eight had been scrubbed from the list. Three went the next day, followed by two more on 2 August. When the rest were subjected to an actual sea trial in one of three SBs, extricated with great difficulty from a Melbourne-bound ship a few days later, some hopefuls, including Hodges, could not cope with the claustrophobia and asked to be withdrawn.

John 'Lofty' Hodges, whose problems with claustrophobia during SB training eliminated him from the final Rimau team

Unlike Britain, where there was a lengthy period of familiarisation at well-equipped and specialised bases, training at the makeshift camp was difficult. Not only was the time frame far too tight but Careening Bay did not have proper facilities and there was a shortage of trained instructors. Lieutenant J F Lind-Holmes, who was actually a technical officer, and Lieutenant David Davis, whose students knew more about an SB than he did despite twenty-five years spent handling small craft and some knowledge of diving, did their best, but it was not until 'test pilot' Grigor Riggs arrived from England via the United States on 7 August, accompanied by Bobby Ross, that things improved – a little. Riggs knew how to trim the craft – a function which had eluded the best of them – but although he was an undoubted expert his teaching skills were poor, forcing his pupils to learn the hard way, by trial and error.

There were now forty-five trainees left and some managed better than others. While carrying out a simulated raid on HMAS *Adelaide* on 17 August, Sergeant Harry Browne found his SB was sinking rapidly. He was rescued by Davidson, but decided to give underwater warfare a miss. On the other hand, Private Douglas Warne displayed great natural talent. Finding himself in a similar predicament, he simply drove his craft out backwards, to resurface with relative ease.

Unlike Operation Jaywick, potential recruits knew what to expect. After explaining Jaywick's achievements, Lyon briefed them on Rimau, using a large sand and cement model of the target area. And, like Jaywick, security was extremely tight, with trainees isolated from technical and camp staff to prevent fraternisation and a special officer appointed to enforce other rigid security measures. It was not easy to maintain secrecy away from the camp – the sight of oddly attired English officers wearing strange regimental badges in Fremantle and Perth led to awkward questions, which required adroit fielding. While the trainees were kept on a fairly short leash, some of the bachelors managed, with the help of mates who covered for them, to make frequent forays to a nearby searchlight battery to enjoy the company of the army girls stationed there.

On 10 August, when *Porpoise* arrived from Trincomalee, Ceylon, Commander Marsham was astonished to discover that SOA's planning department expected him to depart within eight hours for a 25-day reconnaissance voyage to the target area (there being no other subs available), return to Fremantle, load the J containers, stores and equipment and then leave on the mission within four days. Fortunately this 'fantastic program' was abandoned when the J containers failed to arrive. Although they had a fast passage to Ceylon on board HMS *Howe*, at Colombo they had been transferred as deck cargo to an incredibly slow merchant ship whose captain obstinately refused to surrender them when the vessel docked in Fremantle. No amount of smooth talking by Lyon could secure their release – they must be delivered to Melbourne, the port listed on the manifest. Until they could be transported back it was not possible to plan the stowage, modify the submarine casing or have a dress rehearsal. On 18 August, with no containers in sight, a dummy version was knocked up by Walter Chapman so that some work could proceed. Thirteen days later, when the elusive containers finally arrived, they were found to be in a deplorable state. The axles and the wheels, which were supposed to run easily along the mine rails, had rusted solid and, in any case, being only 9 centimetres in diameter, were far to small to take the load. The friction created by each container's 2.5 tonne weight was so great that it took eight men, using a double block-and-tackle, to make them budge at all. Even if they were freed, after a few days in salt water they would be completely rusted again. Chapman, not unfairly, was criticised for both the poor design and his failure to realise that steel and salt water are not a good combination. The anticipated departure day was 14 September. Unless some alternative plan could be devised, Rimau would have to be cancelled.

Hubert Marsham came up with the solution – slide the SBs through the submarine's forward hatch and stow them in the empty torpedo compartments, the normal method employed when transporting folboats and canoes. Furthermore, he told an astounded Lyon, who had been informed months ago that such a thing was impossible, should they need to make an emergency dive the hatch could be shut within one minute of the alarm being sounded. The expensive J containers did not go to waste – on the suggestion of a talented Australian engineer, Warrant Officer Alf Warren, eight were recycled into handy storage containers by welding them to the mine casing. This bit of innovative thinking, on the tail of Chapman's fiasco, impressed Marsham, who declared that Warren exhibited 'the finest mechanical flair, for which his countrymen are noted, and, when confronted with a problem he quickly provides a solution so simple that it's a wonder no one thought of it before'.

On 26 August Lyon and Davidson received the final operational plans, which were split into five sections and covered many pages. They were fortunate the instructions were not longer. Had Rimau not been so delayed, they would be diverting to Java to drop off an agent organising another SOA mission, Operation Binatang.

Rimau's plan, unlike Jaywick's, had been worked out to the last detail. Small, densely wooded Merapas Island had been selected as Base A. The most easterly island in the Riau group, Merapas was located off Bintan Island, about 110 kilometres from Singapore. Apart from its good cover and probable lack of habitation, Merapas was within island-hopping distance of the target, with the longest single stretch of open water not exceeding 24 kilometres. Should Merapas not prove suitable, they were to set up an alternative base on one of the nearby islands.

As soon as the 3.5 tonnes of stores had been secreted on Base A, *Porpoise* was to proceed to a shipping channel which ran between southern Borneo and the Riau Archipelago. In the vicinity of Pedjantan Island they were to seize a junk, tow or sail it to a secluded cove and, over the next two nights, unload 11 tonnes of equipment and stores. A derrick, the responsibility of Major Ingleton, would be used to lift the heavy SBs to the deck of the junk.

With the transfer complete, *Porpoise* would return to Australia, refuel and restock, and return to Merapas to pick up the raiding party fifty-eight days from the date of Rimau's original departure. If *Porpoise* did not return on that date, the party was instructed to wait thirty days. If there was still no sign of the submarine, they were to make their own arrangements for an escape. To cater for this eventuality, enough stores to sustain twenty men for three months were to be hidden on Merapas.

Once *Porpoise* had departed, the Rimau men were to sail the junk to Singaporean waters, via the Temiang and Sugi Straits, a distance of 400 kilometres, in six days. At Kapala Jernith, off Batam Island, the vessel would anchor in a bay while two folboat teams under the command of an officer carried out a reconnaissance of Pulau Labon, where it was planned the junk would wait while the attack took place. While one of the recce teams returned to the junk to report on the suitability of Labon, the officer and his partner were to proceed to Subar, the hot little island used as the Jaywick observation post, to observe shipping movements in preparation for the raid that night. As soon as it became dark, this team would paddle back to the junk. Following a final briefing, the SBs would disperse in all directions to attack six main objectives, from Sambu Island to Singapore. Those attacking Bukom wharves, the Western Anchorage, Keppel Harbour and the Mosquito Fleet would use SBs for the entire journey. The four men assigned to the Eastern Anchorage were to tow two folboats to Subar, and hide them there ready for the return journey. This meant that all but five SB operators would make their way back to the junk. The four raiding the Eastern Anchorage would return to Subar, while the sole man attacking Sambu wharves would head for Dongas where his folboat partner (not part of the attack) would be waiting. From there they would begin a long, solitary journey back to Merapas, around the east coast of Batam Island. When the Subar quartet had retrieved their folboats they and the junk group, after sinking the junk and splitting into three parties, would paddle back to base by whichever route they thought best. If all went well, they would all be safely back at Merapas within a fortnight to await the arrival of the submarine.

The logistics to support this ambitious program were immense. Every single item had to be listed, counted, checked and rechecked, measured, weighed and packed, from food to drinking water, clothing to toothpaste, weapons to condoms (to keep rifle barrels and small items dry). There were Bren guns, silent Stens and pistols; metres of flannelette to clean them; an anti-tank gun to repel any attacks on the junk; plastic explosive and limpets; thousands of rounds of ammunition; Boston Mark II radio stations and walkie-talkies; folboats and folding engineers-boats; stoves; kerosene; compasses; maps; knives; binoculars; ordinary rations, iron rations and comfort rations; hammocks; fishing lines; parachute cord for tying up prisoners; medical kits; skin stain; sunglasses; mosquito nets; and dozens of sundry other items, including a substantial amount of money in various currencies suitably crumpled by the Manderson children. The maintenance stores for the SBs, including a vast array of spare parts, had also been carefully worked out, right down to the last drop of oil.

Nothing was left to chance. The latest enemy intelligence had been collated and a Dutch captain carefully quizzed on climatic and maritime conditions. Bobby Ross had even managed to organise some conversation practice with a party of Malays, who had been moved down from Broome and were now attached to Army Water Transport at nearby Sulphur Bay. Lyon's final task was to organise a signal plan. One had been worked out, and was included in Hornbill's documentation, but Lyon had no intention of using it. After listing the times of the listening watch, and the frequencies and other instructions regarding procedures, the memo issued on 12 August stated that the cipher keys and tables would be given to the party leader prior to departure, and that he and whoever he nominated would be briefed personally.

Rejecting the usual cipher keys and tables, even a simple one such as that used on Jaywick, on the grounds they were too risky, Lyon and SOA's cipher clerk Staff-Sergeant Mary Ellis decided on a far simpler method – a one-off code, impossible to break. Selecting two copies of the same book, they chose a page at random and, starting at the top left-hand corner of that page, eliminated every third word. The remaining letters were then assigned chronological numbers. If a message needed to be sent, a number was substituted for each letter, with no breaks to signify the end of any word or any punctuation. It was fast and foolproof. The transmitted signal was nothing more than a string of jumbled numbers, which could easily be deciphered provided the recipient had a copy of the book, the relevant page and the strike-out pattern.

It was now time to select the final team members. The six Jaywick officers and men and Bobby Ross were automatically included as operatives. Right behind them was Grigor

Lieutenant Bobby Ross

Riggs, the cherubic-looking SB expert who had decided it was time to put his skills to a real test. Named James after his father but always known as Grigor, the blue-eyed, fair-haired Riggs was born in Inverness, Scotland in 1923. After obtaining his Leaving Certificate, he joined the Royal Navy and entered Dartmouth Academy. In early March 1943, aged only nineteen, he came to the attention of SOE and four days later was on the payroll.

It was cool-headed Doug Warne's expertise with the SB which ensured he too made the final cut. Warne, a powerfully built exponent of unarmed combat, was described

Left: *Sub-Lieutenant Grigor Riggs, Sleeping Beauty expert* Right: *Private Doug Warne*

by Harry Browne (who had been trapped in the sinking SB) as being 'built like a brick shit house and just as hard to punch a hole through'. A former stationhand whose family came from Ballina on the north coast of New South Wales, Warne was living with his wife's family in Maitland in the NSW Hunter Valley at the time of his enlistment in an armoured regiment in 1941. Tall, and as powerfully built as Falls, he was teaching unarmed combat at the Canungra Jungle Training Camp in Queensland when he was recruited for Rimau in April 1944. Still a private after three years in the army, his lowly rank was no reflection on his talents but the result of his habit of absenting himself without leave for extended periods to visit his then fiancée, resulting in at least two demotions.

Next on the list was the fifth officer operative, Lieutenant Albert Leslie Sargent, a broad-shouldered, tow-headed soldier originally from the Victorian town of Wangaratta. 'Blondie', who was married, had enlisted in the militia in May 1940. Transferring the AIF, he had seen action in the Middle East and on the Kokoda Track in New Guinea before joining SOA at the end of 1943. Like many SOA recruits, he was a trained parachutist. He was also the inventor of the Sargent Adaptor – an ingenious device which produced air bursts at any height, using a 3-inch mortar. Tough and talented, with a warm smile that lit up a ruggedly handsome face, as Sergeant Sargent he had been one of the last soldiers to be commissioned in the field.

Heading the list of NCO operatives was the newly promoted Jeffrey Willersdorf of Essendon, Victoria. Of average height and with a strong build, the fair-haired soldier was a former clerk. He had been in the army for two years when he joined SOA in November 1943,

Lieutenant Albert 'Blondie' Sargent

Warrant Officer Jeffrey Willersdorf

completing his parachute training shortly afterwards. Although under age when he enlisted, his youthful, fresh-faced complexion had gone unquestioned by the recruiting officer. Also

Corporal Pat Campbell

selected were two army corporals, Archie Gordon Patrick Campbell (known to his family as Pat, and his army friends as Paddy) who came from Dalby, Queensland, and Dublin-born Roland Bernard Fletcher.

An excellent horseman, Campbell had joined 11 Light Horse (militia) Regiment commanded by his father, a highly decorated World War I soldier, and had spent about eighteen months jackarooing in the outback before enlisting in the AIF in June 1940. In September 1942, while fighting at the battle of El Alamein in North Africa with 2/15 Battalion, he sustained a superficial bullet wound to his lower back. After serving in New Guinea, he volunteered for covert operations on learning that his brother was a prisoner of the Japanese. He joined SOA in

Corporal Roland Fletcher

November 1943, three days after Warne and, like him, was also a qualified parachutist. Campbell, aged twenty-four and now a very experienced soldier, was one of the many to be captivated by Lyon, describing him as 'the most wonderful man I have ever met ... not only did he appear to know everything but he could do everything associated wit the job for which we were trained – perfectly'. Before leaving on the mission he confided to his family that, while he could reveal nothing about what he was doing, he could say with complete confidence that Ivan Lyon was 'a leader for whom every one of us would be willing to die'.

Pat's fellow corporal, 'Ron' Fletcher, had entered special operations in a slightly less conventional fashion. One of seven children, he was the third son of a talented English writer and actor and his Irish born-wife, an equally talented singer and artist who happened to be working in Dublin when Roland was born. The Great Depression hit the family hard, and in November 1929 three of the four younger boys emigrated from Liverpool to Fairbridge Farm at Pinjarra, Western Australia, under the sponsorship of the Child Emigration Scheme. Ron, described as 'fearless', was a well-built lad, bright, well-educated, intelligent and not yet fourteen years old. Like his brothers, all of whom had acting experience, he had no trace of an Irish accent and his voice was not only well modulated but beautifully rounded.

The farm to which the boys were sent was named after a Rhodes Scholar, Kingsley Fairbridge, who conceived the idea in 1912 to provide poor children with a way of life. Unlike some other establishments the Fairbridge Farms were well run by compassionate and caring staff, who housed the three Fletcher boys in the one cottage so that they could be together. Twelve months later they were joined by their youngest brother, aged eleven. In 1932, when Ron was fifteen, the farm arranged employment for him on Karratha Station near Roebourne in the northern part of the state, where he remained for three years until transferring to nearby Warrambie Station. Although obedient and well-behaved, Ron was not cut out for farming, something the Fairbridge Farms principal recognised by helping him enrol in a commercial art course with Stott's Correspondence School in Melbourne. He was partway through his first year of instruction when he obtained employment with a storekeeper in Cossack, the port for Roebourne – a position which suited him and which was financially far more rewarding than farming. He was also far busier. Although keen, and determined to succeed in his art course,

Members of the Northern Australia Observer Unit, also known as the Nackeroos

Ron was thwarted not only by his workload but also by the remoteness of his situation, where mail arrived by sea only every six weeks. After a year of frustration he quit his studies, for which he had shown considerable talent. In 1937, now aged twenty-one, he left the protection of Fairbridge and joined the merchant marine. After four years at sea he jumped ship in Sydney and reported to Victoria Barracks in Sydney, where he and his brother Terry enlisted in the AIF, two days before Christmas 1941. The following August he was recruited to the Northern Australia Observer Unit, more commonly known as the 'Nackeroos'.

Having spent years of his life in the outback, the job appealed to Ron's adventurous nature. These hand-picked men patrolled the northern coastline of the continent on horseback with orders to watch for signs of enemy activity and to remain behind the lines in the event of an invasion. Armed with Bren guns and rifles, they were the country's only protection, apart from the garrison at Darwin, in a line which stretched from the Gulf of Carpentaria to the Kimberly coast in Western Australia. Forced by erratic supply lines to live off the land, the Nackeroos became extremely self-reliant, remaining isolated for months in locations described by Fletcher's CO as 'the arsehole of the world', until the threat of invasion passed. Unfortunately, this band of practical and hardened individuals, who could have been put to excellent use at SOA, was disbanded in 1943.

Corporal John Hardy

Another pair of corporals, John Thomas (Jack)

Hugo Pace, a keen rower

Hardy and Hugo Pace, filled the last two places in the operational team. Twenty-three-year-old Hardy, born in Narrabri in country New South Wales, had been earning his living as a lorry driver and boot repairer when he joined the militia in November 1941. Posted to the Army Service Corps, he found that his exciting new job was driving lorries. Nine months later while serving in the Northern Territory he requested a transfer to the AIF, this time describing himself as a 'storeman'. The subterfuge did him no good – his new job was driving lorries with 140 Australian General Transport Company. Finally in November 1943, after somehow managing to undertake parachute training, he fulfilled his ambition to see some real action by joining SOA.

Unlike Hardy, Hugo Pace's life had been fairly exciting. Born in Port Said to French-Egyptian parents, Hugo grew into a fine-looking young man with an excellent physique, honed to a high level by rowing and playing soccer. He had been working as a clerk in a travel agency when in 1934, aged twenty-one and inspired by his father's stories of Australian soldiers he had met in World War I, he had taken a clerical post at Kooincal, an outback station near Biloela, Queensland. After war broke out in Europe his family, whom he was visiting, had begged him to stay in Egypt and not get involved in 'somebody else's' war but by March 1941 he was back in Rockhampton, Queensland, where he enlisted in the AIF. Six months later he was on his way to the Middle East, where he served with 2/12 Battalion before returning to Australia in mid-1942 for redeployment in New Guinea. In January the following year he was wounded in action, sustaining bullet wounds to his lower arm, thigh and buttock. After a period of convalescence, he returned to New Guinea where he was detached for special duty in October 1943 and flown south to join SOA, on the same day as Pat Campbell. Of above average height, the olive-skinned, dark-eyed Pace was a favourite with the searchlight girls. Noted for his smart appearance and his exceptional fitness, which included a 16-kilometre run before breakfast, he traded on his somewhat exotic background, telling anyone who cared to ask that the large scar on his thigh, actually caused by a Japanese bullet, was from a wound

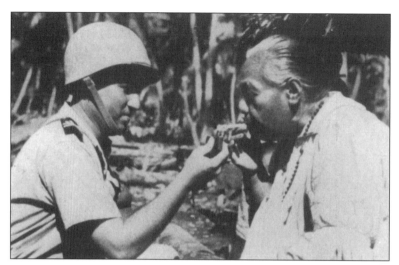

Lieutenant Bruno Reymond lights a cigarette for a newly liberated Gilbert Islander while on secondment to the US Navy's Amphibious Force, 1943

sustained while serving with the Foreign Legion.

The remaining five members of the team were all specialists. The most important by far was Gilbert Islander Bruno Philp Reymond, navigator and master mariner. Born in 1914 at Tetabuki on the island of Makin to an islander mother and a Swiss doctor-turned-merchant-mariner father, Bruno had joined the merchant marine in 1930 at the age of sixteen. By 1943, with thirteen years' experience behind him and a first mate's ticket, he was shuttling war equipment and troops on the Australia–New Guinea cargo run, operated by his namesake and his father's previous employer, Burns Philp. It was by no means plain sailing. On one trip, between Lae and Port Moresby, his ship was attacked and the captain killed, giving Reymond the responsibility of bringing the vessel and the troops on board back to Australia.

In October 1943, with the Americans preparing to invade the Japanese-occupied Gilbert Islands, he was recruited by Australian-born Lieutenant-Commander Gerhard Heinrich Heyen, RAN, a friend of the Reymond family who had lived in the Gilbert Islands pre-war. Mentioned in despatches while serving on HMS *Kanimbla* in 1941, the lieutenant-commander was now attached to the American forces who would later award him a US Legion of Merit. Bruno and fifteen other foreign seamen and civilians, recruited by Heyen to act as pilots, nautical advisers and interpreters for Admiral Richmond Turner's US Amphibious Force, were dubbed 'the Foreign Legion'.

Operation Galvanic, which began on 21 November 1943, resulted ten days later in the successful reoccupation of the Gilberts and the liberation of the islanders, including Bruno's parents, whom he presumed had been killed or taken prisoner – the fate of most Europeans. But by displaying his tattered Swiss passport and greeting the Japanese with a 'Heil Hitler', Bruno's ageing father Maurice, now almost blind from malnutrition, had convinced the occupying enemy force that he was friend, not foe. After a joyful reunion with his family,

Warrant Officer Alf Warren

Sergeant Colin Cameron

Reymond moved to Pearl Harbor in preparation for the reoccupation of the Marshall Islands in February. On his return to Australia, he obtained his master's certificate in May and the following month was seconded to SOA. His first appointment as ship's captain was in late July to HMAS *Alatna*, a sea-ambulance launch retained for SOA work in Darwin. Shortly after his arrival Bruno went down with mumps, and as soon as he had recovered was transferred to Careening Bay to join Operation Rimau.

He was to replace Lieutenant Richard Cox (one of those who had escaped with Lyon on *Sederhana Djohanes*), who had arrived with Ross and Riggs to take up the post of navigator and captain of the junk but had proved unsuitable. Reymond's late arrival on 6 September, just five days before departure, meant he had to cram a two-month folboat and training course into just four days. Every morning at 8 o'clock he was hustled off by Lieutenant Walter Carey, brother of *Scorpion*'s notorious Sam Carey, returning eighteen weary hours later at 2 am. It was a great shock to Reymond, who enjoyed his creature comforts, but Carey's tactics worked and his pupil was pronounced fit. With his extensive maritime experience, dark part-islander looks and intimate knowledge of the waterways to Australia's north, Bruno was the answer to Lyon's prayers.

So too was Port Pirie's talented engineer, 31-year-old Warrant Officer Alf Warren, whose resourcefulness was so admired by Hubert Marsham. Warren was not only resourceful, he was a highly qualified mechanic, having obtained 87 per cent in both his written and practical exams at the end of a tank course, a score which gave him a 'distinguished' grade, qualified him as an instructor and prompted the additional endorsement 'mechanical knowledge is extensive'.

Junior to Warren, but almost as good a technician, was 21-year-old Colin Cameron. Born in Wedderburn, Victoria, he had spent much of his youth at Hamilton in the state's beautiful Western District. Cameron, seconded to SOA on 1 July, the same day as Warren, had given up his job as electrical powerhouse assistant to join the militia in December 1940. He was posted to 26 Machine Gun Regiment but in July 1492, on enlisting in the AIF, was transferred to 227 Light Aid Detachment, a unit dedicated to keeping equipment and trucks in repair. The 180-centimetre, strapping young man enjoyed army life so much he had announced his intention to sign on after the war.

Sergeant David Peter Gooley, born in Terang in southern Victoria's sheep district, was an out-of-work woollen worker living in Melbourne when he joined the militia in 1940. After attending an instructors' course at Bonegilla he was sent to the Guerrilla Warfare School near Foster in May 1942. Four months later, now citing his occupation as an 'iron moulder', he enlisted in the AIF and transferred to the Commando Training School at Canungra four months later. In June 1944, after trying for almost two years to take on something more challenging than instructing, he was finally seconded to SOA and the following month travelled from Fraser Island to Fremantle with Fletcher and Warne. Gooley was considered a 'good bloke' but, being very religious, took a dim view of lewd jokes and the vivid recounting of female conquests by some of his companions. When the conversation turned too blue for his liking, he would turn the photograph of his fiancée face down on the bed, remarking, 'I don't think you should hear this, dear'.

Two signallers from Western Australia occupied the last two places on the Rimau team. The most senior, in age if not in rank, was 35-year-old Clair Mack Stewart, who should not even have been in the armed forces – his age, married status and a reserved occupation working for the State Railways being sufficient to keep him out of the war. Stewart, however, had other ideas. Rejected by the air force because of less than perfect eyesight, he tried the AIF, which was please to sign him on in August 1941, reading glasses and all. Stewart trained as a signaller, attaining such proficiency that SOA, ignoring his spectacles, recruited him on 19 November 1943, the same day as Doug Warne. Like Warne, Stewart was in superb physical condition, his body hardened by years of hard outdoor labour and his neck muscles threatening to burst his collar buttons. Stewart arrived for SB training at Careening Bay on 31 July, after completing parachute training with Pace, Campbell and fellow signaller, Colin Craft.

Quiet and exceptionally even-tempered, Corporal Craft, aged twenty-five, had given up his job of schoolteacher to enlist in April 1941. On completing his signals course he was looking forward to embarking on an exciting new career as a signaller in the field – but found that when he wasn't criss-crossing Australia from one state to another, attached to sundry units, he spent most of his time mowing grass. Bored witless, he had jumped at the chance

Corporal Clair Stewart *Corporal Colin Craft*

of joining a 'different and dangerous outfit', resulting in his secondment to SOA in December 1943. The son of a well-known Perth organist, Edwin 'Cheddar' Craft who spent many years teaching music at Wesley College, Colin was an accomplished pianist and violinist. Although no longer able to play with the ABC orchestra once he joined the army, Colin became a well-known figure at Careening Bay where he wandered around playing tunes on his rather battered violin, from which he was inseparable.

Apart from Warren and Cameron, who were listed as 'experts', all the army personnel, including Corporal Ron Croton who had not made the final cut, were classified as 'Special Raiding Section, on loan to Westops' (SRD). There were also four men on standby: Captain W Edgar, Sub-Lieutenant D H Jarvis and two 'local' operatives, Corporals Mohamed Sharif and Abu Kassim. The twenty-two men finally selected for the mission were to be accompanied to Merapas by two 'conducting' officers, Major Walter Chapman from SOE HQ and Captain Walter Carey, the SOA instructor who had pummelled Bruno Reymond into shape in record time. Their task was to report on the submarine sortie, familiarise themselves with Base A for the pick-up phase, photograph the crew of the pirated junk, take charge of any papers seized and escort the captives back to Australia.

Chapman's colleague, Wal Carey, spent his early childhood on a small, poverty-stricken farm at Campbelltown outside Sydney, and his adolescence in the suburb of Hurlstone Park where his mother ran a corner store. In 1931, at the age of eighteen and working as a clerk, he joined the militia, serving for just under a year with 56 Battalion. In 1935, then aged twenty-

Lieutenant Walter Carey, Rimau's conducting officer

two, he was lured to Aitape, New Guinea where he worked in Charlie Gough's Trade Store before trying his hand at planting. Four years later, in July 1940 he joined the AIF and within seven months was on his way to Malaya with 2/19 Infantry Battalion. After undergoing jungle warfare training with the rest of his brigade, he volunteered for special service in China as a member of Mission 204, known as Tulip Force. Despite high hopes, this somewhat elite unit saw no action and Carey returned to Australia in November 1942, the incursion into China saving him from capture when Singapore fell. In August 1943, after spending some months at Canungra with a training battalion, interrupted by a short stint at the Allied Geographical Section preparing terrain manuals for New Guinea, he was posted to 2/2 Infantry Battalion as lieutenant and, within three months, on his brother Sam's urging, joined SOA. Known as 'Massa' because of his colourful reminiscences of his life in New Guinea, the brown-eyed, lean and wiry lieutenant was filled with the blarney that sets the Irish apart. His capacity to tell the most outrageous but utterly convincing tales with a completely straight face was legendary. So was his dry sense of humour, which gave him perhaps his most admirable trait – the ability to see the funny side of everything.

The team had barely been selected when something occurred which was no laughing matter. Someone had talked. It was the age-old problem – loose talk by a person who should have known better, in this case Lieutenant-Commander Geoffrey Branson, head of SOA's naval directorate. Now aged forty-three, Branson had served in the Royal Navy until his retirement in 1929, but had signed on again in 1939 with the RAN, serving with distinction in the Persian Gulf and at Milne Bay in New Guinea. In November 1943 he joined Naval Intelligence and the following February was temporarily 'loaned' to SOA to carry out 'special duties'. SOE chief Sir Colin Gubbins held him in high regard, doubtless impressed by his long naval service and the MID awarded in 1942 for 'courage, enterprise and devotion to duty'. SOA's Spencer Chapman, also impressed by Branson's 'good grasp of his profession', predicted that he would be 'invaluable' as SOA's naval commitments increased.

He was wrong on both counts. Although Branson's courage had not recently been put to the test, the other attributes mentioned on his citation most certainly had, and were now found to be woefully lacking. Not only had he been loose-lipped on the troop train about the limpets for Rimau which he and Denis Emerson-Elliott were escorting to Perth, but on arrival he had committed two serious breaches of security in a very short space of time. Knowing that Rimau was soon to leave he had strolled up to Commander Marsham, standing on the dock alongside *Porpoise*, and announced, 'I hear you are off to Singapore'. Marsham, stressed and war-weary from too many patrols, went immediately to his commanding officer, Captain Shadwell of 8 Submarine Flotilla, who then informed Lyon, staying with Admiral Christie at the US naval officers' mess. When it was learned there had been a third, and far worse, security breach, Shadwell announced that Rimau would have to be cancelled.

It had occurred in Perth's Peppermint Grove Hotel when an American woman, whom Branson had just met, asked him about Ivan Lyon. Ignoring the wartime slogan, 'loose lips sink ships', he had disclosed everything, including the location of the target. The woman informed her boss, Admiral Christie, and the panic was on. Confronted by SOA's Captain John Ellis, who ran him to earth at the officers' quarters in Perth's Esplanade Hotel, Branson confirmed his indiscretion. Shadwell's and Marsham's immediate reaction was to scrap the entire mission. However, Lyon's persuasive reasoning that Branson's secondment to SOA required him to know about Rimau and that the information to the American had definitely stopped with his close friend and ally Admiral Christie, finally won the day. On 6 September, with 'considerable misgivings', Shadwell, acting on behalf of Mountbatten, gave the operation its final approval. Had he known that about a week later, yet another breach by Branson would be uncovered, he would never have given his consent.

This fourth indiscretion had occurred when a naval officer, later identified as Branson, visited the Navy's boat yard at Williamstown where *Tiger Snake*, the first of the specialised country (or snake) craft was being outfitted. In the course of idle chatter, Branson had told one of the workers about raids on shipping using limpet mines – information so secret that Jock Campbell personally pursued the source and extent of the leak. After considerable agonising it was decided not to recall Rimau, as the information did not affect the operation directly. Branson, in disgrace, had his 'loan' to SOA terminated – but not before he tried to implicate both Bob Page and Donald Davidson in the whole sorry mess.

On 5 September, with news of the Williamstown breach not yet known to SOA and while the current security question was still unresolved, Lyon confidently confirmed a trial run scheduled for that night. As soon as it was dark, all the stores required for Base A were transferred from the submarine in folding engineers-boats and hidden ashore – an exercise which took a total of two and a half hours, the actual unloading from *Porpoise* accounting for just twenty minutes. The following two nights, with the mission now confirmed, they practised offloading the SBs and the stores for the junk using the vessel *Nicol Bay* as a stand-in for the native craft. The exercise went without a hitch and Lyon was delighted with the timing – less than two hours. The third night they carried out a dummy raid, using *Porpoise* as the target when winds whipped up the seas, making it impossible to attack HMAS *Adelaide* as planned.

With the dress rehearsals an outstanding success the departure date was fixed for 11 September, giving the team time to write letters home and for Stewart, the only one who lived nearby, to slip away to see his wife Juanita and farewell his peacefully sleeping children. Hugo Pace made a visit to the searchlight battery where he had his photograph taken with a girl on each arm, while Andrew Huston sent a message to his family, telling them that he was going away for a lengthy training exercise but to have everything ready, including a cake, to celebrate his twenty-first birthday on Christmas Day.

With two days to go, Lyon, Chapman, Shadwell and Marsham discussed the timetable and the pick-up procedure from Merapas, as outlined in 'Fremantle Submarine Operational Order No. 1'. When Marsham, still worrying about the security breach and possibly in the hope that Rimau might yet be cancelled, announced that the submarine might not be able to pick them up, Lyon replied, 'In that case, we shall find some other method of getting back.' Such was Ivan's air of quiet confidence, Shadwell never doubted for one minute that he would not be able to do it.

That night, with the operational stores loaded, there was a party. Held in a large marquee filled with tables groaning with good food, the Rimau team was farewelled by the crews of *Porpoise* and the visiting submarine *Sea Wolf*, the staff from the Garden Island Naval Base, SOA officials and the girls from the searchlight battery. When the evening had reached the lively stage one of the guests, Lieutenant Williams, produced a white handkerchief from the pocket of his naval uniform and invited Lyon and his tigers to record their names for posterity with the aid of an indelible pencil, moistened in puddles of beer. Not to be outdone, another guest produced a Dutch bank note, which was similarly autographed. The following morning, with instructions from Hugo Pace and Rimau's other Lotharios to their shore-based mates to 'look after the girls on the hill', and recovered from the good cheer of the previous night, the men boarded the submarine where Dr Balforth, Royal Marines, issued each one with a small bakelite capsule containing a lethal dose of potassium cyanide. The officers hoped they would not need to be used. Rather than order anyone to take cyanide, they would do what they had planned for Jaywick, had anything gone wrong – shoot 'the boys' and then kill themselves.

At 20 minutes past noon on 11 September the great grey submarine slipped silently and unobtrusively from her mooring and into Cockburn Sound. Within her massive iron hull were twenty-two men committed to serving King and Country. Completely unaware that Operation Rimau was primarily a means to a political end, and that they were mere pawns in a game played for high stakes, it was just as well that they could not read the thoughts

Hugo Pace with two of the searchlight girls,
Lorraine Taylor (left) and Kath Derby,
September 1944

of Hubert Marsham, plagued by doubts and grave misgivings. The entire operation reminded him of a similar raid, centuries before, when swashbuckling Englishman Sir Francis Drake under the patronage of Admiral Hawkins had sneaked into Cadiz harbour and, to the lasting humiliation of the hitherto invincible Spanish Navy, had set fire to the Spanish Fleet. After 'singeing the King of Spain's beard', as Drake's daring feat became known, he destroyed the entire Armada.

While the colourful Sir Francis had earned for himself a lasting place in British history, Marsham was a seasoned warrior, an old campaigner who knew that in war coups such as the Rimau men were attempting required more than raw courage and great daring. They needed an element of luck, a foolproof plan and a fail-proof back-up system. Recalling the dramas, the plan alterations, the make-do solutions and the many problems which had beset the mission to date, the submarine captain recorded:

The whole business smacks of the days of Drake and Hawkins, an ambitious, daredevil scheme proposed by a band of very gallant gentlemen; support and backing from high places and senior officers afloat but hopelessly marred by muddle and inefficiency [and by] self-seeking and obstruction from those locally responsible for the supply and transport of stores and equipment.

These thoughts would haunt Commander Hubert Marsham for the rest of his life.

11
To Singapore

11 September–11 October 1944

After the dramas and uncertainties of the preceding few days, the six-day voyage up the coast of Western Australia and into the Java Sea was entirely uneventful. The submarine followed a zigzagging course, submerging only when in range of enemy aircraft. Apart from a lone junk which they spotted as they passed through the northern narrows of the Lombok Strait, they saw nothing of interest, and there was no sign of the patrol boat which had paced *Krait* the year before. Indeed, there was no sign of the enemy at all until they neared the Kangean Islands, where a few aircraft flew overhead from the direction of Surabaya.

If Ivan Lyon gave any thought to this ramshackle, rather grubby little Javanese settlement, it was most likely passing – his attention only drawn to its existence by the presence of the aeroplanes. He had no idea that, less than 160 kilometres to the south, rotting in the sandy soil of a carelessly filled, hastily dug grave, lay the mortal remains of his friend William Roy Reynolds.

In November 1943, at about the same time as Ivan and his team were partying in Brisbane and toasting their success, the man who had been the catalyst for Operation Jaywick had headed north, following the route taken by *Krait* only weeks before. Unaware that his old fishing boat had even left Australia, Bill Reynolds entered a world which, to him, was completely alien. The invigorating tang of a salt-laden breeze and the rhythmical slap of waves against *Krait's* timber hull had been replaced by stale, warm, recycled air, the almost indistinguishable purr of far-off diesel engines and clammy, confining, iron walls running with condensation. Bill Reynolds, secret agent, was in the bowels of USS *Tuna*, an American submarine.

Safe and anonymous below the surface, *Tuna* had headed for Borneo's south-easterly tip, surfacing at the entrance of the Macassar Straits. About 3 kilometres to the west was Laut Island, Reynolds' destination. In the guise of procuring a junk loaded with quinine and rubber for black-market operations, Reynolds' mission was to make contact with Chinese agents operating in the area. Once he had obtained vital information and intelligence using the vast amounts of money placed at his disposal, he was to make his way back to Exmouth Gulf in the trading vessel. Reynolds was not the slightest bit fazed that this was a solo mission, and a risky one at that, evidently dismissing it as no more dangerous than any other task he had undertaken since the fall of Singapore. At 10.20 on the night of 14 November a handful of openly admiring submariners had watched as the lone Australian who, at fifty-one was older than many of their fathers, stepped into his small dinghy and paddled into the night without a backward glance. Three days later, his presence betrayed to the Japanese by local collaborators, he was captured at the village of Kota Bahru.

He was taken 270 kilometres north of Laut to Balikpapan, on the mainland, where he was imprisoned in Sentosa Barracks, a small building converted into a gaol. During the next three months, aware that his prospects were not bright, he had carefully and methodically scratched into the painted door jamb of his cell his personal details as well as a sketch of a slouch hat, evidently in the hope that someone would recognise this very Australian icon. His last entry was dated 10 February 1944 when, in chilling contrast to his normally meticulously neat printing, he hastily scrawled the message that he was being taken to Surabaya.

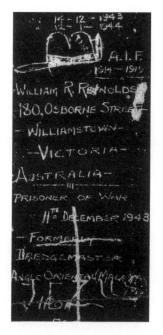

Details scratched onto the door jamb of Bill Reynold's cell in Balikpapan. He included the slouch hat to readily identify himself as Australian

On arrival he was handed over to the Rikkei Tai (Land Garrison Unit) which conducted its unsavoury business at 116 and 118 Sumatrastraat. For the next six months, apart from a period between May and June while undergoing interrogation, Reynolds was confined to Guben Prison, formerly part of the Dutch Naval Barracks and now a detention centre for 21 Special Base Unit, part of 2 South Seas Fleet. Because of his fluency in Malay and Chinese, Reynolds was allowed no contact with any person, Indonesian or European. His command of Malay was so fluent that the Japanese guards believed he was of mixed race.

Accommodation in the gaol was limited and arrests frequent. On 8 August orders were issued to clear the cells in the usual way – by executing the prisoners. At 8 that morning, without any trial whatsoever, Reynolds, and a number of Indonesians found guilty of stealing telegraph wire from the Eastern Fort and the nearby Naval Garrison Unit, were hustled out of the gaol and bundled into a truck. Thirty minutes later they and a second truck carrying a detachment of guards arrived at the execution ground – a stretch of wasteland about 200 metres from the Eastern Fort of the harbour, which the Japanese had renamed Higashiguchi Battery.

The prisoners, handcuffed and blindfolded, were ordered to squat down in front of a hut and wait. Shortly afterwards three Europeans, also bound and blindfolded, arrived from the stockade accompanied by an interpreter and three guards. Despite their frequency, executions always aroused considerable interest, so there was a good-sized gallery. Among the fifty or so onlookers were Lieutenant Yoshimoto who had issued the execution order; his assistant Ensign Okada, one of those who had accompanied Reynolds from the gaol; the legal officer representing the court which had sentenced the Indonesians; interpreter Senuma; Warrant Officer Ikeda; five armed soldiers; officers from the Surabaya Naval Base and a hotchpotch mixture of officers, NCOs and ordinary troops passing through Surabaya who had decided to while away some time. To one side of the spectators was a freshly dug pit about 2 metres wide and 2 metres deep.

After Sumida read out the death sentence in Malay, all but one of those who understood the language had been reduced to a state of shock verging on collapse. Numbed by terror, the first batch of Indonesians kneeled meekly beside the pit while eager volunteers from the rank and file cut off their heads. With rank amateurs volunteering, the executions were neither swift nor clean. The volunteer assigned to the third or fourth prisoner was so inept that his victim was only partially decapitated. Annoyed by the display of extremely bad swordsmanship, Lieutenant Yamamoto ordered Yamashita, a clerk attached to the naval unit, to finish off the unfortunate prisoner with a spear resting against the wall of the hut. His hand trembling uncontrollably, Yamashita failed miserably at the first attempt, succeeding only in inflicting a wound below the left shoulder blade. Forced to continue, he finally manage to deliver a coup de grace by spearing the writhing victim through the heart.

The three remaining Indonesians were by now incapable of standing or squatting. Unable to carry out any further decapitations without reducing the proceedings to an even more bizarre spectacle, the Japanese shot them where they had collapsed. With the three Europeans soon dispatched, the Japanese turned their attention to the remaining prisoner, Bill Reynolds. Dressed in tattered shirt and shorts, his hair and beard long and grey from his lengthy incarceration, the 'elderly' Australian stood rigidly at attention, making it abundantly clear that he, uncowed after months of privation, had no intention of assisting his captors with their grisly task. With the eyes of a now very interested gallery upon him, Yamamoto was forced to reassess the situation.

Clearly, here was a man who would not concede an inch – a prisoner who, even in the face of death, was so iron-willed and fearless that he would never bend before captors who, standing fully erect, scarcely reached his chest. Mindful that the botched executions had already caused a humiliating loss of face, Lieutenant Yamamoto issued fresh orders to a detachment of six guards. Forming a line, they raised their rifles and opened fire. Alone on that open killing ground, watched by an audience which expected him to crack at any moment, Bill Reynolds outfaced his enemy. Unyielding to the end, he crumpled only when the volley of shots forced the life from his body.

As it would be five years before anyone had any inkling of Reynolds' fate, and another forty-six before the true circumstances of his death were uncovered[1], Ivan Lyon, unaware that his old comrade had even left Australia, glided on, past Surabaya.

The following day, 20 September, Marsham sighted three small merchant ships but refrained from firing his torpedoes as the targets were of little consequence and they were also too close to the Karimata Strait. Once through the strait, they saw some local vessels but not, Lyon and Davidson observed, in the numbers of the previous year. When *Porpoise*, now travelling on the surface, approached one junk in the same way as an enemy submarine by crossing its bows, the crew responded by giving a demonstration of the local boat drill. Up went the Port Registration of Singapore Flag (a white pennant with grey lines, a red star and oriental characters) and the more familiar 'poached egg' of the Japanese ensign, confirming that the flags Rimau had brought with them, sewn from fabric dyed in the family bathtub by the dextrous Mrs Manderson, were spot on. Davidson, taking a long hard look at the vessel, its sails and rigging, cargo and crew, made an annotated sketch in his diary for AIB intelligence.

After two days spent locating and rectifying troublesome oil leaks which threatened to betray their presence when submerged, they reached Merapas on the afternoon of 23 September, right on schedule. While *Porpoise* circled the island about 2000 metres offshore, Lyon and Davidson conducted a reconnaissance through the periscope. Apart from what appeared to be a couple of crude huts near a small plantation, two small canoes and a sole figure wandering along the western shore, the island did not seem to be permanently inhabited. As it was far too risky to surface in daylight to allow a party to go ashore and explore further, the submarine headed out to sea to wait until dark.

At 6.45 pm, to his great disappointment, Marsham spotted an 8000-tonne tanker. As their proximity to Merapas prevented any attack, he observed wryly that Rimau's score was now 8000 tonnes in arrears. An hour later they surfaced off Merapas. However, as no one had realised that the new Australian folboat, being larger than the English model, could not fit through the hatch while erected, there was a delay of twenty minutes while an unassembled boat was passed to Davidson and Stewart, who erected it on the hull. As soon as this task was completed *Porpoise* dived and the pair paddled off, with just twenty-four hours to complete a detailed examination of the island.

Thwarted by strong rip tides, ninety precious minutes passed and they still had not reached the shore. They eventually succeeded in edging the boat towards the northern coast which, although rocky and with a good-sized swell running, was an improvement on the windy western approach, where breakers were pounding on the beach. After slipping and sliding across glassy black boulders, they slung their hammocks between a couple of dead trees which had toppled against each other to form a wigwam-like arrangement. Sleep, however, eluded them – the 'scented peace of the island' with the aroma of 'flowering trees and lily palms more delicate than any scent that ever came out of Paris' being far too abrupt after the close confines of the submarine. When the new day dawned they began their exploration, moving in a clockwise direction from the Hammock Tree, midway along the northern shoreline.

The distinctively shaped triangular island, 8 kilometres from Pulau Mapur, has roughly the shape of the head and neck of a greyhound, with the rugged northern coast representing the animal's flat nose and forehead, the eastern side the back of its neck and the long curving south-western shore the lower jaw and throat. Davidson dubbed the northern side, which rose steeply from the rocks, Invasion Coast, with the rocky bump which could be the greyhound's ear becoming Oyster Point. The hundreds of land crabs scuttling behind the three eastern beaches – one sandy, one coralline and the third a mixture of the two – gave the bay its name, while the rocks at the southernmost point were named in honour of Corporal Stewart. Behind Stewart Point was a banana plantation and a little further round, on the first of the south-westerly beaches, a small, abandoned dwelling. Midway along this coast, which offered the gentlest terrain and easiest approach, were the two small huts and canoes which Davidson and Lyon had seen through the periscope. As the mooring stakes inside a small reef appeared to be permanent fixtures for the canoes, they named it Kolek Bay. Immediately behind the huts on a large area of flat land was a coconut plantation and alongside it a large depression filled with tussock grass and extremely thick undergrowth, covered with a blanket of creepers. It appeared to be an old swamp, so choked with vegetation it was no longer marshy but still providing fresh water from the now underground stream. Mosquito-free, it was an ideal place to hide and so became Cache Swamp. Adjoining the swamp area was another small coral beach, backed by a grove of wild sago palms, whose large hairy trunks and low-sprouting fronds created an excellent place to secrete the folboats. Beyond the beach the rocks returned to form a point they named Punai, the Malay name for a pigeon or dove. As they made their way along the northern coast towards the Hammock Tree which marked the end of their circumnavigation, they saw a kingfisher sitting near a large overhanging tree, which gave rise to Kingfisher's Rest.

Apart from the flat area behind Kolek Bay, the interior was far more elevated. The highest point, about 90 metres above sea level, was home to a stumpy-tailed Malayan wild cat which prompted the unimaginative Wild Cat Hill. From the summit the terrain shelved gently towards Punai Point in one direction, passing through an old coconut grove which Davidson pronounced an excellent night camp, while a long arm ran towards Stewart Point in the other.

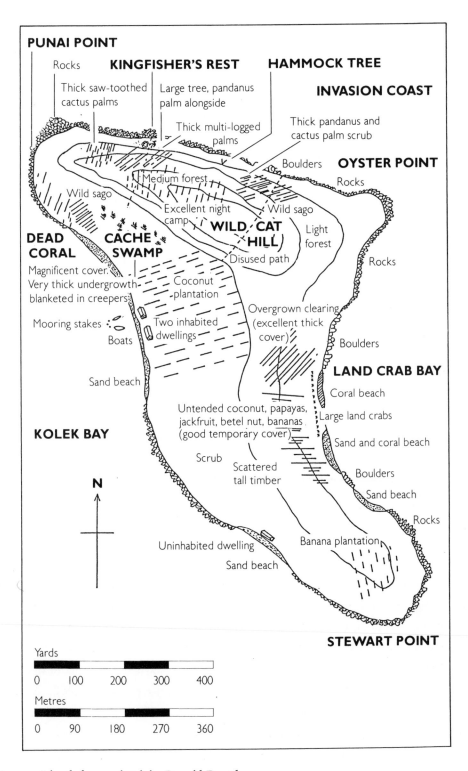

Merapas Island, from a sketch by Donald Davidson

On the ridge behind Land Crab Bay was an overgrown clearing providing very good cover, with the vegetation thinning to scattered tall timber near the banana plantation at Stewart Point. Between this more sparsely forested area and Land Crab Bay was a veritable Garden of Eden, filled with betel nut trees, banana and coconut palms, jack fruit and papayas. Best of all, it was inhabited only by flying foxes.

Their reconnaissance complete, they returned to the Hammock Tree at sunset to await the return of the submarine. Although dark, they had no trouble spotting her silhouette as she surfaced off Invasion Coast. Twenty minutes later, smelling strongly of the jungle, they were reporting their discoveries to Lyon. On learning that locals were visiting the island, he made an amendment to the plan. To preclude any possibility of anyone stumbling on stores, Conducting Officer Wal Carey, armed with a silent Sten and a pistol, would remain on the island while the raiding party was away.

The briefing over, Sargent, Gooley, Campbell, Craft, Fletcher and Warne went into a well-rehearsed drill to erect the two engineers-boats which, being so heavy that they needed ten men to lift and six to paddle them, had been folded flat and secured to the hull of the submarine. While everyone else waited below, the six men stood on the heavy wooden base and erected the boat around themselves. The submarine submerged, allowing the boat to drift off. The crew rowed back to the submarine, which had now resurfaced, and repeated the procedure with the second boat. The rest of the team then began the task of unloading the J containers.

The men moved efficiently, but not fast enough for Marsham. Accustomed to his submariners moving on the double, the Rimau men's 'leisurely manner in emerging from the conning tower' and 'sloping away to their appointed places' drove Marsham into 'an absolute frenzy'. His anger, exacerbated by the feeling of vulnerability which the non-submariners evidently failed to appreciate, was compounded by the discovery that friction during transit had created a hole in the second boat. Worried that the stores would now take twice as long to move, he was relieved when the hole was plugged successfully with a wad of cotton waste. Finding that the J container doors opened easily mollified him somewhat. He had expected the deep-sea pressure to have tightened them considerably but they popped open with no difficulty, the cool Fremantle air having expanded in the tropical heat.

Less than forty minutes after the unloading had commenced, *Porpoise* towed the boats to within 400 metres of Kingfisher's Rest. With the assistance of the tide, sixteen men in the less heavily laden boat towed the second, containing three more men and the bulk of the stores. Lyon, Ingleton, Reymond and Falls remained on board *Porpoise*, along with Chapman. As Davidson had calculated that unloading the stores would take about two hours, Marsham had elected to remain on the surface, close by, rather than put to sea. If the submarine should have to retreat suddenly, the five men on board could spend the time until the danger passed by locating a junk, returning to collect the others when the coast was clear. The decision to keep five of the team on the submarine was unfortunate. Firstly, the labour force ashore was cut by one-fifth. Secondly, since Carey was now to remain on Merapas, the conducting officer for the pick-up would have to be Chapman who, having never set foot on the island, was, and would remain, completely unfamiliar with the layout and terrain.

Carey had been fully briefed on the arrangements for the rendezvous with the raiding party before he went ashore. From the night of 15 October, the earliest the others could be expected to return, he was to sling his hammock at the Hammock Tree and wait until dawn.[2] The distinctive shape of the bleached, dead trunks showed up well in the darkness, while the dark hammock was invisible against the equally dark background. The returning raiders were to approach the island with caution. Avoiding Kolek Bay, the easiest place to land, as it was too close to their hiding place in Cache Swamp, they were to come ashore at Land Crab Bay, whose beaches provided a safe landing place in all but an easterly wind. Leaving the others concealed in the thick patch of undergrowth behind the beach, one member of each group was to make a reconnaissance of the Hammock Tree. If Carey was not there, they would know the base had been compromised.

The same procedure was to be used by the pick-up team – Chapman and SOA's Corporal Ron Croton, who had served with Carey on Mission 204, trained with the Rimau men, and knew them well. At dusk on 7 November, the first pick-up date and, if necessary, every night for thirty nights until the submarine returned, a watch was to be mounted until dawn by the raiding party at the Hammock Tree. It was likely that the lookout would see Chapman and Croton clambering over the rocks long before they reached the tree, since Davidson and Stewart had spotted *Porpoise* as soon as she had surfaced. If there were no one waiting at the tree, Chapman would know something had happened to all of them, Carey included.

The first repercussion of the decision to split the group was soon in evidence. Not only was the working party undermanned, but moving the stores across the slippery boulders was proving very difficult and time consuming. The containers and bags, hauled laboriously from the boats and across 10 metres of rocks, then had to be secreted inside a thicket of stilt-legged palms near Kingfisher's Rest before being lumped up and over the hill to Cache Swamp. One hour passed by, then two, and then three, and still the task was nowhere near complete.

With the submarine's batteries running very low, Marsham's anxiety was increasing by the minute. Just after midnight, unable to see any of the shore party and concerned that they could have been washed away by the tide, he flashed a red torch in the hope of attracting someone's attention. Davidson, to whom the submarine had been in plain view for the entire time, interpreted this as 'hurry up' and much to Marsham's relief all, with the exception of Carey, returned to *Porpoise* within thirty minutes. On the way the reconnaissance folboat and one of the engineers-boats, which were impossible to repack, were sunk in deep water. The other was sunk on reaching the submarine.

Davidson was not happy with the unexpected recall. The work was only half complete, giving Carey the unenviable task over the next three days of moving the remainder of the stores from the palm thicket to Cache Swamp. However Davidson also knew that the stores at Kingfisher's Rest were reasonably well hidden and that Carey would be fastidious in obliterating any tracks that might betray their presence with a small rake, included for that very reason in the Base A stores list. Leaving him to his lonely vigil, *Porpoise* headed out to sea to recharge her batteries, plotting a course for Pedjantan Island, 270 kilometres away. At 3 pm, 26 kilometres off Pedjantan, the submarine dived and approached at high speed to allow Davidson to complete a reconnaissance of the northern coastline before dark. He was ecstatic. Beyond the sandy beaches, where a group of monkeys gambolled about, the jungle-covered land rose steeply, providing cover for hundreds of men. There was no sign of human habitation so, satisfied that Pedjantan was ideal for phase two of the mission, Rimau set off to indulge in a spot of pirating.

Like taxis in wet weather and buses at peak hour, there was not a junk to be seen. Throughout the whole of 26 and 27 September they cruised about the shipping lanes to the east and south of the island without sighting a single, solitary vessel. It was not until 9.20 on the morning of the 28th, while scouting round the Borneo coast near the Pontianak River estuary, that they finally spotted two sails, some distance apart. Selecting the one to the east, *Porpoise* submerged to periscope depth. Conditions were not good for observation as there was considerable haze and the sea was muddy and fouled with driftwood and scum from recent heavy rain. Persistent peering through the periscope eventually revealed a handsome Bughis prahu, unfortunately about 100 tonnes and therefore too large for Rimau's needs. They altered course to follow the second boat but it had disappeared. When they eventually relocated it about an hour later, 11 kilometres from the Pontianak Roads, it was heading towards the shore. Marsham altered course for Pulau Laut[3], but they had not travelled far when they spied a two-masted junk at anchor. *Porpoise* dived and began to close in, but at that very moment the vessel raised its anchor and got under way, leading Marsham to believe that the periscope had been spotted. At 2 pm, after chasing the quarry for well over an hour, the submarine surfaced alongside the junk, near the island of Padang Tikar (Malay for plaited mat).

When there was no resistance from the startled crew, who actually threw a mooring line to *Porpoise*, Lyon, Davidson, Ingelton, Warren, Cameron, Ross and Page went on board while Marsham, his submarine once again vulnerable upon the surface, anxiously counted off the seconds. Thirteen minutes later, the successfully pirated junk was sailing for Pedjantan.

The ship they had selected was an 18-metre, 40-tonne vessel from Ketapang whose name, *Mustika*, was probably a corrupted version of Masa Tiga – a small island near Pontianak. Marsham, who had preconceived ideas of how a junk should look, thought the choice appalling.

Sketch of the pirated vessel, Mustika

Not so Lyon and Davidson, who had seen many vessels like it before the war and, like the Jaywick men, had encountered similar craft the previous year. Unlike the rather lumbering, top-heavy profile associated with Chinese junks, the Indonesian prahus or tonkans were extremely streamlined, with raked timber hulls either oiled or painted white. *Mustika*, with a white stripe running above a brown oiled hull, a painted evil eye to keep away bad spirits, a white-painted deckhouse, two masts and lateen (concertina-type) sails, was typical of the many traditionally built vessels plying the waters of Malaya, Singapore and Indonesia.

Crewed by eight Malays under the leadership of skipper Mohamed Juni bin Haji Abdullah, *Mustika* traded between her home port of Ketapang, where all the crew lived, and Pontianak. The Indonesians told Bobby Ross that life under the Japanese had become difficult. Far from attaining equality under the much-vaunted Greater Asia Co-prosperity Sphere, as promised by the conquerors, the locals were generally ill-treated and forced to bow to the Japanese in the streets, the penalty for failing to do so being a sharp whack on the head. Large numbers of citizens had been thrown into gaol, many of the chiefs and rajas executed and the sultanates completely disrupted. Trade had also suffered. Pre-war, *Mustika* had shuttled between Java and Pontianak, carrying timber on the outward leg and returning with a load of sugar. With food shortages now forcing people to grow rice on all available land, sugar and rubber production had all but ceased, and trading prahus reduced to coastal work, carrying loads of wood. *Mustika* had just offloaded a cargo of roofing timber at Pontianak when *Porpoise* intercepted her, en route for Ketapang. Believing the submarine was Japanese the crew had offered no resistance. It was not until they saw the white faces and berets of the boarding party that they realised their mistake. The fact that their vessel had been hijacked did not upset them. In fact, they were quite pleased. It was owned by a notorious Japanese collaborator, their uncle. Neither were they fazed by their unexpected trip to Australia, apart from their concern that, since they were all related, the family would be worried about their sudden disappearance.

The prahu handled extremely well, outdistancing the submarine which was following at periscope depth. As soon as it was dark *Porpoise* surfaced and, using a deceptively frail-looking but very strong grass rope, took *Mustika* in tow. When the rope parted at about 5 am, the prahu continued to Pedjantan under sail and, aided by a fresh monsoonal breeze, reached the island well ahead of *Porpoise*. *Mustika* anchored in a cove while the submarine conducted a thorough periscope reconnaissance of the island before heading out to sea to recharge her batteries. The unloading was to be split over two nights but when Marsham returned shortly after midnight he discovered that the purchase for the derrick, the responsibility of Otto Ingleton, had been mislaid. As he had taken the precaution of arriving with four SBs on the casing to save time, he was very angry. The derrick problem was overcome by some innovative improvisation but, far from calming down, the submarine commander was even more infuriated to discover that the SBs would not fit through *Mustika*'s hatch using the equipment they had brought with them. Pointing out that the Rimau team could have spent the waiting hours enlarging the opening, thereby solving the problem, Marsham lost his temper completely. Fortunately someone came up with a solution and, after further improvisation and modification, seven SBs, one more than planned, were successfully stowed below decks. Marsham, cooling down a little, later apologised for his outburst, conceding that one hour and thirty-six minutes had not been such a bad unloading time, after all. With peace restored he took *Porpoise* out to sea until after 7 o'clock that evening.

The Rimau team enjoyed a day of rest and relaxation. After a revitalising sleep on *Mustika*'s deck, a welcome change from the stuffy, confined berths of the submarine, they organised the stowage of their gear and equipment before Lyon, Chapman, Page, Stewart and four of the prahu's crew went ashore to explore.

Running along a small coral spit extending beyond the sandy point were the remnants of a long-abandoned rail line, evidently built in the early 1900s to transport copra from a large and now very overgrown plantation stretching from the beach to the mountainous interior. While Lyon and Page followed the railway lines inland, Chapman organised the Indonesians to cut coconuts, leaving himself and Stewart free to explore the beaches either side of a small prominence which they dubbed Crab Rock. Unlike the shallows with their brilliantly coloured fish and stingrays which had darted away as the boat approached, the beach held nothing of interest apart from some bales of rubber and a large quantity of timber washed ashore by the tide. The pair turned inland where the rail track, after passing through the plantation, wound in easy stages up the hill to the ruins of a large building with scattered rusted machinery lying about. Meeting up with Page and Lyon, they agreed that Pedjantan Island, with its tinkling mountain stream, abundant marine life and shellfish and mouth-watering tropical fruit, was close to paradise. Returning to the prahu to allow the others to have time ashore and to collect more coconuts, they rectified the problems with the derrick and hatch before Marsham returned.

It was a good move. When *Porpoise* drew up alongside *Mustika*, four SBs again lined up on the hull, the transfer was completed with a minimum of fuss. The remainder of the J stores were loaded into the last remaining SB which Marsham, anxious to avoid being on the surface for any longer than necessary, had floated off in advance. By 10 pm, less than two hours after the submarine had returned, everything was stowed on the prahu, including 125 loaves of bread baked by the submarine's chef as a parting gift. In return, Rimau handed over a large number of coconuts.

While the stores were being transferred, Lyon, Davidson and Ross had questioned *Mustika*'s crew to obtain information about shipping routes and sailing regulations in the Singapore area. Captain Mohamed Juni explained that as this was a coastal trip, *Mustika* displayed no flags, as none was required. Before venturing further afield, say to Java, the necessary flags would have to be obtained from Japanese authorities in Pontianak. He also stressed that if a Japanese vessel approached they must follow three rules – make sure that there were no more than three men on deck, display no flags or signals, and keep on sailing.

To assist the Rimau men with their disguise, *Mustika*'s obliging crew handed over a selection of singlets and sarongs. They also assured Lyon that with the steady monsoon breeze blowing, sailing time to Singapore would be three days and three nights. Already one day ahead of schedule, since the unloading at Merapas had been completed in one night instead of two, and with the attack date set for 10 October, Ivan now had ten days to reach Singapore. Even without a favourable breeze, by sailing at an average rate of 1.8 knots per hour they would cover the 380 kilometres in less than six days, leaving three or four days to spare. Always erring on the side of caution, Lyon stuck with his conservative estimate, telling Chapman that they would spend the extra time at Pedjantan before leaving for the target area.

It was now 10 o'clock on the night of 30 September and time for the submarine to leave. Assuring Lyon that he would be back at Merapas to pick them up in forty days, Marsham gave the order for *Porpoise* to cast off. As they drew away, Marsham and the men on watch, hats raised above their heads, gave three rousing cheers for 'this extremely gallant body of officers and men', before the submarine headed for the Karimata Strait, and home.

Porpoise had not been gone long when Ivan Lyon, after some thought, revised two aspects of the operation that were not satisfactory – Carey was alone on Merapas without a boat, and there was no emergency escape plan should Merapas become compromised or the submarine fail to return. Leaving Carey behind had been a last-minute, stop-gap measure to prevent the coconut workers stumbling across the stores. While Davidson considered it unlikely they would leave the plantation area, to keep watch was a round-the-clock task, beyond the resources of one person. Instead of remaining at Pedjantan, Lyon decided to return to Base A and drop off three more men to assist Carey. Although Merapas was 270 kilometres away, it was still in the general direction of Singapore, and the detour would add a mere 80 kilometres to the length of the trip.[4]

The team chosen to assist Carey needed to be reliable, level-headed and not involved in any task vital to the mission. As fifteen SB operators were needed for the raid, and navigator Bruno Reymond could not be spared, the Merapas party would need to be culled from the junk crew, consisting of Ingleton, maintenance men Warren and Cameron, signallers Craft and Stewart, and the SB reserves. Gooley, whose dual role as stores expert as well as SB operator could have put him in contention, was kept on *Mustika*, probably to maintain the organisation of food and equipment. Tormented for weeks by a premonition that he would not survive the raid, Gooley may have been the one person not to raise any objection at being left behind.

Ingleton was not vital to the mission's success but, being the SEAC observer, he evidently resisted the suggestion that he remain on Merapas. This left Hugo Pace, a tough, experienced infantryman, and two men who had back-ups – resourceful Alf Warren, who was the more senior NCO of the two maintenance men, and Signaller Colin Craft. Splitting the signallers also allowed Lyon to have a signaller at Merapas and one on *Mustika*.

In a few months' time Mary Ellis, the operation's cipher officer, would discover Lyon had left his copy of the 'one off' code book, along with his personal effects, in his room at the Botanical Hotel in Melbourne where he was normally billeted. She always believed it to be a deliberate act. With all the delays and troubles which had threatened to cancel Rimau, Ellis concluded that Lyon had decided to make it impossible for them to be recalled once the submarine had left Pedjantan. What she did not consider was that there was no need for him to take the whole book. With the radio their sole life-line, Lyon would most certainly either have copied out the vital words needed to establish the code or, more likely, since he did not keep written records when in the field, committed it to memory. To whom he imparted the vital words and the strike rate is not known – probably to Craft, in case anything untoward occurred at Merapas, and possibly to Davidson and Stewart.

Mustika arrived at Merapas without incident on 4 October to disembark Warren, Craft and Pace, and to plan an emergency escape route, including a supply dump at a secure base. The question of supplies for the new base was solved by siphoning some from the huge Merapas stockpile, and of a hideout by selecting the one island that met all the necessary criteria: uninhabited with a water supply; close enough to the target route so they could drop off supplies; within island-hopping distance of Singapore; near a junk route if they needed to pirate a boat to take them to India; and known to at least some of them. It was Pompong, a little over 100 kilometres to the south-west.[5] Perched on the northerly end of the Lingga Archipelago, it was easily accessible from both Merapas and Singapore by any one of a number of routes. Since five of the Jaywick men had already paddled from Singapore to Pompong and the sixth, Fred Marsh, knew the island well, it was an excellent emergency rendezvous.

Mustika sailed from Merapas on or about 5 October, leaving two folboats with the stay-behind group. Instead of going through the Telang Strait, the most direct route, Reymond plotted a course through the islands hugging the south-easterly coast of Bintan Island. The prahu looked innocuous enough and as the vessel displayed no flags was unlikely to come under scrutiny. Should a plane look as if it might attack, Mrs Manderson's excellent copies of the Japanese ensign and the Osame Gunsai Kambu were kept at the ready to display. The latter was similar to the rising sun flag in design, but had additional lines and six Japanese characters signifying Shonan (Singapore) Military Administration Headquarters.

Mustika had now sailed into an area frequented by fishermen and villagers moving constantly between the islands but no one gave the prahu a second look, especially since the crew, from a distance, no longer appeared to be white. Berets and badges of rank had been discarded and all exposed skin dyed brown. Lyon, Davidson, Page and five others had adopted a complete disguise, trading their jungle greens for the sarongs and singlets donated by *Mustika*'s crew and donning wide-brimmed, oriental-style straw hats. Using the strategy employed on *Sederhana Djohanes* and following the advice of Captain Mohamed Juni, Lyon allowed only three of those in local garb to be on the deck at any one time. Ingleton, whose size made it impossible for him to be inconspicuous in this land of small, finely-boned people, was kept out of sight at all times.

Although most of the team were confined below decks, there was plenty to do. As the gathering of intelligence on Jaywick had proved most useful, observation was split into recording, sketching and photography. Davidson, always a copious note-taker, was responsible for the written reports, Ingleton for the sketches and Page for the photographs. Lyon, who was busy overseeing the running of the prahu, filed his information in the usual place – his head.[6] As they sailed along the inner channel, close to the south-eastern tip of Bintan Island, Ingleton sketched the bauxite mines, easily identifiable by the great red scars marring an otherwise green landscape. Page took several photos, including one of Davidson in his sarong and straw hat and another of Lyon, also clad in singlet and sarong but smoking a pipe.

Passing the southern entrance of the Riau Straits they had a fine view of the Japanese fleet at anchor there, promoting a flurry of sketching, note-taking and photography. Ingleton, with the aid of Lyon's high-powered telescope, was able to add many fine details to his ships, recording guns, turrets and any peculiarities. Turning south towards Pompong, all three observers noted more bauxite mines on Lingga Island. Nothing escaped their attention, from the location and strength of enemy defences and installations to the appearance and apparent demeanour of villagers.

Back on Merapas, Wal Carey was also passing the time by recording as much as possible. Although he had no need of a disguise, he occasionally shed his trousers and shirt in favour of a much cooler sarong. As he wandered around the island he recorded the wind strength and direction, shipping movements and the description and flight paths of aircraft flying overhead. The other three contributed items of interest for Carey to note in his diary, which he hoped would be of use to Allied intelligence as well as providing him with a souvenir of the mission.

One day, something occurred which unexpectedly broke the boredom. They had a visitor. In making his prediction that none of the locals would venture beyond the plantation, Davidson had forgotten that small children, especially boys, are universally curious beings. It was not long before 10-year-old Karta wandered away from the beach and into the old coconut plantation selected by Davidson as a night camp, where he had been most intrigued to find a palm with strange hieroglyphs gouged into its soft trunk. Undoubtedly the work of Walter Carey, leg-puller extraordinaire, the unintelligible symbols would cause much head-scratching in years to come. Carved more than 2 metres above the ground, the marks were believed by some to be some kind of survey mark, while others were completely stumped. Despite hours spent puzzling over a possible meaning, the riddle remained unsolved for forty-five years.

Like many people who travel outside their home territory, Carey had evidently decided to leave his mark for posterity – but nothing as crass as his name or initials. Something far more subtle – graffiti that would leave any visitors to the island, especially Japanese, completely mystified. With the aid of his basic phrase book, the Australian had reached above his head and neatly carved two bold Japanese characters into the trunk of a coconut palm. What the short-statured Japanese troops made of this lofty message when they eventually arrived on uninhabited Merapas is anyone's guess. The symbols simply and inexplicably read 'Japanese tree'. Young Karta, unable to read or write Japanese or English and interested only in recognising the handiwork of his newly found friend, coined a phrase for the palm that would last for decades – The British Coconut Tree.[7]

While Carey was leaving his joke for posterity, *Mustika* was weaving her way through one of the numerous small straits leading to Kapala Jernith. SOA Intelligence had warned that surveillance and patrols had been increased after the Jaywick raid, so a close eye was kept on the shoreline and the skies. However, the prahu and her occupants had attracted not the slightest attention, apart from a navy pilot who had banked his aircraft for a closer look but, on spotting the flags Bob Page was waving vigorously from the bow, had wiggled his wings and flown off.

Fortunately, there had been no need to call on the contingency plan. While marginally better than the fantastic scheme dreamed up by Davidson for Jaywick using a dinghy, underwater breathing tubes and suicidal limpets, Contingency Plan II, devised by SOA's Planning Department, was still very risky. Once again, its success depended on the ability of the Rimau men to carry out a prolonged and convincing masquerade as Malays. This time, should an enemy patrol wish to board, a decoy party was to lure the Japanese below, swiftly garrotte them and remove their uniforms. Some of the Rimau men, dressed in these uniforms and with forage hats pulled well over their faces, would then hustle *Mustika*'s 'natives' to the patrol boat, as if carrying out a normal arrest. Using weapons concealed beneath their sarongs, the 'natives' would dispatch the remaining Japanese and steer the boat smartly away from *Mustika*. It was hoped that any witnesses to this pantomime would assume that local fishermen had been apprehended for questioning. Once out of sight, the patrol boat would be sunk, taking the bodies of the Japanese with it. Since the only men who had the remotest chance of passing themselves off as local fishermen were Lyon, Huston and Reymond, the most sensible approach would be to pray that Contingency Plan II, like Plan I, was never put to the test.

Despite the diversions to Merapas and Pompong, *Mustika* arrived at Kapala Jernith at the southern end of Phillip Channel right on schedule. While the prahu anchored in a quiet cove, two recce parties under Lieutenant Ross paddled off to Pulau Labon, about 11 kilometres away. The reconnaissance completed, Ross and Huston moved to Subar, another 11 kilometres distant, while the other team returned to *Mustika* to report to Lyon.[8] For the second time in just over a year Andrew Huston was to endure a swelteringly hot day on rocky, exposed Subar, observing shipping through a telescope. Ross had never been to Subar but his knowledge of pre-war Singapore was good and he spoke Malay well, should they encounter any trouble. While the pair lay sweating in the scant shade *Mustika* weighed anchor and left Kapala Jernith. With Japanese naval vessels anchored at the southern entrance to the Riau Straits and ships from a Japanese Task Force about to leave for an operation, there was constant movement between the anchorage and Singapore, making the waters near Phillip Channel a risky spot to linger for very long. Sailing in a north-westerly direction, by mid-afternoon *Mustika* was off northern Batam, threading her way through the myriad mangrove-ringed islands to Kasu, a small jungle-clad island that was home to a village of simple fishermen.

The kampong houses, precariously erected on poles above the water, were clustered along the edge of a bay, sheltered from the wind by a grove of banyan trees growing on a hill behind the village and by a small cape jutting into the water at the southern end. From the centre of the densely packed dwellings ran a bamboo jetty, long enough to straddle the extensive

The village on Kasu Island, where Rimau's cover was blown

mud flats exposed at low tide and tall enough to clear the high-water mark. Opening out onto the jetty and for a considerable distance along both sides, until the increasing height above the mud put a stop to development, the fishermen's wood and atap huts created a spiderweb-like network, with one dwelling linked to the next by narrow walkways. In one of the more affluent houses lived the headman. Another, commandeered for use as water police post, was staffed by village collaborators, known as the *heiho*, who operated under the control of the Kempeitai. Following a proclamation in April 1943 by Japanese 7 Area Army HQ in Saigon, more than 40,000 Indonesian youths, lured by Japanese propaganda that they would be serving their homeland and nation, would by war's end join this auxiliary force.

Not exactly popular with the locals, the heiho threw their weight around, enforcing their authority by wearing uniforms identical to those worn by the Japanese army. Among the villagers, the intimidating effect of the uniform, which included regulation boots and cap with a red star, was lessened to some extent by the fact that the realistic-looking weapons carried by these quasi-policemen were actually fake. However, the wooden rifles served their purpose, enabling the heiho to bully anyone not in the know.

From their small post, situated about halfway down the jetty, the heiho had an uninterrupted view of the waterway and of any local boat or fishing vessel which, unlike naval vessels, came under their jurisdiction. The observation post was well positioned to strike at passing craft. Facing the small channel which separated Kasu from Batam, this sleepy, quiet backwater with its long, spindly jetty was well hidden from the south by the small cape – so well hidden that strangers approaching from that direction were upon the settlement before they realised it. At about 4 o'clock that afternoon, *Mustika* rounded the point.[9]

Sidek bin Safar, who revelled in the lofty title of 'police inspector', was on duty.[10] The tide was still low and the incoming current sluggish. There was not the slightest hint of a breeze, although the heavy, leaden clouds signified that a storm might soon break, bringing relief from the oppressive heat and humidity of the late afternoon. Suddenly, an unidentified prahu came into view. As the wooden boat, its sails limp, drifted towards the end of the jetty, Sidek idly lifted his gaze. This was no ordinary prahu. The people on deck were not indigenous Malays, but *orang putehs* – white men. There was no doubt about it. The prahu was a mere 20 metres away. It was now so close that he could see there were definitely Europeans on board, badly disguised as northern Indians.

Alerting his underlings Yunus, Yahya and Atan, Sidek ran to fetch the only man in the village who could speak English – Ati, a Singaporean Chinese who had sensibly moved back to the island when the Japanese occupied Singapore. Shoving their military caps on their heads and grabbing their imitation wooden rifles, the four heiho, accompanied by Ati, scrambled down a rickety ladder to where the police boat was moored. About 7.5 metres long, the motor-driven launch was made of rough, oiled timber planks. In the stern was a small, box-like deckhouse, open at the front and with large, unglazed windows on either side. Watched by the entire village, the police boat chugged towards *Mustika* with Ati, the heiho's unwilling human shield, positioned on the bow. As the onlookers wisely elected to remain within their own homes, those whose houses lined the channel had prime seats. Watching from the door and window of two of these dwellings were 18-year-old Arafin bin Akup and Mahat Kunil, a 33-year-old fisherman.

To the men on board *Mustika* the heiho, with their Japanese-style uniforms and convincingly realistic rifles, looked as if they meant business. As soon as the alarm had been raised on *Mustika* with the call 'Patroller, Patroller', everyone below took up action stations, Brens and Stens trained on the launch through holes in the hull. For the moment, Rimau could do nothing more than follow Captain Mohamed Juni's advice – no more than three men on deck, no signal flags and keep going. Lyon, with the others, waited in silence. There had been no indication from the patrol boat as to its intention, and no one had hailed *Mustika*. As it was now raining there was a possibility that the launch might return to shore. If it did not, they would be in grave danger. The launch closed the gap to a distance of less than 20 metres. Would the Japanese board? Would Rimau be able to implement the contingency plan? Would the mission, due to begin in only three hours' time, be over before it had begun?

At this stage, Lyon must have cursed the labour disputes which had put the country craft so far behind schedule. With a diesel engine, they would not be at the mercy of the wind and tide, and could have made a fast getaway, to disappear among the thousands of islands before the alarm could be properly raised.

Someone shouted something unintelligible, the signal for a tall man standing on *Mustika's* deck to order his companion to bend down and level a Bren gun across the edge of the decking, presumably in an effort to cover the enemy launch. The atmosphere below decks was electric, with sweat streaming from very pore and muscles aching from the strain. As the patrol boat drew nearer, an 'English engineer' panicked and opened fire.

What made Ati realise that he was in danger before a shot was fired is not known. Perhaps the abnormal stillness as the launch neared the prahu alerted him that it could be a trap. Whatever it was, it saved his life. In a deft move he threw himself sideways into the water before the bullets thudded into the launch. Exposed upon the bow, their human shield now inconveniently overboard, the heiho tried to turn their boat away, but it was too late. Before they could follow Ati's lead, Rimau's firepower wiped out two of them. Realising that Ati was a Chinese civilian, the guns on *Mustika* concentrated their fire on the uniformed figures now in the water. Within seconds, it was all over. The bullet-riddled body of a third man lay floating face down in the water beside the boat while the fourth had disappeared.[11] Sidek, however, was very much alive. Demonstrating a remarkable talent for survival, he had not made for the shore but had clung instead to the stern of the launch, shielded from the bullets spraying from *Mustika's* deck by the solid wood of the timber deckhouse. And there he stayed, hanging on grimly, long after the launch, its engine still running, became trapped among the stilts of the village houses. Inside their homes, safe from the barrage of fire directed at the heiho, the villagers continued to watch the action unfold with great interest. Although the rain was bucketing down they could still see what was happening on board the prahu, which had made barely any headway during the confrontation.

On board *Mustika*, Ivan Lyon told his men that the raid was aborted. Estimating that it would be no more than three hours before enemy reinforcements arrived from Singapore, he ordered twelve of his men to assemble the folboats and make for Merapas by whatever route they chose.[12] Before the six folboats pulled away Davidson, who was still on board, grabbed the two flags and threw them to one of the men, realising that if it became necessary to pirate a junk they might prove useful.[13]

As the six folboats paddled off, the villagers took to the jungle-covered hill behind the village, lest they be next on the visitors' hit-list. Although the skirmish they had just witnessed was very exciting, and the loss of the unpopular heiho an unexpected bonus, the sight of twelve well-armed white men making in their direction was a most alarming development. Peering from their hiding place, Arafin and Mahat could still make out the shape of the prahu, despite the driving rain and premature gloom brought about by the storm but, as the wind picked up and the prahu floated downstream, they were not longer able to see what was happening on board. A terrified Sidek bin Safar, still clinging to the back of the launch, now had a prime position.

The prahu had finally begun to make some headway so Sidek was surprised when it suddenly stopped and anchored mid-stream. Launching an engineers-boat from the deck, five men loaded it with three unassembled folboats, a rubber raft, large supplies of ordnance material, ammunition, food and medical supplies, and paddled off.[14] Almost immediately there was a loud explosion and the prahu slid slowly beneath the water. This was followed by another, far more muffled bang and then, absolute silence.

While Sidek recovered his composure and the startled villagers made their way cautiously back to the village to collect the dead and bury them before nightfall, as their religion demanded, Lyon, Davidson, Campbell, Warne and Stewart paddled hard for Subar where Ross and Huston were waiting, unaware of the disaster that had befallen the mission. Heading in the opposite direction were twelve bitterly disappointed men, their energies now focused on reaching Merapas alive. They realised there was no turning back. The explosions could only mean one thing – Lyon had scuttled *Mustika* and their precious SBs were now a mass of tangled wreckage. Had the storm arrived just a few minutes earlier, they would have slid by Sidek bin Safar undetected and would now be well on the way to victory. It must have seemed unbelievable – almost as unbelievable as hearing Lyon announce that the raid was aborted.

But it was not. The limpet mines, far from lying in the mud, 14 metres under water, were stowed on the wooden floor of the engineers-boat at Lyon's feet. He had been forced to destroy *Mustika* and the SBs, but he was not going to allow a few Japanese patrolmen shot dead on an isolated Indonesian island to deter him from his task. He may have been temporarily thwarted, but it did not mean that the situation was hopeless. All that was required was a quick revision of the plan, using Jaywick as the blueprint. Once they had collected Ross and Huston from Subar, the seven men assembled their folboats. With the recce kayak, they had a total of four. Three of the boats were paired by men who were either officers or Jaywick veterans. Doug Warne, a very strong paddler who had demonstrated the ability to keep a cool head in a crisis, was to go it alone. The heavy engineer's boat, having now served its purpose, was exchanged for the rubber raft which could not only hold all their equipment and stores but was much lighter to tow. The fact that the Japanese would soon be aware of Rimau's presence did not enter Lyon's calculations. Each and every man knew that the mission was more important than the life of any individual.

Furthermore, Keppel Harbour was filled with ships, unable to leave port owing to enemy submarine activity. For the past month, vessels bound for Japan had been loaded by POW labourers, only to return a few hours later. It was too good an opportunity to miss. In the early hours of 11 October, the raiding party penetrated the outer defences of Singapore Harbour.

12

For God, King and country

11 October–21 November 1944

For the second time in a little over twelve months, the Japanese were astounded to hear the sound of explosions echoing across the water. Some hours later, they heard several more.[1]

After leaving Subar the seven men had paddled their folboats towards targets already identified by Ross. At 3 am all except Warne who, for all his strength and expertise, could not combat the rip tide alone, placed their limpets on shipping anchored in the Roads and the waters off Sambu Island. With the time fuses set, the saboteurs beat a retreat well before the limpets exploded. They then observed the results, probably from the safety of Dongas Island, which had plenty of cover nearby for their raft and supplies.

Meanwhile, the villagers within earshot of the target areas were abuzz with speculation. Who was responsible for the loud bangs and what had been blown up? No one seemed to know and in the absence of any telltale signs, such as great palls of smoke, they were unable to satisfy their curiosity.

Neither the war nor Japanese occupation had made the slightest difference to the inter-island communication system, which was hopelessly outdated. As the police post at Kasu was not equipped with either a radio or telephone, Sidek was forced to travel by boat to the heiho's HQ on Belakang Padang Island to report the skirmish and the deaths of his comrades. His information that some orang puteh, after shooting three of his native policemen, had then sunk their prahu near his village aroused some interest, but not enough to bother informing Water Kempeitai Headquarters in Singapore – at least, not just yet. Of far more interest, at this stage, was the possibility that the scuttled prahu and whatever it contained might be salvageable.

When Sidek returned to Kasu he had with him a number of heiho skilled in the use of diving equipment, probably workers from the shipbuilding yards on Sambu, who provided the villagers with non-stop entertainment throughout that day. After donning strange helmets which Arafin and Mahat noticed were attached to some kind of machine, they disappeared under water for up to thirty minutes at a time. The prahu was located but, to the intense disappointment of the searchers and their audience, the divers came up empty-handed.

It was not until Friday 13 October, three days after Rimau's confrontation with the heiho, that Belakang Padang HQ, the attempted salvage operation now complete, finally contacted their superiors. After Sidek, now the centre of attention, had made a full statement, the police transmitted a message to Singapore Kempeitai HQ that there had been a 'defensive stand' by about twenty people, including Caucasians, earlier in the week. As the message evidently carried no indication of urgent priority, on receipt it was put aside for the attention of military headquarters until after the weekend.

In the meantime, a report was received on 14 October that an American B-24 had been observed circling Bintan Island for over two hours on 13 October and had apparently made contact with someone on the ground. Assuming that members of the tiresome stay-behind parties were involved, Singapore telegraphed Major Fugita Hujime, head of the Bintan Island garrison, with orders to begin an immediate search of the area. The Kempeitai, after dispatching its own task force in the hope of making contact with the culprits, then turned their attention to what they believed was another, completely unrelated matter.

In spite of their Number One Work, which had continued its brutal investigations for exactly twelve months, the sabotage in Singapore had not stopped. Not only had there been two separate attacks on shipping in the space of twelve hours on 11 October, but there had also been recent air raids by American bombers, including an attack on the naval base. Coming at time when Japan was feeling the effects of American submarine activity, resulting in the loss of precious ships, this latest sea-borne attack provoked outrage. As at least three vessels had been sunk, the loss of face was immense. Determined to put a stop to the activities of the saboteurs, for once and for all, the Kempeitai began a new reign of terror, extracting from the civilian population a hideous price for this latest humiliation. Before many days had passed, the heads of innocent Chinese and Malay civilians, thrust upon sharpened stakes, were on display at every major street corner.

The noise from the explosions at Sambu had not reached Singapore, but those from the Roads were clearly audible – loud enough to be heard by some of the POWs working in and around Singapore City. It didn't take long for Australian prisoners labouring near the wharves to put two and two together. Private Roy Bliss, who was with a party quartered at the River Valley Road Camp, reported that the Japanese had created 'a big stir', shooting and then beheading a large number of civilians. Seeing the heads of the unfortunate victims 'stuck on stakes all over the place', Bliss assumed that the purge had to be connected with the attack on cargo ships in the Singapore Roads.

The Kempeitai, busy terrorising the civilians in Singapore, remained blissfully unaware of the action at Kasu until 16 October, when the message from the Belakang Padang police was finally decoded and read, to the effect that a prahu full of white men had wiped out three-quarters of Kasu's local police force. Consequently the frantic search, which Lyon had envisioned would take place within three hours of the fight at Kasu, had not eventuated. Locally, police interest had extended no further than an undersea search for loot, while in Singapore the Kempeitai were focused entirely on proving that the latest sabotage was another inside job.

By this stage the raiders could have been expected to call it a day. But instead of returning to Merapas they paddled to Pulau Pangkil, an elongated island in the Riau Straits straddling the entrance to the Tiung Straits. Barely rising from the sea and ringed by extensive rocky reefs at low tide, Pangkil was not particularly inspiring, being covered in occasional patches of jungle, and lallang grass dotted with nondescript trees and scattered groves of coconut palms. Of no strategic or economic significance, the island was inhabited only by fishermen and coconut workers who lived in two kampongs straggling haphazardly over the water at either end. The Japanese had taken no interest in Pangkil, and neither would Ivan Lyon have done, had it not been such a convenient place to hide during the daylight hours of 14 October.

By rights, he should have been nowhere near Pangkil. The safest route to Merapas from the attack area was to the east across the top of Bintan Island, or to the west, down the old Jaywick route and then through the Dempo Straits. The Riau Straits were no place for men on the run. With a large naval fleet anchored at the southern end near Mantang Island, the entire area was bristling with Japanese. Lyon, from previous intelligence and personal observation from *Mustika*, knew this, and yet he had chosen to paddle over 100 kilometres, dragging a rubber boat loaded with equipment, into the proverbial lion's den. He can have had only one possible motive – to blow up the ships in the Riau anchorage. They had plenty of time to size up the situation. The submarine was not due back for another twenty-five days.

Pangkil was well sited for his reconnaissance. It is within easy paddling distance from Tapai (Fisherman's) Island, a small cone-shaped hill rising steeply from the sea a few kilometres to the south and providing an excellent view of the ships near Mantang Island. Believing that the villagers who, according to SOE intelligence had become disenchanted with their 'liberators', might be able to supply some useful information, the seven men left their hiding place at about 4 pm, unaware that Major Fugita was about to initiate a search for the B-24's ground contacts from his base on Bintan Island. Carrying a supply of sweets, cigarettes and chocolates to exchange for information and possibly a little fresh food, the Rimau party split into two groups. Lyon, Ross and Stewart headed north, and Davidson, Campbell, Huston and Warne paddled to Tanjung Kramat, the main settlement on the south-western tip of the island. Here they met the village headman, Raja Rool. Standing nearby, watching, was Raja Rool's second son, Raja Muhammad.[2]

The tallest of the four strangers, who spoke some Malay, explained that he and his companions, all dressed in jungle greens and each armed with a Sten gun, pistol and a number of hand grenades, were 'Australian officers' who had come by submarine and had been on

Pangkil since midnight. Casting an interested gaze over the visitors' two folboats, the black inflatable raft and their strange 'necklaces' (identity discs), 18-year-old Muhammad assumed that the submarine must have dropped them off in the deep water channel between Pangkil and Karas islands.

It was evidently a satisfactory meeting all round. By the time the discussion finished Raja Rool had a swag of goodies and Davidson had learned something new – there were other ships anchored to the north-east, between Dompak and Penyengat islands. Meanwhile, 5 kilometres away at the other end of Pangkil, Lyon, Ross and Stewart were making the acquaintance of another headman, Raja Mun, who lived at neighbouring Penyengat. After being reassured by the strangers that there was nothing to fear from them he was friendly enough, happily accepting cigarettes and learning that the foreign soldiers, armed with two Bren guns and three pistols, had come to Pangkil in small, two-man canoes.

Evidently confident that the headmen were trustworthy, the Rimau men spent all the next day on Pangkil, although in light of Raja Rool's information about the new anchorage, now the preferred target, they realised that Pangkil was useless as an observation post. Blocking the view to the north-east is a flat coral atoll named Soreh, so tiny that it can be circumnavigated on foot in less than an hour. With its green palm-filled centre ringed by pure white beaches Soreh, also known as Evening Island, was idyllic. Apart from the denser patch of vegetation in the middle of the island, there was no undergrowth, just scattered ru trees, a species of tropical fig whose open, multi-branched canopies and convoluted buttress roots provided a striking contrast to the grey-green backdrop of the slender coconut palms. Although useless as a hideout, as it was possible to see clearly from one side of the island to the other, and with only a limited water supply, Soreh had one redeeming feature – a perfect view of the deep-water anchorage near Dompak Island.

On the night of 15 October, Lyon, Ross and Stewart left Pangkil and paddled off to Soreh to carry out a reconnaissance of the target area. Within hours Raja Rool was urgently contacting the other Rimau men: they had been betrayed and must leave Pangkil at once, before the Japanese arrived. At 4 am, Raja Muhammad watched from the kampong as Davidson and Campbell headed for Soreh to warn Lyon's party and Warne and Huston, rubber raft in tow, made for Tapai.

The informant who had betrayed them was collaborator Raja Mun, one of the few local people in the pay of the Japanese. After farewelling Lyon, Ross and Stewart he had gone by boat to Tanjung Pinang, Bintan Island's principal town, to report the presence of the white men to District Police Officer Mahamit. His reward of $20 was increased to $70 when Mun, accompanied by Mahamit, arrived at Tanjung Pinang's Kempeitai headquarters where he repeated his story to Yap Chin Yah, a most unpopular police inspector brought in from Dabo on Singkep Island to investigate locals who had worked for the Dutch. On receipt of Mun's information, Singapore ordered all naval forces to maintain a strict watch on the Durian Straits and Riau Archipelago.

The following morning Abdul Latif, an Indonesian coconut cutter aged in his early twenties, was quietly stoking a fire inside the hut on Soreh where he lived with his wife and infant child. Part of his job as caretaker for Soreh's owner Tengku Haji Ahmad Tabib was to extract oil from the coconuts growing in abundance all over the island. With no one else on the island, apart from some long-forgotten king buried in a nearby tomb, Latif's life was one of peaceful tranquillity until 8 o'clock on the morning of Monday 16 October 1944.

He was hacking open coconuts about 50 metres from his hut when he first saw them – four bare-headed men, dressed in green and khaki trousers and shirts. All had rope lanyards on their shoulders and each was armed with a Sten gun and pistol. Two were taller than the others and two were older but all four had an 'army badge' (most likely a Rising Sun beret badge) attached to the fronts of their shirts. As Latif saw only four, the fifth was almost certainly guarding their rear, and the folboats loaded with their equipment and Bren guns. Their sudden appearance did not alarm Latif, who had seen some of the strangers on Pangkil in the past day or so. Speaking passable Malay, they asked the young Indonesian if he would climb one of the palms and cut them some green coconuts. After slaking their thirst with Ivan Lyon's favourite tropical drink and scooping out some of the soft juicy meat, they disappeared into the centre of the island, the only evidence of their presence the empty coconut shells discarded upon the ground.

While Lyon, Davidson, Ross, Campbell and Stewart were keeping out of sight on Soreh, 12 kilometres away Pangkil was now the scene of frenetic activity. Although Raja Mun's information had been passed to Yap Chin Yah the previous day, all available men had been out searching Bintan Island for anyone connected with the B-24 incident. Consequently, a full twenty-four hours had elapsed before Major Fugita managed to assemble a force large enough to take on the enemy band reported to be on Pangkil. As the Japanese considered that safety lay in numbers, their search patrols tended to be very large – usually 30 to 40 men, supplemented by heiho and a few locals impressed for the task if necessary. This desire for group travel made for very slow going, took a great deal of organisation and was a logistical nightmare. As result, the pursued frequently had a reasonable chance of eluding the pursuers, who preferred to stick to paths and had an absolute horror of entering the jungle, other than by well-defined tracks. In the absence of any path, they stuck to the coast and moved around the perimeter.

Late that morning, unaware that the quarry had decamped to Soreh and Tapai during the night, Major Fugita and his entourage arrived at Pangkil in two landing barges. They certainly looked a formidable force. In addition to a large number of troops, Fugita had brought along light machine-guns. The transport could not be beached owing to the low tide, so Sergeant-

Major Chizu Takeo of the Bintan Kempeitai made his way across the exposed reef to question the headman, Raja Rool.

In response to the repeated demands that he reveal the whereabouts of the white soldiers, Rool stated, quite truthfully, that there were no white men on the island. Thwarted by what he believed was a failure to cooperate, Chizu applied further pressure, announcing that he would take Rool's son away for questioning. Unmoved by the prospect of Raja Muhammad in the clutches of the dreaded secret police, the headman stuck to his story, leaving the officer with no option but to carry out his threat.

By this time the tide had come in. Chizu's decision to have his hostage row them both out to the waiting landing barges in a small sampan was ill advised, for the young man knew every inch of the waterway. Altering course, he deliberately hit a submerged rock, throwing the officer overboard into deep water. As a most unrepentant Muhammad sat in the partially submerged craft, and Chizu swam back to shore, another landing barge loaded with excited Kempeitai and heiho arrived with the sensational news that some of their party had been killed in a fierce battle with white men on Soreh Island.

While the Pangkil fiasco was unfolding, Abdul Latif and his wife were inside their house on Soreh, rendering coconut oil. Early in the afternoon, on hearing a strange noise coming from the beach, Latif had poked his head outside the door to investigate. To his consternation he saw a Japanese landing barge, filled with Kempeitai and heiho, nose its way onto the beach near the king's tomb, scarcely 50 metres away. They were reinforcements who had come from Singapore in response to the message regarding the fight at Kasu, which had finally been decoded and read, and the follow-up message from Major Fugita reporting white men on Pangkil Island. After arriving at Bintan to join the search of the nearby islands, the Singapore contingent had been led to Soreh by the ever-helpful local spy, Raja Mun, who told them that if anyone were on Soreh island, Latif would know about it.

What Latif knew was that the Kempeitai spelled trouble. Ordering his wife to stay hidden inside the house, he watched as about twenty-five troops made their way towards him from the beach. As they passed through the coconut grove they spotted the empty coconuts upon the ground – irrefutable proof, they believed, that strangers had visited the island. On reaching Latif, clad only in his shorts and singlet and carrying his parang, they demanded to know if there were any white men on Soreh. Although Latif, through interpreter Raja Ibrahim and a member of the local heiho, denied any knowledge of any white men, the Kempeitai were not convinced. Switching to a more persuasive method of approach on the advice of Raja Mun, they offered to reward Latif for any information. For the second time in the space of a few hours the Kempeitai learned that large numbers of local people, unlike Mun, were incorruptible. Latif told them nothing. After another hour of unproductive questioning, the officer in charge finally lost patience and ordered fifteen members of the group, including

Ibrahim, to escort Latif to the barge to await transfer to headquarters for more intensive 'interrogation'.

As the rest of the force fanned out, the stillness of the hot tropical afternoon suddenly exploded with the sound of concentrated gunfire. Unable to see what was happening, those on the barge prudently kept their heads down, aware from the staccato chatter of Bren guns that the white men meant business. The Japanese returned the fire and the fight continued for about two hours until around 5 pm, when the search party was forced to retreat. When they finally reached the safety of the barge, Latif was most gratified to see that five or six were either dead or injured.

The barge, after completing a circuit of the island, headed for Pangkil, arriving shortly after six o'clock. En route the Kempeitai resumed their interrogation of Latif, who managed to withhold the fact that his wife and child were still on Soreh but was forced to admit that his elder brother lived on Pangkil. While Major Fugita organised his troops, Jalil was rounded up and taken to the barge to join his brother and the unfortunate Muhammad, whose little episode with the sampan had not been forgotten. The three men would not have been at all pleased to discover that also on the barge was the person directly responsible for their arrest – collaborator Raja Mun.

Back on Soreh, all was quiet. As soon as the barge left, Mrs Latif had crept from the hiding place where she had huddled, terrified but safe while the battle raged outside. Threading her way through the coconut palms, she found the white men. Two were unhurt, but the other three had been shot. As she bent to help them, one spoke to her in Malay, urging her to 'run away and hide, before the Japanese come back'. Aware of the danger to herself and the baby, she returned to the house, her only place of refuge.

The situation for the Rimau men was serious. The Japanese would most certainly be back, probably in less than two hours, and with reinforcements; Lyon had been wounded, but not too seriously; Davidson and Campbell had sustained quite serious wounds to chest and shoulder; and there was still an hour or so to go until dark. Had all five been unhurt, they may have made a dash for it but there was not enough time, with three men wounded, to find cover on another island. The only option was for Lyon and the able-bodied to stay and fight, while the other two tried to get away. What Lyon needed was time – enough time for Davidson and Campbell to reach jungle-covered Tapai, 10 kilometres away, where Huston and Warne were waiting with a stack of food, ammunition and medical supplies. Furthermore, with the Japanese on the offensive, Huston and Warne must be warned to wait no longer but to return to Merapas. As soon as it was dark, Davidson and Campbell, their pain and shock almost certainly lessened by shots of morphine, set off for Tapai. As they paddled south-east Major Fugita, having left a task force on Pangkil to undertake a thorough search, was heading north-east to Soreh with two barges containing a force of about a hundred men. One hundred

Japanese against three Allied soldiers. The odds, as Lyon might have remarked, were a bit steep.

As Soreh had little cover, Lyon knew that to even the odds, at all, clever tactics and subterfuge would need to be employed if they were to keep the enemy at bay long enough for Davidson and Campbell to escape. The silent Stens, highly effective over short range and almost impossible to detect, were the key to his plan. Positioning Stewart and a swag of hand grenades in a wide, stone-lined ditch about 30 metres from their rear right flank, Ross and Lyon, his wound bandaged and fortified by morphine, climbed a ru tree growing about 50 metres from the north-east beach. Inside the tree canopy, the numerous, upward spreading branches provided an excellent firing platform and well-concealed position. The king's tomb was roughly 130 metres to their east. Latif's house was about the same distance away but more to the south, ensuring that Mrs Latif and the baby would not be caught in any crossfire. Each man had his silent Sten and a large supply of ammunition.

The trio did not have long to wait. Some time after 7 pm, just on dusk, Major Fugita's troops began moving cautiously from the landing barges which had come ashore on the northern beach. For the first thirty minutes, as the Japanese crept inland, everything was quiet. Then without warning the night erupted into chaos as soldiers dropped in their tracks, victims of unseen but lethal weapons. While Ross and Lyon raked the area, the powerfully-built Stewart, hidden completely from sight in the grass-edged ditch, lobbed his hand grenades with practised and deadly effect. Taken completely by surprise the Japanese, now pinned down and without adequate cover, faced an impossible task. With the flashes from the exploding grenades lighting up the scene, Lyon and Ross pressed their advantage, picking off the enemy one by one. The dazzlingly brief flashes of light were of no use whatsoever to Fugita's troops, who were unable to detect from which direction the firing and grenades were coming. For the next four hours, completely bewildered by the lack of sound and unaware that Lyon and Ross were high above them, the Japanese, unable to fight back, sustained heavy losses.[3]

Although the watchers on Latif's barge saw the muzzle flashes from the guns, no one was the slightest bit interested in venturing any closer to deliver this information before the barge departed, as ordered, to collect reinforcements from Karas Island, about 13 kilometres away. Impressed by the cunning of the foreign soldiers, Raja Ibrahim told Raja Muhammad, 'The white men are very smart. They hang like bats from the tree and shoot the people from there.'

Their tactics were certainly clever, but also suicidal. When Lyon and Ross had hauled themselves into the tree, they knew they had chosen a position from which there was no possible retreat. Unless a miracle occurred, death was the only outcome, for they could not possibly be taken alive. For over four hours, they fended off the Japanese attack, killing or wounding over sixty men and pinning down forty more in the hope that the others might yet escape.[4] As midnight approached, on this 16th day of October 1944, their time was up. Someone in the task force finally spotted the muzzle flashes.

A well-aimed Japanese hand grenade soared through the air and, in that split second, it was all over. The ru tree, illuminated in a violent eruption of light, revealed for just an instant the figures of Ross and Lyon, held like flies in a grotesque spiderweb. As deadly shrapnel spewed forth into the balmy tropical night there was a deafening explosion, followed by two dull thuds. And absolute and utter silence. Crumpled on the grass beneath the tree lay the limp and lifeless bodies of Lieutenant-Colonel Ivan Lyon and Lieutenant Bobby Ross.

By the time Latif's barge returned to Soreh it was all over. But the Japanese troops, far from mounting an attack, had retreated to the safety of the landing barges, too terrified to move forward in the dark in case another dozen such warriors were concealed behind or in the trees. Somewhere, hidden among the denser foliage in the centre of the island, was Corporal Stewart. He was safe enough, for the Kempeitai had no intention of checking out the bodies or beginning another search until daylight.

At about 1 am a barge carrying Latif, Raja Muhammad, Jalil, and some of the dead and wounded left for Karas, where Muhammad and Jalil were beaten up by the Kempeitai in an effort to ascertain the whereabouts of Mrs Latif. The savagery of the beating given to Jalil probably saved his life. His unconscious body was thrown into a room with Muhammad who, being in much better condition, managed to escape, steal a boat and get them both to Pangkil. Although Muhammad found a place to hide, Jalil was recaptured and re-interrogated, this time about the escape. Unable to obtain a satisfactory answer, the Kempeitai were in the process of beating him to a pulp when Muhammad, now also re-arrested, arrived and was able to provide a plausible explanation regarding their 'release'.

Latif escaped the attentions of the Kempeitai for the time being, but at about 10 am he and Raja Mun were taken back to Soreh to confirm if the white men lying at the foot of the tree were the same men they had seen previously. Scattered near the corpses, now stripped of everything except clothing and identity tags, were a number of used syringes and empty morphine ampoules. Not only were identities of the two dead soldiers known, but the search party was very impressed that Lyon, in order to continue the fight, had applied field dressings to his wounds and injected himself with morphine. Despite Lyon's obvious bravery, the Kempeitai did not bother to bury the corpses. Leaving the bodies to rot where they lay, they carved the name of their unit into a nearby tree before taking Latif, and the two folboats they had found, back to Tanjung Pinang. Their search of Soreh, if indeed there had been a search, was at best superficial. Not only did they fail to find Mrs Latif and the baby hiding in the house, they also failed to find Stewart who, with his folboat now in Tanjung Pinang, was stranded. He did however, have shelter, the food that the Latifs had left behind, a small well to provide him with water, and an endless supply of coconuts.

Back on Bintan, Major Fugita reviewed the situation. Two folboats, some equipment and two dead white soldiers did not compare well with the loss of forty-four men and more than twenty wounded by shrapnel. Although all but seven of the dead were local heiho, and therefore of little consequence, among those killed was Lieutenant Muraroka from the Singapore Kempeitai. To add to this loss of face, the other three white soldiers known to have been on Soreh had vanished. With the situation far from satisfactory, Fugita continued the search and, by the next morning, found two of them. Both were dead.

By a fantastic feat of determination and endurance, Davidson and Campbell had reached Tapai only to find that Warne and Huston were no longer there.[5] With no sign of Lyon and the others, and the sounds of grenade explosions and gunfire on Soreh clearly audible, the pair had fled to Merapas, leaving behind the rubber raft filled with ordnance and supplies. The decision to leave the equipment and stores, with the risk of the Japanese finding them, must have been difficult. To slash the rubber and sink the boat would have been the best option, had they known for certain that the others, whose lives might depend on finding the raft, were no longer alive.

On reaching Tapai, Davidson and Campbell managed to summon enough strength to pull themselves up and over the boulders. Selecting a large, flat rock about 6 metres above the water line they rested their weary bodies against it. Their wounds, which had stopped bleeding, had formed dark, rust-coloured stains, barely discernible against the dark green of their saturated clothing. They had their pistols, but no ammunition and only one hand grenade. In the darkness, they had evidently been unable to find the rubber raft, or perhaps they were simply too exhausted to look for it.

In daylight, from Tapai it was possible to see all the way to Soreh, and by dawn on 17 October there was every indication that all was not well. As there had been no shooting since midnight and no sign of Lyon, Ross or Stewart, the two wounded men settled back against the rock and waited. Twenty-four hours later, shortly after 7 am on 18 October, two boats carrying a Kempeitai search party, Abdul Latif, Raja Mun and Raja Rool, approached the island. Alerted by Mun that white men had been spotted heading towards the island, the searchers were not surprised to see two men sitting side by side on a rocky ledge, well above the waterline. Always mindful of their personal safety and not anxious to be on the receiving end of any more of the white men's tricks, the Kempeitai pushed Raja Rool from the boat and ordered him to move toward the figures, still resting motionless against the rock. Cautiously, the elderly headman made his way across the rocky shore line towards the two men, who had given no sign that they were aware of his presence.

It was some time before he realised they were dead. They certainly didn't look it. Although their clothing and pistols were soaked from the rain, their skin, although dirt streaked and grimy, appeared pink and healthy. They had been dead for only a very short time, for they were still warm and the voracious ants and other insects had not yet invaded the bodies. But why were they dead, at all? There had been no fighting here. Raja Rool could not understand it.

Neither could Latif when he was brought from the second boat to identify the bodies. They were definitely the same men he had seen on Soreh – one tall and one short, the same combination as the two who lay dead beneath the ru tree. When Mun came forward to give his opinion, his inscrutable face did not betray his surprise that he had never seen either of these white men before. Evidently unwilling to complicate his life any more than necessary, he told the Japanese that they were two of the men who had spoken to him on Pangkil.

Puzzled, Latif took a closer look at the corpses, trying to determine the cause of death. Although there were gunshot wounds to the chest and shoulder, the blood was dried and it did not seem possible that these wounds had been fatal. Perhaps they had killed themselves, or each other, but with what, and how? As the pistols Raja Rool had noticed had by this time been souvenired, the only weapon Latif could see was the hand grenade. In any case, as there were no fresh bullet holes, they could not have shot themselves, or one another. It was an absolute mystery.

If either of the Indonesians smelled the distinctive odour of bitter almonds, they had no idea of its significance. The Japanese, however, most certainly knew. 'ANYTHING IS PREFERABLE TO FALLING INTO ENEMY HANDS', had warned AIB intelligence. This instruction, printed in bold upper case on intelligence summaries distributed to SOA personnel, had been heeded by both Davidson and Campbell. Wounded, without sufficient arms or ammunition and therefore unable to offer anything other than token resistance, they had faced the inevitable with great courage. To ensure the safety of their comrades hiding on Merapas, Donald Davidson and Pat Campbell, deliberately, and with full knowledge that they were committing an irrevocable act, had crushed the glass ampoules containing the fatal dose of potassium cyanide between their teeth.

Confiscating the folboat, the rubber raft packed with sundry items such as clothing, rations, wrist watches, binoculars, weapons, money and sunglasses, the search team returned to Major Fugita with the news that two men were now dead on Tapai Island. They had to report there was no sign of the fifth man, but this was offset to some extent by the discovery of a rather waterlogged but still legible notebook on the body of the officer, whom they identified as Lieutenant-Commander Davidson. If it contained useful information, this unexpected windfall might help mollify their superiors at 7 Army HQ, who had been very annoyed that not only had the message regarding the Kasu incident taken three days to reach them, it had also spoilt their lunch break by arriving right in the middle of their noonday meal.

Believing that the rest of the soldiers involved in the fight at Kasu were still hiding out on Batam Island, the Kempeitai continued the search and, to ensure that the locals understood the consequences of helping them, decided to make an example of Abdul Latif and his wife. Mrs Latif, rescued from Soreh by Tambi Sukar, a Penyengat islander, had arrived at Penyengat hoping to be reunited with her husband, but he was no longer there. He was at Kempeitai Headquarters at Tanjung Pinang, hanging by his wrists from the torture room ceiling. His tormentor Yap Chin Yah, the unpopular Chinese import from Singkep, was keen to obtain a result but Latif was made of stern stuff. When a beating failed to extract the required confession, the coconut cutter, his hands tied behind his back, was hoisted by a rope attached to the ceiling, until he was dangling by his wrists. This tactic failed to produce a confession, but the pain was so intolerable that Latif begged to be put out of his misery. Yap denied his request for an immediate and merciful death, informing his victim he would be hanged in due course. After another five days of torture, the still unbroken Latif was transferred to Pulau Buau, an island at the northern end of the Riau Straits. After surviving six months on a starvation diet and still dressed in the same shorts and singlet, he was transferred to the Singapore Water Kempeitai HQ at Tanjung Pagar.

His wife did not remain free for long. Penyengat Island, being Raja Mun's territory, was a very poor choice as a hiding place. Unable to break her husband, the Kempeitai, with Mun's assistance, arrested Mrs Latif. She too remained silent, despite a hefty dose of the same treatment. Meanwhile, the search for the elusive white men continued; as the days merged into weeks, with not a single report of any sighting, the searchers became dispirited. It was as if the white men had vanished from the face of the earth.

All those still alive, except Stewart, were now at Base A. The twelve men ordered to flee from Kasu had reached Merapas where they were reunited with the party guarding the stores. Huston and Warne arrived a few days later, bringing the number of men hiding on the island to eighteen. When the possibility of any of the others still being alive appeared remote, especially as there had been no signs of any land or sea search, Bob Page, the only officer who had knowledge of the area, assumed command.

The end of October came and went. Despite Major Fugita's headquarters being a mere 50 kilometres away, there had been no sign of any enemy activity. With only a few days until 7 November, the date the submarine was due to return, the Rimau men had no reason to believe they would not be rescued. And they would have been, had a Japanese aircraft bound for Singapore not developed engine trouble on 3 November.

It made an emergency landing at Kidjang, where a Japanese garrison was guarding a bauxite mine, on the south-east coast of Bintan Island, 25 kilometres from Merapas. The two passengers on board, one of whom was Mr Tanabi, manager of the mine, were not injured but they were very interested in the cause of the forced landing: a drop in oil pressure due to a punctured oil line, which the mechanics believed could have been caused by a bullet. To avoid any possibility that enemy agents hiding on the islands to the east of Kidjang had fired at the plane as it passed overhead, Singapore HQ ordered Captain Fujimura and 2nd Lieutenant Orzawa, of the local garrison, to take a search party to Mapur Island, about eight kilometres to the north-west of Merapas.[6]

The news that enemy agents might be in the area ignited considerable excitement at the Kidjang garrison, especially for 14-year-old Aloysius Hayes Weller, a Eurasian of Indian descent. Only a fortnight or so before, Aloy, as he was known, had been standing near Captain Fujimura's office when the radio operator came running from the wireless shack, shouting that a police boat had been blown up at Kasu and that the European soldiers responsible had escaped by boat among the islands. To his great joy, Aloy had been permitted to ride in the landing craft with the soldiers while they carried out a search around Bintan but, to his disappointment, no trace of the enemy had been found.

A favourite with the Japanese, especially Captain Fujimura, whom Aloy regarded as his 'boss', in 1942 the young Eurasian had been living in Telok Anson, Malaya, with his schoolteacher father and the rest of the family when the Japanese occupied the town. With food scarce, he and his friend Shangamungan had carried out odd jobs at the barracks in return for leftover rice from the army kitchen, which they were allowed to take home to their families. When the troops moved to Ipoh and then to Singapore, Aloy, who could now speak Japanese quite well, was invited to go with them. By early 1944, when the regiment was transferred to Kidjang to guard the mine, Aloy had become indispensable as an errand boy and interpreter – but he was not that indispensable. To his chagrin, Captain Fujimura did not invite him to join the search party about to leave for Mapur. He took instead an Indonesian with extensive local knowledge – 24-year-old Abdul Rachman Achap, who worked in the office of Mr Frey, the Dutch harbour master.

Two lightly-built wooden landing barges containing about fifty Japanese troops and heiho arrived at Mapur on the morning of 4 November to interrogate the headman, Abdul Wahib. When he stated categorically that no reports had been received of Europeans in the area, Achap was certain that Wahib, an informant whose loyalty to the Japanese was ensured by a sack of rice every month, was telling the truth. Had he any idea that eighteen white men were hiding on Merapas he would have betrayed them long ago, and pocketed an extra 200 or 300 rupiah for his trouble.

For some reason the Japanese were not convinced. Taking the headman with them, the search party headed for Merapas, where they immediately apprehended a local man fishing from his kolek off the south-west tip. Although he must have known from young Karta that strangers were on the island, the fisherman did not betray them, despite being severely beaten. Evidently satisfied that the fisherman knew nothing, Fujimura left half his force on the landing barges with Lieutenant Orzawa and sauntered across the beach.

Hidden by the dense growth, Page and a group of men watched his every move from

Wild Cat Hill. About to have lunch when the alarm was sounded, they had grabbed their weapons and taken cover there. Another eight, eating their lunch in small shelters they had been repairing in Cache Swamp, also went to ground. From the casual manner in which Fujimura's landing craft approached the beach, Bob Page believed that the landing was routine and that enemy suspicions had not been aroused.

His reasoning was sound. Kolek Bay was a poor choice for troops on the offensive. Military logic dictated that, had the search party intended to storm the island, the troops should have landed on Invasion Coast, which was far more difficult to defend. Fujimura's seemingly very casual approach suggested that the visit was a low-key affair and it might well be that the Japanese, who were never keen on entering thick jungle, would make a superficial search along the beach and leave. What Page did not know was that Fujimura had every intention of searching the island. The troops had come ashore at Kolek Bay only because their lightly-built wooden landing barges could not handle the choppy seas along Invasion Coast.

Fujimura, accompanied by his men, started to move off the beach towards the coconut grove. Tension among the Rimau team on the hill was high – so high that one of them inadvertently discharged his silent Sten. This might not have been such a disaster had the bullets not found their mark, killing Captain Fujimura instantly and mortally wounding his batman, Private Toban, in the head. For the first second or two the Japanese were completely bewildered. It was not until they realised the pinging sounds they could hear were bullets ricocheting off the rocks that light dawned – someone was firing at them. To a man, they hit the ground.

Lieutenant Orzawa, watching from the landing barges, immediately assumed command and ordered his troops to spray the hillside with machine-gun and rifle fire. The fire was returned but, as there was no counter-attack and the firing had become sporadic by 4 pm, Orzawa deduced that the enemy's numbers were not great. With daylight soon to fade, he decided to send one of the barges with the wounded batman and Fujimura's corpse back to Kidjang for reinforcements so that he could mount a concentrated attack on the hill in the morning. Unwilling to expose his men to enemy fire, he ordered the fisherman and his wife to carry Private Toban and Fujimura to the barge, where they were beaten by enraged troops and detained for further punishment. By this time, night was closing in. As it would be many hours before reinforcements would arrive from Kidjang, Orzawa set up his headquarters in one of the huts before splitting his available troops into two groups. With one lot circling the island in the remaining barge, and the other keeping watch on the beach, he was confident that the white men could not escape. Unfortunately for him, he had underestimated the resourcefulness of his quarry.

Once their cover was blown, Page had accepted that Merapas was no longer tenable. If they could get to Mapur, however, just 8 kilometres distant, they might be able to hide out until the submarine returned on 7 November, just three days away. While their comrades provided heavy covering fire, a number of the group quickly retrieved their folboats, made their way to the deserted Invasion Coast and paddled off to Mapur. The remainder ensured the Japanese were kept at bay with sporadic fire. Although the folboats were seen leaving Invasion Coast, evidently by a fisherman who had then reported to Orzawa, they were not pursued. With his troops pinned down on the beach, darkness about to descend like a thick cloak and only one landing craft left, Orzawa decided to defer any search until the following day.

The remainder of Page's group waited until it was dark. Sending a wireless message to Australia to alert SOA of their predicament was evidently not an option. Craft, even if he knew the one-off code, was with the other party, which Page assumed was either hiding somewhere else on the island or had fled. Having ascertained that it took the water patrol two hours to circle the island, Page and his men smashed the radio to deny it to the enemy, recovered their folboats, packed them with available stores, including two of the four long-range walkie-talkies, and headed for Mapur. Probably to make more room for supplies, some of the men were towed behind the folboats, using improvised water-wings made from trousers stuffed with buoyant coconut fibre to provided additional flotation.

The next day at around noon about a hundred troops, most of whom were Kempeitai and heiho reinforcements from Tanjung Pinang, arrived from Kidjang to find about half the original force out searching for Page's group. With them was young Aloysius Weller who, although he had been allowed to tag along, was under strict instructions to remain on the beach when the search party eventually moved off. Abdul Rachman Achap, who had spent the night in one of the huts, was also ordered to remain on the beach near Stewart Point. From their vantage points the pair watched as Orzawa's expeditionary force split into two groups to storm the hill – one from the north and the other from the south-west – and moved off.

On the other side of the island Colin Campbell and Grigor Riggs waited in silence in two small forts, or sangars, built from rocks gathered from the foreshore and positioned either side of the track leading from Kingfisher's Rest to Cache Swamp. Hurriedly constructed, these crude fortifications had no firing steps, or slits, through which a gun could be aimed. Since the walls tapered inwards, there was only room for one man.

While Aloy and Achap watched the search party moving inland from Kolek Bay, the remaining Japanese, ordered to attack the hill from the rear, moved around Punai Point to Kingfisher's Rest. With a limited field of fire and only short-range weapons to defend themselves, the two Rimau men defending Invasion Coast had not stood a chance. They emptied a Sten and then their pistols into the advancing troops before Cameron was hit in the chest. As the Japanese closed in to deliver the coup de grâce to the back of his head, execution style, Riggs dropped his now useless pistol. Leaving the protection of his fort he ran towards

Wild Cat Hill in an effort to draw the enemy to the opposite end of the island, away from the other six Rimau men. He must have had a reasonable start on the Japanese, who were below him on the slippery rocks or advancing through the coconut grove.

For some time, Aloy and Achap had heard nothing. Then, from the far side of the island came the sound of heavy firing. Aloy could not see beyond the coconut grove but Achap, who was in a better position, caught a glimpse of a European soldier racing frantically between the trees on the skyline. Across the top of Wild Cat Hill he ran, down the spur towards Stewart Point, with the Japanese in hot pursuit. By the time Achap saw him, Riggs had run the best part of 300 metres, most of it uphill. He might have outdistanced his pursuers had the beach party not taken up the chase. Achap stood transfixed, watching Riggs' erratic progress as he ran for his life. When he reached the end of the spur, he ran out of land. With nowhere to run, the unarmed man faced his pursuers.

Three shots rang out, striking him in the chest. As he rolled down a rockface, to lie spread-eagled at its base, Achap ran forward. Cradling the badly wounded white man in his arms, the Indonesian looked into eyes that showed no fear. Quite calmly, without uttering a single word, Sub-Lieutenant Grigor Riggs crossed himself and died.

With all attention now on Riggs, the searchers on Wild Cat Hill out of sight, and no one left on the beach at Kolek Bay, the six remaining Rimau men – Blondie Sargent, Bruno Reymond, Doug Warne, Jeffrey Willersdorf, Colin Craft and Hugo Pace – took the opportunity to implement Lyon's contingency escape plan, apparently part of a strategy worked out with Riggs and Cameron the night before. While they created a diversion, the other six would grab two koleks lying on the beach, and head for Pompong Island, leaving Riggs and Cameron to follow in a folboat, if they could. The main group was well organised. Not only did they have rations readily to hand, but Reymond also had his sextant and charts. Grabbing the two koleks, each equipped with sails, paddles and an outrigger, they headed south-west towards Pompong. The koleks, being local craft, were suitable for open water and, unlike the folboats, had the added advantage of blending into the scenery.

As the Japanese closed in on Riggs, Abdul Achap looked closely at the dead body he held in his arms. Around one wrist was a beautiful silver bracelet, emblazoned with some kind of emblem, beneath which was engraved, in block letters, the name of its owner. Achap's English was limited, but he did notice that the name began with a G and ended with an S. His hopes of pocketing this valuable piece of jewellery came to naught. When the Japanese arrived, that was the end of the matter.

A search of the island revealed no sign of the remaining Rimau men. It was not until the koleks were found to be missing that the Japanese realised that the man they had shot on the run had allowed others to escape by deliberately drawing the searchers to the eastern end of the island. There was no attempt to try and follow the escapees. The seas were too rough for

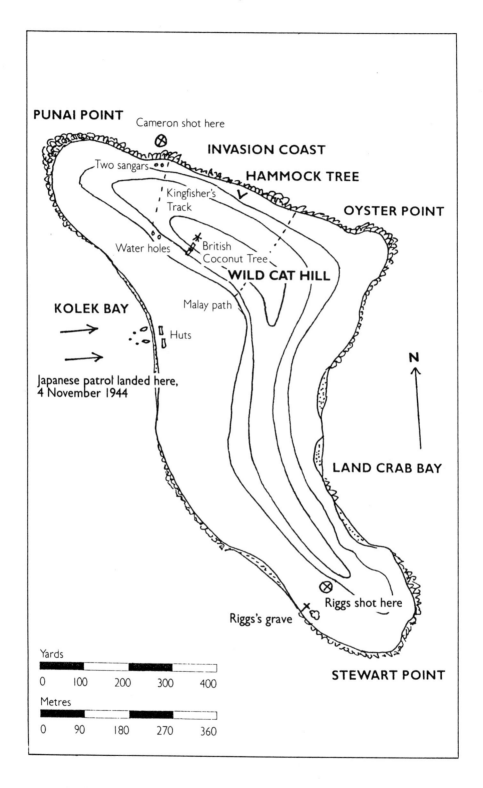

Merapas Island, showing the places at which various actions occurred

the flimsy landing barges to mount a pursuit, fuel was limited and, in any case, no one had any idea in which direction they had fled.

The Japanese normally left enemy corpses where they lay, or threw them into the sea or a nearby ditch. Captain Orzawa, impressed by Riggs' bravery, gave orders to bury him. When Achap saw that the grave was to be simply a pile of rocks heaped randomly on the body, he suggested that the soldier, who was obviously Christian, should be buried in the ground. Finding himself appointed gravedigger for his trouble, Achap lay Riggs to rest at the foot of the hill, in sandy soil near the beach at Stewart Point. The Japanese, who later claimed the credit for the burial, described the grave as 'very fine'. Aloysius Weller who, now that the action was over had left the safety of the beach area, was told about the white man's bravery and shown the grave, marked with a cross 3 metres tall made from two saplings. The Tanjung Pinang search party, keen to demonstrate their one-upmanship over the Kidjang group, bragged about their previous encounter with the white men on Soreh Island, referring constantly to another brave soldier they had encountered – a 'Major Rion' who, although wounded, had injected himself repeatedly with morphine and fought to the death.

With Riggs buried the Japanese, now feeling more confident – especially with Achap walking well ahead as their human shield – undertook a more thorough search of the island. In the clearing Achap found two walkie-talkie radios, one of which he hid under his shirt; bundles wrapped in sacking; two guns; a pistol; and a considerable amount of food. He was so busy tucking into the lunchtime rations abandoned by the Rimau party that he made the mistake of ignoring the Japanese when they called. After a thorough beating they sent him further up the hill to check if there was anything of interest. He found the smashed radio transmitter, situated well up the slope to maximise transmission and reception. Impressed by the fact that it had 'Australia' written on it (Amalgamated Wireless Australasia) and also that it had a short-wave frequency, he hoped that when the Japanese heard the radio was wrecked they would not bother to climb the hill to see it. Unfortunately, they wanted it, broken or not, so Achap had to content himself with the walkie-talkie, still hidden beneath his shirt.

Aloy, after inspecting and admiring the grave, accompanied some of the troops to the forts where Cameron's body lay. By this time he had been dead for some hours and the Japanese soldier souveniring his pistol had to prise it from his stiffened fingers. The soldiers, also much impressed by his bravery, showed Aloy the empty chamber. They also recovered an empty Sten gun, whose silencer was inspected with much interest, and Riggs' discarded revolver.

The searchers remained on the island overnight. To supplement the rations, Aloy was allowed to join a group of local fishermen who had arrived in two large sampans. Luring some very large fish to the surface with bait balls made from chopped sweet potato mixed with boiled fish, they soon had enough of a catch to satisfy everyone. The next day, when the search of the island resumed, Aloy received an unexpected windfall when they stumbled

One of two stone forts where Riggs and Cameron made their last stand

on the cleverly concealed emergency stores – dehydrated vegetables, chocolate and tobacco. Sufficient to last a month, the four-gallon sealed tins had been tied together, twelve at a time, and lowered into the sea on the end of a rope, the other end secured to a submerged tree root. For Aloy it was like a treasure hunt as he searched among the roots for more tell-tale ropes. The Japanese had no interest in the dehydrated meat, cabbage and carrots, or tins of Havelock brand pipe tobacco, and allowed him to take what he wanted. He was allowed to sample some of the chocolate, the first he had tasted in almost three years. What was denied him was an item found in the main camp which generated by far the most interest – a small, watertight brass tube containing a list of twenty-two typewritten names. There was much excitement when Aloy, who was fluent in English, Malay and Japanese, told the Japanese sergeant that the name on the top of the list was the name of the man they had all been talking about – Lyon.

It was obvious that the white men had decamped in a hurry. Further searching located the hammocks, well hidden among the trees further up the hill, three folboats, a camouflage hood and another walkie-talkie. Ransacking the men's belongings, the Japanese recovered Carey's notebook, Ingleton's sketch book, Page's camera (including exposed film), Mrs Manderson's flags and, from one of the huts near the beach, a document written in English. It is likely, from the brutal punishment later inflicted on the hut's occupants, that it was a testimonial written by the Rimau men in the hope that the islanders who had helped them would be rewarded after the war. Leaving a small force of mainly heiho to remain on the island, the Japanese loaded their booty into the barges and departed for Kidjang, taking Achap, Wahib and the Merapas islanders with them. En route, and much to his annoyance, Achap was relieved of the precious walkie-talkie by a keen-eyed Japanese soldier who had noticed him pocketing it while in the clearing. The young Indonesian arrived back home with nothing to show for his outing, other than some large, painful bruises and an unexpectedly but nevertheless satisfyingly full stomach.

Although Abdul Wahib, who had stated no Europeans were on Merapas, was lucky to return to Mapur unscathed, the Malays who had refused to betray the Rimau men were not so fortunate. For three weeks they were mercilessly beaten. The fisherman's pregnant wife miscarried, and her husband was so badly treated that twelve months later he was still unable to speak above a whisper. To compound their misery, when they finally returned to Merapas they found that the Japanese had torched their house.

When the documents, flags and camera recovered during the search of Merapas were examined in Singapore, the Kempeitai turned up the heat. The translated notebooks, the names in the brass tube and Ingleton's sketches, along with the developed photographs, convinced them that there was far more to this enemy party than had previously been thought. While Hiroyuki Furuta, a civilian interpreter attached to the Army's Intelligence Branch, wrestled with the meaning of cryptic written entries, such as 'SB treatment over', Kakoshima Nasaki, Chief of 29 Naval Kempeitai, ordered more Kempeitai troops into the area.

The Singapore Kempeitai's special force was still investigating the incident in which ships had been sabotaged the previous month. When the summary execution of a number of Malays and Chinese and the public display of their remains failed to produce any useful information, they turned their attention to the list of European suspects believed to be implicated in the attack the previous year. The two most prominent were Shell Oil employee John Long, who had just been released from gaol and was now back with the other internees (transferred in May to a new camp at Syme Road) and Captain Cornelis Woudenberg, the Dutch officer accused of espionage, breaching military security and assisting the enemy to attack, who was still in Kempeitai custody awaiting trial. To the Japanese it appeared an open and shut case. Both men must be implicated. To speed up the process and bring about a satisfactory conclusion to the investigation, Woudenberg was hastily brought to trial on 26 November. For John Long, there was no such refinement. As this second outrageous attack had taken place just four days after his release from gaol, the Kempeitai required no further proof of his guilt. On November 25 he was re-arrested. Two days later his captors drove him to a rubber plantation off Reformatory Road, and cut off his head. Back in Australia, twelve months after the raid, the top brass was still congratulating itself on Jaywick's success. In a report dated 24 October, referring to intercepted signals which showed that the Japanese were still blaming local elements, Colonel Roberts had remarked that 'the enemy's ignorance of the form of attack is interesting'.

The real culprits were still free. Page and his men were on Mapur and Sargent's group on the high seas. The latter were having a dream run for, although they had been spotted at various islands, no one had informed the Japanese. While the contingency plan – to make for Pompong, hijack a junk and sail for home – appeared somewhat ambitious, fate could have not selected a better team: Sargent and Willersdorf, both experienced soldiers, as was Pace; cool-headed Doug Warne; the highly intelligent Craft and, last but by no means least, Bruno Reymond, master mariner and expert navigator who, as soon as they had grabbed the koleks, had pointed them in the direction of Beruan Island, their first port of call. While Sargent's group was fleeing towards Pompong, Page and the other nine Rimau men waited patiently at Mapur for the submarine to return. But when Major Walter Chapman finally arrived at Merapas Island on 21 November, thirteen days late, they were nowhere to be seen.

13

Abandoned

21–22 November 1944

HMS *Porpoise* had returned to the Garden Island Base from Panjang Island on 11 October. Although the voyage was blessedly uneventful, both the vessel and her commander required attention. Overtaken by old age and with a singing propeller heading a list of mechanical complaints, *Porpoise* was in need of an overhaul.[1] So too was Marsham. Although he had promised Lyon he would return, he knew he was not the man to do it. War weary and emotionally burnt out by this latest sortie, he asked to be relieved of his command.

Realising that *Porpoise*, even with a new commander, might not be ready for sea in time to make the rendezvous at Merapas, Captain Shadwell cast around for an alternative. Although it had been suggested that an American submarine from Admiral Christie's Task Force 71 might be available, this option was not pursued – the military chiefs preferring not to invite the United States to join what had been up to this point an entirely British–Australian affair. Instead they selected HMS *Tantalus*, a T-class submarine which, although scheduled to undertake a patrol, could perform a dual role and make the pick-up. The sub's commanding officer, since April 1943, was Lieutenant-Commander Hugh Stirling Mackenzie, also known as 'Rufus' or 'Red Mackenzie', to distinguish him from another submarine commander, 'Black Mackenzie'. While commanding HMS *Thresher* in the Mediterranean during 1942, he had covered himself in glory and was awarded a DSO after sinking 40,000 tonnes of enemy shipping while on six patrols. His next command was *Tantalus*, a modern submarine of just over 100 tonnes, armed with one four-inch gun and ten 21-inch torpedo tubes and with a top speed of 10 knots. Mackenzie was itching to add to his tally of 'kills'. He had not had much chance lately, his most recent patrols being around the Malacca Straits where, to his chagrin, his sorties had included dropping off and picking up SOE agents attached to Force 136 – a task which he despised. 'Forever landing people in little canoes and picking them up again' was, to put it bluntly, 'a pain in the neck'. As he subscribed to the unshakeable view that 'the most important task of a submarine is to sink enemy shipping', he was most displeased to discover that *Tantalus* had been assigned as Rimau's taxi.

On 16 October, about the same time as Lyon was making his acquaintance with Latif on Soreh Island, *Tantalus* left Fremantle on her dual mission, carrying Rimau's rescue team, Walter Chapman and Ron Croton, and a full load of seventeen torpedoes. A far cry from *Porpoise* with her ungainly profile and lumbering ways, *Tantalus* was a streamlined hunter, captained by a man determined to live up to, and enhance, his reputation. With more than three weeks to go before he was due to divert to Merapas, Mackenzie had high hopes of sinking quite a few enemy ships.

Unfortunately for him, with the Americans having had free rein in the area for months, targets were now few and far between. After following a zigzagging course for twelve days, which took them to within sight of Merapas on October 28, he spied a ship only to see it scuttle into the safety of the Singapore Straits. Frustrated, Mackenzie resumed his search, the reports of the mauling the Japanese Fleet was receiving near the Philippines at the hands of the Americans serving to make him envious as well as annoyed.

He had to wait five days before another opportunity arose. When finally alerted by a signal from USS *Gurnard* that two large ships were headed for Singapore, *Tantalus* lay in wait, only to have visibility reduced to zero by a fierce rainstorm. The following afternoon, after stalking a convoy of four small merchantmen and sinking one of them – the 2,000-tonne freighter *Taga Maru* – Mackenzie was ordered to call off the chase and take up rescue duties in the waters off Singapore. Although this was designed to save the lives of downed airmen who were routinely beheaded if captured, Mackenzie disparagingly referred to his task as 'life guard duty'. On this occasion, they were to keep a lookout for air crew forced to bail out of B-29s dropping bombs on Singapore. To Mackenzie's disgust, they did not even see an aeroplane, let alone a downed airman. Finally released from the purgatory of rescue duty, Mackenzie resumed his patrol on 8 November.

Although only 60 kilometres away at the time, the submarine commander made no attempt to land Chapman and Croton at Merapas on the night of 7 November, nor did he attempt to do so on the following two days when *Tantalus* was still within 100 kilometres of the island. Without consulting his superior officers or sending any messages seeking an amendment to Operation Order No 44, Mackenzie had decided to delay the pick-up. The official reason, according to the log book, was because there were '15 torpedoes still remaining' and 'further targets had to be found'. He later tried to rationalise his decision by stating that, as he had sufficient fuel and stores for fourteen days and believed his main objective was 'offensive action against the enemy', it would be 'improper' to abandon his patrol in order to pick up the party. Evidently, in an effort to cover himself for what could be construed as a blatant disregard for orders, he 'consulted' Major Chapman. Chapman, a fairly mild-mannered fellow, was no match for Mackenzie, who had been massaging the conducting officer's ego by treating him as a valued member of the crew rather than as a passenger. Chapman, his position now compromised, allegedly accepted Mackenzie's proposal to defer the pick up and 'concurred'.

Despite his protestations, Mackenzie's line of reasoning was indefensible. Everyone including Major Chapman knew that the pick-up date was 7–8 November. Although the Rimau party had been instructed to wait thirty days should the submarine not turn up on time, this fallback position did not absolve Mackenzie of the responsibility of making every effort to keep the original rendezvous, as his orders demanded. The date agreed upon by Lyon, Chapman, Shadwell and Marsham had been explicit, and Operation Order No 44 plainly stated that 'subject to patrol requirements, HMS *Tantalus* will leave her patrol at dark on 7 November and proceed to the vicinity of Merapas Island'.

Patrol requirements at this stage were nil. Despite scouring the ocean they had found no masses of shipping whose destruction was vital to the war effort, which was hardly surprising, since by this stage enemy vessels in the waters *Tantalus* was patrolling were mostly junks. Indeed, the patrol was considered to be such low priority that *Tantalus* had been ordered to assist in 'life guard duty'. Furthermore, there was no practical reason why *Tantalus* could not have returned to her home port with fifteen torpedoes still intact. Conditions on a T-class sub were rather cramped but Rimau's accommodation did not depend on using the space occupied by the six reserve torpedoes. Even if it had, the warheads, although expensive, could have been dumped. After all, what was the loss of a few torpedoes – torpedoes which were often wasted when they misfired, or missed the target – against the lives of twenty-three men?

Tragically, although enemy signals were being constantly intercepted, no one had any idea that the lives of all those who had reached the safety of Merapas were now in very great jeopardy. On the night of 21–22 October the Japanese had sent a four-part message from Singapore, giving details of the action at Kasu and advising, in part, that:

> about 1700 on 10 October, in the vicinity of Kaso Island in the north-west part of the Rio Islands south of Singapore, Sea Police Unit staff members ... discovered a tonkan of about 100 tons acting suspiciously and were about to board it when we were fired on by the crew which had several white men in it. Three men were killed and after that [unintelligible] to nine enemy rubber boats.

Allied personnel intercepting enemy signal traffic sorted them for decoding on the basis of priority. As all the signals of 21–22 October had been classified by the Japanese in Singapore as 'routine', on interception they were put aside as non-urgent translation. Normally this would not have had any real impact, since 'routine' signals were generally decoded within a week of receipt. But with the Americans inflicting staggering losses on the Japanese at the Battle of Leyte Gulf in a campaign to retake the Philippines which began on 23 October, Japanese signal traffic not only soared, but was flooded with high priority messages. The signals which would have alerted SOA that Rimau was in dire trouble were not decrypted until 12 February, 31 March and 10 April 1945, many months later.

Had these signals been classified by the Japanese as urgent, SOA and therefore Chapman would have known by 7 November that the mission had been compromised and the situation at Merapas was critical. There would certainly have been no possibility of Mackenzie deferring the pick-up. Sadly, human weakness and the submarine commander's need for personal glory triumphed. To return home with only one small freighter to his credit, when the United States Navy had been eliminating enemy shipping around the Philippines at an admirable rate, was evidently too much to expect from a man like Rufus Mackenzie. With his own pride, as well as that of the Royal Navy if not the British Empire at stake, the ambitious submarine commander could not resist the opportunity to strut his stuff.

For three days he found nothing. Then, on 11 November, a target was finally spotted. It was a tiny wooden coastal trader carrying Captain Mohammed bin Serim, Assistant Engineer Mohammed Daud bin Saleh, nine Malays and one Chinese, guarded by a lone Japanese soldier. Stuttering across the sea to the north-east of Merapas, *Pahang Maru*, loaded with seventy-five drums of fuel oil and nine drums of lubricating oil, was on a voyage from Kuantan on Malaya's east coast to Bangkok. It was obvious from the trader's stop-start progress that the captain was experiencing serious engine trouble. *Tantalus* soon caught up with the ailing vessel, travelling at a speed of just three knots, and surfaced.

Anxious to capture the scene for posterity, Major Chapman clambered up the ladder to the submarine's conning tower. Without firing a single warning shot against the unarmed merchantman, *Tantalus's* four-inch guns let loose at a range of 540 metres. The first round ignited a fire amidships, the next four killed the captain and his assistant engineer and set the engine room alight. When the firing stopped, the remaining members of *Pahang Maru's* crew were observed hanging over the railings, peering anxiously at the holes in the hull. Although they showed no inclination to flee, *Tantalus* closed in, allowing the gunners to resume firing from a range of only 180 metres. The vessel, now well ablaze and breaking up, began to sink.

As the water reached deck level, nine of the crew abandoned ship and were picked up, clinging to wreckage. Alerted by the prahu's chief engineer that the Japanese guard was making for the shore, the submarine aborted the rescue of the last crew member, still standing on the burning deck, and chased after the soldier, who attempted to drown himself by holding his head under water. After being subdued with a blow to the head with a lead weight he was taken on board *Tantalus* and ushered below where, contrary to his expectations, his burns were treated and he was well looked after. Despite having begged for his life when capture was imminent, he was now so dispirited that he went into a major decline and spent the remainder of the voyage huddled miserably in a corner.

Fortunately the remaining crewman, who was an able swimmer, had sensibly jumped overboard. He simply paddled around in the water awaiting rescue while the drama with the Japanese took place. When he and his fellow crew members had recovered from the trauma of being blown out of the water, they were handed over to the captain of a Chinese junk who, after being hailed by the Chinese crewman, agreed to relieve Mackenzie of his unwanted passengers in return for a tin of biscuits.

With the handover successfully negotiated Mackenzie reassessed his position. Arguing that 'the most useful thing the submarine could do would be to continue on her patrol until the remaining torpedoes had been used up', he decided to delay the pick-up even further – for another week. As this would be pushing his 'patrol requirements' to the limit, at 10.36 pm on 11 November, Remembrance Day, Mackenzie transmitted a signal to Captain Shadwell requesting an additional seven days' deferment. The precise contents of this message are not known but whatever was said must have been persuasive. Against all logical explanation Captain Shadwell, who had once been so worried that Rimau's safety had been compromised with the security leak that he advocated cancellation of the entire mission, gave Mackenzie the permission he sought.

For the next nine days *Tantalus* patrolled the waters between Singapore and the Natuna Islands without success, sighting only three targets – none of which was attacked. November 18, the 'new' pick-up date, came and went. The following day the submarine carried out another round of life-guard duty off the Malayan coast, during a strike on Singapore by China-based Allied aircraft. This mission was as uneventful as the first. Finally on 21 November, three days after the deferred pick-up date and fully two weeks after she was expected, *Tantalus*, her fifteen precious torpedoes still intact, arrived at Merapas.

At 7 that evening the submarine completed a lengthy periscope reconnaissance of the island. As they cruised along, 1500 metres from the shoreline, Chapman was satisfied that, from Davidson's description and map, he had identified the Hammock Tree. On the south-western coast he spotted four figures, believed to be Malays, walking along the beach near the huts, and a kolek, tied to the mooring stakes. The uninhabited house appeared to be still uninhabited and, indeed, the only sign of occupation, apart from the beach wanderers, was a fire burning in the banana plantation behind Stewart Point. It all seemed perfectly normal. There was no sign of the Rimau party, but that was only to be expected.

The pick-up orders, drafted by someone who had paid scant attention to either the topography of the island or to Davidson's detailed notes, had actually directed that the folboat land on the south-western, or lee side, which was about as far away from the Hammock Tree as it was possible to be. Mackenzie, however, decided that conditions were favourable enough to attempt a landing on the northern ('invasion') coast, thereby cutting the distance to be negotiated on foot by about half. At about 1 am Tantalus, with the folboat and stores lashed firmly to the casing, stopped about 450 metres north-west of Oyster Point. Had Chapman and Croton come directly ashore at this point, they would have been about 300 metres from the Hammock Tree, but 300 metres to the west – the wrong direction.

As the approach was supposed to be from the east it is obvious that no one, least of all Chapman, had bothered to consult Davidson's instructions. He had been most specific. When approaching the island the pick-up team was to come ashore at Land Crab Bay. While one man waited in the dense growth behind the beach, the other was to continue on foot in a westerly direction until he reached the Hammock Tree.

Launching their folboat from the submarine's fore hydroplanes, Chapman and Croton paddled towards a small stretch of sand, aided by a calm sea and cloudless sky. As they neared Punai Point, even further to the west, Chapman became alarmed by what he thought was the sound of waves smacking against the rocks and decided to land around the point, on the lee side. It was not far – about 300 or 400 metres – but with the stroke of each paddle they moved further away from the Hammock Tree, which had to be reached well before daybreak. After some difficulty with a breaking sea they touched bottom about 5 metres off Dead Coral Beach. It was now almost 2 am. Concealing the folboat in thick foliage behind the beach, they headed for Punai Point. In selecting this route, it is obvious that Chapman had no idea that the fastest way to the Hammock Tree was to cut inland, across Wild Cat Hill. The coastal route he selected was hopeless. Between Dead Coral and the Hammock Tree were 600 metres of slippery black rocks.

Had Walter Chapman gone ashore when the stores were offloaded from *Porpoise* he may have had some idea of just how difficult the boulders were to negotiate in the dark. Varying in size from 20 centimetres to almost a metre in diameter and as treacherous as polished glass, this route was for the fit and sure-footed. Chapman, a technical expert, was neither. In the past seventy-one days he had spent just four on dry land. Coupled with the need for silence, Chapman's wobbly legs reduced them to an agonisingly slow pace. After two and a half hours of slipping and sliding, covering a distance of just on 300 metres, they finally reached the small patch of sand where they had intended originally to land. As they cleared the point, Chapman switched on a torch to light the way. Horrified that anyone could be so stupid, Corporal Croton cocked his Sten and informed Chapman that he would shoot him if he did not extinguish the light. Exhausted, and convinced that they had reached Kingfisher's Rest despite there being no trace of the track leading inland, Chapman called a halt.

About an hour later, when he was ready to set off again, the pre-dawn light was beginning to flood the horizon. As he glanced seaward, he froze. Three large naval vessels appeared to be anchored off the coastline. His alarm subsided when a closer look revealed that they were simply some small, rocky islands dotted with isolated trees which looked like masts, but this provoked a new concern. Perhaps they might be seen by someone on the islands – a notion dismissed by Croton, who could not see what all the fuss was about and refused to keep low, as ordered. By the time they reached the Hammock Tree, about 300 metres further on, it was almost daylight. When Chapman looked for the hammock slung between the tree trunks he found, to his consternation, that the space was empty. It was little wonder. They had arrived far too late. Not only had they come from completely the wrong direction, they had missed the rendezvous by at least one, possibly two hours. The arrangements were crystal clear. If the rendezvous was not kept, the shore party would leave the tree at first light and take cover during the daylight hours.

The pair searched the area but found nothing except a few small pieces of silver paper beneath a bush. Tracks they did not expect to find, for the men had been trained to remove all signs of their presence. Deciding to carry out a search of the island they avoided the path running up the hill from the tree, striking off a little to the east and up a steep slope covered with palm trees and creepers. They were scaling the hill without any problem when Chapman's boot dislodged a small boulder. It went rolling away with what seemed to be an incredibly loud noise, giving him his second fright of the day. His nerves were obviously on edge. Croton, who was nearby, took absolutely no notice.

On reaching the summit they turned east to explore the remainder of the ridge. It was not very interesting – just an overgrown banana plantation filled with rotting fruit and some spiky sago palms. They had passed the sago patch when they saw a lone Japanese, followed by a small skinny pi-dog trotting along about 50 metres behind. Flattening themselves against the nearest coconut trees, Croton and Chapman watched as the man crossed their field of vision at right angles and disappeared over the rise, followed by the dog.

Ron Croton had no doubt that the man was Japanese. He had seen Japanese soldiers during Mission 204 in China and, like Chapman, had just spent ten days observing the prisoner on board *Tantalus*. Unlike the locals, who dressed in sarongs or shorts and singlet, this man was wearing a proper shirt and long trousers. Too tall for a Malay, his skin was pale and his features oriental. Croton was keen to take him prisoner but, as Chapman pointed out, they had neither rope for securing his hands and feet, nor a suitable gag and, since it was so early in the morning, his absence would be noted long before the submarine returned.

Somewhat shaken by the encounter, Chapman had Croton cover him while he worked his way down the slope, parallel to the path taken by the man and dog, which led to the native huts. As they neared Cache Swamp they turned west and skirted the northern side, to keep well away from the hut area. Reaching its western end, near Dead Coral, Chapman ordered Croton to check that the folboat was well hidden while he sat beneath a tree to rest. The corporal, obeying under protest what he considered an unnecessary order, reported on his return that the folboat, as expected, was still properly concealed and that his errand had been 'a bloody waste of time'. They resumed their search, discovering two paths leading up the hill from a couple of small, rock-lined waterholes, each containing about 30 centimetres of water and concealed beneath some bushes. Observing the weathered piles of earth from the excavation, Croton estimated the 45-centimetre deep holes had been dug six to eight weeks previously. Noting a sweat rag and bandage hanging from a tree and four makeshift bailers on the ground, they proceeded along the nearest path. It led to a recently cut clearing which not only showed ample evidence of occupation, but also that whoever had been there had left in a tearing hurry.

Dominating the area was a crude shelter about 7.5 metres long and 3 metres wide, with a palm frond floor. Similar to a bush lean-to, it had been constructed by suspending a pole between a fork in a tree and an overhanging branch and then partially covering the framework with interwoven palm leaves. Nearby, half-filled with stagnant water and sitting on the remains of a small fire, was a large and very heavy iron wok of the type used by *Mustika's* crew. Four or five Commando cookers containing partially cooked meals rested on the charred sticks of much smaller fires. Although the food was now putrid, it was evident that it had come from Rimau's 'compo' rations and, on closer inspection, it was apparent from the crushed charcoal that the fires had been hurriedly stamped out. Under some cut, dried-out brush, the eagle-eyed Croton spotted a rubbish heap containing fifty empty tin cans, while another heap about 5 metres away held another thirty. Quite obviously, a number of the party had been here. The question was, where were they now?

Further searching revealed other odds and ends – an empty beer bottle, an oil can from the SB maintenance kit, Davidson's small rake, which Carey used to eliminate footprints, empty Three Castle brand cigarette packets, some lengths of rope, a cotton tag inscribed with the name Watanabe Takehiro in oriental characters, a bunch of green bananas, some mostly rotten paw paws, yam roots, a very ripe coconut and, quite inexplicably, a set of unintelligible symbols carved into the trunk of a coconut tree, well over 2 metres from the ground.

Bewildered, Chapman and Croton extended their search and found three paths running from the hill towards the Invasion Coast. The first, leading to Kingfisher's Rest, showed no signs of recent use and was not explored further. The second, which led towards the Hammock Tree, was partially investigated, yielding some more fragments of silver paper and a broken drinking bowl. The third track, which led nowhere in particular, yielded nothing.

They then turned along the ridge to the east where, without actually venturing down to Stewart Point to check the area thoroughly, Chapman came to the conclusion that the missing men were not hiding anywhere in the vicinity. Finding nothing apart from the overgrown banana plantation which they had already visited, they returned to Cache Swamp to find more evidence of Rimau's occupation. Scattered amid the undergrowth were six well-constructed and sturdy wood and palm-leaf shelters. Large enough to accommodate two men, each contained tins of half-cooked food resting on the ashes of long-dead fires. Nearby were two similar but lower structures, which looked as if they might have been built to conceal folboats. Near the small waterholes was a thin rope that could have served as a clothes line, but otherwise they found nothing – no weapons, no clothing, no note and definitely no sign at all of the three tonnes of stores and equipment.

Chapman, satisfied that the Rimau men were not on the island, called off the search. The submarine was not due for many hours so he and Croton sat in the clearing to wait, and think. With few clues on which to base his assumptions and clouded by evidence which did not seem to add up, Chapman concluded that the Rimau men had returned to Merapas, perhaps in the junk, and that they had been surprised and captured without a fight. To aid his investigation he briefly considered taking one of the locals for interrogation, but decided this idea was impracticable, as well as dangerous – and dangerous it most certainly would have been, for the Merapas natives had been supplanted by an enemy patrol. Resigning himself to the fact that Rimau had disappeared, the Major fervently hoped that whatever had happened had taken place before 7 November, the date on which the submarine should have returned to rescue them.

Chapman and Croton remained in the clearing trying to figure out where everyone was until the onset of dusk, when they moved down to Dead Coral, retrieved their folboat and settled down on the rocky shore to await the arrival of the submarine. At 9.50 pm, after four rather anxious hours, Chapman was relieved to see the reassuring silhouette of *Tantalus* round Punai Point in the moonlight.

Rufus Mackenzie had experienced a rather trying day. At six that morning the submarine had been fired upon by a Japanese patrol vessel and forced to dive. Two hours later they had again submerged to avoid detection by a Jake seaplane and other aircraft, evidently alerted by the patrol boat. Consequently, after spending almost the entire day under water Mackenzie was more than pleased to see the figures of Croton and Chapman waiting on the rocks. At 10.20, after experiencing some difficulty in coming alongside in the heavy swell, the reconnaissance party was helped back on board.

Chapman reported to Mackenzie that the rescue operation was a lost cause – although there were signs that the party had been there, they had obviously left at least a fortnight before. Chapman was so adamant on this point that Mackenzie concluded there was no point in returning the next night to try and make contact, as his orders specified. Indeed, he decided that to hang about any longer might unnecessarily jeopardise the safety of his submarine. With 'practically a full outfit of torpedoes remaining', Mackenzie left Merapas in search of richer pickings.

Still waiting patiently on Mapur, and now utterly abandoned, were Bob Page and his men. As they had been unable to contact the submarine with the long range walkie-talkies, and with their only hope of rescue dependent on keeping the rendezvous, every night since 7 November two members of the group had paddled across to Merapas as soon as it became dark to maintain their vigil at the Hammock Tree.

That the two parties failed to meet on the night of 21 November was due to a number of tragic and avoidable errors. Firstly, Rimau had been expecting *Porpoise*, the submarine specifically assigned to the mission, not *Tantalus*, to arrive on or soon after the night of 7–8 November. Secondly, the submarine should have approached from Stewart Point, allowing the pick-up party coming from Land Crab Bay to reach the Hammock Tree well before first light. Thirdly, and most importantly, if contact were not made, the orders stated very clearly that the rescue party was to return on successive nights. Not one of these things occurred.

The substitution of *Tantalus* for *Porpoise* would not have been a consideration had the submarine surfaced in the correct position. Even with her streamlined hull well trimmed down to facilitate the launching of Chapman's folboat, the Rimau lookouts could not possibly have missed seeing her had she lain off Land Crab Bay. Had Major Chapman, late as he was, approached the tree from the east as expected, the Rimau men would have spotted him scrambling over the rocks. In the unlikely event of the men at the Hammock Tree failing to see either of these things, they would have had a second chance to establish contact on the night of 22 November, had *Tantalus* not picked up Chapman and Croton out of sight on the other side of the island. Needless though these mistakes were, the factor which tipped the balance was Chapman's insistence that the Rimau men were no longer on the island and, indeed, had been long gone. Had the rescue party attempted a second rendezvous as ordered on the night of 22–23 November, they would have found the Rimau men waiting in the darkness.

Furthermore, had Chapman carried out the search of the island as thoroughly as he later maintained, he could not have failed to find either the forts or Cameron's rock-covered grave, just five metres away. Nor could he have missed the freshly turned earth surmounted by the sapling cross, marking the burial place of Riggs. While the discovery of the remains and the grave might not have altered Chapman's decision to abandon the search and leave Merapas, it would have removed part of the mystery and gone some way towards establishing the fate of the Rimau men.

With the pick-up abandoned, Mackenzie decided against returning immediately to Australia. He headed towards Java, hoping to find worthwhile targets among convoys sailing south. Despite high hopes, none was located until the morning of 27 November, when a small merchantman with two escorts was spotted. Four torpedoes were fired but, in Mackenzie's words, it was a 'rotten attack'. The first two exploded prematurely, the second pair missed the ship completely. With the enemy alerted to her presence, *Tantalus* beat a retreat for Lombok. Nine days later they were back at the base in Western Australia.

As a rescue mission, the 6th War Patrol of HMS *Tantalus* was an abject failure. As a patrol it had not been much better. The expenditure of six torpedoes, four of which were wasted, 1500 rounds of ammunition and almost 260,000 litres of fuel did not stack up well against the destruction of one small freighter and a nondescript native vessel, two innocent Malays dead and the capture of one dejected prisoner of war. The best spin that could be placed on this very expensive, 52-day patrol, which had covered 18,400 kilometres, was that it was the longest wartime patrol by any British submarine. In the complete absence of anything else about which to boast, it was a claim that assumed disproportionate importance.

On their return, both Chapman and Croton reported to SOA for debriefing. Croton was questioned only briefly. Chapman, being in command, was required to compose a written report. By 12 December he had produced a lengthy written account of the entire operation, including details of the incidents which had occurred while on the submarine. Included in his narrative were some interesting details which had been omitted, or differed, from those which appeared in the report submitted by Mackenzie and information later provided by Croton.

There was no reference by Chapman that Mackenzie had 'consulted' him about the pick-up date, or that he had 'concurred' with the deferment. Although he remembered the little pi-dog with absolutely clarity, he did not mention that Croton had threatened to shoot him, that they had seen the Japanese man or that Croton had suggested taking him prisoner. Despite these apparent memory lapses, he did not forget to submit to his superiors an Adverse Confidential Report on soldier Ron Croton.

It can only be assumed, from the way in which he presented the reasons for the mission's failure, that Major Chapman was now consumed by doubt and guilt. Included in his report to SOA was a two-page copy, typed by Chapman, of Mackenzie's Patrol Report Appendix 1 which gave the submarine commander's version of the pick-up – a sortie which, according to Mackenzie was 'a very bitter disappointment to Major Chapman, and a blow to us all'. He also 'hoped that the delay in carrying out the operation was not the cause for the loss of this gallant party, but it must be considered as a possibility'. In the retyped version, this statement had been altered to 'It is unfortunately very possible' [that the loss of the party was attributed to the delay]', thereby absolving Chapman of any responsibility for the deferment of the pick-up date. Many years later, when confronted with the evidence that he had delayed the pick-up in order to chase after targets, Mackenzie claimed he had asked for, and had received, permission before he did so. But the *Tantalus* log book, which records, in detail, every aspect of the voyage including signal transmissions, does not support this latter-day claim.[2]

In what appears to be a further attempt to mitigate the sickening thought that he might be held accountable in some way for the late arrival, Chapman presented his evidence piece by piece, to 'prove' that, even if the submarine had turned up on the right date, it still would have been too late. The mangoes, the coconuts, the cut brush and the decaying food were all deemed to be at least two weeks old. He even decided that the unripened bananas had been cut fourteen days previously, obviously unaware that in the tropics green bananas ripen at a much faster rate than they do in England and, furthermore, that had they been two weeks old they would have been a blackened, overripe mess. However, to anyone reading the report there seemed to be no doubt – Rimau could not possibly have been on the island in the two weeks prior to 7 November and, judging by Chapman's allegedly thorough search, they were not anywhere in the vicinity.

To add weight to his case, Chapman fancifully suggested that the most likely scenario was that:

> Lieutenant Carey was taken off the island by the enemy, his presence having been given away by the Malays, before the main party started arriving. The main party was then picked up individually as they arrived on the island. The enemy removed the stores at the same time as removing Lieutenant Carey.

The astute intelligence officer who examined this report was unimpressed by either the contents or its conclusions. Convinced that many stones had been left unturned, he began a campaign to mount a secret rescue operation code-named Rimexit. His unshakeable conviction that the Rimau men might still be on Merapas was well founded. Although the party had quit the island as a permanent base sixteen days before Chapman arrived, for thirty anxious days they kept the rendezvous each night, watching and waiting for the submarine to come.

On 5 May 1964, not long after this fact became known to him during an interview with writer Brian Connell, Walter Chapman, aged forty-nine, was found in his car outside the Amersham Hospital in Buckinghamshire, England. He was dead. In his pocket, Constable David Whitehead found an empty bakelite capsule, of a type not seen since World War II. Dr R W Harries conducted an autopsy, as the law required, but even to a layman the cause of death was obvious. Radiating from the pink-cheeked corpse was the unmistakable scent of bitter almonds.

Twenty years on, Operation Rimau had claimed yet another victim.

14

In enemy hands

27 November 1944–30 April 1945

W hen thirty days had come and gone with no sign of the submarine, Page decided to move his men to Pompong Island. Initially, when the pick-up team failed to arrive on the expected date, the men waiting on Mapur had not been disheartened. Japanese boats were still scuttling about the area and Bob Page believed that the submarine commander had simply deferred the pick-up until things had quietened down. But now they had given up all hope of being rescued. Not only were the thirty days up, there had been no response from the submarine via the long-range walkie-talkies. What they did not know was that the walkie-talkies were useless for this purpose (it would not be until mid-1945 that this problem would be ironed out). Leaving Mapur, the Rimau men worked their way south during the following week, skirting the southern entrance of the Riau Straits as they retraced the route taken by *Mustika*. Although they made contact with a Chinese man as they threaded their way to Buton Strait, they were not betrayed.

Blondie Sargent's party, which had opted for a route via Beruan, Borus and Lina islands, a little further east, had also been fortunate that not a single word of its progress had reached the ears of the Japanese now stationed on all islands which were inhabited. However on 27 November, ten days before Page left Mapur, Sargent's group was spotted at Temiang, a short distance from Pompong. From here they had moved south to Sebangka Island and then down the west coast of Lingga Island, stopping off at Lima Island and at Tanjung Datu on December 1 before heading towards the junk routes near southern Sumatra. Although the Japanese had lost contact with the fugitives at Sebangka, the Kempeitai and local collaborators remained very much on the alert. They were to watch out not only for koleks but also for larger vessels which might attempt to penetrate the area – a possibility which, following the fight at Kasu, had been reduced with the introduction of new regulations regarding the identification of friendly vessels, including fishing boats.

When Page's group reached Pompong the men split up – Page, Falls, Gooley and Fletcher in one group and Ingleton, Carey, Warren, Huston, Marsh and Hardy in the other – the composition providing each group with at least one officer and two Jaywick men who were familiar with the area. They were unaware that the Japanese were using the walkie-talkies recovered at Merapas to monitor the radio traffic between the fugitives. Through the Tjempa Straits they paddled, right into the heart of the Lingga Archipelago – and right into the arms of the Japanese.[1]

On December 15, after informants had reported seeing Sargent's group on nearby Lima Island, a search party consisting of Japanese naval personnel, a village headman named Engku Haji Said Nuh, and two heiho – one of whom was called Sukarti – arrived at Selajar Island with orders to look for white men. About 11 am, after forcibly extracting information from locals living in Kampong Penuba, Engku's party surprised Page, Falls, Fletcher and Gooley as they were cooking a meal. The Japanese opened fire. Wally Falls, bending over the fire, was wounded in the right hip and captured. The other three, unhurt, split up and fled.

That same day, but further to the north, between the islands of Pompong and Buaja, and dangerously close to the seaplane base at Tjempa Island, Ingleton's party ran into a group of Kempeitai and heiho. While attempting to escape, the folboat manned by Huston and Marsh was holed by enemy gunfire and sank. Fred Marsh managed to extricate himself from the sinking craft to seek refuge on Tjempa with Carey and Warren, but 'Happy' Andrew Huston, the determined young sailor who learned to swim so that he could go on Jaywick, was caught in a ferocious rip tide, and disappeared. The following day the Kempeitai found his drowned body, washed up on the southern headland of Buaja, a place where many a sailor had finally come to rest. It was 16 December, nine days before he would have celebrated his twenty-first birthday. Two days later, at 5.24 pm, the Kempeitai caught up with Ingleton and Hardy, who had been wounded in the shoulder, on nearby Gentung Island.

December 18 was a most satisfactory day for the Japanese. Thirty-six minutes after Hardy and Ingleton were captured, Bob Page, utterly exhausted, was found hiding in a native hut on Selajar. For three days after Marsh's capture he had been on the run and now, bone-weary and hungry, could run no more. Helped by a local family, he was lying in bed with a local girl pretending to be asleep when the Japanese arrived. The enemy troops approached cautiously on tip-toe, taking what seemed an eternity before they finally pounced. Page could have dispatched one or two of them with his pistol but he was too tired to bother. In any case, he had accepted that capture was inevitable.

The next day Fletcher and Gooley, the last remaining members of Page's party, were also captured on Selajar. Headman Engku Haji Said Nuh watched as all four, along with their folboats, were loaded onto a boat for transfer to Dabo Police Station, a low white Dutch colonial building of indeterminate age on nearby Singkep Island. Shortly afterwards Ingleton and Hardy arrived from Gentung. All six, all charged with being 'an enemy of the state', were objects of great interest to the locals until 23 December, when they departed in two fishing boats for Tanjung Pinang where they were handed over to the Japanese navy.

They arrived in Singapore in two groups – one on Christmas Eve and the other two

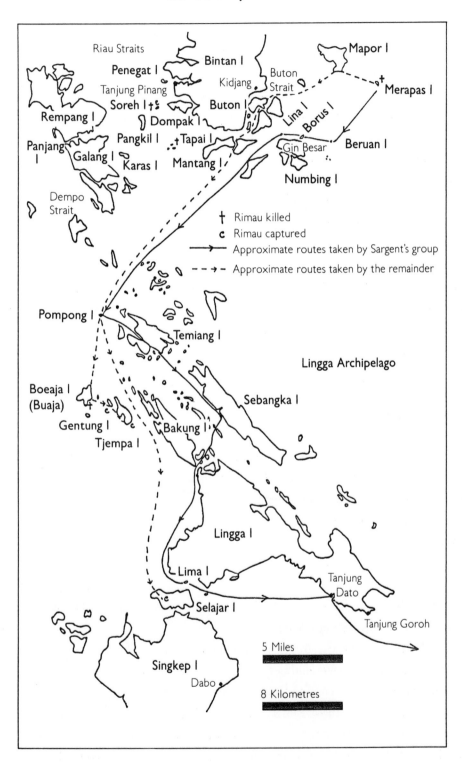

Riau and Lingga archipelagos, showing the routes taken by the Rimau men and places where they were either killed or captured

days later. The group which arrived on 26 December, having spent the interim at Tanjung Pinang, certainly made a memorable entrance. After his return from the Burma-Thai railway, Australian POW Sergeant James Flaherty of 2/1 Fortress Engineers had been sent to River Valley Camp, where he had been placed on a draft with Convoy H184 bound for Japan. Having spent ten tedious days on board the cargo ship *Awa Maru*, packed with tin, rubber and 525 POWs, waiting for the all-clear for the eight-vessel convoy to depart, he and his mates watched with interest as three European men were escorted from a naval vessel by armed sailors, indicating that they were certainly more than ordinary prisoners.

The following day, 27 December, three days after discovering the remains of the supply dump at Pompong, the Japanese cornered the last three fugitives on Tjempa Island. Although there had been no reports since early that month regarding the whereabouts of Sargent's party, the Japanese waited another ten days, presumably in case they reappeared, before sending Carey, Warren and Marsh, suffering from a bayonet wound to the upper chest, to join their comrades in Singapore. Under heavy guard, they made the trip by gunboat, spending the night in the Kidjang Police Station where they became the centre of attention for the local villagers. By now Marsh was so desperately ill that a rumour circulated he was dead.

By the time they arrived at the Tanjung Pagar headquarters of the infamous Water Kempeitai, housed in the Chinese YMCA building off Palmer Street, Marsh was close to death. Suffering from a raging fever, he was so weak that he was carried in on a stretcher. For two fever-racked days he lingered, his cries clearly audible to the others, locked in a nearby room. On 11 January, the moans ceased. Fred Marsh, the sailor for whom life had been a carefree, fun-filled stage, was dead. Whether the actual cause of death was the severity of his wound, a rampant infection, or illness is not known. The Japanese, predictably, declared he had died from malaria.

Most people who died in custody were said to have died of malaria. In nominating this virulent disease, the Kempeitai had hit upon a most convenient method of explaining away deaths which should not have occurred. They also claimed that Marsh had been visited by a doctor but, regrettably, nothing could be done for him. That a doctor had been in 'attendance' was undoubtedly true. One usually turned up at a Kempeitai establishment when it appeared that a prisoner might inconveniently expire while still in custody. The system worked well. The medico looked, the patient died, and the official records were kept in order.

As soon as the first three Rimau men arrived in Singapore on 24 December, the commandant of the Water Kempeitai, Lieutenant Hinomoto Norio, had summoned several men to his office. One who hurried through the streets bright with Christmas decorations to answer the call was 37-year-old Furuta Hiroyuki, the Japanese civilian interpreter who had been translating, and puzzling over, Rimau's notebooks. At the Tanjung Pagar HQ Furuta was joined by Captain Noguchi, also from Garrison HQ, Warrant Officer Imanaka and two other interpreters.

Lieutenant Hinomoto had convened the meeting to seek advice on how to handle the prisoners – members of a party which seemed to be superior to ordinary soldiers. As two of them had fought to the death and another two had taken poison to avoid capture, he had concluded that the Kempeitai's usual methods of persuasion would be ineffective. His belief that violent interrogation would elicit little or no information had already been put to the test. Corporal Stewart, captured on Soreh with the help of Raja Mun on 18 October, had kept his mouth firmly shut for almost ten weeks, despite constant torture.

Furuta, who was well travelled and had spent five years in Europe and England before the war, agreed that violence and systematic starvation would be unproductive. Realising that, since they had not been captured during combat, the prisoners' main concern would be their status, he shrewdly suggested that they could be made to feel at ease by a combination of gentle treatment and reassurance that the interrogators were not trying to gather evidence to convict them as spies.

The three prisoners, one of whom was Page, were paraded before Hinomoto. They were exhausted, the strain of three months of being constantly on the run evident from their drawn, bearded faces and eyes glittering with nervous tension. Their tattered clothes were filthy and their unwashed bodies caked with grime and sweat. To their astonishment, Hinomoto announced not only were they to have a bath and a shave, but their interrogation would not begin until after Christmas.

Although Hinomoto, who also wished them the compliments of the season, claimed that the latter concession had been granted out of respect for their Christian religion, it is far more likely, since the next three prisoners had not yet arrived from Singkep, that he wished to defer any questioning until they were all together. Considering the reputation of the Kempeitai, his cordial Christmas Eve reception must have been almost beyond belief to the prisoners. When the bath and shave materialised, along with clean clothing, it is surprising that the cynics amongst them did not wonder what the Japanese were up to. What they failed to realise was it was part of a cleverly orchestrated plan to gain their confidence and catch them off guard. Unfortunately it worked.

The Kempeitai certainly had a head start. Immediately after Christmas, armed with information extracted from Davidson's notebook, the skilled interrogators divided the prisoners into three groups. Aware that the security of the SBs must be maintained at all costs, each of the men studiously avoided any mention of them, sticking more or less to the cover stories prepared by SOA.

The use of cover stories created a conflict for those undertaking covert missions. On the one hand they were exhorted to avoid capture at all costs, to the extent of committing suicide. Should this not be possible it was stressed that, as the enemy was adept at extracting intelligence, the only information given should be name, rank and serial number. On the other hand, each man had been presented with a cover story to be learned by heart in the unreasonable expectation that he would be lucid enough to stick to it. Some stories, as was the case with Rimau, were extremely complicated. The men had three separate versions, each containing some element of the truth, with the choice dependent on the place of capture. Unfortunately, as no one in SOA's planning department had thought beyond the pick-up date, there was no specific cover story to be regurgitated when the men were finally captured. With three different stories and nine men, plus a possible fourth version concocted at the last minute, the combination of fact and fiction was almost endless. The final result, when added to the entries in the notebooks and the document found in the brass tube, was most illuminating. At the end of each day, Hinomoto, Noguchi and Imanaka compared notes, pooling snippets of information and planning their next move.

It was not long before the interrogators discovered that some aspects of the prisoners' stories did not gel. Why, asked Lieutenant-Colonel Kuwarbara, to whom Furuta reported, did they blow up the prahu, their best means of escape, when all they had to do to preserve the secret of the limpets was to drop them overboard? Furuta's suggestion that the prahu was an obvious target for pursuers did not allay Kuwarbara's suspicion that the prisoners were hiding something – a notion that Furuta, who had built up a good rapport with them, dismissed as impossible.

Hinomoto was more astute. The prisoners had all volunteered that the attack involved the use of folboats. When Furuta and the others noted discrepancies in the folboat pairings for this part of the operations, they did not take much notice. Hinomoto figured it must mean something, but what? Within twenty-four hours they had their answer. On receiving a note from Imanaka which said, 'These people seem to be using some kind of special boat. Please verify', Furuta remembered the puzzling 'SB' entries in the notebook. Taking a punt he asked Bob Page, 'What did you do with the SBs?' Believing that the Japanese knew all about them, Page inadvertently spilled the beans.

It is not known if this benign process of intelligence gathering was speeded up in the early part by the judicious application of selective torture. A well-known tactic, it was used to good effect by the Kempeitai on prisoners confined in Outram Road Gaol, where inmates referred to it as the 'cigarettes and lolly' racket. If friendly overtures did not bring the desired result, the interrogators tried more physical types of persuasion before reverting once more to kinder, even indulgent treatment. As they used two sets of interrogators – one for beatings and the other to play the role of fairy godmother – the psychological effect on prisoners who knew as soon as they saw their interrogator what kind of day was in store, was most effective, probably achieving better results than consistent treatment, good or bad.

While it is impossible to assess how much intelligence was gathered from the prisoners, gleaned from the captured documents, given away with the cover stories or extracted by more forceful measures, one thing is absolutely clear. By 9 January the Kempeitai in Singapore knew almost everything: the date Rimau had left Australia, the mode of transportation, the date of arrival at Merapas, the number in the group, their names, the operational plan, SOA's training system, and the fact that the Allies had a new, secret weapon – the underwater submersible canoe.

And within five days the SOA top brass, as well as a handful of others including Denis Emerson-Elliott, knew what the Japanese knew. Part of an enemy signal, transmitted on 10 January and decrypted on the 14th, revealed (verbatim): 'they got into rubber boats and escaped. After that, pursuing with army and navy co-operating and exterminated them for the most part'. It was devastating news. SOA which, on 22 December had completed the planning for Rimexit, realised there was no hope of rescuing any of them. Rimexit was cancelled. With a heavy heart Brigadier Ken Wills broke the news to an already very anxious and worried Bettina Reid: the chance of Ivan or any of the others being alive was virtually nil. Because this information was top secret, neither she nor Jock Campbell could tell anyone. Any hope that might have still flickered was extinguished as more and more intercepted messages were decoded, revealing the extent of the disaster.

Despite Japanese assertions that the Kempeitai at Tanjung Pagar were at all times kind and benevolent during their handling of Rimau, it does not seem possible that Major Ingleton, for one, would have revealed some of his information to Captain Noguchi voluntarily. Within days he had given details of SOE and SOA plans for the future and outlined methods by which they expected to infiltrate enemy territory.

Irrespective of how this information was extracted, it was of little consequence. The Japanese were already very familiar with SOA organisation, personnel, training, aims and plans, collected by espionage agents and from interrogating previously captured Allied personnel such as Sergeant Leonard Siffleet, an Australian signaller seconded to the Allied Intelligence Bureau and attached to a NEFIS (Dutch) team infiltrated into Dutch New Guinea. Before he and his companions were beheaded Siffleet, like Ingleton, had 'volunteered' details of his mission and training.

So had Blondie Sargent.

By the time the Japanese had flushed out Page's party from the Lingga Archipelago, Sargent, Reymond, Craft, Willersdorf, Warne and Pace were far away. On 1 December, a week before the others had even left Mapur, they were at Tanjung Dato on Lingga's southern tip where Go King Riaz, a native from nearby Tanjung Goroh, repaired one of their koleks. To increase their chances of finding a junk to replace their small wooden boats which, being coastal craft equipped with a tiny triangular sail, were not the ideal choice of ocean-going vessel, they had then set off for the southern coast of Sumatra. For the best part of three weeks they moved south until, after hatching a cunning plan, they managed to pirate a prahu manned by several Chinese on or about 19 December.

The captured boat was sailed east towards the Pelapis Island group, a pick-up point just off the south-west tip of Dutch Borneo established by NEFIS for the rescue of downed airmen. Pelapis was evidently not a destination which appealed to the Chinese, who were not pleased to have been hijacked by a band of European men. As they neared the island on the second night of their capture they staged a revolt during the evening meal. Bruno Reymond, hit over the head with a club, fell over the side and disappeared, along with Craft. Sargent, who had by this stage been relieved of his weapons, escaped by jumping over the side.

After swimming about for some time Sargent was rescued by a fishing boat, only to be pitched into the sea once more when the vessel capsized. Clinging to a large log, he drifted with the current for the next ten hours until washing up against a fishing pagar in the sea at nearby Maja – an island 144 kilometres from Pontianak and separated by a narrow waterway from the mainland. Utterly exhausted, suffering from immersion and minus his trousers, he dragged himself onto the platform above the stakes where he clung for twenty-four hours until rescued by local fishermen. But alas, his luck had run out. Having saved him from a slow and certain death from thirst and exposure, the fishermen informed the Japanese. Two of Sargent's comrades also reached the shores of Maja. At Satai Cape, the benevolent tide that had carried him to the fishing pagar delivered up the drowned bodies of Bruno Reymond and Colin Craft.

The local collaborators and Japanese garrison wasted little time in handing over their prize to the Kempeitai, who took delivery of the prisoner in Pontianak on Christmas Day. The following evening at about 9 o'clock Sargent was in the police station entering his personal details – name, age, serial number, birthplace, military unit – onto a standardized

A fish trap of the type on which Blondie Sargent sought refuge

form when he was seen by Captain Ozaki Chizuki, an anti-sabotage naval officer attached to the Intelligence Section of 2 South Seas Expeditionary Fleet HQ, Surabaya. Although in Pontianak for the Christmas festivities, Ozaki decided to question the prisoner who, having lost all his hair from the effects of his ordeal, was looking decidedly 'aged'.

Debilitated by his recent experiences, Sargent was in no condition to resist the persuasive powers of an interrogator as skilled as Ozaki or invent a plausible story and stick to it, with or without torture. Within ninety minutes Ozaki had extracted a great deal of information about Rimau, including the death of two men on Merapas, the escape of the others, the number of ships blown up by the raiding party and the technical specifications of the SBs. Believing the latter to be of great importance, Ozaki returned to his quarters where he prepared a report for his superiors by candlelight. Two days later, escorted by a naval lieutenant, Sargent was put on a plane and flown via Bandjarmasin to Surabaya. Upon his arrival on New Year's Eve he was confined to Gubeng Prison, where Bill Reynolds had been held.

By the middle of January the Japanese in Surabaya had learned that information similar to that extracted from Sargent had been obtained from other Rimau prisoners. As a result, Staff Officer Tachino of Fleet HQ ordered Ozaki to re-interrogate the prisoner, paying particular attention to the expedition's equipment. This time it was not so easy, for Sargent was now much stronger, mentally and physically. After one and a half frustrating hours Ozaki had accomplished nothing for Sargent, in his haughtiest manner, refused to be drawn. Further interrogation led to a similar result.

Shortly afterwards, Tachino received orders to send Sargent to Tokyo's Ofuna Internment Camp on the first available aircraft. Owing to a shortage of planes, the orders were promptly amended to transportation by the first available means. As this meant a boat of some kind and an armed escort, Sargent was left to cool his heels in the stockade. In mid-February he was still there. When a car arrived one day to transport him to Commander Tatsuzaki's office in the court martial buildings for another round of interrogation, Blondie was startled to find that he was not the only passenger. Seated in the vehicle, somewhat weatherworn but very much alive, was Doug Warne.

Sargent had last seen Warne on the prahu, shortly before he dived overboard to escape the Chinese. Somehow, Warne, Willersdorf and Pace had managed to regain control of the boat, apparently disposing of the Chinese in the process. From Pelapis they had navigated the small vessel around the southern coast of Borneo, past Tanjung Puting to Kadapongan Island, where disaster had struck. Here, far from medical help and surrounded by a hostile enemy, Warne had become very ill with malaria. With his delirium bordering on madness the other two realised they could not take him any further. Possibly believing he had a better chance of survival in the hands of villagers or in the custody of the Japanese, Willersdorf and Pace left him at Kadapongan, a speck in the ocean off Borneo's south-eastern tip.

Doug Warne lived up to his 'brick shit house' reputation. Far from fading away, debilitated by illness, he recovered and left Kadapongan in one of the small koleks which the others evidently had the foresight to leave with him. With no charts, and no navigational equipment except perhaps his army compass, he had spent several weeks island-hopping in the Macassar Straits until betrayed by the locals to Japanese stationed at Bandjarmasin, in Borneo. From here, he had been flown to Surabaya.

Considering his ordeal Warne was in reasonable shape, apart from a pain in his abdomen just below his ribs on his left side – most likely an enlarged spleen, the legacy of malaria. He was interrogated by Tachino and Ozaki for an hour but they extracted little in the way of information. Both he and Sargent were re-examined several times by Ozaki, again with little result.

Transportation had been finally arranged for Sargent and it was now time for him to move on. Escorted by Warrant Officer Shirawaka and Lieutenant Nakamura, both of whom were being transferred back to Japan, he was taken by train to Batavia (now Jakarta) where he was to board a ship bound for Tokyo, via Singapore. The trio had just reached Batavia when Nakamura was recalled to Surabaya to answer questions about the loss of documents for which he had been responsible. The documents must have been important. Instead of reporting as ordered, the lieutenant committed suicide by shooting himself with a pistol in a Surabaya restaurant.

Shirakawa took Sargent to Singapore alone, and passed on instructions that he was to be sent to Japan. But with nine Rimau members already in custody, 7 Area Army and the Kempeitai were not about to relinquish the tenth who had so fortuitously fallen into their hands. Sargent was removed from the ship and taken to Outram Road Gaol.

Following Sargent's departure, Warne was taken by car to the court martial buildings in Surabaya where he was paraded, in a generally dishevelled state, before the members of the court. His appearance lasted only a few minutes and he was asked no questions before being transferred to the custody of Petty Officer Noguchi Naotaki. Warne, who had no idea of what had just transpired, had in fact just appeared before a military court. He also had no inkling that a navy policy, already well-established in Surabaya, to 'dispose' of prisoners, with or without trial, had been further boosted by a message transmitted to all units on 10 February. Having decided that anyone connected to Rimau was an enemy of the state, 7 Area Army had advised:

We want to punish the sabotage units which infiltrated from Australia and were captured in the Singapore area recently. Although the matter will in each case be left up to the unit concerned, we wish the investigations to be that such that no one is left to do harm afterward.

Consequently, anyone captured and whom the Japanese believed to be even remotely associated with the Rimau raid was doomed. This included two Australians who, on about 15 March, had the misfortune to fall into enemy hands near Surabaya while attempting to carry out a mission for SOA

Lieutenants John Sachs and Clifford Perske, members of a combined American/British operation known as Politician/Optician, had left Fremantle on 11 March in US submarine Bream. Although from vastly different backgrounds, Clifford Perske, a farmer from Queensland, and John Sachs, an oil representative of German/Australian descent, were bound by the same single-minded ambition - 'to kill the enemies of the King'.

Perske was not only the less war-like of the two, he was also an incredibly even-tempered and sunny natured individual. Born in Maryborough in 1917, he was an enthusiastic sportsman, with a penchant for boating, swimming, tennis, football and cricket. The summers of his youth were spent with his best mate Norm Dean (the same Norm Dean who had heard the Jaywick explosions) in and around the waters of Ceveland Bay, not far from the family's small farm at Thornlands. When Cliff was about fourteen years of age, his world, along with that of his two sisters and brother, was shattered when their father, Ludovic, while carrying out his duties as a marshall at his Masonic Lodge sports day, was hit on the head by a shot putt and killed.

In October 1939, within a month of the outbreak of war, Perske, now working on the

Left: *Lieutenant John Sachs, Operation Politician*
Right: *Lieutenant Clifford Perske, Operation Politician*

farm, joined the militia. The army medical officer assessing his fitness noted his 'particularly fine muscular development' and that the teeth on his lower jaw were perfect. After serving with 15 Battalion, during which time he met his future bride Betty Stammers, daughter of the regimental sergeant major, he enlisted in the AIF in July 1941 and was assigned to the Armoured Corps. Within two months he was promoted to Sergeant and, obviously earmarked as officer material, was sent on a series of courses. By May 1943, he had received his commission and in November the following year was seconded to SOA, where his steady temperament, superb athleticism, swimming ability and expertise with water craft, developed to a high level on his eight-metre craft Lollypop, singled him out as an ideal candidate for hazardous missions.

His folboat partner John Sachs, aged 31, was the son of Fritz Sachs, a successful German immigrant who had embraced the concept of the British Empire with passionate fervour. Raised in an atmosphere of unquestioning love of King and Country, John, like Ivan Lyon, also revelled in all things military. After completing his secondary education at The King's School in Sydney, a prestigious private establishment run on quasi-military lines, he joined 15 Heavy Battery, a militia unit based at South Head on Sydney Harbour, rising to the rank of gun sergeant after eight years. A crack shot, Sachs had won many trophies for sharp-shooting including the much coveted Aggregate Cup which he held for three consecutive years, 1935-37. He was also in great demand at parties and functions to perform various tricks, including the bull's eye penetration of a coin tossed into the air and splitting a business card held edgewise from a distance of 25 paces. But his piece de resistance was shooting four pieces of chalk, in quick succession, from between the fingers of his accomplice Sergeant Ken Todd – by candlelight and while standing on his head.

When not engaged in artillery drill and target practice, Sachs indulged his other passion – flying. When scarlet fever prevented him from accompanying pilot Captain Travis Shortbridge on a flight to Melbourne in the famous *Southern Cloud* in March 1931, his disappointment turned to shocked relief when he learned that the plane had disappeared over the Southern Alps, with the loss of all on board.

Because of his love affair with aircraft, Sachs had volunteered to join the RAAF on the outbreak of war, but found that his colourblindness rendered him ineligible. Undaunted, he enlisted in 2/1 Field Regiment as a gunner, sailing for the Middle East with the first convoy of troops in January 1940. In April 1941 his skill with firearms was put to good use in Greece during a desperate rearguard action, fought over ten days and nights against an enemy which at times was so close that the great artillery guns, designed for long-range warfare, were fired at point-blank range.

On reaching Kalamata the exhausted gunners were awaiting evacuation when the entire area came under heavy aircraft attack. Learning that an advance unit of German troops, dispatched to prevent any further evacuations, was almost upon them, Sachs sprang into action. In what amounted to almost a one-man army, he single-handedly wiped out a machine-gun nest, captured and rendered a large gun useless, killed an untold number of the enemy and, after joining forces with a tall New Zealander, rounded up a score of prisoners. Shot three times and knowing, with huge enemy reinforcements due, that his capture was inevitable, Sachs had finally allowed himself the luxury of lying down in the back of a truck and passing out.

When he came to, he was a prisoner of war – but not for long. As soon as his wounds had healed he escaped, was recaptured, escaped again and then, disguised as Cypriot peasant, spent five months fighting with the Greek resistance. Fed up with living a hand-to-mouth existence, he managed to gain access to an enemy airfield but, clambering into the cockpit of one of the planes, quickly clambered out again. This was one plane he could not fly. Although the son of a Berliner, he was unable to read the names on any of the controls, as they were all in German. Finally, he stole a boat and made his way back to Cairo via neutral Turkey.

Although fever-ridden and suffering from malnutrition, his reappearance created a sensation. Since the last anyone had seen of John Sachs was in Greece – a blood-soaked and apparently lifeless corpse on the back of a truck – the general opinion was that he had been killed in action after feats of exceptional bravery, and the wheels were already in action to recommend him for a posthumous Victoria Cross. Unfortunately, the recommendation for the VC was lost when the officer, who was returning to London by ship with the paperwork in his uniform pocket, placed his jacket over a stretcher patient who had been rescued from the water. With the precious paperwork irretrievably lost when the medics evacuated the patient, along with the jacket, Sachs did not receive any recognition for his heroic stand at Kalamata.

As soon as he had regained his strength, Sachs returned to Greece by submarine and extracted a number of key Allied personnel, earning a well-deserved Military Medal in the process. He then transferred to the infantry and fought in New Guinea where, after being commissioned in the field, he again covered himself in glory by concocting a huge gelignite bomb to eject some well-dug-in Japanese holding up the Australian advance on the Komiatum Ridge.

Such single-minded determination and innovative techniques on top of his earlier conspicuous efforts, all of which had been reported prominently in the press, did not go unnoticed by SOA. In May 1944, after a short spell instructing at Canungra, Lieutenant Sachs was seconded to covert operations. Later that year, under the auspices of SOA but under the direct control of America's Admiral Christie, Sachs was attached to Operation Politician to assist in the rescue of downed airmen, ferry personnel for emergency evacuation, carry out reconnaissance duties and blow up ships and installations whenever the opportunity arose.

In early February Sachs completed a patrol on *Bream* to Ita Ubi Island. He found it so boring that, in the hope of adding some spice to future missions, he concocted a wild scheme on his return, aimed at detecting whether Japanese 'hospital' ships, which were suspiciously prolific in the seas between Borneo and Singapore, were carrying wounded men or combat troops. His proposal was for a submarine with all torpedoes trained at point-blank range to surface close to the suspect vessel. Sachs and his partner would board the ship, establish its bona fides and signal the result to the submarine. If the ship was not what it claimed to be, the torpedoes would be fired at the portion of the hull furthest from the operatives, who would abandon ship and await rescue. After working out the finer details, Sachs submitted his plan and anxiously awaited the verdict. It was not approved.

On 11 March he and Clifford Perske, who was undertaking his first mission, boarded *Bream*, bound this time for the South China Sea to carry out Politician 7. During the afternoon of 14 March while proceeding to the patrol area, *Bream* attacked a Japanese convoy sailing from Bandjarmasin to Surabaya. After sinking one vessel, the sub tracked the convoy to the eastern tip of Great Masalambo Island, just to the north of Java, where the convoy had sheltered for the night.

Grasping the opportunity to do some more damage, at 11.45 pm Sachs and Perske set off in a folboat to attach limpet mines to their targets, some 4 kilometres away. Conditions were ideal – dark and rainy, with little wind. They had paddled only half the distance when the submarine's crew noticed that the folboat was, inexplicably, well to the east of the intended destination. Unable to make contact, *Bream* submerged, waited until the appointed time and then surfaced at the pre-arranged rendezvous. Sachs and Perske were nowhere to be seen. Unbeknown to anyone on *Bream*, an unsuccessful attack by a British submarine on the same convoy at 5 pm had placed the Japanese on full alert. Before the Australians had time to leave their lethal calling cards, they were captured by a naval patrol.

Despite being harassed by depth charges dropped by destroyers from the Surabaya Naval Base, *Bream*'s commanding officer did not call off the search. Fully aware of the terrible risk he was taking, he continued to comb the sea to the north and east of the island. For two days he searched but found no sign of the missing men. Then, at 2.56 am on 17 March, they picked up a radio signal on the allotted frequency. Although the Americans thought the voice sounded like that of Lieutenant Perske, the authenticator code word was not given and the commander, fearing a trap, did not proceed.

It is almost certain that the Americans had summed up the situation correctly. One of the first questions asked of the captured Australians would have been the wireless frequency for contacting the submarine. By giving this information, but withholding the authenticator, they gambled that *Bream*'s commander would realise they had been captured and the submarine's situation was perilous, as indeed it was. Badly damaged by the heavy depth-charging, it was with great difficulty that *Bream* made her way back to Australia safely.

After their capture, Sachs and Perske were transferred to Gubeng Prison where Tachino, the naval officer who had questioned Sargent and Warne, sought permission to interrogate them. Sachs, being the operational leader, was questioned first. It is doubtful that torture, which was often employed by naval personnel from Captain Shinohara's Special Base Unit, was used by Tachino. Indeed, Shinohara's techniques were a contentious issue between the two men, since Japanese Fleet orders expressly forbade the use of torture during interrogations.

Whatever his methods, Tachino did not fare well. After two hours of questions, which were written as the interrogator was not proficient in spoken English, Sachs had revealed only that they had left Fremantle by submarine and that their intention had been to blow up shipping at Masalambo with magnetic mines. As all attempts to induce Sachs to reveal the codes and frequencies for communication with Australia failed, Tachino bothered to ask Perske only his name, rank and serial number, then informed Shinohara that he wished to question both prisoners at a later date.

Shinohara, who was conducting his own investigation, was given a free rein by his superiors and was evidently a law unto himself. The brutality of his interrogation of the Australian officers was such that he almost came to blows with an extremely angry Tachino, who remonstrated in the strongest possible terms that such treatment was expressly forbidden. To this Shinohara haughtily replied, 'While they are under my care, I can treat them as I wish. I can eat them if I wish, either boiled, or roasted.'

In the latter half of March word circulated that all prisoners in naval custody, and from whom all useful information had been extracted, were to die at a date to be fixed. This included Warne, Perske and Sachs; two American airmen held since the previous November; two American merchant mariners; and nineteen Indonesians and Chinese condemned to death for the machete murder of a Japanese civilian on Lombok Island. The merchant sailors had been shipwrecked in the Indian Ocean when their oil tanker *Fort Lee*, en route from Persia to the huge American naval base on Manus Island, New Guinea, was sunk by a German U-boat on 2 November. After drifting in a life-boat for several weeks they had come ashore near Membora on Sumba Island where, malnourished and suffering from exposure, they were rescued and treated by locals at a naval outpost, only to be sent to Surabaya.

When he heard that all prisoners were to be killed Dr Nakamura, a naval captain attached to 2 South Seas Fleet, became very interested. With anti-tetanus serum impossible to procure, the doctor had been searching for an alternate substance with which to inoculate his troops. The death rate among wounded Japanese, ten in every 100,000 cases, was extremely high compared to the deaths of sixteen men, nine of whom were not immunised, in the entire US Navy and Army for the same three-year period. When his colleague, bacteriologist Commander Natase Ide, evolved a new and revolutionary substance described as a 'denatured anti-toxin', Nakamura believed it might be a suitable substitute. As it was derived from tetanus bacteria, the dosage was critical: too much, and the patient would die. Nakamura had tested his discovery on monkeys but, as he had little time to carry out a series of controlled experiments on humans – increasing the dosage and observing the results – what he really needed were some expendable 'volunteers'. Urged on by Nakamura, Commander Tatsuzaki was persuaded to release all prisoners to the Naval Hospital's medical staff, with certain provisos: the locals were to be injected with the toxin and the others with a vitamin or saline solution. He stressed that care must be taken to ensure the injections were not muddled.

As soon as permission had been granted all prisoners at Gubeng, Caucasian and Asian, were lined up for their inoculations. Two days later a second injection was administered. As interpreter Saito Junya could not remember the Malay word for 'tetanus', he was instructed to tell the prisoners that they were being vaccinated against typhoid and that they might suffer a very high fever as a result.

Within days, Doug Warne and all the local people became ill. Warne was admitted to the Naval Hospital at Darumo, about an hour's drive from Surabaya, suffering from a complaint to one of his legs – evidently the first stages of a muscle paralysis similar to that experienced by tetanus victims. As the illness progressed and the paralysis began to affect his ability to swallow, he was taken off normal rations and fed soup and rice gruel.

Also gravely ill as a result of the injections were the two merchant seamen. Nakamura, who was supposed to have ensured that they too received a placebo, went to extraordinary lengths to keep them alive, informing the guards that 'as these prisoners of war are very important, they must not be permitted to die'. It was to no avail. About a fortnight after admission Warne's guard, Petty Officer Noguchi, reported his charge could no longer move.

Tetanus is a disease for which there is no cure. Those who survive probably owe their lives to a strong constitution and constant nursing care, designed to help lessen the excruciating pain and violent seizures that wrack the victim's body. Towards the end, Warne, now pale, thin and desperately ill, was placed on a soft bearskin rug in an attempt to ease the unbearable pain which now affected his entire body. But the constitution that had kept Warne from death's door at Kadapongan could not hope to combat the effects of Dr Nakamura's preventative medical technique. He lapsed into unconsciousness, finally dying about fifteen days after his admission to hospital. On the orders of Ozaki his body and those of the castaways were removed for burial in an unmarked grave in a nearby Christian cemetery, thereby effectively removing all trace of them.

The Japanese, who later claimed Warne was in good health before he became inexplicably ill, declared he had died from the combined effects of 'stomach trouble', exposure and malnutrition. Not surprisingly, the merchant sailors and the seventeen local people were also deemed to have died from 'other' causes.

Perske and Sachs, along with two Indonesians and the two American airmen, had not become ill. Whether routine inoculations before they left home, their fitness, the administration of a lesser amount or toxin or none at all, as had been instructed, saved the Europeans is not known. What is known is that the experiment provided Nakamura and Ide with an excellent guide to the correct dosage, for they went on to inoculate their troops successfully.

The patients who had escaped the toxic effects of the doctor's hideous experiments had no hope of survival. When it became obvious that these prisoners had suffered no ill effects from the injections, Captain Shinohara, evidently on the orders of his superiors, announced their immediate execution. At about 11.30 on the morning of Friday 30 April, fourteen days after their arrival in Surabaya, Perske and Sachs, along with the remaining Indonesians and the two airmen, were removed from their cells.

The two Americans, Flight Officer Mason Schow and Sergeant Donald Palmer, were now the sole surviving crew of a B-24 which had crash-landed on 24 October at Macassar while returning to base from a bombing raid over Sandakan, Borneo. They never had any chance of surviving their capture. Since August 1942, in retaliation for a bombing attack by American aircraft on Japan in April, known as the Doolittle Raid, all captured Allied airman could be put on trial and executed, under regulations laid down by General Tojo in the 'Enemy Airmen's Act'. Although the Japanese at Surabaya had been ordered to transport all fliers to Tokyo, these orders had been ignored. As was the case elsewhere, airmen were executed out of hand, with some subjected to horrific procedures including vivisection. Now, blindfolded and handcuffed, Schow and Palmer were placed on a truck with the others for the 30-minute journey to the Eastern Fort execution ground.

Many of the naval base personnel had no idea that an execution was imminent until they saw about twenty armed men ranged around a truck outside the guardhouse. Alerted by the unusually large escort, Mike Kazuyuki watched as the prisoners were loaded into the vehicle. Mike, who had given the airmen chocolate and had attended the interrogations of Sachs and Perske, was in no doubt of their identity, blindfolded or not. Dashing John Sachs, lean, dark-haired, dark-complexioned and with a high-bridged nose (the legacy of a German bullet which had slightly rearranged his features in Greece), stood almost 183 centimetres tall. Perske was about seven or eight centimetres shorter and equally good looking but lighter in hair and skin colour. The Americans were also easily recognisable. The older one, who appeared to be about thirty, was reasonably tall, heavily built and sported a massive red-blond beard; his fresh-faced, much younger companion was by far the shortest of the four. The Australians were dressed in khaki, Schow and Palmer were wearing white cotton undershirts and brown pants. When Mike realised all were bound for the killing ground he enquired about the sudden decision, but was unable to obtain any satisfactory answers.

Down at the fort a large crowd was gathering around a pit dug by members of the

291

Special Attack Group (Sword Unit), who had been ordered to demonstrate their skill in swordsmanship. On disembarking from the truck, which came to a halt about 10 metres away, the condemned men were taken into a small hut where they waited for an hour, as the grave-digging detail had not dug the pit deep enough. It was some time after 1 pm (Tokyo time) before the interpreter was ordered to inform the Indonesians that their death was imminent. Nothing was said to the Europeans.

An officer named Ikeda executed the first Indonesian, then John Sachs was led away. He can have been in no doubt of what was in store. By throwing his head back as he walked, and aided by the bump on his nose, he was able to see from beneath the blindfold. Kneeling before the pit, he was beheaded by Lieutenant Okada.

Thousands of kilometres away in the Sachs family home in the Sydney harbourside suburb of Double Bay, at precisely 2.30 local time on the afternoon of Good Friday, 30 March 1945, Lieutenant John Sachs' framed Army Commission crashed to the floor. While Fritz Sachs, who had no idea his son was even missing, stared at the shattered glass with a feeling of great foreboding, the officer in charge of the execution glared at Sachs' lifeless body in absolute fury.[2]

It was typical of John Sachs that even in death he was able to cause a ruction. In executing him, Lieutenant Okada had not performed his task well, nicking his sword and thereby incurring the wrath of Lieutenant Yoshimoto who, after a great deal of yelling, ordered Petty Officer Tamura to produce more youthful volunteers. When no one offered he ordered that 'men of the lowest rank shall cut', which caused Seamen Norimura, Nakauchi, Nakayama and Hashimoto to inherit the job.

Nakayama's victim, the youngest American airman, and Hashimoto's, the remaining Indonesian, kept segregated from the others, had been roped to prevent their bodies from pitching into the hole. The reason for this was not obvious until several white-coated medical officers appeared on the scene for an on-the-spot dissection. While Yoshino removed the hearts, livers and gall bladders, Officer Konishi pointed out items of anatomical interest to the onlookers, including a spleen affected by malaria and the fact that the stomach of the mostly grain-eating Indonesian was larger than that of the meat-eating American. The dissected organs were placed in a metal box, packed in a wooden crate and sent to the laboratory, where the hearts were preserved in formalin. An attempt to dry the livers and gall bladders using copper sulphate was unsuccessful.

The reason for this sickening and pointless procedure had been to satisfy the whim of one man – Captain Shinohara, a chronic asthmatic. Unable to obtain the bile of a bear which he, like many Asians, believed was a cure for chronic wheezing, he had opted for the human variety. Ironically, while the executions, being carried out without trial, were illegal, cannibalism was not. Under current orders it was permissible to eat the flesh of the enemy dead. To consume parts of a fellow Japanese, however, was a capital offence.

While Shinohara's contemporaries may have been overawed by his behaviour, they were untroubled by the fact that prisoners of war were executed, since specific orders had been issued by the Fleet Commander allowing for the disposal of POWs who were regarded as being of little consequence. Although they were supposed to be tried, this was rarely, if ever, done – especially since all prisoners captured other than in combat were deemed to be spies.

The distribution of the signal ordering that all units punish anyone connected to the sabotage in Singapore had given the Japanese in Surabaya an even freer hand. Had this message not been issued, it is quite possible that Warne, Sachs and Perske might have been dispatched to Tokyo and even have survived the war. When the Japanese in Surabaya had informed their superiors of Sargent's capture, they had been ordered to transfer him immediately to Japan – an order which would have been carried out had the Kempeitai in Singapore not removed him from the ship. Although the navy was not obligated in any way to carry out orders issued by the army, the extreme stance taken by 7 Area Army allowed the Japanese personnel based at Surabaya, whose record of wholesale execution was already well established, to look upon the request as an even greater licence to murder with impunity.

Warne, having confessed that he had been a member of the party which had blown up three ships in Singapore Harbour, was doomed. So were Sachs and Perske who, apart from being 'spies', had been caught attempting to carry out a mission that was indistinguishable from Rimau's. As far as the Japanese were concerned, Sachs and Perske were as much Rimau men as the twenty-two who had set off from Australia on 11 September 1944 with Ivan Lyon.

A few days after Lieutenants John Sachs and Clifford Perske met their bloody fate on the Eastern Fort execution ground, Tokyo, having learned the prisoners were being executed without trial, rescinded Singapore's order.

15
Judicial murder

February 1945–7 July 1945

Towards the end of February, the nine Rimau prisoners in Singapore whose deaths were so desired by 7 Area Army were still alive and, despite eight weeks in detention at Tanjung Pagar, in good shape. They had been permitted to cook their quite adequate food ration and to mix freely in two large cells assigned to them on the second floor, exercise occasionally on a large lawn and even take part in a ju-jitsu contest with their gaolers. This seemingly benign treatment was not due to any change of heart by the Kempeitai, but to three quite disparate reasons – Hinomoto's decision that torture would achieve little; the illuminating data recorded in the notebooks; and, very importantly, information from the prisoners that Ivan Lyon was related to Queen Elizabeth, consort of the King of England. Although this relationship was distant, it was so widely believed that Ivan was often referred to as Ivan Bowes-Lyon. The Japanese, who could never have envisioned anyone in Emperor Hirohito's family actually taking up arms and going to war, were exceedingly impressed and, without a doubt, decided to tread very carefully.

Despite the fact that it was strictly forbidden to keep personal records while on a mission, the diaries of Davidson and Carey (in common with the diary kept by Young on Jaywick) were extraordinarily detailed. The Japanese even knew the name of the operation, which they preferred to call 'Tora Kosuku Tai' or 'Tiger Operation Party', rather than Rimau. As result the investigators, aided by the unassuming civilian interpreters and Hinomoto's clever tactics, had managed to glean most of their intelligence without having to resort to more violent methods.

By the first week of February, 7 Area Army had added to this intelligence some other quite startling information that had arrived from Timor where Willersdorf and Pace had finally been captured: Ivan Lyon's men, not internal saboteurs, were responsible for both the Jaywick and Rimau raids. The Japanese hierarchy now realised they were sitting on time bomb. Something would have to be done about Rimau – fast.

Desperate to keep thousands of POWs and indeed, their own troops, from knowing that the war was not going well, Japanese commanders in Singapore had the option of either executing recently captured enemy personnel, as was the case with airmen, or placing them in solitary confinement in Outram Road Gaol where, apart from being isolated, they might conveniently die from disease, malnutrition or ill treatment, thereby saving their captors a great deal of bother. But Rimau presented a special problem. Whereas airmen could be disposed of without any trouble, the summary execution of such a large number of Allied soldiers would be difficult and imprisonment in Outram Road Gaol, long term, too risky.

The problem posed by Rimau was the immensely complex problem of 'face'. From the moment the Japanese learned that the raids on shipping in Singapore Harbour were not inside jobs, the surviving members of Rimau were doomed. Should it ever become known that a few men had come thousands of kilometres to thumb their noses at the enemy, not once, but twice, the Japanese would be a laughing-stock. And, should it ever be revealed that the Kempeitai, under the auspices of the Imperial Japanese Army, had tortured and murdered untold numbers of Asian and European civilians, in the mistaken belief that internal saboteurs had been at work, the shame would be unendurable, especially since the most recent execution had taken place less than a fortnight earlier.

The victim was Captain Cornelis Woudenberg who, on 31 January, had been taken to the same rubber plantation as John Long and beheaded, not because the Japanese believed he was actually guilty – the verdict passed down after his hastily arranged trial the previous November – but because the Kempeitai could not possibly disclose that they had made a mistake. To admit that the entire judicial system, from the investigators, to the prosecutors, to the judges, had been wrong and that Japanese justice was flawed was absolutely unthinkable. In order to save collective Japanese face, all the Rimau men would also have to die. So too would a number of Malays, already tried and sentenced to death.

Once Rimau's fate had been decided, 7 Area Army transmitted the fatal signal, requesting all commanders to deal with the matter in such a way that 'no one is left to do harm afterwards'. While this demand was carried out promptly in Surabaya, and would lead ultimately to the deaths of Willersdorf and Pace in Timor, a little more discretion was needed in Singapore. To avoid any repercussions, it was decided to pursue the line that the Rimau men had committed an international war crime, which would call for them to be punished 'firmly and strictly' – in effect, executed.

As the prisoners had been lulled into a sense of security by the low-profile methods of interrogation at Tanjung Pagar, it is not surprising that none of them noticed a change as the questioning progressed. Indeed, it was not until 'severe' re-interrogations began three weeks later in Outram Road Gaol, in order to collect 'evidence' for their trial, that both Page and Ingleton noticed the distinct shift of emphasis. Despite this, neither they nor the interpreter Furuta, who had realised for some time that the questioning had ceased to be benign, voiced their suspicions to the others.

Furuta's association with Rimau had begun long before they had ever met, for he had been present at lunch at the Army's Raffles College HQ on 16 October when word had arrived that *Mustika* had been scuttled and three Malay heiho killed. When the recovered diaries and papers, along with Mrs Manderson's flags, had arrived in Singapore it was Furuta who had been assigned the task of examining them. But it was not until Christmas Eve, when the first of the prisoners arrived, that he had come face to face with the personnel mentioned in the various documents.

Since then, being in attendance at many of their interrogations, he had built a rapport of sorts with the men, especially Page, Carey, Ingleton and Stewart. In common with anyone who had ever met Bob Page, Furuta had fallen under the spell of his warm personality and ready smile. To the somewhat plain Japanese interpreter, the handsome features of the tall Australian rivalled those of the most dashing movie star.

Always keen to improve his English, Furuta engaged the prisoners in conversation at every opportunity. Stewart told him about his wife and children and Page about his medical studies, while Fletcher reminisced about his life on the stage. True to form, Carey could not resist pulling Furuta's leg, assuring him that he was related to every Carey in the Sydney telephone directory and that, since he had been in the army for so long, he must now surely be 'promoted' to captain and therefore should be addressed as such. Acceding to a request to draw plans of an SB also smacks of Wal Carey's jokey larrikinism; it is perhaps indicative that, despite their best efforts, Japanese engineers were unable to produce a prototype of the craft, based on these 'plans', before the war ended.

It is also odds-on that it was Carey who announced that only small Australians had been selected to go on the Rimau mission. What Furuta made of Wally Falls, who was a well-built 90 kilograms or, for that matter, any of the others, most of whom towered over the Japanese, is not disclosed. It is also evident that the remark made by Ingleton that he 'had never eaten so much rice in his life' and 'didn't know rice could be so tasty' was also lost on Furuta, who believed that conventional English taste buds had adapted to oriental food with amazing rapidity. By the time Sargent arrived from Java in March and told Furuta that all his hair had fallen out as the result of a high fever, Furuta didn't know whether to believe him or not.[1]

As his relationship with the Rimau men deepened, Furuta was torn between his allegiance to Japan and his growing friendship with men who were, in fact, his enemies. Haunted by the knowledge that their interrogations were leading them inexorably towards death, he was not brave enough to warn them of the danger, yet fantasised that somehow he might be able to spirit them off to Changi Camp where they could be hidden – an action far beyond the capabilities of such a mild-mannered civilian. Tormented, Furuta trod a shaky path as he attempted to serve his country and his Emperor while coming to terms with his conscience, but it was not until Bob Page made an unexpected confession that Furuta's divided loyalties were really put to the test.

Apart from the most senior army officials, who had themselves just discovered this amazing fact, no Japanese had any idea that the raids on shipping were anything other than the work of local saboteurs. Rumours, even at this high level, flew thick and fast, among them the ludicrous theory that the Kasu heiho were part of a sabotage team, shot by mistake. Although he knew a great deal, Furuta had not learned anything about either raid from the prisoners, since no one had breathed a word about Jaywick, and none of those who had attacked Rimau's targets and were still alive (apart from Stewart who had told the Japanese nothing) had been interrogated in Singapore. Since any disclosure of the facts would have weakened the spying case they were trying to construct, the Japanese Command, which always suppressed unfavourable news, ensured there was complete security clampdown. Consequently, Furuta knew nothing about the raids, neither did he have any idea of why the army was so anxious to rid itself of Rimau.

One day he quite casually mentioned to Bob Page that a large number of Malays were to be executed for blowing up ships in the harbour 'last year'. Assuming Furuta was referring to Jaywick, Page consulted the others who, after a heated exchange, decided that he should come clean. The following day, fully aware that admitting to the 1943 sabotage might do him and his companions immeasurable harm, he told Furuta that the Malays were innocent, and why. When Furuta, who had not been in Singapore for long, checked on the details for Jaywick, he discovered that Page was telling the truth.

Furuta was now in a real bind. Not knowing that his superiors already knew the facts, he wrestled with his conscience. If he passed on this information, Captain Page would be in an even worse situation. If he did not, he himself might land in serious trouble. He eventually confided in Colonel Nagayaki Koshida, his Divisional chief who, being a very senior officer, was cognisant with all the facts. An astute man, he told Furuta to forget the incident, reminding him that as the Malays had confessed, the trial had been held, the papers signed and the execution arranged, the loss of face for the investigators and judiciary would be too great to contemplate.

Convincing himself that he had done everything possible to save the lives of the condemned men Furuta took the advice, telling Page to keep quiet and leave everything to him. Although the unfortunate Malays were regarded as expendable and were executed, Furuta was consoled by the thought that at least he had done something to prevent Page from getting himself into more hot water for, by this stage, he knew all the prisoners were in dire trouble. He also knew there was little he could do about it.

As a mere civilian interpreter, a job ranked by the army as lower than that of a carrier pigeon, Furuta was in no position to voice any opposition when he realised the army intended to pin a capital charge on the Rimau men. In fact, by interfering, he ran the risk of being replaced by someone far less kindly disposed towards the very prisoners whom he sought to protect. Realising that stalling for time could help, he received permission for the prisoners to help him compile a military dictionary and compose propaganda messages for Japanese radio broadcasts to Australia. Telling Page not to worry about the accuracy of the details, they produced a number of scenarios which evidently satisfied Furuta's superiors. But these delaying tactics were not enough. In about mid-February, after the Kempeitai had finished its preliminary investigation and the army had decided that Rimau must be eliminated, the nine prisoners were moved from Tanjung Pagar to Outram Road Gaol. Conditions at the prison had marginally improved in the past year but, as the tide of war started to turn against the Japanese, it was still a place of great misery and suffering.

As the Kempeitai wished to keep the Rimau men isolated from the rest of the inmates, they were placed two to a cell, according to rank, in a special section partially below ground level reserved for 'spies' and airmen, including four Americans forced to bail out from a B-24 over Malaya during a bombing raid on Singapore. Above these lower ground-floor cells were two identical floors, previously condemned by the British as being unfit for habitation, each containing about sixty-eight cells. Even under ideal conditions the cells, which measured approximately 1.5 by 2.4 metres, with a 3 to 4 metre ceiling, could never have been called comfortable. Thick stone walls, covered in plaster, rose from a concrete floor, on which rested the bed – two 20-centimetre wide, thick wooden planks supported by two pieces of timber 60 centimetres long and roughly 5 by 10 centimetres. The pillow was a piece of thicker timber. The so-called blanket was about two-thirds the size of a normal single blanket and about the same thickness as a sheet. In one corner stood a wooden bucket with a lid – the latrine, which the Japanese called the *binkei* or *benjo* bucket.

Fresh air was via an iron grille about 60 centimetres by 45 centimetres set into the rear wall, 2.5 metres from the ground and shielded from the outside by a metal awning installed at a slope of 45 degrees, effectively shutting off most of the light and reducing airflow to a minimum. On the lower floors, covering the four vertical and four horizontal bars of the grille was a heavy wire mesh, making it impossible to pass anything in or out of the cell. The only other link with the outside world was a door, 7 centimetres thick and just under a metre in width, composed of a sheet of steel sandwiched between two stout wooden layers and fitted with a Judas hatch so the guards could spy on the prisoners.

The cells were perpetually damp, and infested with lice, cockroaches, bed bugs, mice, rats and various lizards. Directly over the door was a naked electric-light globe of about 15 watts which was kept burning from six at night until eight in the morning. Food – three meals a day, trundled along the corridors on a wooden cart and delivered via a flap-covered slot in the door – generally consisted of a small bowl of rice, another of some indeterminate vegetable matter and a cup of weak black tea.

Although conditions had improved slightly, the methods of the gaolers had not. Furuta, who later made much song and dance about the good treatment at Tanjung Pagar, was suspiciously tight-lipped about the conditions at Outram Road, as well he might be. John MacDonald, one of the American airmen, had learned that life in Outram Road could be extremely unpleasant. From the time of his imprisonment there, about a month before Rimau arrived, routine bashings, psychological and mental torture and almost total absence of medical attention were standard. Many of the guards, 'bomb-happy' soldiers sent from the front for a spell of 'recreation', were fanatics whose first act on taking over guard duty was to give each prisoner a thorough going-over. Not only was torture commonplace, but brutal punishment could result for any infraction of the rules, including communicating with fellow prisoners and not sitting to attention during daylight hours.

Segregated from the rest of the inmates, the Rimau men's lives would have been even less tolerable had the small gestures of kindness from Furuta, already extended to them at Tanjung Pagar, not continued. In the guise of working on the military dictionary, he visited Rimau regularly in Outram Road, keeping them supplied with occasional cigarettes and a considerable amount of his own reading matter, a kindness he extended to John MacDonald and the other American fliers who were nearby. Ingleton, a voracious reader, shunned crime writer Damon Runyon but devoured Furuta's entire collection of P G Wodehouse before moving onto the complete works of William Shakespeare, also a favourite of Fletcher. Perhaps these attempts to bring a touch of humanity into a world that was otherwise bereft of any trace of civilised behaviour helped Furuta to cope, for he was in an invidious position. On the one hand, confronted daily with the awfulness of Outram Road and other Kempeitai establishments, he could not help but see the results of brutal treatment, even though he did not actually witness it. On the other, he was one of the few who knew that steps were in train to charge the Rimau men with espionage – a secret he must share with no one, least of all the prisoners.

On 1 March 1945, shortly after the prisoners had been transferred to Outram Road, a report based on the Tanjung Pagar interrogations was referred to the Judicial Department for confirmation that it was legitimate to classify the Rimau men as spies. Consequently, the investigation passed from the Kempeitai to the Judicial Department's Major-General Otsuka, who ordered prosecutor Major Kamiya, a lawyer in civilian life, to pursue the matter.

By the end of March, having studied the report closely, Kamiya informed Otsuka that there appeared to be several violations of law under which the prisoners could be tried. When General Itagaki, the new Commander-in-Chief of 7 Area Army, ordered Kamiya to organise a trial and to ensure that a sentence of death was handed down, the prosecutor began in earnest to lay the foundations of a case that confirmed Furuta's worst fears. He knew that by the time the major had finished, every Rimau member would be facing the executioner.

Kamiya was progressing quite well until a few days after the executions of Sachs and

Perske on 30 March when Tokyo, concerned that as the war was not going well certain individuals might one day have to account for their actions, ordered that executions without proper trial were to cease. Kamiya and Otsuka had concluded there was sufficient evidence to proceed with a trial under Japanese law but were now somewhat apprehensive about its validity under international law, the yardstick which would be used by the Allied forces at any trial. On 20 April, Kamiya travelled to Japanese HQ in Saigon for consultation with his superiors.

Although Saigon's Major-General Hidaka agreed with Kamiya's opinion, he wanted more evidence, particularly in relation to Rimau's clothing, since a charge of espionage could not be levelled under either Japanese or international law if personnel collecting information were in military uniform. After a period of 'severe' interrogation which lasted a month, Otsuka extracted the information he required. On resubmitting the evidence to Saigon, Kamiya was instructed that the offences were to be tried under Japanese law and the subsequent death sentence must be handed down by a judge.

This meant that the accused had no hope of acquittal. Under Japanese law, the very fact that the prosecutor had made out a case and taken it to court meant that the verdict was almost invariably 'guilty'. As the decision was worked out in advance, it required very powerful evidence to overturn it. Quite unknown in English law, which presumes innocence unless proven otherwise, this procedure followed the European system and was used in Japanese criminal and military courts. As the judge's role was to rubber-stamp the prosecutor's opinion, it had the distinct advantage for the prosecution of achieving the desired outcome.

Securing a verdict which would satisfy the prosecution was ensured when Kamiya's colleague Major Jifuku Mitsuo was appointed one of the judges and handed all the papers pertaining to the case. At the end of May he began a close examination of the documentation. By this time the war in Europe was over and Germans were being rounded up in large numbers to face war crimes trials – a factor that was a very sobering consideration for the Japanese. After a week's careful deliberation Jifuku decided that although the paperwork was excellent he would seek further evidence from additional witnesses to back up the statements extracted from the accused. The fact that the trial was delayed for several weeks in an effort to obtain these additional statements underlines the extraordinary lengths to which the Japanese were prepared to go. In the past, executions had been carried out without any formality at all. Indeed, it was a rare occurrence for the accused to face even the most rudimentary of trials.

The Japanese case rested on the charges of perfidy and espionage. The perfidy related to the allegation that Rimau had not worn proper uniforms and that *Mustika* had breached international law by displaying a Japanese national flag when it attacked the police boat at Kasu. The charge of espionage concerned the information in the notebooks, the sketches and the photographs, some of which had been collected while in disguise. Although the prisoners had admitted to removing their berets and badges, to carrying Japanese flags which they had waved once, and to taking notes on military installations and the like, Jifuku wanted additional statements from eyewitnesses at Kasu and Merapas to prove that international law, as well as Japanese law, had been breached and to forestall any accusations that the prisoners had been found guilty on confessions obtained under duress.

On 5 June he ordered the Kempeitai to obtain the necessary statements within seven days. On 20 June he received an affidavit from Sidek bin Safar, who had been very cooperative. In his statement was an account of the attack on the police boat, a description of *Mustika* and of the clothing worn by Rimau. Most conveniently, he had come up with a new 'fact' – the Japanese national flag had been 'marked' on the stern of the prahu.

Ordered by Otsuka to expedite the date of the trial, Major Jifuku decided he could wait no longer for further evidence to be obtained from Merapas. Since in the opinion of both the local and chief judiciary departments the case was clearly evidenced and must not be delayed any longer, on 28 June he gave the go-ahead for the trial to proceed.

With a trial date now imminent, Kamiya busied himself with the task of finding two more judges prepared to hand down the correct verdict. The senior judge had to outrank the accused – someone with the rank of lieutenant-colonel at least. As he also had to be serving with a combat unit, Kamiya was forced to look outside his own very cooperative department.

He ran into trouble almost immediately. Furuta's superior Colonel Yoshida, who knew the trial was a sham and that he would be expected to endorse the demand for capital punishment, refused to have anything to do with it. Fully conversant with the facts, he informed Furuta that he would not be used 'as a tool of the judiciary department just to read out the death sentence prepared by that department'. Declaring that, should he have a free hand, he would find the Rimau men 'not guilty' and send them all to a POW camp, he also confided to Furuta that he considered them heroes, not war criminals.

His view that they should be accorded POW status was shared by other, lesser ranked officers who, from the fragmented information available to them, did not believe the prisoners were guilty of war crimes. Unfortunately Yoshida, knowing that in the light of orders issued at a high level it would be impossible to go against the wishes of the prosecution, took the line of least resistance and dissociated himself from the affair.

If Colonel Yoshida refused to be party to a trial which he knew was nothing more than a device to sanction judicial murder, Colonel Towatari Masayoshi of Garrison HQ had no such qualms. Considered by Furuta to be a 'swaggerer and a general nuisance', he accepted the position as President of the Court on 1 July. The third place on the tribunal was filled by Staff Officer Major Hisada Myoshi, who accepted the appointment the same day. As soon as the arrangements had been confirmed, Jifuku met his fellow judges and explained what was required of them.

*Raffles College,
Singapore, where
the Rimau men
were tried*

Around noon on 3 July, the Rimau men were removed from their cells and taken to the trial venue – a former professor's residence in the grounds of Raffles College, a beautiful colonial building situated at the opposite end of the padang from the Singapore Cricket Club. The court was packed. Colonel Towatari as presiding judge was positioned in the centre of the dais, with Jifuku on his right and Hisada on his left. Seated at the same level was prosecutor Kamiya, while off to one side was the official court recorder, Warrant Officer Asuka Rikichi. In front of Kamiya, but below the dais, was Furuta who, in deference to the occasion, was wearing the uniform of an army lieutenant instead of his usual civilian clothing. In the gallery was Major-General Otsuka, flanked by scores of military personnel resplendent in full dress uniform and with campaign ribbons emblazoned upon their chests who had come to watch the interesting and unusual spectacle of Allied prisoners being put through the motions of a full military trial. Lined up ominously in a rack beside the door were dozens of ceremonial swords belonging to the officers in attendance. Had a Western observer been present, he would have been struck forcibly by the fact that one person considered vital in an English court of law was absent. In accordance with Japanese court procedure, there was no defence counsel.

At 1 pm the prisoners, dressed in Japanese military clothing and with their normally bare feet squeezed into Japanese army boots, were escorted into the courtroom and lined up before the judges, right to left, more or less according to rank. Ingleton, the most senior officer was first, followed by Page, Carey, Sargent, Warren, Stewart, Fletcher, Gooley, Hardy and, at the very end, the lone sailor Wally Falls. Being dressed in enemy uniforms, they wore no badges of rank and displayed no insignia. However, their hair had been cropped crudely with shears and their faces were clean shaven.

After each prisoner had given his name, rank, age, birth place and military unit, Major Kamiya read out the charges. The first, that of perfidy, had several strands. It alleged that the Rimau men, dressed in green shirts and trousers, had removed their berets and badges of rank; all had applied stain to their skin and some, including Page, Lyon and Davidson, had worn sarongs. While wearing these clothes, on a prahu flying a Japanese flag belonging to the original Indonesian crew, they had entered Singaporean waters and killed four members of the local police. They had then fled to Merapas, where they had engaged in battle with the Japanese. As a result of the fighting on Soreh and Merapas, eight Japanese had been killed. Because of these activities, the accused were charged with 'engaging in hostile activities without wearing uniforms to qualify them for fighting and also using the vessel which lacked qualification for fighting'. The charge of espionage centred on the allegations that Davidson, Ingleton and Page had collected information while in disguise and that Carey had made observations at Merapas. Had a defence lawyer been present, he would have objected strenuously: the 'crimes' of the dead, such as the fighting at Soreh and the wearing of sarongs by Lyon and Davidson, had been cleverly intermingled with those of the living, thereby allowing all those on trial to be regarded as accomplices for acts in which they did not take part.

When Kamiya had finished speaking, he handed to the tribunal a weighty volume which contained he evidence he had gathered – the statements made by the prisoners during interrogation, Sidek's affidavit, a report made by the chief of the Singapore garrison and five pieces of physical evidence: a Japanese national flag, Carey's notebook, Ingleton's sketch book and Page's camera and photographs. For some reason, Davidson's notebook, although it contained a great deal of information, was not admitted as evidence. As all the judges had seen this file and Major Jifuku himself was responsible for collecting some of the evidence in it, the review of the contents was superficial. After flicking through it, the judges were ready to proceed.

In trials such as this it was usual for the tribunal to ask questions of the accused. This was not to assist in deciding the guilt or innocence of the person, but to make sure that the prosecution had not doctored the evidence – a sensible precaution if the Kempeitai were involved. In Rimau's case, as the trial was a carefully orchestrated act, the judges simply went through the motions.

Ingleton was brought forward first. When asked if he had any objection to the facts read out, he replied that he had not. It is no wonder. His only chance to assess the validity of the charges was as Furuta made the translation, a task that would have been extremely difficult. While Furuta seems to have had some degree of fluency in English, translating military jargon may not have been his strong point. In June 1944 he had interpreted at the trial of James Bradley and three others who had been charged with 'deserting' from their working party on the Burma-Thailand railway. Saved from immediate execution by the intervention of a Japanese-speaking English major named Cyril Wild, and Colonel Dillon (the same Colonel Dillon of Lyon's escape route), Bradley had been brought to trial. He had no idea what was going on and had actually thought, from Furuta's translation, that he was being charged with 'keeping within him cholera germs'.

Given what appear to be severe limitations with Furuta's translation, if it not surprising that Ingleton did not challenge statements made by the prosecutor that *Mustika* had been flying a Japanese flag belonging to the Malays or that four (not three) policemen had been killed at Kasu. Neither did he point out that jungle green clothing was the uniform worn by Australian soldiers serving in the tropics.

The discrepancy in the number of deaths at Kasu was of little consequence, but the accusation that they were flying a Japanese flag from *Mustika*'s stern was a complete and utter fabrication. Although Mrs Manderson's flags had been kept handy so that they could be produced and waved if necessary, *Mustika*, which was not masquerading as a Japanese vessel as *Krait* had done but as an Indonesian prahu on a coastal trip, was displaying no flags at all. As the crew had not needed them for their trip, they had been, and still were, securely locked in the Japanese port office at Pontianak in Borneo.

After confirming that Ingleton had no objection to the charges, the judges continued with their questioning. The prisoner was asked one or two questions about his job and the composition of the Rimau party before his inquisitors finally got down to the nitty-gritty – the clothing worn on board *Mustika*.

They did not accept Ingleton's explanation that badges of rank had been removed as the party all knew each other well. In fact, the tribunal actually had Ingleton agree that rank identification was to enable outsiders to recognise them as military personnel. Since badges of rank in the Australian army were not obtrusive, often being little more than a simple white tape, it appears that 'badges of rank' as a term was being interchanged with 'regimental emblems'. If this was the case, the judges had just asked Ingleton, a Royal Marine with scant knowledge of the Australian military system, a loaded question.

British Army uniforms, unlike those of the AIF, often featured highly polished, ornate badges which identified at a glance the regiment to which the soldier belonged. The Australian Army was far less flamboyant, issuing only two small metal badges to its personnel – the 'rising sun' and the word 'Australia', both coated in non-reflective black paint which made them indistinguishable, except at very close range. Therefore, while the British Army may have used badges to enable others to identify its personnel, the Australian Army most certainly did not. Had this notion been put to anyone but Major Ingleton, it would have met with an emphatic denial.

The topic of the badges covered, the tribunal moved on to the subject of camouflage dye and the facts that berets had not been worn. Ingleton was forced to concede that, while some of the men were dressed in shirts and trousers, the application of the skin dye and lack of headgear did not make them readily recognisable as Australian soldiers. Unfortunately, he did not know enough about military law to realise that, since this was allowable under international law, it was a perfectly legitimate ruse. After asking Ingleton to identify a sarong-clad figure in a photograph as Davidson, the judges moved back to *Mustika*'s flag.

Ingleton, who had no idea what was really going on, was unaware that Kamiya was about to introduce a choice piece of 'evidence' – the revelation by Sidek, after his memory-jogging visit by the Kempeitai, that a Japanese flag was 'painted' on *Mustika*'s stern. Failing to grasp the significance of the unquestioning, Ingleton conceded that, although he could not recall seeing one, it was possible that this may have been the case. In response to further questioning, he also stated that they had not displayed either Mrs Manderson's flag or a British flag at Kasu.

Significantly, if the issue was raised regarding *Mustika*'s original flag, something which Ingleton could have categorically denied, it was not recorded in the court proceedings, even though this was part of the charge. A number of questions were then asked about the fight at Kasu, the owner of the sketchbook and the reasons why the sketches were made. Satisfied with Ingleton's answers, the judges called Bob Page.

He had nothing to add during his brief examination, except to state that he had once seen Lyon wearing his badges of rank on the junk. In response to questions put by the judges, he admitted he had worn a sarong while taking his photographs and that he had fired at the police boat at Kasu. When asked 'Did you yourself kill any Japanese soldiers?', Page allegedly replied in clear and deliberate tones: 'I am an officer in the British army and I know that my aim is good.' After identifying the camera and admitting to fighting at Kasu and Merapas, he was replaced on the stand by Carey.

Apart from stating that he had always been on Merapas Island with the stores and was never on board *Mustika*, Carey did not challenge the charges. He admitted he had worn a loincloth on Merapas as it was cooler and had taken notes of enemy shipping and aircraft that came near the island. He also admitted that, although Warren and the other two had not taken notes, they had supplied him with items of interest to include in his report. After confirming he had engaged in fighting at Merapas and another island (near Buaja), he too was dismissed.

The others, headed by Sargent and Warren, had little to add or subtract. Warren pointed out that he had been on Merapas, Sargent confirmed that the flags which the Japanese produced in court had been brought from Australia and had been waved at enemy aircraft, and the others admitted that they had been on the look out for useful information. Wally Falls challenged the question of badges of rank by stating 'I am a navy man and therefore do not wear badges of rank'. The judges smartly came up with the obvious question: if jungle green uniforms were recognised army dress, why was a navy man wearing one? If Falls replied that the RAN wore tropical combat kit that was almost identical with that of the army, the answer, like the judge's question, was not formally recorded.

After the questioning was complete, each of the accused was asked to voice any objections about statements made by any fellow accused. There being none, the statements made by the prisoners to the Water Kempeitai and to Major Kamiya were read out. As there were again no objections, the prosecutor read out the affidavit of Sidek bin Safar. Except for disputing that a flag was painted on the stern, the prisoners confirmed that his statement was correct. Sidek's evidence was followed by the report of the garrison chief and the identification of each of the exhibits. With no objections lodged and no one wishing to add anything or emphasise any point of evidence advantageous to him, it was time for the prosecutor to address the court.

The contents of this fairly long dissertation came as no surprise to the judges or to Major-General Otsuka, who had already reviewed and sanctioned it. After running through the facts and evidence, Kamiya began to consolidate his case. The accused, he stated, had been proven guilty of displaying the Japanese flags they had brought from Australia and of wearing Malay dress. Although he conceded it had not been proved conclusively that *Mustika* had a flag marked upon the stern, he evaded the question of whether Rimau had attacked the police boat while flying a Japanese flag by stating there was no doubt whatever that no British flag had been hoisted before the shooting took place. This, said Kamiya, was in direct contravention to the Hague Convention of 1907.

It most definitely was not. According to the Hague Convention, flying the flag of the enemy and even dressing in his uniform is classified as a legitimate ruse and is therefore not forbidden. The Hague Rules do, however, prohibit its 'improper use'. Although this is not actually defined, to open fire while employing the ruse is recognised unanimously as being 'improper'. Despite Kamiya's assertions, there does not appear to be anything in the Hague Convention which insists that the aggressor's own national flag must be shown when attacking the enemy. This is clearly demonstrated by the fact that ambushes and surprise naval bombardments are legitimate and that submarines and aircraft attack without warning, although international judges such as Heaton and Oppenheim have ruled that if approaching under the enemy's flag, the attackers must reveal their true identities before hostilities commence. As *Mustika* was flying no Japanese flags and the Rimau men were not masquerading as Japanese soldiers, this rule cannot have been breached. Kamiya was therefore on very shaky ground.

In assessing Rimau's dress he carefully evaded the issue of whether jungle green was a recognised uniform and did not mention that Japanese badges of rank, being scarlet and gold collar tabs, were quite unlike the Australians' nondescript epaulette tapes. He also asserted that, since the quite definitely dun-coloured clothing of the Japanese army was so close in colour to Rimau's distinctly jungle green, badges of rank should have been displayed. In making this claim, he ignored the Hague Convention's ruling that removal of badges from uniforms was a legitimate ruse.

This lapse of memory and allegation of similarity of colour enabled Kamiya to level the accusation that, although Malay clothing was worn by some of the party for some of the time, all had participated in hostile activities while wearing a uniform that was a de facto disguise. Had he been able to prove that the Rimau party was dressed in Japanese uniforms, he would have had a case under international law. Since he could not, he simply disregarded the fact that engaging in battle while in disguise is punishable only if the enemy's uniform is worn, or if military personnel masquerade as civilians without being ordered to do so by their commander or government. With disguise an integral part of Plan Rimau, the entire party should have been safe from retribution since, under the Hague Rules, those issuing the order, not obeying it, were answerable.

Having 'proved' that everyone was illegally in disguise, the espionage charge was easier to tackle. Interestingly, although the prisoners were being tried under Japanese law, Kamiya when it suited him referred constantly to the Hague Convention of 1907 which, unlike the Geneva Convention, was recognised by Japan. It would appear that Kamiya, in attempting to validate the charges under international law, was already planning for the future. After the war, it was the Hague Convention, not the Geneva Convention, that was used as the yardstick when assessing if a war crime had been committed.

Kamiya now declared that, according to the Hague Convention, 'a spy is defined to be a person who is mainly engaged in the collection of informations' while in disguise and that 'such action is not illegal on his part but the country which capture such a spy can punish him'. Although these words are basically correct, Kamiya's definition of what constituted an illegal disguise was not. According to Article 29, in the section pertaining to spies of that same Convention he was so fond of quoting, anyone clandestinely collecting information, including soldiers not in uniform, can be classified as a spy. One of the few exceptions is military personnel dressed in uniform.

Had the Australian uniforms, badges or not, been accepted as correct military dress, Kamiya could only have pinned his espionage charge on those who were disguised as Malays. The only person still alive who was known, beyond all doubt, to have collected information while dressed in this manner was Bob Page. Indeed, the Kempeitai themselves had established that Ingleton, because of his size, had never abandoned his military clothing in favour of a sarong.

Having convinced the court that the Rimau men were spies and that the punishment of spies was legal, Kamiya broached the subject of punishment for those who had participated in hostile activities while in disguise. Employing logical sleight of hand, he announced that, since he found nothing in the Hague Convention which prohibited it, punishment was therefore permissible. In stating that punishment was not prohibited, he was quite right. What he did not say was this: since the Hague Rules do not recognise that these activities constitute a crime, there is, naturally, no mention of this non-existent breach of military law.

By this time, the accused were completely enmeshed in a tangle of lies, half-truths and judiciously selected fact, so intricately and cleverly woven it was impossible for any of them to escape. By decreeing that the uniform was not a uniform but a disguise, Kamiya had made the tricky aspect of who was, or was not, wearing Malay dress completely irrelevant. All were spies, including those who had not recorded observations. Although Carey and Warren were not on board *Mustika*, Carey was included as he had worn a sarong while collecting information on Merapas. Warren too was a spy, as he had not replaced his beret and badges of rank, removed on the voyage between Pedjantan and Merapas, before supplying verbal information to Carey.

With everyone now a known spy, Kamiya solved the problem of who had actually taken part in any hostile activity by declaring that, since all had a common objective, all were equally guilty. He then stated that as the Hague Convention allowed spies to be punished, and did not prohibit the punishment of those engaged in hostile activities while disguised, Japanese law could be used in deciding the penalty.

Having wrapped up his case so neatly, Kamiya launched into an inspired oration, declaring that the Rimau men, being supplied with poison which they had intended to use, were obviously heroes whose intentions had been thwarted. Was it permissible to execute such men? A precedent, he reminded the court, had already been set. After citing the case of two great Japanese heroes, Oki and Yokogawa, who had been executed by a Russian court for blowing up railway bridges in the Russian-Japanese war, Kamiya went on to say:

Comparing the heroes of Operation Rimau to both heroes Oki and Yokogawa, the two parties are identical with each other in their action viewed from the standpoint of international laws and in the value of patriotism to their respective countries.

It has been proven to the court beyond all doubt that the accused are guilty of the charges. When the guilt is so clear, it would be disgracing the fine spirit of those heroes, if we tried or thought of saving their lives.

When they left their homeland, they put aside the matter of their lives. All they cared about was the success of [their] mission; lives were nothing in the face of heated patriotism.

When their action deserved death, I am sure they would rather die than save their lives at the mercy of the captor, because dying gloriously is the way to immortalise their names on the history.

We are told that our two heroes who attacked the Port of Sydney in a tiny submarine were given a cordial funeral ceremony. The Australians are people who have a real sense of honour. They respected our heroes because they found true heroism in death.

Let us pay them the same respect, same admiration to the heroes, and send them to the glory of death to glorify the last of the heroes.

Let us not disgrace their spirit by supposing that they may want to be alive. Sending them to death is the only way to send them to an eternal glory. Let us do this.

With that, Kamiya formally demanded the death penalty.

Before handing down judgement, the President of the Court asked the accused if they had anything to say. It must have been a very shocked Ingleton who now rose to his feet. After thanking Kamiya for the remarks about his being a patriotic hero he stated that, although he realised that Rimau's modus operandi may have been an unfair method of warfare, he did not know until this present moment that they were such grave offences – thereby confirming that he had no idea he was on trial for his life. The others, probably too stunned to think, echoed the sentiments of their senior officer.

Six hours after the trial began, it was all over. After a short adjournment, the presiding judge handed down the verdict of the court. Guilty. At a time and place to be fixed, all would be executed.

Chief Judge Towatari's conscience must have been bothering him. Before the prisoners left for Outram Road, he spoke privately to them in an attempt to explain that, as a military man acting under orders, he had no alternative but to find them guilty. Page and Ingleton accepted the explanation, but it must have been a bitter blow to know that the President of the Court knew they were not guilty. Furuta, completely taken in by the elaborate courtroom drama that had just unfolded, believed the judge's reluctance to condemn them to death stemmed not from the fact that they were innocent, but from the fact they were heroes. It was a fallacy to which he clung for the rest of his life.

Back at Outram Road, the Japanese acceded to the prisoners' request to be together by transferring them to a large cell on the upper floor of the condemned block. To prevent any contact with other prisoners, the front of the cell, which was composed entirely of bars, was draped with blankets.

Now that they had been condemned to death, their treatment changed dramatically. The food, which in common with the rations of all the inmates had been even more miserable of late, assumed feast-like proportions. They were given cigarettes, tins of condensed milk and blankets on which to sleep in relative comfort. Furuta was also permitted to visit them.

As he was the only Japanese whom they trusted, Page and Stewart gave him messages for their families, which he promised to deliver to the Allies when the war had ended. He also undertook to look for Bob Page's father whom Bob, not knowing he was long dead, believed was still a prisoner of the Japanese. In return, Page and the others handed Furuta a testimonial in the hope that he would be exempted from any reprisals after their deaths. Some of the men also told Furuta of their anger at not being told by SOA that their activities, if caught, might result in execution – a rather odd viewpoint, considering all had been issued with cyanide with the instruction to use it. However this anger most likely stemmed from their belief that, after their trial, they would be sent to a regular POW camp. None had been aware he was facing a capital charge until the sentence was handed down.

Furuta, who had by this time developed an even greater rapport with the men, especially Page whom he described as 'a slender-faced, handsome youth with a fine moustache', was devastated by the verdict. Horrified that all were to die, he felt compelled to do something. Unaware that General Itagaki had specifically ordered the death sentence, he asked Otsuka to appeal to Itagaki for clemency. Otsuka, who had known for months that there could be only one outcome told Furuta that, being a civilian, he did not understand the psychology of the warrior and that his persistent requests only made him look ridiculous. Rebuffed, but sure that Otsuka had refused to intervene because he was a weak-minded intellectual, Furuta made another, if somewhat feeble and completely futile attempt, to solicit help from two other senior officers.

On 6 July, five months after ordering Rimau to be eliminated, 7 Area Army finally achieved its objective. General Itagaki, the very person on whom Furuta, in his naivety, had pinned his last hope, gave orders to execute all ten men.

The elaborate precautions taken to seal off the condemned prisoners from the rest of the gaol did not stop Australian Bert Rollason from managing to snatch a few words with them as he passed by on binkei duty – a highly prized job, as it allowed those collecting the latrine buckets to act as eyes and ears for the entire prison community. It wasn't much of a conversation, simply that they were now being better treated and were receiving good food and cigarettes. The last time Bert spoke to them was on 6 July, when he learned that they were to be executed the following day. As with the date of the infamous Double Tenth, there was an ominous ring about the seventh day of the seventh month.

The next morning the rest of the inmates were alerted that something was up by the huge kerfuffle which erupted as the guards tried to prevent anyone from seeing the condemned men as they were led outside. Dressed in jungle green shirts, with trousers or shorts, the ten barefooted prisoners were securely fastened in single file to a central chain. Later, as they were loaded into the two vehicles that were to take them to the execution ground, they were seen fleetingly by Rollason, whose guard had been less than vigilant. If any of them were frightened, or even nervous, that they were about to keep an appointment with death, they certainly didn't show it, putting on an outstanding performance for the benefit of the Japanese by laughing and joking as if they didn't have a care in the world.

By 10 am they had arrived at the killing field, situated on the crest of a ridge to the east of Reformatory Road. It was a desolate place. The sandy soil, little more than a wasteland, was pitted with half-filled and open graves, which were scattered among scrubby, stunted bushes. With plenty of flies about, a carnivorous plant known as Dutchman's pipe flourished.

In common with most executions, there was a good-sized gallery. The army top brass was represented by Chief Judge Towatari, Major-General Otsuka, the commander of Outram Road's military gaol, Major Kobayashi Shuzo, and his civilian counterpart Major Mikizawa Koshiro, who had expressed the wish to witness a decapitation. The actual executions, under the direction of Major Hisada, once their judge, now their executioner, were to be carried out by Corporal Hirata and Sergeants Nibara, Tsukudu, Okamura and Shimoi. There was nothing special about these five men, who were simply Kempeitai personnel known to the prisoners by such nicknames as Woof Woof, Cookhouse and Boofhead. Standing by, ready to fill in the three pits that had been dug to a depth of four feet, were four Japanese convicts from the gaol, one of whom was known as Kadino or Convict Warder No 6.

The only person missing was Furuta Hiroyuki. Unable to face the thought of the execution and the fact that he would have to translate the final order, he had asked another interpreter, Yoshimura, to take his place while he waited in his quarters in Nassim Road. However, at the eleventh hour the suspense became overpowering and, jumping into a car, he drove to the killing field where he found himself unable to come face to face with the men he had come to regard as friends. He watched from behind a bush.

Once the prisoners were assembled it fell to Major Kobayashi, as gaol commandant, to formally announce that they were to be beheaded. Although the official record would state, as it invariably did, that the executions had been by firing squad, the Japanese used this method rarely. Not only did decapitation save on ammunition, which was now in short supply, it was also whisper quiet. The echo of rifle shots could be heard far away. The sound of a sword swishing through the air was almost negligible.

Furuta, peering from his hiding place, saw that the prisoners, temporarily released from their bonds, were smoking cigarettes. Still demonstrating the bravado which had filled the onlookers with admiration as they left Outram Road, they were laughing and joking, determined that the Japanese would not break them. When the rest period was over they still displayed no emotion. Shaking hands, they simply wished each other 'good luck'.

Ingleton turned to face the throng as he made his final speech. After asking Kamiya and Kobayashi to thank those responsible for the recent good treatment, he said: 'We have one regret. This is that we cannot see at this place Mr Furuta who has been so kind to us. We all wanted to thank him once more, but I suppose he has his duty. Please tell him we thanked him before we died.'[2]

Furuta was close enough to hear every word; he was almost blinded by tears and incapable of movement. As an officer shouted 'Ki-o-tsuke' (attention), followed by 'Ichi-ni-tsuke' (take your position), Major Ingleton, his hands tied behind his back, was escorted at bayonet point and forced to kneel at the edge of one of the pits. When the swordsman raised his weapon in both his hands, its finely honed blade glinting in the brilliant sunlight, Furuta's nerve gave way. Covering his ears so that he could not hear the shriek of the executioner as he brought down his sword, he ran from the scene.

It was as well for someone as civilised as Furuta that he did not witness the proceedings. After the four officers had been beheaded, the other six were brought forward, only five of them blindfolded. All were bound. Far from being a ritualistic Samurai-style execution, befitting the heroic status of the prisoners that Kamiya had so impressed upon the court, the proceedings were no different from any of the hundreds carried out by the Japanese during the war. The executioners were not high-born swordsmen but common soldiers whose expertise left a great deal to be desired. The execution of two victims was botched, so much so that the decapitation of one was incomplete. And when it was all over, the three pits containing the bodies, piled one on top of the other – four in one grave and three in each of the other two – were hurriedly filled in, like those of common criminals. Far away, in the family home in Casino, New South Wales, the framed photograph of Wally Falls displayed in the living room toppled over. That night, in Western Australia, Mrs Stewart was woken by a vivid nightmare. She dreamed that she had seen her husband, and that his head was covered in blood.

Back at Outram Road the gaol's 300 prisoners were aware that the executions had been carried out. Before he had left for the execution that morning, Kobayashi (nicknamed 'Major Felix' owing to his habit of poking his head over walls to spy on inmates, in much the same way as the popular feline cartoon character), had ordered everyone into the courtyard, where he told them that ten Allied prisoners were to be executed. Although the convict gravediggers had been forbidden to talk to rest of the prison population when they returned, further details were about to emerge.

In the warder's room were two Korean prisoners, Noh Bok Kun and Kim Kyong Soon. Conscripted by the Japanese, they had been employed as POW guards until falling foul of the Kempeitai. While ostensibly engaged in cleaning the room, they overheard the executioners laughing and joking about the task they had just performed and taunting Nibara for being so unskilled that he had required two or three cuts to completely sever both his heads. Barely a month later, when atomic bombs were dropped on Hiroshima and Nagasaki, ending the war with a suddenness that took everyone by surprise, Noh was interested to learn that a Japanese prisoner by the name of Noburo Yamane had been dispatched in great haste to stick six wooden crosses on the three common graves at Reformatory Road.

By the time the Japanese surrendered, all was in order. Although there had been no time to rid themselves of witnesses by executing all Allied prisoners as planned, the Kempeitai were well prepared. With the last resting places of the heroes reverently and Christianly marked, those responsible for the deaths had only to ensure that the paperwork was impeccable. In this they succeeded beyond their wildest dreams. When the Allied investigating teams arrived in Singapore a few weeks later they swallowed the Kempeitai's story hook, line and sinker.

As the Kempeitai later so rightly recorded, 'because of the kempei's proper management, no one was accused as war criminals'.

16
Forgotten heroes

August 1945–June 1951

In August 1945 the nations of the world, still recovering from the shock of the Nazi holocaust, once more recoiled in horror. It was hard to credit that the skeletal creatures liberated from jungle huts, euphemistically described by the Japanese as POW camps, could ever have been normal human beings.

Japan had not intended that anyone should ever learn of the many acts of inhumanity inflicted on their POWs. As early as 1 August 1944 the High Command had ordered the massacre of all prisoners 'as the situation dictates' and to 'annihilate them all, and not leave any traces'. Twelve months later, with defeat inevitable, mass graves had been dug at jungle camps and measures taken to ensure that by the end of August all would be destroyed 'individually or in groups by mass bombing, poisonous smoke, poisons, drowning, decapitations or what'. Some prisoners had just six hours to live when, at noon on 15 August, Emperor Hirohito stunned his nation by announcing Japan's unconditional surrender.

Not until Allied troops had liberated all the camps did the enormity of the situation hit the Australian people. Day after day the death figures rolled in, accompanied by graphic descriptions and photographs of men, barely more than spectres, lying by the thousand on bamboo slats awaiting rescue and rehabilitation. Even more horrifying, to a society where women were treated with respect, was the revelation that nurses and female civilian prisoners had been subjected to the same dreadful conditions. Australia, a small nation whose citizens had volunteered to defend the Empire for two consecutive generations, was so appalled that the need to punish those responsible was overshadowed, at least temporarily, by a greater need – to bring her people home.

There is no question that for both the ex-POWs and their families, who had fretted about their welfare for three and a half years, repatriation was the only sane course of action. However, as each ship and plane load headed south the eyewitnesses to Japanese atrocities all but vanished, dispersed into homes and convalescent hospitals across Australia. Although there was a concentrated effort to distribute questionnaires on the repatriation vessels and some superficial debriefings were conducted, follow-up work was extremely difficult. By the time many of the deponents were tracked down by investigating teams seeking further

Major Cyril Wild, war crimes investigator

information to identify the perpetrators, many of those responsible had disappeared.

Those Japanese who did not flee had a fair chance of evading retribution, for the workload of the investigating teams was immense. In an attempt to establish the whereabouts of tens of thousands of POWs, the investigators worked round the clock for the best part of three months, processing cases at the rate of 700 a day. But because this work was often carried out by personnel whose talents lay elsewhere, it was by necessity superficial, the actual fate of many prisoners was never determined, and many war crimes remained undetected. Indeed, it was often only by the remotest chance that investigators had any idea that a war crime might have been committed.

Major Cyril Wild, the Japanese-speaking officer who had the unenviable task of carrying the white flag at Singapore's surrender, and later as a POW had saved James Bradley from certain execution, had been seconded upon his release from the Changi Camp to investigate the fate of missing pilots, most of whom had simply vanished on capture. A tip from a Malay driver named Samson, who recalled that he had driven his Japanese master to an execution

Cyril Wild questioning Outram Road Gaol commandant, Colonel Mikizawa in an attempt to establish the identity of victims buried off Reformatory Road

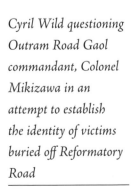

315

ground out near Bukit Timah in July, pointed Wild in the direction of Outram Road Gaol and Mikizawa in particular.

The civilian gaol commandant, doubtless in an attempt to mitigate the fact that 1200 Asians in his custody had died from starvation during the last fourteen months of the war, decided to cooperate. Leading Wild to a lonely stretch of wasteland off Reformatory Road, he poked about in the scrub until he found three newly made mounds with six wooden crosses which, he declared, marked the graves of Chinese and perhaps 'one or two Europeans' whom he had seen executed. Wild, on viewing the distinctly Christian markers, was immediately suspicious. Despite close questioning, Mikizawa protested that he knew nothing more and Wild, unable to obtain permission to exhume the bodies there and then, was forced to let the matter rest.

About a week later the Malay chieftain Amir Silahili arrived in Singapore searching for Ivor Salmond, one of the evacuees whom he had helped after the ships were bombed near Pompong Island. When Salmond had farewelled the amir to make his way up the Indragiri, on what was to be a futile attempt to escape with Colonel Dillon's party, he had vowed that 'when the day comes I shall return from Singapore with the British Navy to drive out the Japanese'. To which Silahili had replied, 'No, Tuan. I shall come to Singapore to meet you and we shall return together with the British Navy to liberate my people.'

After three years of Japanese occupation the young chieftain, stripped of his titles and deposed by the Japanese, had managed to steal a motor tonkan and sail to Singapore to call in his debt. Salmond was only too willing to oblige and took him to Wild, who listened with great interest to his story, and to two facts in particular. Firstly, a garrison of heavily armed Japanese, twenty-seven of whom were Kempeitai wanted for the Double Tenth massacre, was still terrorising the Lingga Archipelago. The second piece of information was that in December 1944 about ten Australian and British soldiers, members of a raiding party, had been taken to Singapore after being imprisoned on Singkep Island.

Tantalising though this information was, the authorities, swamped by the huge task of reoccupying Singapore and Malaya, were not in a position to act until 1 October when four motor launches, carrying naval personnel, Wild, Salmond, the amir, two civilians investigating the Double Tenth incident and half a platoon of paratroops, set out for Singkep to help Silahili liberate his people.

On arrival the party split into four groups to undertake its various tasks, which were completed to the satisfaction of everyone, except the Japanese – the amir was restored to power; the Kempeitai, including Miyazaki, who had interrogated and tortured Bishop Wilson, were in custody; a great deal of information about the capture of European men in the Lingga Archipelago was collected; and Wild had in his custody the Dabo Police Admission Book and a scrap of paper on which were written the names Warren, Carey and Marsh.

The Police Book was a mystery, for it showed that six 'white men' had been admitted to Dabo Gaol on 18 and 19 December and three more on 28–29 December, for crimes described as 'enemy of the state'. Their identities, except for 'R M Ingleton, Royal Marines, British' were not clear to Wild as their surnames had been omitted. A column alongside the entries showed, however, that almost all were Australian. With this scant information Wild returned to Singapore to begin a search for the nine men. To his consternation, he discovered there was no evidence that any had ever been in a POW camp. Furthermore, the Japanese would tell him nothing.

It was about this time, mid-October, that another group of investigators returned to Singapore from Bintan Island. They were members of an Australian POW inquiry team, which had been asked to follow up reports received in India that 6000 Allied prisoners were on Bintan. When the team's observers, peering from the doorway of a reconnaissance plane, reported they had seen no sign of any Europeans, a ground party was sent in with additional instructions from SOA's Captain John Ellis to make enquiries about Rimau, whose disappearance had been confirmed. On arrival at Kidjang on 8 October some of the team members questioned the locals while others tackled Major Fugita and his men, who had been rounded up by British paratroops. In establishing that their information was incorrect and that no POWs, let alone 6000, had ever been incarcerated on the island, the investigators inadvertently stumbled on two other, very disturbing incidents.

Shortly after Singapore had capitulated about thirty-four Australians who had surrendered to the Japanese at Tanjung Pinang had been taken to a tennis court, where they were bayoneted, shot or beheaded. The dead, and some who were still living, were thrown into an air-raid shelter and down a well in the grounds of the local hospital. One officer who escaped the initial massacre was subsequently decapitated on the beach. While the investigators were collecting this evidence, three men had come forward – Abdul Wahab, the headman of Mapur; Alexander Ouvarow, an English-speaking Russian planter from the island of Numbing who had interpreted for the Japanese; and Mr Tobing, a Malay employee of the Dutch Administration at Tanjung Pinang. They alleged that a number of white men, after being involved in a battle with Japanese troops on Merapas Island, had been pursued down the Lingga Archipelago and that three white men, captured on Singkep, had been lodged in the Tanjung Pinang Police Station overnight while en route to Singapore.

While the civilians were pouring out their tale, Major Fugita, head of the Tanjung Pinang garrison, had decided to tell everything he knew about the incidents at Kasu, Soreh, Tapai and Merapas. Yap Chi Yah, who had been responsible for Latif's torture, was rounded up, along with Chizu of the Kempeitai, and transferred with Fugita to Singapore for further questioning on board HMS *Caprice*, a British destroyer. Collaborators Raja Mun and Mahamit, along with Raja Rool, the loyal headman of Pangkil, were also brought in. By the time all had made

Major Fugita boards HMS Caprice *after his arrest on Bintan Island*

their statements the investigating team knew of the various fights that had taken place, that some men had been killed and that prisoners had been taken to Singapore. Incredibly, all this information had been known to SOA for months but, as it had been obtained from intercepted signals, its distribution had been restricted to those at the highest level.

A search of Bintan, Mapur and Merapas yielded nothing except a set of dentures and Riggs' grave (thought to be that of a Japanese) on Merapas, and irrefutable evidence that Rimau had been on the island. For some reason, no attempt was made to visit the easily accessible islands of Soreh and Tapai, where the skeletal remains of Lyon, Ross, Davidson and Campbell still lay.[1] The additional information from Abdul Wahab that five men had been seen on the nearby uninhabited island of Sentut in July 1945 raised hopes to such an extent that a search party was sent to investigate. They found nothing apart from a length of rubber hose, apparently used to divert smoke from a fire, long since dead, and indications that several small saplings had been sawn down, possibly to construct a raft. (Forty years later it would be discovered that the five men were slave labourers who had escaped from the bauxite mine, betrayed to the Japanese by Abdul Wahab himself.)

When the results of the Australian investigation were brought back to Singapore and added to what Wild had discovered, the main investigation was stepped up. From the Koreans Noh and Kim, Wild learned that ten European men had been taken from Outram Road in early July and executed. When it was discovered that the officers and the Kempeitai responsible, with the exception of Commandant Kobayashi who had fled, were already in custody for other crimes, it did not take long for the story to emerge.

Unable to deny what had occurred, Major-General Otsuka and Major Kamiya produced their trump card – the trial documentation. When Wild read through the contents he released Furuta from gaol and questioned him. By the time the Japanese interpreter had finished delivering his heavily embroidered mixture of fact and hearsay, Wild was convinced that the Rimau party had committed crimes contrary to the Hague Convention of 1907 and that the Japanese, after giving them the best of care, had reluctantly executed them in a manner befitting heroes.

If Furuta had witnessed any violence during Rimau's imprisonment, he now erased it from this mind. As was pointed out in later war crimes trials, the Japanese were very adept at structuring their thinking in such a way that unpleasant thoughts could either be pushed into the background or disappear completely, as if the unpleasantness had never occurred. By the same token, small gestures of kindness could be blown out of all proportion, allowing one of two incidents to become the rule, rather than the exception. As a mature, well-educated, fairly cultured and much travelled man, it is doubtful that without employing this device Furuta would have been able to come to terms with violence of the type usually doled out to prisoners by the Kempeitai, and with which he was familiar.

During his interviews Furuta handed over the two messages which he had promised to deliver for Page and Stewart. Bob's stated, 'I trust my father will approve the way I took in giving up my studies and joining the army', while the message from Corporal Stewart read, 'I hope my wife will excuse me for not saying a special good-bye when I saw her the night before I left for the operation. I did not want to worry her with my danger.' Having committed these poignant messages to memory and recorded them verbatim, Furuta felt satisfied that he had at last fulfilled the dying wishes of two men whom he respected greatly. He might as well not have bothered. The army did not take the trouble to deliver them.[2]

When Cyril Wild and his Australian counterpart in Singapore, Colonel Pritchard, viewed the trial papers, they were extremely impressed, as well they might be. By Japanese standards it was an exceptionally detailed document. Normal trial summaries, if they existed at all, were very perfunctory and did not contain the details or examples of cross-examination which appeared in Rimau's paperwork. With Furuta confirming everything that appeared in the written record, and SOA HQ failing to pass on the information that the message ordering Rimau's execution had been intercepted and decoded in February 1945, five months before the actual deaths, it is no wonder that the investigators had no idea that the entire trial was a sham.

The decision to withhold the intercepted message was deliberate. Although the war was over, SOA, like many other covert organisations, was paranoid about keeping the breaking of the enemy codes a closely guarded secret. This cloak of secrecy was so effective that it was not until the 1970s that the public learned what a phenomenally useful weapon the intercepted material had been.

During the actual hostilities, the knowledge gained from intercepts proved so valuable that drastic measures were taken to safeguard secrecy. Fully aware that Coventry was to be bombed, Winston Churchill had been unable to do anything to warn either the city or its people and, as Japan's diplomatic code had been broken long before war erupted, it has long been accepted that President Roosevelt knew for certain that the Pacific bases would be attacked. In 1989 it was learned from the wartime diary of Australian cryptanalyst Eric Nave that Japan's naval code had been broken in November 1941 and that Churchill had known of the impending attack on Pearl Harbour. Although the question of whether this information was passed to Roosevelt was unresolved, many believe that the fortuitous removal of the aircraft carriers out to sea, just prior to the raid, was not as 'coincidental' as it appeared. From Nave's diary it seems that by sacrificing the lives of 2400 sailors on the ships still in port, the secret of the intercepts was preserved and an outraged United States was at last brought into the war without jeopardising Roosevelt's presidency.

Unaware that highly ranked SOA officers had known for a long time that Rimau's execution had been ordered, the investigators in Singapore tackled the question of whether or not a war crime had been committed. That ten men had been beheaded was irrefutable. According to the Japanese the executions had been carried out in grand style, in keeping with their status as heroes. Furuta confirmed that after the execution, in attempting to bolster the morale of his own men, Otsuka had raved about the bravery of his victims, with words such as 'flowers of chivalry' flowing easily from his lips.

Wild was mightily impressed by this, because it was the embodiment of all he had ever learned about the Samurai way of death and the legendary code of the Knights of Bushido. Unfortunately, it appears that Wild's love of Japanese mythology had coloured his judgement, enabling him to accept some of the atrocities he had witnessed and the beatings he had endured in the belief that the behaviour was based on 'a living, honest thing, that belonged to the Samurai warrior – the code of the Warrior'. Although various other investigators were also fooled by elaborate Japanese cover-ups, it was perhaps his colleagues' mistaken belief that Wild had a great understanding of the Japanese mind that caused them to accept his opinion without question.[3]

Consequently, after a half-hearted attempt to verify whether uniforms had been worn, Wild and Pritchard accepted that the Rimau men had been legally executed as spies who had opened fire on the enemy while in disguise and while flying the enemy flag. No effort was made to find any of the many witnesses to the Kasu incident, nor to make independent investigations at any of the other islands.[4] The investigators also ignored the evidence of RAMC Captain Roderick Ross who, with Lieutenant-Colonel Bowes and Captain William Kerr, from an Australian Contact and Inquiry team, supervised the exhumation by Japanese labourers of the decapitated and semi-decapitated bodies on 22 November 1945. That same day, near Pasir Panjang Estate, about 2 kilometres to the south-east, they had also exhumed the remains of John Long and Cornelis Woudenberg, buried side by side. As was the case with the Rimau men, each of these graves had been marked with a brown wooden cross.

Ross's report made it clear that the botched executions and subsequent burials of the Rimau men had definitely not been fit for heroes. Incredibly, in the face of this damning evidence, which was supported by the statements of Noh and Kim, the investigators believed the story of the Japanese rather than the testimony of the Koreans and the forensic evidence of Ross. The decision to accept that each Rimau man had been accorded a hero's death, in keeping with the code of the Knights of Bushido, was ultimately responsible for suppressing the truth and subverting the course of military history.

When the various reports on Rimau and the Bintan massacre arrived, army personnel in Australia were not nearly as gullible. They cabled Singapore to enquire if either or both were war crimes and, if so, what was going to be done about it. The answer, which included the trial documentation, was forwarded with several opinions stating that in Rimau's case no war crime had been committed and intimating that, because of lack of evidence, the Bintan massacre was virtually a lost cause. In this correspondence, sent on 29 January 1946, the personnel in Australia who were being asked to give an opinion on the matter were also reminded that no suspect was to be brought to trial unless conviction was assured. The reason was allegedly twofold – firstly, there was a backlog of cases requiring attention and, secondly, anything more than an occasional acquittal would adversely affect public morale. Summing up, Lieutenant-Colonel R Smith, Officer Commanding 1 Australian War Crimes Section, stated he had been advised that the executions 'did NOT constitute war crime and it is not proposed to arraign any member of the Imperial Japanese Army ... unless instructions to the contrary are received from you'.

This reply appears to be a very liberal interpretation of a policy laid down by Mountbatten. As soon as hostilities ceased he had declared:

> The Japanese should be tried on criminal charges only, that is to say, brutality, etc.
> ... no one should be charged unless there is very strong prima facie evidence that
> he would be convicted on evidence which could clearly be seen to be irrefutable ...
> nothing would diminish our prestige more than if we appeared to be instigating
> vindictive trials against individuals of a beaten enemy nation.

Consequently, the premise on which the British judicial system had operated satisfactorily for centuries – presumption of innocence until proven guilty – was brushed aside by the fear that Japanese public opinion might view the British Empire's pursual of war criminals as something which was not altogether 'cricket'.

The explanations proffered did not satisfy some of the investigators. On 16 February 1946, the validity of the executions of the Rimau men and also of Douglas Hatfield, beheaded in 1942 for trying to escape, was questioned. It was not until 7 June, almost four months later, that the Director of Prisoners of War and Internees (DPW&I) found the time to reply. During this period, Legal Service's Brigadier Allaway had examined the documentation and reached the same conclusion as Wild's advisers.

The much-delayed opinion from the DWP&I dealt with the matter in some depth. He advised that although decapitation was abhorrent to the Western mind, it was perfectly legal if the prisoner had been tried in accordance with Japanese law. Members of a court could only be classified as war criminals 'if they acted without jurisdiction … or if the trial was not conducted bona fide or was unfair'. If this occurred, 'the members of the court, and the officer who confirms the proceedings are blameworthy and may be charged with an offence as war criminals'. As there was no way now of establishing that the Japanese, having deliberately set the Rimau men up, had committed these offences, those agitating for further action were effectively silenced.

Nevertheless, it is astounding that the Singapore investigators did not suspect that skulduggery may have taken place. On 27 December they had discovered that nine British and New Zealand airmen on a mission code-named Meridian had been summarily executed and the whole incident covered up. Captured in January 1945 during an air strike on Palembang, Sumatra, they had been sent to Outram Road Gaol, much to the annoyance of several junior Japanese officers who had advocated their immediate execution, only to have their request refused by their superiors, Colonels Sato and Ichiba. On 15 August, following the news the atomic bombs had been dropped on Japan, smouldering resentment had erupted into fury. With the apparent blessing of Commandant Kobayashi, all nine had allegedly been removed from the gaol by three army officers, taken to Changi Beach, beheaded and the bodies sunk in a weighted boat in deep water. However, gaol inmates sent to clean the airmen's cell later stated that it was awash with blood and the floor strewn with blood-soaked clothing. Other prisoners reported that they had observed shrouded bodies, placed on boards, being removed from the gaol.

As the officers responsible for the executions – Lieutenant Mayashita, Captain Ikeda and Major Kataoka – left written confessions and then committed suicide, the precise place of death is unclear. It may well be that, with the war over, the Meridian airmen were secretly beheaded in their cell. If this were the case, no one was talking. With repercussions inevitable, the less said, the better.

When a very worried Colonel Ichiba broke the news of the illegal executions carried out by these junior officers to Colonel Sato, they decided that in the case of 'the former' beheading incident, it would be prudent to keep the matter quiet. Accordingly, Sato reported to his superior, General Kinoshita, that 'a boat sailed from Singapore carrying these nine British airmen to Japan and the boat met aerial bombings off Camoulahan [Cam Ranh] and was lost, together with the entire personnel on board'.

Five days after the Meridian airmen met their deaths, the exhumed remains of eight American airmen were being incinerated on the parade ground at the naval base. Shot down during July by the destroyer *Kamikaze* while attacking the base, the fliers had been taken ashore where they came under the jurisdiction of Vice-Admiral Fukodome Shigeru. They had no hope of survival. Beheaded at the Nee Soon Rifle Range on about 4 August, they were buried alongside the corpses of another fourteen airmen, captured while attacking Singapore and executed at the same spot earlier in the year. After being cremated at the base, the charred remains of all twenty-two men were thrown into the Straits of Johor. With war crimes investigators unable to determine who had given the order, those found guilty of this atrocity (the former beheading incident) were sentenced to just three years' imprisonment.

Although no one was ever brought to trial over the deaths of the Rimau men, fate (or the War Crimes Commission) eventually caught up with almost all of them, for their many crimes against POWs had extended well beyond the executions at the Reformatory Road killing field. Corporal Hirata, one of the executioners, committed suicide. General Dihihara, who had issued the 10 February order, was hanged. So were General Itagaki, who had authorised the trial and insisted upon the death sentence, Major-General Otsuka, responsible for the legal proceedings, and the two commandants from Outram Road Gaol, Majors Kobayashi and Mikizawa. Major Kamiya, who had so brilliantly manipulated the 'evidence' to prove Rimau's guilt and so bring about their deaths, was himself sentenced to life imprisonment. The remaining four executioners were gaoled for between five and ten years.

Those responsible for the Double Tenth massacre were, however, brought to trial in March 1946. Seven Kempeitai, including Colonel Sumida, were sentenced to death, along with Chinese collaborator Toh Swee Koon. Six others, including Interpreter Miyazaki whom Cyril Wild ran to earth on Singkep Island, were sentenced to terms of imprisonment ranging from eight years to life.[3]

One person delighted by the news that Otsuka was to die was Furuta. He had never forgiven Otsuka for refusing to intercede on Rimau's behalf, and had been even more disgusted when he turned informant in an attempt to save his own skin. Ironically, although he detested Otsuka, Furuta believed that Outram Road's Kobayashi was essentially a 'fair and kind man' who 'could not give prisoners as much comfort and treatment as British authorities expected him to give'. This lack of understanding, said Furuta, had 'caused him death'. He also clung tenaciously to the delusion that Major Kamiya had been forced to place the Rimau prisoners on trial very much against his will. Furuta himself was absolved of any complicity and given a job – translating for the British at the trials of the Japanese.

By June 1946 SOA had been dissolved for over six months and all interest in Rimau had evaporated, despite irrefutable evidence that the raid had succeeded, at least in part: on 26 January 1945, the Japanese had transmitted OKA Staff Message 62 from Singapore. Although some words were indecipherable owing to lack of clarity in transmission, the message, decoded just a few days later, was plain enough.

The 23 English and Australian officers and men, led by Lt-Col …… of the British Army …… a Special Reconnaissance Duty (abbreviated as SRD) at Melbourne, under direct control of Australian Army headquarters … were personnel from …… They left Garden Island, Australia, by a large submarine on the night of 11 September and going by way of the Lombok Straits, Java Sea, and Karimata Straits, they infiltrated into Merapas Island.

After this they divided into small boats … which can be concealed in darkness and approached ships at anchor in Singapore harbour at about 0300 and attached magnetic rivets (time limit of about six hours). The following day, after confirming the results of their work, each group sailed about, waiting around for darkness. Although there seems to have been a plan by which they were to return [home] again by submarine from [Merapas], when they were midway in their work, our longtime resident patrollers discovered them and in the long run they did not succeed.

A second intercepted signal, transmitted from Timor on 3 February 1945, had stated 'Lt Col Lyon and six men in September 44 penetrated to the vicinity of Singapore and succeeded sinking 3 ships at anchor in the harbour'. This information was distributed by SOA in a memorandum on 6 April 1945 which advised, 'it appears that at least three ships were sunk, although the party has been captured by the enemy'.

From intercepted signals it also appeared that the captured men had given away information, and that someone on *Mustika* had panicked and fired. As early as January 1945, a committee comprising General Blamey, General Northcott, Brigadier Lloyd and SOA's Colonel Chapman-Walker had met for high-level and secret discussions to discuss the material gleaned from the intercepts. Although the intercept naming Ingleton and the information he had revealed was deleted from an intelligence summary before it was circulated any further, the fact that other information was known to the enemy and that someone had fired prematurely resulted in a decision that no awards or honours could be considered. However, on 7 December 1945 Jock Campbell, who had taken over as Director of SOA from Chapman-Walker in June, recommended a Posthumous Mention in Despatches for each of the men. None of the Australians received any citations but, within ten days of Campbell's telegram being dispatched, all the British – Lyon, Ross, Davidson, Riggs and Ingleton – were awarded MIDs on the recommendation of SOA. In England, SOE senior officers had 'tried without avail' to have Lyon awarded a Victoria Cross or George Cross for Gallantry, a recommendation which could not succeed as it was believed no witnesses had survived. Had SOE known that not only had Lyon and Ross fought to the death, but that Lyon's bravery in particular had been witnessed by scores of enemy troops, they may have made some attempt to find them.

On 19 August 1945, the silence surrounding Operation Jaywick was broken with a press release issued by Brigadier Ken Wills and on 8 November the *Daily Telegraph* in Sydney reported that Lyon had been captured and 'beheaded' while on another raid. It was not until August 1946, following the announcement of the gallantry awards for Jaywick, that full details of that mission, including a large number of photographs, were made public. Three weeks later, on August 22, the Minister for the Army, Francis Forde, revealed that there had been a second raid which had taken the lives of all twenty-three men. In relating the tragic details he stressed that the Japanese had been 'profoundly impressed' by the bravery of the executed Rimau men, so much so that a Japanese major-general had concluded a lecture to the General Staff in Singapore by stressing that 'the Japanese Army could not hope to win the war unless it learned to imitate the courage and patriotism of the captured men.'

On 27 March the following year, when Corporal Jack Hardy's mother wrote to Forde's successor Cyril Chambers, asking what recognition would be conferred upon her son and what punishment had been meted out to the Japanese responsible for his death, she was in for a shock. She was informed that the party had given up their uniforms and spied on the Japanese on their own initiative, that they had displayed Japanese flags and when finally captured were not wearing any uniforms or badges of rank to suggest that they were members of any fighting force. The Minister stated that, by being clad in non-military attire, 'these intrepid Australians voluntarily deprived themselves of the right to be treated as prisoners, according to the customs and usage of war' and had been 'tried before a legally constituted Japanese court'.

By asserting that the adoption of a disguise was voluntary, when it had actually been an integral part of the plan; by not conducting any proper investigation; and by regurgitating the 'facts' supplied by the Japanese, the Australian Government had neatly distanced itself from any potentially embarrassing questions about Operation Rimau, for which it was answerable. In less than two years, the fabrications of the Japanese, aggravated by the poor assessments of investigating officers and distortions of the truth, had turned Operation Rimau from a testament of courage and tenacity into an episode which was both shameful and humiliating. Through ignorance and apathy, a terrible slur had been cast upon all twenty-three men. Swept under the carpet, they and their mission were all but forgotten. Indeed, the term 'war crimes' in connection with Rimau would probably not have surfaced again had it not been for a message scrawled upon the wall of a cell in Surabaya.

Following the cessation of hostilities, investigation teams had arrived in Surabaya and discovered not a single prisoner, European or Asian, in custody. Nor was there any evidence of the mass graves at the Eastern Fort – all remains had been hurriedly exhumed and cremated on sheets of corrugated iron, leaving only small, isolated bones scattered below the sand. The destruction of evidence was so thorough that preliminary questioning elicited no information about any Australians, and no hint whatsoever that Allied prisoners had been executed without trial, some of them after Japan surrendered. With the murder in April 1946 of three team war crimes investigators, who were conducting enquiries about POWs said to have been placed in bamboo pig baskets and thrown to the sharks in Surabaya Harbour, the Japanese based in Surabaya were confident they would evade retribution – especially those involved in the pig basket case, since the Japanese who had murdered the investigators had then committed suicide. But for those involved in the killings of Perske, Sachs, Warne and the Americans, fate was about to overtake them.

In late July 1946 Dutch Private G L Bakker was imprisoned in Surabaya for thirty days for a misdemeanour. Reading the graffiti scribbled on the walls of his cell by former occupants, he came a cross a message written sixteen months before by Lieutenant Mason (Bob) Schow, one of the American airmen:

After the war – whoever reads his send a postcard with this on it to Mr M R
Schow, P.E.D. I Fluverenk, Jamestown, New York, U.S.A.
    Dear Dad, It is 25 February 1945 and I have been a prisoner here Soerabaja, for about three months. What will happen from now on I don't know. Love Bob.

At some later date he had added:

PS. Donald Palmer. Clif Peask [sic], Aussie, Brisbane, Australia. John Sachs – Australia. Same cell. God bless whoever sends his message for me.

As soon as he was released, Private Bakker responded to the airman's plea. When the postcard arrived in the United States, Martin Schow, Mason's father, informed the authorities who then contacted their counterparts in Australia. On 18 June 1947 a Dutch judge by the name of van Beek began a preliminary investigation at Surabaya. The cell walls had by this time been whitewashed in a fit of spring cleaning by the Dutch, effectively destroying any other clues, so his enquiry raised more questions than it answered. As a thorough investigation was obviously needed, in the latter half of 1947 Captain Jack Sylvester was appointed to 2 Australia War Crimes Section (2 AWCS), based in Tokyo, to investigate the disappearance of Sachs and Perske, still officially classified as 'Missing – Believed Prisoner of War'. Although SOA knew that both men had been captured and, if intelligence sources could be believed, most probably executed, post-war investigations had not shed any light on their fate.

When Sylvester arrived in Japan he was confronted by a conspiracy of silence. Nobody, it seemed, had either seen or heard of any Allied prisoners ever being held at Surabaya. Determined to get to the bottom of the story, Sylvester chipped patiently away until various Japanese, in an effort to disengage themselves from the investigator's clutches, began dropping names of people who might be able to help him. For two long years Sylvester interrogated and re-interrogated suspects, probing and worrying at every detail until the whole shocking story emerged.

He was aided in his quest by the fact that almost all the Japanese affected by total amnesia in 1947 had, by the end of 1949, made a miraculous recovery, recalling various events and dates with utmost clarity. Under Sylvester's persistent questioning, one suspect who had stated categorically that no prisoners had ever been held in Surabaya was able to remember that not only had prisoners been confined in the naval stockade at Gubeng, but that they had been executed. Moreover, in a flash of total recall, he suddenly remembered that he himself had been one of the executioners.

In 1948, unaware that almost all of the remains had been cremated, war graves recovery teams dug up the entire Eastern Fort searching for the bodies. After sifting through tonnes of sand, they found only small bones and part of a lower jaw, believed to be that of Perske. Sylvester continued with his investigations, inadvertently uncovering many crimes besides the fate of the two Australian commandos. Some were horrendous and clear cut, others were equally horrific but unsolvable because of their complexity and the amount of misinformation mixed with factual evidence. Without realising it, Sylvester discovered the fate of both Bill Reynolds and Doug Warne. Although Reynolds' death was more or less established later by other investigators assessing the evidence, Doug Warne was identified as an SOE operative with a similar name – Lieutenant-Colonel Douglas Richardson, who had worked behind the lines with Freddie Spencer Chapman in Malaya and who had survived the war. A New Zealander by birth, Richardson had never been listed as missing and had never been in Java. Not one of the people examining Sylvester's file, all of whom had a list of all missing SOA men, realised that the name given by the Japanese as 'Douglas Richardson' was actually Douglas Richard Warne.

Although he was not familiar with the names of all the Rimau men, Sylvester knew of the fate of some of them, since by this time the executions in Singapore were common knowledge. Consequently, when he learned that the signal calling for their executions had been received in February 1945, he realised that the death sentence had preceded the trial by five months. In 1949, shortly before this independent evidence came to light, 2 AWCS again raised the question of whether a war crime had been committed. With Major Wild killed in an air crash in Hong Kong in September 1946 and all his papers lost in the resulting conflagration, the enquiry was finally passed to the Army Legal Section in Singapore. The old file was located and the original opinion transmitted to Tokyo, effectively putting paid to any further speculation by the investigators. In any case, with more startling revelations about other crimes emerging from Sylvester's investigations, his staff were too occupied in taking down statements to press the Rimau matter any further.

One previously undetected crime which took up a great deal of their time was the massacre of 250 Allied prisoners on the prison ship *Suez Maru*. While being transferred from Ambon to Surabaya, the vessel had been attacked and sunk by an American submarine. Far from rescuing the prisoners from the water, the Japanese crew of Minesweeper No 12 had machine-gunned every one of them.

Although the perpetrators of many of the crimes Sylvester uncovered would never be brought to trial, he did manage to amass sufficient evidence to ensure that in 1951 those responsible for the deaths of Sachs, Perske and Warne were arraigned before a Military Court at Los Negros, on Manus Island off the north coast of New Guinea. Although some of the accused were acquitted, the court demanded that Rear Admiral Tanaka, executioners Yoshimoto, Okada and Ikeda, Doctor Nakamura and his accomplice Tatsuzaki, medical officers Yoshino and Konishi, and the evil Shinohara, be punished.

Fortunately for the accused, and unfortunately for people like Sylvester who had worked so hard and for so long to see that justice was done, Australia by this was entering into an anti-communist alliance against China and Russia with her former wartime Allies and old enemy Japan. For this reason, the British and Americans had been handing down much lesser sentences or reducing them following appeals for clemency – a point raised by the defence lawyer handling the Surabaya case. Consequently, the executioners and the medical staff (some of whom had only been accused of injecting the Indonesians with toxin, a crime to which they admitted), were given sentences ranging from one to seven years, while Tanaka, who claimed to have no knowledge of any policy to kill prisoners, had his death sentence commuted to fifteen years by Australia's General Sturdee, in whose hands alone lay the responsibility for confirming or mitigating sentences.

While very senior officers, despite their culpability, would escape the executioner, for Shinohara there was no reprieve. On 11 June 1951, he and four others also convicted of heinous crimes were hanged. Their dying wish to have their remains cremated and sent home to Japan was thwarted by torrential rain of such intensity that the bodies were eventually wrapped in canvas and unceremoniously dumped out to sea.

With the death of Shinohara, and the sentences handed down to the others (not one of whom, following various petitions for mercy, would remain in custody beyond 1958), the deaths of Perske, Sachs, Warne and Bill Reynolds might have been considered to be more or less avenged. Yet the very people who might have gained some grim satisfaction in justice at least being seen to be done – their families – were not only unaware that any trials had taken place but were never given any details on the fate of their relatives. In Australia, John Sachs' brother Peter wrote scores of letters to the army and the government, begging for information. None was ever forthcoming. In a misguided but nevertheless benevolent attempt to shield grieving relatives from even more heartache, the Australian Government and the army had agreed to allow only the barest outlines of atrocities perpetrated by the Japanese to be published, and definitely nothing at all which might identify the victims – a policy to which the press, although no longer constrained by any wartime censorship considerations, voluntarily agreed.

So, while the front pages of newspapers throughout Australia reported in graphic detail the crimes of Nazi Germany, those of Japan were usually restricted to a couple of columns, generally towards the rear of the publication. The trial of Shinohara was reported, but there were no clues as to the identity of his victims. It was not until 1989 that the current author, after a chance meeting with John Sachs' nephew and namesake, was able to inform the family of all the details surrounding the arrest and execution of Sachs and Perske. On learning the full story Peter Sachs remarked, 'I am not a vindictive man, but it would have given our family some measure of comfort to know that John's murderers had been punished.' In Brisbane, Mrs Perske had waited in vain for her husband to come home, clinging to the remote possibility that he might be marooned on some uninhabited island, awaiting rescue. By the time she gave up hope and remarried, she was beyond child-bearing age. 'I can forgive the Japanese for what they did to Cliff', she said, 'because that is what happens in war. What I cannot forgive is that their actions and attempts to cover it up denied me the chance to become a mother.' And in Jamestown, New York, Mrs Schow lit a candle in the front room of their house night after night for years to welcome her son home. It was not until 1951 that the candle went out.

While the facts surrounding these deaths at Surabaya were being suppressed on compassionate grounds, further to the east, on the island of Timor, the fate of Jeffrey Willersdorf and Hugo Pace, the last of the Rimau men, had become inextricably enmeshed in a matter so sinister that, had it been made public, would have created an immense scandal and undermined the confidence of the nation. It was one of the deadliest secrets of the war, and its name was Operation Lagarto.

17

The Timor affair

August 1943–August 1945

Australia's closest Indonesian neighbour, Portuguese-Dutch Timor, was invaded by the Japanese in early 1942. An infantry battalion, sent into Dutch territory to fulfil a promise made to the Dutch by the Australian government, had fought valiantly against overwhelming odds. All those not captured took to the hills where, with the help of loyal locals, they continued the fight only to be evacuated when their position was no longer tenable.

The politically neutral, adjoining Portuguese territory had also been forced to accept Japanese occupation, but many pro-Allied Timorese and Portuguese bands had continued to resist until reprisals against their countrymen dramatically diminished aid to the rebels and pushed them deep into the mountainous interior. In July 1943, when their position also became perilous, Australia dispatched Lieutenant M de J Pires – a Portuguese army pilot, former administrator of Sao Domingos province and now SOA agent – to organise their evacuation and to set up a covert operation.

When the evacuees, numbering more than seventy men, women and children were successfully evacuated on 3 August 1943, SOA's Sergeant Alfred Ellwood, an Australian signaller, joined the undercover party. Since Pires' English was not altogether fluent and as he was a rather volatile, highly-strung type, 21-year-old Ellwood, who had fought in Dutch Timor, was instructed to keep an eye on him. Although there was already a signaller, Patricio Luz, assigned to the covert team, SOA was anxious to be kept properly informed of the activities of the party, given the codename Lagarto – Portuguese for 'lizard' or 'cunning fellow'.

Unfortunately, Pires resented Ellwood's presence, refusing to relinquish any of the signalling work and completely rejecting any organisational advice. Ellwood's concern over his rather gung-ho attitude to the operation was exacerbated by the discovery that Pires allowed Lagarto to be accompanied by an enormous entourage. Apart from the eight-man party there were twelve servants, thirteen assorted carriers and Timorese chiefs, who had simply attached themselves to the group, and two women, one of whom was pregnant and constantly ill – companions of Pires and his offsider Matos da Silva.

The logistics of feeding, hiding and moving this monstrous retinue were overwhelming. The day after Ellwood's arrival the party was forced to keep on the move by the unexpected arrival of pro-Japanese locals, who also prevented the retrieval of stores from the beach. With all available rations soon exhausted and friendly villagers loath to help for fear of reprisals, the group was reduced to a hand-to-mouth existence as it tried to keep one jump ahead of the Japanese. After two months, with Pires refusing to split the party into smaller, more manageable groups and preferring to rely on his intuition, rather than military strategy, Ellwood informed SOA that unless it organised an immediate evacuation, capture would be inevitable. By the time SOA had made up its mind to accept Ellwood's suggestion, it was too late. On 29 September, aided by hostile Timorese and the confessions of tortured villagers, the Japanese closed in.

Only eight of those who survived the machine-guns regrouped. This small band, including Pires and Ellwood, made for the beach where the Australian, being without dry matches to burn his cipher, signal plan and papers, buried them in the sand. When an exhausted Pires announced he could go no further, Ellwood, unlike wireless operator Luz and two others, did not abandon his superior officer. Although Pires had been issued with suicide pills, the pair surrendered.

They were taken by truck to Dili, the capital of Portuguese Timor and HQ of the Japanese Army's 48 Division, for interrogation by the Kempeitai. When a softening up period of no sleep, paralysingly tight bonds and beatings failed to loosen Ellwood's tongue, he was given salty food and water and kept awake. Maddened by thirst, his mind numbed by lack of sleep and his body bruised and battered, he begged the Japanese to execute him or allow him to shoot himself. When the interrogators found the suicide pills on Pires, it made matters worse. Unable to withstand the torture, which included being strung up by his thumbs, Pires declared he was pro-Japanese and that Ellwood had intended to poison the Kempeitai. This 'confession' resulted in treatment so brutal that Ellwood once more called for merciful release.

Meantime Pires, who had lost control completely, had given the Kempeitai a message enciphered in his emergency code and which the Japanese now wanted Ellwood to transmit to SOA. When he refused, he was subjected to bouts of re-interrogation and returned to a filthy, fly-and-mosquito-infested cell beneath the verandah of the kempei building, where his bonds cut into his rapidly swelling flesh, producing running sores, and his feet began to rot inside his boots. Finally, on 5 October, after six days of virtually non-stop interrogation, his resolve weakened by sleep deprivation and mental and physical torture, Ellwood's resistance broke.

The experienced Japanese wireless officer who, like his fellow officers, spoke English, could easily have transmitted the signal, but in order to subject Ellwood to further degradation held his hand on the transmitting key, forcing him to tap out the message Pires had prepared:

From A.B.C. [Pires] to H.B.M. [Manderson, head of Timor Section]. Continue big pursue against us. In this moment our H.Q. stay in Waqui Mountain where we are hiding. Our operator Patricio Luz run away. We lost cipher book.

Had anyone bothered to take basic security precautions, the authenticity of this message could have been immediately verified by SOA's sending back in its reply a prearranged authenticator word. To confirm he was not in enemy hands, the field operative would then make sure he included this word in his next message. Ellwood had no idea what his authenticator was, because SOA had not provided him with one, or any cover story. Improvising, he had withstood his interrogation for as long as possible, only to discover, too late, that his resistance was futile. Pires had sung like a bird and the Japanese, who already possessed many ciphers, messages and documents captured from other areas, as well as the documents Ellwood had buried on the beach, had been in the box seat from the very beginning.

As there was no answer to Pires' message, the following day Ellwood was ordered to compose another. When he signalled that the party was now at Obaqui, it was with the expectation that SOA which was, after all, an intelligence organisation, might actually use some. Since they knew from previous messages that Lagarto's capture was imminent, it is incomprehensible that, on receiving the Obaqui message, someone did not realise that the party had been caught. Obaqui was not only 32 kilometres from Lagarto's last reported position, it was also 32 kilometres into the heart of an area which SOA knew was full of Japanese patrols and hostile Timorese. There is no doubt that SOA consulted a map for, in response to the rest of the signal, it replied that a food drop would be made.

While failing to pick up this warning was bad enough, SOA HQ committed an unforgivable breach of security by mentioning the names of other operatives in Timor. Referring to the message they believed Pires had sent, they asked, 'ABC say Luz run away. Is this fact or precaution. Are you with ABC or separated. Who is operating.' The next day, when the Japanese had Ellwood reply, 'Confirm ABC lost cipher book during pursuit by Jap patrol. At same time Luz run away. I am with ABC and am operating wireless', they paved the way for the total control of Operation Lagarto.

Ellwood knew that as long as he transmitted, Lagarto's lives might be spared. His problem was how to indicate to SOA that he was compromised. Fearful that allowing signals to be transmitted with glaring errors would bring about an over-reaction from Melbourne, resulting in instant liquidation, Ellwood vetted the Japanese signals, trying to make them as boring, bland and colourless as possible in the hope that the stream of trite information would set off alarm bells. Expecting that someone at Operational HQ would question his motives, he stubbornly refused the offer to extract him, although this had been a firm arrangement before he left Australia.

Both ploys failed miserably. On Christmas Eve, with a complete and utter disregard for security, SOA signalled that it intended to insert another party, code-named Cobra. It capped this appalling security breach a few days later by transmitting the details of MacArthur's 'island-hopping' strategy to regain control of the South-West Pacific. In a further fit of enthusiasm SOA also decided, on receiving a glowing reconnaissance report from Lagarto on the suitability of Cobra's operational zone, to change Cobra's intended role – that of a three-week reconnaissance – to a semi-permanent base.

Ellwood's despair can only be imagined. His messages so far had resulted only in his being forced to accompany the Japanese to collect regular supply drops. While it was sickening to know that the enemy was the beneficiary of a large amount of equipment, stores, food and gold coins, it was unthinkable to allow his countrymen to be captured without trying to warn them.

The arrangements for Cobra's insertion at Edemomo were perfectly straightforward. On 29 January, after the correct signals had been flashed from shore to ship, the party would be escorted to safety by three Lagarto Timorese. Apart from substituting three pro-Japanese Timorese for the Lagarto personnel, the kempei intended to stick to this plan. However, any hopes Ellwood may have harboured of warning the Cobra party were dashed when the Japanese elected to keep him in a hut at Edemomo, under lock and key, instead of taking him to the beach with the signal party. Determined to warn the Cobra men before they left the ship, he managed to appropriate enough material to make a simple lamp. When zero hour approached he asked to visit the latrines, where he swung a violent punch at his guard. Unfortunately, the guard ducked and, while he suffered broken teeth and fell to the ground, he was not rendered unconscious. As he shouted the alarm, Ellwood ran, pursued by Timorese and Japanese who came from all directions. With his pace slowed by the effects of beri beri, a vitamin deficiency disease, he was caught and hit over the head with a metal sword scabbard. Saved from immediate decapitation by the number of people thronged about him, he was trussed securely, kicked and beaten senseless and left in the broiling sun without food or water for two days. Ellwood's misery was absolute when, during a lucid period, he heard the voice of an Australian, signifying that Cobra had been captured. Roped behind a horse and forced to move at a trot until he collapsed, he was taken back to Dili, where he was subjected to further punishment before being once more put to work transmitting bogus messages.

After being successfully dropped off by an Australian Navy fairmile at 8 pm and making contact with their three 'guides', the Cobra party, comprising Captain Cashman, radio operator Lieutenant Liversidge, and three native Timorese, had buried their stores on the beach and moved inland. After about an hour, when the leading Timorese pretended that he had lost the way and asked Cashman for a torch, the Japanese sprang their trap. When Cashman, knocked senseless by a blow to the head, regained consciousness, he found that Liversidge and one of

Cobra's Timorese were also captive, and that all were securely bound. After a preliminary bout of questioning, accompanied by the usual kicks and blows, all three were taken to Dili, where they were subjected to even worse treatment than that meted out to Ellwood.

Part of Cashman's early interrogation was aimed at discovering the meaning of the phrase '2926 Slender Silk key' – Cobra's code and authenticator which, contrary to all regulations, Liversidge had recorded in his notebook. Although Cashman was able to satisfy the Japanese with a plausible explanation, he was not able to prevent them from sending SOA a message on 5 February. Such was the euphoria in Melbourne that Cobra had arrived and was on air, that for eighteen days no one bothered to carry out a security check. Even then, it was not prudence which prompted the challenge but the decoding of an intercepted signal on 26 February which revealed that Cashman was in Japanese hands.

While the security check was simple, it was also almost useless. The arrangement for SOA to transmit the authenticator word – in Cobra's case, 'slender' – was an entirely random procedure, unlike the arrangement for SOE which had a check built into every signal. In an attempt, now that this disturbing information about Cashman's capture had been received, SOA issued the challenge 'Slender girl sends greetings'. As the authenticator was not included in the reply, two days later SOA tried again, using a more oblique 'Please acknowledge in last sentence from this particular girl. It will relieve her feelings and ours. We do not know her name but she is not, repeat not the fat repeat fat one'. The Japanese, who could make neither head nor tail of this strange communication, sought clarification from Cashman who again offered a plausible explanation. As, from their point of view, there was no sensible answer to this latest message, the Japanese did not bother to reply to it.

When four days passed with no news from Cobra, an alarmed SOA sought help from Lagarto. After informing Ellwood that it appeared all was not well, and that the challenge had not been answered, SOA called for suggestions. Lagarto replied noncommittally, but offered to send Matos da Silva to 'investigate'. Before this suggestion was acknowledged, SOA again signalled Cobra, this time with no subtlety whatsoever. After a preamble containing war news from Rabaul, the message concluded with 'Jap chances escape encompassed troops very slender, repeat slender, repeat slender'.

This time the Kempeitai finally realised that there was a connection between the entry in Liversidge's notebook and the message just received. Under torture, Cashman revealed the secret. It did not matter that his resolve was broken. The very next day, 3 March, SOA signalled Lagarto, ordering 'Matsilva to go to Edemomo at once. If he finds Cobra to be OK tell 452 [Cashman] to work slender repeat slender as authenticator in message confirming his safety'. These instructions to Ellwood concluded with the useful information that Lagarto now had an authenticator – 'compact'.

With this great flood of information, the Japanese had no trouble sending an authenticated reply. But before this was received in Australia, SOA, which must have been verging on panic, dispatched yet another message to Cobra. The contents were designed, should Cobra indeed have been captured, to lure the enemy into the open. Out of the blue, SOA advised that £10,000, in gold, was available for Cashman's use, provided a safe method of delivery could be arranged. As the Japanese could not work out what this message was about, Cashman underwent another round of violent interrogation.

Meanwhile, the Cobra signal with the correct authenticator in its reply was received in Melbourne. This created such a sense of relief that SOA threw all caution to the wind, replying that an intercepted Japanese message had claimed Cashman's capture. This was followed by another signal, divulging Lagarto's authenticator, and then yet another, disclosing that the offer to deliver the gold had been nothing but a ruse.

Luckily for the security of the entire Allied intelligence network, the Japanese refused to believe that their signals had been intercepted and decoded, reasoning that if their code had been broken, no one would be stupid enough to disclose it. Their overestimation of the level of intelligence of those running SOA prevented the destruction of the Allies' ultimate secret weapon.

The Japanese were possibly so busy being incredulous over SOA's 'intercept' information that they failed to notice that on 16 March Lagarto had been challenged with a security signal asking, 'Is Matsilva back. Send us compact signal to assure us finally re safety 452'. Ten days later Lagarto finally replied, 'Matsilva not yet returned. Will send required signal when he returns'. That this message failed to contain the authenticator word 'compact' went unnoticed by SOA which, having sent the check, went back to the matter at hand – sending information about personnel it intended to insert to relieve Lagarto.

Despite SOA's obtuseness, Ellwood did not abandon his attempt to warn Australia that he, and therefore Cobra, had been captured. His messages became ridiculous, giving inane 'information' about completely irrelevant matters such as village fiestas and offering weak excuses as to why he and his party could not be extracted. Eventually, this extraction issue could no longer be sidestepped, but when messages began to arrive at SOA insisting that a submarine would be the best method – a clever but vain attempt by the Japanese to lure a submarine into range – no one wondered about the change in Ellwood's attitude, let alone suspect there might be an ulterior motive. Never once did SOA question how Lagarto had managed to evade capture or query how the hideout, surrounded by hostile locals, remained unchanged for over twelve months. Neither did anyone think it odd that the drop zones were in country known to be populated, or that Ellwood never stirred from his base except to receive substantial amounts of stores. For almost two years, not a single person ever questioned the value of his alleged intelligence or asked him precisely what he was doing. SOA, with the assistance of the RAAF, kept up the regular supply drops of a vast amount of valuable material, including arms and ammunition to equip a fictitious army, and continued to break security by needlessly giving information which led to the deaths of six other operatives. It was the same story for Cobra. Before six months had passed, Cobra's wireless, with the help of SOA, would lure two unsuspecting men to their deaths.

Although Cashman, unlike Ellwood, was not actually transmitting, he was originating many of the signals and enciphering and deciphering all of them. With no way of alerting SOA to his predicament, now that the secret of the authenticator had been blown, Cashman sent a stream of 'intelligence' just as stupid as that sent by Ellwood, only to have someone compile this puerile information into official AIB 'Information Reports', bearing the signature of Brigadier Ken Wills, its director.

Ellwood's other attempt to warn SOA, by giving the right location name but the wrong navigational references for drop zones or insertion points (thereby placing an easily identifiable geographical feature into, say, the middle of the ocean), was equally futile. The navigational information, which was evidently not checked for accuracy, was merely passed to the RAAF which, believing an error had occurred during transcription, simply corrected it to suit the geography. It is also apparent that no attempt was made to check on either Chapman or Ellwood by comparing the 'fingerprints' of their transmission idiosyncrasies with a master copy, held on graphically interpreted tapes in Melbourne.

Shortly after the wireless links had been established with Cobra, SOA began planning the insertion of another party. Code-named Adder, it consisted of three Portuguese Timorese and two Australian soldiers, Captain John Grimson (one of Sam Carey's Scorpion men) and signaller Sergeant Jack Shand. Although no arrangements had been made through Cobra or Lagarto to 'welcome' the party, the Japanese knew from signals sent by SOA that the landing point at Cape Ile Hoi had been reconnoitred.

On the night of 20 May the party attempted a landing, only to be swamped in heavy seas and lose all their stores. A second attempt in mid-June was thwarted when enemy aircraft spotted their ship en route from Darwin, and a third was aborted when Shand crushed his finger at the Melville Island base. Eventually, with Sergeant Ernest Gregg replacing Shand, Adder was inserted on 22 August. Two days later they were ambushed. In the ensuing struggle, Gregg and one of the Timorese were killed. That same evening, about 300 metres away, there was a second skirmish. The following day the body of Captain Grimson was found.

The Japanese knew that the cause of death was not the slight wound to his left eye. The bullet which had passed between his lower right jaw and the left side of his head clearly showed that rather than fall into enemy hands Grimson, like Davidson and Campbell, had obeyed his orders absolutely. In a rare show of respect, the Japanese buried the Australians together, marking the place with a wooden pillar, in traditional fashion.

Meanwhile, SOA's suggestion to withdraw both Ellwood and Cashman for consultation

Sergeant Ernest Gregg, Operation Adder   *Captain John Grimson, Operation Adder*

was evidently causing the Japanese some concern, for they began to employ delaying tactics. It was perhaps this sudden evasiveness, and the lack of correlation between intelligence sent by Cobra and the RAAF's reconnaissance information, that prompted SOA on 9 October to seek assurance that Cobra was not in enemy control.

It was not before time. Not a single challenge had been issued since 30 April. Security was so lax that, when SOA became concerned at the lack of communication from the Adder party, it gave details of Adder's insertion to Cobra without conducting any security check and asked Cobra to investigate – a request which the Japanese countered by saying that there was too much enemy activity in the area. Shortly after this message was received, SOA finally made a security check. On 11 October, in answer to SOA's Signal 34, Cobra dutifully transmitted 'slender', allowing SOA to relax once more.

The apparently comatose state which had afflicted SOA from September 1943 may have continued indefinitely had the organisation not been jolted awake on 10 March 1945 with the realisation that at least one party seemed to be in enemy control. Consequently, orders were issued to halt plans to supply either party with new codes and frequencies, suggested by Seymour Bingham, a security-conscious SOE major.[1]

On reviewing the Timor operations shortly after taking over SOA's Darwin-based Group D, which had assumed partial control of Timor in December 1944, Bingham had become concerned that the signal plans, ciphers and wireless frequencies for both parties had been in use for far too long and therefore were a security risk. Although he asked repeatedly for access to copies of all previous signal traffic between Timor and Australia, his request to view the material, which would have alerted him that Cobra had already been the subject of a security scare, was denied. Bingham's caution was born of experience, for the unfortunate major had already had his fingers burnt in the matter of operational security, when he was made the scapegoat for the failure of an SOE operation in Holland which had resulted in the capture of sixty-four agents.

Although innocent of any complicity, Bingham had been banished from SOE HQ to the antipodes in much the same way as unwanted citizens had been expelled from the mother land 150 years before. His distress can only be imagined when, on 10 March 1945, he learned that security in Timor appeared to have been breached and that Cobra and/or Lagarto was believed to be compromised.

It had taken SOA six weeks to reach this conclusion. On receipt of an early February report, based on an intercept which indicated that 'some chaps in hiding' had been captured in Timor, SOA accepted without question a suggestion from the Department of Intelligence that they could be the Adder men. This was in spite of the fact that the same top-secret report repeated the previously intercepted Japanese information that 'Lt Pirusu [Pires], who is an agent, landed on the south coast of Timor on 3 July [1943] from an Australian submarine'. Indeed, it was not until the evidence became overwhelming that light began to dawn on SOA that something was amiss.

On 19 January and 4 February a memorandum listing items of intelligence required by AIB had been dropped to Lagarto and Cobra. Five weeks later, on 10 March, SOA learned that a copy of this document was in Japanese hands in Timor. Four days later, a wide-awake radio operator maintaining a listening watch in Australia reported that he had eavesdropped on signal traffic between two parties, one of whom used Cobra's call sign to send Q signals – a secret code meaning 'very urgent, come on air', which had only been recently dropped to Lagarto and Cobra. After some discussion, SOA dismissed the wireless operator's information as impossible. No one considered that the mystery signals were most likely transmitted by Cashman and Ellwood trying to alert SOA, or sent at the direction of their handlers, who were simply amusing themselves by playing around with the newly captured codes.

Having missed the significance of the wireless transmissions and the earlier information, SOA was undisturbed by the implications of the March intercept mentioning the intelligence memorandum, since eleven days passed before guarded questions were asked of either party. When further signals enquiring whether they still had all their copies of the memorandum finally elicited an affirmative reply on 2 April from Cobra, SOA decided that only Lagarto was in enemy control. This deduction must have been sickening, nevertheless.

Not only was Ellwood captured, but SOA realised that four pages of closely typed secret plans, written in plain language, containing 'crack' codes, passwords, and the most exacting details for Lagarto's extraction, all dropped by parachute in March, were also undoubtedly in Japanese hands.

Despite harbouring grave doubts about Lagarto, no one at SOA considered that Cobra might also have been compromised. It appears that Cobra's satisfactory reply about the memorandum had been so reassuring that SOA took no notice of a report compiled on 6 May which pointed out that every single drop-zone reference point given by Cobra had been incorrect.

In June 1945, as a result of an enormous upheaval in the upper echelons of SOA, both Chapman-Walker and Bingham were replaced.[2] No reasons were given, but it seems almost certain that Lagarto had something to do with it. The mishandling of Timor may also have provided the perfect excuse to install Jock Campbell in place of Chapman-Walker who, in common with former Director Edgerton Mott, did not enjoy cordial relations with everyone, including AIB's Brigadier Ken Wills. Whatever the cause of Bingham's sudden departure, it was a case of déjà vu. For the second time in just over twelve months he had been innocently involved in a scandal of monstrous proportions.

While SOA was being reorganised, the plan to investigate Lagarto ground on at an interminably slow pace, for no other apparent reason than SOA's inability to come to terms with the fact that the party was actually in enemy control. While doubts were still being voiced, signal traffic went on as usual. Perhaps it was this failure to face reality that was responsible for an act of incomprehensible stupidity which occurred on 27 June. Four days before the check on Lagarto was to be made, yet another party was inserted into Timor.

Within hours of its arrival the presence of the party, code-named Sunable, was reported by hostile locals. For the next week it was dogged by Japanese patrols and ambushed three times before party leader Lieutenant Des Williams, during a fight on 5 July, was fatally wounded. The other three, Sergeants Jack White, Jack Shand (his finger now healed) and Francis Curran, evaded their pursuers for another week until lack of food and water forced them to surrender. During the various encounters, four Japanese were killed and several wounded.

It may well be that the unfortunate Sunable party diverted attention away from Sunlag, which had parachuted into Timor on 29 June to investigate Lagarto. Having ascertained that the three-man party – Captain Arthur Stevenson, signaller Sergeant Roderick Dawson and Timorese guide Celestino dos Anjos – had arrived without mishap, SOA signalled Lagarto that a relief party was confirmed for the evening of 1 July. Right on schedule, unaware that three pairs of eyes were watching their every move, Ellwood and his Japanese guards appeared at the drop-zone to provide the 'welcoming' committee. Because of wireless problems it was not until 3 July that Stevenson was able to inform SOA that its worst fears were confirmed, and another eighteen days before he could report in person – due to 'inexcusable incompetence', Sunlag's seaborne rescue party failed to pick up them up.

The vessel assigned to this farcical episode was *Krait*, which after the Jaywick raid had been commissioned into the RAN. Now glorying in the title HMAS *Krait* and crewed by a succession of hopeful young sailors (including Bruno Reymond) on the lookout for adventure, she was based in Darwin in expectation that she could be used for other covert missions. Despite a harebrained scheme dreamed up by Commander 'loose lips' Branson to use her as a Q ship, she saw little action. After setting up stores dumps along the Kimberley coast for Operation Mugger, an SOA mission which was subsequently cancelled, the vessel suffered a series of mechanical complaints which had her declared as unfit for service outside sheltered waters. However in June 1945, with no other vessels available, she was fitted with machine-guns and given the task of evacuating Sunlag, a mission code-named Lagartout. As the extraction point was a considerable distance from the party's current position, a rendezvous was arranged with *Krait* for the night of 15 July and, if necessary, for the next three nights, between the hours of 10 pm and 2 am.

The date chosen for *Krait*'s departure from Darwin – Friday the thirteenth – was, from an astrological point of view, ill advised. As the ship approached the Timor coast on the night of 15 July, weather conditions deteriorated alarmingly. Deciding that poor visibility and rough seas would greatly limit the possibility of sighting Sunlag's signals, let alone allow the rescue team to manoeuvre a rubber dinghy to the shore, *Krait*'s skipper, Sub-Lieutenant Harry Williams, aborted the rendezvous and took the ship out to sea.

The next night they tried again. This time as *Krait* approached the coast, several lights were spotted. Wishing to cut engine noise to a minimum, Williams reduced the ship's speed to dead slow. As a result *Krait* failed to reach the rendezvous position in time and again put out to sea without any contact being made.

The third attempt on the night of 17 July was no better. Although the weather was initially good, by 1 am a sea fog rolled in, reducing visibility to less than 30 metres and making it impossible to see Sunlag's signals. *Krait* once more put to sea. Mindful that the next attempt would be the final chance to make contact, the crew tried again the following night. At 1.40 am, with only twenty minutes to go until the time limit ran out, they were rewarded by the sight of Sunlag's Morse signal (the letter R) flashing from the shore. Williams eased the ship to within 300 metres of the beach. They were so close to land that not only could they quite plainly see enemy vehicles travelling up and down the coastal road, they could also hear the sound of music and voices wafting across the water. As *Krait*'s engineer, Seaman Sid O'Dwyer, later recalled, it was like being 'Peeping Toms at a window'.

The gravity of the situation had failed to make an impression on the SOA rescue team. Despite having hours to prepare, the party was nowhere near ready. For a start, the rubber boat had not been inflated and sixteen vital minutes passed before they were able to launch it. There was then a lengthy delay while party leaders Major T C Johnson (British Army) and Lieutenant J W Jeffray (RNVR), who had been asleep on the engine-room housing, organised themselves. While an incredulous Sid O'Dwyer watched the major bedeck himself with enough equipment, hand grenades and other weapons, including a dagger stuck down the side of his sock, to storm the beaches at Normandy, the lieutenant scrabbled around, trying to find his gear in the dark.

Since O'Dwyer had taken the precaution of ensuring that the ship remained blacked out by removing all the light fuses, Jeffray decided that some alternative form of illumination was required. Before anyone could stop him he whipped out a torch, which he proceeded to flash around in an effort to locate his equipment. Seeing the light, O'Dwyer burst out of the engine room like an enraged bull, pitched the torch over the side and let forth a stream of abuse which left no one in any doubt as to what he thought of the lieutenant's parentage.

With all the delays it was after 2.30 am before the rescue team was ready to leave the ship. Major Johnson, festooned like a Christmas tree and with bandoleers of ammunition slung across his chest, stepped off the deck and straight into the water. Hindered by the weight of his assorted ironmongery, he sank like a stone and was saved only from a watery grave by his Australian underling Warrant Officer Doddrill, a practical and cool-headed member of SOA's instructional staff, who jumped in after him and hauled him to the surface with a rope. It was not until 2.40 am, forty-four minutes after launching the dinghy, that the rescue team actually left the ship's side.

Despite a desperate and risky attempt at 2.15 am, Harry Williams had been unable to attract Sunlag's attention. Two minutes after the dinghy left, the shore signals stopped and contact was lost. Forty minutes later, after narrowly missing being blown out of the water when Johnson failed to answer *Krait's* recognition signals, the dinghy returned to the ship minus the Sunlag team.

With no shore signals to guide them, the boat party had lost its sense of direction and had not even made it to the shallows. Paddling around in aimless circles, it was only by sheer chance that they had relocated *Krait* in the darkness. At 3.25, when a further signal attempt failed to raise Sunlag (which, having no idea that *Krait* was just off the beach, had long since retreated from its perilous position), the ship left for Darwin.

With barely any food remaining from their eight-day ration pack, the Sunlag party spent the next eighteen days dodging Japanese and scrounging food from villagers until the RAN took the initiative and mounted a rescue from Darwin. At 6.15 on the morning of 5 August, Harbour Defence Motor launch 1324 commanded by Ray Evans showed how it should have been done. With corvette HMAS *Parkes* under the command of Lieutenant N O 'Paddy' Vidgen standing off the coast, and a fighter aircraft on immediate standby in Darwin, the launch approached the rendezvous point. Thirty minutes later the rescue team was back on board, having extracted the entire party, plus a local whom Sunlag wished to interrogate, in a rubber dinghy, without mishap. Although it was later claimed that the operation had been hindered by poor weather and the efficiency of the rescue personnel impaired by drenchings from 'spray and sea water', SOA HQ, in what was a case of the pot calling the kettle black, denounced the bungling as 'inexcusable'.

Unfortunately the long delay in extracting Sunlag had tragic consequences. Two days after arrival in Darwin Sergeant Dawson died from kidney failure – the result of an obscure infection contracted through injuries to his feet when the party, in order to leave no trail for the pursing Japanese, had been forced to remove their heavy boots and go barefoot.

It was also *Krait's* operational swan song. According to Harry Williams the voyage had been a calamity from start to finish: the generator had packed up; the bilge pumps had failed; water had entered the wireless room hatch, temporarily knocking out communication; the propeller shaft had developed an alarming vibration; and the wheelhouse had begun to disintegrate, allowing rain to enter. To top it off, the ventilation in the engine room, a long-running and contentious issue, was so poor that diesel fumes had rendered both stokers prostrate.

Despite the debacle, at least Stevenson and Celestino retained their freedom. Suncob party's Captain Wynne and Corporal Lawrence, sent to check on Cobra, were not nearly as lucky. SOA, in another display of exceedingly poor judgement, had ordered them to parachute into Cobra's area on 2 July, without waiting to hear from Stevenson if it was safe to do so. From the very beginning, things began to go wrong. The pair became separated by the wind, both parachutes hit trees and their arrival was witnessed by large numbers of excited locals. Helped by some of them, Wynne evaded capture until 16 July when he was surrounded by Japanese and felled, not by one of the bullets they fired but by a rock, thrown by someone who exhibited far better marksmanship than the riflemen.

Lawrence did not fare as well. Captured on 5 July, he was taken to Lautem and Baucau where, during sixteen days of torture which sickened even the Japanese interpreter, he told his captors nothing. His resolution was such that he attempted to bite off his tongue and dash out his brains on the cell wall. But it was all for naught. When Captain Wynne was brought in for interrogation he offered little or no resistance.

With the capture of Suncob, SOA was still not certain that Cobra had been compromised. Apparently incapable of accepting that this was the case, SOA sent another 'slender' signal which was, of course, correctly acknowledged. By this time however, personnel at SOA's forward base at Morotai had voiced the opinion that this latest 'evidence' that Cobra was still free was highly suspect. Against their better judgement, they allowed the next drop to take place and agreed, for the time being, that it would be best not to inform the Senior Air Staff officer that Lagarto, and possibly Cobra, were under enemy control.

With Suncob and Sunable as well as Lagarto and Cobra in the bag, the Japanese tally of captured prisoners was impressive. Unfortunately, there was plenty of room for the newcomers. From the Lagarto party, only Ellwood and Luz, who had managed to evade capture completely, were still alive. Lieutenant Pires had died, insane, in February 1944 and the others, except for one who was killed in a cliff fall, had perished from maltreatment, illness and starvation, were crucified or buried alive. Of the Cobra party of five, only two survived – Cashman and Santo da Silva, brother of Matos. Lieutenant Liversidge died on 20 November 1944 from a combination of malaria, beri beri and starvation. The two remaining Timorese were murdered by the Japanese, as were the two surviving members of the Adder party.

The entire SOA effort in Timor had achieved nothing but death and suffering. Every attempt to insert parties had ended in disaster, including the loss of all those aboard a Liberator aircraft, shot down in May 1945 while attempting to insert Sunbaker, another party which SOA, despite the security fears, had decided to sent to Timor. The tally of Allied dead which can be attributed directly or indirectly to SOA's massive incompetence is thirty-one. The number of loyal Timorese tortured to death or massacred for helping members of SOA parties is incalculable.

As if this death toll was not enough, the way in which the Japanese put an end to the Cobra/Lagarto charade really rubbed salt into the wound. On 12 August, three days before the Japanese surrender was announced, SOA received two messages. From those controlling Cobra came:

> For ABC from Nippon. Thanks for your information this long while. Herewith present a few words to you. Quote. Control enemy thousands of miles out by preparing tactics within. Unquote. Nippon Army.

And from Lagarto:

> Nippon for LMS [the SOA section in Darwin which supplied transport for supplies and personnel]. Thanks for your assistance this long while. Hope to see you again. But until then wish you good health. Nippon Army.

After some debate an enraged SOA sent off two carefully worded replies, warning Lagarto's Japanese in the strongest possible terms that no prisoners must come to any harm and expressing disbelief that Cobra was in enemy hands, stating: 'We are most surprised your information. Can you tell us whether our soldiers are safe and well?' There was no reply, but as soon as was practicable Captain Stevenson was dispatched to Timor to ascertain the whereabouts of all missing personnel. He arrived at Kupang, Dutch Timor, too late to catch up with those still alive. The Japanese, in an effort to prevent early identification of those responsible for war crimes, had sent them to Bali on the pretext that Allied troops would pick them up there.

Stevenson arrived in Portuguese Timor on 22 September to find that no investigation into war crimes would be permitted by the governor until a proper mission, complete with visas, was organised between the Australian and Portuguese governments. However, 'unofficial enquiries' of the sole witnesses available, Francisco Madiera and his father, revealed that three Australian prisoners had died in Dili Gaol – two from malnutrition and beatings and the other allegedly in an air raid. Three other airmen who had parachuted from the crashing Liberator were said to have been shot on landing but, as he was unable to investigate further, Stevenson had to make do with inspecting the aircraft's wreckage.

When he returned to Kupang and questioned some of the Japanese who had been rounded up with the permission of the Dutch, Stevenson was very puzzled. According to his list of Timor agents, only three Australians – Gregg and Grimson from the Adder party and Cobra's Liversidge – were missing. As he had reports of three dead men in Dili, the matter would have ended had the Japanese not insisted that the two Australians from the Adder party had been killed on arrival in Timor, giving Stevenson five dead bodies but only three names. Statements from Ellwood and others simply added to the confusion. From the information of Sancho, Ellwood thought that the Dili victims must be Gregg and Grimson – which was very odd, as both he and Cashman had been told by Japanese officers in August 1944, and again when they left for Bali, that the two Adder men had been killed at the entry point.

To establish the identity of the men who had died in the gaol, Stevenson began an investigation, only to be hamstrung by the withholding of information by SOA, obtained from intercepts in January, that a warrant officer and a sergeant from the Rimau party had been captured and taken to Dili for interrogation. Also, he had not been given the names of the missing Rimau men, although Lieutenant-Colonel J E B Finlay, Director of Plans, noted in a September intelligence summary that members of the Rimau party had been captured in the Timor area. Although Stevenson's enquiries about Perske and Sachs, who were on the list, naturally brought no result, he did learn from Indonesians on Nila Island that two Australians – one long and thin and one short and stubby – had been captured on Romang Island. Believing they could be Rimau survivors, Stevenson requested photographs of the entire Rimau party for identification purposes. It appears that the request was ignored and, since the identity of the five bodies was never resolved, that Stevenson did not pursue the matter any further.

It also appears that the General Staff Officer Intelligence, Advanced Headquarters, Australian Military Forces, one Lieutenant-Colonel Charles H Finlay, was unaware that information on Rimau was known to his namesake J E B Finlay. In February and March 1945, a signal transmitted from Dili to Singapore in several parts on 24 January had been decoded. Although Pace's rank (lance-corporal) was not correct, there was no doubt that the signal referred to the capture of two Rimau men who had reached Romang Island, not far from Timor:

> We captured one warrant officer and one sergeant of the Australian army who
> infiltrated Romang Island on 17 January. We are now investigating details.
> According to the confession of the above [men], they [left by submarine] from the
> vicinity of Perth on 11 September of last year, with the objective of destroying ships
> anchored in Singapore Harbour.

Yet on 13 November 1945, a considerable time after J E B Finlay had received sufficient information to more or less establish the fate of the two Rimau men, Charles Finlay was vainly trying to rationalise the information volunteered by the Japanese about the deaths of Gregg and Grimson. The best he could manage was that it had been simply an attempt by the interrogators to impress or frighten their prisoners. In making this deduction, Charles Finlay was evidently unaware that Stevenson (now busily investigating Lagarto and Cobra) had passed to his superiors an urgent cable. Received on 10 November, it was from a Japanese intelligence officer, Captain Goto, and contained a blow-by-blow description of Gregg's and Grimson's deaths and details of their burial place.

Although high-ranking officers withheld vital information, it is surprising that the identity of those who died in Dili Gaol was not uncovered by less senior army officers reviewing the information that *was* available. Stevenson had made some useful deductions, Captain Goto had verified the fate of Gregg and Grimson, and Sancho da Silva had given the name of one of the men who had died in the Dili Gaol as 'Peace'. Had anyone bothered to compare this name with the list of missing men, he could not have failed to realise that the name was a corruption of Pace.

The superficial nature of the Timor investigations combined with the inability of supposedly mentally alert army officers to put basic evidence together was one of two reasons why the fate of Willersdorf and Pace remained unknown to all but a select few for the next four decades. The other reason was the Lagarto cover-up.

When the whole sorry story began to emerge from Ellwood's and Chapman's candid statements and frank operational reports, submitted to SOA on 23 and 24 October, it was obvious that if the facts became public, heads would roll – not the heads of the rank and file, but those of various directors of military intelligence, highly placed SOA personnel and indeed, Lieutenant-General Thomas Blamey, to whom SOA had been directly answerable. There was only one solution – keep the truth about Timor under wraps.

When SOA selected Arthur Stevenson to investigate the Lagarto affair, it had picked a good man. Although he had arrived too late to prevent Ellwood and Cashman from making any statements to investigators regarding their treatment, he had been able to see their reports and several Japanese confessions which were now in the hands of Timforce – the team rounding up Japanese who had tortured the SOA prisoners. These particular documents, as Stevenson pointed out in his final report of 29 November, had been carefully perused by him and fortunately 'contained no reference which would cause derogatory comments in a military court'. He went on to observe that:

> It would not be surprising if during cross examination at the trials, the activities of Cashman and Ellwood under duress came out, but since it is completely irrelevant to war crimes, and my opinion is that Timforce [being interested only in war crimes] would not be interested in the other aspect [the Cobra and Lagarto fiasco], it is doubtful if any enquiry will ensue.

These assurances about the likelihood of the story leaking out were not required. Within a week of penning this report, a top-level directive was issued to SOA and to Z Special Unit administrators that 'no member of this organisation will be used as witnesses in war crimes trials'.

This caused immediate problems for those collecting evidence in Timor, since some of the witness statements already taken down lacked vital information or were unsigned. Timforce, which could not understand why such an extraordinary directive had been given, was so incredulous that it asked for confirmation, pointing out that the matter was urgent as some statements from SOA personnel were now questionable as evidence.

Had the deponents been allowed to appear as witnesses for the prosecution, any irregularities in the statements could have been resolved with a few pertinent questions. Although rules for war trials were far more relaxed than for an ordinary criminal trial (allowing diaries, unsigned documents, letters, etc. to be admitted as evidence, even though the authors of such documents were unavailable for cross-examination), Timforce was worried that the existing evidence against Japanese who had tortured and mistreated prisoners might not stand up in court.

Except in cases where the evidence was overwhelmingly clear, Australian war crimes trials generally took many months, and in some cases years, to get to court. Considering that no SOA witnesses were allowed to appear, the documentary evidence needed to be of the calibre of that collected by Jack Sylvester who, in bringing Shinohara and his gang to justice, took two years to amass the evidence and another two to assess it.

No such concession was allowed for Timor. No allowance was made for the fact that the Portuguese Government, by insisting that various diplomatic procedures must be adopted, had disrupted and delayed the war crimes investigation. In February 1946 the prosecution was forced to go to trial without the benefit of vital and corroborative evidence, much of which was not collected until June that year.

As Timforce had feared, without witnesses to cross-examine, without evidence essential to the case, the trial was a sham. It was also not properly constituted, since to expedite the process it had been decided to try all nine accused together. Had they all belonged to the same unit, this would have been no problem but, as they did not, the President of the Court, Lieutenant-Colonel Brown, ruled that some aspects of the trial were invalid. Even then, the hard-pressed prosecution might have succeeded in making some charges stick had Brown not dismissed five pieces of vital evidence on the grounds that the statements were unsigned (allowable under conditions laid down by a charter set up for the trials of Far East war criminals), and had the admissible evidence of Ellwood and others not been merely a watered-down version of their frank reports made to SOA. With the defendants admitting to only minor tortures or none at all, with no witnesses to testify to the contrary and a great slab of documentation disallowed, it is little wonder that the court acquitted all but three of the accused.

The trial was conducted in Darwin. Scheduled so soon after the war and being the only war crimes trial to be held in Australia, it attracted great interest, particularly from members of 8 Division, which had suffered hideously at the hands of the Japanese. As had already been agreed, all war crimes reports appearing in the press were self-censored by editors to omit the more violent forms of torture and to prevent the identification of any individual victim or unit. But the newspapermen had no idea that evidence had been disallowed or that key witnesses vital to the prosecution case had not been permitted to testify.

When the verdict was announced, the Australian public was astounded. So too were the Japanese, whose incredulity was clearly visible on nine otherwise inscrutable faces as the judge read out the findings. They were even more stunned when they learned that the sentences for those found guilty ranged from one to three months' imprisonment. As all had already spent 106 days in custody, all were free to go. Saiki, the most culpable of the three found guilty, was so disbelieving that he immediately sought reassurance from the interpreter that the sentence was three months, not three years.

Astonishment in Australia quickly turned to outrage. Lieutenant-General Gordon Bennett was so infuriated the he publicly declared 'it was difficult to conceive that such brutal crimes should result in such absurdly small sentences. Either the accused were innocent and should be acquitted or they were guilty and must be heavily sentenced'. To underline the leniency of the court, Bennett added that punishment for being absent without leave in the Australian Army was one months' detention, while the President of the Ex-Serviceman's Legion observed that cruelty to a dog incurred a similar penalty.

These attacks and the vehement protests of others achieved nothing. Lieutenant-Colonel

Brown merely stated that he was 'absolutely happy' about the outcome of the trials, and that 'when the public knows the full facts as we do, they [sic] too will be quite happy with our verdicts'. But the public was never given the chance. All public debate on the matter ceased immediately. The press was also strangely quiet. It was if the Darwin trials had never taken place.

With the trials over, all those implicated in the Timor Affair were safe. Ellwood and Cashman, who might have expected at the very least a military enquiry to take place, were given leave and demobbed, thereby eliminating any possibility that their frank and forthright reports would be made public.

The quiet and quick disposal of the key figures in the Timor scandal is significant, particularly as others were brought with alacrity to answer questions about incidents which were far less serious. In one case, Major Charles Cousens was hounded for taking part in a Japanese propaganda broadcast while under duress, while Group Captain Clive 'Killer' Caldwell was stripped of his rank after a very public hearing in which he was found to have used an aircraft belonging to the RAAF to supply liquor to the Americans. Yet the army made no move to investigate the conduct of Ellwood and Cashman, whose activities, in some quarters, might have been regarded as treason. With the facts unknown to the public, the part played by Ellwood in particular was taken out of context in later years. As a result, he remained under a cloud for much of his life, while those responsible for his predicament kept their reputations intact.

Of all those involved in the Timor affair, the person with the most to lose if the truth came out was General Blamey, whose conduct had landed him in hot water in the 1930s while serving as Victoria's Police Chief. Not only had he managed to get himself mixed up in a sex scandal, in 1936 he had also lied to a Royal Commission, forcing his immediate resignation. The reason for the perjury, according to Judge Macindoe, who lamented his inability 'to steer him to the true story', was that 'being jealous of the reputation of the force he commands, he thought that that reputation might be endangered if the whole truth was disclosed'.

Far from fading into obscurity, Blamey had grown in stature, power and influence in the decade following this incident. In the Great War, he had served as a brigadier-general on the General Staff, resigning from the permanent army in 1925 to take up the post of Police Chief, but had remained in the citizen forces, commanding 3 Militia Division (army reserve), a post he had relinquished in 1937. Consequently, despite the public scandal and the damage to his reputation, he was still well connected in political and military circles. At the outbreak of World War II he was appointed commander of the AIF's 6 Division by his old friend Robert Gordon Menzies, who had not only served as Victoria's Attorney-General during Blamey's turbulent reign as Police Chief but was now the Prime Minister.

In March 1942 Blamey was appointed Commander-in-Chief of the Australian Military

Forces, a position he held until the cessation of hostilities. Autocratic by nature, during this period he had created powerful alliances and also made a considerable number of enemies. Surrounded by many who would not have grieved at his downfall, including troops who had served under him and who had dubbed him 'Brothel Tom', Blamey must have been relieved that he was not called to answer for the actions of SOA, over which he had ultimate control.

He must also been relieved that clever filleting of secret files and censoring of substantial amounts of material, clearly marked 'not to appear in the official history', successfully prevented other SOA disasters from being made public. The worst by far had occurred in British North Borneo, where poor decision making and faulty intelligence gathering had ultimately led to the cancellation of a mission to rescue almost 1000 starving POWs from Sandakan in April 1945. By the time SOA realised its mistake, it was far too late. Of the 2434 Allied POWs incarcerated at Sandakan, there were just six survivors. In 1947, when asked by one of the highly trained paratroopers selected for the mission, code-named Operation Kingfisher, why the rescue had not taken place, Blamey claimed that at the last minute General MacArthur had refused to supply the necessary aircraft – a monstrous lie which persisted unchallenged until 1998, when Blamey's duplicity and the full extent of SOA's complicity and bungling was exposed with the publication of the book *Sandakan – A Conspiracy of Silence*.

Any enquiry into SOA's activities post-war would not only have ruined Blamey, it would have contaminated his politically influential friends, including Liberal Party leader and former Prime Minister Menzies, who had high hopes of ousting the Chifley Labor government in the coming election, and also put paid to Blamey's involvement in a right-wing, fiercely anti-communist 'secret army'. Formed eighteen months after the war ended this organisation, known as The Association, was privately funded and controlled by a core of high-ranking military and intelligence officers, headed by Blamey himself, who were committed to the suppression of communism. In its own words, one of the aims of The Association was to 'organise the civil population to meet the unexpected, sudden emergency caused by a communist uprising'. It was intended that this uprising, which was spelled out in suitably lurid language, would be met by the determined resistance of The Association's thousands of members, including many pillars of society, aspiring politicians and ex-servicemen. The secrecy of this clandestine army was strictly maintained and it seems that it was prepared, if necessary, to organise a right-wing coup should the Labor Party, which intended to nationalise the banks, again retain power in the 1949 election.

Blamey's loyalty was just one reason among many why Menzies, who fulfilled his ambition to regain the office of Prime Minister in 1949, chose to bestow on the retired general a high and great honour. On 16 September 1950 he was created Field Marshal. To achieve this elevation in rank, fiercely resisted by Labor, Menzies created a precedent by restoring Blamey, who was on his death bed, to the Active List.

The expeditious nature of the Darwin trials effectively put an end to any further interest in Timor. Any additional information, collected far too late for inclusion in the court proceedings, was therefore of little consequence. As the file on the whole sorry mess was closed, and with SOA reports locked up for at least the next thirty years, any chance of uncovering the fate of Willersdorf and Pace was lost. Like the other Rimau members, whose mission had been officially decreed a failure and whose story was lost in a maze of military bungling and ineptitude, they were destined to become forgotten heroes.

18

Latter-day sleuthing

1981–1994

When Jeffrey Willersdorf and Hugo Pace had left Warne, delirious and raving, at Kadapongan in December, they had continued sailing in an easterly direction. Aided by a steady monsoonal breeze, they navigated their way towards the Dutch pick-up point at Nila Island with extreme accuracy, finding and noting the names of islands that were little more than dots on Reymond's navigational charts. From Kadapongan they had called at Mesalima, Doangdoangan, Dewakang and Kadjuadi islands, reaching Romang Island by 17 January. Away to the north-east, only 230 kilometres distant and a little over two days' sailing, lay Nila, and safety. Equipped with automatic weapons, as well as their pistols and binoculars, they landed at the village of Parao, on Romang, unaware that the headman was pro-Japanese. They must have felt safe, for they made no attempt to leave. Two days later, on the morning of 19 January, the Japanese swooped on their hiding place.

When Willersdorf and Pace arrived in Dili from Lautem, the closest Japanese base to Romang, they were in a pitiful state. Both had been beaten. In addition to two large bayonet wounds to his legs, Willersdorf's hands and feet were a mess, with the webbing between every finger and toe sliced through. Pace was suffering from general ill-treatment and was tightly bound, apparently with telephone cable, which the Japanese were fond of passing through, rather than round, the wrists. The torture had been such that by 23 January the interrogators had managed to extract from these two very tough and resolute men the purpose of their mission. Some time later, further questioning elicited the fact that they had been forced to leave Warne, whom the Japanese were told had 'gone mad', at Kadapongan Island. They also gave up details of their route and revealed that their prahu had been repaired by Goh King at Tanjung Dato.

By 10 February, when 7 Area Army ordered that all Rimau men were to be 'dealt with', Jeffrey Willersdorf was no longer a problem. Denied medical treatment, his fly-blown wounds had mortified, resulting in his death a week after his arrival in Dili. Pace was simply allowed to waste away, his wounds infected and his body so emaciated by starvation and wracked by disease that he too died – but not until June. They were buried in the Christian cemetery on a hill at Tiabesse, about 200 metres south-east of the old Dili Power Station which had

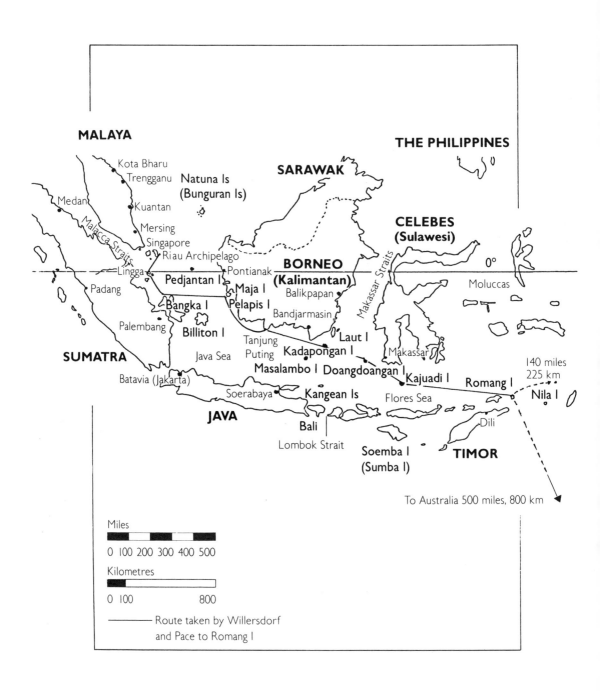

MALAYA

Kota Bharu

Trengganu

Medan

Kuantan

Mersing

Singapore

Riau Archipelago

Lingga

Padang

Natuna Is
(Bunguran Is)

SARAWAK

THE PHILIPPINES

CELEBES
(Sulawesi)

0°

Pedjantan I

Pontianak

BORNEO
(Kalimantan)

Moluccas

Maja I

Pelapis I

Balikpapan

Bangka I

Billiton I

Palembang

Bandjarmasin

Laut I

Tanjung
Puting

Kadapongan I

Makassar

SUMATRA

Java Sea

Masalambo I Doangdoangan I

Kajuadi I

Romang I

140 miles
225 km

Batavia (Jakarta)

Soerabaya

Kangean Is

Flores Sea

Nila I

JAVA

Bali

Dili

Soemba I
(Sumba I)

TIMOR

Lombok Strait

To Australia 500 miles, 800 km

Malacca Straits

Makassar Straits

Miles

0 100 200 300 400 500

Kilometres

0 100   800

——— Route taken by Willersdorf
and Pace to Romang I

Route taken by Willersdorf and Pace to Romang Island

Left: *Rimau's execution site near the intersection of Reformatory Road (now Clementi) and Dover Road (pictured)* Right: *In 1993, a wire fence and a sign signifying that the execution site was under the control of the Ministry of Defence (MINDEF)*

served as their gaol. Since their fate was unknown their bodies, unlike those of Lyon, Ross, Davidson, Campbell and the Outram Road group, were not recovered post-war.

In February 1946 the skeletal remains of those who had died at Soreh and Tapai were recovered by the Dutch and transferred in wooden coffins for burial in Singapore. The bodies of the Singapore victims, exhumed in November 1945 with the help of Japanese labour, were wrapped individually in black blankets and reburied in shallow pits until such time as a more fitting place could be prepared.

Paperwork identifying the location of the Reformatory Road killing field was unavailable to the public for thirty years. Although released in 1975, it was not until 1992, using documentation collected by a retired army major, Tom Hall, that an effort was made to pinpoint the exact site. The catalyst was a letter from Peter Macmillan, an Australian commercial airline pilot based in Singapore, who wrote to me, after reading my book *The Heroes of Rimau*, published in 1990, which included Hall's research.

The location, in broad terms, was known and had been plotted onto a specific wartime map, using the six-figure coordinates (759113) cited in the Rimau investigation and body recovery files. This, in turn, had been transposed onto a modern-day map of Singapore, which showed that the killing field was in the vicinity of the Warren Golf Club, near the intersection of Clementi Road (formerly Reformatory Road) and Dover Road, which in 1945 had been an unnamed dead-end track. However, the coordinates were only accurate to a 100-yard square, radiating from a central point. To find the exact location, someone needed to 'sniff the ground'. Peter Macmillan was more than willing. On 21 October 1992 he called at the Warren Golf Club, having concocted a somewhat vague story as to why he wanted to enter the grounds. To his surprise, in the course of their conversation the manager mentioned that 'some soldiers had been killed nearby'. He did not know the precise location but knew that this was the case, as there had been enquiries about it in the past.

Guided by the contours of the wartime map, Macmillan homed in on an area of a hectare or so, surrounded by barbed wire and with padlocked gates, on the ridge immediately to the rear of the clubhouse. Speaking to an elderly resident who had lived nearby for many years, he learned that the area was under government control and the undulating part along the road was where those killed were buried. The government authority, as evidenced by a sign propped against the fence, was MINDEF – the Ministry of Defence. Despite exhaustive enquiries, no one at the Ministry was able to shed any light on why this particular piece of land had been fenced off, but the general consensus was that it had been done in the days of the British by some official who knew that the area had been a killing field and, aware of the way local people, Chinese in particular, felt about places of death, had put the area aside.

In September 1993 this location was disputed by a group of ex-servicemen, who had served with SOA and Z Special Unit administration during the war and who wished to mark the site during a commemorative visit to Singapore for the 50th anniversary of Operation Jaywick. Evidently unaware that the site had already been located and that archival material was readily available to the public, they sent a wartime map to Dr Roderick Ross, the British army doctor who had performed the exhumations. With nothing else to guide him, other than his memory – almost fifty years after the event – he placed a cross on the map which the ex-servicemen then had surveyed. According to the survey report, the place the doctor had marked was on the north side of Dover Road, down in the grounds of the Singapore Polytechnic. Ross, who had made only the one visit to the site, obviously believed his memory was good enough to identify the place by simply looking at a map on which few geographical features were evident. He also made the amazing claim that the victims, whose butchered bodies he had exhumed, had been beheaded with honour, samurai style.

The location determined by the surveyors was not only outside the boundaries of the specific map reference, it was also in a hollow and bore no resemblance whatsoever to Ross's written description or to wartime photographs which showed that the graves exhumed were on top of a ridge. Despite this, the 'discovery' was announced in the Singapore and international press and permission sought to mark the spot with a red circle. The principal of the Polytechnic, not at all pleased to learn his educational facility was occupying part of a killing field, grudgingly gave his permission but, fortunately, refused to consider the installation of a bronze plaque. The only person apart from myself to question this bizarre location was Tan Yong Meng, a well-informed and senior journalist with the *Straits Times*. Because of the wide dissemination of the misinformation, it would take sixteen years to clear up the confusion.

There is no doubt that the execution site is on the southern side of Dover Road, at the entrance to what now forms part of a university campus occupying the old Warren Golf Club. Because of the controversy created in 1993, in 2008 Mr Ayadurai Jeyathurai ('Jeya'), Director of Changi Museum, independently reassessed the wartime evidence and arrived at the same conclusion as Peter Macmillan. With the location now clarified, it is the intention of local authorities to erect some kind of marker on the site to honour the Rimau men who were killed there and, most importantly, the many civilians who died as a result of both raids.

Recognition for the local people will not be before time. The bloody price paid for Jaywick and Rimau is something which Australians have preferred to ignore. Although some details regarding this tragic outcome were included in *The Heroes of Rimau*, it was not mentioned at all during the commemorations held by the ex-service group in 1993, nor were any floral tributes laid in the memory of the local victims – omissions which Singaporeans found offensive but were too polite to remark upon. Indeed, the only reference to the suffering endured by the local population at the time of the 50th anniversary was in the *Sydney Morning Herald*, in an article entitled 'After the *Krait's* bite the poison kept spreading', written by senior journalist Tony Stephens. He took the opportunity on 3 September to tell the other side of what was becoming a rather over-worked story. His efforts were not entirely appreciated. According to some ex-servicemen, by raising the subject of the Double Tenth massacre Stephens had 'taken the gloss off the 50th anniversary commemorations'.

In the ten years which followed, the plight of the Singaporeans continued to be ignored by Australians, both generally and at memorial services for the Jaywick and Rimau men. In 2003, in response to a question put to him during an interview, asking if he knew of any reaction from the Japanese regarding the Jaywick raid, Jaywick operative Arthur Jones remarked: 'I've never heard [of] any reaction.' That same year, when asked by Special Forces to produce a booklet and to assist in special events to mark the Jaywick 60th anniversary commemorations, I agreed, on one condition – that the Australian public attending these events, and those reading about them, must be made aware of the terrible price paid for Jaywick's success. The army was in complete agreement.

In September that year, for the first time, the Australian Government laid a wreath to honour the civilians in Singapore who had suffered and died, and Mr Jeyathurai was invited to share the podium with me to deliver two keynote addresses – one on the planning and execution of the raid, the other on the consequences. The much-belated recognition of the Singaporean Chinese did not go unnoticed. A grateful High Commissioner took the time at a VIP function commemorating the anniversary to personally convey to me the gratitude of the people of Singapore for ensuring that their story and their sacrifice had at last been officially acknowledged. Although touched by this tribute, my reaction was one of acute embarrassment that it had taken so long for these brave people to be honoured.

The ten Rimau men who were executed and those who died in the Riau Archipelago did not have to suffer such indignity, thanks to the Commonwealth War Graves Commission, which makes sure that our war dead are honoured and revered. In late 1946, the remains of the Rimau men were reburied in Kranji War Cemetery, a grassy hillside overlooking the spot where the Imperial Japanese Army stormed the shores of Singapore Island on the night of 8 February 1942. Dominated by a simple bronze sword superimposed upon a towering white marble cross and surrounded by lush, well-laid out gardens, Kranji is far removed from the hustle and bustle of Singapore City.

The beheaded were separated and buried in single graves, with headstones erected left to right alphabetically, since it was not possible to determine who was who. The four who died on Soreh and Tapai Islands were recovered by the Dutch in early 1946 with the help of Abdul Latif, the coconut cutter who lived on Soreh. Lyon and Ross, whose identities were known, were placed in marked graves in Kranji, but the remains found at Tapai were buried nearby as 'unknown' – an extraordinary situation since one of them was named as Davidson by Major Fugita and also referred to by the Japanese as a 'lieutenant-commander' in subsequent intercepted signals. Furthermore, a report by the War Graves unit which had taken custody of the remains from the Dutch for reburial had recorded that each 'could be a member of the Clandestine Party under command of Lt-Col Lyons [sic]. Found with remains were portions of khaki and uniforms and a broken tooth denture which may help identify one body'. The denture was forwarded to Australia – a futile exercise since few army dossiers included complete dental charts. What became of the denture is not known, but it certainly was not used to help identify the remains. The two 'unknown' were not identified until 1991 when, alerted to Latif's information, the Commonwealth War Graves Commission located paperwork to isolate the graves at Kranji in which the remains from Tapai had been reburied. With the recovery paperwork located, the old headstones, inscribed with the words 'A soldier of the 1939–45 war. Known unto God' were removed and replaced with new ones bearing the details of Donald Davidson and Pat Campbell. The remains of Huston, Reymond, Craft, Warne, Willersdorf and Pace have never been found, but those of Cameron and Riggs were located, many years after the war had ended.

The information from Latif was collected by Hall in 1981 when he travelled to Indonesia to undertake research for the South Australian Film Commission, which was intending to make a film about Rimau. On this trip Hall also visited Merapas, where he viewed the two stone forts and met Karta, the boy befriended by Walter Carey, now very much a grown man and the island's owner. Before his visitor left, Karta had handed over a cardboard box. It contained a skull from the rocky grave which he had finally located in 1976, following an unsuccessful search by an Australian army team in 1971. The skull had been stored under his bed ever since, in the hope that the soldiers would return.

Hall's attempt to bring the remains, purchased from Karta for 98,000 Indonesian rupiah (about $12 in 2009), back to Australia for forensic analysis was a rather stressful journey, involving his arrest by Indonesian marine police keen to exploit an opportunity to supplement their income. Fortunately they did not discover the remains stowed under the seat of the small boat, which were subsequently smuggled into Singapore by members of a local 'gang'. Carried on board a Sydney-bound flight in a backpack, the skull arrived safely in Australia, where Hall had intended to declare it to Customs, along with a bottle of liquor. Just as he reached the head of the line, there was a change of personnel. The new official, a friend from old army days, recognised the passenger and, after exchanging pleasantries, glanced at the bottle and waved him through.

The skull, which had fallen apart from less than optimal handling, was handed over to Inspector Mervyn Beck of the NSW Police, who sent it to Dr Godfrey Oettle (pronounced Ottley), a forensic pathologist at the Institute of Forensic Medicine in Glebe, Sydney. When examination revealed that many of the facial bones were missing, including the entire lower jaw and most of the upper jaw, shot away by a bullet which had entered the back of the skull, Oettle sent the fragments to Bert Bailey at the School of Anatomy at Sydney University. Using only two points of reference, he was able to glue the pieces together. There were some upper teeth still intact, two of which had an overlap.

After Oettle had established that the victim was male, Caucasian and aged between twenty and thirty years, he sent the repaired skull to the Criminal Investigation Bureau (CIB) Ballistics Division, where experts confirmed that the bullet hole had been made by a Japanese military wartime round, fired from behind the victim at a slightly downward angle. It was not possible to determine the range, but the angle of entry was consistent with a shot possibly fired by the search party advancing from the rear, and also consistent with the type of wound found in people executed by the German SS.

A short list of possible Rimau victims was drawn up. Relatives were located and Defence files in the United Kingdom and Australia combed to obtain dental records or photographs showing the men's front teeth. A process of elimination left two possibilities – Cameron and Riggs. Unfortunately, Cameron's relatives did not have a photograph of him smiling (possibly he was self-conscious about the uneven alignment of his teeth), and Riggs' family had only a half-smiling studio portrait. Some years later Dr Ken Browne of Adelaide University was able to determine from cranio-facial superimposition that, while the skull was not that of Riggs, the results were absolutely consistent with it being that of Cameron. These various processes took quite a long time to complete, and the remains were entrusted in the interim to Oettle for safekeeping.

In 1989, as part of the process of assessing Hall's evidence for *The Heroes of Rimau*, I travelled to Indonesia and Singapore to see the various places where the action had taken place, and to undertake further research myself. One aspect in particular which needed to be cleared up by Latif was the state of the bodies at Tapai. Because Hall is very hard of hearing, he had taped all his interviews in 1981, which I then had independently translated, where necessary. On listening to the original interpreter, and the back-up translator, it was obvious to me that Latif was very confused about the cause of death – the men at Tapai were clearly dead, but how?

It was not until I sifted through information provided by the Japanese that I discovered the claim that two men had taken a powerful poison – a claim which had not been taken seriously, even though it had been mentioned at the trial. It seemed to me that as neither Davidson nor Campbell had suffered fatal wounds, this was exactly what they had done – a viewpoint shared by Dr Oettle. 'To be certain,' he said, 'your eyewitness will need to answer two questions. Firstly, what colour were they? Secondly, had the insects invaded the bodies? If they had taken cyanide, they should look very pink – life-like, in fact. As for insects, well, in the tropics, infestation is very fast. If there are no insects, death must have only just occurred.' With Latif confirming that they didn't appear to be dead, were a good colour and there were no insects, I concluded that they must have used their cyanide capsules, as the Japanese had always claimed. With that settled, it was time to undertake further ground reconnaissance.

At Kasu, after clambering up the jetty where Sidek had spotted *Mustika*, and appreciating just how close in the vessel had been, Hall and I located two new eyewitnesses, Arafin bin Akup and Mahat Kunil. The latter was now quite elderly and, somewhat to his embarrassment, was still dressed in his pyjamas when we called. Seated at a wooden table in Mahat's small house,

Eyewitnesses to the action at Kasu and the scuttling of Mustika. *Mahat Kunil (left) and Arafin bin Akup (aged 33 and 18 in 1944) at Kasu Island after being interviewed by the author in 1989*

they recounted their story before a wide-eyed audience of villagers who crowded into the stiflingly hot room, or leaned through the unglazed window openings and door. After sketching the police boat which had confronted the white men's prahu, they walked us through the action, step by step, and pointed out the spot where *Mustika* had been scuttled.

The next stop was Subar, which was just as hot and just as barren as when the raiding parties had used it as an observation post. And, just as it had in 1943 and 1944, it afforded a good view of Singapore. From here we travelled to Dongas Island, still uninhabited, still jungle-clad and still a superb observation post. But it was at Merapas that the most startling new information emerged – Abdul Achap recounted to Hall the story of Riggs' death, pointing out the rock on which he had died and the place where he had

Villagers who cannot fit into Mahat's house, listen to his first-hand story of the Kasu action through the open window

been buried, in the shade of a distinctively shaped tree. Asked to describe the bracelet the dead man had been wearing, Achap did so, and also drew a sketch, including the first and last letters of the name inscribed on it, all that he could recall – 'G … S', Grigor RiggS. With the identity of the dead man buried beneath the tree confirmed, the skull, by a process of elimination, had to belong to Colin Cameron – a fact confirmed by Dr Browne in 1994.

When *The Heroes of Rimau* was published the story of Riggs' death was included, along with a map of the island showing his burial place. In late 1993 this information came to the attention of the Royal Naval Funeral Society, which in May that year asked Colonel Brian Nicholson, Defence Attaché at the British Embassy in Jakarta, to investigate the matter. Nicholson immediately began to liaise with the Indonesian Government for permission to locate the grave and recover the remains. While the lengthy negotiations involving several governments were under way, there was a new development. I found another eyewitness.

In May 1993, an article about the Rimau mission which mentioned my name appeared in the *Straits Times*. It was read by retired railway engineer and former army lieutenant Aloysius Hayes Weller who, as a 14-year-old, had gone with the Japanese troops to Merapas Island and was now on an extended visit to Hong Kong. Anxious that I should know that the body of one of the Rimau men was buried on Merapas, and unaware that a book had already been published containing this information, he asked Russell Matieu, a New Zealander now living in Australia and whom he had met in Hong Kong, to contact me.

A phone call soon established contact with Weller, who revealed that not only had he seen Riggs' grave, he also had a great deal of new and valuable information which, among other things, gave insight into Lyon's last stand and clarified the action which had taken place at Merapas. Prior to this, the available evidence seemed to indicate that all of Page's group had left for Mapur during the night; that Sargent's group, unable to reach the folboats, had been forced to flee in the koleks the next evening; and that Cameron's and Riggs' deaths had not been related to Sargent's escape. Weller's information made it clear that some of Page's group, at least, had left in daylight under covering fire; that Sargent's choice of koleks had not only been deliberate, but was part of an orchestrated plan; and that Cameron and Riggs had sacrificed their lives to allow their comrades to escape. Weller explained that although Sargent's party had escaped in daylight, the koleks had not been pursued since the light wooden Japanese landing craft were not designed for prolonged use in open water, the Japanese had no idea of which direction the fugitives had fled and, in any case, had insufficient fuel to take up the chase.

By May, Colonel Nicholson had obtained permission from General Mantiri, Chief-of-Staff of the Indonesian Armed Forces, to travel to Merapas Island and exhume the remains of Riggs – an expedition which I and my husband Neil were invited to join. While the colonel finalised details, including the provision of an armed naval escort as protection against pirates, and Neil learned to operate a highly sophisticated metal detector in the hope that Riggs had been buried wearing something metallic, I occupied my time absorbing advice from three forensic experts – Dr Oettle, Professor John Hilton and Professor Denise Donlon, an anthropologist – on how best to carry out the search.

So it was that on the last day of May 1994 we found ourselves on Merapas Island – a place of stunning tranquillity and peace. Apart from Nicholson, my husband and myself, the main party consisted of Aloysius Weller; businessman Julian Manning, whose company's luxuriously appointed motor cruiser provided the transportation; Colonel Antonius Suwarno, head of the Indonesian Armed Forces Foreign Liaison Staff; and Abdul Achap who, with Hall, had joined us at Tanjung Pinang. On board the escort vessel were eight Indonesian labourers and several Indonesian officials.

It took little time for Achap and Weller to identify, independently, the approximate burial

Merapas Island, looking towards Riggs' burial site, May 1994

site, which was marked by two readily identifiable features – a distinctively shaped tree and the rock against which Riggs had died. A rectangle measuring approximately 10 metres by 6 metres was cleared of the thick, ribbon-like grass which carpeted the ground around the coconut palms, and work commenced.

The fine sandy soil made it impossible to dig a series of narrow test trenches, as advised by the forensic experts, so the only option was to remove all the soil to a depth of one metre within the designated search area. There were no readings from the metal detector, so the entire area would have to be searched. A local labour force had been provided, but Julian Manning and Neil Silver, inspired by the nature of the mission and determined to get a result, added their muscle power to that of the less than enthusiastic Indonesians. As they sweated and toiled in the broiling sun, the two Europeans jokingly called on Riggs to give them a sign. But he offered no assistance. Despite their best efforts, in oppressively high temperatures and humidity, from which there was no respite other than that provided by the occasional tropical downpour sweeping in from the South China Sea, nightfall approached with nothing to show for their exertions.

In an attempt to escape the worst of the heat, work recommenced early next morning.

Lynette Silver discusses the plans for the field operation with Julian Manning who, with Neil Silver, took over the bulk of the digging. Eyewitness Abdul Achap (seated) is on the far left, while the other eyewitness, Aloysius Weller chats to Karta (far right), the island's owner who recovered Cameron's skull.

With the workers making slow although steady progress, and with no indications of imminent discovery, Hall, who was not involved in the digging, decided to go with me to visit the remains of the little forts built by Cameron and Riggs, the only tangible evidence that the Rimau men were ever on Merapas.

As we were forced to negotiate Cache Swamp, which was knee-deep in water and overgrown with vines, plough through dense undergrowth and then scramble over the slippery black volcanic rocks, already heated to an almost unbearable level by the morning sun, our excursion took much longer than expected. We returned to the news that in our absence the searchers' efforts had been rewarded. After two more hours' digging, Colonel Nicholson declared himself satisfied with the outcome and called a halt. At 11 am on 1 June, watched by those of the Muslim faith, who stood reverently to one side, the remainder of the party conducted a short but moving service, after which a small bag brought by Nicholson to hold the remains was taken by naval vessel to Tanjung Pinang to begin the journey to Kranji.

At 8.30 am the following day – the anniversary of Riggs' birth – a small casket was handed over with full military honours to Colonel Suwarno by the Commodore of the Indonesian Naval Base at Tanjung Pinang. From here Nicholson and Suwarno flew to Jakarta in an aircraft provided by the Indonesian Fleet Arm, where the casket was placed in a coffin draped with the Union Jack. At 9 o'clock on the morning of 3 June, General Mantiri handed over the coffin to Charles Grey, Deputy Head of Mission at the British Embassy, whose task

Military funeral for Riggs and Cameron, Kranji War Cemetery, 27 August 1994

Left: *Headstone on the grave of Grigor Riggs*
Right: *An Australian soldier from the Armoured Corps, in traditional slouch hat and emu feathers, mounts guard over the flag-draped coffin of Colin Cameron*

was to liaise with his colleagues in Singapore for a military funeral to be held in Kranji War Cemetery. Cameron's remains were still at the Institute of Forensic Medicine in Sydney, and the Australian Army agreed that they too should be properly interred, arranging for them to be transferred in a small casket to Singapore for burial at a joint funeral service.

Just after dawn on 27 August 1994, as an early morning mist enveloped the hillside at Kranji, the silence was broken by the slow, rhythmic beat of a single muffled drum. The mourners, assembled around the Cross of Sacrifice, turned towards the north as two long ranks of solemn, khaki-clad Australian soldiers emerged slowly from the mist. Behind them, draped with the flags of the United Kingdom and Australia, were two coffins, borne by six British sailors and six Australian soldiers. A naval officer and an army officer, and two bearers carrying campaign medals on red cushions, followed.

As the cortege moved through the rows of white marble headstones, past the honour guard and up the hill, the voice of the padre intoning prayers for the burial of the dead floated on the moisture-laden air. When the cortege reached the Cross of Sacrifice it stopped, and the catafalque parties took up their silent vigil which they maintained, statue-like, throughout the religious service which followed. The ceremony and committal were intensely moving, but it was the sight of the jaunty emu feathers on the slouch hats of the honour guard, so reminiscent of another war, which brought a lump to the throats of the many Australians assembled.

The graves of Colin Cameron and Grigor Riggs are at the very top of the hill. About midway up the slope, united in death as they were in life, lie those who lost their lives at the killing ground on Reformatory Road. On the opposite side of the cemetery, buried side by side, are Ivan Lyon and Bobby Ross. Pat Campbell and Donald Davidson lie nearby. For the others, at Buaja and Maja islands, Java and Timor, there are no known graves. Like Bill Reynolds, John Sachs and Clifford Perske, their mortal remains are in a place 'known unto God'.

Let these words serve as an epitaph for them, and for all those who gave their lives, no matter where they lie.

Greater love hath no man than this, that a man lay down his life for his friends.

John 15: 13.

EPILOGUE
Fabrications, fallacies and fakes

In the almost fifty years since the story of Jaywick and Rimau became better known to the public, a number of myths have arisen. Some are the result of assumptions, based on too little knowledge. Others were spawned by rumour or, in some cases, were deliberate distortions either to make up for lack of information or to present a particular spin. Once film-makers stepped in, the distortions increased in the name of dramatic licence, or to create a better role for some particular actor.

Writers and historians reconstructing past events are dependent on the material available at the time, and the extent to which they are willing to undertake further research. However, while reconstruction of the past by a writer is perfectly legitimate, it should always be made clear (unless the book is a novel) how a particular conclusion was reached, either in the text itself, or by way of references and endnotes.

The disclosure of facts which upset the status quo during the reconstruction process is not always welcome, particularly where an entrenched mythology has evolved. When the long-forgotten massacre of an Arab village and Bedouin camp, involving the legendary Australian Light Horsemen who had fought at Beersheba, was resurrected in July 2009, many Australians squirmed uncomfortably. Although the incident, which occurred after the war ended, had been published in some detail in the official history five years later, few people aware of it, allowing the light horsemen, who had been immortalised by Charles Chauvel in the 1940 film *Forty Thousand Horsemen*, to enjoy an unsullied reputation.

To challenge well-entrenched myths of more recent events, where those involved are still alive, or if deceased are well remembered, can be very confronting for both the researcher and the public. Furthermore, there is a tendency by those who are far more comfortable with a sanitised or fictionalised account to 'shoot the messenger', no matter how strong the evidence might be. When well-known historian and parliamentarian Dr Barry Jones revealed that atrocities perpetrated by Australian soldiers against local people on the Kokoda Track had been covered up and ignored, he was inundated not with letters expressing shock and horror, but with letters filled with vitriol from people in denial. As journalist Fenella Souter, commenting on this issue, wryly observed, 'unpalatable truth is rarely a welcome ingredient in making myth'.

While the aim of a non-fiction writer should be simply to present an accurate and readable account, films are made primarily for entertainment and to provide a financial return to investors. A degree of dramatic licence is to be expected, but this does not absolve film-makers of their obligation to ensure that the portrayal of characters and events is as factual as possible. This is especially true if the subject matter is breaking new ground. Unfortunately, as Mr Justice Athol Moffitt pointed out in his 1993 paper, *A Legend Endangered*, in the case of Jaywick and Rimau the facts were not allowed to get in the way of a good story.

Writer Ronald McKie was the first to set the wheels in motion with the 1960 publication of *The Heroes*, written from official documents made available to him by the government and augmented by the recollections of three Jaywick members, with input from Furuta and from McKie's own imagination. It is therefore a 'factionalised' account, containing fictitious dialogue, a substantial number of factual errors, unreliable dates and outright fabrications.

In McKie's hands, Camp X became Camp Z, dates were scrambled and places muddled. People who had not yet enlisted, such as Jack Sue, or were not at ZES in early 1943, appear in the narrative, while Carse, eager to give himself a larger slice of the action, claimed *Krait* was handed over to him in Cairns in March 1943, long before Jaywick was back on track and names submitted for the position of navigator. By 1967, when he was interviewed by the Army newspaper, Carse's story had become even more highly coloured, containing grave factual errors and omissions. Interestingly, Carse stressed that there had been no consumption of alcohol on board until the raiding party returned, a statement supported by Young but refuted by both Morris (who traded his rum ration for cigarettes) and Berryman. McKie's failure to interview Morris, a most reliable witness, not only allowed Carse's biased and fanciful version of events to go unchallenged to the detriment of Lyon, but also led to the erroneous story that Morris, who left Sumatra on an official evacuation ship, sailed with Lyon across the Indian Ocean in *Sederhana Djohanes*. However, it is not simply Jaywick which suffers from distortions. With limited documentation and no eyewitnesses at his disposal, McKie was forced to indulge in creative writing in relation to Rimau, particularly in regard to the various actions which took place.

Unable to find an island named 'Sole' (a mistranslation of So-reh, pronounced So-leh by the Japanese, and then further distorted), McKie created a fictitious island near Mapur, named it Sole and then arranged the action to suit. He also included fanciful details, taken from an article by Furuta entitled 'The Harimu Party Sleeps Here', published in February 1957 in the Japanese magazine *Bungei Shinju*. Written for a literary competition, it contained fabrications and distortions which Furuta actually corrected and emended during protracted correspondence with McKie, but which the latter chose to ignore. Since the one thing which Furuta did not witness were the actual executions, carried out by lowly guards from Outram Road Gaol, McKie's description of this event is pure invention:

Epilogue

Then the executioners – ten of them so that there was one for each prisoner, for this was a ceremonial execution – formed up facing the prisoners and ten yards from them. They were in full uniform, with ribbons, and, holding their swords in their right hands they came to attention, bowed to the prisoners, then turned and marched off in single file along the track which led through the bushes, to the execution place. They were all officers or warrant officers from 7th Area Army Headquarters, all men who had seen battle, and all expert swordsmen.

A most puzzling reference to the Rimau executions also surfaces in the war diary of Edward 'Weary' Dunlop, a famous Australian POW doctor who spent many months on the Burma-Thai railway. In referring to the events of 4 November 1943, Dunlop recorded that the evening was

> enlivened by some grim accounts of kempi [sic] torture, conduct of Nipponese trials and a sad account of Page, my old rugby-playing friend, following capture in the second long-range heroic raid on Singapore. Page's courage and bearing won him respect, and a senior officer after this trial recommended that his life be spared. However, the Commander said 'No', and – in effect – that such an heroic exploit in the tradition of the Samurai code could have one appropriate end; beheading. The sentence was carried out respectfully.

It is not simply the date on which Dunlop asserts this discussion took place (almost two years before the executions in July 1945, and three before details were released) which strikes the reader as extraordinary, but also the reference to playing rugby with Bob Page. Dunlop was born in 1907, and Page in 1920. In 1927, when Page was just seven years old, Dunlop, aged twenty, entered Melbourne University and in 1931 switched from Australian Rules to rugby. A brilliant player, he was selected to represent Australia against New Zealand the following year and again in 1934, the year of his graduation from medical school. Bob Page was now fourteen years old. In 1938 Dunlop left Australia for England where, following the outbreak of war, he managed to pull strings to enlist in the AIF and join the Australian forces in the Middle East.

With Bob Page enlisting in Australia in 1941 before his medical studies were complete, and not venturing overseas until Jaywick, there is no possibility that Dunlop, a player of international standing, played rugby with Bob Page, a Sydney schoolboy. However, a New Zealand All Black, James Russell 'Rusty' Page, born in Dunedin in 1908, did represent his country in a number of tests against Australia, including the two tests in 1932 and 1934 played by Dunlop. While it seems amazing that Dunlop could possibly muddle the extremely youthful Bob Page with the New Zealand All Black and 1934 test captain, the inclusion of this information, along with the mention of the executions in an entry dated November 1943, must cast doubt on the credibility of other material appearing in this diary.

In 1982, writer and producer Lee Robinson faithfully reproduced McKie's version of the execution in a joint Australian/Japanese film production, originally entitled *Beneath the Southern Cross* (for Australian audiences) and *The Highest Honour* (for the Japanese). With the ending for the Japanese version showing Roma Page forgiving the former enemy for the execution of her husband, it is small wonder newspapers in Tokyo reported that Japanese cinema-goers were moved to tears. A book entitled *Secret and Special* by John Laffin, published in 1990 as part of the Time-Life series *Australians at War*, features a number of stills taken from this movie, which gullible members of the public believe are actually captured wartime photographs. The most notable images depict Lyon being dramatically shot down on 'Sole Island', the captured Rimau men being driven through Singapore in the back of a truck, the courtroom scene and, finally, ten white-gloved samurai swordsmen, standing at attention, respectfully acknowledging the men they are about to behead. Not surprisingly, the text accompanying these photographs and also that dealing with Jaywick is unreliable. A few years later, when a mini-series dealing with Rimau was released, the Robinson film was recycled on television as *Heroes of the Krait*.

Another long-standing fallacy, also attributable to McKie, is that Willersdorf and Pace paddled a folboat all the way from Lingga Archipelago to Romang Island, near Timor, a distance of some 4000 kilometres. Ironically, it was this unlikely tale which inspired Tom Hall, back in 1958, to spend the best part of three decades trying to establish the names of the two men, believing it to be a feat of exceptional endurance and seamanship.

In 1981 this same story indirectly inspired another film-maker to enter the scene – the South Australian Film Corporation. Since there was insufficient detail then available to make a film, a substantial amount of additional material was collected by Hall and others over the next two years. When the project was eventually shelved, owing to irreconcilable differences between Hall and story editor Harold Lander, a box of Hall's incomplete research material, along with a number of fictitious and contentious film scenarios written by Lander, were deposited with the Archives and Historical Studies Section at the Department of Defence. Among the papers was material which had been misheard and passed to Lander by Hall before the interviews he had recorded were properly assessed and the misconstrued material corrected. Since all the valid research material, along with the scenarios, had been retyped on paper bearing the SA Film Corporation letterhead, prior to being handed over to the Defence Department, it was impossible for an outsider to determine what was true and what was not.

In 1988, believing that contents of the box including the film scenarios were entirely factual, the Defence Department's Myriam S Amar produced the wordily entitled *Historical Monograph No 76, Operation Rimau 11 September to 10 October 1944, What went Wrong?* While this publication included a number of Lander's fictitious story lines, the one which featured a Sikh guard sodomising Bob Page in an effort to have the others confess was fortunately not included. A protest by Hall about other material which did appear in the monograph eventually saw it recalled, but not before military historian David Horner, who believed McKie's book to be 'an excellent account of Jaywick and Rimau', had included Amar's monograph as a source for his book, *SAS Phantoms of the Jungle*, published in 1989.

In 1990 a revised version of the monograph was issued, this time to an even wider circle. Some errors persisted, however, such as fictitious folboat pairings, again concocted for the film. As Lander had created two different scenarios to account for Davidson's death (neither of them correct, one being with Lyon, and the other with Huston), the confusion created by the conflicting factual and fictional material resulted in Amar concluding that Davidson and Lyon had actually died together, and that Davidson's remains were therefore wrongly buried in the grave marked with Ross's name.

The release of the amended monograph brought considerable distress to the families concerned, including Pat Campbell's brother Walter, then the Governor of Queensland. In an attempt to have the monograph withdrawn, a letter was forwarded to Senator Robert Ray, Minister for Defence, enclosing a statement from the Office of Australian War Graves (OAWG) which, with the Commonwealth War Graves Commission, had already assessed the evidence in regard to the place of death and subsequent reburial of Davidson and Campbell. OAWG stated:

> In view of the weight of evidence presented by the work of Major Hall and
> Lynette Silver, supported by our own research, both here and in the UK, the
> Commonwealth War Graves has concluded that it is now sufficiently confident
> of the burial places of the two servicemen in question that it intends erecting
> two Commission headstones over the graves of 23D 19 and 23D 20 in Kranji
> War Cemetery. The headstones will bear the names of Corporal Campbell and
> Lieutenant-Commander Davidson, respectively.

Although distribution of the 1990 version of the monograph was limited to forty copies, it was not withdrawn and therefore remained in public repositories such as the Australian War Memorial, the Joint Services Staff College and Special Forces Association. As it has the imprimatur of the Defence Department, it continues to be used as a resource, and the material included in it continues to be recycled.

The Heroes, a mini-series on Operation Jaywick based on the book of the same name and produced for TVS Films UK, was released in 1988 featuring teenage heart-throb Jason Donovan as Andrew Huston. Although a mass of archival material had been released 1973 following the end of the 30-year closed period, in this production the RAN (the only organisation willing to back Lyon) was depicted as being extremely hostile. As had been the case in McKie's book, Carse again emerged as the key figure while Lyon was portrayed as highly strung and obsessive. In an unfortunate case of miscasting, actor John Ewart, short and stocky in stature, played the long, lanky Bill Reynolds.

The year 1991 saw the release of the sequel – *Heroes II The Return* – which concentrated on Rimau. Although Operation Hornbill was formulated by SOA's planning department, Rimau was depicted as a harebrained scheme devised by a 'driven, obsessive and dangerous' Lyon who, motivated by his own personal agenda, had gone over the heads of his senior officers and appealed to SOE and Winston Churchill, who sanctioned it.

As the Department of Defence had made public the material deposited by Harold Lander, some of the research undertaken by Hall between 1958 and 1983 was included in the mini series. So too was Lander's fictitious scenario which saw Davidson and Huston dying together, evidently in the belief that, as this paperwork was 'on the public record', it was true. However, the veracity of the Samurai execution, as described by McKie, had been questioned and viewers were now confronted with two versions from which to chose – Samurai style with individual graves or outright butchery, with the Rimau men being dragged, bound, from a truck and screaming for mercy as they were beheaded where they lay – a distortion which was far more offensive than McKie's 'death with honour' scenario.

With McKie's book providing little or no detail regarding the events which took place in the Riau Archipelago, and with Lander's film scenarios accepted as a true account, the on-screen action depicted in *Heroes II* bears little relationship to the facts: Rimau buying fish from local people with gold coins, which leads to their betrayal; fierce firefights with unsilenced weapons at various places; Lyon and Ross, after being surrounded on an unnamed, jungle-clad island (which bears no resemblance to Soreh), deliberately emerging from between the buttress roots of a huge tree to be mown down by enemy fire; Davidson, having sought refuge on an unspecified island with a fatally wounded Huston, dying in a blaze of automatic fire after leaping from a tree and dispatching two Japanese with two knives, one of which is hidden in his sock. Other scenarios, such as Lyon threatening to kill a rebellious and uncooperative Indonesian junk crew, whose willingness to assist the Rimau team is well documented, are equally fictitious. McKie's old claim that two of the men paddled to Timor is also included.

The 1990 publication *The Heroes of Rimau*, which contained a vast amount of new research, all of it backed by detailed references, was launched just before production of the mini-series commenced. Although this new material was not written into the script, copies were obtained by the series' executives, used by members of the cast to study their characters and sent to the London-based script executive, who was also in contact with Lyon's former colleague, Geoffrey Rowley-Conwy, now the Lord Langford. Concerned about the way Lyon had been portrayed in the first mini-series, Rowley was anxious to ensure that there was no further character assassination in the sequel. On discovering that the new production intended to portray the Rimau raid as a failure, Rowley pursued the matter with the Australian producer. Although Lyon's character was much truer to type in this production, Rowley was only partially successful in regard to the successful attack on shipping for which the evidence, he assured the script executive, 'is so strong that I am surprised you are not prepared to give them full credit for this'. While it was made clear on screen that limpets had been placed on three ships, the question of whether they had exploded was left unresolved.

There is no doubt that an attack took place and was successful. Apart from the very detailed intercepted signal transmitted by the Japanese on 26 January 1945, there was the second intercepted signal, transmitted from Timor on 3 February 1945, stating 'Lt Col Lyon and six men in September 44 penetrated to the vicinity of Singapore and succeeded sinking 3 ships at anchor in the harbour' – information which was then distributed via AIB's April memorandum.

The five men whom Sidek saw leaving *Mustika* shortly before it sank and the two on Subar formed this seven-man raiding party (Lyon, Davidson, Campbell, Stewart and Warne, and Ross and Huston). 'September' refers to the date on which they reached the Singapore area. There is no question that the Japanese confused Rimau with Jaywick, which used six men, blew up seven ships and was conducted while Lyon was a major. Apart from the signals, there were the explosions heard by local people; the report by Australian POW Roy Bliss, who immediately linked the attack to the subsequent beheadings of civilians; the sudden and summary execution of prime suspect John Long followed by the trial and execution of Cornelis Woudenburg and, very importantly, three wartime wrecks in the harbour and near Sambu Island, for which maritime authorities in Singapore cannot account. All this evidence was on the public record in 1990.

Although a good portion of *Heroes II*, being heavily reliant on McKie's book, is a fictionalised account, more attention could have been taken to detail. Japanese patrol boats were not streamlined, white-hulled pleasure cruisers, with the word 'POLICE' prominently displayed in English on the roof, and the Rimau men did not use three-man folboats with double paddles, but two-man craft with single paddles – a fact stressed in the easily accessible training diary and a detail observed in the first series. Possibly fearing legal action, the film-makers also let Rufus Mackenzie off the hook with the receipt of fictitious 'battle orders' instructing him to seek out Japanese ships allegedly limping back to port from the Philippines. There was no mention that only two signals were sent by Mackenzie during the patrol – one after the rendezvous date had come and gone, and the other after he had abandoned the search for the Rimau men. This partial exoneration of Mackenzie not only allowed the submarine commander to exploit the situation to prove his 'innocence', it also allowed the blame for the loss of the Rimau men to be deftly shifted to the Americans, who are accused of not passing on decoded enemy signals indicating that all was not well – signals which were not decrypted until long after the pick-up date. In 2003, the book *Kill the Tiger*, written largely from secondary sources by Peter Thompson and Robert Macklin, devoted an entire chapter to this so-called 'betrayal', despite the fact that the readily accessible decrypts clearly show the dates of translation. This publication also reproduced McKie's map showing the fictional Sole Island, as well as the now much-recycled story that Willersdorf and Pace paddled to Timor in a canoe. This claim was proved to be a fallacy in 1990, not only because of the sheer impossibility regarding distance and time (4000 kilometres in twenty-six days, or over 150 kilometres a day, paddling for twelve hours a day non-stop at an average speed of about 13 kilometres an hour), but because Japanese signals referred to a prahu, an ocean-going vessel.

Not all the myths surrounding Jaywick can be attributed to McKie. Some appear to have simply evolved, such as the incredible tale that *Krait's* new engine (actually dispatched by sea by Bert Bevan-Davies) had been flown to Cairns in a DC3 and was so heavy that the plane's undercarriage had collapsed on landing. How the aircraft had ever managed to take off, with a full fuel load, was not questioned. Another widely circulated story stated that the greatest contribution of the Jaywick mission (classified as top secret until after the war), was to raise the spirits of the Australian public at a time when Allied victories were few and far between.

In August 1946 another myth had emerged when the Minister for the Army, Francis Forde, evidently in an attempt to soften the blow that six of the Jaywick men had lost their lives, told the Australian Parliament that 'the disorganisation caused to Japanese transport in Singapore by this heroic group, I believe, shortened the duration of the war, and this saved the lives of many other Allied servicemen'.

While a large number of fallacies about Jaywick and Rimau continue to circulate, it is the reputation of Ivan Lyon which has suffered most. The perception of a man driven by a personal agenda was created initially by one of McKie's informants and exacerbated by lack of further basic research. His informant (referred to only as 'a woman who must remain nameless') was Donald Davidson's wife Nancy, who claimed that in July 1942, while working for Naval Intelligence, she had met Lyon at Government House in Melbourne and had helped him plan the Jaywick raid. She further claimed that, after showing her Wavell's letter, Lyon had said, 'You see the irony of it. My wife's a prisoner in the very place I'm going to attack'.

According to a letter written to the Navy in late 1945 seeking information on her husband, and which found its way into Donald's SOE file, Nancy had worked as a secretary in Melbourne. At no time was she attached to, or working for, Naval Intelligence or any secret organisation, and was not a member of the Australian armed forces. She had no information at all on Operation Rimau, apart from some details given to her by Admiral Sir Guy Royal, whose acquaintance she exploited to try to obtain further information in England. Although Colonel Mott, to whom her letter was referred, was aware that one of the men killed at Tapai was Davidson, this information was not given to her.

In accepting Nancy's fabrications at face value, McKie laid the groundwork for the widely held belief that Ivan Lyon planned both Jaywick and Rimau in an attempt to rescue his family. McKie began compiling his story in 1957, only twelve years after the war had ended. A basic check of newspaper files would have revealed that the true story of Gabrielle and Clive was reported in the *Daily Telegraph* in Sydney on 8 November 1945 at the height of the Jaywick publicity and again, with more detail, on 14 February 1946 as a follow-up article.

Nancy's fabrication was not only included in McKie's book, it was also expanded in the mini-series, with a distressed Gabrielle Lyon lamenting that Ivan 'did it for me' and an investigating officer referring to Rimau as 'one man's obsession'. So entrenched is this myth that many ex-servicemen and, indeed, ill-informed relatives of the Rimau men, still lay the blame for the deaths of the twenty-two men squarely at Lyon's feet. The detractors include Jaywick's Arthur Jones who, having described Lyon as a 'death and glory' type was, as late as 2003, publicly promoting this indefensible viewpoint.

The indisputable facts are that Jaywick had its genesis when Lyon met Reynolds on the Indragiri River in February 1942, by which time Ivan knew that his family was safely in Australia. With the plan receiving Wavell's support, Gabrielle left for India to join her husband, only to have the ship *Nankin* intercepted by a German raider. With no news of either the ship or its passengers, Ivan believed that Gabrielle and Clive were dead. Operation Rimau, a product of SOA's planning department, evolved from Hornbill and was well advanced before Lyon learned from Commander Long that his wife and child were alive, and in an internment camp in Japan. Lyon's sole motivation for the Singapore raids was to strike back at the Japanese.

Nancy Davidson's fabrications did not stop with the claim that she had planned the raid with Lyon and that Gabrielle was in Singapore. In 1947, under the pseudonym Noel Wynyard (a mythical person portrayed as an additional member of the Jaywick party), Nancy penned *Winning Hazard*, a 'first-hand' account of the operation written from Davidson's training and personal diaries, which created the distinct impression that Davidson was the 'real' leader of the mission.

In later years Nancy's lies became more elaborate. No longer content to masquerade as an intelligence officer who had planned the raid with Lyon, she now claimed she had written Jaywick's training manual, that her husband was the co-leader of the mission and that she, with her face blackened, had trained with the men at Refuge Bay and taken part in night raids. These delusions were not an issue until they were published in London in the Autumn Edition of the *Special Forces Journal*, in a statement written by a Mr Chillingworth on behalf of Nancy, who had remarried and was now known as Mrs Noel Heath. Obviously regretting that she had spoken so candidly to Hall about her personal relationship with Donald during a taped interview in 1981, she now retracted her statement that, after deciding she 'would change the course of events', she 'went out and got married to him [Donald]' within hours of her arrival (in either Penang or Bangkok). This story, she said, had been invented by Hall.

The only woman involved with Operation Jaywick was Bettina Reid, who had been cleared at the highest level and given the details of the mission at a meeting with Jock Campbell and Lyon at the Potts Point flat. Nancy Davidson, who had her small daughter to care for, was never part of the Jaywick team and most certainly took no part in the planning, much less the training. She never visited Camp X. The only woman to set foot in the camp at Refuge Bay was Reid, who was taken there by an impulsive Gort Chester, much to Lyon's annoyance. After climbing to the top of the cliff she was given only the most peremptory look, before being told 'Time to go – this is no place for a woman'. Nancy, however, fancied herself as a spy. On occasion she visited the flat at Potts Point, where she was given short shrift by a hostile Jock Campbell, who could not tolerate her and had labelled her a 'mischievous woman'. Ivan was far kinder, saying, 'Oh she exaggerates, but there were so many like her in Singapore whom I dealt with as an I O [intelligence officer] and who liked to play the part of the big spy, that I don't mind.'

As the Jaywick raid became well known, other opportunists jumped on the bandwagon, citing the *Official Secrets Act* as the reason they could not speak openly or in detail about their 'secret' war service. The unsuspecting public, unaware that any secrecy surrounding the raid had long since vanished, did not question these impostors. Sailors who were assigned to *Krait* in Darwin in 1944–45 and who begged to return to normal service when they discovered they were manning a rundown vessel moored in mosquito-ridden mangroves, now claimed to have gone on the Jaywick and/or Rimau raid. So did others who had never served with SOA. As late as 2003, a Sydney man named Ron Morris convinced a neighbour that he was Ron 'Taffy' Morris – a subterfuge which only came to light when the neighbour, believing that the Jaywick hero, now confined to hospital, should be receiving better government support, contacted the Army who referred him to me.

However, perhaps the most-widespread misconception concerns the status and role of Z Special Unit.

With the term SOA used only at the highest level, those seconded to Special Operations Australia were unaware of the correct name of the organisation and often of its cover name, SRD. With Australian soldiers 'posted' to Z Special Unit not realising it functioned as a purely administrative body, Z Special Unit has taken on the persona of the operational unit.

Epilogue

This confusion extends to those handling service dossiers of SOA operatives, who assumed that the unit at time of demobilisation or death was Z Special, instead of the parent unit of the soldier, who had remained on that war establishment throughout his secondment to special duties. This in turn resulted in the CWGC inscribing headstones with 'Z Special Unit', instead of, say, in the case of Bob Page, '2/4 Pioneer Battalion, KIA while serving with Special Operations Australia'. Because of the sheer impossibility of altering headstones, and more especially the stone or bronze inscriptions on the Memorials to the Missing, a practical decision was made in 1994 prior to the reburials of Riggs and Cameron to maintain the current but incorrect status quo in the interests of uniformity.

The adoption by post-war Z Special Unit Associations of a dashing insignia, depicting a dagger through a Z, and the promotion of the terms 'Z Force' and 'Z men' has further submerged the true identity of the parent organisation. Had the term SOA been used, it would have been as well known in Australia as SOE is in Europe. Persistent efforts to ensure the correct terminology have been only partially successful. While Australian Army historians now insist on the use of the term Special Operations Australia, or SOA, a request in 1998 to have the Australian War Memorial also adopt the correct terminology prior to the refurbishment of the World War II galleries was rejected. The response from the senior historian at the Memorial, an institution regarded by Australians as the authority on all matters relating to war and one which should be setting the standard, not blindly following the masses, was that Z Special and Z Force 'are the terms used by the general public'.

While the term 'M Force' has fortunately not yet entered the vernacular, personnel who were seconded to various organisations controlled by AIB are referred to as 'M Special Operatives'. Such is the general level of ignorance surrounding AIB operations that one enterprising ex-serviceman managed to convince his organisation that he had served with 'S Special Unit', which was duly added to the group's letterhead. At the same time, the Z (and M) symbols of the purely administrative bodies have also achieved such status that they have been incorporated into the Double Diamond patch of the true commando unit associations – the Independent Companies – which operated as part of the AIF and had absolutely nothing to do with covert operations.

Because SOA and AIB were secret organisations, they have spawned a larger number of fallacies and attracted more 'pretenders' than other military units. In 1978, the general level of ignorance regarding SOA enabled 'Sergeant' John Gardner to not only ascend to the presidency of Z Special Association NSW but also, on the strength of his 'secret' war work, to lead the Anzac Day march in Sydney that year – the first civilian to do so. It took ten years for his duplicity to be discovered by his colleagues, none of whom questioned his alleged service with SOA. He had certainly served in World War II, but not in any covert organisation. He was an aircraftsman in the RAAF, engaged in airfield construction. During his ten-year misrule as

MV Krait, following her return to Australia

president, he was responsible for promoting the term 'Z Force', endorsing B-grade war films as entirely factual, and attributing a large number of missions and decorations to 'Z' and 'Z men'. These figures, which are still bandied about, refer not to SOA missions but to every covert operation carried out by the Allies behind enemy lines, the lion's share of which, along with the gallantry awards, belong to the Coastwatchers.

The outing of Gardner did not deter those who *had* served with SOA from embroidering their own war stories. One, who was in the field in Borneo, has written himself into missions in which he did not take part. The skilful use of the 'royal we' by another, whose two SOA operations consisted of a survey of islands in an American submarine just before the war ended, and a mopping-up mission in Borneo some weeks afterward, left the audience attending a lecture he gave with the distinct impression that he had placed limpet mines on enemy ships – an activity restricted solely to Operations Jaywick and Rimau. Amazingly, this same man, speaking of war service in general when interviewed on an ABC Radio current affairs program on Anzac Day 1997, observed that ex-servicemen were 'telling bigger and better lies as the days go by. We all think we won the war and no one else did. We really bask in the glory of our comrades who are no longer here'. One of his colleagues, who joined the lecture circuit, certainly lived up to this assessment by entertaining audiences with an account of his service behind enemy lines in the latter half of 1944. What he failed to disclose was the wireless relay station he was manning was on Manus Island, one of MacArthur's island-hopping bases, which had been under total control by the United States long before the relay station was established.

Krait too has her share of fabrications and fallacies, including disputes over who actually captured her in December 1941 (see Appendix 2). Although her missions following Jaywick were reduced to ferrying stores along the Kimberley coast, and the disastrous attempt to pick up the Sunlag party from Timor, vague references to fictitious covert operations deep into enemy territory continue to emerge, along with stories of drug-running post-war.

Restored to her wartime configuration after years of neglect in Borneo, *Krait* is now part of the heritage fleet moored at the Australian National Maritime Museum in Sydney. The most interesting thing about this nondescript, rather ungainly little ship is that the salvage claim lodged with the Admiralty by Bill Reynolds in 1943 has never been resolved. On the instructions of the Admiralty the vessel was supposed to be returned to Singapore for a Prize Court hearing as soon as the Civil Administration in British North Borneo (BBCAU), which had 'borrowed' her from SOA for post-war reconstruction, had completed its work. Despite a solemn undertaking by BBCAU's Brigadier C S C Mackaskie, a former Deputy Governor of British North Borneo, to obey this instruction, in 1947 or 1948 she was sold, illegally, by the Marine Department (under the control of Chief Secretary R B Blade) to River Estates, a large timber company based at Sandakan on Borneo's north-east coast. In 1958 her whereabouts were discovered through the efforts of Dick Greenish, who had married Bob Page's widow, Roma. Now named *Pedang* (Malay for sword), she had been used for various tasks ranging from fish carrier to log hauler to mail boat. By 1964 enough money had been raised by public subscription to buy her back at a vastly inflated price from the owner of River Estates, an Australian by the name of R G Barrett. The vessel, which was in a deplorable state, was brought back as deck cargo to Brisbane, where repairs were effected in time for her triumphal entry into Sydney Harbour on Anzac Day that year.

With the celebrations over, and no one interested in assuming responsibility for an expensive-to-maintain and ageing wooden ship, she was finally taken over by the Royal Volunteer Coastal Patrol (RVCP), which used her for safe boating courses. For the next seventeen years the RVCP did its best to maintain *Krait* but in 1981 the financial burden became overwhelming. With her custodians facing the prospect of having the ship sink at her moorings, the executive producer of the popular TV program, *This is Your Life*, offered to make *Krait* the subject of one of his shows. The resultant publicity attracted donations from all over Australia, more than sufficient to fully repair and refit the ship and, in 1984, she proudly led the Royal Yacht *Britannia* up the Brisbane River for the opening of the Commonwealth Games by the Queen.

Restored to better than her former glory, *Krait* was now a very desirable object, so desirable that an unseemly and very public argument broke out between the RVCP and Z Special Unit Association NSW over who 'owned' her. Fed up with the dispute, the RVCP eventually relinquished its de facto ownership of the vessel to the Association, which then 'gave' *Krait* to the Australian War Memorial – a donation which attracted howls of outrage from members of the public who had donated money to keep her in the water, in Sydney. However, as the Memorial was unable to accommodate or care for the ship in land-locked Canberra, *Krait* was 'loaned' to the Sydney Maritime Museum in 1985 and then, in 1988, to the newly opened National Maritime Museum at Sydney's Darling Harbour.

Since then she has attracted a great deal of attention and is the focus for various commemorative ceremonies, including one held in November 2009 to mark the return of

Krait *in Sydney, Anzac Day 1964, with the newly 'donated' bell. (L to R) Harold Nobbs (RVCP), Moss Berryman, Horrie Young, Arthur Jones, Ted Carse*

The bell, stolen from Krait *in 1945, 'donated' back in 1964, 'reclaimed' in 1983 and finally returned in 2008*

the much publicised 'Krait bell'. In a newspaper article published in *The Australian* on 11 November, it was claimed that the origins of a brass bell, with the word 'KRAIT' crudely etched along one side, dated back to 1944, when it was 'liberated' from a visiting merchant ship by 'commandoes' on board *Krait*. It appeared that one of those involved in the heist was a William Malcolm McLean, a former Wallaby Rugby Union captain, who had served in World War 2. The whereabouts of the bell for a 40-year period dating from 1944 was not disclosed, but McLean's son Ian stated that in the early 1980s his father, as head of Queensland's Commando Association, had taken the bell for safekeeping, allegedly worried that it would be pilfered while the ship sat in dry-dock in Brisbane. He would, he had stated, return it to the ship when she was finally assigned to the care of a museum.

However, having been 'rescued' or 'liberated' for an apparent second time, the bell was not returned to the ship when she came under the control of the Australian War Memorial in 1985. It remained in the hands of McLean, who rang it in his Clarence Corner Hotel in Brisbane to awaken sleeping drunks slumped over the bar, before transferring it to Ballymore Oval, where it was used at rugby union matches to signal half and full time. When McLean retired to the Gold Coast, the bell also moved on – firstly to his home and then to Lions Haven, an aged-care facility where World War 2 ex-servicemen would queue up to ring what was, by this time, regarded as *Krait's* original bell. After his death in 1996 the bell was retained 'for safe keeping' at her home by the matron of Lion's Haven, who later retired. Following some local publicity regarding the ship, she unexpectedly surfaced, along with the bell, in mid-2008.

Unfortunately for the myth makers, this story does not stand up to close examination. There were no SOA 'commandoes' on *Krait* in 1944. Although now classified as HMAS *Krait*, the ship's poor state of repair ensured she was confined firstly to routine coastal work and then to the inner waters of Darwin Harbour, during which time she was serviced by a skeleton crew, drawn from the Australian navy. An operational team was not assigned until July 1945 – for the disastrous Timor mission.

Since it was planned, after *Krait's* return from Jaywick in 1943, that she should continue to masquerade as a Japanese fishing boat, working behind enemy lines and in total silence, it is inconceivable that a clanging brass bell, much less one which was inscribed in English, would have been allowed on board. Had this been permitted, or had it been considered that some protection might be afforded to those on board in the event of capture, the bell would have been engraved with HMAS KRAIT. In any case, had the bell been purloined from a merchant vessel, as claimed, it should have been inscribed with the name of that ship.

Further research has revealed a far more likely scenario regarding the origins of the bell.

Since family members of Bill McLean recall seeing the bell in their home late 1940s, it seems certain that he was in possession of it post-war, by which time *Krait*, now renamed *Pedang*, was in British North Borneo. The question is, how and where did he gain custody of the bell? Captain William McLean was not a 'commando' serving with SOA, or a naval captain assigned to *Krait*. SOA records show he had no association with either the ship or any facet of covert operations. However, his war service dossier reveals that, as a member of 2/3 Independent Company (also known as 2/3 Commando Squadron), he was in Morotai shortly after the cessation of hostilities and, most significantly, at the same time as *Krait*, which had been to Ambon for a surrender ceremony before being loaned to BBCAU. This was an unexpected move for the ship, and a proud mission for the current crew. It seems extremely likely that, with *Krait* assigned to take part in the ceremony, and no official bell, the crew members obtained a spare from the stores of AIB's Lugger Maintenance Section in Darwin, where *Krait* was based, and then either had it inscribed, or inscribed it themselves, using rudimentary tools and in great haste, hence the extremely crude lettering.

Shortly before McLean's arrival in Morotai, Jaywick became headline news. There was not a member of the armed services, or indeed any member of the Australian public, who was not marvelling at the exploits of the Jaywick team. For anyone based in Morotai who was interested in 'souveniring' a little piece of history from the very ship which had made it all possible, here was the perfect opportunity. Far from *Krait's* commandoes 'liberating' a bell in 1944 from 'a visiting merchant ship', it appears that McLean himself, perhaps assisted by fellow commandoes, stole the bell from a 'visiting merchant ship' – *Krait* herself – after she arrived from Ambon.

Information from McLean's post-war associates reveals that in 1964, while the ship was being refitted at the Army Water Workshops in Brisbane, following her successful purchase from River Estates in Borneo, McLean returned the bell to the ship. Polished to a high shine, and resplendent with a newly-plaited bell-rope, the long-lost artefact had pride of place in the wheel-house, And there it remained, for almost twenty years, until it was time for the ship to undergo extensive restoration.

During the refit McLean, as president of the Queensland Commando Association, visited the Ballina shipyards to inspect the progress. During one such visit, he claimed ownership of the bell, on the basis that he had 'donated' it in the first place. By this time, there was no love lost between the RVCP and the Association – the irreplaceable original brass snake purchased by Reynolds (and now the ship's mascot), which his family had donated to the ship in 1964, having been stolen, along with valuable charts and other items, while *Krait* was on loan to the Queensland Commando Association for fund-raising purposes. Despite the RVCP's best efforts, along with those of the current author and others, these items have not been recovered and are 'missing' to this very day.

The acquisitive McLean may have not succeeded in his bid to regain possession of the the bell if members of Z Special Association NSW, which claimed (wrongly) to be the trustees of the ship, also had not clashed swords with the RVCP. Consequently, instead of anyone in 'authority' insisting the bell remain with the vessel, McLean was allowed to take it – but not before six new bells were cast from the original and inscribed in more formal lettering. Five were given away to various people, including Horrie Young. The sixth stayed with the ship. Evidently unaware that the bell of this increasingly famous vessel was a replica, someone stole it a few months later, while *Krait* was moored off HMAS Penguin, on Sydney's Middle Harbour.

As *Krait* has been restored to her authentic wartime configuration, the bell taken by McLean in Morotai will not be returned to the ship, but it will be placed on display in Canberra by the Australian War Memorial. However, despite the vessel's iconic status and the various claims which doubtless will continue to be made, a most intriguing core issue remains. Is Reynolds' outstanding salvage claim, recognised by the Admiralty in 1943, still valid and, if it is, who actually owns the ship? Some say the claim is invalid. Others say that that there is no statute of limitations on fraud and that, like a stolen art work, *Krait* belongs to her original owner. Is this the Fugisawa family? Should *Krait*, having been impounded, have been returned to Japan after the war by the Controller of Enemy Property? Or was the ship, in a poor state of repair, regarded as 'abandoned', and therefore claimable as salvage under maritime law? If so, is the rightful owner, until a court decrees otherwise, Reynolds' legitimate heir, Mrs Margaret Reynolds? Or, with the passage of time, has ownership passed by default to the current custodians? Unfortunately, although an offer made by Margaret Reynolds in 2003 to publicly relinquish any rights she might have in order to clarify the situation, had the support of the army, it was stymied by members of Z Special Association NSW, which dismissed the idea as 'farcical'. Farcical or not, it is a lost opportunity which many believe could have so easily resolved the issue, especially for the 'current' owners, the Australian War Memorial and, therefore, the Australian public.

Whoever the legal owner might be, the loser in this story is, of course, Bill's wife Bessie. With the secrecy surrounding SOA, she was never informed that her husband had lodged a salvage claim against the ship, his most valuable asset. Left without financial support following his disappearance, Bessie travelled from Melbourne to Canberra in the hope of obtaining a war widow's pension. She was out of luck. The Australian Government informed her that since Reynolds had not been a member of any regular armed force, she was not entitled to any remuneration. Bessie, who had never had to work in her life, was forced to keep body and soul together by performing menial tasks until she was old enough to receive an age pension.

Krait and the high-profile Operation Jaywick have become the shining jewels in the 'Z Force' crown. Although Jaywick's status as an SOE/RAN mission, funded directly by SOE London, planned by one man and backed by the RAN, makes it unique, it is popularly regarded as an SOA/SRD operation since, by the time Jaywick actually left Australia, the new covert organisation had been established. For 'Z Men' to claim Jaywick as a 'Z Special' mission is understandable. Not only was it brilliantly executed with great daring, it was the only operation of its type to achieve its objective without losing a single man. However, the heavy loss of life in Singapore following the raid must be weighed up against this success, especially since Jaywick's value as a propaganda tool was zero and the two ships which remained sunk were of no military significance.

A sobering aspect of Special Operations Australia is the inescapable fact that many fine men who volunteered for hazardous service died while carrying out flag-waving missions that were politically, rather than militarily, motivated. Plagued by ineptitude, poor decision making and inexcusable mismanagement at the highest level, many SOA missions failed to fulfil their objectives or were aborted. Others, on which high hopes had rested, were made redundant by the tide of war.

Even more sobering is the fact that too many of these operations, including Jaywick, Rimau, the Timor missions and the bungled POW rescue operation in Borneo, achieved nothing but death, misery and suffering. Others put the lives of the operatives at risk by sending them on missions that were ill-advised and poorly planned.

There is no doubt that the sacrifice and bravery of those who served behind the lines with SOA are worthy of great admiration and respect. However, the Australian Army's assessment of the organisation to which they belonged, published in *The Oxford Companion to Australian Military History*, is not only uncomfortably and unpalatably honest, it is also brutally frank:

> Despite the glamour attached to SOA it cannot be said that SOA missions achieved anything of significance ... In the final analysis SOA operations were characterised by inefficiency, inappropriate objectives and unreliability. They did not greatly hamper the enemy and did not shorten the war by a single day.

As Ivan Lyon might have said, 'War is a grim business, isn't it?'

APPENDIX 1
About *Krait*

Specifications

Built: 1934, Nagahama, Japan

Owner: Kotaro Fugisawa and family

Construction: Teak wood

Length: 21.3 metres (70 feet 8 inches)

Breadth: 3.6 metres (12 feet)

Draught: 1.5 metres (5 feet) for'ard, 2.3 metres (7 feet 6 inches) aft

Gross tonnage: 68 tonnes

Original engine (1934): Deutz PMV 230 model, 4-cylinder, 2-stroke diesel, 430 rpm, 100 hp. Maximum speed 8.5 knots. Engine number 171583-586. One of 188 engines manufactured by Deutz, Koln, Germany between 1927 and 1930

Replacement engine (1943): Gardner 6L3 model, 6-cylinder diesel, 450 rpm, 110 hp. Maximum speed 6.5 knots. Engine number 54512. Range 8000 miles. Manufactured by L Gardner & Sons, England

Names

Between February 1942 and the end of World War 2, *Krait* had the following names:

Kofuku Maru 2283 (1934–March 1942)

British Privateer *Suey Sin Fah* (March 1942–April 1942)

MV *Krait* (April 1942–14 April 1944)

MV *Audacious* (used by RAN only, January–October 1943)

HMAS *Krait* (15 April 1944–12 December 1945)

MV *Krait* (13 December 1945–1947)

Pedang (1947–March 1964)

MV *Krait* (April 1964–present day)

Colours

She sailed under the following flags:

Japanese (1934–February 1942)

Chinese (February 1942–March 1942)

pseudo-Japanese (September–October 1943)

Royal Australian Navy (April 1944–December 1945)

British (December 1945–April 1964)

Australian (April 1964–present day)

'Owners'

Fugisawa Family, Japan (original owners 1934–8 December 1941)

Controller of Enemy Property, Singapore (8 December 1941–10 February 1942)

William Roy Reynolds (10 February 1942–present day? Salvaged from Telok Ayer Basin, Singapore)

SOA ('borrowed' from January 1943–December 1945. Commissioned into RAN April 1945–December 1945)

50 Civil Administration Unit, a division of British North Borneo Civil Administration Unit, or BBCAU. ('Borrowed' in December 1945 by Brigadier C S C Mackaskie, Chief Judge and Deputy Governor of North Borneo, Chief of BBCAU, who then 'loaned' the ship to British North Borneo's Marine Division, under the control of Chief Secretary R B Blade. In use until 1947)

R G Barrett, owner of River Estates Sandakan, BNB (illegally sold to Barrett by Marine Division *c.* late 1947)

Trustees of *Krait* Public Museum Fund (illegally sold by Barrett in 1964)

Royal Volunteer Coastal Patrol (as no legal trustees of the vessel had been appointed, RVCP was de facto owner 1964–1984, and custodian 1964–1985)

Australian War Memorial (ship 'given' to AWM by 'owner' Z Special Unit Association NSW in 1984, after RCVP relinquished fight for 'ownership'. AWM financially responsible, but vessel still under custodianship of RVCP)

Sydney Maritime Museum ('on loan' from AWM 1985–1988)

Australian National Maritime Museum ('on loan' from 1988 to present day by AWM)

Note: The legality of the 1943 salvage claim lodged by William Roy Reynolds has never been resolved. His heirs are Mrs Margaret Reynolds and her family.

Function

Krait has served as a Japanese fish carrier, an Allied rescue ship, a spy and relief vessel, a British Privateer, an escape craft, a special operations ship, a mail carrier, a log hauler, a supply boat, a training vessel, a Volunteer Coastal Patroller, a floating war memorial and a public museum.

Krait Crew List

February–March 1942

William Roy Reynolds (master)

Alec A Elliott (engineer)

Harold Papworth (able seaman)

Ah Tee and seven Chinese (deserted at Pulau Koendoer)

Looi Pek Sye (stewardess/deputy helmsperson)

Ah Kwai (motorman; deserted at Bengkalis)

Ah Chung (motorman; deserted at Bengkalis)

Saitaan bin Abdulamid (deck hand)

Frank McNeil (also listed as Frank McGrath, dismissed at Tambilahan)

Looi Lam Kwai (aged three, daughter of Looi Pek Sye)

January 1943–July 1943: Original Jaywick team

Ship's crew

William Roy Reynolds (ship's master, left the ship in Cairns)

Leading Seaman Kevin P Cain (joined the ship in Brisbane)

Stoker Manson (engineer, left the ship in Brisbane)

Leading Stoker J P McDowell (engineer, joined the ship in Brisbane)

Leading Telegraphist Donald Sharples (wireless operator, left the ship in Cairns)

Seaman A Hobbs (cook, left the ship in Cairns)

Additional staff

Corporal Ronald G Morris (medical orderly)

Operatives

Major Ivan Lyon (Commanding Officer and party leader)

Lieutenant Donald M N Davidson (2IC)

Captain Francis G L Chester (left mission in Cairns)

Sub-Lieutenant Bert T Overell (explosives expert, left mission in Cairns)

Able Seaman Arthur W Jones

Ordinary Seaman Mostyn Berryman

Ordinary Seaman Walter G Falls

Ordinary Seaman L K Hage (left mission in Cairns)

Ordinary Seaman Andrew G Huston

Ordinary Seaman Frederick W Marsh

Ordinary Seaman Donald W Russell (left mission in Cairns)

Ordinary Seaman Norris R Wright (left mission in Newcastle)

Note: Leading Seaman Johnson was 'on loan' at Refuge Bay and did not join the operation. E E Kerr and J C McKay also remained at Refuge Bay on 17 January, when *Krait* sailed. For other personnel eliminated during training see Additional Notes to Chapter 6.

September 1943: Final 14 Jaywick team

The ten officers and men who remained from the original team were:

Operatives: Lyon, Davidson, Berryman, Jones, Falls, Huston, Marsh (Berryman, Falls, Huston, Marsh now Acting Able Seamen)

Crew: Cain, McDowell

Additional staff: Morris

Newcomers:

Lieutenant Hubert Edward Carse (navigator)

Lieutenant Robert C Page (operative)

Leading Telegraphist Horace S Young (wireless operator)

Corporal Andrew Crilly (cook)

1944–45: Darwin (HMAS *Krait*)

Since records for this period are not complete, the following list may contain omissions. Some dates of commencement may also be approximate.

February 1944

Lieutenant Walter King Witt (CO)

ERA F Brown-King

ERA R W Mathers

Sergeant Hoffie

Sergeant Russell

June 1944

Skipper T N Naylor (CO)

Lieutenant Key

Mate Davey

Able Seaman C A Halgren

Able Seaman Turner

Seaman Harris

Seaman Hurren

Appendix 1

Seaman Mather
Stoker Aarons
Stoker Wilson

August 1944
Seaman S O'Dwyer

October 1944
Sub-Lieutenant T F Wayland (CO)

December 1944
Sub-Lieutenant Dann (CO)

February 1945
Sub-Lieutenant Harold Williams (CO) RANVR
Petty Officer Godfrey
Sergeant J Flinders (W/T–AIF)
Stoker G W Myringe, RN
Able Seaman Tanner
Able Seaman Taylor

July–August 1945
Sub-Lieutenant J M Brooke, RNVR
Able Seaman C Borland, RANVR
Able Seaman J C Burton, RANVR
Able Seaman R H Eason, RANVR
Able Seaman N Moore, RANVR
Able Seaman L J O'Dwyer (engineer) RANVR
Seaman D P J von Steiglitz, RANR

No starting date available
Leading Seaman Frecker
D A Campbell
Lieutenant A R Chapman

APPENDIX 2

The Capture of *Kofuku Maru*:
A case of mistaken identity

On 8 December 1941, *Kofuku Maru* was impounded by Denis Emerson-Elliott in the Telok Ayer Basin, Singapore, on the orders of Dickie Dickinson. However, as this fact was not known until the publication of this book, the question of who captured her has long been disputed.

In 1971, there appeared in the press a statement by a former RAN Petty Officer, L M 'Sandy' Boxsell, that the ship had been captured by the corvette HMAS *Goulburn* during a routine patrol of the waters near Singapore, shortly after the commencement of hostilities with Japan. The corvette's commanding officer, Basil Paul, who was interviewed in 1974, attested to this fact and before long this statement, along with the claim that *Kofuku Maru* was the first Japanese ship captured by the RAN in the Pacific Zone, became fact. Both these claims have appeared in publications world-wide and were repeated on the television program *This is Your Life?* which featured *Krait*, and on which some of *Goulburn's* crew members, who allegedly captured her, appeared. Although the various sources disagreed on the date, it was widely accepted that this event occurred on either 8, 11, 12 or 13 December 1941 and that *Kofuku Maru* was towing either four or six barges at the time of her capture.

Although the papers confiscated by *Goulburn* clearly showed that the name of the Japanese vessel was *Shofuku Maru* (Small Fortune), the disparity in the names was dismissed as a clerical or transcription error, in the belief that the ship was really *Kofuku Maru*. It is not to be wondered that such a mistake in identity was made. With the claims made by *Goulburn's* crew that she had captured *Kofuku Maru* accepted at face value, and unchallenged for almost twenty years, fiction had inevitably become fact.

The issue became even more confused with the oft-repeated statement that *Kofuku Maru* was the first ship captured by the RAN in the Pacific Zone. Since the crew members of *Goulburn's* sister ship, HMAS *Maryborough*, knew without doubt that this honour belonged to them, *Goulburn's* claim had been hotly disputed. No one however, had managed to prove the claims either way.

On 8 December 1941, HMAS *Maryborough*, together with HM Australian Ships *Goulburn*, *Burnie* and *Bendigo* of 21 Minesweeping Flotilla, additional corvettes and various other Allied vessels (including two Yangtze river-boats, *Grasshopper* and *Dragonfly*, and a Yangtze River gunboat, the 700-tonne *Scorpion*), was patrolling the waters off Singapore. All ships in this rather diverse fleet were under the control of *Maryborough's* Lieutenant-

Fukuyu Maru, *following her capture by HMAS* Maryborough

Commander Cant, RAN. At noon, when about 40 kilometres from Singapore and only hours after war with Japan had been declared, *Maryborough* intercepted a vessel named *Fukuyu Maru* (Fortune of Excellence), registration number 2163. After shots were fired, the vessel surrendered and a boarding party from *Maryborough* took her over. *Fukuyu Maru* was then taken in tow to Singapore waters, where she was impounded at the naval base and destroyed. Three hours after the capture of this vessel, in keeping with the policy of checking on all shipping, enemy or otherwise, *Goulburn* stopped a launch towing a junk. After the vessels had hove to, a party was sent in the ship's whaler to examine the other ship's credentials.

At 11:50 am on 11 December 1941 (three days after Denis Emerson-Elliott had impounded *Kofuku Maru* and all other Japanese fishing vessels in port, and three days after *Fukuyu Maru* had been apprehended by *Maryborough*), HMAS *Goulburn*, which was patrolling with the rest of the flotilla about 65 kilometres from Singapore, was ordered to proceed to the Horsburgh Light to take over a Japanese fishing vessel, *Shofuku Maru*, and four barges (registered numbers 2205, 1597, 500, 133 and 284), which had been captured by the US destroyer *Edsall*.

One minute after this signal was received, *Burnie* signalled *Goulburn* that she had made contact with a submarine. At 12:10, ten minutes after placing a boarding party and prize crew on board *Shofuku Maru*, *Goulburn* also detected a submarine, about 450 metres distant. Leaving Gunnery Officer N O 'Paddy' Vidgen, First Lieutenant Jack Langley, Petty Officer Sandy Boxsell, three armed sailors (able seamen Donald Johnston, Bertram Towner and the engine room artificer) and the ship's multi-lingual Chinese steward, on the Japanese vessel, *Goulburn* took up the chase for the submarine. After an hour's fruitless search by the two corvettes, during which time four depth charges were dropped, *Goulburn* broke off the attack to retrieve Vidgen, Langley and the steward from *Shofuku Maru*. Boxsell and the three armed sailors were left on board to see that the enemy ship reached Singapore.

When Vidgen returned to *Goulburn* in the ship's whaler he brought with him two brass tubes containing *Shofuku Maru*'s confiscated ship's papers. Included among them were the identity papers of her captain, Suburo Izimi, and crew member Eikichi Nagamine. To make matters even more confusing, Nagamine's papers showed he had been on another ship besides *Shofuku Maru* – *Fukufu Maru* (Fortune of Wind). None of these papers were surrendered to the RAN: Vidgen kept the identity papers, and *Goulburn*'s captain, Lieutenant-Commander Paul, retained the others. At 3.30 pm, with her crew once more on board and the whaler restored, *Goulburn* rejoined *Burnie* to seek further submarine contacts for half an hour, when the search was called off.

Just on dusk at 6.40 the following evening, *Goulburn* was again ordered to proceed to the Horsburgh Light, this time to take over an unnamed Japanese fishing vessel towing six barges, recently captured by the British destroyer HMS *Encounter*. By 8:15 a boarding party from *Goulburn* had been lowered in the ship's whaler to relieve *Encounter*'s party, which then returned to the destroyer.

By the time Singapore fell on 15 February 1942, the tally of fishing vessels taken into custody was considerable. Indeed, for the month of December alone, there had been many small craft apprehended by Lieutenant-Commander Cant's flotilla, nineteen being captured on 16 December – fourteen by *Bendigo* and another five by *Dragonfly*.

It was therefore not surprising that, more than thirty years after the events of December 1941, incidents which occurred during the many patrols of HMAS *Goulburn* became telescoped and the identity of *Kofuku Maru* confused with that of *Shofuku Maru* and, occasionally, the other Japanese ship captured by *Encounter* on 12 December. Moreover, it appears, from the hand-lettered label on the brass cylinder which held the papers retained by *Goulburn*'s commander, that Paul himself (despite the fact that the papers were clearly marked *Shofoku Maru*), believed them to be those of *Kofuku Maru*.

With Denis Emerson-Elliott, Department of Naval Intelligence and other documents proving that *Kofuku Maru*, registered number 2283, was taken into custody in Singapore on 8 December; *Maryborough*'s Letter of Proceedings and photographs taken at the time by one of her crew members proving beyond all doubt that the Japanese vessel captured by *Maryborough* that same day was *Fukuyu Maru*, registered number 2163; *Goulburn*'s Log recording that *Shofuku Maru*, registered number 2205, was apprehended and taken as a prize on 11 December; Vidgen's confirmation that papers were retained by him and Paul;

and the internal configuration and paintwork of the ships being quite different (the single-masted *Kofuku Maru* having four fish-holds and white paint around the wheelhouse doors and windows; the single-masted *Fukuyu Maru*'s wheelhouse being painted a dark uniform shade, and the apparently twin-masted *Shofuku Maru* having one very large fish-hold situated between the foremast and the wheelhouse), it is obvious that *Kofuku Maru*, *Fukuyu Maru* and *Shofuku Maru* are three quite distinct vessels. It is also obvious that the honour of capturing the first enemy ship in the Pacific Zone must belong to HMAS *Maryborough*.

Honour Roll

Operation Jaywick

Major Ivan Lyon, MBE, DSO, Gordon Highlanders, SOE and SOA

Lieutenant Donald Montague Noel Davidson, DSO, Royal Naval Volunteer Reserve, SOE and SOA

Lieutenant Robert Charles Page, DSO, Australian Imperial Force, SOA

Lieutenant Hubert Edward Carse, MID, Royal Australian Naval Volunteer Reserve, SOA

Leading Stoker James Patrick McDowell, Royal Australian Naval Reserve, DSM, SOA

Leading Telegraphist Horace Stewart Young, MID, Royal Australian Naval Reserve, SOA

Corporal Andrew Anthony Crilly, MM, Australian Imperial Force, SOA

Corporal Ronald George Morris, BEM, MM, Royal Army Medical Corps, SOA and SOE

Acting Leading Seaman Kevin Patrick Cain, MID, Royal Australian Naval Reserve, SOA

Able Seaman Arthur Walter Jones, DSM, Royal Australian Naval Reserve, SOA

Acting Able Seaman Mostyn Berryman, MID, Royal Australian Naval Reserve, SOA

Acting Able Seaman Walter Gordon Falls, DSM, Royal Australian Naval Reserve, SOA

Acting Able Seaman Andrew William George Huston, DSM, Royal Australian Naval Reserve, SOA

Acting Able Seaman Frederick Walter Lota Marsh, MID, Royal Australian Naval Reserve, SOA

Operation Rimau

Honour Roll
(in order of rank and service priority)

Lieutenant-Colonel Ivan Lyon, DSO, MID, MBE, Gordon Highlanders, SOE and SOA, killed in action at Soreh Island, Riau Archipelago, Indonesia, while on Operation Rimau, 16 October 1944, aged 29

Lieutenant-Commander Donald Montague Noel Davidson, DSO, MID, Royal Naval Volunteer Reserve, SOE and SOA, died at Tapai Island, Riau Archipelago, Indonesia, while on Operation Rimau, 18 October 1944, aged 35

Honour roll

Major Reginald Middleton Ingleton, MID, Royal Marines, SOE and SOA, beheaded at Reformatory Road, near Bukit Timah, Singapore, while on Operation Rimau, 7 July 1945, aged 29

Lieutenant Bruno Philp Reymond, Royal Australian Naval Reserve, SOA, drowned off Satai Cape, Borneo, while on Operation Rimau, 21 December 1944, aged 31

Captain Robert Charles Page, DSO, Australian Imperial Force, SOA, beheaded at Reformatory Road, near Bukit Timah, Singapore, while on Operation Rimau, 7 July 1945, aged 24

Sub-Lieutenant James Grigor Mackintosh Riggs, MID, Royal Naval Volunteer Reserve, SOE and SOA, killed in action at Merapas Island, Indonesia, while on Operation Rimau, 5 November 1944, aged 21

Lieutenant Walter George Carey, Australian Imperial Force, SOA, beheaded at Reformatory Road, near Bukit Timah, Singapore, while on Operation Rimau, 7 July 1945, aged 31

Lieutenant Harold Robert Ross, MID, British Army General List, SOA, killed in action at Soreh Island, Riau Archipelago, Indonesia, while on Operation Rimau, 16 October 1944, aged 27

Lieutenant Albert Leslie Sargent, Australian Imperial Force, SOA, beheaded at Reformatory Road, near Bukit Timah, Singapore, while on Operation Rimau, 7 July 1945, aged 26

Warrant Officer Alfred Warren, Australian Imperial Force, SOA, beheaded at Reformatory Road, near Bukit Timah, Singapore, while on Operation Rimau, 7 July 1945, aged 32

Warrant Officer Jeffrey Willersdorf, Australian Imperial Force, SOA, died while POW in Dili, Timor, while on Operation Rimau, February 1945, aged 22

Sergeant Colin Barclay Cameron, Australian Imperial Force, SOA, killed in action at Merapas Island, Indonesia, while on Operation Rimau, 5 November 1944, aged 21

Sergeant David Peter Gooley, Australian Imperial Force, SOA, beheaded at Reformatory Road, near Bukit Timah, Singapore, while on Operation Rimau, 7 July 1945, aged 25

Corporal Archie Gordon Patrick Campbell, Australian Imperial Force, SOA, died at Tapai Island, Riau Archipelago, Indonesia, while on Operation Rimau, 18 October 1944, aged 24

Corporal Colin Montague Craft, Australian Imperial Force, SOA, drowned off Satai Cape, Borneo, while on Operation Rimau, 21 December 1944, aged 25

Corporal Roland Bernard Fletcher, Australian Imperial Force, SOA, beheaded at Reformatory Road, near Bukit Timah, Singapore, 7 July 1945, aged 29

Corporal Clair Mack Stewart, Australian Imperial Force, SOA, beheaded at Reformatory Road, near Bukit Timah, Singapore, while on Operation Rimau, 7 July 1945, aged 35

Able Seaman Walter Gordon Falls, DSM, Royal Australian Naval Reserve, SOA, beheaded at Reformatory Road, near Bukit Timah, Singapore, while on Operation Rimau, 7 July 1945, aged 25

Able Seaman Andrew William George Huston, DSM, Royal Australian Naval Reserve, SOA, died off Buaja Island, Lingga Archipelago, Indonesia, while on Operation Rimau, 16 December 1944, aged 20

Able Seaman Frederick Walter Lota Marsh, Royal Australian Naval Reserve, SOA, died while POW at Tanjung Pagar, Singapore, while on Operation Rimau, 11 January 1945, aged 20

Lance Corporal John Thomas Hardy, Australian Imperial Force, SOA, beheaded at Reformatory Road, near Bukit Timah, Singapore, while on Operation Rimau, 7 July 1945, aged 23

Lance Corporal Hugo Joseph Pace, Australian Imperial Force, SOA, died while POW at Dili, Timor, Indonesia, June 1945, while on Operation Rimau, aged 32

Private Douglas Richard Warne, Australian Imperial Force, SOA, died while POW at Dili, Timor, Indonesia, while on Operation Rimau, April 1945, aged 24

and also honouring

Captain William Roy Reynolds, MBE, Master Mariner, SOE, SOA and US Bureau of Economic Warfare, executed at Surabaya, Java, while on a special mission, 8 August 1944, aged 52

Lieutenant Clifford Perske, Australian Imperial Force, SOA, beheaded at Eastern Fort, Surabaya, Java, Indonesia, 31 March 1945, while on Operation Optician, aged 27

Lieutenant John Sachs, Australian Imperial Force, SOA, beheaded at Eastern Fort, Surabaya, Java, Indonesia, 30 March 1945, while on Operation Optician, aged 31

The Double Tenth Massacre

Honour Roll
Names of some of those known to have been taken into custody and interrogated.

*   died during or after interrogation

**   known to have been sentenced to Outram Road Gaol

From Changi Civilian Internment Camp

Birse, A L	Bryning, H E W*
Blackstad, G C C	Buchanan, A* **
Bloom, Mrs Elfrieden (Freddy)	Buckley, T A
Bowyer, Dr T H* **	Burns, R

Calderwood, Robert**
Cherry, William Thorpe**
Chettle, A
Clark, Mr Justice Adrian J*
Coulson, Norman*
Curtis, Walter S V**
Dalton, J
Dawson, R M
Day, W H
Dunlop, J W
Earl, Lionel Richard Franklin**
Fisher, Dr O E
Francis, Mr
Fraser, Sir Hugh*
Gibson, F H
Gilmour, C C B
Goodall, Lionel Arthur
Grosuch, L H
Hagger, S A*
Hardman, J
Hebditch, E G
Hill, H L
Hilterman, Charles Eric
Jackson, Clarence Cyril
Jelany, S M S

Johns, Dr B M
Ker, A W W* **
Little, W R
Long, John Spurrier*
MacIntosh, James
McIntyre, H
Middlebrook, Stanley Musgrave* **
Milne, J A
Nixon, Dorothy
Penseler, W* **
Perry, D V P*
Rendle, Hilary Cameron R*
Scott, Robert H**
Sidney, R
Smith, F J
Stanley, Dr C A*
Stanley, R E
Stevens, E S
Stevenson, W L*
Travis, Samuel Eric
Wardle, R A
Williams, Dr Cicely D
Wilson, Bishop John L
Worley, Mr Justice N A
Yoxall, Walter Thomas

From Singapore

Ah Chan
Chan Soo Chen**
Chan Yeng Fong
Choy, Mr**
Choy, Mrs Elizabeth
Clarke, Dr Fowlie*
Cornelius, Mr S*
Cornelius, Mrs
Drysdale, Mr

Eason, H J
Ebert, R Edward**
Ebert, Reginald Victor**
Ellow, Mr
Fernando, T Ernest
Gelani, Dr
Ho Tak Chiang
Hoffman, Leslie**
Joseph, Frances

Kathay, Mr

Khoo Fook Tan

Koo Hock Choo, Dr

Lean, Mrs Ah Beck

Lia Sia

One Lin Seong

Royston, Lewis

Sheppard, C F

Sim Keng Yong

Singh, Mahinder

Swee Lye Huat

Tan Yew Cheng

Webb, Guy

Wee Eik Teck

Wong Cheong Khin

From POW Camp

Redy, Charles**

Woudenberg, Cornelis*

Zaayer, J W**

Burial and Commemoration Roll

Burials

KIA Soreh Island, 16 October 1944
Lieutenant-Colonel I Lyon, grave 27 A 14
Lieutenant H R Ross, grave 27 A 15

KIA Tapai Island, 18 October 1944
Lieutenant-Commander D M N Davidson, grave 23 D 20
Corporal A G P Campbell, grave 23 D 19

KIA Merapas, 5 November 1945
Sub-Lieutenant J G M Riggs, grave 32 E 4
Sergeant C B Cameron, grave 32 E 2

Executed Singapore, 7 July 1945
(names left to right, alphabetically in graves 28A 1–10)
Lieutenant W G Carey
Able Seaman W G Falls
Corporal R B Fletcher
Sergeant D P Gooley
Lance Corporal J T Hardy
Major R M Ingleton
Captain R C Page
Lieutenant A L Sargent
Corporal C M Stewart
Warrant Officer A Warren

Commemorations

Memorial to the Missing

Kranji, Singapore
Corporal C M Craft, column 118
Corporal H J Pace, column 118
Private D R Warne, column 118
Warrant Officer J Willersdorf, column 117
and
Lieutenant C Perske, column 117
Lieutenant J Sachs, column 117

Naval Memorial, Plymouth, England
Able Seaman A W G Huston, panel 92 column 3
Able Seaman F W L Marsh, panel 95, column 3
Lieutenant B P Reymond, panel 92, column 2

Commemorative Roll—Merchant Navy

Australian War Memorial Canberra
Captain W R Reynolds

References and Explanatory Notes

Abbreviations

AAHUA: Australian Army History Unit Archives

ANMM: Australian National Maritime Museum

AWM: Australian War Memorial, Canberra, ACT

GL: Guildhall Library, London

IWM: Imperial War Museum, London

LFP: Lyon Family Papers

ML: Mitchell Library, Sydney

NAA: National Archives of Australia

NAK: UK National Archives, Kew, London (previously Public Record Office)

NHR: Naval Historical Records, Canberra

SP: Silver Papers

USNA: United States National Archives, Washington

For full citation of published books see Bibliography.

Chapter 1: War Comes to Singapore

Emerson-Elliott family experiences

Emerson-Elliott family papers

Singapore before the war

Books: Morrison; McKie's *This was Singapore*

Papers: Emerson-Elliott family papers

War situation in Malaya and Singapore

Archival material: HMAS *Burnie*, Reports of Proceedings, AWM 78 79/1(AWM); Log of HMAS *Goulburn*, Navy Hydrographic Service, Log Books of HM Colonial Ships, HMS and HMA ships SP 551 Bundle 238 3/12/41-5/3/42 (NAA); HMAS *Maryborough*, Reports of Proceedings, AWM 78 218/1 (AWM); Squadron-Leader T C Carter, History of RDF organisation in the Far East 1941-1942, Carter Papers TCC2/1 (IWM)

Despatches: Brooke Popham, Maltby, Percival

Interviews/correspondence: Geoffrey Rowley-Conwy (SP)

References and explanatory notes

Books: Allen, Barber, Bennett, Callahan, Churchill, Day, Falk, Gough's *Escape*, Hall, Leasor, Maxwell, Montgomery (contains quotes from the diary of Sir Shenton Thomas), Morrison, Penfold et al., Percival, Reid, Silver's *Rimau* and *Parit Sulong*, Simpson, Skidmore (actually a personal account of the experiences of Geoffrey Rowley-Conwy), Smyth, Stewart, Warren, Wigmore.

Additional chapter notes

1   Casualties: It is estimated that at least 9000 Chinese died in Singapore as a result of the bombing

Chapter 2: Secret Business

Secret services

Private papers: Emerson-Elliott Family papers; List of Oriental Mission personnel, compiled by Jonathan Moffatt (Moffatt papers)

Articles: Morris, Nigel, *The Special Operations Executive 1940–1946*, on line at http://www.bbc.co.uk

Books: Comber, Cookridge, Cruikshank, Dourlien, Elphick's *Far Eastern File*, Foot, Garden, Gough's *SOE*, Murray, Spencer Chapman

Documentary: *Arms and the Dragon* (BBC 1984)

Code breaking, intercepts

Books: Ballard, Bleakley, Kahn, Pfennigwerth, Rusbridger & Nave, Thomson

Chapter 3: Exodus

Emerson-Elliott family experiences

Emerson-Elliott family papers

Situation in Singapore

Interviews/correspondence: Jeremy Atkinson; Geoffrey Brooke; Robert Mullock

Books: Bennett; Brooke's *Alarm Starboard*, Gough's *Escape*

Final withdrawal from Malaya

Books: Brookes; Gough's *SOE*; Rose; Stewart

Empire Star

Archival papers: Bennett to Sturdee, 19 January 1942, Document 54, 553/2/3 (AWM); *Empire Star*, Papers relating to attack by Japanese aircraft, MP 1587/1 157A (NAA); Service dossiers of James and John Bowman (NAA)

Private Papers: Emerson-Elliott; Papers relating to *Empire Star* (Ross Woods); Redmond Faulkner papers (newspaper clippings, etc); Report by Captain Capon (copy in SP); Diary of Charlie Johnstone (copy in SP)

Interviews/correspondence: Atkinson; Betty Bradwell, an Australian nursing sister from 10 AGH; Roy Cornford; Denis Emerson-Elliott; Derek Emerson-Elliott; Redmond Faulkner; Archie Mitchell Mitchell (AASC *Empire Star*); Cyril H Scriven (AASC, *Empire Star* – see also original correspondence in MSS 1450 AWM); Captain George Wright, copy of transcript of ABC interview with Bruce Miller, *Singapore Pilot: The last trip*, March 1944; copies of letters from Anthony J Higgins (crewman *Empire Star*) to Ross Woods

Articles: Redmond Faulkner, various items and news clippings relating to *Empire Star* (SP); George F Heads (ship's cook, *Empire Star*), *The Australian* 20/02/1992; A J Higgins, *Escape from Singapore* (copy in SP); Dr Peter Last, *Empire Star* (typescript from book, *The Repat*); Sister Margaret Selwood, unidentified newspaper article 1942; Lynette Silver, *Scapegoats for the Bloody Empire*, Australian Broadcasting Commission website, 4 Corners; *War Cry* 14 March 1942

Books: Brook's *Singapore's Dunkirk*; Elphick's *Singapore*; Hodder; Reid; Ross; Docker & Silver; Taffrail

Websites: Blue Star Line's MV *Empire Star*, http://www.bluestarline.org; *Heroines of the Empire Star* (various contributors), http://www.angellpro.com.au

Evacuation ships

Archival papers: Malayan Research Bureau Papers (Excerpts from Memoires of Mrs Edith Stevenson; Memoires of Marjorie de Malmanche) (IWM); Papers relating to attack by Japanese aircraft, MP 1587/1 157A (NAA)

Interviews/correspondence: Brenda McDuff; Marjorie de Malmanche, Robert Mullock

Books: Gough's *Escape*; Brooke's *Singapore's Dunkirk*

Allegations of desertion

For a full account of the various allegations levelled at Australian troops, and their rebuttal, see Docker & Silver, *Fabulous Furphies*; also *Scapegoats for the Bloody Empire* on ABC website

Dalley and Dalforce

Books: Allen; Elphick's *Far Eastern File*; Gough's *Escape* and *SOE*; Warren

Documentary: *Arms and the Dragon*. Archival footage shows the Dalforce men with Martini Henry rifles and a converted version of the same weapon.

References and explanatory notes

Secret services
Books: Comber, Cookridge, Cruikshank, Dourlien, Elphick's *Far Eastern File*, Foot, Gough's *SOE*

Bowden's death
Bowden, VG, death of, Report by A N Wootton, 19 October 1945, A1066 H45/580/6/4 (NAA)

Additional chapter notes
1 The vessels were *Derrymore* (loaded with ammunition), *Redang, Ipoh, Ampang, Jalakrishna, Jalavihar, Jalarantna, Oriskany, Ashridge, Hong Kheng, Sin Kheng Seng, Aquarius* and *Lee Sang*.
2 The Salvation Army officers were Major W Blaskett, and Adjutants W Witney, J Kinder and G Woodland. All reached Australia safely.

Chapter 4: Escape
Reynolds
Archival papers: Admiralty files relating to Operation Jaywick, XC/3197 ADM (NAK); Lloyd's Lists, 8 October 1923, 4 September 1924, 18 August 1943(GL); Malayan Research Bureau Lists, ML 984/62 (ML); Malayan Research Bureau Papers (IWM); Merchant Navy List MF 18 568 Vol 1 2A, M/F 18 569 Vol 32 (GL); *Shofuku Maru*, papers of (ANMM)
Private papers: Emerson-Elliott Family papers; Reynolds Family papers
Interviews/correspondence: Ted Buckler; Marjorie de Malmanche; Brenda McDuff; Margaret Reynolds
Articles: John Hellman, 'Australian Capital in South East Asian Tin Mining, 1906', *Australian Economic History Review*, vol 45, issue 2
Books: Coates and Rosenthal; Pratten, Silver's *Krait* and *Rimau*

Kofuku Maru/Suey Sin Fah
Archival papers: Brigadier L E C Davis, WW 2 Papers (IWM); *Krait*, drawings and plans, by crewman Sid O'Dwyer AWM 3 DRL 7530 (AWM); Malayan Research Bureau Papers; Memorandum *Krait* AA 1981/155/1 605/2D/1 (NAA); Naval Papers relating to HMAS *Krait*, Department of Navy, Classified general Correspondence Files, multiple number series 1923-50, MP 1049/5 2026/27/296 (NAA); exterior and interior photographs of *Krait* (AWM); Admiralty report, XC/B 3197 (NAK); Memorandum 'Krait' DNI 9 February 1943, AA 1981/155/1 605/2D/a (NAA)
Interviews/correspondence: Peter Loosen of Deutz Australia Pty Ltd; Manager of Klockner-

Humboldt-Deutz, Koln, Germany; information from Fugisawa Family and archivist of Nagahama township Shichiro Kubo, collected by Yoshio Shimuzu, and translated by Yoshi Tosa; Ron Morris; Nippon Kaiji Kyokai re Japanese ownership; Ray Williamson of Ruston Diesel; Greaves Cotton Bombay; M Mosley of L Gardner and Sons, Manchester

Private papers: Reynolds papers; Report on Deutz Diesel engine PMV Model 1927-30 (SP); Correspondence, various, re *Krait*, papers of Bill Cockbill, RVCP

Books: Bostock; Silver's *Krait* and *Rimau*; Wynyard

Fate of escapers/evacuees

Archival papers: Report on activities of 2 Aust Contact and Enquiry Unit (SEAC) AWM 52 (AWM); Malayan Research Bureau; Service dossier of Lt Gordon Keith RAN (NAA)

Interviews/correspondence: de Malmanche; McDuff; Robert Mullock; Geoffrey Rowley-Conwy

Private papers: Papers of Dr Albert Coates (copy in SP); Reynolds Papers;

Articles: Cyril Wild, 'Expedition to Singkep', *Blackwood's Magazine* no 1572, vol 260, October 1946

Books: Australian War Memorial, *HMAS Mk IV*; Brooke's *Escape*; Coates & Rosenthal; Gough's *Escape*; Hall; Silver's *Krait, Rimau*; Skidmore; Baldwin (Dr Marjorie Lyon article)

Sinking of *Kuala, Tien Kwang, Kung Wo*

Archival papers: Malayan Research Bureau papers

Articles: Lieutenant Franklin Caithness, RNR, edited account of the loss of HMS *Kuala*, to Commander H V Creer, *Naval Historical Review*; Frank Man, account of his escape (copy in SP); Brian Napper, article on line, http://www.bbc.co.uk/ww2peopleswar

Books: Brooke's *Singapore*; Gough's *Escape*

Ivan Lyon meets Bill Reynolds

Lyon Family papers; correspondence with Clive Lyon; interviews/correspondence with Ron Morris

Chapter 5: A Meeting of Like Minds

Ivan Lyon and Lyon Family

Archival papers: Lyon's SOE Dossier, HS 9/9563/2 (NAK); Shipping lists, on line, (NAA)

Private papers: Information on Lyon, compiled from information from Clive Lyon, Francis Moir-Byres, Ron Morris, Bettina Reid (SP); Emerson-Elliott Family papers; Lyon Family papers (including letters from Ivan to Gabrielle)

Interviews/correspondence: de Malmanche

References and explanatory notes

Articles: Ivan Lyon, 'Malaya to Indo-China', *The Yachting World*, 11 November 1938, G F Moir-Byres, 'Malayan Sailing', *The Yachting World*, 7 October 1938; Diary (anon) *Down the Danube by Canoe*, July–August 1935 (Lyon papers)

Patrick Heenan
Interviews: Denis Emerson-Elliott
Articles: Silver's *Scapegoats*
Books: Elphick's *Odd Man* and *Far Eastern File*; Docker & Silver

SOE activities in Singapore and escape route
Archival papers: Robert John Patterson Garden, SOE file HS 9 562/2 (NAK)
Private papers: Emerson-Elliott Family; Gordon Grimsdale to General Lyon re Ivan's secret activities (LFP)
Articles: Michael Pether, 'Account of the evacuation ship HMS *Scott Harley*' (copy in SP)
Interviews/correspondence: Ron Morris
Books: Brooke's *Alarm Starboard*; Cruikshank; Elphick's *Far Eastern*; Foot; Garden; Gough's *Escape* and *SOE*; Silver's *Krait* and *Rimau*; Skidmore; Spencer Chapman
Documentary: *Arms and the Dragon*

Jock Campbell
SOE dossier HS 9/ 260/3 (NAK); additional information from Jonathan Moffatt and interviews/correspondence from Morris and Reid (SP)

Vanrenan party
Books: Silver's *Parit Sulong*

Reynolds in Sumatra, India
Archival papers: Memorandum *Krait* by DNI 9 February 1943, and *Krait* Defect list, Brisbane 6 February 1943 AA 1981/155/ 605/2D/1 (NAA)
Private papers: Log book of *Suey Sin Fah* (copy in SP); Reynolds papers; Coates papers
Book: Coates and Rosenthal; Silver's *Krait* and *Rimau*

Additional chapter notes
1   Campbell served in Federated Malay States Volunteers 1931–37, Kedah Volunteer Force from 1937–40, Johor Volunteer Engineers 1940–41, and British Army 1941–45. Post-war he returned to Malay to take up his former post as Inspector of Palm Oil Estates, effective from 17 October 1945.

Chapter 6: A Plan Evolves

Indragiri escape route
Interviews/correspondence: Morris
Books: Brooke's *Singapore* and *Alarm*; Gough's *Escape*; Silver's *Rimau*; Skidmore; 2/19 Battalion's *Grim Glory* (Appendix 4)

Rooseboom
Books: Brooke's *Singapore's Dunkirk*; Gibson; Lim

Situation in Padang
Books: Gough's *Escape* and *SOE*

Voyage of *Sederhana Djohanes*
Private papers: Reid correspondence with Gabrielle Lyon, 13 December 1948 (LFP)
Interviews/correspondence: Reid; Rowley-Conwy
Books: Brooke's *Alarm Starboard*; Silver's *Rimau*; Skidmore

Gabrielle Lyon/*Nankin*
Private papers: Jock Campbell to Brigadier Lyon 9 March 1942 (LFP); Reid (SP); Reynolds; Malayan Research Bureau papers; Reynolds Family papers
Books: Muggenthaler

Naming Jaywick/*Krait*
Private papers: Reynolds (re naming *Krait*)
Books: Silver's *Rimau* and *Krait* (information of Francis Moir-Byres)

Jaywick plan
Archival papers: Jaywick preliminary papers, A3269 E2 (NAA); Wartime Ops and Reports, ref 85-35927, File 405/4/123 (held at ANMM)
Private papers: Governor Duggan's secretary to General Lyon, 8 March 1946 (LFP)
Interviews/ correspondence: Morris; Reid
Books: Fergusson; Silver's *Rimau*
Documentary: *Snakes and Tigers* (BBC 1984); *This is Your Life* (7 Network, 25 April 1981)

Donald Davidson
Archival documents: Davidson, D N M, SOE dossier HS 9/397/5 (NAK)

Private papers: Profiles on Davidson, Interviews/correspondence with Morris and Nancy Davidson (SP)
Books: Silver's *Rimau*

SOE (Australia) and AIB

Archival papers: Official History of the Operations and Administration of Special Operations Australia conducted under the cover name of Services Reconnaissance Department (compiled in 1945 by Sergeant D J Fennessy, Official Historian SRD, 1945, never published) A3270 (NAA); Operations of the AIB SWPA, GHQ, A3269 O 12/13; AIB Activities 1942–1945, Press release AWM PR 85/325 8 (AWM); Paper concerning SRD matters etc, Papers of Field Marshal Sir Thomas Blamey, 3DRL 6643 45/56.3 (AWM); Wartime operations and reports in relation to Operation Jaywick, Naval File 405/4/123 (ANMM)
Private papers: Emerson-Elliott (List of Australian secret agents); Profile on Colonel Mott (SP)
Interviews/correspondence: Reid
Articles: 'Z Force Home for Sale', *Australian*, 28 October 1977
Books: Horner's *Commanders* and *High Command*; Ind; Silver's *Krait* and *Rimau*; Thomson; Winter

Commander R M Long/DNI

Archival papers: Long's RAN Service dossier (NAA)
Private papers: Emerson-Elliott
Articles: Commander J M Wilkins, 'A Short History of Naval Intelligence and the Royal Australian Navy Intelligence Department, Part 2 1942–1945', *Navy Reserve News*, 24 June 2002
Books: Winter (Long's biography)

Bettina Reid

Archival papers: Reid's Service Dossier (NAA)
Interviews/correspondence: Reid
Articles: 'Barton's Creative Attitude', *Daily Telegraph*, 9 January 2008

Additional chapter notes

1   Also present at the meeting were Valentine Killery, Andrew Findlay (Head and staff member of Oriental Mission), John Galvin and Ted Sayers (propaganda, OM), Squadron Leader Mallery (Combined Operations intelligence Centre), Charles Drage ('MI6's Mr D', of SIS Hong Kong), and Gerald Wilkinson (SIS Manila)

Chapter 7: Jaywick Begins

Jaywick plans, training

Archival papers: File A3269 E2, including Training Log and Davidson's Diary (NAA); Wartime Ops and Reports

Private papers: Reid papers (correspondence from Lyon); Reynolds

Interviews/correspondence: Davidson; Moss Berryman; Morris; Reid; Don Russell; Instructors Clarrie Willoughby, Arthur Suters (all SP); interview by Arthur Jones, 2003, Australians at War (National Film Archives); interview by Horrie Young *c.* 2003, Australians at War (National Film Archives)

Books: Silver's *Rimau*; Wynyard

Documentaries: *Snakes and Tigers*; *This is Your Life*

Photographs: various photographs of Camp X and environs, 1942 and 1995 (SP)

Krait

Archival papers: Motor Vessel *Krait* Defect list; *Krait* 'Memorandum'; Appendix on *Krait*

Personal papers: Emerson-Elliott; letters from Lyon to Reid, Reid papers

Interviews/correspondence: Don Ramsay; Bert Bevan-Davies; Emerson-Elliott

Cleopatra

Private papers: Lyon to Reid, 31 January 1943 Reid papers

Interviews/correspondence: Morris

Books: Silver's *Rimau*

Documentary: *This is Your Life*

United States Bureau of Economic Warfare

Private papers: Reynolds' papers; correspondence with Margaret Reynolds, Ted Buckler; and Notes on E Farrell (all in SP)

Krait's **new engine**

Interviews/correspondence: Bevan-Davies, Emerson Elliott

Books: Silver's *Krait*

Scorpion and Carey

Archival papers: Operation Scorpion, A3269 C11 (NAA); Operation Scorpion, Operation Rimau, Minutes of final planning conference, 7 July 1944, A 3269 E 4 (NAA); Correspondence between Mott, Blamey and others, Papers of Blamey, Field Marshal Sir Thomas, 3DRL 6643 45/56.3 (AWM); Papers relating to Operation Scorpion, including letters by Carey, Blamey

and Mott, AWM 3/6643 2/58 (AWM); Service dossier, Asher Joel (NAA)
Interviews/correspondence: Carey
Books: Silver's *Rimau*

Restructuring of AIB and formation of SOA
Archival papers: A3270; A3269 O 12/13, Z1; AIB Administrative Adjustments, 16 April 1943, MP 729/8 20/431/53; Blamey papers 56.3. For AK numbers, see SRD cards, A3269; Papers of Field Marshal Sir Thomas Blamey, 3 DRL 6643 45/56.3 (letter from Mott re 'bumping off missionaries,' statements re SOA's political status, Mott's letters regarding his treatment etc)

Jaywick/*Krait* in Cairns
Archival papers: Memorandum Jaywick Operation (Chief of Naval Staff to Flag Officer Commanding, Royal Indian Navy, Calcutta); Revised Jaywick Operation, A3269 E2; Report by B/B 187, Jock Campbell, 8 April 1943; Memo by R E M Long, 'Motor Vessel *Krait*'); Davidson's *Krait* Log (reprinted in Wynyard); Davidson's SOE file
Interviews/correspondence: Walter Witt
Books: Wynyard; Silver's *Rimau*

Jaywick personnel
Profiles compiled on each member of the team from service and SOE dossiers (NAA and NAK), Jaywick training Log, interviews/correspondence with Emerson-Elliott, Reid, Jaywick crew members, friends and family members (SP) and letters from Crilly to Brigadier Lyon (LFP)

Additional chapter notes
1   The recruits who were discharged in Melbourne on 24/8/42 were R S Abrahams, N R Granit and R B Lamerton. Recruits eliminated during training at Refuge Bay were P Cameron, S F McCabe (to *Penguin*), C A Monk (to *Warramunga*). E E Kerr and J C McKay were discharged on 17 January 1943. For list of those on board *Krait* when she left Refuge Bay, see Appendix 2.
2   The RAN referred to the ship as *Audacious*, see Davidson's service record (NAA)
3   In April 1943, Davidson was transferred to HMAS *Assault* (see SOE file)
4   Carey in later years claimed that Mott had given him the nod for Scorpion. However, Mott had been removed from his post in February 1943 and replaced by Oldham. All paperwork is signed by Oldham, as acting Director of SRD, with copies of correspondence from Roberts also directed to him. Carey's claim that Scorpion had occurred on 19 June 1943 is also incorrect. The letters regarding the breached security of the port on 16 April

are clearly dated 17 April.

5   It was widely believed that Crilly was suffering from such poor health that he was about to be medically discharged. Although he had recently had his appendix removed, after his convalescence he had been posted to 2/14 Battalion and according to his service record, was in good health.

Chapter 8: The Jaywick raid

Krait's voyage from Thursday Island to Panjang Island

Archival papers: Davidson's *Krait* Log; Jaywick Log; Navigational Log, A3269 E2 (NAA); Jaywick Admiralty report; Operation Jaywick Report 21 July 1944, Collated Intelligence all in A3269 E2; Diary of Horrie Young Exhibition Document 154 (AWM)

Private papers: Emerson-Elliott; H B Manderson to Brig. Lyon 5 January 1948 (LFP)

Interviews/correspondence: Reid; Morris

Books: Connell; Silver's *Rimau*; Wynyard

Photographs: Photographs taken by Donald Davidson (AWM, IWM and SP)

Jaywick personnel

See reference for Chapter 7

Jaywick at Potshot

Archives: Davidson's *Krait* Log; Young Diary; Specifications of stores, Report by Davidson 1 September 1943 and Signal from Admiral Royal to Radio Potshot, 301132 August 1943, A3269 E2 Copy 1(NAA)

Private papers: Admiral Christie to Brig Lyon 11 April 1946; Thomas de Pledge to Brig. Lyon 10 January 1946 (LFP)

Interviews: Jones, Young (Film archives)

Books: Wynyard; Silver's *Rimau*

Documentaries: Snakes and Tigers; This is Your Life

Contingency plan

Interviews: Young (article 'Duty First', *Journal of NSW RAR,* vol 4, no 2, 2005, and Film archives); Jones (film archives)

Documentaries: This is Your Life

Books: Silver's *Rimau*; Wynyard

Jaywick Raid

Archival papers: Admiralty Reports, Operation Jaywick Report, Report 'Confidential

References and explanatory notes

Operation X' 21 July 1944, Operation Jaywick Report 25 October 1943, Collated Intelligence reports, Reports by raiders, Stores Lists, all in A3269 E2
Books: Wynyard; Silver's *Rimau*
Documentaries: *Snakes and Tigers*
Photographs: AWM, IWM and SP

Krait's voyage Panjang Island–Pompong Island
Archival papers: Navigational Log, *Krait* Log, Young's diary
Interviews/correspondence: Berryman, including information regarding Carse; Reid; Emerson-Elliott; Rae Grimwade, Andrew Huston's sister (regarding problems with Carse)
Books: Silver's *Krait*; Silver's *Rimau*

The wheelhouse incident
Interviews/correspondence: Emerson-Elliott's Report of meeting at DNI, between Long, Lyon and Davidson; Emerson-Elliott's interviews; Reid; notes re Rae Grimwade statement re Cain, Cain's statement backed by Morris and Berryman held by Tom Hall; Berryman statement re Carse's drinking; file note re statement made by Glenn Darlington, Perth 1993, regarding information on wheelhouse incident given to him, prior to 1988
Books: Silver's *Rimau*

Krait's return voyage from Pompong
Archival papers: *Krait* log; Navigational Log; Davidson's diary; Young's diary; July Jaywick Report; Operation X; Jaywick Admiralty report
Books: Silver's *Rimau*; Wynyard
Documentaries: *Snakes and Tigers*; *This is Your Life*

The unauthorised signal
Interviews/correspondence: Emerson-Elliott's Report of meeting at DNI, between Long, Lyon and Davidson; Emerson-Elliott's interviews; Reid
Articles/statements: Statements by Young in 'More About *Krait* – The ship's operator tells the story', *Amateur Radio*, January 1991 and 'Duty First'; Statements made by Young and Jones, Film Archives; H Young, *Fourteen Days, a Sequel to My Recollections of Operation Jaywick*, c. 2003, in which Young defends Carse as being 'an inspiration'

Gallantry awards
Archival papers: Proposed awards to Jaywick personnel, A816 66/301/523 (NAA); Chapman Walker to Commander-in-Chief (no date) and to Admiral Sir Guy Royle 11

January 1944, A3269 E2; Lyon's SOE file HS 9/953/2; Davidson's SOE file HS 9/397/5; Admiralty file XC/B 3197 ADM 1/16678 (NAK)

Private papers: Letters from Lord Shelbourne and Prime Minister Curtin to Clive Lyon, re recommendation for VC (LFP)

Additional chapter notes

1 According to Wynyard, the lights of Sambu Island were seen from Kapala Jernith. However, the raiders did not go via Kapala Jernith as the plans were amended (see official reports and maps). It appears that Wynyard's statements were based on notes from the original plan.

2 'Hill 120', the original site chosen, is about 13 kilometres from Dongas. The first mention of Dongas Island appears in Jaywick Admiralty Report Part I and Part II.

3 Morris turned down the offer of £5 cash per bottle for his rum (about a week's pay including danger money), and insisted on trading it for cigarettes.

Chapter 9: The Double Tenth Massacre

This chapter is based largely on transcripts of *The Trial of Sumida Haruzo and Twenty Others*, WO235/891 (NAK), reproduced in Sleeman & Silkin, and Mallal's *The Double Tenth Trial*, with additional sources as indicated below.

Details on Changi internees

List of internees, database on Changi Museum website, Bell's *Destined Meeting*

Elizabeth Choy

Germaine Foo-Tan, 'The Double Tenth Massacre: The Elizabeth Choy Story', *This Month in History*, vol 7, issue 10, October 2003; 'Survivor can forgive – but never forget', *The Australian* 14/2/1992

Robert Heeley Scott

Gough's *Escape*

Camp conditions

Interviews/correspondence Sheila Bruhn (nee Allan) and Elizabeth Ennis (SP)

Operation Cleanup

Documents: Transcripts of International War Crimes Tribunal, Tokyo (ML)

Interviews/correspondence: My Wartime Experiences in Singapore, interview of Mamoru

Shinozaki by Kim Yoon Lin, Institute of Southeast Asian Studies, Singapore 1973

Articles: Salt Vol 11, No 5, 5 November 1945, statement by J M Brodie

Newspapers: Straits Times 27 May 1947

Books: Low, Sidhu, Shinozaki, Ward

Outram Road Gaol

Documents: Details on Long and Woudenberg, Investigations on Bintan Island, B3856 144/14/118 (NAA); AIF and British POWs admitted to Outram Road Prison, B3856 144/1/358; Statements of various deponents AWM 54 554/11/1 (AWM);

Books: Daws; McGregor; Young

Additional chapter notes

1   Shinozaki believes the death toll among the Chinese was close to 17,000. The Chinese estimated it at 30,000. The Japanese confessed to 5,000 but later revised this to 25,000

Chapter 10: Lyon's Tigers

Mountbatten's appraisal

Memorandum on Operations in SEAC, 20 September 1944, A3269 N 1 Pt 1 (NAA)

Political situation

A J Wilson to General Northcott, 20 May 1944, A3269 H 14; (NAA); Silver's *Rimau*

Hornbill plans

Archival papers: Memorandum on Hornbill, A3269 E4; Lieutenant-Colonel Chapman-Walker, Signal 55 S/6, 3 November 1942, A3269 E 2 copy 1; Memorandum on SOE operations; MacArthur to Chiefs-of-Staff, A3269 N1 Pt 1; Major Walter W Chapman's Technical report on Operation Rimau 4 April 1945 A3269 E4; Chapman-Walker to Roberts 19 September 1944 A3269/1 H13 (NAA)

Books: Connell (statements by Chapman)

Hasler

Book: Philips' *Cockleshell Heroes*

SBs/transportation/J containers

Archival papers: Chapman's technical report; Hubert Marsham to Captain 8 Submarine Flotilla 29 September 1944; Captain Shadwell to Commander-in-Chief, Eastern Fleet, 30 October 1944; Memo M 0583292/44 6 January 1944; XC/B 3197 ADM 199/513 (NAK)

Interviews/correspondence: Reid
Books: Connell (Chapman statements); Davis; Hampshire

Lieutenant Ross
Archival papers: Ross's SOE dossier HS 9 1283/6 (NAK); Oppenheim, HR, Diary of, British Association of Malaya Collection, Royal Commonwealth Society, London
Private papers: Additional profile on Ross compiled from family and material supplied by Johnathan Moffatt (SP)

Gallantry awards
Jaywick decorations, XC/3197 ADM 1/16678 (NAK)

Gabrielle Lyon
Private papers: Gabrielle Lyon's diary; Jock Campbell to Brigadier Lyon 9 March 1943; Red Cross message; Jane Lyon to Reid (LFP)
Interviews/correspondence: Reid

Country craft
Archival documents: SOE memorandum; Chapman's technical report; Chapman-Walker to Roberts; Memo by NID (Q) 24 December 1944 XC/B3197 ADM 199/154 (NAK)

Operation Rimau, plans and training
Archival papers: Kookaburra papers, A 3269/1 E8; Plan Rimau; SRD Intelligence Report, A3269 E4; Roberts to Chapman-Walker 22 August 1944 A3269 H13 (NAA); Papers re Operation Rimau, XC/B 3197 ADM 199/513 (NAK); SRD Intelligence Report
Book: Silver's *Rimau*

Major Ingleton
SOE dossier HS 9/776/4 (NAK); Profile on Ingleton (SP); Minutes of Final Planning Conference, 7 July 1944 A3269 E4 (NAA)

Fraser Island Commando School
Archival papers: Lynette Silver *Special Operations Australia and the Fraser Island Commando School* MSS 1540 (AWM)

Personnel involved in Rimau
Archival papers: Progress reports – groups, A3269 H6 (NAA)

References and explanatory notes

Private papers: Profiles on each member compiled from service dossiers (NAA) family, friends, newspaper clippings, interviews and documentary *Snakes and Tigers* (SP)
John Lofty Hodges: Interviews with Hodges (SP)
Mary Ellis: Interview with Ellis (SP)

Nackeroos
Books: Walker; Preston & Silver

Security breaches
Archival papers: SRD papers on Breach of Security A3269 V7; Special Operations Activities Organisation A3770 Vol 1 (NAA); Branson's service dossier (NAA)
Interviews/correspondence: Emerson-Elliott; Tom Argyle to Brigadier Lyon 17 February 1946 (LFP)
Articles: Weekend Mail, 25 June 1960
Book: Silver's *Rimau*

Farewell party
George Astley to Gabrielle Lyon 14 December 1944 (LFP); Silver's *Rimau*

Submarine patrol
Marsham's report 15 October 1944 of 28th Patrol of HM Submarine *Porpoise*, ADM 199/1877, and Monthly Report, entry for 11 September 1944, ADM 173/18592 (NAK)

Additional chapter notes
1   Operation Frankton consisted of six two-man teams, but the canoe of W A Ellery and Eric Fisher (*Cachalot*) was so badly damaged while being unloaded from HM Submarine *Tuna* on the night of 7 December that they were unable to take part in the mission. Two men who drowned on 7 December after their canoe (*Conger*) was swamped were George Sheard and David Moffatt. Samuel Wallace and Robert Ewart (in *Coalfish*) were captured on 8 December en route to the target and executed. James Conway and John Mackinnon (in *Cuttlefish*) were also captured. They were executed on 23 March 1943 with Albert Laver and William Mills, who had reached the target in *Crayfish*, along with Hasler and W E Sparkes in *Catfish*, only to be captured while trying to flee. Hasler and Sparkes were the sole survivors.

Chapter 11: To Singapore

Voyage to Merapas and Padjantan islands

Archival papers: Davidson's Diary, 11–30 September 1944, A3269 E4 (NAA) [Note: the poor quality of the type makes the original difficult to read. The retyped version has omissions and no record of the sketches or plans]; Marsham's Report; Shadwell's Monthly Report 30 October 1944 and Letter to C-in-C Eastern Fleet, XC/B 3197 ADM 199/513 and Monthly Log of *Porpoise*, September 1944, ADM 173/18519 (NAK); Chapman's Report on first sortie of *Porpoise*, 19 December 1944 A3269 E4 (NAA)

Private papers: H B Manderson to Brig. Lyon (LFP)

Books: Silver's *Rimau*

Fate of Reynolds

Archival papers: Sworn statements of Hirai, 17/3/48, Takahashi 20/5/48, Moriyama 24/5/48, Uchida 15/6/48, Hamada 3/9/48, Ozaki 13/9/48, Yamashita Ginichi 28/12/48, Bunyu 31/5/48, Hirokawa 28/6/48, Yamashita Tatsukichi 12/7/48; Report by Van beck, 19/6/47; Interrogation of Uchida 15/6/48; 2 AWCS SCAP Missing personnel SWPA 12/11/48 and Appendix A 16; Signal A140 File 153/2 18/5/49 – all in MP 742/1 336/1/1939 (NAA)

Pick-up plan

Plan Rimau, Personnel List and Signal No 99, FCS 7 July 1944, and Report of Attempted Pick-up by Chapman, 12 December 1944 A3269 E4 (NAA)

Mustika and crew

Report by Ripley on interrogation of *Mustika* crew, 12 October 1944 A3269 E4 (NAA); Log of *Krait* (re ships seen in 1943); Davidson's diary; Chapman's 1st sortie report; Statement by Mohamed Juni, 9 January 1945, Rimau Report Copy II A3269 E4

Code book

Interview with Mary Ellis (SP)

Mustika voyage from Merapas to Kasu, situation on Merapas

Archival papers: Interrogation of Furuta, 21 October 1945 Appendix A ADM 1/18596-3231 (NAK); Translations of Proceedings of Military Court of 7 Area Army MP 742 336/1/755 and Full Account of Australian Special Operations party, Judicial Department 7 Area Army (NAA); Japanese I Staff message No 211 9 January 1945 (USNA); Translation of Kempeitai documents and Kempeitai war diary (original in Japan); Furuta statement to R

McKie 1957 (AAHUA)

Articles: Furuta Hiroyuki, 'The Harimu Party Sleeps Here', originally published as part of a literary contest in *Bungei Shunju* February 1975, and also corrected version of the original (copy at AAHUA), mentioned in the references of the current work, along with correspondence to McKie, as 'and docs'. Note: Some of the facts altered by Furuta for dramatic effect for the original publication were later corrected. The two versions are not identical, with additional details appearing in one or the other; 'A Report on Exercise Jaywick', *Army Journal 1981*, statement by Karta to Lieutenant R W Lowry

Books: Silver's *Rimau*

Flags

Archival documents: Furuta statement; Furuta interrogation; Judicial Dept account; Kagayaki Staff 2 Signal 227, 25 January 1945 Box 38 J 21138A, B, C in SR 29841/2 and 3 (USNA)

Articles: Furuta's 'Harimu' and docs

Kasu incident

Archival documents: Furuta's interrogation; Furuta statement; Military Court translation; Judicial Account; translation of Kempeitai documents; Report by Colonel Pritchard on missing personnel 13 October 1945, E Group South SACSEA, ADM 1/18596 3231; Japanese signal 227 and Oka Staff No 2 Message 799, 21 October 1944 Box 45 J 250251 A/B and D, SR 35040-42 (USNA)

Articles: Furuta's 'Harimu' and docs

Interviews: Arafin bin Akup and Mahat Kunil

Private papers: Personal observations, photographs made by L Silver 1989

Books: Silver's *Rimau*

Ships in harbour

MP1587 Box 1 File 20s, Appendix 3 (NAA)

Additional chapter notes

1   In 1949, the Australian government established that Reynolds had been executed in August 1949, information which was not passed to his family. His fate and the manner of his death were not made public until 1990, with the publication of *The Heroes of Rimau*.

2   Although fourteen days at 8 km per day was the allowed time, it was expected that strong canoeists such as Davidson would over the distance in much less time, possibly as little as five days. Therefore the raiders were expected back between 15 and 24 October.

3   Pulau Laut should not be confused with the island on which Reynolds was captured, which lay further to the south.

4   The events after *Mustika* left Merapas have been reconstructed from Indonesian eyewitness accounts and from written Japanese reports. As Japanese versions are sometimes telescoped in time and confused by hearsay, they have been extensively cross-checked with other available sources. When Japanese versions do not agree with other proven evidence or are obviously inaccurate (dates, time, numbers, etc.) they have been disregarded. The process of elimination in order to deduce which Rimau member was present at any particular scene has been made possible by knowledge of their roles, their place and time of death, the evidence of the Military Court Proceedings and the operational plan.

5   Translation of Kempeitai documents revealed that equipment belonging to Rimau was found at Pompong.

6   No notebooks were found on Lyon's body. His reports were always succinct and exceptionally brief (see Jaywick report and report on Endurance Test, Jaywick file). It was an aspect of his work noted by Harry Manderson in his letter to Gabrielle Lyon, 25 September 1947 (LFP). In comparison, Davidson recorded everything of military, geographical or scientific interest, as well as making notes on personnel and specific aspects of the operation. These notes were so exhaustive for Jaywick that his wife was able to write a book about the mission immediately after the war.

7   Japanese characters translated by L Silver 1989. Karta, who lives on Merapas Island, identified the British Coconut Tree.

8   The officer at Subar went on the raid. The three officers who took part in the raid (Lyon, Ross and Davidson) were all killed. As Lyon and Davidson were on *Mustika* (both named at court martial), they were not on Subar. Neither were any of the officers present at the court martial, since all admitted they were at Kasu, and Reymond must have been on *Mustika* at all times as he was the navigator. Ross was therefore the only possible candidate. An operative, he had the added advantage that he could speak Malay and had been in Singapore before the war. His companion, by necessity, also went on the raid. As all other ranks at the court martial said they were at Kasu, the OR on Subar must have been either Huston, Campbell, Cameron, Warne or Marsh. Cameron's job as SB technical expert precludes any possibility of his being on Subar, and he was also non-operative. The best person from the remaining four was Huston, who knew Subar and Singapore Harbour.

9   The Japanese worked on Tokyo time, so 5 pm local time was 4 pm.

10 In Military Court translation, Sidek bin Safar is named incorrectly as bin Shiapell. No one by that name ever lived on Kasu. In the Judicial Department account, Sidek is correctly identified as Ende (a corruption of Sidek) bin Safar.

11 The Military Court translation stated that four heiho were killed. Three is the number confirmed by Sidek, Arafin and Mahat, and also Japanese signal 227 and Oka Staff 2 message 799.

12 The statement in Pritchard's report that there were thirteen men in six folboats is incorrect and perhaps a typographical error. As there were four men at Merapas, two on Subar and four with Lyon, a total of eleven, twelve must have left *Mustika* in the first group, comprising six folboats with two men in each. Later, in Staff message No 2, the Japanese stated that the escape from the junk was in nine folboats. This was correct from their viewpoint – the six seen by Arafin and Mahat and also mentioned by Pritchard and the three recovered in the Riau Archipelago between 17–18 October. Later, when the Japanese can account for eleven folboats, the number is raised.

13 Although, according to the judicial account, only one flag was produced in court, Furuta stated he examined two flags – one the Japanese national flag and the other the Administration flag, both made in Australia. Neither flag was flying at the time of the Kasu incident.

14 Kagayaki Signal 227 relayed information that a large amount of material and supplies was recovered, along with a rubber raft and folboat on 18 October 1944, the date on which the Japanese found the bodies of Campbell and Davidson on Tapai; see Statement by Major Fugita, B3856 144/14/118 (NAA).

Chapter 12: For God, King and Country

The attack

Archival papers: Japanese signal, 48 Division (Timor) Staff Message 4024, 3 February 1945, A3269; Japanese Oka Staff 2 signal No 62, 25 January 1945, Box 39 J 21468 A to H, SR 30295-30298 (USNA); Report on Interrogation of Shizuo Tachino 28-31 December 1947 MP 742/1 336/1/1939 (NAA)

Books: Bliss statement, *Grim Glory*; Silver's *Rimau*

Activity at Kasu

Archival papers: Judicial account; Military Court translation; Japanese signal, Commander Special Base Force 10 Singapore, 15 October 1945, No 15129, Box 73 SRN 58234 RG 457 (USNA)

Interviews: Arafit, Mahat

Books: Silver's *Rimau*

Articles: Furuta's 'Harimu' and docs

Riau Archipelago
Archival papers: Statement by Sgt Major Chizo, Tanjung Penang Kempeitai, ADM 1/18596 (NAK); Base Force 10 Signal
Articles: Furuta's 'Harimu' and docs

Kempeitai reaction in Singapore
Books: Sleeman & Silkin; *Grim Glory* (Bliss statement); *Report of Joint Army/Navy Assessment Committee* (details of enemy vessels sunk)

Pangkil Island
Archival papers: Statements by Major Fugita, Raja Mun to John Ellis, B3856 144/14/118 (NAA); Report from HQ E Group South, file 40 Appendix B ADM 1/18596 3231 (NAK); Staff message 227; Base Force 10 signal 15 October; Summary of information 'Food', SRD Intelligence summaries A3269 H9 (NAA)
Books: Silver's *Rimau*

Soreh Island
Archival papers: Fugita's statement; Mun's statement; Statement by Yap Chin Yah to John Ellis 11 October 1945, Statement by Sgt Major Chizu Takeo to F/Lt Gardner, in B3856 144/14/118 (NAA); Special Base Force 10 Signal; Summary of information, Tactics (re Japanese searches); Furuta interrogation; Pritchard report; Kayagaki Staff 2 message; Translation of Kempeitai documents; Translation of Military Court proceedings; CWGC grave registration cards (NAA)
Interviews/correspondence: Aloysius Hayes Weller
Books: Du Quesne; Silver's *Rimau*

Tapai Island
Archival papers: Statements by Major Fugita, Raja Mun; message to Admiralty February 1946, A3269 E4; Furuta interrogation; Pritchard report; Instructions, security, SRD Intelligence Summaries A3269 H9 (NAA); Stores List Plan Rimau (for details of items recovered); Kagayaki Staff message 227
Articles: Furuta's 'Harimu' and docs

Merapas Island
Archival papers: Statement by Abdul Wahab to Major M L Shephard 10 October 1945, ADM 1/18596 3231 (NAK); Chapman's Pick-up report; Umi San message 228, in Information about Operation Rimau; Fugita's statement; Chizu's statement; Furuta interrogation;

Report by Lieut L G Palmer, 12 October 1945, AA 1981/155/1 505/2D/1 (NAA); Ellis report 13 Oct 45, B3856 144/14/118; I Staff message 211 9 January 1945, J16625 A-I, L-O (USNA); Translation of Military Court proceedings; Furuta's additional statements; Translation of Kempeitai records; re-interrogation of Ozaki Chikari, 4-5 March 1948 MP 742/1 336/1/1939 Pt 1 (where Ozaki tells Sargent that 2 or 3 Australians were killed on Merapas); Statement by Mr Ouvarow to Captain John Ellis 11 October 1945 MP 742

Private papers: Achap and Karta information; Forensic and ballistics reports by Dr G Oettle and police expert 1993 (SP)

Interviews/correspondence: Abdul Achap and Aloysius Weller (SP)

Articles: Furuta's 'Harimu' and docs; Karta's statement *Army Journal* 1981, Lowry, *Army Journal* 1972

Fate of John Long

Archival documents: Details on Long and Woudenberg, Investigations on Bintan Island, B3856 144/14/118 (NAA); AIF and British POWs admitted to Outram Road Prison, B3856 144/1/358; Exhumation report by Captain R Ross RAMC, B3856 140/1/51 (NAA); For remarks by Roberts, see A3269 E2, Report of 24/10/44 to DMI, DNI and Director SRD

Additional chapter notes

1   Admiralty charts for Singapore list three wrecks, off Sambu and in the Roads, for which the Port of Singapore Authority is unable to account. The Japanese Research Division, US Forces 29 August 1956; Information Room, Historical Section, Admiralty, Royal Navy 3 August 1956 and Cabinet Office UK Foreign Office Historical Section, 1 August 1956 are also unable to offer any explanation as to why these ships were sunk. In his Jaywick report, Lyon noted that there was intense activity at Sambu day and night and, from the sound of machinery and arc lamps, he was certain there was a shipbuilding and repair yard on the island. For this reason Sambu was one of the targets for Operation Rimau.

2   The identification of personnel has been established as follows: the seven men on the raid went to the Riau Archipelago. The two men who went directly to Tapai from Pangkil were not killed and went to Merapas. They were Warne and Huston. Raja Mun saw three men at Pangkil, two of whom he identified as having died on Soreh (Ross and Lyon). The two found dead on Tapai were unknown to Mun. The other man seen by Mun, who was not one of the Tapai victims, was Stewart, later captured on Soreh. Two of the men seen by Raja Muhammad at Pangkil went to Soreh, where they joined the three whom Raja Mun had seen. (The other two men seen by Muhammad at Pangkil were Warne and Huston, who went to Tapai.) The four men whom Latif met on Soreh were all killed –

two on Soreh and two on Tapai. The only possible combination which makes all of the above possible is for Lyon and Ross (killed at Soreh) and Stewart to meet Raja Mun; Davidson, Campbell (dead at Tapai), Huston and Warne to meet Raja Muhammad; and for Latif to meet Lyon, Ross, Davidson and Campbell.

3 Since, in addition to the enemy dead, over twenty were injured by hand grenades (Muhammad), quite a number must have been thrown. Military experts advise that it is almost impossible to throw a hand grenade from a tree because of the instability and the proliferation of branches. Therefore the grenades must have been thrown from the ditch. As Stewart was not detected, it is possible he may not have fired his Sten gun.

4 Number of dead: The Japanese version 'six officers and men of one battalion were killed here' (Oka staff message 799) and 'Lieutenant Muraroka and seven other army personnels' (two of whom were fatally wounded/killed at Merapas), stated in Military Court translation, is at variance with the eyewitness accounts of Latif, who was on Soreh at the time of the first fight and counted at least twelve dead bodies at the end of the second. It appeared the Japanese only reported the deaths of Japanese nationals, and did not bother to record the deaths of heiho who, according to Latif and Muhammad, formed the bulk of the search parties. This is also evidenced by the fact that the deaths of the heiho at Soreh at the first fight did not rate an official mention.

5 Had Warne and Huston been on Tapai they would have taken the wounded men with them or, failing that, left them in a good defensive position with adequate weapons and ammunition.

6 Achap had named the Japanese commander in 1981 as Sungarno. However, according to Weller, who spoke Japanese and English and was under the personal protection of the officer, his name was Captain Fujimura.

Chapter 13: Abandoned

Porpoise, Tantalus, **Marsham and Mackenzie**

Archival papers: Report on 28 War Patrol of *Porpoise*, Section L, ADM 199/511 (NAK); Minute by A H Taylor for DNI, 19 February 1945, and Shadwell to C-in-C East Indies Station, 9 January 1945 XC/B 3197 199/513 (NAK); Signals re new submarine, and Wilson to Northcott 20 May 1944 A3269 H14 (NAA); Annex D to Operational Order No 44, A3269 E4; Monthly log of *Tantalus* October 1944, and November 1944 ADM 173/18950 and 18952 (NAK); Report of 6th War Patrol of *Tantalus*, including Chapman's report, ADM 199/1862-3186 (NAK)

Books: Mars; Silver's *Rimau*; Trenowden; *Report of Joint Army/Navy Assessment* (for comparison of US and British submarine attacks)

References and explanatory notes

Intercepted messages
Oka Staff message No 2

Search of Merapas
Archival papers: Report on attempted Pick-up of Rimau party by Major WW Chapman, 12 December 1944 A3269 E4 (NAA); Appendix 1 of *Tantalus* patrol report; Davidson's diary for 11–30 September 1944, and sketch of the island; Wahab statement (re Japanese patrols); Report of Interrogation of Lance Corporal Croton, 11 December 1944 Rimau Report C, A 3269 E4 (NAA); Memos and Minutes by senior naval officers, annexed to Appendix 1 of *Tantalus* Patrol Report
Private papers: Personal observations at Merapas Island by L Silver 1993 (SP)
Books: Connell (for additional statements by Chapman); Silver's *Rimau*

Rimexit
Pick up Sortie, Deductions and remarks upon facts and evidence – Merapas Island; and statement of Juni January 1945 A3269 E4 (NAA); Papers associated with Rimexit, A3269 E5 (NAA)

Chapman's suicide
Archival papers: Notes of Evidence, Inquest on Walter William Chapman, 8 May 1964, evidence of Police Constable Donald Whitehead and Doctor R W Harries and Post Mortem Report by Harries at Amersham General Hospital, Amersham, England.
Articles: Report of Chapman's suicide, *Daily Mail*, London, 9 May 1964

Additional chapter notes
1   When a war-weary Marsham returned to Australia, he was replaced by Commander H B Turner. A few months later, in early 1945, *Porpoise* disappeared while laying a minefield in the Malacca Straits. Reports indicate that after being forced to dive to evade enemy aircraft, *Porpoise* was sunk by an anti-submarine vessel which tracked the submarine's oil leak, thereby giving *Porpoise* the dubious honour of being the 74th and last submarine sunk in WW II, see Alastair Mars, *Submarines at War*.
2   Only two signals were sent from *Tantalus* during this patrol – see Log entries for 11 November (after agreed pick-up date) and 2 December (after leaving Merapas).

Chapter 14: In enemy hands

Page's group

Archival papers: Investigation regarding missing Personnel, Appendix C, Statements by Amir of Senengang [sic], Soekarti, Said Abdullah, Boeang a Malay policemen (heiho), and Extracts from Dabo Police Book ADM 1/18596/3231 (NAK); Pritchard report; Umi San message 228; translation of Kempeitai documents; statements by Furuta

Interviews/correspondence: Weller

Articles: Furuta's 'Harimu' and docs; Wild, Cyril, 'Expedition to Singkep', *Blackwood's Magazine*, October 1946

Kempeitai deaths in custody

For examples of how these were covered up, see books by McGregor, Russell, Sleeman & Silkin

Rimau men's arrival in Singapore

Statement by Sergeant James Flaherty (SP), Flaherty's service dossier (NAA) and Michnow's *The Hell Ships*

Interrogation tactics

Memo – Securities, Prisoners of War A3269 H8; Furuta's 'Harimu' and docs; McGregor's book (cigarettes and lolly racket)

Cover stories

Cover – Plan Rimau 14 July 1944 A3269 E4; Furuta's 'Harimu' and docs

Information known to enemy

Top Secret report, 13 February 1945, Enemy information on Inter-Allied Services Department, Z Special Unit, and Services Reconnaissance Department [collated from intercepted signals and other intelligence] A3269/1 H10 Pt 3 (NAA). This 12-page report contains only a fraction of the information in enemy hands.

Intercepted signals

Oka No 2 message 799 of 22 October 1944, I Staff 2 messages 211 and 238 of 13 January 1945, Umi San message 158 of 21 January 1945, message 171 of 23 January, 228 of 3 February, Kagayaki Staff 2 message 227 of 25 January, and Oka 2 Staff message 62 of 25 January (USNA)

References and explanatory notes

Sargent's group

Archival papers: Ozaki interrogation; Ouvarow statement; Umi Staff message 228; SRD Project Summaries by Lt-Col J E B Finlay A2369 E4; I Staff 2 Message 238 13 January 1945 Box 37 J 20187 A-F SR 228578-82 (USNA); ATIS Bulletin 730, copy of PW Examination Report, Document 3/6643 2156.9 (AWM); Information on Sargent and Warne, contained in Investigation into the Disappearance of Lts Sachs and Perske, MP 742/1 336/1/1939 Pt 1 and Trials of Vice-Admiral Shibata and fourteen others and Captain Shinohara and two others A471/1 81961 and 81966 (NAA). For itemisation of these documents, see Silver's *Rimau*, endnotes for Ch 14.

Lieutenant John Sachs

Sachs Family papers, including signed memo by Fritz Sachs, 2.30 pm 30 March 1945

Operation Politician

Special Operations Australia, Vol II Part V, Politician-Optician, A3270; and An account of Operation Optician-Politician A3269 O8 Vol 2 (NAA)

Mason Schow

Correspondence between John Erickson (Schow's neighbour), Don Munro and L Silver, 1995–2003. Also MP 742/1 336/1/1939. For itemisation of these documents see endnotes Chapter 14, Silver's *Rimau*

Sumba castaways

MP 742/1 336/1/1939 and A471/1 81966. For itemisation of documents, see endnotes Chapter 14, Silver's *Rimau*

Tetanus experiments

Various statements MP 742 336/1/1939, Shibata and Shinohara trials (for itemisation of documents see endnotes Chapter 14, Silver's *Rimau*); *Sydney Morning Herald* 22 March 1951

Fate of Sachs and Perske and American fliers

Investigation into the disappearance of Lts Sachs and Perske, MP 742 336/1/1939 (NAA) and A471/1 81966 (NAA). For itemisation of documents, see endnotes Chapter 14, Silver's *Rimau*

Dissections
MP 742/1 336/1/1939, and A471/1 81966. For itemisation of documents, see endnotes Chapter 14, Silver's *Rimau*. For reaction to Shinohara's cannibalism, see Kinoshi, 10 September 1948 in A 471/ 81966

7th Area Army message
10 February 1945, Box 4, Magic Far East Summaries, SRS 339 of 22 February 1945 (USNA)

Execution of prisoners/spies without benefit of trial
Statements, interrogations, reports of Tachino, 14, 18 September 1945; Nomaguchi, 6 November 1948; Shibata 24 February 1948; Furuno 4 March 1949, all in MP 742 336/1/1939. In trial LN5, A 4781945 (NAA) expert witness General Imomura admitted that most subordinates would interpret 'punish strictly and firmly' as 'punish by death'.

Additional chapter notes
1   By intensively cross-referencing the clues in the Dabo Police book, eyewitness statements and translated Kempeitai records coupled with knowledge of the distances between Buaja and Singkep islands, it has been possible to reconstruct the movements of the party and sequence of events which led to their capture. There has been confusion in the past as hearsay evidence had incorrectly stated that six men went to both Buaja and Selajar, and further complicated by post-war Kempeitai accounts which listed fourteen people either killed or captured in the Lingga Archipelago. The discovery of two bodies at Merapas, and information from eyewitness Engku Haji Said Nuh, who stated that four men were on Selajar and that three small folboats were 'sunk' near Pompong (in reference to the fight which took place with Ingleton's subgroup) has enabled the number of men in each subgroup to be fixed at four and six.

2   Fritz Sachs was so disturbed by this event that he wrote a signed account it with the date and time (2.30 pm Sydney time, which was 1.30 Tokyo time). He died in September 1945, before he even knew his son was officially 'missing'.

Chapter 15: Judicial Murder
Note: Furuta's 'Harimu' needs to be read in conjunction with his corrected versions and other statements

Tanjung Pagar interrogations
Archival papers: Umi Staff message 228; Staff Area Message 10 February

References and explanatory notes

Books: Silver's *Rimau*
Articles: Furuta's 'Harimu' and docs

Lyon as Bowes-Lyon
Furuta docs; Palmer to POW Liaison Officer 21 November 1945 and Cdr Long to SRD 22 October 1945 AA 1981/155/1 605/2D/1 (NAA)

Keeping of records on missions
SRD Intelligence Summaries Part III Security, A3269 H9 (NAA)

Loss of face
Furuta's 'Harimu' and docs; statements by interpreter Miyazaki, Double Tenth trial

Outram Road Gaol
Archival papers: Testimony of Sgt John A MacDonald, USAF, for War Crimes Office, USA (USNA – copy in SP); Statements by Chris Neilson, John Wyett, Alexander Weyton, Roderick Wells, Walter Blee and others in AWM 54 1010/4/79, and Conditions in Outram Road Gaol, AWM 54 544/11/1 (AWM)
Interviews/correspondence: Outram Road inmates sent from Sandakan Borneo: Bert Rollason, Bill Young, Carl Jensen, Rod Wells, Frank Martin
Books: McGregor; Silver's *Rimau*
Articles: Furuta's 'Harimu' and docs; *Expedition to Singkep* (re Rimau in gaol)

Japanese attitude to torture
Furuta docs; Sleeman's *Gozawa*

Executions without trials to cease
Shuzio statement

Trial, preparations for, legal system
Archival papers: Judicial Account; Translations of Proceedings of Military Court; Interrogation of Major General Ohtsuka [sic] and Major Kamiya by Major C Wild, 19 October 1945, Appendix D, and Decisions passed at 7 Area Army Court Martials, Appendix F, ADM 1/18596 (NAK)
Private papers: Detailed notes on trial and rules of warfare (SP)
Articles: Furuta's 'Harimu' and docs
Books: Shinji (re legal proceedings); Silver's *Rimau*; *Hague Convention of 1907*; *Australian*

Manual of Military Law; Bradley (re Furuta's fluency); Moffitt (re use of Hague Convention as yardstick, not Geneva Convention, in war crimes trials)

Flags

Juni's statement re flags left in port office

Treatment post-trial

Archival papers: Interrogation of Noh Bok Kun and Kim Hyong Soon, 14 October 1945 Appendix G and interrogation of Furuta Appendix A, of ADM 1/18596; Furuta statements

Interviews/correspondence: Neilson, Rollason, Young, etc.

Articles: Furuta's 'Harimu' and docs

Execution

Archival documents: Interrogation of Noh and Kim; Furuta interrogation and statements; List of Japanese War Criminals Implicated in War Crimes against Australians DOC 422/7/8 (AWM); photographs of exhumation (AWM Collection); Exhumation Report by Ross; translation of Kempeitai documents

Interviews/correspondence: Rollason, Young

Private papers: Notes on Falls' photograph, Mrs Stewart's dream (SP)

Articles: Furuta's 'Harimu' and docs

Additional chapter notes

1 Furuta only knew what the prisoners had told him. Although Willersdorf and Pace had mentioned Jaywick in their interrogations (Umi Staff message 228) and Warne revealed that he had been on the Rimau raid (Shizuo interrogation), this information was only known to the top echelon. Furuta did not know about Rimau's involvement with Jaywick until Page told him, or anything about Soreh, Tapai or the attack on shipping by Rimau. He had no idea that Lyon had been killed until 1957 and believed he was the author of the book written by Davidson's wife about Jaywick.

2 Furuta corrected his original version of events, stating that Ingleton had made the final speech. Previously, for dramatic effect, he had attributed it to Page.

3 The sentences were: Sergeant Sugimoto Kozo and Chan Eng Thiam, 8 years; Miyazaki Kasuo, 15 years; Warrant Officer Sakamota, Sergeant Kasahara Hideo and Nigo Masayoshi, life imprisonment; Lieutenant-Colonel Sumida Haruzo, Warrant Officer Monai Tadamori, Sergeant Majors Makizono Masuo, Terada Takao and Morita Shozo, Sergeants Nozawa Toichiro and Tsujio Shigero, and Toh Swee Koon, death by hanging.

Chapter 16: Forgotten Heroes

Final solution

Archival papers: Document 2701, 1 August 1944, translated and quoted in Edwards;
Interview: Dr Ian Duncan, ex-POW (SP)

Collating information from ex-POWs

Archival papers: Report on Activities of 2 Aust Contact and Enquiry Unit by Maj A McKinnon, 15 November 1945 AWM 52 (AWM); War diaries 25/1/9 (AWM)
Books: Wigmore (Appendix 6)

Investigations into Rimau's disappearance

Archival papers: Reports and statements from E Group South ADM 1161/5665 044233 (NAK); Information regarding missing Australians, 10 Oct 1945 MP 742 336/1/755 (NAA) and ADM 1/18596 (NAK); Reports by Mackinnon, Sweeney, Burnett, Lloyd 2 Aust contact, etc; Reports and statement from Investigations on Bintan Island B3856 144/14/118 (NAA); Signal from Morotai re missing personnel, A3269 V16 (NAA); statement by General Finlay 13 June 1984, re fate of Rimau known to SOA, PC/5353 (AAHUA)
Private papers: Detailed notes on statements, interrogations, etc. (SP)
Interviews/correspondence: Dennis Harman RN (on board HMS *Caprice*)
Articles: 'Expedition to Singkep'
Books: Silver's *Rimau*

Pearl Harbor intelligence

Books: Prange, Rusbridger, Stevenson

Samurai culture

Russell's *Knights of Bushido*

Exhumations

Ross's report

Rimau's execution – a war crime?

Archival papers: Signal 18 January 1946, 1 AWCS to HQ AMF 29 January 1946, DPW&I 7 June 1946 to 1 AWC, Minute paper by Col Allaway, all in MP 742 336/1/755
Books: Sleeman (re Mountbatten quote)

Execution of airmen

Archival papers: Execution of Nine new Zealand Airmen without trial, ADM 116/5665 044233; Trial of Fukudome Shigeru WO 235/1102 (NAK); MacDonald's testimony

Interviews/correspondence: Rollason, Young

Success of raid

Archival papers: Oka staff message 62, J 21468 A, Box 39 (USNA); Umi San message 228, 3 February 1945, Information about Operation Rimau (USNA); Memorandum 6 April 1945, A3269 V5 (NAA). Also see Epilogue, current work.

Awards for Rimau

Archival papers: Finlay statement; telegram 7/12/45 re awards A3269 V16. [For evidence of censorship, compare Information about Operation Rimau with original I Staff 2 message 211, parts 9–15, 9 January 1945, J 11625 I-L, M, N, O (USNA)]; Cyril Chambers to Mrs J S Hardy, 27 March 1947, MP 742 336/1/755; British awards see SOE files for Lyon, Ingleton, Ross, Davidson and Riggs. For Lyon's possible VC/George Cross, see Lyon's SOE file.

Investigations in Surabaya

Archival papers: Report by Sylvester (n d) referring to evidence from Nomaguchi that all remaining POWs were executed after the cessation of hostilities, Witsell to Commanding General US Armed Forces California (n d); G l Bakker to Mr Schow 21 August 1946, Extract from 2 Echelon letter 6 January 47, Signal of 28 February 48 from RAAF HQ to Manila, W L Jinkins to SRD 31 August 1945, Report by L Talbit 10 October 1945, memorandum MIS-X Section 23 October 1945, Rear Admiral James Fife to Adjutant General AMF HQ 22 November 1946, DWP&I memo January 1947, Report by Judge van Beek 18 June 1947, all in MP 742/1 336/1/1939 Pt 1

Interviews/correspondence: John Erickson (Schow's neighbour) and Don Munro

Books: Silver's *Rimau*; Spencer Chapman (re Richardson); also documentary *Arms and the Dragon*

Executions without trial

Report by Sylvester (nd), statements of Tachino 9/11/48 and 16/11/48, Nomaguchi 6/11/48, Furuno 3/3/49, Shibata 2/2/49 all in MP 742/1 336/1/1939 Pt 1

Surabaya – was a war crime committed?

Lt Col Evans to AWC Tokyo 8 April 1949, MP 742 336/1/1939 Pt 1

References and explanatory notes

References and explanatory notes

Suez Maru

Fujimoto statement 13/7/49 MP 742/1 336/1/1939 Pt 1 [*Minesweeper 12* was torpedoed on 12/4/45 by USS *Besugo*, see *Report of Joint Army/Navy Assessment Committee*]

War crimes trials

Archival papers: Trial of Yaichiro Shibata and fourteen others, Trial of Tamao Shinohara and two others A471/1 81961 and 81966 (NAA)
Articles: *Sydney Morning Herald*, 15 February; 13, 22 March; 3 April; 1 June 1951

Additional chapter notes

1   No one visited Soreh or Tapai until 1946, when the Dutch recovered all four bodies for reburial in Kranji.

2   The messages were finally delivered in 1981 by Hall.

3   For examples of cover-ups see Executions at Matupi A 703/614/1/7 (NAA) and Kavieng Massacre AWM 1010/6/134 (AWM).

4   No local people were questioned regarding incidents at Kasu, Soreh, Tapai or Merapas until 1981. The only island searched in 1945 was Merapas. Although Pritchard's information differed somewhat from that of Ellis, and Lloyd wanted further investigations carried out (see Palmer's report 21/11/45 in AA 1981/155/1), no further enquiries were made.

Chapter 17: The Timor Affair

Preliminary situation

Archival papers: History of SOA Operations Vol II: Partisan Phase and Lizard I, II, III A3270 Vol 2 (NAA)

Operation Lagarto

SOA Operations Vol II, Lagarto; Sworn statement of Alfred James Ellwood Doc 1010/4/48 (AWM); Summary of examination of Antonio Augusto dos Santos, 28 June 1946 and Statement of Chung Hui Cheng, MP 742/1 336/1/1724 (NAA); Sworn statement of Minoru Tad 11 December 1947, MP 742/1 336/1/2073

Operation Cobra

SOA Operations Vol II, Cobra; Captain J R Cashman's report on Cobra Party 23 October 1945 A3269 V7; Examination of dos Santos, da Silva 27 June 1946 MP 742/1 336/1/1724; Statement by S Kamimoto, The Case of Captain Cashman, MP 742/1 336/1/1213; Exhibits 2, 5, Saiki Trial, A471/ 80708 (NAA); Cobra signals A3269/1 D3; Information reports compiled by Brigadier Wills in Cobra Signals; telegram Hollandia to SRD 6 May 1945, Cobra signals

Operation Adder

SOA Operations Vol II, Adder; telegram from Captain Goto (Japanese Intelligence) 10 November 1945, A3269 D26, Groper copy II (NAA)

Seymour Bingham

See Appendix II, Silver's *Rimau*

SOE security checks

Statement by SOE agent H M G Lauwers in Giskes' *London Calling North Pole*; Cookridge's *Inside SOE*; Statement by SOE coding expert Leo Marks, on BBC documentary *England Speil*. For more details on the latter, see Silver's *Rimau*, Appendix II

Operation Sunable

SOA Operations Vol II Sunable; Final Report by Stevenson, 29 Nov 45, A3269 D26; Report by Sgt J R White and amplifying report by White 20 Oct 45, Report by Sgt J A Shand 20 Oct 45, A 3269 V17 (NAA)

Operation Sunlag

SRD Operations Vol II, Sunlag

Operation Lagartout ('rescue' by *Krait*)

Archival papers: SOA Operations Vol II, Lagartout and Brim; Report, proceedings HMAS *Krait*, March–August 1945, AWM 78 193/1 (AWM)

Interviews/correspondence: O'Dwyer Family; Ray Evans; N Vidgen

Operation Suncob

SRD Operations Vol II Suncob; Report on Suncob Operation by Capt P Wynn 22 Oct 1945 and Corporal B Lawrence 19 Oct 45 A3269 V17 (NAA); Groper Final Report; Lawrence statement, AWC questionnaire, Statements by Mori 1 Dec 45, Haraguchi 1 Dec 45, Naruta 15 Nov 45, all in Saiki trial. Another copy at MP 742/1 336/1/1213; Report by Wynne, Treatment of SRD prisoners while in Japanese hands, and statement by Saiki, MP 742/1 336/1/11213

Fate of SOA personnel

Cobra report; Casualty reports for Lt Liversidge, Paulo da Silva and Appendix A, A3269 V17; Signals on missing personnel, A3269 V16; Report on investigations of war crimes made at Dilli [sic] by Capt A D Stevenson, 2 Oct 45 AWM 1010/2/29 (AWM); Timforce Report 8 October 1945 AWM 571A/4/3 (AWM); SOA Operations, Lagarto, Cobra, Adder; Ellwood's report and sworn statement

Operation Sunbaker
SOA Operations Vol II Sunbaker, Suncharlie

Final signals
Cobra, Lagarto Signals; Lagarto operational report. For debate deciding what answer should be sent, see all signals 12–13 August between Morotai, Darwin, SRD, and Timor, in Cobra signals.

Covering Cobra's and Lagarto's tracks
SOA Operations Vol II, Groper; Lagarto operational report

Investigating missing personnel
SOA Operations Vol 2 Groper; Stevenson's war crimes report; Weekly report by Stevenson 9 Oct 45 A3269 V16; Casualty reports of Gregg, Grimson from interrogation of da Silva by Ellwood 4, 9 Oct 1945 A3269 V17; Cobra report; Lagarto report; letter from Finlay to 2 Echelon 13 Nov 1945 A3269 V16; Goto's telegram; NEFIS interrogation report, quoted in Groper summary of missing personnel A3269 D26; note at foot of Gregg's casualty report (Peace)

Suppression of evidence, trial preparations
Signal from Landops to Landforces 6 December 1945 MP 741/1 336/1/1213; Signal from Timforce to Landops Z Special Unit 27 December 1945 MP 742/1 336/1/1213; Charter of the International Military Tribunal for the Far East, Article 13

Timor trials
Archival papers: Minute paper Director of Legal Services 28 Mar 46, Exhibits 2, 7, statements by Cashman and Ellwood, Record of Military Court first schedule records, and minute paper, all in Saiki trial
Newspapers: Argus, *The Age, Sydney Morning Herald* 1–16 March 1946

Corroborative evidence
Examination of dos Santos, statement of Tada, Ellwood statement; Examination of Patricio Luz 28 June 1946 and Sancho da Silva 27 June 1946, all in MP 741/1 336/1/1724

Reaction to sentences
Argus, The Age 16 March 1946; *Sydney Morning Herald* 18 March 1946

Cousens, Calwell publicity
Argus, The Age, Sydney Morning Herald July 1946–March 1947 (Cousins), January–February 1946 (Calwell)

Ellwood's reputation
For example see Dick Horton's *Ring of Fire*, which claims Ellwood went to the beach and lit the fires which lured Cobra to its doom

Blamey's character/status
Articles: David McKnight, 'A Very Australian Coup', *Sydney Morning Herald* 11 November 1989
Books: Hetherington; Horner's *Commanders*

Additional chapter notes
1 SOA operations states that the date was April 1945. However, as signals were promptly translated and as a summary of missing personnel in A 3269 V16 states that Lagarto was reported captured on 29 January 1945, this April date appears to be incorrect. On 10 March, Bingham was informed that new ciphers were not to be included in the next drop to Cobra and Lagarto.
2 Bingham was replaced by Lieutenant-Colonel Holland and Chapman-Walker by Jock Campbell. See also Chapman-Walker to General Blamey, 4 July 1945, 3 DRL 6643, 56.4 (AWM).

Chapter 18: Latter-day sleuthing
Fate of Willersdorf and Pace
Umi San messages 158, 171, 228; NEFIS Interrogation Report No 2055/III by Ibrahim, A3269 D30; Summary of examination of Sebasrao Graca, 25 June 1946, MP 742/1 336/1/1724; Examination of da Silva, Luz (*note*: Luz unfortunately muddled Adder, Cobra, Willersdorf and Pace. The men of whom Luz spoke must be Rimau as no Australians in Cobra were tortured in this manner and both Adder men died on insertion);Casualty reports of Gregg and Grimson (actually Willersdorf and Pace)

Graves at Kranji
Graves registration cards, Kranji War Cemetery (NAA); CWGC website; WO concentration List, 26/6/47, Malaya 16/133E, set 9/32 Sheet 26 (CWGC records)

References and explanatory notes

Execution site
Archival papers: Ross's exhumation report; Pritchard's reports 18, 23 October 1945, MP 742/1 336/1/755 and ADM 1/18596 3231; Graves registration cards for ten executed; wartime map of Singapore (AWM)
Private papers: Personal examination of site, photographs (SP)
Interviews/correspondence: Peter Macmillan
Articles: Silver, *Operation Rimau: The Final Chapter*, and *Postscript to the Epilogue*, written for publication in various journals, March 1993

The polytechnic site
Correspondence: Journalist Tan Yong Meng
Newspapers: 'Veterans: Allied soldiers were buried at poly site', *Straits Times* 27 September 1993 and 'A Matter of Honour', *The Scotsman* 28 September 1993, for account by Dr Ross regarding his role in 'identifying' the Polytechnic site, and also that the Rimau executions were samurai.

Recognition for Double Tenth
Private papers: Program, promotional material for 60th Jaywick Anniversary Commemoration, file notes of meetings; thank you by Singapore High Commissioner at ANMM official function (SP)
Interview: Arthur Jones (National Film Archives)
Newspaper articles: 'After the *Krait*'s bite the poison kept spreading', *Sydney Morning Herald* 3 September 1993

Merapas remains
Account of recovery of skull, forensic examination, attempts at identification, etc. (SP); Interviews with Dr Oettle; Copies of official forensic, ballistics documents prepared by Oettle and police, 1994 (SP); Lowry, *Army Journal 1972*

Visit to Singapore, Indonesia 1989
Private papers: Notes on investigations, photographs (SP)
Article: Silver, 'Unravelling the Mystery of Operation Rimau', for publication in various journals, 1992–93

Expedition to Merapas, 1994
Private papers: Correspondence between Colonel Brian Nicholson and L Silver; notes relating to trip, photographs; Interviews and correspondence with Aloysius Hayes Weller (SP)
Article: Silver, 'In Search of a Hero', June 1994, for publication in various journals

Military funeral
Articles: Account in *Straits Times* 28 August 1994; Silver, 'Military Funeral in Singapore for Two WW2 Heroes', for publication in various journals, September 1994

Epilogue: Fabrications, fallacies and fakes
Unpalatable truth
Gullett's *Sinai and Palestine*; Fenella Souter, 'Death on the Track', *Good Weekend* 11 July 2009; Moffitt, Athol, 'A Legend Endangered', *Royal United Services NSW Journal*, 1993

Carse's claims
Archival papers: Service details of Jack Sue show he did not enlist until 25 September 1943
Interviews/correspondence: Reid; Emerson-Elliott; Berryman; Glenn Darlington; Morris
Books: McKie's *Heroes*

Execution myth
Books: McKie's *Heroes*; Dunlop; Laffin; Jenkins (details of rugby teams)
Films: Highest Honour/Beneath the Southern Cross/Heroes of the Krait; Heroes II the return
Websites: http://www.scrum.com/newzealand/rugby/player

Willersdorf and Pace paddle to Timor
Books: McKie's *Heroes*; Amar, Dennis et al; Dunlop, Horner, Jenkins, Thomson & Macklin

Film scenarios become fact
Archival material: Documents, film scenarios deposited by H Lander with AAHUA
Private papers: Correspondence re withdrawal of monograph; Silver and Senator Ray 1991; Walter Campbell and OAWG; Walter Campbell and Silver (SP)
Books: Amar

Various Rimau myths
Archival papers: Copies of correspondence between Furuta and McKie; film scenarios (AAHUA)
Correspondence: Geoffrey Rowley-Conwy, The Lord Langford and L Silver, November 1990–January 1992, including copies of letters and memos of telephone conversations between Langford and Anthony Buckley, and Langford and Corine Cartier; notes by a cast member of *Heroes II* found in a copy of Silver's *Rimau*, loaned by SOA's Kelvin Wright
Articles: Furuta's 'Harimu'
Books: Amar; McKie's *Heroes*; Thompson & Macklin

References and explanatory notes

Films: *The Highest Honour etc.*; *Heroes II The Return*

Ivan Lyon's 'private agenda'
Correspondence: Reid; Clive Lyon
Interviews: Arthur Jones (Film Archives)
Books: McKie's *Heroes*
Films: *The Heroes*; *Heroes II The Return*

Intercepted messages withheld
Books: Thompson & Macklin
Films: *Heroes II The Return*

Nancy Davidson's claims
Correspondence: Reid; Emerson-Elliott; Editor, *Special Forces Journal*
Article: Statement by Chillingworth, *Special Forces Journal* Autumn 1992
Books: Wynyard; McKie's *Heroes*
Films: *The Heroes*; *Heroes II The Return*

Military 'Fakes'
Archival papers: Service dossier, John Napier Richmond Gardner (NAA); SOA Operations Vol II, Semut IV
Private papers: File note, I Cdo Regiment to L Silver, September 2003, regarding investigation of claims by Ron Morris, of Normanhurst
Papers/correspondence/dossiers: relating to war service of Rowan Waddy and Gordon Morris with SOA; Notes on lecture by Rowan Waddy; Account of Operation Crocodile by US submarine crew; statement by Rowan Waddy, on ABC AM program 25 April and 26 April 1997; Investigation into war service of an 'Agas operative' 1945; Service dossier of John Gardner; Claims by SA veteran re S Special Unit (SP); Correspondence with editor, Special Forces Journal (SP)
Articles: *Sun* newspaper, 25 April 1978

Krait myths
Archival documents: Minutes and Status Reports of *Krait* Public Museum Fund Raising Committee, 1981–83 (Chief Secretary's Department, NSW); Minutes of the *Krait* Appeal Fund Committee and *Krait* Public Museum Fund Committee, 1962–1985 (Chief secretary's Department, NSW); Miscellaneous notes on *Krait*, RHR File 52y (NHR, ACT); Naval papers, etc MP 1049/5 2026/27/296 (NAA); Papers relating to BBCAU, AWM 54

376/5/29 (AWM); Reports, Proceedings, HMAS *Krait*, March–August 1945, AWM 78 193/1 (AWM); War diary of BBCAU HQ, AWM 52 1/10/8 (AWM)

Books: Silver's *Krait*

Reynolds Papers: Family papers; Legal and other papers relating to salvage claim for *Krait*

Royal Volunteer Coastal Patrol: Legal papers relating to the ownership and trusteeship of MV *Krait*; Papers relating to the maintenance, care, control and usage of MV *Krait* from 1963–1985; Minutes and Reports of the RVCP *Krait* Division, 1977–78

Krait bell: *The Australian* newspaper 11 November 2009; ABC Radio North Queensland website; information/photographs on website 'Follow the *Krait*'; service record of William Malcolm McLean (NAA ACT); notes re statements of various members of '*Krait* Fund' (SP); Silver's *Krait*; various media interviews/press releases by Allan Miles (Follow the *Krait*) 2008 (SP); correspondence with Peter Woods, RVCP Archivist (SP)

Newspapers: see Silver's *Krait* for full list

Appendix 2: The Capture of *Kofuku Maru*: A Case of Mistaken Identity

Archival papers: HMAS *Burnie*, Reports of Proceedings; HMAS *Goulburn* Log; HMAS *Maryborough*, Reports of Proceedings; *Shofuku Maru* papers

Private papers: Emerson-Elliott Family; Reynolds Family; Vidgen to Silver (SP)

Books: Ogle

Photographs: Capture of Japanese fishing vessel by HMAS *Maryborough* (Barney Ogle).

BIBLIOGRAPHY

Books

Allen, Louis, *The Politics and Strategy of the Second World War, Singapore 1941–1942*, London 1977

Arneil, Stan, *One Man's War*, Melbourne 1988

Australian War Memorial, *HMAS Mk IV*, Canberra 1945

Bell, Leslie, *Destined Meeting*, London 1959

Baldwin, Suzy (ed.), *Unsung Heroes and Heroines of Australia*, Melbourne 1988

Ballard, G St V, *On Ultra Active Service: The Story of Australia's Signal Intelligence Operations during World War II*, Richmond 1991

Barber, Noel, *Sinister Twilight*, Glasgow 1968

Barker, A J, *Japanese Army Handbook 1939-1945*, New York 1979

Bennett, Lieut-Gen. H. Gordon, *Why Singapore Fell*, Sydney 1944

Bleakley, Jack, *The Eavesdroppers*, Canberra 1992

Bostock, John, *Australian Ships at War*, Sydney 1975

Braddon, Russell, *The Naked Island*, London 1952

Bradley, James, *Towards the Setting Sun*, NSW 1982

Brooke, Geoffrey, *Alarm Starboard*, Cambridge 1982

Brooke, Geoffrey, *Singapore's Dunkirk*, London 1989

Browne, Courtney, *Tojo the Last Banzai*, London 1967

Budden, F M, *The Chocos*, Sydney 1987

Caffrey, Kate, *Out in the Midday Sun*, London 1973

Callahan, *The Worst Disaster*, London 1977

Chapman, F Spencer, *The Jungle is Neutral*, London 1949

Churchill, Winston S, *The Hinge of Fate*, The Second World War Vol 4, London 1951

Churchill, Winston S, *The Onslaught of Japan*, The Second World War Vol 7, London 1951

Coates, Albert & Risenthal, Newman, *The Albert Coates Story*, Melbourne 1977

Comber, Ian, *Malaya's Secret Police 1945–1961: The role of the Special Branch in the Malayan Emergency*, Institute of Southeast Asia Studies 1961

Connell, Brian, *Return of the Tiger*, London 1960

Cookridge, E H, *Inside SOE*, London 1966

Cruikshank, Charles, *SOE in the Far East*, Oxford, 1983

Davis, Sir Robert H, *Deep Diving and Submarine Operations*, London n.d.

Daws, Gavin, *Prisoners of the Japanese*, 1994

Dennis, Peter, Grey, Jeffrey, Morris, Ewen, Prior, Robyn with Connor, John, *The Oxford Companion to Australian Military History*, Australia 1999

Docker, Edward & Silver, Lynette, *Fabulous Furphies: Ten Great Myths from Australia's Past*, Burra Creek NSW 1997

Dourlein, Pieter, *Inside North Pole*, London 1953

Drea, Edward J, *MacArthur's Ultra, Codebreaking and the War against Japan, 1942–1945*, Kansas 1992

Dunlop, Sir Edward, *The War Diaries of Weary Dunlop*, Melbourne 1997

Du Quesne, Bird Nicholas, *The Observer's Book of Firearms*, London 1978

Edwards, Jack, *Banzai You Bastards*, privately published, n.d.

Elphick, Peter, *Far Eastern File: The Intelligence War in the Far East*, London 1997

Elphick, Peter, *Singapore the Pregnable Fortress*, London 1995

Elphick, Peter & Smith, Michael, *Odd Man Out*, London 1993

Falk, Stanley L, *Seventy Days to Singapore*, London 1975

Feldt, Eric, *The Coastwatchers*, Melbourne 1946

Fergusson, Bernard, *Wavell: Portrait of a Soldier*, London 1971

Foot, M R D, *SOE: The Special Operations Executive 1940–46*, London 1984

Frost, Ted, *From Tree to Sea: The Building of a Wooden Drifter*, Levenham, Suffolk 1985

Garden, R J P, *Survival in Malaya, January to October 1942*, Dunedin, 1992

Gibson, Walter, *The Boat*, London 1974

Gill, Herman, *The Royal Australian Navy 1939–1942*, Canberra 1957

Gillison, Douglas, *Australia in the War of 1939–1945: The Royal Australian Air Force, 1939–1942*, Canberra 1962

Gough, Richard, *The Escape from Singapore*, London 1987

Gough, Richard, *SOE Singapore 1941–42*, London 1985

Gullett, H A, *Official History of Australia in the War of 1914–18, Vol VIII, Sinai and Palestine*, Sydney 1923

Hague Convention of 1907

Hall, Timothy, *The Fall of Singapore*, Sydney 1983

Hampshire, Cecil A, *The Secret Navies*, London 1978

Hetherington, John, *Blamey: Controversial Soldier*, Canberra 1973

Horner, D M, *The Commanders*, Sydney 1984

Horner, D M, *High Command*, Sydney 1982

Ind, Allison W, *Spy Ring Pacific*, London 1958

Jenkins, Peter, *Wallaby Gold: 100 years of Australian Test Rugby*, Sydney 1999

Kahn, David, *The Codebreakers*, London 1973

Kirby, Major-General S Woodburn, *Singapore: The Chain of Disaster*, London 1971

Ladd, James J, *SBS: The Invisible Raiders*, Glasgow 1983

Laffin, John & Badman, Peter, *Australians at War: Special and Secret*, North Sydney 1990

Leasor, James, *Singapore*, London 1968

Lim, Janet, *Sold for Silver*, London 1958

Low, N I, *When Singapore was Syonan-To*, Singapore 1973

McGregor, John, *Blood on the Rising Sun*, Perth, no date (c 1960).

McKie, Ronald, *This was Singapore*, Sydney 1942

McKie, Ronald, *The Heroes*, Sydney 1960

Malla, Bashir A, *The Double Tenth Trial War Crimes Court*, Malayan Law Journal Office Singapore (nd)

Manchester, William, *American Caesar: Douglas MacArthur 1880–1964*, London 1979

Bibliography

Manual of Military Law, 1941

Mars, Alastair, *Submarines at War*, London 1971

Maxwell, Sir George, *The Civil Defence of Malaya*, London 1943

Michnow, Gregory F, *The Hell Ships: Prisoners at Sea in the Pacific War*, Annapolis MD 2001

Moffitt, Athol, *Operation Kingfisher*, Sydney 1989

Montgomery, Brian, *Shenton of Singapore*, London 1984

Mooney, James l (ed.) *Dictionary of American Naval Fighting Ships, Vol VII*, Washington 1981

Morrison, Ian, *Malayan Postcript*, London 1942

Muggenthaler, Karl August, *German Raiders of WW II*, London 1978

Murray, Jacqi *Watching the Sun Rise: Australian Reporting of Japan 1931 to the Fall of Singapore*, 2004 (published PhD thesis)

Norman, Diana, *Road from Singapore*, 1967

Ogle, Barney, *The History of HMAS* Maryborough, Wahroonga NSW 1992

Penfold A W, Bayliss W C, Crispin, K E, *Galleghan's Greyhounds: The Story of the 2/10th Australian Infantry Battalion*, Sydney 1979.

Percival, Lieut-Gen A E, *The War in Malaya*, London 1949

Pfennigwerth, Dr Ian, *A Man of Intelligence: the Life of Captain Eric Nave, Australian Codebreaker Extraordinary*, Dural 2006

Phillips, C E Lucas, *Cockleshell Heroes*, London 1956

Prange, Gordon W, *Pearl Harbor: The Verdict of History*, New York 1986

Pratten, Herbert Edward, *Tin Mining in Malaya* (online book)

Preston, Mark & Silver, Lynette, *Australia's Special Operations 1940–2003*, Sydney 2003

Reid, Carline, *Malayan Climax: Experiences of an Australian Girl in Malaya, 1940–1942*, Melbourne 1944

Report of Joint Army/Navy Assessment Committee, Washington, DC 1947

Rose, Angus, *Who Dies Fighting*, London 1944

Ross, Squadron Leader J M S, *Royal New Zealand Airforce*, Wellington 1955

Rusbridger, James & Nave, Eric, *Betrayal at Pearl Harbor*, London 1991,

Russell, Lord, of Liverpool, *The Knights of Bushido*, London 1958

Shinji, Menemija, *The Account of the Legal Proceedings of the Court for War Criminal Suspects*, translated by Yoshioko Kazuo, Japan 1946

Shinozaki, Mamoru, *Syonan: -My Story, the Japanese Occupation of Singapore*, Singapore 1975

Sidhu, H, *The Bamboo Fortress: True Singapore War Stories*, Singapore 1991

Silver, Lynette Ramsay, *The Heroes of Rimau*, Sydney 1990

Silver, Lynette Ramsay, *Krait: The Fishing Boat that Went to War*, Sydney 1992

Silver, Lynette Ramsay, *The Bridge at Parit Sulong: An Investigation of Mass Murder, Malaya, 1942*, Sydney 2004

Simson, Ivan, *Singapore: Too Little Too Late*, London 1970

Skidmore, Ian, *Escape from the Rising Sun*, London 1973

Sleeman, Colin, *The Trial of Gozawa Sadaichi and Nine Others*, London 1948

Sleeman, Colin & Silkin, S C, *The Trial of Sumida Haruzo and Twenty Others (The 'Double Tenth' Trial)*, Edinburgh 1956

Smyth, Sir John, *Percival and the Tragedy of Singapore*, London 1971

Stevenson, William, *A Man Called Intrepid*, London 1976

Stewart, Brigadier I, *History of the Second Argyll and Sutherland Highlanders*, London 1947

Taffrail (Captain Taprell Dorling), *The Blue Star Line at War 1939–45*, Foulsham, London 1973

Thomson, Judy, *Winning with Intelligence*, Loftus NSW 2000

2/19 Battalion Association, *The Grim Glory: The History of 2/19 Battalion AIF*, Sydney 1975

Trenowden, Ian, *The Hunting Submarine*, London (nd)

Walker, Richard & Helen, *Curtin's Cowboys: Australia's Secret Bush Commandos*, Sydney 1986

Ward, Ian, *The Killer They Called a God*, Singapore 1992

Warren, Alan, *Singapore Britain's Greatest Defeat*, South Yarra, Victoria, 2002

Wigmore, Lionel, *Australia in the War of 1939–1945: The Japanese Thrust*, Canberra 1957

Winter, Barbara, *The Intrigue Master*, Sheldon Queensland 1995

Wynyard, Noel, *Winning Hazard*, London *c.* 1948

Yacob, Shakila, *The United States and the Malaysian Economy* (on line book)

Young, Bill, *Return to a Dark Age*, Allawah NSW 1991

Documents

Australian Archives

Australian War Memorial (AWM)

National Archives of Australia (NAA), NSW, ACT and Victoria (VIC)

Bennett to Sturdee, 19 January 1942, Document 54, 553/2/3 (AWM)

Empire Star, papers relating to attack by Japanese aircraft on, MP 1587/1 157 A (AA VIC)

Blamey, Field Marshal Sir Thomas, papers of, correspondence between Mott, Blamey and others, 3DRL 6643 Item 45/56.3 (AWM)

Bowden, VG, death of, Report by A N Wootton, 19 October 1945, A1066, Item H45/580/6/4 (AA ACT)

Chapman, Major Walter W, Technical Report on Operation Rimau 4 April 1945, A3269 Item E 4

Chapman-Walker, Lieut-Colonel, to Colonel Roberts Controller AIB, 19 September 1944, A3269/1 item H 13 (AA ACT)

Chapman -Walker, Lieut-Colonel, Signal No 55 S/6, 3 November 1942, A3269 Jaywick E2 Copy 1

Holmes, Lieutenant J Lind, Weather report, A3269 Item E 4 (AA ACT)

Krait Log, Exhibition Document 154 (AWM)

Krait memorandum by DNI, 9 February 1943, including defect list, AA1981/155/1 Item 605/2D/1 (AA ACT)

MacArthur to Chiefs-of-Staff, AIB Correspondence, A3269 Item N1 Pt 1 (AA ACT)

Operation Hornbill memorandum, 1 May 1943, A 3269 Item E 4 (AA ACT)

Opertaion Hornbill, Security, A 3269/1 Item E 8 (AA ACT)

Bibliography

Operation Jaywick, Decoration, recommendations of Chapman Walker to General Blamey and Sir Guy Royal, A3269 Jaywick E1 Copy 1 (AA ACT)

Operation Jaywick, Preliminary Papers (including Training Diary) A3269 Item E2 (AA ACT)

Operation Python A3269, SP87/2574 (AA ACT)

Operation Rimau, Plan Rimau, Fremantle Submarine Order No 1, 9 September 1944, A 3269 Item E 4 (AA ACT)

Operation Rimau, Plan Rimau, Folio 1, A 3269 Item E 4 (AA ACT)

Operation Scorpion, Operation Rimau, Minutes of final planning conference, 7 July 1944, A 3269 item E 4 (AA ACT)

Operation Rimau, Papers on Breach of Security, A 3269 Item V 7 (AA ACT) and also Special Operations Activities Organisation, A 3770 Vol 1 (AA ACT)

Papers relating to, including letters by Carey, Blamey and Mott AWM 3/6643 Item 2/58 (AWM)

Perske and Sachs, Disappearance of, MP742/1 336/1/1939 (AA VIC)

Roberts, Colonel to Colonel Chapman-Walker, 22 August 1944, A 3269/1 item H13 (AA ACT)

SEAC and SOE, Memorandum on Operations in SEAC, 20 September 1944, A3269 Item N Pt 1 (AA ACT)

SOA, Official History of, compiled 1945 (not published), A3270 Vols I–V (AA ACT)

SOA Intelligence report, report of interview with Captain H J Ahgers KPN, 5 July 1944, A 3269 Item e $ (AA ACT)

SOE, Memorandum on Operations, A 3269/1 Item E8 (AA ACT)

SWPA, map showing zones of responsibility, A3269/1 item E8 (AA ACT)

War Cabinet Minute, 2 March 1942, notes on discussion with Major-General Gordon Bennett, A2673, Vol II (AA ACT)

Wilson, AJ to General Northcott, 20 May 1944, A3269 /1 Item H 14 (AAA ACT)

Young, Horrie, Diary (AWM)

Relics

Door jamb with information scratched on it by W R Reynolds (AWM)

UK Archives

Public Record Office (PRO)

Imperial War Museum (IWM)

Guildhall Library (GL)

Carter, Squadron leader T C, Papers of, *History of RDF Organisation in the Far East 1941-1942* (undated), TCC2/1/ (IWM)

Cooper, Duff to Winston Churchill, 18 December 1941, enclosure in Tennant to Churchill, 6 January 1942, PREM3, 161/1 (PRO)

Davis, Brigadier l E C, WW2 Papers of (IWM)

Lloyd's Lists, 8 October 1923, 4 September 1924, 18 August 1943(GL)

Malayan Research Bureau, Records of, including papers of Mrs G Howell, with correspondence from W R Reynolds, May–July 1943; Excerpt from Memoires of Mrs Edith Stevenson; Memoires of Marjorie de Malmanche (IWM)

Marsham, Commander Hubert to Captain 8 Submarine Flotilla, 29 September 1944, XC/B 3197 ADM199/513 (PRO)

Marsham, Commander Hubert to Senior Officer (submarines) Eastern Fleet, 18 August 1944, and 29 September 1944, XC/B 3197 ADm 199/513 (PRO)

Memo M 0583292/44, 6 January 1944, re carrying supplies on submarines, XC/B 3197 ADM 199/513 (PRO)

Merchant Navy List, MF 18 268 Vol 12A and M/F 18 569 Vol 32 (GL)

Operation Hornbill, Kookaburra Papers, A3269/1 Item E8

Operation Hornbill, memo by NID (Q) re problems with plans, 24 December 1944, XC/B 3197 ADM 199/153 (PRO)

Operation Jaywick, Admiralty Files relating to, XC/B 3197 ADM 1/21966150; XC/B3197 ADM 1/16678A (PRO)

Operation Jaywick, Decorations for personnel, XC/B 3197 1/16678 (PRO)

Oppenheim, HR, Diary of, British Association of Malaya Collection, Royal Commonwealth Society, London.

Porpoise, Monthly Reports, 11 September 1944, *ADM 173.18592 (PRO)*

Porpoise, Report of 28th War Patrol, ADM 199/1877 (PRO)

Shadwell, Captain to Commander-in-Chief, Eastern fleet, 30 October 1944, XC/B 3197 ADM 199/513 (PRO)

United States Archives

USS *Tuna*, 22 December 1943, Report of Landing of Allied intelligence Personnel in Vicinity of Balik Island during Ninth War Patrol (Department of navy, Naval Historical Centre, Washington DC)

Despatches

Brooke-Popham, Air Chief Marshal Sir Robert, 'Despatches to the British Chiefs of Staff, May 28 1942', The London Times, Supplement 22 January 1948

Maltby, Air Vice-Marshal Sir Paul, 'Despatches to the Secretary of State for Air, July 26 1947', The London Gazette, Third Supplement 26 February 1948

Percival, Lieut-Gen A E, 'Despatches to the Secretary of State for War, 25 April 1946', The London Gazette, Second Supplement 26 February 1948

Private Papers

Silver Papers

Correspondence with Keith Andrews; Jeremy Atkinson; Moss Berryman; Geoffrey Brooke; Andrew and Muriel Buie (Riggs' family); Sir Walter Campbell; Capon; Deutz Australia Ltd; Ray Evans; Captain Redmond Faulkner; the Fletcher family; the Fujisawa Family, Japan; L Gardner and Sons ltd, England; Senkichi Hamagami, Japan; Dennis Harman; Schichiro Kubo, Japan; Colonel the Lord Langford (Geoffrey Rowley-Conwy); Clive Lyon; Brenda McDuff; Marjorie de Malmanche; Ron Morris; Nippon Kaiji Kyokai; Brian Ogle; the Pace Family; RAN Archives; Bettina Reid; Ruston Diesel Ltd, UK; Yoshio Shimizu, Japan; Tai-O Fishing Company, Japan; N O Vidgen; Special Forces Club, London; the Warne Family; Kelvin Wright; Horrie Young; Captain Selwyn, report (copy)

Emerson Elliott, Anthony, sketch of *Empire Star*

Emerson Elliott, Denis, account of evacuation on *Empire Star*

Emerson-Elliott, Derek, recollections of Singapore

Faulkner, Redmond, various items and news clippings relating to *Empire Star* (SP)

Jaywick personnel, profiles (SP)

Johnstone, Charlie, diary (SP)

Rimau personnel, profiles (SP)

SOE personnel, profiles (SP)

SOA personnel, profiles (SP)

Other private collections

Atkinson, Kenneth, papers (Atkinson Family)

Bevan Davies, Bert: Correspondence including letters from Paddy McDowell, L Gardner & Sons England; Hawker Siddley, Victoria

Emerson-Elliott Family: Papers relating to Denis Emerson-Elliott's life

Lyon Family: Correspondence from Andrew Crilly, Paddy McDowell and families of Jaywick and Rimau men; Tom Argyle; Admiral Christie; Prime Minister Curtin; Eric Gannon; Thomas de Pledge; Bettina Reid; Lord Selbourne; and army colleagues of Ivan Lyon etc. Also correspondence from George Astley and Harry Manderson to Gabrielle Lyon, and Red Cross message re Gabrielle Lyon to Herve Gilis, Gabrielle's brother-in-law.

Reid, Bettina: Papers, various correspondence, to and from Ivan Lyon and Gabrielle Lyon.

Reynolds, William Roy: Papers (copies in SP) including Logs of *Suey Sin Fah*; legal papers, Marriage Certificate; Master's Certificate; MBE citation; Article 'How an Australian Tin Miner won the MBE'; RN statement of service; newspaper clippings related to war service; Naval commissions; Naval signals; Papers relating to *Krait*; personal memos and notes; photographs

Sachs Family: Papers, diaries, photographs, memorabilia

Wood, Ross: Papers relating to *Empire Star*

Interviews

Arafin bin Akup, interview at Kasu with L Silver, 1989

Bradwell, Betty, Australian nursing sister from 10 AGH, interview with L Silver 8 June 1996

Cornford, Roy (2/19 Battalion *Empire Star*), interviews/correspondence with L Silver, 2 October 1994–April 1995

Davidson, Nancy (taped interview)

Ellis, Mary, interview with L Silver, 1993.

Emerson- Elliott, Denis, interviews with L Silver, various dates 1996–1997

Emerson-Elliott, Derek, interviews with L Silver, various dates 1996–2009

Jones, Arthur, interview for *Australians at War*, 2003

Mahat Kunil, interview at Kasu with L Silver, 1989

Mitchell, Archie (AASC *Empire Star*), interview with L Silver 31 January 1995

Scriven, Cyril H (AASC, *Empire Star*), correspondence with L Silver, 2 and 17 February 1993 (original correspondence in MSS1450 AWM)

Shinozaki, Mamoru, *My Wartime Experiences in Singapore*, Institute of Southeast Asian Studies Oral History Programme, Japanese Occupation Project, interview by Kim Yoon Lin, Singapore 1973

Weller, Aloysius Hayes (Merapas eyewitness), interviews/correspondence with L Silver, 1993

Wood, Ross, various correspondence, discussions with L Silver, 1997–2009.

Wright, Captain George, transcript of ABC interview, March 1944

Yamada, Kojiro, correspondence/interviews with L Silver, 2009

Young, Horace, interview for *Australians at War c.* 2003

Newspapers and articles

Army newspaper, 6 September 1967 (contains highly coloured account of Jaywick according to E Carse)

Blue Star Line's MV *Empire Star*, http://www.bluestarline.org

Caithness, Lieutenant Franklin, RNR, edited account of the loss of HMS *Kuala*, to Commander H V Creer, *Naval Historical Review*

Furuta, Hiroyuki, 'The Harimu Party Sleeps Here', two versions

Heads, George F (ship's cook, *Empire Star*), *The Australian* 20 February 1992

Hellman, John, 'Australian Capital in South East Asian Tin Mining, 1906', *Australian Economic History Review* vol 45, issue 2

Heroines of the Empire Star (various contributors), http://www.angellpro.com.au

Higgins, A J, *Escape from Singapore*

Last, Dr Peter, *Empire Star* (typescript from book, *The Repat*)

Lowry, Lieutenant R W, 'A Report on Exercise Jaywick 8/9 September 1971' *Army Journal No 272*, January 1972

Lyon, Ivan, 'Malaya to Indo-China', *The Yachting World* 11 November 1938

Man, Frank, *The Fall and Evacuation of Singapore* (eyewitness account, August 1942)

Moffitt, Mr Justice Athol, 'A Legend Endangered', *RUSI NSW Journal*, 1993

Moir-Byres, G F, 'Malayan Sailing', *The YachtingWorld* 7 October 1938

Owen, Gwilym (eyewitness) The Bombing of the *Tien Kwang* and *Kuala*

Bibliography

Salt (Army magazine), vol 11, no 5, 5 November 1945, statement by J M Brodie, 2/9 Australian Field Ambulance

Selwood, Sister Margaret, unidentified newspaper article 1942

Silver, Lynette, *Scapegoats for the Bloody Empire*, 1993, ABC website, 4 Corners

War Cry, newspaper of the Salvation Army in Australia, 14 March 1942

Weekend Mail, WA, 25 June 1960, article on Colin Craft

Wild, Cyril, 'Expedition to Singkep', *Blackwoods Magazine* no 1572, vol 260, October 1946

'World of Tin', *Time* magazine 7 May 1934

'Z Force Home for Sale', *The Australian* 7 October 1977

Films and Documentaries

Arms and the Dragon (BBC, London) 1984

Snakes and Tigers (Channel 10, Australia)

This is Your Life, Anzac Day 1983

Beneath the Southern Cross (aka *The Highest Honour/Heroes of the Krait*) 1982

Heroes 1988

Heroes II The Return 1993

List of illustrations

INDEX

Index

Index

Index

Deadly Secrets